D0850409

Illusions of Emancipation

THE LITTLEFIELD HISTORY
OF THE CIVIL WAR ERA

Gary W. Gallagher and T. Michael Parrish, editors

*This book was supported by
the Littlefield Fund for Southern History,
University of Texas Libraries*

This landmark sixteen-volume series, featuring books by
some of today's most respected Civil War historians, surveys
the conflict from the earliest rumblings of disunion through
the Reconstruction era. A joint project of UNC Press and
the Littlefield Fund for Southern History, University of Texas
Libraries, the series offers an unparalleled comprehensive
narrative of this defining era in U.S. history.

Illusions of Emancipation

The Pursuit of Freedom and Equality in the Twilight of Slavery

JOSEPH P. REIDY

The University of North Carolina Press
Chapel Hill

The University of North Carolina Press has been a member of the
Green Press Initiative since 2003.

Library of Congress Cataloging-in-Publication Data
Names: Reidy, Joseph P. (Joseph Patrick), 1948– author.
Title: Illusions of emancipation : the pursuit of freedom and equality in the
     twilight of slavery / Joseph P. Reidy.
Other titles: Littlefield history of the Civil War era.
Description: Chapel Hill : University of North Carolina Press, [2019] |
     Series: The Littlefield history of the civil war era | Includes bibliographical
     references and index.
Identifiers: LCCN 2018024859| ISBN 9781469648361 (cloth : alk. paper) |
     ISBN 9781469648378 (ebook)
Subjects: LCSH: Slaves—Emancipation—United States—History. | Slavery—
     United States—History—19th century. | African Americans—Social
     conditions—History—19th century.
Classification: LCC E441 .R35 2019 | DDC 305.896/07309034—dc23
     LC record available at https://lccn.loc.gov/2018024859

Jacket illustrations: front, *Emancipation* by Thomas Nast (courtesy of the
Library of Congress Prints and Photographs Division, LC-DIG-pga-03898);
back, *Fugitive African Americans Fording the Rappahannock River, Va.* by
Timothy O'Sullivan (courtesy of the Library of Congress Prints and
Photographs Division, LC-DIG-cwpb-00218).

For Patricia, our children, and our grandchildren

Contents

Figures

Illusions of Emancipation

Introduction

Phantoms of Freedom

On December 18, 1940, the distinguished Howard University historian Charles H. Wesley delivered a lecture commemorating the ratification of the Thirteenth Amendment to the U.S. Constitution. This was seventy-five years to the day after Secretary of State William H. Seward announced that slavery was officially abolished. Wesley spoke at the newly opened Founders Library, named in honor of the thirteen men responsible for establishing the university, which Congress had chartered in 1867. That same year, the institution's namesake, Oliver Otis Howard, the Civil War hero and commissioner of the Freedmen's Bureau who was often referred to as the "Christian General," purchased the land where the campus stood from John A. Smith, a prominent resident of the District of Columbia. Five years earlier Smith had received $5,146.50 in compensation from the federal government for fourteen enslaved persons under the act that abolished slavery in the District of Columbia.[1] Smith's 150-acre farm, "The Hill," was located slightly more than one mile north of the White House, the Washington Monument, and the U.S. Capitol building, just beyond Boundary Street, which separated rural Washington County from the city of Washington. Several blocks east of the Capitol in Lincoln Park stood *Freedom's Memorial*, the noted sculptor Thomas Ball's famous work commemorating Abraham Lincoln as emancipator (see figure 1.1).[2] Wesley referenced the memorial in his remarks.

Wesley focused particularly on the stylized portrayals of Lincoln and the black man who also occupied the pedestal. He noted that Ball's original design, sculpted shortly after the president's assassination, depicted the freedman "kneeling in a completely passive manner, receiving his freedom at the hands of Lincoln, his liberator." In response to criticism, Wesley explained, Ball altered the model "so that the slave, although kneeling, is represented as exerting his own strength to break his chains." "Nearer to historical truth" than the original, the final version of the statue nonetheless still failed to represent accurately the enslaved people's role in emancipation. In the spirit of the day they commemorated, Wesley invited his audience to imagine the influence that black freedom seekers had on Lincoln and on the development of emancipation policy more generally.[3]

One of the persons most responsible for *Freedom's Memorial*, William Greenleaf Eliot, a prominent St. Louis minister and foe of slavery who helped found the Western Sanitary Commission during the Civil War, offered reflections similar to Wesley's more than fifty years earlier. Acknowledging that the figures portrayed "President Lincoln in the act of emancipating a negro slave, who kneels at his feet to receive the benediction," Eliot observed that the slave's "hand has grasped the chain as if in the act of breaking it," suggesting "that the slaves took active part in their own deliverance." Eliot's comments reflected an insider's knowledge; in fact, he had convinced Ball to use the "likeness, both face and figure," of Archer Alexander as the model for the freedman. Alexander had escaped from slavery in 1863, and Eliot offered him shelter and employment and even helped thwart an attempt to reenslave him. Eliot published an account of Alexander's life in 1885.[4]

The African American artist Edmonia Lewis also portrayed emancipation through design elements and classical motifs similar to Ball's in her 1867 sculpture *Forever Free* (see figure I.2). Like Ball, Lewis employed two figures, one standing and the other crouching, and the freedman depicted in both wore clothing only around his waist. The similarities in composition ended there. Whereas Ball's second figure was Lincoln, dressed in a suit, standing above the kneeling freedman with arm outstretched symbolically freeing him, Lewis's second figure was a woman, clothed in a dress but, like the man, wearing broken shackles. It was she who knelt and he stood next to her, his right hand resting on her shoulder and his left arm raised in triumph. Both gaze skyward. Although critics have variously interpreted Lewis's symbolism, none has doubted her intention to depict freedom as the product of struggle and to suggest that escaping slavery constituted only its initial phase.[5]

Wesley, too, rejected the notion that freed people were passive recipients of freedom at Lincoln's hand. To make the case, he drew on Frederick Douglass's remarks at the dedication of *Freedom's Memorial* on April 14, 1876. The veteran abolitionist strained to rebalance not just the images that Ball's statue conveyed of Lincoln (the liberator) and Alexander (the liberated) but also the broadly popular stereotype that the artist had tapped into for his initial inspiration. Douglass spoke against a backdrop of the increasingly fragile Republican governments in the former Confederate states and the increasingly brazen violence against freed people everywhere. The audience included the sitting president, Ulysses S. Grant, and a host of other government officials and dignitaries as well as a number of the most distinguished black leaders in the land. The front of the memorial bore a plaque with the caption "Freedom's Memorial in Grateful Memory of Abraham Lincoln," which acknowledged that the freedwoman Charlotte Scott's initial contribution of five dollars, "her first earnings in freedom," had set the project in motion. Tell-

Figure 1.1 Emancipation Monument, Lincoln Park, Washington, D.C.—Thomas Ball, Sculptor. Courtesy of the Library of Congress, Prints and Photographs Division, LC-USZ62-53278.

ingly, the commemorative program altered the inscription on the plaque to read "the Freedmen's Memorial to Abraham Lincoln."

An earlier elision transformed the nature of the occasion itself. In March, when John Mercer Langston, the renowned abolitionist and attorney, and his fellow members of the national committee on arrangements petitioned Congress to declare the day "a general holiday" for all government employees in the city, they recommended holding the event on April 14 in honor of two anniversaries. Besides Lincoln's assassination, they wished to mark "the emancipation of the slaves in the *District of Columbia*" on April 16, 1862. The newspaper report that ran in the Washington *Republican* and that was reprinted in the commemorative pamphlet referenced only "the eleventh

Figure 1.2
Edmonia Lewis,
Forever Free.
Courtesy of the
Howard University
Gallery of Art.

anniversary of the death of Abraham Lincoln." This effectively separated Lincoln the martyr from the broader struggle for freedom, which long predated his birth, much less his assassination.[6]

Fully aware of the delicacy of the situation, Douglass nonetheless recast the history of the struggle against slavery in terms that acknowledged Lincoln but placed his contributions within the context of the social movement. Douglass surely turned the heads of listeners when he observed that Lincoln was "pre-eminently the white man's President, entirely devoted to the welfare of white men" and that black Americans were "at best only his stepchildren, children by adoption, children by force of circumstances and necessity."[7] He frankly admitted that many of Lincoln's early actions left black Americans "stunned, grieved and greatly bewildered; but our hearts believed while they ached and bled." "Despite the mist and the haze that surrounded him; despite the tumult, the hurry and confusion of the hour," Douglass explained, "we saw him, measured him, and estimated him," concluding "that the hour and the man of our redemption had met in the person of Abraham Lincoln."[8]

After Lincoln's announcement of the Emancipation Proclamation, Douglass elaborated, "we were thenceforth willing to allow the President all the latitude of time" necessary to achieve "liberty and progress." The process was bound to be convoluted and perhaps halting as well. When "viewed from the genuine abolition ground," he concluded, "Mr. Lincoln seemed tardy, cold, dull, and indifferent; but measuring him by the sentiment of his country, a sentiment he was bound as a statesman to consult, he was swift, zealous, radical and determined."[9] Arguing that "few great public men have ever been the victims of fiercer denunciation" than was Lincoln, Douglass predicted that "the silent judgment of time" would vindicate the sixteenth president: "Whatever else in this world may be partial, unjust and uncertain, *time! time!* is impartial, just and certain in its actions," Douglass insisted. Wesley followed suit, quoting the abolitionist: "No one can tell the day of the month, or the month of the year, upon which slavery was abolished in the United States"; rather, "the chains of slavery were loosened by degrees." Indeed, in a summary assessment of the "results of emancipation" two years after the close of the war, Salmon P. Chase, Oliver Otis Howard, and other members of the American Freedman's Union Commission observed that "emancipation in the United States was a growth rather than an enactment. The first act of war gave new vigor to the already strong anti-slavery sentiment of the North."[10]

Casting emancipation in these terms served a twofold purpose. First, it acknowledged the antislavery struggle that abolitionists and enslaved people had waged for decades. Second, it debunked the common myth that President Lincoln's Emancipation Proclamation of January 1, 1863, abolished slavery in a single stroke. Wesley theorized emancipation from the enslaved people's perspective. He characterized as "voluntary" those actions "in which the enslaved, working within their own framework of activity, sought freedom for themselves." "Involuntary" actions featured "individuals and social forces from without [that] operated to advance the cause of freedom." He parodied the conventional language that speakers and writers employed when addressing the subject—"'When Abraham Lincoln struck the shackles from the slaves', or 'Seventy-five years ago, when the Thirteenth Amendment brought freedom to the Negro'"—labeling such formulations as "oratorical outbursts" rather than statements of truth. He also dismissed "the stereotype of the suppliant slave who did not desire freedom and who would not strike a blow for his freedom" as an outdated approach to "writing the history of the Negro people."[11]

———

Most historical writing during the early decades of the twentieth century, in fact, gave short shrift to the notion that African Americans, whether enslaved or free, influenced the course of the nation's development as self-conscious and principled actors. A wave of recent interest in the phenomenon of historical memory has revealed how the late nineteenth- and early twentieth-century proponents of sectional reconciliation aimed to erase the importance of slavery in the events leading up to secession and war and of emancipation as one of the most significant results of the contest. Instead, these partisans depicted the loss of more than 600,000 lives as the product of a lamentable misunderstanding between Northerners and Southerners—white men, that is—that could best be remediated by nostalgic appeals to shared trials on the battlefield and a commitment to let bygones be bygones. Lurking just beneath the veneer of this reunited brotherhood was the nation's recent armed incursions onto the world stage that, among other things, resulted in the annexation of the Philippines and Puerto Rico after the Spanish-American War. Children of abolitionists joined forces with black and white anti-imperialists to protest American expansionism, elements of which looked strikingly similar to the imposition of racial segregation and disfranchisement in the American South. But for the advocates of sectional reconciliation, the apparent relationship was far from coincidental: many viewed empire and segregation as two sides of the same coin, a compromise in which the once-warring sections might reconcile. Then, as earlier, oppressed groups of persons with dark complexions at home and abroad became pawns in larger geopolitical schemes played by white men in the United States and Europe.[12]

During the Civil War, as enslaved people began asserting freedom and influencing the course of development of the Union's evolving emancipation policy, commentators from varying backgrounds and with varying motives explored the root causes of slavery's downfall. Then, as later, most showed little interest in understanding how enslaved and free African Americans contributed as historical actors in their own right rather than as passive objects of other people's actions. The wartime debate is instructive. Then, as later, a growing chorus of observers, who included clergymen, editors, elected officials, and political activists, black and white, credited President Lincoln with abolishing slavery. In April 1862, for instance, Illinois representative Owen Lovejoy spoke in favor of the revised Confiscation Act that was then under review. "If Abraham Lincoln pursues the path evidently pointed out for him in the providence of God," Lovejoy declared, he will become "the emancipator, the liberator" and thus commend himself to lasting fame on earth and in heaven.[13] The African Methodist Episcopal (AME) minister Henry McNeal Turner, like many other black leaders, also lauded Lincoln's role in charting slavery's course to extinction. From the time of the preliminary emancipation proclamation, Turner was convinced that Lincoln intended "to wage the war in favour of freedom, till the last groan of the anguished . . . slave shall be hushed."[14]

With due deference to Lincoln, a number of his contemporaries hoped that history would also acknowledge their parts in dismantling slavery, perhaps none more so than the prominent congressional Republicans who helped clear the path toward emancipation. Chief among them was Massachusetts senator Henry Wilson, a strong abolitionist known as the "Natick Cobbler" for his earlier stint in the shoemaking trade. Wilson published *History of the Antislavery Measures of the Thirty-Seventh and Thirty-Eighth United-States Congresses* in 1864, with an updated edition in 1865. Practically a day-by-day digest of debates over such key measures as the Confiscation Acts, the bill ending slavery in the District of Columbia, and the Thirteenth Amendment to the U.S. Constitution, Wilson's compilation explained what Republican lawmakers did to destroy slavery during the Civil War. Henry Wilson created one of the first chronologies of emancipation.

Given its origins and purpose, Wilson's account placed Congress rather than the president in the leading legislative role in abolishing slavery. To be sure, Wilson quoted liberally from the testimonials to Lincoln's leadership that his Republican colleagues delivered from the floors of Congress. Wilson also delighted in hoisting by their own petard congressional conservatives, particularly the senators and representatives from the Border Slave States that had remained within the Union (Delaware, Maryland, Kentucky, and Missouri), who worked so cunningly to protect slavery from criticism much less from any adverse legislation. Yet for all its value as a chronological record of official government actions, Wilson's account was a largely self-contained story of what happened within the Capitol, with only passing hints at the role of constituents' opinions in the stances congressmen and senators took on these pressing issues. *History of the Antislavery Measures* said nothing of African American influence on the legislative process, not even by such prominent activists as Frederick Douglass and other black abolitionists. It did not even reference the "Memorial Discourse" that the noted abolitionist and Presbyterian minister Henry Highland Garnet delivered before Congress in February 1865, the first such appearance by an African American speaker since the founding of the nation.[15]

Union generals extolled their roles in destroying slavery. For years after the war, General Benjamin F. Butler defended his "authorship" of the concept of "contraband of war" as the "theory of disposing of such captive slaves" as came into Union lines.[16] In mid-1864 General William T. Sherman casually remarked—somewhat immodestly, but no doubt correctly—that the armies under his command had "conducted to safe points more negroes than those of any General Officer in the Army." In the same breath he contended "that the treason and Rebellion of the Master, freed the Slave."[17] Many of Sherman's contemporaries agreed with his assessment. In April 1862, for instance, the Missourian John Brooks Henderson took the floor of the U.S. Senate amid the debate over the proposed Second Confiscation Act, which, among other things, proposed to free the slaves of all rebel sympathizers and not just those who had labored directly on behalf of the rebellion. "The shells that passed from rebel batteries to Fort Sumter twelve months ago," Henderson argued, "wrote [slavery's] doom in living letters upon the southern skies." The "authors of the war" set in motion the "sudden change in the labor and social systems of the country," for which they would have none but themselves to blame.[18]

General Daniel Ullmann, a prewar Whig politician from New York who had affiliated with the Know-Nothing movement during the nativist backlash of the 1850s, insisted that "the first gun that was fired at Fort Sumter sounded the death-knell of slavery." As he set about recruiting a brigade of black soldiers in Louisiana during the summer of 1863, he described the gunners as "the greatest practical abolitionists this nation has produced."[19] Robert Dale Owen, in the final report of the American Freedmen's Inquiry Commission (AFIC) issued a year later, cautioned his fellow Northerners not to "take credit to ourselves for generous philanthropy," for, by severing the Union, the Southern slaveholders "became the abolitionists of slavery." "Thus, in the providence of God," he insisted, "the very effort by armed treason to perpetuate an abuse has given us the will and the right to effect its eradication."[20]

Shortly before New Year's Day, 1863, General Nathaniel Banks addressed the people of Louisiana—a varied group whose Unionist segment consisted of persons of varying complexions, ethnic backgrounds, and degrees of loyalty to the United States—on the subject of emancipation. The president's much-anticipated proclamation had everyone on edge, but for different reasons. Unionist slaveholders took heart from Lincoln's earlier promise to exempt from the final decree states or parts of states that were no longer in active rebellion, but they wondered if federal authorities would continue to uphold slaveholders' rights. Free persons of color (the *gens de couleur libres*) and enslaved persons, who also supported the Union, feared that the exemption would grant a new lease on life to the wobbling institution of slavery thereby stymying their own aspirations for full freedom and citizenship rights. Mixing politics, history, and philosophy, Banks situated contemporary events in a providential context. Although "the War is not waged by the Government for the overthrow of slavery," he explained, "violence and war will inevitably bring it to an end":

> The first gun at Sumter proclaimed emancipation. The continuance of the contest there commenced will consummate that end, and the history of the age will leave no other permanent trace of the rebellion. Its leaders will have accomplished what other men could not have done. The boldest Abolitionist is a cypher when compared with the leaders of the rebellion. What mystery pervades the work of Providence! We submit to its decrees, but stand confounded at the awful manifestations of its wisdom and power! The great problem of the age, apparently environed with labyrinthic complications, is likely to be suddenly lifted out of human hands. We may control the incidence of the contest, but we cannot circumvent or defeat the end.[21]

The Virginian John M. Washington, who escaped from slavery at Fredericksburg and took refuge with the Yankees in April 1862, described the Confederate bombardment of Fort Sumter as "the Death-knell of Slavery."[22]

In January 1865, the freed citizens of Memphis held a parade to celebrate the second anniversary of the Emancipation Proclamation; one of the banners read: "Jeff. Davis, the great Abolitionist."[23] At a Union meeting in New York two months later, Congressman Gilbert Dean distinguished between theoretical and practical abolitionists, saying that "for thirty years" the theorists "talked and never acted," whereas the "practical abolitionists residing south of Mason and Dixon . . . by their madness and folly, [and] their crimes" essentially destroyed slavery. "Since Moses, four thousand years ago, stood upon the cliffs of the Red Sea, with his 2,500,000 Hebrews rescued from bondage," Dean concluded, "there has been no abolitionist in history, equal to Jefferson Davis." Lest his sarcasm disguise his true intentions, Dean added that "this is a Government of white men, and should not and shall not be destroyed for the sake of the African."[24] In his view and that of many of his white fellow countrymen, abolishing slavery threatened the future of the very same white republic that the secessionists had hope to preserve by placing slavery beyond the reach of government action. The possibilities circled back on themselves, like the proverbial snake eating its own tail.

A former U.S. congressman from Virginia used similar terminology to capture the frustration that he and other slaveholding Unionists experienced as they watched the bitter fruits of secession mature. John M. Botts described the antislavery stalwarts William Lloyd Garrison and Wendell Phillips as mere "*theoretical abolitionists.*" "The *practical abolitionists,* who have done more in *three years* for the abolition of Slavery, than the theoretical abolitionists could have done in *three thousand*," were Jefferson Davis, William L. Yancey, and Robert Toombs. They and other such champions of secession were "the great *Aarchitects* of *mischief and ruin*."[25] Unionist slaveholders could do little more than shake their heads in disbelief.

From the start, most Northern observers understood the link between secession and the outbreak of hostilities, but they hesitated to admit that saving the Union might require making war on slavery. At the extremes, Conservative Democrats rejected emancipation even out of military necessity, while the most radical Republicans welcomed the prospect. Middle-of-the-road Unionists accepted abolition as a by-product of the conflict, a necessary step to quash the rebellion. By the end of the war, persons of all political persuasions acknowledged the role of black soldiers in achieving victory, but the public mind remained divided as to whether that service purchased full citizenship including the right to vote. For their part, former slaveholders and the staunchest supporters of secession rejected both the premises of emancipation and its concrete manifestations. By the 1870s, as Northerners' interest in supporting political, economic, and civil rights of the freed people waned, proponents of intersectional peace gained political ascendancy. By the turn of the twentieth century, even white progressives in the South acquiesced in the conservatives' legislative program of racial segregation and disfranchisement, and white Northerners looked the other way, effectively agreeing that Reconstruction was a failed experiment in "Negro rule," to which the legally sanctioned subordination of African Americans was the appropriate fix.

————

In his 1940 remarks about the end of slavery, Charles Wesley's reference to the proper manner of "writing the history of the Negro people" struck a sympathetic chord among his listeners at Howard University, who were well aware of the work of black authors who contested popular racist myths with meticulous historical scholarship. Two particularly notable examples were W. E. B. Du Bois, the erudite scholar-activist who edited *The Crisis* (the monthly organ of the National Association for the Advancement of Colored People [NAACP]), and Carter G. Woodson, the prolific author and editor of the *Journal of Negro History*, which he founded in 1916. Du Bois's masterful *Black Reconstruction* (1935) affirmed the role of black Southerners in helping to undermine slavery and defeat the Confederacy by engaging in a "general strike" and enlisting in the U.S. Army. The book also challenged the work of the two leading scholars of Reconstruction, the historian William Archibald Dunning and the political scientist John W. Burgess, both of Columbia University. With their students, the two portrayed Reconstruction as a time when opportunist Northern carpetbaggers and Southern scalawags led impressionable freedmen in an orgy of incompetence, greed, and corruption. Like Woodson and his protégés, such as Alrutheus A. Taylor, Du Bois intended to overturn the prevailing public orthodoxy about Reconstruction; he emphasized the positive contributions of the Republican coalition governments in the former Confederate states and credited black Americans with helping to save the Union and advance the cause of freedom. Wesley also contributed to the revisionist work with insightful monographs on black labor and the collapse of the Confederacy.[26]

In short, by the eve of World War II, black scholars had established the foundation for understanding emancipation as central rather than peripheral to the war. Without disparaging the roles of other historical actors, such as Lincoln, Republican congressional stalwarts such as Charles Sumner and Thaddeus Stevens, and the military strategists Grant and Sherman, these revisionists highlighted the contributions black people made to achieving victory and destroying slavery. Viewed properly, they insisted, emancipation was a social movement involving unheralded thousands of enslaved people. After World War II, the pace and volume of antiracist scholarship increased exponentially, buoyed by the success of the struggles against segregation in the United States and against European colonialism in Africa, Asia, and the Caribbean. John Hope Franklin's *From Slavery to Freedom* (1947) constituted a major milestone in that effort.[27] Franklin proposed a framework for conceptualizing all of African American history, from the pre-enslavement experience in Africa to the contemporary United States, the unifying theme of which was the quest for freedom and equality. The struggle that Franklin chronicled achieved notable success during the Civil War and Reconstruction, only to endure the setbacks of disfranchisement and segregation by the turn of the twentieth century. After the defeat of Germany and Japan in 1945, the struggle against racial oppression in the United States gained momentum, buoyed in part by the active participation of African Americans in the armed forces during the war and by the worldwide anticolonial movement.

As the sesquicentennial of Lincoln's birth in 1959 and the centennial of the Civil War in 1961 approached, this scholarship began to bear on the official commemorations being planned to mark those anniversaries. Somewhat ironically, during the centennial observance of Lincoln's birth in 1909, black activists bucked the national tide of sectional reconciliation and insisted that a proper acknowledgment of his legacy required understanding his role as emancipator, but the claim fell on deaf ears. Fifty years later, the postwar world presented a different configuration of political ideas and imperatives. The appearance of Benjamin Quarles's *The Negro in the Civil War* (1953) and *Lincoln and the Negro* (1962), as well as John Hope Franklin's *The*

Emancipation Proclamation (1963), respectfully yet firmly suggested that the view of the Civil War as a contest between persons of European ancestry who disagreed over states' rights would no longer suffice. Slavery was the heart of the matter, they argued, and black people, free and enslaved, threw their collective might into influencing the outcome.[28]

The Allied victory in World War II also gave new life to the belief that the United States was unique, favored by God as an example for all the world—a city on a hill—destined for greatness. From that vantage point, the entire national history could be cast within the single framework of progress unfolding in linear fashion through time. Although Franklin's *From Slavery to Freedom* appeared to endorse this view, it did so with a twist, describing how advancement often came at the expense of African-descended people and how their recurring struggles for freedom and equality contradicted the simple view of never-ending improvement. In short, his work signaled an inflection point wherein postwar historians examined the nation's past as something more than a chronicle of glory etched in the actions of the Founding Fathers and presidents. They argued instead for understanding the historical process as a democratic enterprise in which "anonymous" persons contributed as actors and not just as objects.[29] This approach soon came to be characterized as "history from the bottom up" or "social history."

One of the major byproducts of this new approach to historical interpretation was the creation in 1976 of the Freedmen and Southern Society Project (FSSP), a research and publication effort focused on Civil War emancipation as revealed in government records preserved at the National Archives. Most notable were those of the War Department, which, besides the documents generated by field armies during the war and Reconstruction, included the voluminous records of the Bureau of Refugees, Freedmen and Abandoned Lands, or Freedmen's Bureau. Material that documented the actions of other executive agencies, including the Treasury Department, as well as the legislative and judicial branches of government, also held the promise of creating a rich portrait of slavery and its demise during the rebellion.[30] Under the original direction of Ira Berlin and more recently that of Leslie S. Rowland, the FSSP has decisively shaped scholarship on the subject thanks largely to six letterpress volumes published under the general title of *Freedom: A Documentary History of Emancipation, 1861–1867* and several other derivative works.[31] Combining interpretive essays with annotated documents, each volume of *Freedom* explores a facet of emancipation, illustrating both the complexity of the process and the central role that formerly enslaved people played. Among other things, the volumes of *Freedom* offer strong support for points that Wesley and Du Bois, Woodson and Taylor, and Quarles and Franklin had articulated decades before and that the revisionist scholarship inspired by the Civil Rights Movement was busy reaffirming. The work of the FSSP has inspired hundreds of publications that stretch interpretive boundaries surrounding the collapse of slavery in directions that could hardly have been predicted forty years ago. And the work continues to inspire.

————

My analysis begins with the simple assertion that emancipation was a complex and uneven process rather than a specific event, and that it drew into its vortex as historical actors from all regions of the country and backgrounds, most significantly enslaved Southerners and free African Americans in the North as well as the South. Although the appearance of the early volumes of *Freedom* understandably prompted a foray into clarifying "who freed the slaves," this preoccupation has not fully spent itself despite having reached the point of diminishing returns exactly where Charles Wesley summarized the case in 1940.[32] Finding meaning in what individuals and groups did in the midst of these unsettling changes requires an appreciation of contingency in the human experience and the imperfect reliability of individual and collective memory.[33]

Attempts to describe the process may benefit from a conventional chronological approach that identifies signs of change over time and then seeks to understand the explanatory causes. As recent work on emancipation demonstrates, there is still much to learn this way.[34] But some promising recent scholarship has departed fruitfully from those strictures. By crossing traditional boundaries chronologically, geographically, or conceptually, this work—which includes important contributions by veterans of the FSSP—has produced new levels of understanding with regard to the war and its consequences and the role of African Americans' political action in influencing the course of their own history and that of the entire nation.[35] Even such a niche area as the black military and naval experience has proved a fertile source of new approaches and conclusions.[36]

I remain fascinated with the comparative study of emancipation, which continues to yield the rich insights that it has since the debut of the journal *Slavery & Abolition* in 1980.[37] An intriguing array of comparative models that scholars have recently devised offers new ways to conceptualize events throughout the North American continent during the Civil War era. On the one hand are those that examine communities on either side of the boundary lines dividing the United States from the Confederate States, and on the other hand are those that compare developments on the Great Plains and in the far West with the those within the conventional framework of the Northern Union and the Southern Confederacy. These works not only require reassessing the meanings of emancipation in light of the experiences of Native Americans, Mexican Americans, and Chinese immigrants in the territory between the Mississippi River and the Pacific Ocean but also call for a fresh look at the process of national consolidation following the Civil War.[38] Recent works on the literature and imagery of war also provide fascinating insights into the period and the overriding issues, as have recent examinations of such iconic events as Lee's surrender at Appomattox and Lincoln's assassination.[39]

The recent scholarship most relevant to the perspective I have adopted here stretches beyond, while not necessarily abandoning, the FSSP's concentration on the breakdown of slavery and the development of compensated labor. The prevalence of disease and death offers one such window, as does the focus on time, personal mobility, the physical and environmental destruction wrought by the war, the legacy of violence that derived from slavery and emancipation, and risk.[40] Some of the most fascinating examples of this work address emancipation from oblique angles as represented, for instance, by collections of essays on "weirding the war" and "disrupting the history of emancipation."[41]

For twenty-first-century observers, understanding the customs and habits from 150 years ago requires suspending conventional beliefs, particularly with regard to appreciating the depth and breadth of slavery's influence in the nation at that time. In the slaveholding states, apologists for the institution included enslavers, factors, politicians, scholars, editors, and ministers, most of whom stoutly defended it as a positive good and not simply a necessary evil.[42] Even non-slaveholding whites had long since dulled their senses to the sights and sounds of human bondage. Slavery, after all, was a given feature of the world into which they had been born and socialized. Northern visitors to any one of the slave states might have encountered slavery on full, even violent, display. Residents of various places in the Northern states, including the border cities of Philadelphia and Cincinnati, and visitors to the resorts and military installations that dotted the region from the Atlantic Ocean to the Mississippi valley heartland and beyond might have observed enslaved servants attending to their owners on business or on vacation. Yet for most white Northerners, slavery remained an abstraction, at least until Harriet Beecher Stowe's *Uncle Tom's Cabin*, which portrayed the institution in terms that resonated as real. Its appearance in serial form in 1851 and in book form the following year created a sensation. Stowe brilliantly captured the growing sense of discomfort with slavery that many white Northerners had begun to experience for reasons that ranged from the religious to the political.

Despite the growing polarization between the two sections, neither the outbreak of war nor the destruction of slavery was its preordained outcome. Events unfolded within parameters shaped by existing circumstances, which in their constant changes presented new opportunities and constraints. Had the Confederacy succeeded in fighting to a standstill, or had the 1864 Democratic candidate for president, George B. McClellan, defeated Lincoln, slavery would likely have persisted for years, maybe decades, beyond 1865 within an independent Confederacy or a reconciled Union. And the questions that began to arise in 1863 regarding "a new birth of freedom" and the prospects of black citizenship would have generated very different answers.

It is sobering to recall that more than two-thirds of the 4 million enslaved persons in 1860 remained unfree at war's end. Of the one-third who had escaped slavery, perhaps 1.1 million enjoyed direct federal protection: nearly 400,000 persons (including soldiers) in Union-held areas of the rebel states, another 500,000 in the Border States, Tennessee, and southern Louisiana where they had gained legal freedom late in the war; and perhaps 200,000 as servants and laborers with armies in the field. It is likely that at least another 200,000 enslaved persons died during the war. The estimated 2.6 million still in bondage constituted 66 percent of all enslaved persons in 1860 and more than 80 percent of the 3.5 million in the states that left the Union. Moreover, slaveholders in out-of-the-way places often succeeded in keeping their laborers in slave-like conditions for months thereafter until federal authorities succeeded in rooting out the last surviving pockets of the old order. Some of these persons had interacted with federal armed forces during the war, perhaps even tasting freedom for a time. But even those who never laid eyes on the Yankees understood that a Northern victory would mean drastic changes in their lives. In any case, they had little practical experience with freedom before the collapse of the Confederacy. They began to acclimate themselves to changes with which their counterparts in the Union-occupied portions of the Confederacy had grappled for several years to various ends. In that process, they, too, learned how decisively local conditions shaped the encounters between the past and the future.

The effort to extract patterns and to assign meaning must be sensitive to the fact that the several million enslaved persons who gained freedom in the process of emancipation each had a story. At the same time, the full picture was more than just the sum of the parts. Secession and the ensuing rebellion set loose a many-sided struggle in which all participants hoped to achieve objectives that, whether they coincided or clashed, remained in flux. In pursuing their goals, historical actors often risked their lives and, indeed, hundreds of thousands lost theirs, not all on the fields of battle.

In the pages that follow, I propose three overlapping frameworks whereby members of the Civil War generation attempted both to understand and to help chart a way through the extraordinary events that swirled around them daily. The first two were time and space, which historians no less than historical actors routinely employ for interpretive purposes. Mid-nineteenth-century Americans—like human populations everywhere—observed and recorded the passage of time in several ways. They relied on the ancient technique of noting the movements of celestial bodies by day and by night and from one day to the next. They also used modern devices such as clocks and calendars. They understood that events in the world around them followed an inexorable chronology, which mimicked the linear trajectory of living things from birth to death and, for Christians, the history of salvation from Adam and Eve to the anticipated second coming of Christ. But time might also be tracked cyclically—by the succession of seasons that accompanied the earth's annual revolution around the sun—rather than linearly. Time could even behave erratically, appearing to slow down, speed up, and even stop. War and social revolution proved to be the nurseries of erratic time.

Mid-nineteenth-century Americans oriented themselves spatially in multiple ways as well. First, they relied on known features of the natural and built environments. That approach worked best in their local communities and in adjacent regions with which they were familiar. Beyond such comfort zones, they had to rely on more generic markers such as the position of objects in the night sky, the lay of the land, patterns of natural and cultivated vegetation, and such human modifications to the landscape as turnpikes and railroads. Literate persons might also resort to maps. Yet in the context of war, even the most familiar spaces from which persons may not have wandered often took on new meaning and significance, fraught with peril and promise. Effective navigation of open spaces relied implicitly on knowledge of the social environments that coexisted with the physical ones. Nowhere was this clearer than in the second variety of spatial awareness—that which concerned the restricted spaces in which enslaved persons interacted with the persons who claimed them as property. In the planter's big house, the small farmer's cabin, the merchant's stock room, or the artisan's workshop, masters and mistresses exercised close oversight, and both short-term and long-term interests of the enslaved people required a nimble awareness of the changing dynamics. Finally, like time, space might possess malleable properties that the war exposed and that emancipation magnified. A specific parcel of land might be a scene of oppression, liberation, or death based on which party exerted armed jurisdiction over it. Bodies of water assumed new significance as gateways or barriers to freedom.

The third strategic framework or reference point was home, which teemed with literal and figurative meanings. The concept of home promised a sense of familiarity and stability to counterbalance the swirling sensations of time and place set loose by the war.[43] Through the interpretive lens of home, historical actors could view their actions within contexts that radiated throughout society: from the individual and family, through the neighborhood, to the social and political institutions that constituted the national fabric. The term "home" had particular relevance for enslaved people. Prior to the war, it consisted of the land and the buildings in the possession of the "master" as well as the patriarchal household that was the social foundation of the master-slave relationship. The antebellum home might also refer to a dwelling, which, however spartan in its construction and appurtenances, might still offer some respite from the oppression of the surrounding world. Home might also signify memories of childhood or of loved ones left behind in Maryland, Virginia, or the Carolinas. But, like time and space, home could also prove to be an insecure mooring. As wartime circumstances threatened homes in both literal and figurative senses, opportunities to seek a new home presented themselves, but rarely without associated challenges. Breaking free of slavery's chains required fending for oneself (and perhaps for other family members as well) without the "master's" protection. It meant venturing into unknown and potentially dangerous space.

In communities throughout the South, residents knew of individual cases and sometimes entire families that had made the transition from slavery to freedom.[44] Local lore also recorded the names of persons who had freed themselves and followed the North Star to the North or Canada. With the start of the war, advancing armed forces of the United States presented the possibility for an entirely new conception of home, one that combined personal freedom, compensated labor, and, with that, the chance to achieve self-sufficiency. Even without a clear pathway to full citizenship, the prospects of federal protection alone redefined the relationship of black persons to the national government. The United States might yet prove to be a national home instead of simply a site for the continuing oppression of its residents of African descent.

After the war, the South's antebellum ruling elite refused to abandon the goal of confining African Americans to the status of perpetually subordinate laborers—its vision of an ideal home that secession aimed to realize. When former slaveholders did not actively resist the effort of federal authorities to establish a system of compensated labor and to secure life and property and protect the citizenship rights of the freed people, they bided their time for what they confidently predicted would be the Yankees' return to the North.

Often assuming the posture of prodigal sons and daughters they feigned contrition and regained much of their prewar property (particularly the land) and many of their prewar prerogatives. Long before the end of Reconstruction and the cessation of federal oversight, they set about devising new methods of exploitation and oppression. As a result, most freed people and their descendants remained propertyless laborers whose quest for economic independence, political influence commensurate with their share of the population, and an equal chance in the race of life faced an uphill battle at best. This "counter-revolution of property," as Du Bois characterized the post-Reconstruction compromise, re-created a culture of exploitation and oppression that has dogged African Americans in the states of the former Confederacy and in the Northern and Western states to which they relocated during the great migrations of the twentieth century. It has exerted a racially inspired, deeply conservative influence on local and national politics for the 150 years since the end of slavery.[45]

———

Given the emphasis I place on the testimony of formerly enslaved people in understanding wartime emancipation, a few words of explanation about some of its forms are warranted here. The documents produced by the federal government (particularly those of the armed forces and administrative agencies that operated in the Confederacy and the Loyal Border States during and immediately after the war) contain a treasure trove of information about black Southerners. In addition to their sheer volume, their proximity to the events they describe, and their wealth of personal information, these records also possess another virtue. When taking testimony from African American informants, many bearing the fresh marks of slavery, agents of the federal government generally rendered the transcriptions using standard grammar, syntax, spelling, and punctuation without any embellishments designed to portray Southern black dialect.

Such transcriptions contrast sharply with those of contemporary newspaper reporters, who, like antebellum visitors to the South, frequently employed the stylized conventions of nonstandard English, with which the popular press and minstrel shows had lampooned African Americans for generations. During the Great Depression of the 1930s, the Federal Writers Project breathed new life into those conventions in its typed transcriptions of conversations with thousands of formerly enslaved people. All but a handful of the writers and editors used contrived spellings ("wuz" for "was," to cite a common example) and other such devices to create a visual image of inferior speech that the spoken words themselves did not convey. In quoting from such documents, I have at times made slight alterations to minimize the possibility of distracting from the larger value of the observation, in which case I describe the change in the corresponding note. For most such quotations, I have left the grammar and spelling that appears in the source document unchanged.

Documents produced by literate black correspondents present a related but not identical challenge. Although almost always employing conventional forms to open and close their letters ("I seat myself and take my pen in hand to drop you a few lines . . ." and "Your most humble and obedient servant . . ."), the writers often used nonstandard spelling and punctuation that suggests their newness to communicating via the written word. If at times the words appear strange to the modern eye, reading them aloud adds the reinforcement of the voice and the ear to get the gist of the writer's intention, an exercise that rarely goes unrewarded. The combined senses of eyes, voice, and ears also reveal the cadence of mid-nineteenth-century speech and the similes and metaphors that speakers routinely employed. I draw liberally from such documents, and particularly those published in the *Freedom* volumes, following the editorial conventions regarding spelling and punctuation that guided the preparation of the original manuscripts for publication.[46]

I note here, too, my dependence on certain individuals for consistently insightful observations on the rapidly changing world around them. Especially notable in this regard are Edward L. Pierce, the young Boston attorney who figured prominently in the early experiments in compensated labor that federal authorities undertook at Fort Monroe, Virginia, beginning in the summer of 1861 and at Port Royal, South Carolina, beginning in the fall of 1861, and the Reverend Henry McNeal Turner, a freeborn South Carolinian who affiliated with the AME Church during the 1850s and who served as chaplain of the First U.S. Colored Infantry from its organization in 1863 through its demobilization two years later. Throughout his long career, Turner stood as one of the nation's most outspoken advocates for African American rights. Two formerly enslaved persons who left postwar memoirs also provide key insights into emancipation's complexity and uncertainty. The first is Louis Hughes, a Virginia-born man who was sold to a Mississippi planter when a young adult; and the second is Mattie J. Jackson, who at the start of the war was an enslaved teenager in St. Louis. Both of these narrators left detailed, often heart-stopping, accounts of their struggles to become free amid the dangers and uncertainties of war. The experiences of Turner, Hughes, and Jackson provide checkpoints and counterpoints to the linear chronology of emancipation depicted by official government actions.

I also return for various interpretive purposes to several key areas of the Union-occupied Confederacy that presented different ideological and operational challenges to the federal program of revamping the slave South and that have long served scholars who wish to understand the associated histori-cal processes. Besides the small enclaves of Fort Monroe and Port Royal, the vast expanse of the Mississippi valley between Memphis and New Orleans also figures prominently. Not coincidentally, the region drew the special at-tention of members of the AFIC. The rich documentary evidence from all the regions under U.S. administrative authority invites analysis from various per-spectives; imagining it as the multicolored pieces inside a kaleidoscope, I explore the different interpretive possibilities that result from a simple turn of the wrist. Twisting further, I also peer into what enslaved people experi-enced in areas under Confederate authority where the old order continued to function, even if not strictly according to prewar conventions.

———

Longtime participants in the antislavery struggle knew that perseverance required faith. After all, the struggle for freedom, as John Hope Franklin noted in a related context, could produce "illusions of equality."[47] Only in ret-rospect from the day that Charles Wesley commemorated—December 18, 1865—did a constitutional amendment abolishing slavery throughout the nation appear to be the outcome of what began at Fort Sumter four years earlier. In between, participants may or may not have witnessed what looked like the end of slavery. If they did, the collapse did not necessarily occur in one fell swoop but in a series of incremental movements, backward as well as for-ward, some more fleeting than others. Few, if any, pointed unmistakably to the Thirteenth Amendment's declaration that "neither slavery nor involun-tary servitude, except as a punishment for crime whereof the party shall have been duly convicted, shall exist within the United States, or any place subject to their jurisdiction."[48] Staring into the future from December 18, 1865, pre-sented equal uncertainty: the challenge of implementing the freedom that the amendment referenced only indirectly as the presumed antithesis of "slavery" and "involuntary servitude." This book examines the collapse of slavery through the sometimes clear and sometimes foggy lenses with which con-temporaries saw their world. It explores the illusory aspects of emancipation that often perplexed participants and witnesses at the time and later observ-ers alike.

As years passed and the Civil War generation reflected back on events of that time, their memories often left them confused at how the nominal vic-tors so quickly shied away from the implications of the victory and their ob-ligations to the hundreds of thousands of black warriors whose loyalty helped ensure that outcome. Persons born after the war, who did not experience the long-repressed joy and seemingly endless promise associated with the dawn of freedom, had to rely on the memories of prior generations. Collectively they strove to see through the distortions of segregation and disfranchisement to preserve awareness of the time when the federal government stood as the champion of freedom and equality and not just an idle spectator to lynching and other unspeakable acts of injustice. Those who had not witnessed the early fruits of emancipation might well have presumed that a regime of violent oppression over millions of nominal citizens had been present for all time, a seamless continuation between nineteenth-century slavery and twentieth-century segregation. Little wonder that the question repeatedly arose whether the Union's victory over the Confederacy left any lasting accomplishments or whether it, too, was an illusion.

As to whether the Civil War destroyed slavery, the following pages will show that the answer is a qualified yes. The defeat of the rebellion abolished slavery but neither exploitation nor discrimination based on race. By the same token, Radical Reconstruction achieved some notable success in guaranteeing the political rights of all citizens, but not, as events soon showed, in placing them beyond assault. And the revolutionary momentum stopped well short of redressing the unequal distribution of wealth between black and white Americans that began with slavery and continues to this day. As a result, the expectations associated with what freedom meant in principle and what it constituted in practice gave rise to a recurring cycle of hope and frustration. The gains that were achieved and then lost, the promises that were made and then broken, and the pleasant dreams that devolved into nightmares could appear as surreal. These were the phantoms of freedom, the illusions of emancipation.

PART I

Time

At first glance, time appears as a natural framework for understanding emancipation. Like the other significant milestones of the Civil War era—Abraham Lincoln's election, the firing on Fort Sumter, Robert E. Lee's surrender—key events in the history of slavery's demise, such as the Emancipation Proclamation and the Thirteenth Amendment to the U.S. Constitution, may be usefully depicted along a chronological time line. Time lines display events in linear relationship with each other along a continuum that extends from the past through the present and into the future. They contain discrete units (hours, days, months, years) of agreed-on lengths, which follow each other methodically. The time-keeping conventions that are taken for granted today are the product of several thousands of years of development, during which societies found the need to track time ever more carefully for liturgical and dynastic purposes. Such conventions also served to record the births, the deaths, and other such milestones in the lives of individuals. In the context of Civil War emancipation, the personal narratives whereby enslaved people recalled their deliverance from slavery to freedom often employed conventions of linear time.

The ability to reckon time accurately and to situate events in temporal relationship to each other gained value during the Age of Revolutions that began in the late eighteenth century. Understanding time and carefully measuring its passage, like other advances in knowledge that characterized the period, enabled the politically marginalized middle class (whose members included scientists as well as businessmen) to challenge the monopoly of knowledge that the clergy and the nobility had possessed for centuries. The full flowering of these scientific advances late in the eighteenth century helped usher in the era of industrial capitalism. During the twentieth century, harnessing the minute movements at the level of individual atoms enabled accuracy far beyond what mechanical or electric timepieces were capable of achieving. The search for ever greater precision continues.[1] Yet clocks and watches are not the only way to observe and record the passage of time.[2]

The apparent linearity of time undergoes cyclical or seasonal variations, which early humans learned from observation long before subsequent generations developed scientific explanations. Most of North America, including the areas of the southern latitudes that witnessed most of the clashes between the armed forces of the United States and the Confederate States, experiences seasonal differences in ambient temperatures and hours of sunlight as the earth rotates around the sun. Over the four seasons of spring, summer, autumn, and winter, these changes affect the circadian rhythms of all living things. Whether in cities or on farms or amid the open plains and mountains, the continent's flora and fauna no less than its human inhabitants respond to these seasonal changes. Measuring and recording the passage of time by the meteorological seasons antedated both calendars and clocks, and the practice continued even as the practitioners carried watches on their persons and tacked mass-produced calendars onto walls.

Emancipation in the context of war generated revolutionary changes that made mincemeat of both linear and cyclical concepts of time. The mobilization for war and its prosecution created personal and social dislocations that the breakdown of slavery often magnified. This produced a widespread sensation that time behaved erratically, alternately speeding up, slowing down, even stopping, amid unprecedented events that seared themselves into participants' and observers' memories forever. Seeing through the distortions requires looking not just backward in time but also sideways into time—in laboratory terminology, cutting cross sections into it. These views reveal that time did not conform to the expected pattern of uniform units following one another in linear fashion even though time often displayed such characteristics. In short, time may be irregular, messy, and unpredictable as well as straightforward and evenly paced. No wonder that the concept of time lends itself to so many idiomatic and metaphorical uses. One of the most common examples, *tempus fugit*, a staple of Latin-influenced languages and cultures for more than two millennia, suggests time's apparent ability to fly.[3] At once precise and vague, linear and circular, fast and slow moving, the passage of time also bore the influence of such powers as secular spirits of the age and of Divine Providence. Over the course of the war, participants and observers alike increasingly viewed human events in the context of providential time described in the Old and New Testaments of the Christian Bible. Present-day studies have begun to reveal that not only in metaphorical terms did time appear to behave erratically: biochemical processes, particularly those related to the circulation of hormones in times of stress, create real sensations of time behaving erratically. What many observers then and since have seen in simplistic terms as a series of events that played out in sequential, chronological time misses how time awareness affects human actions, how human beings account for the passage of time, and how they record into memory events that occur during extraordinary periods such as disasters, wars, and social revolutions.[4]

Understanding emancipation requires more than abandoning the still-popular belief that it consisted of a single event, such as Lincoln's Emancipation Proclamation, or even a process that involved a series of related events that occurred in a linear sequence between Lincoln's inauguration in March 1861 and the ratification of the Thirteenth Amendment in December 1865. The three chapters of this section explore the collapse of slavery through the lenses of chronological or linear time, seasonal or recurring time, and erratic or revolutionary time.

Chapter 1

Linear Chronology

Slavery came to an end during the Civil War not in a specific event at a single moment but in a tumultuous process that began before the shooting started and continued long after the Confederate surrender. Yet the main markers along the imagined road to freedom occurred in four years between 1861 and 1865—which contemporaries viewed as either a remarkably short or an agonizingly long span of time. They include Fort Sumter; the congressional Confiscation Acts; the Emancipation Proclamation; the organization of the U.S. Colored Troops; the Union's victories at Vicksburg, Gettysburg, and Atlanta; General Robert E. Lee's surrender; and the ratification of the Thirteenth Amendment. For all their explanatory usefulness, such chronologies of events are inherently prone to mislead, creating a false impression that emancipation unfolded in stepwise fashion, even if unevenly, over the course of the war. To be sure, understanding the past requires the use of appropriate analytical frameworks, not the least of which is the chronological sequencing of events. Linear time—which is marked by clocks and calendars and measured in minutes, hours, days, months, and years—provides a good and, to all appearances, a natural starting point.[1]

The chronology of slavery's collapse between 1860 and 1865 fits into a national and an international context of emancipation that spanned more than a hundred years from the mid-eighteenth century into the late nineteenth. Official actions of government bodies, such as the court orders, laws, and constitutions of the various states of the fledgling United States during the American Revolution and in the years after, offer key markers in this history. In the British West Indies, to illustrate the point further, Parliament accelerated the process that was begun in 1833, declaring a final end to slavery in 1838 in no small measure owing to fears of unrest among the prime beneficiaries of emancipation—sugar plantation workers. When the African-descended population in the French colony of Saint-Domingue took up the revolutionary fervor of the colonial metropole in 1791, few could have predicted that by 1804 the armies of France and Britain would have failed to suppress the rebels and restore slavery and that Haiti would take its place among the independent nations of the world. During the 1870s and 1880s, the tidal wave of emancipation rolled over the last bastions of African slavery in the Americas: Cuba and Brazil.[2]

Observers of a secular mind-set in all the nations of Europe and the Americas described this trend as the progressive spirit of the age. Guided by reason, they posited, human civilization's long struggle to rise above barbarism succeeded in weakening, if not overturning, two institutions with deep historical roots. The first, hereditary monarchy, had been thrown on the defensive during the American and French Revolutions of the late eighteenth century and then assaulted anew in the revolutions and uprisings across Europe during the first half of the nineteenth century that crested in 1848. The second was slavery, the ancient practice that had won a new lease on life during the age of merchant capitalism, which began during the fifteenth century when European nations spread their influence around the world. By the late eighteenth century, a combination of economic and moral critiques of the system placed its adherents on the defensive, but the advent of industrial capitalism enabled the architects of slave-grown commodity production to thrive as never before. Over the next hundred years, abolitionist movements mounted successful campaigns against, first, the Atlantic trade in captured Africans and then race-based slavery throughout the Americas. Meanwhile, the planter classes of the American South, Cuba, and Brazil gained political sophistication commensurate with their economic clout, even as republican movements in Europe alternately flared and fizzled.[3] The path to this outcome was neither direct nor smooth, as those who pursued the goals of power and profits through slavery well understood. To be sure, the liberal economic and political philosophy that underpinned capitalist expansion held firmly to the belief in the superiority of liberty over restraint across a wide spectrum of human behavior, including the social relations whereby owners of capital retained laborers to produce valued commodities and thereby generate wealth. But neither the narrative arc of "The Age of Emancipation" nor the chronology of events in any one of the polities where slavery came to an end during the nineteenth century supports the notion of a steady march to extinction.

———

Perhaps no example illustrates the surface simplicity and the underlying complexity—in short, the strengths and the flaws—of a strictly chronological account of emancipation better than the iconic event that generations of Americans have associated with it: President Abraham Lincoln's Emancipation Proclamation of January 1, 1863. Although contemporary critics faulted its limited immediate impact on slavery in Confederate-held areas, it nonetheless established a new commitment on the part of the federal government to abolish slavery, and Lincoln's words traveled far beyond the reach of federal armed forces.[4] The one hundred days between September 22, 1862, when

Lincoln publicly announced the government's new policy of emancipation, and January 1, 1863, when the policy became official, were filled with anticipation and not just on the part of African Americans. Northern Democrats and not a few moderate Republicans questioned the constitutionality and the propriety of emancipation, even under the pretext of military necessity. Conservatives feared that Lincoln's assault on human property posed a threat to property rights of every kind, everywhere. For others, emancipation raised the specter of a mass uprising of the enslaved that might overspill the Confederate States and inundate the North. Soldiers and sailors might abandon the service rather than risk their lives on behalf of the slaves. Fears of the proclamation's possible impact on Unionism in the Border States—to include not just Delaware, Maryland, Kentucky, and Missouri, where slavery was still legal, but also the tier of states just north of the Mason and Dixon Line and the Ohio River—was not misplaced.[5]

The proclamation unmasked hidden fears about the future of its intended beneficiaries: roughly 3.5 million enslaved persons in the Confederate States. If large numbers of refugees, many of whom were destitute and ill as a result of slavery and the war, decided to move to the North to enjoy the fruits of freedom, a political uproar would certainly result. In a spring 1862 speech denouncing the proposed revised Confiscation Act, Ohio congressman Samuel S. Cox asked rhetorically: "What will be the condition of the people of Ohio when the free jubilee shall have come in its ripe and rotten maturity?" "If slavery is bad," he concluded, "the condition of the State of Ohio, with an unrestrained black population . . . partly subservient, partly slothful, partly criminal, and all disadvantageous and ruinous, will be far worse."[6]

In light of such prospects, many Northerners wondered if Lincoln would shy away from delivering what he had promised. Among the doubters was George Templeton Strong, the New York socialite and diarist. "Will Uncle Abe Lincoln stand firm and issue his promised proclamation on the first of January, 1863?" he asked himself during the final days of December. "It is generally supposed that he intends to redeem his pledge," Strong mused, "but nobody knows, and I am not sanguine on the subject."[7] Frederick Douglass had similar misgivings. In Boston on New Year's Day, he joined hundreds who had gathered "to receive and celebrate the first utterance of the long-hoped-for proclamation." "In view of the past," Douglass worried, "it was by no means certain that it would come."[8]

Anticipating the release, African American church congregations in all the free states (and some slave states as well) organized "watch parties" to keep vigil through the night of December 31, 1862. They planned to gather and pray all night long for the cause of freedom, for the security of the Union, for family members and strangers alike who had been afflicted by the evils of slavery

Ent'd according to Act of Congress, A. D. 1863, by W. T. Carlton, in the Clerk's Office of the District Court of the District of Mass.

Figure 1.1 Watch Meeting, Dec. 31, 1862—Waiting for the Hour. Courtesy of the Library of Congress Prints and Photographs Division, LC-DIG-ppmsca-10980. The original painting is part of the White House Art Collection.

and color prejudice, and perhaps most fervently for President Lincoln. The Massachusetts artist William Tolman Carlton imagined a similar scene in which enslaved people had gathered in a barn to await the stroke of midnight (see figure 1.1). Residents of the refugee camp in northwest Washington, several blocks from the White House, assembled at 8:00 P.M. to celebrate the New Year and to "hold a jubilee in view of the President's proclamation." With the camp superintendent presiding, they offered personal testimonies. One man celebrated: "Can't sell you wife and children any more." "'I have a right to rejoice,' declared another, 'for I am free, or will be in a few minutes, and I shall rejoice, for God has placed Mr. Lincoln in the President's chair, and he would not let the rebels make peace until the first of January.'" Just before midnight they began to pray and sing. After an hour they formed "a procession" and marched through the camp. A hearty few continued reveling "till daybreak."[9] Per the custom of the day, bells in public places pealed at the stroke of midnight. An observer in Camden, New Jersey, noted the particular brightness of the moon that night, clearly looking for a sign that slavery's cloud was lifting.[10]

As the celebrants awoke to the bright sunshine of the new morning, word of the proclamation still had not arrived. The capital city, like most business and commercial centers throughout the country, observed New Year's Day as a holiday. Shops and government offices were closed so that officials and private citizens alike might enjoy the company of their families, friends, and peers. Notwithstanding the holiday, many of these "New Year's hospitalities" had the formality of official events.[11] In the spirit of the holiday, the president and his secretaries mixed business with social obligations. The schedule unfolded this way:[12]

> *Before 10:00 A.M.:* Lincoln placed the finishing touches on the document, the text of which he had discussed with his cabinet repeatedly over the previous several days. He copied the final version by hand from the working draft and then transmitted it to the Department of State, where the heading and the subscription attesting to its authenticity were to be inserted.
>
> *10:45 A.M.:* Secretary of State William H. Seward returned the document to the White House for the president's signature. Lincoln noticed that the wording of the subscription was in the incorrect form for a presidential proclamation and the document was then returned to the Department of State for correction.
>
> *11:00 A.M.:* Lincoln received cabinet officers and representatives of foreign nations.
>
> *11:30 A.M.:* Lincoln received officers of the army and the navy.[13]
>
> *12:00 noon:* Lincoln received the public.
>
> *Around 2:00 P.M.:* Lincoln retired to his study to sign the corrected proclamation. At his writing table he paused to steady his right hand, which had grown weary from shaking the hands of well-wishers for the previous several hours. After the president signed, Secretary of State William H. Seward did too, attesting to its authenticity.
>
> *Before 3:00 P.M.:* The official text of the proclamation was distributed to Washington newspapers, which were braced to rush it into print. At the Government Printing Office, typesetters began to work on the official copies.

Throughout the evening, hawkers distributed the newsprint copies throughout the city and couriers speeded them to the surrounding cities and towns. North- and westbound trains carried bundles to their destinations.

The Reverend Henry McNeal Turner, pastor of the Israel Bethel African American Episcopal (AME) Church in Washington, witnessed the excitement and reminisced about it on the fiftieth anniversary of the event in 1913. After hours of anxious waiting, when word spread late in the afternoon that the *Evening Star* was printing the document, he rushed to get a copy and encountered pandemonium in the streets. "Men squealed, women fainted, dogs barked, white and colored people shook hands, songs were sung, and . . . cannons began to fire at the navy-yard," he remembered. "Great processions of colored and white men marched to and fro and passed in front of the White House and congratulated President Lincoln," who nonetheless "kept at a safe distance from the multitude, who were frenzied to distraction." "It was indeed a time of times," Turner concluded; "nothing like it will ever be seen again in this life."[14] In Boston, where Frederick Douglass and other abolitionists had gathered to witness "the first flash of the electric wires announcing the 'new departure,'" suspense grew as the hours passed. "Eight, nine, ten o'clock came and went," he recalled, "and still no word." Only later did the text of the document arrive, confirming that the president had kept his promise. The War Department telegraph office had begun transmitting the official text only around 8:00 P.M.[15]

Why issuing the proclamation of freedom did not occupy pride of place on Lincoln's agenda for January 1 remains a mystery that the weighty implications of the act only partly explain. To be sure, committing the Union to the revolutionary step that opponents of abolition had railed against from the beginning was bound to change the nature of the war, perhaps even to the point of alienating Northern voters and neutral European nations. Yet after one hundred days, Lincoln apparently needed several more hours to do what he had repeatedly convinced himself was necessary and appropriate. As a result, millions of persons throughout the United States and the Confederate States retired for the night on January 1, 1863, not knowing whether the new epoch Turner was witnessing had actually begun.

In light of the consequences of the new policy, Lincoln made several significant changes to the preliminary document he had issued the previous September. He altered the promise that "all persons held as slaves" in the areas still in rebellion "shall be then, thenceforward, and forever free." Absent the qualifier "forever," January's final proclamation noted instead that such persons "are, and henceforward shall be free." Similarly, whereas the preliminary version explicitly obliged government officials (including the armed forces) to "recognize and maintain the freedom of such persons" and to "do no act or acts to repress such persons, or any of them, in any efforts they may make for their actual freedom," the January document required federal authorities to "recognize and maintain the freedom of said persons" and enjoined the freed people "to abstain from all violence, unless in necessary self-defence." Lincoln clearly intended for the final decree to strengthen and not merely put into action what he had earlier promised, yet by eliminating "forever," he foreshadowed his uneasiness that a proclamation made under presidential war powers could last beyond the war. He clearly also had second thoughts about prohibiting interference with enslaved persons' bids for freedom.[16] But most of all, the final document at last revealed which "States and Parts of States" were now at peace and therefore, as he had promised in September, exempt from the emancipation decree.[17]

———————

At Port Royal, South Carolina, which federal forces reclaimed early in November 1861, military authorities and the Northern missionaries and teachers worked for weeks with local ministers and other community leaders to plan a grand celebration. Port Royal and the surrounding Sea Islands held special significance. The natural harbor would provide shelter for the U.S. Navy's South Atlantic Blockading Squadron and a prospective staging ground for military and naval operations against Charleston. The islands were home to wealthy slaveholders whose fortunes derived from the exotic Sea Island cotton, with long and silky strands, that the rich soil of the region produced and that Liverpool cotton traders prized. Finally, owing to a combination of the malarial environment, the harshness of the slave regime, and the importation of captured Africans into the region right up to (and even beyond) the U.S. ban on the Atlantic trade in 1808, visitors to the region had long characterized the enslaved population as semisavage, as witnessed, among other things, by their peculiar Gullah dialect.

As day broke on January 1, 1863, Charlotte Forten, an African American native of Philadelphia who had come to the islands several months earlier to serve as a teacher, pronounced it "the most glorious day this nation has yet seen." Later, with pen in hand and her journal open before her, she confessed, "I *cannot* give a regular chronicle of the day"; she was "in such a state of excitement" that "it all seemed, and seems still, like a brilliant dream."[18] With the festivities organized to take place at the camp of Colonel Thomas Wentworth Higginson's First South Carolina Colored Volunteers, the program understandably had a strongly military flavor. Higginson presided, and assorted dignitaries, including the former-slaveholder-turned-abolitionist William Henry Brisbane, who served as a tax commissioner for the Treasury Department, and General Rufus Saxton, who was the military governor at Port Royal, made remarks. Brisbane read the proclamation. Two noncommissioned officers in Higginson's regiment, Sergeant Prince Rivers and Corporal Robert Sutton, also spoke. Frances D. Gage, the noted abolitionist and women's rights advocate, addressed the women, "very sensibly" in Higginson's estimation.[19]

By all accounts, the most remarkable feature of the proceedings was entirely unscripted. At one point "there suddenly arose," Higginson recalled, "a strong male voice (but rather cracked and elderly), into which two women's voices instantly blended, singing, as if by impulse" the song "My Country, 'tis of thee." "I never saw anything so electric," he reported, "it seemed the choked

voice of a race at last unloosed. Nothing could be more wonderfully uncon-
scious; art could not have dreamed of a tribute to the day of jubilee that should
be so affecting; history will not believe it." Higginson noted that "tears were
everywhere." "Ah, what a grand glorious day this has been," Forten concluded. "The dawn of freedom which it heralds may not break upon us at
once; but it will surely come, and sooner, I believe, than we have ever dared
hope before. My soul is glad with an exceeding great gladness."[20] Although
the celebrants had good reason to believe that Lincoln would not have spared
a single square inch of South Carolina's soil from the emancipation decree,
they did not know that for sure until days later, when official copies of the
document arrived by ship from Fort Monroe.[21]

Prompted in part by Northern missionaries, black refugees in eastern
Virginia also began planning to celebrate well before the New Year. In Hampton, an advisory committee urged residents to usher in the New Year "on
their knees, before God," and to gather at noon "in thanksgiving to God for
their deliverance from the house of bondage."[22] When the day arrived, hundreds of persons turned out in Hampton, Fort Monroe, and Norfolk to thank
God for deliverance and to express gratitude to the president and to the United
States for this "birth-day of freedom." At Norfolk, the African American missionary John Oliver reported a scene of great jubilation, with "more than
5000" persons gathered from far and wide to celebrate "what they supposed
was their freedom." Their joy was short-lived when they learned soon thereafter that the president had indeed exempted the Union-occupied region of
eastern Virginia. As Oliver observed on the scene, "the slaveholders have
began again to maltreat their slaves, at the same time tell them that no one on
earth has the power to free them." The exemption caused the refugees "in-
tence greaf," he reported, and "human life is most terabely insecure in Norfolk, for the Colored people." Persons residing in the exempt areas could ill
afford to assume that the spirit of the proclamation would grant them what
its words did not.[23]

————

For African Americans in Louisiana, President Lincoln's decision to exempt
from the emancipation decree the thirteen southern parishes under U.S. military control came as no surprise. Despite the much ballyhooed confronta-
tions between Union general Benjamin F. Butler and the Confederate
sympathizers of the region—especially the ladies, the most outspoken of
whom he had infamously likened to prostitutes—a substantial pro-Union
population resided in New Orleans and in the surrounding parishes (the political jurisdictions known as counties in most other states). They were
a mixed group of sugar planters, businessmen, shopkeepers, artisans, and

laborers, and they included the *gens de couleur libres*, free persons of both European and African ancestry. Having weathered the storm of secession and Confederate rule down to the arrival of U.S. gunboats and troops in April 1862, the Unionists cooperated, albeit not always enthusiastically, with Butler's administration of affairs. The sugar planters along the Mississippi River and the various tributary bayous were particularly conservative; they trusted that Butler would protect their slave property in exchange for their professions of loyalty to the United States.[24]

Butler aimed to maintain social order through a combination of what he termed suppressing vagrancy (that is, arresting persons who fled the plantations) and convincing loyal planters to begin paying wages to their laborers. By the late fall of 1862, a significant number of the wealthiest and most influential citizens agreed to adopt this new approach, but many other nominal Unionists did not. When Butler was removed as military commander in mid-December, his successor, General Nathaniel P. Banks, another Massachusetts politician, tried to walk a fine line. Believing that slavery would not survive the war, Banks nonetheless affirmed that "the war is not waged by the Government for the overthrow of slavery." "To correct public misapprehension and misrepresentation," he insisted that the Union-controlled parishes would not be affected by the president's proclamation and, therefore, "all persons" must "govern themselves accordingly."[25]

Before Butler left, and with his full knowledge and approval, the African-descended population of New Orleans had begun preparing for a grand celebration of freedom on January 1 regardless of whether the proclamation excluded the Union-held parishes. Bowing to slaveholders' fears that the holiday would spark a rebellion, Banks suspended "all unusual public demonstrations." In an unconvincing attempt to ease the pain of the enslaved, he advised them "to remain upon their plantations until their privileges shall have been definitely established."[26] Within weeks, Banks issued general orders, which expanded and codified Butler's plan of compensated labor in the areas under federal control.[27] The tug-of-war between landowners and laborers continued, but now a new set of rules required compensation and forbade corporal punishment. Despite the limited reach of federal arms, enslaved people in areas under Confederate control set their bearings for the nearest Yankee outpost. When the official copies of the proclamation arrived near the end of January, the wording confirmed the exemption, and Banks dutifully distributed the text to the people of Louisiana.[28]

––––––––

Lincoln's decision to exclude all of Tennessee is perhaps the most anomalous feature of the final Emancipation Proclamation. Despite pockets of Unionist sentiment throughout the state, federal authorities faced widespread armed resistance from regular Confederate forces as well as rebel sympathizers. What is more, the numerous slaveholding Unionists in Middle and West Tennessee did little to disguise the fact that they expected protection of their enslaved property in return for their loyalty. In Nashville they found a true friend in General Lovell H. Rousseau, the native Kentuckian who commanded federal forces there and made no secret of his opposition to emancipation. Rousseau routinely issued orders requiring military and civil authorities to cooperate with masters who were apprehending fugitive slaves, a blatant "violation of the highest Military authority of the land as set forth in the Proclamation of the President of the United States" in the view of the city's provost marshal.[29] Tennessee slaveholders, however, rejected the provost marshal's emphasis on the spirit of the proclamation, seizing instead on its exact wording.

In east Tennessee the patchwork of competing loyalties and changing military regimes created openings that enslaved freedom seekers could exploit. Chief among these was negotiating terms of working for themselves. In 1863, amid expanding Union military operations, a large slaveholder attempted to refugee his slaves south, moving them deeper into Confederate territory to reduce the likelihood that they would escape to or be captured by the Yankees. When they refused, he struck a deal stipulating "that if they remained on his farm during the war, they should be entitled to all they could make." At the end of the war he returned and sued them for the rent of the farm, receiving judgment "notwithstanding the testimony of 3 white men . . . to the effect that the presence and labor of the negroes on the farm during the war, was worth more than the rents." Early in 1866, thanks in part to a white Union army veteran who intervened on behalf of the freed people, the Freedmen's Bureau agent in Chattanooga succeeded in persuading the former owner to abandon his claim for the rent.[30]

African American Tennesseans faced grave uncertainty about their status, not least because of their owners' determination to keep them enslaved, removing them away from the Yankees or hiring them into Confederate service. For every case in which nominally enslaved persons arranged with refugee owners to stay at home and share the proceeds of what they grew, there were scores of others in which men and women worked for food and shelter without wages, caught in the halfway house where slavery had ceased to function but slaveholders still had legal rights to their human property. In February 1865 the loyal voters of Tennessee approved a new constitution that prohibited slavery but made no provisions for resolving disputes over compensation either awarded or withheld between January 1863 and February 1865. In the Loyal Border States of Delaware, Maryland, Kentucky, and

Missouri, no enslaved person quite understood why the man whom they viewed as their deliverer chose to declare freedom in the states where he had no authority and leave slavery untouched in the states where his authority was secure. In short, the iconic event in the chronology of Civil War emancipation occurred not in an instant at dawn on January 1, 1863. Just as its promulgation extended through the day and beyond, its practical implications remained contested for years.

––––––

This brief chronology of the Emancipation Proclamation's emergence into the world illustrates how a presumably discrete event may possess a complex history that begins before and continues after the event itself. To be sure, government officials, ranging from the president and his executive cabinet, to Congress and the federal courts, to military and naval officers and assorted officials at the state and local levels, all possessed certain authority to promulgate public policy. Yet it was in the prehistory and the posthistory of a policy's promulgation where the larger cast of historical actors that Frederick Douglass, W. E. B. Du Bois, and Charles H. Wesley identified—whose ranks included unnamed enslaved persons, conductors on the underground railroad, and other anonymous ordinary citizens—had the opportunity to affect the historical process. No wonder Lincoln conceded that events controlled him rather than the other way around.[31]

Historians often employ chronology as a framing device for reducing the complexity of historical processes and establishing a degree of interpretive order over incomplete, imperfect, or contradictory evidence. Taking for granted that events unfold through time, they remain cautious to avoid the logical fallacy of "post hoc ergo propter hoc," whose seductive powers might lead a naive interpreter to conclude that simply because one event preceded another in time the earlier event caused the later one.[32] Yet by focusing inordinately on public policy, interpreters of the past risk separating official actions from the circumstances of their origins that lie outside official institutions and procedures. To take one example, President Lyndon B. Johnson deserves credit for his role in enacting the Civil Rights Act of 1964 and the Voting Rights Act of 1965, which outlawed racial segregation and disfranchisement. But such legislation would have been unthinkable without the broader movement that, among other things, sustained the Montgomery Bus Boycott and Freedom Summer.

The apparent order implicit in any chronology of emancipation belies the fitful character of policy making. Of course, the variable winds of public opinion, the direction and speed of which change constantly, affect lawmaking in every representative assembly. Legislative calendars render the process inherently uneven, with cycles of intense activity followed by extended periods of recess. The Constitution obliges each Congress to meet at least once in each of its two years of life. By long-standing custom, the first session of each Congress began in early December of the year after its members were elected. The respective houses remained in session for three to four months, during which time senators and representatives often conducted business six days a week. A recess of eight to nine months followed the close of each session. When Congress was at work, Washington reflected a pace of activity that was markedly more energetic than during recess. Well before the start of the war, the capital city and the nation had become accustomed to the cyclical nature of the official business of the United States.[33]

Legislatures stand apart from other corporate bodies in the complex and often arcane rules under which they operate. At the pleasure of the body, prospective bills properly introduced by a member are referred to a committee, where they may be tabled indefinitely or marked up for consideration and debate before the full body. The almost leisurely speechifying and polite sparring might continue for days before a scheduled vote, with flurries of amendments in the closing hours and minutes. Bills approved in one chamber undergo consideration in the other, where they may be tabled, defeated, or (if both chambers concur) submitted to a conference committee in hopes of reaching accord. When both houses agree on the wording, the bill moves to the president for his disposition; in the event of a veto, two-thirds of both houses must agree to override. Owing to the freewheeling nature of much of this process, it constituted a form of comic relief for participants and observers alike, with the galleries of both houses often packed with interested onlookers, including growing numbers of African American men and women. But at the bottom, the work was much more than entertainment.[34]

Despite holding majorities in both houses, Republicans could not take approval of any antislavery measure for granted and expect a rapid passage through the procedural gauntlet. Little wonder, then, that Massachusetts senator Henry Wilson took such great pride in the antislavery legislation of the Civil War congresses that he memorialized the work in a magisterial compilation titled *History of the Antislavery Measures of the Thirty-Seventh and Thirty-Eighth United-States Congresses, 1861–64*.[35] Each of its twenty-three chapters presented a day-to-day—at times even speaker by speaker—account of the debates, dutifully "tracing the words of the actors in these great measures of legislation" from the pages of the *Congressional Globe*.[36] For all its value, Wilson's *History* also created the false impression that legislative emancipation unfolded logically and progressively, even if erratically, as Congress identified the areas over which it had constitutional jurisdiction and then developed appropriate measures.

————

Evolving federal policy regarding confiscation during the first two years of the war illustrates the complex interplay of forces that affected the prehistory and the posthistory of major public policy actions. At the start of the war, the principle that an army might seize an enemy's assets and employ them for its own benefit had been well established. In May 1861, General Benjamin F. Butler, commander of federal forces at Fortress Monroe, the outpost at the tip of Virginia's Peninsula, encountered three enslaved men who had fled from their owner and sought federal protection. He quickly overcame the apparent dilemma of whether he could accede to their request, reasoning that the rebels' insistence that humans were property entitled him to confiscate such property to prevent it from being used for belligerent purposes. He employed the term "contraband of war" to justify his action, and the concept quickly gained popularity, indeed, going so far in the shorthand form of "contraband" to label every freed person.[37]

Realizing the contribution such fugitives from the Confederacy might make to the Union cause, Butler welcomed not just the men who were capable of productive labor but also their families; Secretary of War Simon Cameron approved.[38] When Congress convened on July 4, 1861, legislative strategists had already been working for weeks on a plan that would enable the national government to respond to the rebellion. Radical Republicans also wished to establish a record of their opposition to slavery. Five days after the start of the special session, the abolitionist congressman from Illinois, Owen Lovejoy, whose brother Elijah had been murdered by a proslavery mob in 1837, introduced a nonbinding resolution that "it is no part of the duty of the soldiers of the United States to capture and return fugitive slaves," which the body adopted after only a short procedural debate.[39] Given that commanders of federal forces in the Loyal Border States and in Confederate Virginia had repeatedly declared that they would protect loyal slaveholders in the enjoyment of all their rights, including property in slaves, the resolution had little direct impact on military operations. But as a symbol of antislavery Northerners' growing sense that the national government need not coddle slaveholders, the resolution appeared as a bolt from the blue.

On July 15, on the Senate side of the Capitol, Lyman Trumbull, another Illinois Republican but one more moderate than Lovejoy, introduced a measure proposing "to confiscate property used for insurrectionary purposes."[40] When the bill reached the Senate floor one week later, it contained provisions that would free any person employed "in aiding or promoting any insurrection, or in resisting the laws of the United States."[41] Since ancient times, peoples and nations have been confiscating the property of their enemies and mobilizing traditionally subordinate social classes as they see fit. And the codified international law of more recent times recognized the liberation of slaves in wartime, as the fledgling American nation learned to its consternation during its war for independence. To be sure, British lord Dunmore's 1775 offer of freedom to the slaves of Virginia's rebels still gnawed at slaveholders' sensibilities nearly ninety years after the fact; so did Alexander Hamilton's acquiescence in the British removal of some 3,000 black Loyalists, most of whom were fugitives from American colonists, at the end of the Revolutionary War.[42] The Kentuckian John C. Breckinridge, a presidential candidate in 1860 whose unvarnished sympathy for the Confederacy soon resulted in his expulsion from the U.S. Senate, feared that such a measure would be but the first step toward "a general confiscation of all property, and a loosing of all bonds."[43] The moderate senator John Sherman from Ohio (General William T. Sherman's brother) hoped to narrow the Union's war aims "to preserve the Union, to defend the property, and to maintain the constitutional authority of the Government."[44]

Just as this debate got under way, news reached the capital "that negroes were in the fight" at the Battle of Bull Run on July 21, and that Confederates had abused, even killed, captured, and wounded Union soldiers.[45] Such reports heightened Republican suspicions that the rebels had employed enslaved black men to support their military operations and prompted them to view the liberation of slaves used for such purposes as an appropriate remedy. New Jersey senator John C. Ten Eyck was willing to suspend his earlier concern over "what was to become of these poor wretches" if they were freed. "God knows," he confessed, "we do not want them in our section of the Union," but the ultimate disposition of the vexed question of what to do with the freed people took a back seat to devising ways to punish the rebels for violating the laws of civilized warfare by employing black men in combat.[46]

Early in August, under the leadership of the Republican congressman from Ohio, John A. Bingham, who chaired the Judiciary Committee, the House of Representatives took up the Senate's bill and began a vigorous debate over the relationship between seizing property and liberating slaves.[47] Bingham locked horns with Kentucky representative Henry C. Burnet, who, like Senator Breckinridge, was soon expelled from Congress for his disloyalty. The bill appeared to apply "to all slaves who may be owned by persons now in this rebellion, and to their services in any wise used in aiding this rebellion, without limitation," Burnet claimed, insisting that if federal authorities were to rely solely on the testimony of the slaves to determine whether they had been employed in support of the rebellion "then, that amounts to a wholesale emancipation of the slaves in the seceding or rebellious states."[48] "The eyes of the world are upon you," declared Congressman John J. Crittenden, author of the unsuccessful 1860 attempt to avert war through a set of compromises over slavery. "You are in the presence of events that will be of deeper interest in history than any that have occurred in a hundred years; of as great importance, it seems to me, as can occur to the human race." Warning that "the pen of the historian will lay all these things open before the world," Crittenden urged his colleagues to avoid "giving an anti-slavery character and application to the war."[49]

The New York Republican congressman Alexander S. Diven posed the question of what to do with the "negroes employed against the country." Acknowledging that they could not be sold "in the Cuban or any other markets," he observed that holding them as prisoners would pose a problem "entirely novel in the usages of war." He questioned whether releasing the captives and invalidating the master's claims to their labor would conform "with the great principles of civilized and humanized warfare": "Is it not rather bringing back the age of barbarism, and inaugurating a barbarous instead of a civilized warfare?"[50] On August 3 the House returned the bill to the Senate with one significant change. Instead of Trumbull's original wording, which broadly referenced "aiding or promoting any insurrection, or in resisting the laws of the United States," the House markup specified "[taking] up arms against the United States" or "[being] employed in or upon any fort, navy-yard, dock, armory, ship, intrenchment, or in any military or naval service whatsoever."[51] The Senate concurred. With some reservations, President Lincoln signed the bill into law on August 6, 1861.[52] His qualms did not include the specific narrowing of the range of actions that would warrant freedom from the Senate's general formulation to the prescriptive list that the House favored.

Four months later, when the second session of the Thirty-Seventh Congress convened, Congress considered expanding the concept of confiscation to weaken the rebel war effort further and punish Confederates and their sympathizers. An African American observer in Washington speculated that Congress was about to "do much for the colored people." Sponsors had already introduced measures to abolish slavery in the District, to lift the onerous requirement that African Americans carry passes when exiting the city heading northward, to abolish the fugitive slave law, and to free the slaves of rebels. These initiatives constituted "four great national movements." With a clear understanding of both the seasonality and ultimate unpredictability of the legislative process, the observer noted that even if the bills "may not succeed this session," at least "they have been started."[53] Yet as practiced Congress watchers knew, a draft measure was a far cry from an enacted law.

As lawmakers in Washington busily pursued legislative remedies for defeating the rebellion, Union forces began offensive operations in Arkansas, Tennessee, Louisiana, South Carolina, and Virginia. In each case, they encountered the work that impressed slave laborers had performed to obstruct their progress and to strengthen Confederate defensive positions. But they also met enslaved people who offered valuable intelligence, including the size and location of rebel forces and the best routes through the often unmapped and always unfamiliar networks of roads.[54] The Second Confiscation Act, which emancipated the slaves of all rebels and not just those who had permitted them to work directly in support of the Confederate war effort, became law on July 17, 1862. The same day, Congress approved and President Lincoln signed the bill that revised the Militia Act, authorizing the employment of black men in the army.[55]

After July 17, 1862, Congress did not return again to refining the tactic of confiscation as a means to cripple the Confederacy. Several considerations help explain why. First, the emerging concept of emancipation focused on the humanity of the enslaved persons, thereby rendering confiscation, and its focus on their attributes as property, anachronistic. Second, despite the theoretical potential for the Second Confiscation Act to have served as the basis for freeing the slaves of rebel sympathizers in the Border States as well as the Confederate states, the bill offered no practical guidance as to how such freedom would be established in law.[56] Third, and most important, by making provision for formerly enslaved men to serve the cause, the Second Confiscation Act and the Militia Act marked a profound shift in the thinking of congressional Republicans. No longer simply pawns to be moved about the chessboard of war, black people were emerging as active participants in the strategy to save the Union by destroying slavery. In such an atmosphere, the term "contraband" (and the related notion of confiscating human property) began falling out of vogue, at least in the arena of public policy. In the culture of minstrelsy, however, "contraband songs" grew in popularity, and in the U.S. Navy the rating of "contraband"—the practical equivalent of "boy," an underage youth whose enlistment depended on the consent of a parent or guardian—marked the men as former slaves for their entire term of service and beyond. When the War Department decided to restrict the pay of black soldiers to the rate of ten dollars that the Militia Act prescribed, freeborn men from the North vigorously opposed the government's demeaning attempt to reduce them to the status of "contrabands."[57]

————

Free black communities in the Northern states and Canada, many of whose residents had escaped from Southern slavery, often framed the issues of the war in chronological terms that often stretched deep into the past. Those who had escaped from slavery looked to enlist in the army and return to the scene of their oppression to liberate loved ones and neighbors and to exact vengeance on the enslavers. But Northern black communities also pursued objectives that were grounded in their experiences as free persons who endured numerous liabilities on account of color. To be sure, persons of African ancestry who lived in New England, where slavery had become defunct several generations earlier and where most black men were able to vote, did not face the same impediments that their counterparts in other states endured. In New York and New Jersey, where legislation decreed the end of slavery in the 1820s and the 1840s, respectively, telltale vestiges of the institution lingered. And in the Midwest, where states that entered the Union were bound by the provisions of the Northwest Ordinance of 1787 prohibiting slavery and involuntary servitude except in punishment for crime, slavery lingered even after statehood. What is more, the states of Ohio, Indiana, Illinois, and Michigan imposed various legal restrictions—generically referred to as "Black Codes" or "Black Laws"—on their black inhabitants.[58]

Despite such barriers, a small but influential class of black property owners, business proprietors, and ministers gained a toehold in these states and began pressing for equality. Beginning in the 1830s, running parallel with the emerging abolitionist movement, they used the print media to voice their opinions and sponsored dozens of state and national conventions to articulate the dual cases of freedom and full citizenship for all persons regardless of color or previous condition.[59] Just as enslaved persons viewed the war as an opportunity to demolish slavery and fulfill their dreams of freedom, free black persons in the North viewed the war as an opportunity both to destroy slavery, the root of popular prejudice, and to improve their status vis-à-vis white fellow citizens.

Black political activists well knew the challenges to passing antislavery legislation long before congressional Republicans took up that work in earnest during the Civil War. While working to achieve many of the same legislative objectives that Senator Henry Wilson did, their sense of urgency generally far surpassed his. What is more, they remained intensely focused on the overall shape of postemancipation society, constantly reminding lawmakers that wholesale transformation, not just piecemeal reform, was required. In short, the African American narrative of emancipation reached back at least to 1619, when the first enslaved Africans landed at Jamestown, Virginia. And it did not end with the emancipation decrees that the various Northern states had enacted between the 1770s and the 1840s. Entire communities had participated in that history-making process, which the public at large often came to understand in terms of the freedom narratives of individuals, thanks in no small measure to the efforts of abolitionists to publish in book form the accounts of persons who had succeeded in escaping from slavery. Most notable was Frederick Douglass, whose ordeals in slavery in Maryland, his escape to freedom in the North, and his eventual rise to international notoriety as an abolitionist were chronicled in two works that he published before the war.[60] Like the authors of other such narratives, Douglass mapped a trajectory from slavery to freedom, which has served as the general framework for conceptualizing wartime emancipation no less than the personal life histories of successful freedom seekers. The tales unfolded through chronological time, from youth to adulthood, with critical incidents along the way. The moment of escape, like the Emancipation Proclamation, marked a definitive moment that both literally and figuratively closed the book on slavery. The newly freed men and women then discovered that the new book of freedom contained mostly blank pages that they would fill with actions and experiences of their own choosing, not those of a putative master.

The life of Frederick Douglass described a heroic individual who through sheer willpower and force of character marched forward through history carrying the weight of thousands, if not millions, on his shoulders. In some respects, his journey mirrored—even surpassed—Lincoln's. The lives of other participants in the struggle against slavery reveal chronologies whose overall trajectories moved from slavery to freedom, but whose individual details reveal repeated setbacks—often accompanied by self-doubt—that belie any prediction of a heroic ending. One such person was Henry M. Turner. The personal narratives of the participants in freedom's struggle pose cautionary lessons to those who would view emancipation as a foregone conclusion after the Confederate gunners opened fire on Fort Sumter in April 1861. Taken together, these narratives plus the running chronology of the war's events that appeared in the black press, particularly the *Christian Recorder* and the *Anglo-African*, constitute a counternarrative to what appeared in the popular press in the major cities of the Union. To be sure, the black press generally contained the same accounts of federal military operations and the same news from Washington that appeared in the white press (often by reprinting material from favored sources). Yet as much as the black press shared the desire to see a return of peace, editors and correspondents did not wish only to reduce the bloodshed or to save the Union. Destroying slavery was their primary preoccupation, and whoever advanced the cause was a hero. The war had meaning chiefly in terms of that goal.

————

Turner was born free in Abbeville, South Carolina, in 1834. His parents apprenticed him to a carriage maker to learn the trade, while a combination of instructors tutored him in the rudiments of reading and writing. During his teen years, he worked for a time as a clerk in a law office, where he further refined his mastery of the skills that would serve him so well later. He also developed a penchant for carousing that remained strong even after he affiliated with the Methodist Episcopal Church, South, in 1848. "I was a wild, reckless boy," he later recalled, until 1851 when he attended a camp meeting that changed his life. Following preparation for the ministry, he was licensed to exhort in 1853. He began preaching and traveled through South Carolina, Georgia, Alabama, Louisiana, and Missouri over the next several years. After an 1858 visit with William R. Revels, a physician, AME minister, and brother of future Mississippi senator Hiram R. Revels, Turner left the Methodist Episcopal Church, South, for the AME Church. Soon he departed for Baltimore to attend Trinity College and prepare for work in the African missions, studying biblical languages and theology. Over the next four years he grew more deeply committed to pastoral work in Baltimore and his interest in Africa waned. The outbreak of the war also helped refocus his attention on the United States.[61]

An avid reader, Turner mixed newspapers with religious treatises in his daily regimen. The local press furnished information along with a heavy dose of each editor's partisan biases. He relied on the abolitionist and black press to frame issues related to the destruction of slavery and the future of African Americans in the United States. As the war began, the *Christian Recorder*'s governing board focused on finances and editorial leadership, but its editor, like his counterpart at the *Anglo-African*, took pains to satisfy readers' curiosity about Haiti and the fate of the recent emigrants there. Events that soon came to a head at Fort Sumter merited scarcely a mention, but that would soon change. Readers of both papers took a strong interest in emigration because its proponents advocated an escape from "the chains of servile degradation" in the United States to enjoy the "untainted air of heaven as free and independent, self-reliant men and women." Yet, the decision to leave never came easy. Apart from understandable fears of the unknown, prospective migrants did not readily concede the absence of a future under the stars and stripes. The deepening political crisis might just offer an occasion to reaffirm the United States as their home and to focus on having the nation live up to its founding professions of liberty and equality.[62]

At first, the *Recorder*'s editor (the Reverend Elijah Weaver), its correspondents, and many of its readers approached the war gingerly, almost as if in deference to the prevailing Northern view that the contest had nothing to do with slavery or people of African descent. In April when Baltimore mobs attacked soldiers from states farther to the north who were on their way to Washington to defend the capital, an anonymous observer in Washington cautioned readers to distance themselves from "this pending crisis" because never before "in the history of this country" had there been a time "so critical to us as a people."[63] Days before, Weaver had proposed that "the soothing and calming Christian influence of the Bible," coupled with "fervent prayer . . . to Almighty God, for his mercy and his holy wisdom," might avert "the impending troubles" and restore peace "to our distracted country."[64]

Although Weaver aimed to focus on church matters and avoid direct criticism of the administration, his editorials gradually took on a sharper political edge with regard to national affairs.[65] But even when his own editorial voice veered toward reticence, he did not hesitate to publish frank commentaries and exchanges from correspondents that focused on the affairs of the state as well as those of the church. By the conventions common in mid-nineteenth-century journalism, the *Recorder* also reprinted items of interest, particularly war news, from other newspapers (with and without attribution) and the wire services. In addressing the special needs of their subscribers, editors of the black press, like their counterparts whose clienteles consisted of national or ethnic groups (the Germans or Irish, for instance) or workingmen, duplicated much of the conventional news that appeared in the major metropolitan dailies but added a distinctive spin.

In their very nature, newspapers impose chronological order on events, but not without gaps. The intervals between press runs interrupt the flow of information, which in return may affect the analytical process. Readers silently fill these voids, but when lectors read the news aloud before audiences of listeners, the dynamic changes radically: the otherwise private exercise takes on a public and collective form. Of course, disadvantaged communities had practiced the art of consuming news in this way for generations (indeed, from the earliest days of printed newspapers), but for African Americans—Northern and Southern, enslaved and free—the war raised the stakes of awareness at a time when the number of literate men and women rose to new heights. In Kentucky, the enslaved man Elijah Marrs read at length to the enslaved people of his neighborhood from whatever printed material he could find.[66] Black persons who wished to keep abreast of the news found ways to do so, in defiance of their owners' wishes to keep them uniformed.

The political persuasion or editorial stance of the newspaper mattered little—a collective perspective adjusted for slants. From early in the war black sailors circulated copies of the *Recorder* and the *Anglo* until they fell apart. A black Philadelphian serving on a U.S. gunboat that had sought shelter from a storm at Port Royal, South Carolina, proudly reported the *Recorder*'s popularity in this news-deprived corner of the world. He noted that nearly one-third of the 300 local men whom the navy had enlisted to work on the U.S.

storeship *Vermont* could read, and they were eager to receive the paper.[67] Once black men were permitted to enlist in the army, they too prized these two publications, looking forward to the arrival of each issue as they would "a precious visitor," Turner later observed.[68]

Although it is likely that Turner had contributed to the *Recorder* under a pseudonym before November 1861, it was then that he began writing under his own name. Over the first six months of the war, his perspective evolved from that of an outsider with a deep interest in national affairs to that of a participant in a larger political project. Following the successful federal assault on Port Royal, South Carolina, early in the month, he blasted the "ridiculous, outrageous, and cannibalistic reports . . . about the conduct of the negroes." Some six weeks after federal forces sent the Confederates flying, General Thomas W. Sherman, the military commander of the expedition, speculated why so few freed people had abandoned their homes to join the Yankees. They were "naturally slothful and indolent," he concluded, so they were reluctant to work, and as long as they could provision themselves on the plantations they did not need government assistance. Turner vigorously disputed these unflattering characterizations, which the major metropolitan newspapers broadcast reflexively.[69] For the rest of the war, his letters constituted a running commentary on current events. He believed without question that God had ordained the destruction of slavery but also understood that such an outcome unfolded on a cosmic scale that did not necessarily accord either with human timekeeping instruments or with the notion of one-directional progress toward the greater good that stood at the center of the American secular creed.

Appreciating human frailty, Turner could forgive the unintended missteps of public officials. But he took them to task relentlessly when they missed opportunities to advance the cause of freedom. His voice was independent, unfettered by allegiance to person or party, as his dissent from the fanfare surrounding President Abraham Lincoln's March 1862 message to Congress demonstrated. Commentators such as Horace Greeley, editor of the *New York Tribune*, praised Lincoln's offer of compensation in the form of federal bonds to any state willing to adopt gradual emancipation.[70] Turner had hoped for the president to act as "a Moses" whose message would sound "the Jubilee trumpet, *Arise, ye slaves, and come to freedom!*" The disappointment did not end there. Rather than offering "hope for a brighter day," the message aimed instead "to pacify the humane and philanthropic hearts of the country." He was particularly frustrated with Lincoln's denial "that Congress has any power to legislate on slavery—leaving it under the absolute control of individual States." And he saw only trouble in the provision whereby the states could dispose of the money at they saw fit.[71] Besides political commentary,

Turner offered his readers object lessons in how to parse the official policy statements of the nation's leaders for clues into the matters that most deeply concerned black Americans.

"It is no strange or uncommon thing," noted one witness to the meteoric rise of Turner's ministry, "to behold in his congregation honorable senators and representatives, and officers of every grade in the army, from the 'stars' to the 'bars,' listening carefully and attentively to . . . this distinguished pulpit orator."[72] He hosted public lectures by leading political figures, scientists, and experts on topics of current interest. Turner began attending congressional debates to observe with his own eyes and ears what he read in the daily newspapers. Not surprisingly, he applauded passage of the measures that he knew would advance the antislavery cause or ease the burden of discrimination that African Americans bore. He noted with pleasure that General George B. McClellan's stalemate on the peninsula had prompted even "exceedingly conservative" senators and congressmen to propose enlisting black men into the army and rewarding their service with freedom.[73] By dint of the strength of his personality and the fearlessness and wit of his commentary on matters of public policy, Turner's stature as a participant-observer in the campaign against slavery grew.

Scarcely had Turner gotten his bearings in the nation's capital when he found himself in the midst of the flap over colonization sparked by President Lincoln's own interest in the topic and by the pledge of funds to support the removal of persons freed by the law ending slavery in the District of Columbia in April 1862.[74] During the House debate, some members of Congress joined voices with critics in the press who faulted Lincoln for not having developed a coherent policy regarding emancipation. Missouri representative Frank Blair, the son of Francis P. Blair (whose notoriety dated from the presidency of Andrew Jackson) and the brother of Montgomery Blair (Lincoln's postmaster general), defended the president, holding up the bill as evidence. The Illinois congressman Owen P. Lovejoy elaborated, noting that the three pillars of "Emancipation[,] compensation & colonization" formed the foundation of "*a policy*" that satisfied "all shades of Republicans."[75]

Under no particular obligation to find coherence or consistency in the president's actions, Turner delighted at seeing the bill's opponents squirm at the prospects of "the universal abolition of slavery" and of a "war of extermination between the races" that would make "the horrors of the French Revolution" appear tame in comparison.[76] He noted approvingly that "the heel of Providence" had stomped "the head of the serpent" by abolishing slavery in the nation's capital, but he refused to bestow "much credit to human agency in this matter." Men, after all, had "sadly mismanaged the whole slavery agitation," with the advocates of abolition and colonization having blasted each other rather than their common enemy, slaveholders. "And now, what is the Providential solution?" Turner asked sarcastically: "Emancipation and colonization both!"[77] While crediting Congress and the president with taking the bold step of ending slavery in the capital, Turner faulted them for bowing to narrow prejudice that coupled exile with black freedom. He would return to this theme repeatedly.

––––––––

Even before the dust of colonization had settled, President Lincoln unveiled his startling preliminary Emancipation Proclamation of September 22, 1862. Turner rushed to the president's defense, dismissing the chief executive's prior interest in "colored expatriation" as a clever diversion for the emancipation proclamation. "Mr. Lincoln loves freedom as well as any one on earth," he concluded, "and if he carries out the spirit of his proclamation, he need never fear hell. GOD GRANT HIM A HIGH SEAT IN GLORY." Turner also viewed the proclamation as a call to action. "We live in one of the most eventful periods of the world's revolutions," he argued. By clearly articulating a policy of freedom, the president ushered in "a new era, a new dispensation of things": "to action, to action, is the cry. We must now begin to think, to plan, and to legislate for ourselves."[78]

Like many of his contemporaries, white and black, Turner viewed these developments within a framework of human progress. "This world is improving," he insisted, and the living generation enjoyed the "great privilege" of "carrying forward these heaven-begotten principles, ordained by God for man's elevation." Through "the general darkness" that still pervaded the land, Turner perceived a star rising in the distance, and with multitudes marching behind the banner of "Freedom to the slaves in all the land. Abraham Lincoln."[79] Confident that "the world is still moving onward," he sensed a growing sentiment among the American people favoring abolition. He faulted blundering generals for stalling "the great freedom revolution," yet he took comfort in knowing that, "as Galileo said, 'it moves, nevertheless.'"[80]

Turner approached discerning God's will as both a historical and a spiritual exercise. He found in the Bible persons aplenty whose stories foreshadowed events of the war. In his commentary "The Plagues of this Country," for instance, Turner sought to explain the various prophecies of some "dreadful calamity" that would befall humanity in the next several years, but he did so with a twist. Rather than portraying the nation as a naive innocent, he viewed its long history of oppression against persons of African ancestry as crying out for divine retribution. President Lincoln was the pharaoh presiding over the latter-day Egypt of "American slavery." Indeed, it was his refusal to heed God's plea to "let my people go" that produced the plagues, which took the form of military losses. Failing to see that God favored freedom over slavery, Lincoln continued to blunder. When General John C. Frémont in Missouri "heard a voice saying from heaven, Let my people go," Pharaoh Lincoln "hardened his heart" and forced Frémont to retract the offer of freedom. Whereas "angels rejoiced" when General David Hunter "declared the mystic Israelites free throughout South Carolina, Georgia and Florida," Lincoln again "hardened his heart, and in one great mutter, furious enough to make hell grumble, precipitantly hurled them back into the darkest caverns of oppression." "The great revolution which is to rack the earth and convulse the nations about the year 1866," according to prophecies of, among others, the Mormon leader Joseph Miller, "is the liberation of the oppressed," Turner concluded.[81]

As the world waited with bated breath to learn which areas of the Confederate states would be exempted from the final Emancipation Proclamation, the war news from Virginia reemphasized the important connection between freedom and federal military victories. The news was far from encouraging. On Saturday, December 13, 1862, at Marye's Heights just outside Fredericksburg, Union general Ambrose Burnside and his soldiers in the Army of the Potomac discovered one of the emerging truths of the war the hard way: frontal assaults against an entrenched enemy risked high casualties.[82] The following day, as Turner conducted Sunday evening services, a report arrived from the battlefront to the effect that Burnside had prevailed. The resulting "stir" left the pastor with no choice but to dismiss the congregation, only to learn the next day that the rumor was false.[83]

———

Like the white volunteer regiments that officials in the states had been organizing from the beginning of the war, the black regiments that the president's proclamation called forth reflected local origins. Men often knew each other as civilians before they volunteered, and they maintained ties to their communities of origin throughout the war, staying informed of happenings there by means of visitors from home and the movement of letters and men on furlough back and forth. To be sure, the nation exerted a strong force field, drawing men together to fight the common enemy, but home communities often pulled hard in the opposite direction.

The start of black enlistment enabled Turner to direct his ministerial work toward military service, which he viewed as the long-awaited opportunity to advance the antislavery cause and create an irrefutable case for full citizenship. He eagerly joined the effort to recruit men for the First U.S. Colored Infantry, which began taking shape in Washington during the spring of 1863, hoping for the opportunity to serve as the unit's chaplain. He began writing to Secretary of War Stanton asking "if there is any possibility of a colored man, being honored with the position." Secretary of the Treasury Salmon P. Chase and Illinois congressman Owen Lovejoy wrote to Stanton in support of Turner's application, which was approved early in November.[84] Soon after the New Year, he contracted smallpox, which incapacitated him until late May and permanently scarred his face with the signature pockmarks of the disease. After rejoining his unit in Virginia, he threw himself into ministering to the needs of the black soldiers among whom he served and of the enslaved people in surrounding communities. He officiated at marriages and planted seeds for AME congregations to take root; and he conducted schools to promote literacy and to prepare the freed people for the responsibilities of self-support and citizenship.

Black regiments organized in the Northern states of Massachusetts, Connecticut, and Kansas, which retained their designation as state volunteers throughout the war, demonstrated the heterogeneity of the black regiments even when their initial core of recruits hailed from a particular state. The same was true of the regiments of U.S. Colored Troops in the other Northern states (the free states of New York, Pennsylvania, Ohio, Michigan, and Indiana as well as the slave states of Maryland, Missouri, and Kentucky) and in the Southern states (Louisiana, Mississippi, Alabama, and Arkansas, for instance). A regiment's point of origin generally masked the disparate origins of the men who had made their way there through the happenstances of war and the interstate trade in humans before the war.

Black soldiers experienced a newfound identification with the federal government unlike anything in the prior history of the nation. For the first time the concept of citizen-soldiers spelled out in the militia acts of the 1790s applied to them, and they seized on that recognition with all their might. This new relationship and the awareness of its novelty also drew in their families and home communities. The association was reciprocal, obliging the government to respect the soldiers as individuals and as men in return for the faithful performance of duties in this time of national need. More than just a symbol, this relationship held deep meaning.[85]

Between the spring of 1863 and the spring of 1865, the military service of black men established the case for full and equal citizenship with all the rights and privileges (including the suffrage) that their white counterparts enjoyed. The military experience quickly became an integral part of the war against slavery, significantly advancing the cause of freedom both by contributing to the defeat of the Confederacy and by destabilizing slavery in the Loyal Border States. The 1989 film *Glory* offers a modern-day retelling of the heroic version of this story, the narrative arc of which began with the initial rejection of the idea that black men could or should participate in the fight to save the Union, then proceeded through the enlistment of approximately 178,000 black men in the U.S. Army following the Emancipation Proclamation, and concluded with victory and vindication. Although the men in Turner's First U.S. Colored Infantry hailed from vastly different circumstances from those of their counterparts in the Fifty-Fourth Massachusetts Volunteers, the story of both overlapped in significant ways.

The Fifty-Fourth Massachusetts Infantry was the first regiment of black men raised in a Northern state. Its illustrious members included Lewis H. Douglass, the son of Frederick Douglass, who served as sergeant major, the highest enlisted rank. Its first commander, Colonel Robert Gould Shaw, was a member of Boston's social elite, who lost his life in the unsuccessful assault on Fort Wagner, South Carolina, in July 1863. Lieutenant Colonel Edward N. Hallowell, who succeeded to command after Shaw died, was a fighting Quaker abolitionist like his older brother Norwood P. Hallowell, who had left the Fifty-Fourth to assume command of the Fifty-Fifth Massachusetts Volunteers weeks before the battle. The Fifty-Fourth's other battle credits included Olustee, Florida, in February 1864 and Honey Hill, South Carolina, in November 1864. Over the course of the war, the Massachusetts men waged several other notable struggles aimed to ensure that the government and the nation accorded them respect appropriate to their status as U.S. soldiers.

The first of these concerned recognition as legitimate prisoners of war in the event of capture. They entered service insisting that the Lincoln administration and the civilian and military leadership of the army treat them exactly as they did white soldiers. They had, in fact, extracted promises of such equal treatment from governor John A. Andrew before enlisting, and Andrew made such professions freely and repeatedly. With scores of their comrades captured at Fort Wagner, they and their families, friends, and supporters at home feared for the worst. Although the War Department's General Order 100, issued on April 24, 1863, under Lincoln's name, bound U.S. forces to the international conventions regarding the proper treatment of captives, the Confederacy pointedly disregarded these standards, viewing black soldiers as insurrectionists and their officers as inciters of rebellion.[86] With the issue of the treatment of captives elevated to new urgency by the events at Fort Wagner, Lincoln issued his famous retaliation order on July 31, 1863, stating that if Confederate authorities carried through their threats to execute or enslave captured black soldiers, the U.S. government would execute or place at hard labor Confederate prisoners on a one-for-one basis.[87]

On the very day Lincoln issued his order, the mother of a soldier who fought with the Fifty-Fourth urged the president to protect the nation's black defenders. "A just man must do hard things sometimes," Hannah Johnson exhorted Lincoln, "that shew him to be a great man." Her words conveyed on behalf of all black Americans this newborn sense that the government was both legally and morally bound to protect all men in uniform regardless of color.[88] Although atrocities continued throughout the war—without any documented retaliation of the kind Lincoln had threatened—the number would have likely been even greater had not the president made emphatically clear that the lives of black soldiers held the same value as those of white soldiers.[89]

Just as they expected equal treatment if captured, black soldiers also expected equal pay. But whereas the former struggle pitted them against the Confederate enemy, the latter placed them at odds with the very government they were fighting to save. Another of the promises that Governor Andrew had made—backed by assurances from War Secretary Stanton himself—to recruiters and enlistees was that the black soldiers would be paid the same as their white counterparts. For private soldiers, that meant $13.00 plus a clothing allowance of $3.50 per month. The recruits for the Fifty-Fourth regiment assembled on the outskirts of Boston during the late winter and early spring and trained in the arts of the soldier without pay. They left Boston early in June without pay, and they fought and died at Fort Wagner in mid-July still without pay. Only in the fall, when the paymaster finally appeared, did they realize that Washington officials overrode the governor's repeated promises of equality. The solicitor of the War Department concluded that the wording of the July 1862 Militia Act required that all black soldiers be subject to its provisions of $10.00 per month pay, less $3.00 for clothing.[90] The men talked of mutiny but settled instead, to a man, on rejecting the paymaster's insulting offer. Firmly supported by their officers and soon joined by men in other regiments, they held firm to that decision, often at great cost to their loved ones at home, until June 1864, when Congress removed the inequality and provided retroactive pay.[91] Like other regiments recruited from the slave states, the First U.S. Colored Infantry did not engage in the boycott. Their families needed their earnings too desperately to be sacrificed on the altar of soldierly honor.

Although the circumstances of particular units' ties to their families and home communities created differences of opinion regarding the appropriate response to unequal pay, men in all black units shared a common belief in the need for men of their own color to hold commissioned office. Turner developed his interest in the subject as early as February 1863, as he witnessed the congressional debates over black enlistment. As he observed the growing sentiment in favor of segregated units—which, indeed, was formalized in May 1863 under the auspices of the War Department's Bureau of Colored Troops—Turner hoped that the corollary proposition would be to "have our own . . . captains, colonels, and generals."[92] Yet when Adjutant General Lorenzo Thomas began to organize units for the U.S. Colored Troops in the Mississippi River valley during the spring of 1863, he made no bones about their intended role as rear-guard forces, a far cry from the images of Hannibal and Toussaint L'Ouverture that must have occupied Turner's mind.[93] In short order, Turner and the men in all the regiments came to realize that for every white officer who harbored sincere antislavery convictions and who worked diligently to prepare the troops for the responsibilities of free men and citizens, there were others whose commitment to the cause was significantly less intense than their quest for authority and the emoluments of commissioned rank. In the worst of cases, men likened the new regime of army life to the old one of slavery.[94]

The wartime history of black military officers had a prequel about which Turner learned more in later months. It began in April 1861, as war clouds gathered over the nation. That month, Louisiana's Confederate officials received a gift from the *gens de couleur libres* of New Orleans: the tender of their services as "Defenders of the Native Land." The free men of color had had a proud tradition of militia service that dated from colonial times and that benefited from the blessing of General Andrew Jackson following their stout defense of New Orleans at the end of the War of 1812. Notwithstanding the black Creoles' offer, Governor Thomas More waited until the fall of 1861 before accepting recruits and offering commissions as company officers to men of African ancestry who raised companies.[95] In March 1862, as federal warships assembled in the Gulf for the expected assault on the city, he welcomed the "Native Guard" into the state militia, even though the men were still unarmed, imperfectly equipped, and only sparingly trained. When rebel officials evacuated the city, requiring soldiers to retreat with their commands, virtually all of the Creole officers and men disregarded both the orders and the accompanying threats against anyone who refused to comply. Free people of color stood side by side with enslaved people in welcoming the Yankee forces into the city.

Beginning in the summer of 1862, when General Benjamin F. Butler gained approval from Washington to augment his ranks with black recruits, the prospect of military service helped create a unity of purpose among all Louisianans of African descent, but it also reopened old sores. The *gens de couleur libres,* for instance, objected to being treated like slaves and demanded that federal authorities respect their rights.[96] And after General Butler reassembled the Native Guard companies, awarding commissions as captains and lieutenants to the men who had previously served in those roles, the men concluded that their chance to parlay loyal service into full citizenship was never brighter. That elation lasted barely into 1863 before a change in military commanders of the department resulted in an about-face. General Nathaniel P. Banks, like his predecessor, a Massachusetts politician rather than a career soldier, considered black officers to be inherently incompetent and systematically began revoking their commissions. Believing "that the appointment of colored officers is detrimental to the Service," in February 1863 he started purging Butler's appointees, deeming their presence in the army "a source of constant embarrassment and annoyance" that "demoralizes both the white troops and the negroes."[97]

The bravery of the officers and the men who fought at Port Hudson, particularly in the unsuccessful assault in late May 1863 in which Captain André Cailloux sacrificed his life and became a local hero, did not dissuade Banks from his course. With a greater urgency to enlist black soldiers than before, Banks transformed Butler's Native Guard into the "Corps d'Afrique," which, he insisted, was "not established upon any dogma of equality or other theory, but as a practical and sensible matter of business." He capped the units at 500 men (half the customary size) "to secure the most thorough instruction and discipline, and the largest influence of the officers over the troops." Blaming the black officers for the atmosphere of "lax discipline" he found in the Native Guard, he viewed white officers as the only remedy.[98] By June, former lieutenant Robert H. Isabelle had resigned his commission in protest against the "prejudice" Banks and other white officers under his command had demonstrated against men of color. Isabelle reported that thirty-nine of the seventy-three line officers and two staff officers that Butler commissioned had also resigned due to their "rights being withheld" under Banks's regime.[99] The Creole officers got no satisfaction, and the War Department silently supported the view that black line officers posed a practical problem best solved by decommissioning them.

———

War Secretary Stanton offered several gestures of accommodation to the numerous requests on behalf of black men who sought commissions, most notably in the case of surgeons and chaplains. Men bearing such commissions held the titular rank of major and captain, respectively, but they held no authority to command soldiers in battle. As a result, white enlisted men and officers alike often failed to respect them, as Major Alexander T. Augusta, surgeon for the Seventh U.S. Colored Infantry learned by experience. Early in 1864, a group of white surgeons serving in the same brigade as Augusta— several of whom were assigned to his own regiment—wrote to President Lincoln protesting "that the *Senior Surgeon* of the command was a Negro." They insisted that they had entered the service under the universal understanding that "*all* Commissioned Officers were to be white men." "Judge of our Surprise and disappointment," they said, when they discovered that was not the case. Claiming "to be behind no one, in a desire for the elevation and improvement of the Colored race, in this country," they nonetheless refused to "compromise what we consider a proper self respect." Being "Subordinate to a colored officer" would bring them "Such degradation" that they begged for a remedy to "this *unexpected*, *unusual*, and most unpleasant relationship." Apparently holding the white surgeon's self-respect in higher regard than Augusta's, the War Department reassigned Major Augusta to recruiting duty in Baltimore.[100]

Early in 1865, with the war virtually won, Washington officials abandoned their categorical opposition against commissioning black officers, beginning with Stephen A. Swails, of the Fifty-Fourth Massachusetts Volunteers. Since early in 1864, Swails had served as a lieutenant, but the War Department refused to muster him out of his enlisted rank of sergeant to assume the rank of lieutenant officially, despite an intense lobbying campaign by Governor Andrew and Colonel Hallowell. The delay had been based solely on his "African descent," an officer of the regiment later explained, "although to all appearances he was a white man."[101] When John Mercer Langston, the noted black attorney and abolitionist from Ohio, sought a colonel's commission after having secured the endorsement of Congressman James A. Garfield, the War Department said no.[102] At that same time, the department made several minor concessions in awarding the rank of major to Martin R. Delany, who had recruited black troops throughout the war, and the rank of brevet lieutenant colonel to Major Augusta, but these cases represented token exceptions to the department's long-standing refusal to commission black officers.

The military and naval service of some 200,000 African Americans contributed significantly to the defeat of the Confederacy and the destruction of slavery. Yet in many respects, military and naval service constituted experiences unto themselves, separating the soldiers and sailors both geographically and experientially from home and family. They functioned daily in a world of regulations and practices that were as rigid as those of slavery and were administered by officers who often acted like slave drivers. Ordinary Seaman George E. Smith, a New Yorker, left his ship out of frustration with "the general treatment men of Color receive" in the navy. In the hope of finding "more scope for [his] personal ambition," he enlisted as an orderly sergeant in a black regiment. But the navy considered him a deserter, tried and convicted him, and sentenced him to five years in prison.[103] A fifty-year-old first sergeant in a Louisiana regiment, William D. Mayo, led a number of his men in refusing to serve any longer under their abusive captain. Mayo was found guilty and sentenced to a term at hard labor, and his ordeal only grew worse. Prison guards confiscated "the Army Regulations that I bought and paid for with my own money," he observed, "and charged me with reading that which a Nigar had no business to know." His appeals for clemency fell on deaf ears.[104]

Mayo did not fare nearly as badly as other perceived troublemakers. Sergeant William Walker, who enlisted in the Third South Carolina Volunteers (later the Twenty-First U.S. Colored Infantry), had worked for the navy as a civilian pilot before enlisting in the army. When on shore visiting his family, he succumbed to "the promise solemnly made" by officers of the regiment that he would receive the same pay and allowances as white soldiers and volunteered for army service. In November 1863, he joined the men of his company in protesting against unequal pay, which officers of the unit perceived as "a general mutiny" instead of "a peaceful demand for the rights and benefits that had been guaranteed them." Fingered as the ringleader, Walker was court-martialed, convicted, sentenced to death, and executed on February 29, 1864.[105]

———

Henry McNeal Turner's Civil War service, which echoes that of the men in the Fifty-Fourth Massachusetts Volunteers, also demonstrates that the heroic narrative oversimplifies the full complexity of the black military and naval experience. As even this brief comparison between the Fifty-Fourth Massachusetts Volunteers and the First U.S. Colored Infantry suggests, the time and place of organization mattered, for from those circumstances followed the demographic composition of the officer corps and the enlisted ranks. Whereas many of the freeborn Massachusetts men could read and write, few of Turner's comrades who had been born into slavery in Washington, Maryland, and Virginia were literate. The profile of the officers followed suit. The early experience of the First witnessed prospective officers (all of whom were white) grubbing for commissions, with only glimmers of the antislavery zeal that the prospective officers of the Fifty-Fourth demonstrated.[106]

Like the history of the black military and naval experience, other strands of the emancipation narrative followed a similar arc. The story began amid the uncertainty of success in overturning the entrenched slave power. Yet, through the combined efforts of public officials, men in arms, freedom seekers, and men and women of conscience throughout North America, the movement for freedom gained momentum and eventually succeeded. Over the long run and in the aggregate, these narratives trace a line from exclusion to inclusion, from inequality to equality, and from slavery to freedom. Over the short run and in the particulars, however, the plot twisted and turned away from as well as toward the final destination.

By accentuating the linear features of the passage of time, clocks and calendars provide a superb way to situate events chronologically in relationship to each other, a necessary first step in understanding causal relationships among events. Yet chronological time can be deceiving and not just because of its presumptions of uniform units (the 24 hours in the day, and the 365 days in the year, for instance). The passage of time can subvert linearity as well as model it, both literally, in such recurring phenomena as the changing seasons and the associated variations in the length of the solar day, and figuratively, in terms of patterns that recurred over time though unpredictably. And when the transmission of information about events depended on inherently flawed media ranging from the human voice to the telegraph, messages could become garbled and events could lose their proper sequence. The enslaved Alabamian Monroe Jamison recalled that, at the end of the war, the report of Lincoln's assassination reached Talladega before the news of the surrender. "Old master was everywhere, cheery and lively" over the president's death, gloating that he had "told you boys you would never be free." The master's "good news," Jamison recalled, "plunged us into the deepest gloom," but the tables quickly turned. Within days, the enslaved man entrusted with carrying the master's mail reported that "the town is full of Yankees, and they told me I was freed."[107] In an instant, the hands on the clock of slavery stopped, and slave time ceased to exist.

Chapter 2

Recurring Seasons

Nature exerts a powerful influence on human perceptions of time. The daily rotation of earth on its axis results in the succession of darkness and light each day, just as the annual revolution of the earth around the sun accounts for the changing seasons. Understanding emancipation requires accounting for diurnal and seasonal time. Except for the southernmost tips of Florida and Texas, the Confederacy lay in latitudes where seasonal changes produced marked fluctuations in hours of daylight and ambient temperatures from summer to winter, with corresponding impact on all living things. Among humans, the seasons affect individual and collective moods, winter and spring most dramatically. "At length, the long dreary winter is gone!" shouted the AME *Christian Recorder* in April 1862. "Spring with its resurrection and life has come. All nature shows signs of renewal and exulting joy."[1]

Seasonal changes affected emancipation in several ways. Military operations followed the seasons, with most new offensives beginning in early spring, when the ground and the roads were dry enough to support the trudging feet of man and beast and the weight of wagons rolling on iron-rimmed wheels. Once begun, campaigning continued through the summer and fall. Clashing armies disrupted work in the fields and, by coincidence or design, appropriated or destroyed crops in the ground or in the barn. The movement of soldiers invariably put civilians in motion. Persons who aspired to be free had to take into account this changing seasonal array of opportunities and constraints.[2]

Just as seasonal changes affected the chances of becoming free, seasons also figured metaphorically into emancipation. Springtimes of hope followed winters of despair, in cycles that often mimicked the seasons of nature. "According to what was issued out in the Bible," explained the formerly enslaved Alabamian Charlie Aarons, "there was a time for slavery, people had to be punished for their sin, and then there was a time for it not to be."[3] Paraphrasing Ecclesiastes, Aarons suggested that for everything there is a season. Abraham Lincoln drew on the same theme in his second inaugural address.

—————

Charles Ball, an enslaved man who was born in Maryland in 1780 and then sold south early in the nineteenth century, left a remarkable account of his escape. Between August 1813 and June 1814, he retraced the steps between

Morgan County, Georgia, and Calvert County, Maryland, that he had taken several years earlier in chains.[4] Success in such attempts required overcoming two major logistical challenges: the escape route and the sources of subsistence along the way. These challenges presented themselves differently at different times of the year, so identifying "a proper season" to commence the bid for freedom was the critical first step.

From the time of his forced departure from his wife and children, Ball was determined to return home to them. During his journey southward he memorized features of the terrain, the names of rivers and towns, and the spatial relationship of each element to all the others. He also kept close track of the passage of days and months. He decided to flee captivity in Georgia after a brutal beating administered by two brothers of his owner's wife who, he explained, "thought a good whipping would be good for me."[5] After much study, he concluded that the proper season was August, when the ripening corn was "fit to be roasted." To facilitate fire building he put together a "fire-box . . . a tin case containing flints, steel, and tinder."[6] He carried additional clothing, coats, shoes, and a quantity of cornmeal. When he first set out he traveled by day, confident that the thick vegetation of woods and forests was sufficient to shield both his movements and his nightly fires for roasting the ears he took from cornfields. After nearly being detected, he began traveling at night by the light of the moon, taking his bearings from the stars.[7]

Through the remainder of the summer, the weather accommodated sleeping outdoors, but by late September he felt the change in the air.[8] During October, the nights turned noticeably cooler, but he was able to supplement the corn ration with sweet potatoes as well as wild fruits and nuts. He also managed to trap the occasional opossum, rabbit, and wild pig for protein.[9] In November, with the last of the corn having been harvested from the fields and the last of the potatoes grubbed from the ground, each day's search for "the means of subsistence became . . . more difficult."[10] December brought regular frost and the occasional storms of snow and sleet. "The fields were muddy, the low grounds in the woods were wet, and often covered with water . . . the air was damp and cold by day, the nights were frosty, very often covering the water with ice."[11] Thence forward he would have to depend on the stores laid up by humans, not the raw fruits of nature, for his food, and he perfected the technique of breaking into barns and corn cribs to access their shelter and sustenance.[12]

Ball's battle against inclement weather continued through March, with each body of water he crossed leaving him cold and wet and needing to build a fire when he reached the other side.[13] He reached Virginia in the spring and passed through Richmond uneventfully. Not far from the Potomac River, the last major obstacle separating him from Maryland, he was captured and jailed.

"This day appeared as long to me, as a week had done heretofore," he recalled, but he was determined to escape when darkness gave him sufficient cover. Commandeering a canoe, he crossed into Maryland and traversed the remaining distance home, reaching his wife's cabin in early June 1814. Remarkably, Ball never requested food or shelter from strangers, and he traveled alone nearly the entire way.[14]

Over the half century that elapsed between Charles Ball's escape and the Civil War, much changed in the Southern states, as the experience of Louis Hughes illustrates. Hughes was born a slave in Virginia in 1832 and was sold at age twelve to a cotton planter from Mississippi. Like Alabama and Louisiana, Mississippi had become the cotton frontier during the second quarter of the nineteenth century. Hughes's new owner lived in Panola County, in the north-central part of the state. The man had married his first cousin and settled near her parents and other relations. Hughes described him "as in some respects kinder and more humane than many other slaveholders," but not so the man's wife, whose persistent cruelty prompted Hughes to long for freedom.[15] After a spat with a neighbor, the planter moved his operations some sixty miles westward to Bolivar County along the Mississippi River approximately fifteen miles downriver from Helena and seventy below Memphis. Railroads employing steam locomotives linked the cotton plantations with the major cities of the region, and steamboats plied the rivers. Twice before the war, Hughes attempted to escape by steamboat. In one of those attempts he got as far as Louisville before being apprehended.[16]

Hughes's wife, Matilda, a domestic servant, yearned for freedom at least as strongly as Louis did. During the mid-1850s, the Mississippi man who held Louis purchased Matilda and her sister, members of a Kentucky family whose freedom had been stolen. Their grandmother had been born free, but their mother was held as a slave, ostensibly to be set free (along with all her children) at a certain date. Instead, unscrupulous members of the owner's family sold them, splitting them apart among multiple buyers.[17] After federal forces regained control over Memphis in June 1862, Matilda and the other servants and the field laborers were refugeed back to Panola County to stay with the owner's family. Louis remained behind on the river place as Union gunboats and transport vessels plied back and forth, stopping routinely at plantations along the way.[18] He twice attempted to reach Memphis by land, following highways and railroad lines, but failed both times. In those attempts Hughes drew on the knowledge of the coachman on a nearby plantation who knew all the roads to Memphis and who comforted Hughes when his "heart was heavy and sore."[19] Before leaving on his first try, shortly after Christmas 1862, Hughes informed Matilda "that the way seemed clear, and that I was going at once. I was bent on freedom, and would try for it again." Insisting that he "would return for her, as soon as possible," they parted "after many tears and blessings."[20] Despite taking necessary precautions, Hughes fell into the hands of a rebel patrol, whose members first thought to hang him. Instead, they carried him home, where a severe flogging greeted his return.[21]

Several months later when mild weather arrived, Hughes tried again, this time along with the coachman, their wives, and another man. They carried few clothes and provisions, hoping to replenish at a town along the way. They remained close to the road—but not too close for fear of the soldiers—and traveled through the woods by night, contending with "briar patches" and "old logs and driftwood" and taking their bearings from the stars. Several nights into the journey, they heard the sound of pursuing dogs, and the coachman oiled everyone's feet with an "ointment made of turpentine and onions, a preparation used to throw hounds off a trail." The ruse failed, the dogs overtook their quarry, and the coachman's owner and the man's son, accompanied by "Williams the nigger-catcher," took the freedom seekers into custody.[22]

Louis and Matilda plotted another escape in the spring of 1865, when they "were held with a tighter rein than ever" due to the Confederacy's flagging fortunes. The plan involved two steps, the first of which involved Louis and another man going to Memphis to ask federal authorities for assistance; this they accomplished in late June. The second step—the actual rescue—appeared to hit a snag when the officer with whom they spoke offered his sympathy but declined to dispatch soldiers lest he "be overrun with similar applications." In consolation, however, the officer advised that U.S. soldiers in the city "would be glad of such a scout," which Hughes and his companion soon found to be true. With a rented wagon, the party returned to Panola and the home plantation. Hughes and his companion gathered their loved ones, who numbered a dozen in all, and confronted their owner's family as they left. In a scene similar to thousands being enacted across the entire expanse of the former Confederate states that spring, the new order confronted the old. With the soldiers berating the proprietors for not having informed the people that they were "free men—that they can go and come as they like," Matilda's sister bade "good luck" to the mistress, who in reply wished them only "bad luck." The refugees reached their destination on July 4, 1865, an appropriate day to celebrate both personal and national liberty but three months—a full meteorological season—after Lee surrendered.[23]

———

Even amateur military strategists who had done nothing more than read accounts of Napoleon's ill-fated 1812 incursion into Russia knew that conducting winter campaigns in hostile territory in the Northern Hemisphere could lead to disaster. When Confederate forces opened fire on Fort Sumter on April 12, 1861, they aligned the fight for independence with the fairest season for doing so. Despite the ardent hopes on both sides for a short war, military planners went about their work with the reassuring knowledge that, even if neither side achieved an overwhelming victory quickly, some eight months of moderate weather lay ahead before winter would force the suspension of operations.

In the flood tide of Confederate nationalism, strategists took for granted that slaves as well as free black persons would support the military mobilization. In late June 1861, the Tennessee state legislature passed "An act for the relief of Volunteers," authorizing the governor "to receive into the military service of the State, all male free persons of color between the ages of fifteen (15) and fifty (50) years" to perform "all such menial service for the relief of the volunteers as is incident to camp life, and necessary to the efficiency of the service." In addition to the customary allotment of one ration per day and an annual clothing allowance, they were to be paid eight dollars per month. The act contained provisions for the involuntary impressment of free black men if sufficient numbers did not present themselves voluntarily, but it also enjoined military officers to ensure that the men did "not suffer from neglect or maltreatment." On a related note, the act authorized the allocation of one daily ration to "any mess of volunteers" that employed a servant "to wait on the members of the mess."[24]

Slaveholders who entered service as officers selected manservants to accompany them, generally from among their own household staff.[25] In May 1861, the young Louisiana diarist Kate Stone, whose family owned a cotton plantation some thirty miles northwest of Vicksburg, Mississippi, noted the departure of her beloved older brother, William, and her "Uncle Bo," accompanied by one of the family's servants, Wesley, "to wait on them." Stone noted that Wesley "was very proud of the honor of being selected to 'go to battle with Marse Will.'"[26] Sam Aleckson, a ten-year-old youth in Charleston, South Carolina, recounted with pride his service as an "officer's boy" to his owner in the spring of 1861. Minutemen "wearing blue cockades on the lapels of their coats" and displaying other signs of support for the cause set his imagination wild. Unversed in the terminology of war, he asked "Uncle Ben" where was the "Front"; the elderly man replied that it was the place where the "young buckra"—the term for white men in the local Gullah Creole—would "ketch de debble."[27]

When federal forces began operations in the slave states, Union officers also displayed the same penchant for employing black men as servants that their rebel counterparts did, and enlisted men followed suit. In the summer of 1862, the federal commander at Helena, Arkansas, lamented the shortage

Figure 2.1 Colored Army Teamsters, Cobb Hill, Virginia [1864]. Courtesy of the Library of Congress Prints and Photographs Division, LC-DIG-ppmsca-11338.

of formerly enslaved men to perform the necessary work at the fort. "Every other soldier in the Army of the South West has a negro servant," he declared.[28] The practice came full circle by the following spring, as private Confederate soldiers took on escaped slaves to work for rations and a place to sleep.[29] Over the course of the war, it is likely that 100,000 or more formerly enslaved men and women cooked for and waited on officers and enlisted men in the armed forces of each of the belligerents.

Military labor employed even larger numbers of black men whom Confederate authorities impressed to fortify the major cities and strategic points along the Atlantic and Gulf coasts and the inland waterways.[30] Officials called on the free black population first, especially in Virginia and in Louisiana, but nowhere could free black men alone satisfy the demand for laborers.[31] Over time, officials at the state and national levels attempted to balance the overarching need to advance the cause of independence with the individual rights of slave owners. What no one quite understood at first was how the mobilization of armed forces would affect the enslaved population, both those who were conscripted for such service and their families who remained on the farms and plantations (see figure 2.1).

At first this balancing act involved little more than agreeing on how the government might access the laborers when needed, with proper compensation to the owners and respect for their property rights. Before long, competing needs emerged, particularly when military commanders conscripted the laborers during a critical phase of the agricultural cycle. In light of the concerns raised by skeptical owners, conscription officers had to tread lightly. Impressed men and their families found ways to influence the terms and conditions of their hire. When treated poorly, they ran away, but not always toward the Yankees. They often went home instead, explaining on their arrival what prompted them to leave and begging not to be sent back. Such flight became the negotiating tool of choice, as impressed slaves pitted masters against Confederate authorities in hopes of improving their own lot and that of their families. For their part, conscription officers and overseers of work parties began to tighten the screws. One man who had been impressed later recalled that the bosses "usually whipped to kill. They were mad at negroes, anyway, about the war, and they whipped cruelly."[32] The experience of impressed labor—for weeks or months or even longer at a time—became one of the defining aspects of the war for both free and enslaved black men throughout the Confederacy.

The Virginia Peninsula nicely illustrates the dynamics that played out everywhere military officials conscripted slaves. General John B. Magruder, a Virginia native and a West Point graduate with more than thirty years of distinguished service, was responsible for planning defensive positions that would hinder the ability of federal forces to advance from Fort Monroe toward Richmond. After being named commander of the newly created Army of the Peninsula in July 1861, he promptly issued orders impressing adult male slaves in the counties north and south of the York River to reinforce Gloucester Point overlooking Yorktown. He similarly scoured the lower peninsula for laborers to rebuild the defensive line—parts of which dated from the American Revolution—along the Warwick River extending from Yorktown in the east to Williamsburg in the west.

Relying "upon the patriotism of his fellow citizens," Magruder called on free black men to present themselves. He also asked planters to relinquish half of their laborers for temporary duty, and they responded favorably.[33] He dispatched patrols to round up formerly enslaved people who had left their home farms and plantations in search of freedom. A Confederate staff officer's black servant reported that "our free town, Hampton" had become home to some 2,000 former slaves, transformed through contact with the Northerners into so many "raging Yankee negroes."[34] Accordingly, Magruder ordered "the whole country scoured to Hampton," which yielded "some 150 negroes." He put the men to work on the fortifications "and the rest [he] delivered to their masters." The commander of a cavalry regiment responsible for the round-up cautioned Magruder that "the negroes taken from the James River side" of the peninsula required close guarding. "They have been constantly in communication with the enemy," he explained, "and evinced the strongest dislike of being taken."[35]

When the absence of impressed laborers began affecting farm operations, slaveholders lost some of the patriotic enthusiasm they had earlier demonstrated. Late in August 1861 former president John Tyler wrote to Confederate secretary of war LeRoy P. Walker complaining that the impressment had produced "some little feeling of discontent" on the part of the affected slaveholders. The absence of the men for nearly six weeks "delayed the threshing of the wheat crop"; moreover, when impressed laborers returned home without authorization they were "followed by a posse to recover" them. Tyler questioned the legality of these proceedings. Walker explained that "in times of war, the necessities of the public service often demand departures from the ordinary rules of administration." Acknowledging that military commanders must subordinate their authority "to the ultimate rights of owners," Walker conceded that in the future officers should issue certificates promising "the return of the negros" and the payment of "reasonable hire."[36] Try as they might, Confederate authorities could not resolve the essential dilemma of impressment: sooner or later it was bound to disrupt critical agricultural operations such as plowing and planting in early spring, wheat harvesting and threshing during the summer, and general harvesting in the fall.[37]

At the same time, federal military and naval officials began to realize the substantial advantage that the ability to mobilize enslaved black laborers gave to the enemy. Even apart from the larger strategic and policy implications of denying such labor to the Confederacy, black men and women could perform useful work that soldiers and sailors would otherwise have to do. In July 1861, at Hampton, Virginia, when General Butler decided to create a buffer protecting Fort Monroe and Newport News, he turned to the "contrabands" to build fortifications, naming Edward Pierce to superintend "the experiment." Pierce was a Harvard-educated attorney, an abolitionist, and the former private secretary to Treasury Secretary Salmon P. Chase who served in a ninety-day regiment under Butler's command. With little more than a week before his enlistment was to expire, Pierce set about convincing a group of some sixty-odd men why they should be willing to work. Curiously, in this first experiment in compensated labor, he offered to furnish rations (for their families as well as the workmen) but not to pay cash wages. He also assured them that they would be respected as human beings and "treated kindly." In short order, their numbers grew with additional "fugitives from the back-country," and they soon displayed a level of workmanship that was superior to that of the soldiers.[38]

Later that fall, when General Thomas W. Sherman, leader of the military force that captured Port Royal, South Carolina, offered wages as the lure to recruit a labor force, he complained that "from the hordes of negroes left on the plantations but about 320 have thus far come in and offered their services."[39] In short, because Union policy makers had not fully analyzed what use they could make of enslaved laborers as their forces gained toeholds in Confederate territory during the first summer and fall of the war, they relied on commanders in the field to stumble into whatever appeared best in the circumstances. Curiously, when operations undertaken during the fall resulted in the capture of cotton plantations, military leaders did not take long to decide that black laborers might pick cotton, using force when the promise of future wages proved ineffective. The Yankee newcomers quickly learned the rhythms of the Southern agricultural calendar: autumn was the season when black hands picked cotton.

———

In the plantation districts of the Confederate states, the initial mobilization of volunteer soldiers did not reduce the number of direct producers so much as it depleted the cadre of supervisors who kept the black workforce subservient and productive. Nonetheless, Confederate agricultural strategists hoped to carry on as before, with enslaved laborers performing their usual tasks at the customary seasons supervised by elderly men and teenage boys or, when necessary, by plantation mistresses and trusted slaves. In 1862, Confederate authorities urged agriculturists to plant corn without discouraging the cultivation of cash crops, particularly cotton. The U.S. naval blockade of Southern ports greatly restricted the Confederacy's international trade and hence its ability to exchange cotton for weapons, but the full impact of the blockade came later.[40]

The inability to market the harvested cotton produced several results. Most planters attempted to carry on as before, baling the ginned cotton as usual, and either attempting to store it in warehouses or hiding it in secluded places in hopes of marketing it later. Hundreds of thousands of bales of such cotton eventually went up in smoke, generally at the hands of either Confederate or Yankee forces who wished to deny its use to their enemies. Planters who wished to avoid such risks reduced cotton acreage and planted grains instead, an approach that leading agricultural journals such as the *Southern Cultivator* advocated consistently by the beginning of 1862. Against the advantage of producing an edible crop that could be disposed of readily after the harvest, the shift away from cotton produced a counterbalancing disadvantage by disrupting the traditional patterns of field labor. Simply put, through the entire agricultural cycle grains required less time to cultivate and harvest than cotton, and plantation workers resisted maintaining the prewar pace of work in any event. Try as they might, the new managers could not enforce the old discipline in the new circumstances. Of course, where a single plantation or a cluster of plantations remained largely unaffected by the military mobilization, with both proprietors and overseers remaining at home, the enslaved people's efforts to work at their own pace did not fully succeed, at least not at first. But over time, as more overseers entered military service, that changed. In sum, the switch from staple crops to grains gave enslaved Southerners a chance to reduce the intensity of fieldwork. Stopping far short of freedom and full control over their own labor, this achievement had other consequences. In the summer of 1862, a Mississippi overseer replied to the question "what will you have your negroes doing" if cotton acreage were reduced by simply noting that he would put them to work on the oft-neglected maintenance of fields and buildings.[41] Military labor directly in support of the war effort and indirectly in the auxiliary services of salt making, mining, manufacturing, and transportation also absorbed the time of laborers who normally would be relentlessly chopping weeds from cotton rows.

Over the winter of 1861–62, Confederate strategists identified the key points whose strategic military location or value as manufacturing or transportation hubs warranted reinforcement, and mobilized enslaved men to perform the necessary work. Given the likelihood of federal operations along the Mississippi, the Tennessee, and the Cumberland Rivers, they focused special attention there, with ramifications that extended across hundreds of square miles. The diarist Kate Stone noted in late January 1862 that Confederate general Leonidas Polk had gathered "hands to complete the fortifications at Fort Pillow," above Memphis. "A great many Negroes have been sent from Arkansas, Tennessee, and North Mississippi," she reported, "and now it comes Louisiana's time to shoulder her part of the common burden."[42] Confederate forces in Tennessee mobilized enslaved laborers to work on Fort Donelson, and when Grant's troops captured the position in February, among the captives were "twelve negro slaves" kidnapped from Kentucky. Upon the appeal of their masters, Grant returned them, to the approval of the conservative Kentucky congressman Charles A. Wickliffe.[43] Confederate authorities impressed slaves in and around Nashville to reinforce the gun batteries there, correctly reasoning that the state capital was Grant's next target.

Such dramatic labor calls in the face of impending federal attacks masked the prosaic daily additions of enslaved persons to the labor force supporting Confederate armies. At established positions, some order was achieved, with slaveholders who were willing to hire their laborers to the army doing so. But armies on the move did not always observe such formalities; instead, they took up persons they encountered on the roads with few questions asked. In the spring of 1862, Confederate authorities attempted to control the allocations of laborers to army units, authorizing the employment of four cooks for each company of soldiers without regard as to whether they were "white or black, free or slave persons" and stipulating the pay and other amenities they were to receive. By that fall, so many reports had reached Richmond about the unauthorized use of enslaved laborers that the Confederate Congress ordered all military and naval personnel to relinquish all slaves captured, arrested, or taken except "by lawful authority" and to forward those unlawfully employed to reception depots to be established in each state. There, officials would determine whether a person's owner had agreed to the hire. Persons whose masters consented were to be assigned where needed; those without such permission were to be returned home. Such orders ultimately proved ineffective. For the rest of the war, Confederate authorities butted heads with officers and soldiers in the ranks, quartermasters, and commissaries of subsistence, who flaunted bureaucratic formalities when they needed work to be done.[44]

———

As the proper season for the start of military operations in 1862 drew near, many Northern observers began to sense that "a new state of things exists . . . and important events seem to be rapidly approaching." Some even strained themselves to see "the blessings of freedom . . . springing up in the path of a war of rebellion and treason."[45] But progress along that front would depend on the progress of Union arms. Events in the western theater gave reason for optimism, but in the east General George B. McClellan, the charismatic but egotistical commander of the Army of the Potomac, dragged his feet. After much prodding from President Lincoln himself, McClellan began to move toward Richmond in March. Reasoning that the peninsula offered the best route to the Confederate capital, he organized an armada of vessels to relocate his men and their equipment by water from their base at Alexandria to Fort Monroe. In the end, more than 400 transports moved some 120,000 soldiers, 15,000 horses and mules, and 4,000 wagons and ambulances, as well as weapons, ammunition, food, and fodder.[46]

McClellan consistently undercounted his own troop strength and moved only reluctantly against the enemy force, whose numbers he consistently overestimated. When Magruder abandoned Yorktown in early May, federal forces rushed in only to discover that the heavy guns that had kept them at bay for weeks were nothing more than logs.[47] As they pivoted toward

Williamsburg, McClellan's troops encountered the work that Magruder's impressed laborers had done along the Warwick River line over the preceding months. Whereas the Confederates continued to employ black men as military laborers, McClellan balked at employing black laborers until late in the campaign when his troops were so exhausted from marching, fighting, and digging that he had little other choice.

Events on Virginia's Peninsula influenced the first springtime of the Port Royal Experiment, some 500 miles by sea to the south on South Carolina's Sea Islands below Charleston. General David Hunter, a West Point graduate with a strong antipathy to slavery who was a personal friend of President Lincoln's, had assumed command of the Department of the South in March 1862, eager to take the offensive. As he contended with the debilitating impact of the coastal climate and its associated fevers on his Northern-born troops, the War Department requisitioned a portion of his force to strengthen McClellan's army in Virginia. To compensate, Hunter began enlisting local black men and then dispatching them to round up every man of military age to serve in his fledgling regiment, using force if necessary to persuade the footdraggers. Officials and employees of the Treasury Department, which had assumed jurisdiction over managing the plantations, joined the men and their families in full-throated protest. From one quarter to the next, the men headed for the woods at the mere rumor that soldiers were in the neighborhood, unwilling to leave their families even for the honor—which they perceived as dubious at best—of donning the uniform of U.S. soldiers. Far from being the mere pawns of the Yankee newcomers, freed people quickly began to calculate their own stake in the federal occupation and to act accordingly. Springtime was the time for planting, not for soldiering, for winter was certain to come again and with it the need for fully stocked larders, war or no war.[48]

When Union forces advanced into Middle Tennessee, northern Mississippi, and northern Alabama, they followed the Confederates' lead and mobilized enslaved men to support their own operations.[49] By seizing the railroad junctions at LaGrange, Huntsville, Corinth, and Holly Springs, they cleared an overland approach to Memphis, which fell to the federals in June. With a combination of black freedom seekers who fled their homes at the approach of the Yankees and the enslaved laborers who were taken up from the plantations, Grant's army had laborers to spare. Fortunes changed with lightning speed, as an enslaved man who was working on an Arkansas cotton plantation learned. When Confederate officials called for laborers to throw up "breast works," the overseer recommended that he and his coworkers "put out to the woods," promising to furnish provisions "till we could get to the Yankees." After achieving that goal, he worked as a deck hand with the marine fleet and then as a woodchopper on an island in the river before enlisting in the U.S. Colored Troops.[50]

In the weeks after the fall of Memphis, Union gunboats defeated Confederate forces at New Madrid, Missouri, and Island No. 10, thereby opening the Father of Waters to Vicksburg. In an early attempt to bypass the impressive guns that the rebels had mounted there, General Thomas Williams devised a plan to dig a canal across a bend in the river. "Between 1,100 and 1,200 negroes, gathered from the neighboring plantations by armed parties, are now engaged in the work of excavating, cutting down trees, and grubbing up the roots," he reported on July 4, 1862. Despite his enthusiasm, the laborers faced the challenge of digging away eleven feet of "hard clay." They needed to expose the sand bed below, he explained, because "the current of the river, however great, will not wash the clay." Although he noted the "highly satisfactory" progress of "the negro force . . . duly organized into squads of 20, with an intelligent non-commissioned officer or private to each, superintended by officers," he also conceded that the labor required was "far greater than anticipated by anybody."[51] But his vision faded before the clay yielded, obliging Williams to abandon the project. From nearby Louisiana, Kate Stone recorded the toll of the Yankees' impressment of "all the Negro men on the river places and putting them to work" on what she termed "a ditch . . . across the point opposite Vicksburg." Reacting to the news that the press gangs had shot men who refused to cooperate, Stone recoiled at the "outrages committed on private property." Her mother, she recorded, summoned "all the men" and "told them if the Yankees came on the place each Negro must take care of himself and run away and hide," adding with at least a hint of doubt, "We think they will."[52]

The slaveholders' fears were only partly justified given the conflicting ways in which federal military and naval officers treated the enslaved people they encountered. The commanding officer of the side-wheel steamer *John P. Jackson*, Selim E. Woodworth, for instance, enlisted men into naval service and gave protection to their families at a large camp at an island near Vicksburg where several thousand refugees had gathered. In July 1862, he communicated with the commander of the Mortar Flotilla, to which his ship was attached, that Commander Thomas T. Craven had collaborated with "the wife of a notorious rebel" to return forty persons whom she claimed as her slaves, among whom were persons Woodworth "had promised . . . immunity from punishment" when he enlisted the men. The colony of refugees, some from "three hundred miles distant," consisted of persons who had been "induced to leave thier masters, by reports amongst them, that they would never again be returned, after once reaching the Aegis of our Flag and guns." The commander of the Mortar Flotilla forwarded the information to secretary of the navy

Gideon Welles, who repudiated Craven's actions. Several months earlier, the secretary had advised squadron commanders to employ as needed the large number of acclimated refugees who were "flocking to the protection of the United States flag."[53]

Camps of black refugees quickly took shape wherever the federal forces lingered for more than a few days. They availed themselves of their former masters' horses, mules, and wagons, which were particularly effective for carrying the elderly, the young, and whatever household possessions might fit. By one later estimate, some 50,000 black refugees had gathered at Grand Junction, Tennessee, by November 1862, when General Grant appointed John Eaton, a chaplain in a regiment of Ohio volunteers, superintendent of contrabands. With clothing and rations furnished by the army, the men and their families had a start toward subsistence. They built shelters from unserviceable tents and scavenged lumber, and villages took shape around camps where the Yankees established permanent garrisons.[54]

From the standpoint of enslaved people who had been waiting for generations to be free from bondage, the success of Union military operations during the war's second spring sometimes produced the opposite effect from what they expected. Nowhere was this more evident than in southern Louisiana. When the presence of federal forces prompted disloyal slaveholders to flee, the black residents of New Orleans and the surrounding plantation districts seized the opportunity to act, shedding the habits of slavery and challenging the restrictions of the old regime. "No one can tell what a Day may bring Forth," observed the unsettled owner of Magnolia Plantation, where the enslaved people constructed a gallows as the first design element in their vision of the new order. On other plantations, however, the residents asserted freedom by taking to the highways bound for New Orleans, the headquarters of federal operations, or Camp Parapet, on the city's western suburbs, where General John W. Phelps, a Vermont abolitionist, had made clear his desire to shelter all freedom seekers.[55]

Owners whose political sympathies lay with the Confederacy often decided to abandon Louisiana rather than take their chances with Butler, and Texas proved to be an attractive destination. On one plantation not far from the city, word of impending relocation prompted the enslaved people to act preemptively. As Stephen Jordon later recalled, the entire workforce of some fifty persons "had a secret meeting at midnight, when we decided to leave to meet the Yankees," then quickly gathered their valuables and departed under a moon that was "shining like day." After several hours of trudging through the woods, they opted for the public road instead. Patrollers soon overtook them and returned them home. Their owner identified Jordon as the ringleader of "all this devilment" and planned to have him executed as an example. While languishing in a cell, Jordon learned that a man from Texas had purchased him, thereby sparing his life.[56] Almost inconceivably, Lincoln's proclamation, which the world anticipated with bated breath, threatened to turn the springtime of hope into a winter of despair in southern Louisiana and the other Union-occupied portions of the Confederacy where slavery had begun to crumble.

Grant's campaign against Vicksburg gained momentum from the Emancipation Proclamation. Under the new policy, federal forces took steps to free black men and women from bondage, mobilizing them in support of military and naval operations rather than simply trying to shelter and subsist those who had escaped from or who had been abandoned by their owners. The operational plans that Grant and Navy Flag Officer David D. Porter developed did not attempt to amass such a huge and ultimately unwieldy force as George McClellan had on the peninsula the spring before. Nor did federal strategists shy away from winter operations, making several preliminary forays—by land and by water—to determine the most accessible route to Vicksburg beginning in the closing days of December 1862. As earlier, the soldiers and sailors who had wielded axes and shovels in support of the advance gladly relinquished a portion of that work to freedmen.[57] But the new strategy encouraged commanders of naval vessels to fill their need for sailors by shipping black men directly on board rather than awaiting the arrival of recruits from the North. In an even stronger signal of the Union's commitment to destroying slavery, Adjutant General Lorenzo Thomas visited the Mississippi valley in March and April, beating the drum for the U.S. Colored Troops. His efforts quickly produced recruits by the thousands.

By exempting Tennessee from the Emancipation Proclamation, Lincoln hoped to bolster the loyalty of slaveholding Unionists there. While this action did not necessarily weaken black Tennesseans' hope in their eventual deliverance from bondage, it created a halfway house between slavery and freedom that lasted for the rest of the war. In areas under federal control, slavery deteriorated regardless of the exemption: owners refused to feed and shelter their slaves, and freedom seekers abandoned their former owners. Both practical and legal ramifications arose when prospective employers encountered persons still nominally held as slaves who wished to work for wages or on some other similar arrangement. Government and civilian employers alike faced the nettlesome question of whether the owners or the laborers were entitled to the pay. Most government employers decided to issue rations and clothing but to withhold the wages. The War Department authorized payment directly to the laborers in November 1863, but the problem persisted despite the laborers' repeated complaints of not being paid for work they had performed. The legal question remained unresolved until after the war.[58]

In April 1863, Assistant Secretary of War Charles A. Dana somewhat ruefully reported from Tennessee that General Stephen A. Hurlbut, who commanded the Sixteenth Army Corps headquartered in Memphis, intended "to settle the negro question here by enrolling for duty as pioneers, teamsters, &c., all who are fit for service in this immediate vicinity and along the line of the railroad he is guarding, taking sufficient bonds for the good treatment and return of the persons." In one fell swoop, Hurlbut intended to ease the loyal masters' concerns about their property and put to work the men who otherwise would require support.[59] Each division employed a pioneer corps, and the laboring units "had negroes attached to them, who had come into our camps," reported the chief engineers of the Department of the Tennessee, who added that these men "proved to be very efficient laborers when under good supervision."[60] In mid-June, a brigade commander who had "but a very limited number of contrabands" available to labor on breastworks requested "about 100 more negroes from the organizing regiments temporarily detached to assist my working party."[61] In short order their numbers grew into the thousands as they supported all the federal operations against Vicksburg. One knowledgeable commentator later estimated that 80,000 African Americans participated in the campaign.[62]

The assistant secretary's ebullience notwithstanding, solving "the negro question" was not a simple task, as Hurlbut himself knew. Late in March he had written directly to the president seeking authority to relocate the thousands of refugees in Memphis and the vicinity to abandoned plantations. Besides those who received support from the government, he estimated that several thousand others occupied "vacant sheds and houses," lived "by begging or vice," and constituted a "fruitful source of contagion and pestilence." Meanwhile, landowners wanted their land to be productive and were willing to hire their former slaves. "It is Spring," Hurlbut noted, "the time to put in crops—either of cotton or of corn," even "garden vegetables," but he felt constrained to act. "In the present anomalous situation" of Tennessee, "neither exactly loyal nor altogether disloyal" yet lacking "the Machinery [of] Civil Government," no one knows for certain "whether the State of Slavery exists or not" because "the law is in abeyance." Despite the state's exemption from the Emancipation Proclamation, Hurlbut informed Lincoln matter-of-factly that "military authorities both from choice and under orders ignore the condition of Slavery," the net result of which was an "incursion of ungoverned persons without employment and subject to no discipline." "Both from feelings of humanity to the people around us and to relieve the Army from this burden," Hurlbut sought authority "to bring . . . together" the vacant land and the idle labor.[63]

In mid-April, Secretary of War Edwin M. Stanton replied on the president's behalf, agreeing that the "contrabands" who were not already in the army "had better be set to digging their subsistence from the ground." He instructed Hurlbut to settle as many refugees as possible on the abandoned plantations and also permit those who "voluntarily make arrangements to work for their living" to do so. Finally, he authorized "loyal men of character in the vicinity to take them temporarily on wages to be paid to the contrabands themselves" on the condition that they "not let the contrabands be kidnapped or forcibly carried away." In the meantime, Hurlbut's superior, General Grant, authorized the hiring of freed people to loyal persons who posted bonds.[64]

Long before federal operations against Vicksburg even began, Confederate strategists had pressed black laborers into making defensive preparations. Early in January 1863, just after his attempt to approach the city from the rear met defeat at Chickasaw Bayou, General William T. Sherman reported having encountered fortifications extending fourteen miles from the city along the Yazoo River, which took advantage of "a natural fortification" that had been "strengthened by a year's labor of thousands of negroes, directed by educated and skilled officers."[65] But by early May, after Grant and Porter's combined operation succeeded in steaming past the batteries at Vicksburg and disembarking downriver to commence an overland approach to the city, the work intensified. Confederate engineers supervised the labor of thousands of slaves to extend the fortified zone, to perfect a system of trenches and tunnels, and to dig underground magazines for ammunition. In the interest of leaving no hands idle, "a working force of 24 negroes from the jail-gang" joined in the digging. If the heat were not enough of a burden, the work itself was inherently dangerous. The commander of a Confederate brigade reported the death of "eight negroes and the overseer in charge" from the premature explosion of a mine.[66]

Thanks to the federal siege, by the time the Confederates capitulated on July 4, 1863, Vicksburg had become a very small place and one that the survivors would never forget. Hundreds of the black laborers were among the captives, and hundreds from nearby plantations who had earlier been impressed into the work returned to the city after the fall. Paroled Confederate officers tried to exploit the ensuing confusion by attempting to take with them black people whom they claimed as personal servants. Union officers became suspicious that the parolees were "abusing" the privilege of removing such persons beyond the lines and began granting approvals only "in cases of families and sick or disabled officers." Recruiters for the U.S. Colored Troops dutifully pursued their work. Isaac Stier was but one of hundreds who had endured the siege as a Confederate officer's servant and then entered the U.S. Army.[67]

It is impossible to exaggerate the importance of the fall of Vicksburg in loosening the bonds of slavery throughout the Mississippi valley. Enslaved people's springtime of hope became a summer of freedom. Although far from a deathblow to either slavery or the Confederacy, Grant's victory succeeded in establishing federal authority in the major river towns from Memphis to New Orleans and on the abandoned plantations that lined the banks of the river. More than soldiers, sailors, and freed people took part in the work; Treasury Department officials, plantation lessees, and cotton speculators, as well as missionaries, teachers, nurses, and clerks employed by benevolent and freedmen's aid societies did too. This unlikely coalition, with differing—even at times contradictory—motives, attempted something new in North America: "the transition of the oppressed humanity of the negro race from a state of forced labor to a condition of voluntary industry," as leaders of the major freedmen's aid societies declared.[68] Meanwhile, "for every mile" of Grant's advance, one observer noted with some hyperbole, "ten thousand freedmen drop their chains."[69]

The Union army's stunning success at Chattanooga late in 1863 set the stage for operations against Atlanta, Georgia, as the major strategic objective for spring 1864. In March, when Grant became general in chief and moved east to join General George G. Meade and his Army of the Potomac in the campaign against Richmond, Sherman assumed command of the Western army. The Northern public sensed the new spirit of aggressiveness, though it remained unclear how well Northern voters would tolerate the accompanying casualty lists in the upcoming fall elections. In February 1864 an observer in Oberlin, Ohio, condemned the practice of retreating to winter quarters and suspending military operations during cold weather. Citing lessons from military history dating back to classical times, the writer noted that "we are in the midst of a revolution whose issue is beyond the ken of mortal." Circumstances called for the relentless pursuit of Confederate armies. "To delay, is but to strengthen the enemy and weaken ourselves." Disregard the "parallels of latitude or change of seasons," he insisted, and "let the coldest weather call us out for a campaign" in which we will throw "our forces like an avalanche upon them." The result would be to drive them "into submission or into the Gulf of Mexico."[70] In February 1864, Sherman's operation against Meridian, Mississippi, signaled his willingness to undertake winter operations. For the next fifteen months, his army paid no heed to ambient temperature, conditions of roads and streams, or hours of sunlight as they pursued victory first across Mississippi and Tennessee, and then through Georgia and the Carolinas.

Sherman's victory at Atlanta in September tipped the balance favoring Lincoln's reelection, which the AME minister Richard H. Cain termed a "great revolution in the political arena." What is more, it enabled Grant and Sherman to execute the plan that they had discussed for some time: bringing the full impact of war to the Confederate heartland. By marching across Georgia to Savannah, Sherman aimed to rain "utter destruction" on the "roads, houses, and people" of the Confederate heartland and, by doing so, to demonstrate that no rebel force could stop the Union's juggernaut.[71] The autumn presented what Charles Ball would have described as a proper season for such a march, in which the army would live off the land. Undeterred by the decreasing bounties of cornfields and potato patches, Sherman's men used their numbers and their force of arms to punish wealthy slaveholders, particularly those with the temerity to resist. They gathered sheep and cattle for slaughter, pulled hams from smokehouses, and helped themselves to every other article that could make a soldier's life comfortable.[72] What they could not consume or carry away, they destroyed.

By following four nearly parallel routes to the seacoast, with General Oliver Otis Howard commanding the Right Wing, Sherman's forces cut a swath of devastation more than sixty miles wide through the heartland of Georgia. The sheer numbers of black refugees who greeted the Yankees along the way, coupled with the gratitude that they expressed and the tales of suffering and hope that they told, softened the hearts of many hardened veterans. The troops soon developed a taste for having the freed people regale them with plantation songs and dances in the evenings.[73] Yet operational imperatives could quickly jolt the revelers back to reality. When a portion of Howard's command reached Ebenezer Creek, a short distance from Savannah, for instance, pioneers constructed a pontoon bridge. After the troops and their supply trains had crossed, their commander, General Jefferson C. Davis, ordered the bridge to be destroyed, leaving hundreds of black refugees at the mercy of pursuing Confederate cavalry. Scores attempted to swim through the chilly waters to avoid capture, and not all reached safety. Those who remained behind fell into the hands of the rebels.[74] Such incidents notwithstanding, an estimated 10,000 freedom seekers arrived in Savannah with the Union army days before Christmas 1864. Upon reaching the coast, the soldiers encountered black communities that had been self-supporting since the flight of the rebel landowners three years earlier. Far from viewing Sherman's legions as liberators, the residents considered them plunderers who confiscated their animals and provisions and destroyed other property with abandon. Instead of distributing Christmas gifts of cloth or shoes, as the planters had traditionally done, the Yankees inaugurated a new custom of taking instead of giving. This not only violated the spirit of the season but also jeopardized the freed people's ability to survive the upcoming winter.[75]

Early in January, Sherman, Secretary Stanton, and other high-ranking officials, including General Howard, met with a delegation of Savannah clergymen who had been chosen to represent the views of the freed people. In a soon-famous "colloquy with colored ministers," Sherman quizzed them about their expectations for the future. Garrison Frazier, the spokesman for the group, eloquently stated the collective sentiment that without land they held little hope for success.[76] Within days, Sherman issued Special Field Order 15, which set aside the Sea Islands of South Carolina, Georgia, and Florida and the mainland to the distance of thirty miles from the coast as a reserve on which freed people would be granted access to small parcels of land.[77]

Although the general did not realize it at the time, by establishing the "Georgia refugees" on these lands he set up the potential for later conflict when the antebellum residents who had spent the war in the interior returned during the summer of 1865. Even before the planters begged President Andrew Johnson for clemency and received it, the freed people who had been involuntarily removed from their homes during the war wondered how the government could grant the land that their sweat and blood had made valuable to a group of strangers.[78] Sherman's order, with its specific reference to the distribution of land to heads of households in forty-acre parcels, reinforced the long-cherished expectation on the part of slaves in the Northern Border States no less than the Southern Confederate states that with the end of slavery would come the gift of land as partial recompense for their years of unrequited toil. Indeed, the Freedmen's Bureau bill that Congress enacted in March 1865 contained a similar reference to parcels of forty acres. In short, the much-maligned notion of "forty acres and a mule" did not simply drop out of the clear sky: its superficial element—cast-off army mules—were easy to come by and capable of rehabilitation in skilled hands. Freed people had some reason to believe that the substantive element—the land—which both military orders and national law referenced, would help repay the debt the nation owed them for more than two centuries of exploitation and abuse.

———

As the year 1865 dawned, the Union soldiers in winter quarters before Petersburg and Richmond looked to resume the fighting and speed the defeat of the rebellion. Thomas Morris Chester, an African American newspaper correspondent for the Philadelphia *Press*, announced with pride "that the past winter has been spent in the most thorough preparation for a vigorous spring campaign" that gives "all the troops the most perfect confidence . . . as to the speedy termination of the rebellion." Late March brought the "refreshing days of spring that give renewed vigor to humanity." Chester also observed that Confederate soldiers were crossing the picket lines with growing frequency and that black residents of Richmond escaped to federal lines daily, often in extended families. They reported a bleak mood in the rebel capital. Confederate partisans who had endured the periodic threat of attack in each of the prior four years packed their valuables feverishly in anticipation of evacuating the city.[79]

Sherman's army rested at Savannah until February before heading north into the Carolinas, where heavy rains had saturated the ground and gorged the rivers. Pioneer battalions, consisting of soldiers and black laborers, constructed corduroy roads through the swamps and built bridges across the waterways.[80] They went about their work relentlessly but with high spirits, flushed with the satisfaction of bringing war to the birthplace of secession at last. In North Carolina they were joined by troops that had been dispatched from Virginia to take part in operations against Fort Fisher the previous December and January and that had occupied Wilmington in February. Among them were regiments of the all-black Twenty-Fifth Army Corps, including the First U.S. Colored Infantry. Chaplain Henry M. Turner's first glimpse of the westerners left him incredulous that this barefooted and unkempt force of destruction could be considered "*the* army of America." Quite simply, they consumed, confiscated, or torched everything in their path. On the occasions when black troops served as the vanguard, Turner observed, they spared poor whites some food that they advised them to hide before Sherman's men arrived.[81] At Goldsboro, North Carolina, Sherman overtook Confederate general Joseph E. Johnston's tattered remnants of the Army of Tennessee, leaving Lee's forces at Richmond bereft of their last hope of reinforcement. The refugees who straggled behind Sherman's supply wagons and ambulances numbered an estimated 8,300, "two-thirds of whom were negroes," according to General Howard. Most were entirely destitute, their provisions having long since been exhausted.[82]

In the late winter of 1864–65, as the Confederacy's life ebbed away and as the proposed antislavery amendment to the U.S. Constitution worked its way through congressional approval and the assent of the requisite number of states, the emancipation process continued to reveal contradictory crosscurrents, which sometimes aided and sometimes stymied freedom seekers. One such anomaly that cut against the grain involved "biding time," or awaiting "a proper season" (in Charles Ball's terminology) to act. The noted Confederate diarist Mary Boykin Chesnut identified this tendency at the very start of the war as she studied the behavior and the facial expressions of Charleston's "negro servants" after the Confederate batteries opened fire on Fort Sumter. Unable to "detect any change in [their] demeanor," she observed that "people talk before them as if they were chairs and tables" yet "they make no sign." "Are they stolidly stupid?" she mused, "or wiser than we are; silent and strong, biding their time?"[83]

In the fall of 1863, an anonymous "Colored man" in New Orleans provided insight into the phenomenon from the standpoint of the enslaved people. Though they desired freedom with every fiber of their being, they also understood that a hasty or false move might lead to catastrophe. "The Collored population is not educated but what Great responcibility has been placed on them," he marveled, in terms of the skilled and unskilled labor they performed. Yet in New Orleans and the surrounding Union-held parishes, they faced a dilemma. Mindful of the biblical injunction that man cannot serve two masters, he observed that "the Collored population" was expected to serve two: "a rebel master and a union master." The rebel masters "wants us to make Cotton and Sugar And the[y] Sell it and keep the money." For their part, "the union masters wants us to fight the battles under white officers and the[y] injoy both money and the union black Soldiers And white officers will not play togeathe much longer." As to the reason for the fighting, "our Southern friend tells that the[y] are fighting for negros and will have them," while "our union friends Says the[y] are not fighting to free the negroes" but rather "for the union and free navigation of the Mississippi river."[84] Risks abounded on both sides.

The smoldering tension between slaveholders and Union authorities coupled with the exemption from the Emancipation Proclamation left enslaved people in a state of limbo. Slavery had deteriorated to the point where a distinguished attorney informed the "Colored Man" that "the Colored population was all free and Had as much liberty in the union as he had," but the man remained skeptical. After all, soon after "the white Preachers" began declaring that "we were all free as any white man," military officials started "taking us up and puting in the lockups and Cotton presses giving us nothing to eat nor nothing Sleep on And haveing negro traders for recruiting officers Drawing his Sword over us like we were dogs." "Freedom and liberty is the word with the Collered people," the man concluded, "nothing Shorter." But because "we have been made fools of from the time Butlers fleet landed hear," the man refused to lower his guard and believe that the day of jubilee had arrived. "I have remained At my old Stand," he explained, "and will untill i See what i am dowing."[85]

Biding time often involved passing back and forth between Confederate and Union lines. Some of this movement occurred within tightly structured circumstances. Louis Hughes's experience provides insight. Yankee transports regularly passed by the Mississippi River plantation where he lived and worked, at times even making landfall and sending parties of soldiers ashore to frighten the slaveholders. Despite the frequency of these visits, the prospective number of liberated slaves was small because the planters had already refugeed their workforces away from the river after federal forces liberated Memphis in June 1862. Men like Hughes who were ordered to stay behind had to balance the chances of escape against their attachments to their absent families. When his owner was arrested and jailed, Hughes carried papers between Confederate and Union negotiators to exchange the man for the crew of a captured transport vessel.[86] He fulfilled his duty without attempting to escape, at least not then. Another man who had been hired to work as a teamster for Confederate forces in Mississippi "was content to bide his time" and "was on several different occasions in the union lines and in conference with union officers" before departing to the Yankees for good.[87]

A man identified only as Charles reportedly was "among the first" to abandon the Louisiana plantation where he resided, but he "soon returned to stay at home," claiming that he had "had enough of Yankees." With the white men all absent in the army, the enslaved people contended only with the wives and children of the owners. "Marauding parties" paid no heed to the "protection papers" issued by a Yankee general, and on the plantation where Charles served as "leader" the people did as they pleased, among other things using "very abusive language" toward their mistress.[88] In the eastern theater, enslaved people moved back and forth between Union and Confederate lines with a similar degree of ease. One man told a federal official in Virginia that with "nobody on the plantations but women" they had little fear. "The white people have nearly all gone, the blood hounds are not there to hunt them and they are not afraid."[89]

The freewheeling circumstances of war and the vagaries of emancipation accounted for the rest of the movement back and forth. In his 1864 year-end report, for instance, Horace James, the superintendent of contrabands in eastern North Carolina, reported a slight decline in the number of black refugees under his charge from the time of his earlier report. By way of explanation, he simply noted that numbers of people had left.[90] Colonel John Eaton, general superintendent of contrabands in the Department of the Tennessee, similarly noted that some unspecified number of the more than 20,000 refugees who had entered the camps under his jurisdiction in western Tennessee "in various ways have gone back to slavery."[91] The line separating Union from Confederate territory was porous, and black people moved back and forth from one side to the other, voluntarily as well as involuntarily. At times these movements had pronounced seasonal components, for instance, in the fall when men at work within federal lines crossed back into the Confederacy to ensure that their families had adequate provisions for the winter. With free-dom as the ultimate goal, the Union's policies of "confiscation" and "emanci-pation" had limitations. So did the Confederate laws of slavery, which, like other laws, were made to be broken.

Emancipation in the Loyal Border States also reflected pronounced sea-sonal changes that overlapped with the ebb and flow of larger wartime events. But whereas in the Confederacy the major consideration was the timing of Union military operations, in the Loyal Border States of Maryland, Kentucky, and Missouri the impetus was recruiting black men to fill the depleted ranks of the federal armed forces.[92] After beginning to recruit enslaved black Mary-landers during the summer of 1863, in October War Secretary Stanton ex-tended the authorization to Missouri as well. Slaveholders there had few illusions about the potentially disastrous impact of this change in policy on the stability of their prized domestic institution of slavery. Indeed, Massachu-setts senator Henry Wilson "gloried" in knowing that a companion act of Congress had "declared tens of thousands of slaves in the loyal States free, upon their own will to become free." It was, he boasted, "incomparably the greatest emancipation measure that was ever passed by the Congress of the United States."[93]

In Missouri, slaveowners dissembled and stalled for several months, which meant that recruits faced the perils of inclement weather in addition to slave-catchers and other outlaws on their way to the recruitment rendezvous points. Unionist masters maneuvered to evade the government's recruiters, in the most extreme cases by fleeing with their human property to the Con-federate states. Those who remained in the state intimidated enslaved men to stay at home, which many did in the interest of safeguarding their fami-lies. The onset of winter gave an unexpected advantage to the masters, who threatened to withhold clothing, shoes, fuel, and provisions from the fami-lies of black volunteers, or, worse yet, to turn them out into the public roads. Martha Glover, the enslaved wife of a recent Missouri recruit, suffered through the Christmas holidays of 1863. "I have had nothing but trouble since you left," she wrote to her husband Richard Glover just before New Year's, citing her owner's verbal and physical abuse and threats not to "take care of our children."[94]

Recruits who left home soon after Christmas often reached the rendezvous point suffering from fatigue and exposure. Men from the tobacco- and hemp-growing region in the central part of Missouri, through which the river of the same name flowed, assembled at Benton Barracks in St. Louis, where they became the Sixty-Second, Sixty-Fifth, and Sixty-Seventh U.S. Colored In-fantry regiments. But army officials were ill equipped to cure all the men's ailments, and hundreds died at the camp and its adjacent hospital. In

March 1864, the men of the three units who were fit enough to take the field were transferred to Morganza, Louisiana, where they continued to experience inordinately high rates of morbidity and mortality due to its swampy environs. In the end, they accounted for some of the highest unit losses due to disease of all regiments in the U.S. Army. Much of their misery and misfortune derived from the exposure they suffered during the winter of their enlistment.[95]

A similar scenario played out in Kentucky in the fall of 1864, by which time not even the determined opposition of the state's officials could postpone the inevitable start of recruiting. Prospective enlistees gathered into bands along the way to keep each other "company," as the recruit Peter Bruner explained, and to realize security in numbers.[96] If the opposition of enslavers were not enough, the men and their families also faced the indifference, or worse, of federal officials. The changing seasons also worked to their disadvantage, as the lamentable case of Joseph Miller and his family illustrates. Miller testified that he left his master to enlist "about the middle of October 1864," taking his family with him after the master asserted that "he would not maintain them." With the permission of an officer in his regiment, Miller's family occupied a tent on the grounds of Camp Nelson, where Miller was stationed and where the families of scores of his comrades had also taken shelter. There they remained peaceably until one evening in late November when "a mounted guard" notified them that none but the soldiers could remain. Despite the "bitter cold," even "freezing" conditions the next morning, the guard commenced forcing the women and children into wagons. Ignoring Miller's objections that he, too, was a soldier and that the move would kill his ailing son, one guardsman threatened to "shoot the last one of them" if they did not follow orders.

That night Miller set out to find his loved ones, finally succeeding in locating them six miles away "in an old meeting house belonging to the colored people." They were suffering terribly from the cold and hunger, and, as he had predicted, his son was dead. In the weeks that followed, the other members of his family also died, one by one. Miller himself succumbed in January 1865, marking an ignominious end to the family's quest for freedom, whose warm prospects during the autumn turned cold under winter skies. Those who were struggling to become free well understood that until the war settled the issue permanently, their goal could be elusive, with seasons of death and despair following those of life and hope.[97]

Joseph Miller and his family did not die in vain. After the abolitionist press published his affidavit, congressmen and other officials in Washington, along with a sizable swath of Northern public opinion, expressed outrage. In short order, military officials in Kentucky not only permitted the soldiers' families to return to the camp but also established a permanent shelter for freedom seekers at Camp Nelson. Many other cases similar to that of the Miller family went unrecorded and indeed disappeared into the ocean of death and suffering that was an integral part of Civil War emancipation everywhere and in every season.[98]

———

"When the Yankees came" was a time that witnesses remembered for years afterward, but the memories, like the soldiers' arrival itself, differed markedly from one encounter to another. Only after the collapse of the Confederacy did the bluecoats spread themselves across the landscape as an army of occupation. Over much of the Confederacy over much of the war, they were a fleeting rather than a permanent presence. Their movements had a seasonal character, associated in part with the warm months from early spring through late fall and in part with the changeability of the seasons. Just as the warmth of the summer sun came and went, so did the Yankees, a lesson that many freedom seekers learned the hard way.

As early as February 1862, following his victory at Pea Ridge in northwest Arkansas, General Samuel R. Curtis led his forces along the White River entirely across the state to Helena, on the Mississippi, issuing certificates of freedom "to negroes who were mustered by their masters to blockade my way." In many ways a precursor to Sherman's much better known foray across Georgia in the fall of 1864, Curtis's army lived off the land rather than relying on a supply base in the rear. But given that his forces were on the move, his freedom certificates had little value for those who were unable to reach Helena to redeem them at face value. Indeed, some bearers of the certificates fell into the hands of Confederates before they could reach the safety of the Union position.[99] From the start of the war until well into 1864, the Shenandoah valley of Virginia represented a similar scene over which the Yankees alternately gained and then lost control.[100]

When the Yankees established a permanent base, particularly at a city or large town, the camp itself became a beacon for fugitives, but it was the arrival of the soldiers that marked "when the Yankees came" and hence gave the freedom seekers confidence to undertake the quest.[101] The prototype of such places was Beaufort, South Carolina, which U.S. soldiers occupied after the naval flotilla that transported them from New York seized the deep harbor at Port Royal and its surrounding islands early in November 1861. On "the day the big gun shoot," as local black residents described the event for years afterward, the guns that Confederate artillerymen fired from recently built fortifications proved no match for the great guns of Admiral Samuel F. Du Pont's warships. With their bags already packed, plantation owners and other rebel sympathizers fled, leaving most of the enslaved people behind. This cleared the way for one of several early experiments in compensated labor.[102]

By the summer of 1862, when Union forces had also established toeholds in New Orleans, Nashville, and Memphis, operations of varying size and composition attacked Confederate positions along the South Atlantic Coast, in southern Louisiana, and in West Tennessee, northern Mississippi, and northern Alabama. Enslaved people who encountered the federals offered valuable information, just as they did in support of George McClellan's Army of the Potomac on the Virginia Peninsula.[103] Many black Southerners had sighted Yankees repeatedly, even spoken with them, with no resulting transformation in their circumstances. Indeed, many masters in areas vulnerable to such patrols devised drills prescribing what to do when the federals entered the neighborhood. Monroe F. Jamison later recalled his teenage years in Talladega, Alabama, during the war. Rumors often determined the actions of slaveholders and enslaved people alike. At the sound of the alarm—"The Yankees are coming!"—carried by criers from plantation to plantation, the overseers would send the slaves into the mountains with the horses, mules, wagons, and provisions, returning only after the threat had passed.[104] Regardless of their frequency or the damage they inflicted, Union patrols helped undermine the stability of the slave regime. The sights of apprehended guerrillas and burned cotton vividly illustrated the power that Lincoln's armed forces wielded and the threat they posed to the authority of the slaveholders once they directed their might toward that objective. But troops of Yankee horsemen alone did not topple slavery.

The Emancipation Proclamation's call to destroy slavery encouraged the fuller development of the budding strategy of "hard war," which proved liberating to Union soldiers as well as to enslaved African Americans. From early 1863 onward, federal forces made concerted efforts to take animals, food, and anything else of value, often destroying what remained. The soldiers who occupied Louisville, Alabama, Wadley Clemens later recalled, seized the mistress's "gold yearings and bracelets" and placed the jewelry on their horses' ears and ankles.[105] Soldiers who swept through the state's piney woods terrified the population, black and white, as they cut a path of destruction. Years later, Cheney Cross, who witnessed the scene from a plantation near Evergreen, recalled the Yankee raid like it was just yesterday. They departed less than a day later, leaving the whole place "strewed wid mutilation."[106] In June 1863, in one of the most notorious episodes of the war, Colonel James Montgomery led men from his own regiment, the Second South Carolina Colored Volunteers, and from the Fifty-Fourth Massachusetts Volunteers in a raid on the coastal town of Darien, Georgia. His order to sack and burn the town caused a national sensation and something of a scandal in Massachusetts because of the strong objections voiced by numerous officers of the Fifty-Fourth, including its commander, Colonel Robert Gould Shaw. Aside from the burning and looting, the raid liberated 800 "grateful slaves," according to one report.[107]

Most enslaved people in the Mississippi valley experienced "when the Yankees came" as a series of open-ended events rather than a single decisive one. Although at times the soldiers assisted black refugees in reaching their base camp, they were also capable of displaying little patience with stragglers, who risked being overtaken by Confederate guerrillas when they could not keep pace with the Yankee soldiers. But after July 1863, the phrase "when the Yankees came" took on new meaning in Vicksburg and elsewhere along the Mississippi River. Beginning then, it referred to the moment in time when they came and they stayed. The occasional campaigns to the interior—Sherman's destructive Meridian campaign of February 1864 and even General Nathaniel P. Banks's bungled Red River Campaign several months later—resulted in the liberation of thousands of enslaved people who accompanied the forces back to Vicksburg and New Orleans.

Yet the confusion of such operations could frustrate hopes for freedom as well as enable them to blossom. Approximately 8,000 freed people followed Sherman's troops from Meridian back to Vicksburg. Officials dispersed the ill-clad and hungry refugees to the already-overcrowded camps in and around the city and to the Hurricane and Briarfield Plantations of Joseph and Jefferson Davis at Davis Bend, a narrow spit of land surrounded on three sides by the Mississippi River, some twenty miles downstream. There they lived with other refugees from slavery in wretched conditions, mitigated only in part by the rations they received from camp officials. Until winter passed, there was little hope for improvement.[108]

Employing the Meridian refugees safely on leased plantations in the spring depended on federal military protection, which, when it came at long last, proved to be inadequate. According to a special agent of the Treasury Department, this state of affairs produced "a most disastrous influence upon many of these Negroes, and is rapidly working their ruin." "They collect in abandoned camps in large numbers," he explained, "and make a precarious living by chopping a little wood [and] stealing Cotton, corn, mules &c on the abandoned Plantations. Many of them are armed with Government Guns, and they not infrequently resort to murder and all manner of personal violence upon unprotected white persons," whose acts of retaliation produced a state of near chaos. In the quest for freedom, the sufferings brought on by the privations of winter multiplied the other difficulties incidental to the war. In fact, as much as they desired freedom, not every enslaved person in the Mississippi valley—the Confederate heartland where more than one million slaves lived in 1860—found the proper season to flee to the Yankees. Indeed, most did not.[109]

————

After Appomattox, the coming of the Yankees signaled not only the end of the secessionists' bid for national independence but also the downfall of slavery. Whereas former slaveowners viewed the federal occupation as a form of death, freed people saw it as a rebirth, coinciding perfectly with the season for new life. African American commemorations of emancipation reflected this rolling tide of Yankee occupation, with the relevant local date that marked the day of liberation coinciding with the arrival of the bluecoats. The popularization of the Juneteenth holiday in recent years, for instance, began in Texas to mark June 19, 1865, the date when Union general Gordon Granger's General Order 3 announced that "all slaves are free."[110]

For the roughly 2.6 million enslaved people who still resided within Confederate lines as of April 1865, both understanding that they were free and being able to act on that dramatic change in status depended heavily on the strength of the Union force in the neighborhood where they resided. When the U.S. Army occupied Wilmington, North Carolina, in February and Richmond, Virginia, in April, the Confederacy was on the brink of collapse. Regiments of U.S. Colored Troops marched at the van of the conquering forces, and they did not disguise the fact that they brought freedom to the enslaved. "I would have loved for you to have had a sight in the City of Wilmington on February 22d, as we marched through," exalted Sergeant N. B. Sterrett in a letter to the *Christian Recorder*. "Men and women, old and young, were running through the streets, shouting praising God. We could then truly see what we had been fighting for, and could almost realize the fruits of our labors."[111]

In areas that had managed to escape the destruction, persons who had bided their time dutifully throughout the war did not readily abandon their caution, even after the federals appeared. Several days after Lee's surrender and not far from Appomattox Courthouse, the planter Tasswood Ward stood with a newspaper in hand and his tearful wife by his side. Ward addressed his former slaves as "men and women," telling them, as one later recalled, that "you are as free as the birds that fly in the air." With the crops already in the ground, he offered to pay wages or a share of the harvest to anyone who would remain through the end of the year. Everyone accepted the terms except for one man, Uncle Fendall. "Massie Tass dis yere thing might be a mistake and den dar rebs might go back fighting again and we might not hab but four or five days freedom," Fendall explained. I'm "going to take de first day" because "I done prayed all my life for it, so goodbye Mr. Tasswood Ward."[112]

While other Confederate partisans refused to give up the fight, clinging to the traditional tools of threats and intimidation as a substitute for legal ownership of the labor force, still others turned quickly to constructing a narrative of denial. In Winnsboro, South Carolina, where Mary Boykin Chesnut had taken refuge, she marked May 4, 1865, as the day "when the Yankees came" and with it "a feeling of sadness [that] hovers over me now, day and night." By July 4 she was repeating the mantra of "the fidelity of my own servants" during the war, and when she returned to the family plantation near Camden, South Carolina, she observed that "our people were all at home, quiet, orderly, respectful, and at their usual work." "In point of fact," she told herself, "things looked unchanged."[113] In voicing this early version of the myth of the loyal servants, she forgot her own musings from four years earlier when she wondered if they were not "silent and strong, biding their time."

Try as they might to cling to this fiction, the former partisans of the Confederacy quickly understood that the arrival of the Yankees changed everything, a reality that they resented in both subtle and overt ways while biding their own time until the seasons changed back in their favor. The Texan Martin Jackson later explained how that dynamic affected at least some formerly enslaved persons. Jackson was a body servant to a Confederate officer, with whom he remained throughout the war but with decidedly mixed emotions. Over time, "lots of colored boys" who were servants escaped to the Yankees, but he could not forget his father's advice that "the war wasn't going to last forever, but that our 'forever' was going to be spent living among Southerners, after they got licked."[114] The springtime of freedom led to the summer of Radical Reconstruction, which was followed by the autumn of Redemption, and the winter of segregation and disfranchisement. After years of careful observation of the seasons, Jackson's father could see the long cold spell in the future casting its shadow before.

Chapter 3

Revolutionary Time

In the United States of the mid-nineteenth century, the term "revolution" overflowed with meaning largely owing to the legacies of revolutionary movements over the prior eight decades. The American Revolution, not surprisingly, presented the positive example of a cause that institutionalized representative government grounded in the principle of restrained liberty. In contrast, the French Revolution epitomized revolutionary excess, perhaps best exemplified by the reign of terror and its signature instrument, the guillotine. Most unsettling to the defenders of hierarchical privilege were political movements in the name of social equality that the French Revolution spawned, particularly the Haitian Revolution. "Revolutions cannot be effected without bloodshed," a black Philadelphian acknowledged in July 1863, and, by way of proving that "black revolutions have not been particularly bloody," he insisted that events in Haiti would "compare favorably with the massacres in Syria, India, or France." Not all of his contemporaries on either side of the Atlantic Ocean would have agreed.[1]

Despite the negative lessons they drew from the French and Haitian Revolutions, white Americans did not condemn the resort to violence when hereditary despots prevented oppressed peoples from governing themselves. In 1853, the son of a Maine farmer who was attending the U.S. Military Academy at West Point devoted considerable thought and study to the subject. "Revolutions are an evil but an evil necessary to the work of reform," he wrote. Praising the recent wave of democratic movements in Europe, he insisted there was no fear that "the world will again be plunged into the barbarism of the middle ages, and anarchy tramp upon the glory of free & republican institutions" because "the march of civilization . . . is under divine direction" and "progress is the *will*—the immutable *law* of the Creator." This student stood out from his peers in certain respects. Older than they, having already completed a course of study at Bowdoin College, he also held views about slavery that differed from those of his classmates, particularly those from the slaveholding states. By no means an advocate for the social or political leveling that revolutions might produce, Oliver Otis Howard nonetheless justified revolution to achieve representative government and its accompanying freedoms. Both divine and secular forces favored democracy, for which the United States of America served as an ideal representation.[2] Many of Howard's African American contemporaries would have agreed, although with one caveat. "The American Republic . . . would be the best governed country in the world," declared Frederick Douglass in April 1861, were it not for slavery.[3]

Secession breathed new life into the concept of revolution as a struggle for national independence that the founding generation had declared in 1776 and then achieved after seven years of warfare.[4] Partisans of the Confederate cause described secession as "revolution," hoping to tap into that historical and political legacy. They also flaunted the term to emphasize their radical departure from the path that the nation had been following since the end of the Mexican-American War in 1848. Secessionists wished to reaffirm the conservative values that they believed provided the only lasting foundation for social stability and economic progress. Slavery was the centerpiece of this value system. Southern slaveholders had a particular understanding of the nation's civilizing mission with regard to people of color in North America and elsewhere in the world, yet they too at times acknowledged the guiding force of a larger secular spirit in the process. Like other conservative social classes in Europe and the Americas, they blasted the spirit of the age of revolution run amok in such developments as abolitionism, feminism, and socialism that threatened the stability of the traditional social order and its main pillar, the family.[5]

Among the rights that they associated with the ownership of human property was their ability to move it across state lines and into the unorganized territories without molestation. When the Republican Abraham Lincoln won the White House in 1860 on a platform opposing the further expansion of slavery into the western territories, slaveholders in the seven cotton-growing states of the Deep South draped themselves in the emblems and rhetoric of revolution and left the Union. By February 1862, when the seceded states formed the Confederate States of America, they elaborated on the revolutionary nature of the act. They adopted a constitution that, for all its similarity to the Constitution of the United States, departed radically from that template in boldly using the term "slave" and making clear that the organic law of the new nation would explicitly safeguard slave owners' property rights. Renegade republics were nothing new, as the Republic of Texas demonstrated in seceding from Mexico in 1836. But to undertake such a venture for the express purpose of placing slavery beyond the reach of executive, legislative, or judicial meddling for all time signaled a jarring pause, if not a complete about-face, in the forward progress of democracy.

The term "revolution" had more ambiguous connotations for the Union's partisans than for the Confederacy's. To be sure, Northerners also wished to associate their cause with the noble one of the Founders. The American experiment was still young, full of unrealized potential at home and an inspiration to the foes of monarchy abroad. Indeed, from early in the nineteenth century, romantic revolutionaries from the United States threw themselves into the various antimonarchical struggles across Europe.[6] Their ranks included such persons as the future physician, reformer, and pioneering educator of the blind, Samuel Gridley Howe, whose republican internationalism first lured him to Greece, where he served in the revolutionary army in the mid-1820s, and later to France, where he mixed advanced medical study with radical politics, returning home after the July Revolution of 1830. But such ventures aimed to spread the American model, not to overthrow it. Like other believers in the nation's destiny, African American leaders had long considered the form of government described in the U.S. Constitution to be a beacon of hope for the entire world, and they praised political movements everywhere that attempted to emulate it.[7]

Conservatives feared that rapid change would undermine the existing social order. They particularly worried that emancipation would undercut two fundamental pillars of every society: property rights and domestic institutions, specifically, the patriarchal household. If government could invalidate property rights in humans, then what of property rights in land and workshops, dwellings and farm animals? And if government could invalidate the master's dominion over his slaves, then what of the household head's authority over his wife and his children? In his message to Congress in December 1861, Lincoln affirmed the hope that the conflict "shall not degenerate into a violent and remorseless revolutionary struggle" and urged Congress to avoid "radical and extreme measures, which may reach the loyal as well as the disloyal."[8] That framework of social beliefs motivated General George B. McClellan's famous July 1862 letter to President Lincoln from Harrison's Landing, Virginia, as his infamous Peninsula Campaign unraveled. "Military power should not be allowed to interfere with the relations of servitude, either by supporting or impairing the authority of the master," McClellan lectured the president. Continue to receive "slaves contraband under the Act of Congress," but "neither confiscation of property, political executions of persons, territorial organization of states or forcible abolition of slavery should be contemplated for a moment." "A system of policy thus constitutional and conservative, and pervaded by the influences of Christianity and freedom, would receive the support of almost all truly loyal men, would deeply impress the rebel masses and all foreign nations, and it might be humbly hoped that it would commend itself to the favor of the Almighty," McClellan continued pedantically. In a final warning, he cautioned that "a declaration of radical views, especially upon slavery, will rapidly disintegrate our present Armies."[9]

Like Lincoln, nearly all white Americans, and many black ones, too, viewed the history of the United States as an extended lesson in national exceptionalism, and, like him, they yearned to predict the ending to the latest chapter that began with the shots on Fort Sumter. Robert Hamilton, editor of the New York *Anglo-African*, viewed the outbreak of the war as "but another step in the drama of American Progress" whose "*tendencies* are for Liberty."[10] What made the exercise particularly challenging was the real stake that numerous Northerners had in settling the difficulties with the Confederacy as amicably and as quickly as possible. Besides slaveholders in the Border States, such Northerners included the businessmen who catered to the Southern market—ship owners who transported enslaved persons from Richmond to New Orleans and cotton from every Southern seaport to Liverpool; cotton and shoe manufacturers that produced "Negro cloth" and "Negro shoes"; insurance brokers who wrote policies protecting investments in human property; and factors who outfitted their planter clients with all the goods and supplies necessary to raise marketable staples employing enslaved laborers. Many Northern Democrats supported secession outright. With some linked by birth or family ties with the South, and others opposed to the war against the Confederacy for partisan or ideological reasons, they constituted a potential fifth column of Confederate supporters in the North. Many more Democrats desired peace, and the vast majority of them remained loyal to the national government despite their distaste for the president and his policies. Lincoln and his fellow Republican strategists stood little chance of harmonizing all these interests, but they hoped at least to reduce the din to manageable proportions.

At the start of the war, when both sides were convinced of the rightness of their cause and the particular favor that God showered on them, Frederick Douglass observed that the Confederates ought not to assume that victory was theirs. Focusing on "a favorite maxim among the slaveholders a few years ago"—namely, that "revolutions never go backward"—he argued that revolution was a two-edged "weapon" capable of cutting "both ways." Against the slaveholders' attempt to preserve slavery, he argued, "the people of the Free States will yet come forth to battle for freedom" with the end result "clearly foreshadowed."[11] Many others besides Douglass held this view. John S. Rock, the promising young attorney who would later become the first African American admitted to the bar of the U.S. Supreme Court, took the occasion of the ninetieth anniversary of the Boston Massacre to invoke the name of Crispus Attucks, the first black hero of the American Revolution, and to observe that "insurrections, when properly planned, may lead to successful revolutions."[12] In making a case for gradual emancipation in the spring of 1863, General Benjamin F. Butler argued that "all natural changes are gradual" while at the same time insisting that "once started" it "will not go backward."[13] B. Gratz Brown, the U.S. senator from Missouri and strong advocate of emancipation, also subscribed to the dichotomous view, noting that the war required "regeneration or death" while at the same time taking heart in the belief that revolutions never go backward.[14]

By early 1865, the abstract predictions of such men as Douglass, Rock, Butler, and Brown began to take on the appearance of reality. In observing the numbers of black men and women occupying seats in the Senate gallery and moving leisurely about the Capitol building, for instance, the Washington correspondent to the *Boston Advertiser* felt confident that "this revolution . . . will not go backward."[15] Yet not everyone agreed. Thomas Wentworth Higginson, the Boston Brahman who had supported John Brown's antislavery cause in Kansas and by 1863 commanded the First South Carolina Volunteer Infantry (Colored), was one such dissenter from the creed of universal progress. The experience of Hungary in 1848, he cautioned, demonstrated clearly that "revolutions may go backward."[16]

Analogies that posited two directions of motion, forward and backward, exhibited the broader trend of viewing the war and human events more generally in terms of polar opposites. The "Manifesto of the Colored Citizens of the State of New York," issued in mid-July 1863, described the war as a clash between "barbarism and freedom—civilization and slavery; it is a death struggle between the feudal ages and the nineteenth century; and every drop of blood shed from Northern veins is a sacrifice on the holy altars of human freedom." The manifesto posited that "if the representatives of human liberty yield the battle, and retire ingloriously beaten, the age will recede a century, and the hands upon the clock of Progress will cease to move across the face of Time."[17] Charles Sumner insisted that passage of the Second Confiscation Act would mark "the change from Barbarism to Civilization."[18] A year later, on the occasion of the flag-presentation ceremony marking the organization of the first black regiment raised in Washington, the prominent African American minister John F. Cook pronounced the war as "a strife between civilization and barbarism, truth and error, right and wrong."[19] Early in the war, fifty-four men and women, "Citizens of West Alexander Pa," petitioned Congress to address the deplorable conditions in the jails of Washington and Alexandria, where enslaved men and women were being held without access to "the comforts of life" in conditions that were "a disgrace to the civilization of the age." They begged for legislation that would render such embarrassments "unknown outside of Pandemonium."[20]

Although few partisans on either side of the contest completely abandoned this dichotomous view of the world, some added additional layers of subtlety.

Henry McNeal Turner, pastor of Israel Bethel AME Church in Washington, for instance, argued that reverses did not contradict but rather reflected the workings of divine providence. In the face of tumult, as "revolution succeeds revolution," he explained reassuringly, "inconstancy marks its progress." For Turner, the "terrible revolution" must endure phases of "progression and retrogression." Indeed, such reverses were "channels of indispensable necessity" to "physical and moral elevation." The *Anglo-African*'s Hamilton noted "the flux and reflux in the tide of Human Progress." And Richard H. Cain, an increasingly influential AME minister in Brooklyn who frequently employed the metaphor of "the revolving wheel of time," insisted that "nations grow to maturity by the inevitable laws of progression," with "age and experience" doing their work to ensure that governments as well as individuals absorb "the accumulated wisdom of centuries."[21]

Amid all the talk of revolution, persons in exalted as well as lowly stations sensed the operation of forces over which they had little control. After the attack on Fort Sumter, Frederick Douglass oscillated "between the dim light of hope, and the gloomy shadow of despair" as he brooded over the uncertain future of the nation. "We cannot see the end from the beginning," he noted, so "we read the face of the sky" for "the signs of the times." "The control of events has been taken out of our hands," and, instead, "invisible forces . . . are shaping and fashioning events as they wish, using us only as instruments to work out their own results in our National destiny."[22] In September 1861, the *Philadelphia Ledger* summed up how rapidly the pace of events overtook conventional wisdom regarding slavery and the political calculations necessary for the Union to achieve victory. Conceding that General John C. Frémont's recent proclamation freeing the slaves of Missouri was premature, the editorial noted that "political policy, in revolutionary or insurrectionary times, has to give way to the stern realities of war." Like many other of his contemporaries, the editor employed the analogy of flowing water, perceiving that "the current of events is rapidly drifting towards the extinction of slavery." "Important changes" were in the offing, but their benefits were indeterminable: "Today, they lead to a proclamation of confiscation of property and freedom to the slaves of rebels in arms. Tomorrow, they may go further, and decree universal freedom to the black." "No government can control events like these," the editor concluded, "when civil war has once stirred passions to their depths, and waked up a fury in the land."[23] In the spring of 1864, Lincoln himself admitted, "I claim not to have controlled events, but confess plainly that events have controlled me."[24]

Missouri's Senator Brown also considered moving water the appropriate metaphor for describing the changes then under way. The current he observed, however, did not flow leisurely but ran swiftly and formed whirling eddies. There could be no returning to "the Union of the past," he argued, because it no longer existed. The nation must move forward, recognizing that the revolution was "the grandest ever yet essayed by man, and destined to give its watchword to other lands and peoples." Brown perceived a new nationality—a "Continental Republic"—in the making and exhorted "all friends of freedom" to embrace the fact "that in this flowing on we are the movement, in this going forward we are the progression, in all this change and alteration and accomplishment, we are the revolution."[25] Moving water offered an image that captured the unpredictable flow of events as slavery began to collapse and as the visionaries of the nation's future destiny looked westward with an eye toward empire.

Time itself appeared to behave erratically in the revolutionary vortex. Observers marveled at how the war appeared alternately to compress time, to accelerate it, to slow it, to stop it altogether, and even to reverse it. Charlotte Forten noted how "time flies," while a correspondent to the *Anglo-African* noted that black soldiers who were performing laborious fatigue duty in Virginia "developed that faculty known by phrenologists as *time*, so that all will come to a halt, or any motion, with a precision which challenges admiration."[26] The signs of the accelerated passage of time appeared to be everywhere, as momentous events followed one after the other. From the earliest days of the war, the military mobilization itself hinted at the sensations that would only become more pronounced. In April 1861, as the Seventh New York Militia departed for Washington, an observer noted: "What a day is this! I hardly recognize myself in this terrible time. I seem to be some one from an age long past, of whom I have read and thought, but who I never expected to be. Hourly we are *living history*. Each day is freighted with events which shall tell on all coming time."[27] A black San Franciscan noted that "great deeds" such as the birth and death of kingdoms and empires and "the inauguration of great reforms in the body politic" are "a rare occurrence" that as a general rule required "the fruition of time to accomplish." But the war created something new, "an age" where long historical cycles "are crowded into a single year."[28] The likelihood that slavery would end over the course of the war warped time and recast everyday processes into world-shattering events.

Romanticism fueled much of this distorted sense of time. Colonel Higginson's *Army Life in a Black Regiment*, the 1870 memoir of his experience with the Colored Troops, bore a decidedly romantic stamp. Hilton Head, the headquarters of federal military operations for the Department of the South, "always seemed like some foreign military station in the tropics" such as

"Jamaica or the East Indies." He described "the dreamy delight" of the regiment's reconnaissance up the St. John's River in Florida in March 1863, "ascending an unknown stream, beneath a sinking moon, into a region where peril made fascination." His language painted a surreal picture: "Since the time of the first explorers, I supposed that those Southern waters have known no sensations so dreamy and so bewitching as those which this war has brought forth." He marveled that "a powerful night-glass" could "change darkness into light," illuminating people and things that would otherwise be invisible. Simultaneously fascinating and disorienting, such experiences also created "a feeling of childish delight." "The whole enchantment of the scene" transported him away, "and had I been some Aladdin, convoyed by genii or giants, I could hardly have felt more wholly a denizen of some world of romance."[29]

Recalling the first such "fascinating experience" a month earlier, when he and his men conducted a raid along the St. Mary's River, Higginson predicted that "its zest . . . will come back to me in dreams, if I live a thousand years." The chorus of one song in the Sea Islanders' repertoire reminded him of "some Romaic song" he had heard years before. "The Orientalism" of camp life among black soldiers had struck up the association. Despite this aura of romance, all these operations dutifully liberated the enslaved people they encountered, ushering them back to Beaufort. And the "hard hand of war" could turn romanticism into reality in an instant. Colonel James Montgomery, a veteran of the Kansas free-state struggles of the 1850s who commanded the second regiment of black troops raised in South Carolina, routinely had his men apply the torch to homes, buildings, and at times even to entire towns during their forays. Higginson sardonically observed that Montgomery had elevated such operations to a "fine art," noting that "his conceptions of foraging were rather more Western and liberal than mine."[30]

"A political sirocco is passing over this country," Richard H. Cain noted in the fall of 1862. "Parties, individuals, and communities are being swept away by the fierceness of the storm. A revolution in politics as well as in arms, is one of God's ways to redeem this nation from its sins." Employing another comparison to natural phenomena, he likened new ideas to glaciers, which "make their way in silence" until "suddenly, the work done in secret reveals itself, and a single day is sufficient to lay bare the agency of years, perhaps of many centuries." "A new era is beginning for this country," he concluded, "and the cause of freedom." "What a change has come over us in two brief years! The nation has been slumbering on a volcano," and now that it has exploded "the interests of humanity are arising." "The revolving wheel of time is to give impetus to these truths," Cain noted.[31] The metaphors of churning waters, swirling winds, smoldering volcanoes, and earth-scouring glaciers offered greater explanatory subtlety than did rigid, bidirectional models of change. What is more, such natural images captured the suddenness with which forces that had been gaining intensity out of sight might unleash their fury in the blink of an eye.

––––––––

As early as November 1861 Lincoln began working with George P. Fisher, a congressman from Delaware, on a bill to abolish slavery in the First State. The bill offered compensation in the form of U.S. bonds if the state would develop a plan for gradual emancipation. The comparatively small number of persons held as slaves in Delaware (1,798 in 1860) held forth the hope of success. Even a modest victory of this sort would give Lincoln an opening to approach the congressional delegations of the other Border States. But the state legislature did not take the bait.[32] In his annual message to Congress the following month, he took a somewhat different tack, proposing relief from a portion of federal direct taxes to states that agreed to let the federal government colonize persons freed under the First Confiscation Act to "some place or places in a climate congenial to them."[33] Once again, the proposal raised some eyebrows but otherwise failed to move lawmakers to action.

Against that background, President Lincoln's message to Congress in March 1862, proposing that the national government provide monetary assistance to states that "may adopt gradual abolishment of slavery," struck like lightning.[34] Horace Greeley described it as "the day-star of a new National dawn." March 6, 1862, he argued, "will yet be celebrated" for marking "the Nation's deliverance from the most stupendous wrong, curse and shame of the Nineteenth century." Even if "years may elapse" before slavery ended, that outcome was no longer doubtful. When "to-morrow's steamer" carries the news to Europe, its arrival "seals the fate of the Rebellion in every Christian land." Greeley pronounced "the Emancipation Message of President Lincoln" as "one of those few great scriptures that live in history and mark an epoch in the lives of nations and of races."[35] Robert Hamilton concurred: Lincoln's emancipation proposal "sent a thrill of joy throughout the North, and will meet with hearty response throughout christendom."[36]

Lincoln's emancipation proclamations of September 22, 1862, and January 1, 1863, prompted similar reflections on the larger relationship among slavery, the war, and the broad sweep of human history. "The world moves," commented the editor of the *Lutheran and Missionary*, after Lincoln issued the preliminary proclamation. "We are living years in days and centuries in years." Though "a war measure," he observed, "it draws fine lines between liberty and slavery, and boldly sets the Government before the world on the side of liberty for all men." "The Sun will never go backward from these points on the dial of our nation's history," he concluded.[37] Union general Ormsby M. Mitchel, who characterized the struggle against slavery as "some great and radical revolution," believed that thanks to Lincoln's preliminary proclamation "the entire subject rises to a dignity, grandeur and importance unsurpassed by any that has ever occupied the attention of mankind."[38] After the announcement of the final proclamation, a white soldier in the Army of the Potomac delighted in the prospect of overthrowing "this barbarous sin" as other nations have done, and stopping the cruelties that should disgrace the nation "in the 19th century, when civilization is triumphant!"[39] In a similar vein, Robert Dale Owen, the social reformer who at the time served as chairman of the AFIC, observed that "a system" such as slavery "has lamentably failed" when it "results in the arrest of human civilization and Christian progress, in injury to the national character, and in disregard, under any circumstances, of the natural and inalienable rights of man."[40]

Weeks before the scheduled release of the final Emancipation Proclamation, Lincoln addressed the nation's legislature as he had the previous December and would again in the following two Decembers in the annual ritual of the president's message to Congress. On December 1, 1862, as his date with destiny drew near, the president attempted to breathe new life into the various offers he had made over the previous year to encourage officials in the slave states—and, by extension, their slaveholding constituents—to adopt gradual emancipation. This time he hoped the proposal would provide a pathway to ending the war and reconciling the disparate interests of the divided nation. Specifically, he proposed three constitutional amendments for Congress to consider, the most important of which was the first, which would make "compensation from the United States" available to any state that abolished slavery voluntarily "at any time, or times, before the first day of January, in the year of our Lord one thousand and nine hundred."[41] If Congress and the states agreed to the president's recommendation and appended such an amendment to the U.S. Constitution authorizing slavery in the stipulated circumstances until 1900, persons born into slavery may have lived into the twenty-first century, perhaps even to the brink of Barack Obama's election as president. But once again the Border Slave States chose to decline the offer of compensated gradual emancipation.

Early in the new year, H. Ford Douglas, who had escaped slavery and become a prominent abolitionist and emigration activist in the Midwest, offered a rare perspective on the meaning of the war and emancipation against the larger backdrop of time. Douglas enlisted in the Ninety-Fifth Illinois Volunteer Infantry in July 1862 and was taking part in the advance against

Vicksburg when he was detached from his unit to recruit a company of black soldiers. "We are on our way to Vicksburg," he boasted to the editor of an Illinois newspaper from "Camp near Memphis." Yet Douglas preached patience. "No thoughtful man," in his view, "can reasonably expect to see the momentous issues which this war has raised to the surface of American society settled in one or two years." While understanding why thoughtful persons would harbor "doubts and apprehensions," he took pride in knowing that "the good old flag . . . now, thank God, means justice and liberty." "Being in the right" did not by itself guarantee success on the battlefield. "In modern times," he explained, "war has been reduced to a science, so that it is not altogether the righteousness of a cause, but the ability of the contending parties to make the right application of these principles, that wins." Caveats aside, he believed strongly that infusing the cause of freedom into the Union's strategic operations pointed unmistakably toward "success in crushing out this infernal revolt."[42]

By mid-1864, Northerners who failed to grasp the full implications of the changes that emancipation had wrought provoked wonder. A fascinating observation that Union Army officer Major Reuben D. Mussey, who supervised the recruitment of black soldiers in Tennessee, made regarding General William T. Sherman illustrates the point. Long after federal officials embraced the concept of recruiting black soldiers, and after such recruits had proved their mettle on the field of battle on countless occasions, Sherman still downplayed their potential effectiveness as a fighting force in his Military Division of the Mississippi. "The Negro is in a transition state and is not the equal of the white man," Sherman insisted. Although he did not rule out grooming selected men "in the art of the Soldier," he preferred employing them "for Pioneers, Teamsters, Cooks and Servants." While not abandoning his admiration for the general, Mussey nonetheless marveled that what Sherman "says of the Negro" was "fully two years behind the times—and when I say two years I mean two of those century like years which we are living."[43]

Falling out of step with the times could affect entire groups of persons and not just individuals. A black resident of New Jersey expressed disappointment but not surprise that voters there did not support Lincoln in the 1864 presidential election, noting that the characterization of his home state as "out of the United States" was "too true, and yet not true enough." The real truth was that "she is behind the times at least one century."[44] In January 1865, the *Christian Recorder* editorialized that the House of Representatives "will be at least thirty years behind the PEOPLE!" if it failed to pass the bill adding an emancipation amendment to the U.S. Constitution, which the Senate had approved the previous April.[45] Individuals, states, and nations could fall behind the times, as, indeed, many were coming to believe the United States had done by not having abolished slavery sooner.

––––––––

The swirling eddies of time especially affected enslaved people's struggles to escape from slavery. Virtually every such attempt presented circumstances in which the freedom seeker experienced fear that could be paralyzing. The perception of time, along with the other mental functions that were so vital to survival, could go haywire, as Charles Ball had experienced half a century earlier. A pack of dogs from which he narrowly escaped, for instance, left him disoriented throughout the following day. "When a man is greatly alarmed, and in a strange country, he is not able to note courses, or calculate distances, very accurately," he reasoned, so he wisely chose to stay put. Pursuit by men on horseback unnerved him even more. "Trembling in every joint, nerve and muscle," he was "so completely bereft of understanding, that I could not tell south from north, nor east from west." The encounter with the horsemen required him to delay for three days before "my brain had been restored to its ordinary stability." Those days were "the most unhappy of my life; for surely it is the height of human misery, to be oppressed with alienation of mind, and to be conscious of the affliction."[46] In the summer of 1864, as the freedom seeker Wallace Turnage attempted to reach federal forces at Mobile, he too "became very much troubled in mind" contemplating certain death if captured.[47] The uncertainties associated with the war and the destabilization of slave society caused tremors of fear among slaveholders as well. "How can one settle down to anything; one's heart is in one's mouth all the time," Mary Chesnut observed about the growing tension around Fort Sumter in early April 1861. "Any moment the cannon may open on us."[48]

Octave Johnson's escape to Union lines in Louisiana during 1863 paralleled Ball's half a century earlier. Johnson was an enslaved barrel maker on a sugar plantation where he worked by the task. Fulfilling his task, he reasoned, did not require him to answer the morning bell that rang "so early that I could not see." He fled to the swamps in 1861 rather than face what he considered an unjust whipping. Johnson found that life in the wild was challenging but survivable. He eventually joined forces with thirty other men and women, who sustained themselves in part by poaching free-ranging cattle and trading meat with "friends on the plantation" for their necessities. Early in 1863, a "master of hounds" set out to break up the settlement. When the dogs discovered the hideaway, Johnson and his companions managed to kill several and escape across a bayou, where, he gratefully noted, the alligators "preferred dog flesh to personal flesh." After reaching federal lines above New Orleans, Johnson worked for a time as an officer's servant and later enlisted, doubtless having many an opportunity later to retell the heart-stopping tale of terror when he escaped the hounds and the alligators.[49] Like Johnson, the thousands of freedom seekers who reached federal lines by outrunning and outwitting their pursuers experienced the rush of adrenaline, which made time appear to accelerate, to slip into slow motion, or to stand still. But unlike Johnson, the many who did not escape their pursuers faced reenslavement, often with horrors more unspeakable than dogs and alligators. The teenager Mattie J. Jackson, whose family was sold from St. Louis to Louisville, Kentucky, early in 1863, likened their ordeal to a "rending tornado." Only after escaping to Indiana was she able to experience the sensation that she "had emerged into a new world, or had never lived in the old one before."[50]

Gordon, the man whose lacerated back became an overnight sensation after it was photographed on his arrival at Union lines at Baton Rouge, told a tale of escape through the swamps similar to Octave Johnson's, but in his case, after the threatened whipping rather than before. The overseer on the plantation where Gordon lived on the Atchafalaya River some sixty miles west of Baton Rouge administered a savage beating two months before Christmas 1862, which in Gordon's words rendered him "sort of crazy" and incapacitated him until after the New Year. Once recovered, he trudged for ten days through "swamps and bayous" with a search party in hot pursuit before reaching the Yankees. When serving as a guide for federal troops, he reportedly fell captive to Confederates who whipped him severely and left him for dead. Returning again to Baton Rouge, he enlisted in the U.S. Army and reportedly fought at the battle of Port Hudson in May 1863.[51] The surgeon who examined Gordon (known as Peter in some accounts) noted that he had personally witnessed hundreds of recruits whose backs were similarly lacerated. Commentators at the time noted Gordon's dignified pose that displayed a certain sense of detachment from the horrors that his back displayed (see figure 3.1). Yet observers also speculated "what must the whipping have been to leave such scars" on a member of "the laboring class . . . a servant of king Cotton; one of the most useful men in the community . . . a man who is nine-tenths production, and only one-tenth consumption."[52] Even without such outward manifestations of slavery's abuses, the refugees who succeeded in reaching Union lines taxed their mental and emotional capacities as well as their physical endurance.

The relatively new medium of photography lent itself nicely to depicting the acceleration of time that the revolution made possible, often through staged displays of sudden transformations. One standard motif that Gordon's story personified was the conversion of a raggedly clad refugee into a smartly uniformed soldier of the United States, armed for combat against the Confederacy.[53] Two vivid images could portray in ways that words might not how

|A TYPICAL NEGRO.|

WE publish herewith three portraits, from photographs by M'Pherson and Oliver, of the negro GORDON, who escaped from his master in Mississippi, and came into our lines at Baton Rouge in March last. One of these portraits represents the man as he entered our lines, with clothes torn and covered with mud and dirt from his long race through the swamps and bayous, chased as he had been for days and nights by his master with several neighbors and a pack of blood-hounds; another shows him as he underwent the surgical examination previous to being mustered into the service—his back furrowed and scarred with the traces of a whipping administered on Christmas-day last; and the third represents him in United States uniform, bearing the musket and prepared for duty.

This negro displayed unusual intelligence and energy. In order to foil the scent of the blood-hounds who were chasing him he took from his plantation onions, which he carried in his pockets. After crossing each creek or swamp he rubbed his body freely with these onions, and thus, no doubt, frequently threw the dogs off the scent.

At one time in Louisiana he served our troops as guide, and on one expedition was unfortunately taken prisoner by the rebels, who, infuriated beyond measure, tied him up and beat him, leaving him for dead. He came to life, however, and once more made his escape to our lines.

By way of illustrating the degree of brutality which slavery has developed among the whites in the section of country from which this negro came, we append the following extract from a letter in the New York *Times*, recounting what was told by the refugees from Mrs. GILLESPIE's estate on the Black River:

GORDON AS HE ENTERED OUR LINES.   GORDON UNDER MEDICAL INSPECTION.   GORDON IN HIS UNIFORM AS A U.S. SOLDIER.

Figure 3.1 Gordon, Harper's Weekly, July 4, 1863. Courtesy of the Library of Congress Prints and Photographs Division, LC-USZ62-98515.

military service changed a degraded victim of slavery into a proud champion of freedom. In July 1863, Frederick Douglass put the matter succinctly: "Once let the black man get upon his person the brass letters U.S.; let him get an eagle on his button, and a musket on his shoulder, and bullets in his pocket" and "no power on earth or under the earth" could deny his claim to citizenship. But verbal descriptions could also perpetrate the very concepts of racial inferiority that the pictorial images helped to invalidate.[54]

One early example of the potential of the new medium for propaganda purposes emanated from Louisiana, where General Nathaniel P. Banks, commander of the Department of the Gulf, joined forces with the American Missionary Association and the National Freedmen's Relief Association to raise funds in support of schools for the freed people of the state. Colonel George H. Hanks, the department's Superintendent of Negro Labor, accompanied a group of eight formerly enslaved persons (three adults and five children) to New York and Philadelphia in an appeal to the hearts and purse strings of the Northern middle class. In studio portraits—which were widely reproduced as cartes de visite—the subjects appeared as neatly dressed models

Figure 3.2 Myron H. Kimball, *Emancipated Slaves Brought from Louisiana by Col. George H. Hanks*. Gilman Collection, Purchase, The Horace W. Goldsmith Foundation Gift, through Joyce and Robert Menschel, 2005. Courtesy of the Metropolitan Museum of Art (https://www.metmuseum.org).

of the transformative influence of freedom (one of the two men wore an army uniform) (see figure 3.2). The key to the appeal, and to the coverage the images received courtesy of *Harper's Weekly,* lay in its leap beyond the conventional opposition between slave and freedman to explore the more politically charged dichotomy of "White and Colored Slaves." Three of the children appeared to be "of unmixed white race," and another, a light-complexioned girl, was described as the daughter of a woman "who is almost white." More than just a plea for support so that formerly enslaved children might enjoy the same educational opportunities as their Northern counterparts, the campaign made a subtle but effective case for the injustice of a system wherein children who looked white were subject to hereditary bondage. The chance to end such injustice justified an antislavery war at whatever the sacrifice.[55]

Another widely circulated set of photographs, those of Hubbard Pryor, offers a cautionary tale regarding the assumptions that lay beneath the stock before-and-after poses (see figures 3.3 and 3.4). As usual, the images conveyed the rapid change that enlistment produced. But they did not—indeed could not—predict a man's subsequent military career. Pryor escaped from slavery in northern Georgia and made his way to federal forces in Tennessee, where he enlisted in the Forty-Fourth U.S. Colored Infantry. He was part of the federal force at Dalton, Georgia, that Confederate soldiers captured in October 1864. Unlike a number of his less fortunate comrades, Pryor avoided being shot or sold into slavery; instead, for the rest of the war he worked under guard repairing Confederate railroads.[56] As Pryor learned, the great transformation from slave to freeman was not irreversible—revolutions could go backward—and a change of fortune could leave a man like him farther back on the path to freedom than when he started. Indeed, when released from his captors after the surrender at Appomattox, he started for home "in a sick, broken down, naked and starved condition," traveling at night, "the country being everywhere full of returned Confederate soldiers" who, he feared, would be only too happy to kill him.[57] Pryor's wartime experience illustrates how in more than just metaphorical terms time could behave erratically. Enlistment photographs capture only a small fraction of the story of Hubbard Pryor's revolution as it moved forward, then backward, and through the cycle again. During the Battle of Brandy Station, Virginia, in June 1863, two black Confederate body servants reportedly captured a "Yankee Negro" whom they then retained as their servant.[58]

Several enslaved servants of Kentucky congressman Charles A. Wickliffe also experienced time's stoppage and reversal, but in circumstances quite different from Hubbard Pryor's. During the chilly days of early spring 1862, as Congress neared passage of the bill to abolish slavery in the District of Columbia, slaveholders worked feverishly to move their human property out of the capital. The pace quickened after the Senate approved the measure on April 3. After numerous attempts by Border State representatives and their copperhead allies from the Northern states to block passage or soften the blow, the House followed suit on April 11. President Lincoln did not sign the bill into law until April 16. His friend Oliver H. Browning, like him a transplanted Kentuckian who had lived since his youth in Illinois and who was then filling the unexpired Senate term of Stephen A. Douglas, explained the reason for the delay.

Apart from Lincoln's reservations about the law's specific provisions—he preferred "gradual emancipation," for instance, because if the change occurred immediately "families would at once be deprived of cooks, stable boys &c" and the persons freed would be deprived "of their protectors

Figure 3.3
Photograph of
Private Hubbard
Pryor, before
enlistment in the
Forty-Fourth U.S.
Colored Troops.
Courtesy of the
National Archives.

without any provision for them"—he confessed to Browning that he intended to sign it, but not before Wednesday, April 16. After doing everything in his power to stop passage, Wickliffe paid the president a visit. Claiming that "two family servants" attending him in Washington "were sickly" and would not benefit from freedom, he "wanted time to remove them, but could not get them out of the City until Wednesday." Lincoln obliged.[59] The president had literally stopped the clock of emancipation between April 11 and April 16 simply by agreeing not to touch the pen. During that interval Wickliffe's two family servants and hundreds of other persons were spirited away to Maryland and Kentucky (and some even to Virginia), where the clock of slavery still ticked strongly.[60]

Figure 3.4
Photograph of
Private Hubbard
Pryor, after
enlistment in the
Forty-Fourth U.S.
Colored Troops.
Courtesy of the
National Archives.

For others, the fear that the revolution might spin too fast led to a similar outcome. If the emancipation bill would require the liberated persons to be colonized, perhaps to Africa or Central America, then the cost of freedom might be too dear. The enslaved woman Alice Addison, her two grown daughters, and her three grandchildren lived in the District of Columbia, and her father lived in adjacent Montgomery County, Maryland. Colonization would create the unthinkable outcome of her father remaining in slavery while she and the children traveled to freedom in a distant land. To escape being "colonized in Africa," Addison persuaded her owner to let the family join the father, and he persuaded his owner to permit them to do so. As Congressman Wickliffe was spiriting his servants back to Kentucky, the Addison family moved to Maryland, forsaking the chance to be free to avoid the prospect of being permanently separated from their patriarch.[61]

––––––––

In the face of these revolutionary forces that were far beyond the ability of any single human to control, maintaining "ordinary stability" of mind proved challenging. Supernatural powers—both spiritual (God's providence) and secular (the spirit of the age)—might serve as counterweights. Of all the explanations for the war's events, and particularly the movement toward emancipation, the "finger of God" or "the visible hand of God" was perhaps the favorite, North and South, among persons of every background and every political and religious belief.[62] God directed human affairs according to an unknown and unknowable plan and according to a cosmic timetable that might bear little relationship to such human timekeeping devices as calendars, clocks, and changing seasons of the year. "In the revolutions of barbarism, no less than in the evolutions of Christianity" the editor of the *Christian Advocate and Journal* could plainly see "the working of a higher law, which sweeps through all time and space, and issues from . . . [the] Lord God Almighty."[63] Ironically, Confederate general Robert E. Lee did not dispute God's guiding hand on the institution of slavery, using words similar to those of the *Christian Advocate* but to very different effect. "There are few . . . in this enlightened age, who will not acknowledge that slavery as an institution is a moral and political evil," he acknowledged in 1856. "The blacks are immeasurably better off here than in Africa, morally, physically and socially," he reasoned, while at the same time offering this caution: "While we see the course of the final abolition of human slavery is still onward, and give it the aid of our prayers, let us leave the progress, as well as the results, in the hand of Him who sees the end, who chooses to work by slow influences, and with whom a thousand years are but a single day."[64]

All but the most irreligious believed firmly that God controlled the affairs of nations as well as individuals, and that the outcomes of particular battles as well as the overall progress of the war mirrored God's will.[65] Even such prominent abolitionists as Frederick Douglass, who held that God helped those who helped themselves, found overwhelming evidence of supernatural influence. In a speech at Philadelphia in January 1862, he explained the war as a result of Americans' having forgotten that nations, like individuals, "are subjects of the moral government of the universe." A lapse in that understanding had resulted in "flagrant, long continued, and persistent transgression of the laws of this Divine Government," which could result only in "national sorrow, shame, suffering and death."[66] As the fortunes of war ebbed and flowed, the respective belligerents saw signs of God's pleasure and wrath. To that end, the presidents of both the United States and the Confederate States called for days of meditation and prayer in thanks for divine blessings already bestowed and in hopes that the good fortune would continue.

Many a freedom seeker experienced God's providence in immediate ways in the form of personal deliverance. W. E. Northcross, an enslaved Alabamian, fell into the hands of rebel deserters who threatened to take his life but decided to rob him instead. "I left loving God and believing in his providence as I had never believed, before," he later recalled.[67] God looked after individuals and nations that believed. Kate Drumgoold, who with her family was held in slavery in the Shenandoah valley of Virginia, told a similar tale of her brother, James, who was pressed into Confederate service but "was determined" to be free. After one unsuccessful try "he was caught and locked up in Richmond"; his family feared the worst, "but God was there to help him." Sent to work "on the breastworks," James relied on the Lord as "his leader" and escaped across the James River to the Yankees. In later years he repeated the tale of "how he walked on the water" and how he "was so scared" that he did not know whether he got wet, no doubt to peals of laughter from his listeners. Neither he nor his sister doubted that "the Lord carried him" across.[68] The youthful Wallace Turnage similarly recalled having "put my trust in the Lord and I walked in the river as though there was no river there" as he made his way from Mobile to federal forces in Mobile Bay during the summer of 1864.[69]

Believing that God moved the universe toward freedom was not incompatible with believing that secular forces might also lend a hand. A remarkable allegory that appeared in the *Christian Recorder* in April 1862 after enactment of the law abolishing slavery in the District of Columbia illustrates what they shared in common. "Observer"—whose style and tone suggest authorship by Henry M. Turner—pictured a hypothetical encounter between "the angels of history and prophecy" who "sit side by side and make their record" of the fulfillment of God's will. The secular angel, History, records April 16, 1862, as the day when President Lincoln announced the "immediate emancipation of the slaves in the District of Columbia." The spiritual angel, Prophecy, writes that before the end of the nineteenth century ("18—") an unnamed chief executive ("President——") "will announce to Congress, that, by co-operation of each of the Slave States with the United States Government in whole, the great and glorious work of emancipation has been consummated, and the entire territory of the Union made free forever."[70]

Allegorical fantasies appeared believable in light of actual events. In one such instance in which human agency played a decisive role, General Edward A. Wild, the Massachusetts abolitionist who commanded the African Brigade in the Department of North Carolina, staged an example of what he termed "Poetical justice." In the spring of 1864, a federal patrol arrested a notorious slave owner named William H. Clopton. When Wild learned that several freed people in a nearby refugee camp had been Clopton's slaves and past victims of his whippings, he staged a ritualized reversal of roles with their assistance. At the general's instructions, a man and three women administered the lash to the rebel's bare back, "settleing some old scores." Wild applauded the "superior humanity" they showed in exercising "moderation," but he had hoped for a blunter demonstration of vengeance.[71] Other cases illustrated the utter inability of humans to influence events. In April 1865, Chaplain Garland H. White along with his comrades in the Twenty-Eighth U.S. Colored Infantry took part in occupying Richmond following Lee's surrender. By chance he met a woman on the street with whom he struck up a conversation. They soon determined that he was her son who had been sold away years before, as it happened, to a Georgia slaveholder named Robert Toombs, an aspiring politician who subsequently served as a U.S. senator and held other elected and appointed posts. White had traveled with Toombs across the South and accompanied him to Washington, whence he escaped to Canada just before the war.[72]

The spirit of the age and God's providence appeared to converge in the cause of human freedom. "It is a fixed fact that the nineteenth century will see the end of slavery in all its forms," pronounced the French abolitionist and advocate of Protestant rights Count Agénor de Gasparin in the spring of 1861, "and woe to him who opposes the march of such a progress!" Gasparin's paean to Lincoln and the United States, *The Uprising of a Great People*, noted that the president's inauguration occurred just as Russian tsar Alexander II issued his manifesto abolishing serfdom. "In such coincidences, who does not recognize the finger of God?" he asked.[73] The editors and correspondents of the black press repeatedly cited the emancipation of Russian serfs as an example of enlightened statesmanship that foretold a similar fate for enslaved people in the United States. *Douglass' Monthly* reprinted Alexander's proclamation in toto, citing it as "a great event." As the one-year anniversary of Russian emancipation and the start of the Civil War drew near, the *Christian Recorder* reprinted a Lutheran journal's opinion that the emancipation of the Russian serfs sealed slavery's fate. "Let our struggle end as it may, the doom of slavery is decided." Restoring the institution to its former status would require "a revolution of all civilization" and would run counter to "the strongest reasons of philanthropy, national economy, and mercantile interests" as well as to the "spirit of the age" and the will of "the God of Love, the Father of Mercy."[74] The end of serfdom in Russia and the continuation of slavery in Cuba and Brazil provided recurring international reference points for the advocates of emancipation in the United States.[75]

To ensure that God's will and the spirit of the age would be fulfilled, human actors could not flinch from their duty. The final report of the AFIC that War Secretary Stanton created in March 1863 concluded that "nothing short of a bloody revolution" could accomplish the "eradication of slavery throughout a country containing 4,000,000 of slaves, estimated by their masters as property worth $12,000,000 or $15,000,000."[76] Early in the war Frederick Douglass invoked Shakespeare's Brutus to remind his fellow Northerners that there is "a tide in the affairs of men," and now that it was full, the nation needed to act.[77] Richard H. Cain echoed Douglass's words and reinforced the need for concerted action to ensure that the "moral and political revolutions" that God had wrought continued to hold promise for "a brighter day." He specifically urged black Northerners "to sustain the Government" and to venture south to minister to the moral as well as material needs of the freed people. Dutifully, he repeated the mantra "Revolutions do not go backwards."[78]

The outbreak of violence against African American residents in urban areas across the North during the spring and summer of 1863 provided additional evidence of how the revolution could spin wildly out of control in spite of supernatural powers and the forward-looking actions of elected officials and ordinary citizens alike. The cities of Boston, Albany, Detroit, Chicago, Cincinnati, and Washington, in addition to New York, experienced such unrest, as did a number of smaller towns in Ohio, Indiana, and Illinois. African American residents of these places fought back when the opposing odds were not suicidal and established self-defense organizations to deter future attacks.[79] But New York was in a class of its own.

Ironically, a company of disgruntled firemen ignited the troubles on the morning of July 13, 1863, when they marched to the place where the lottery for the draft was being conducted. After being joined by other opponents of conscription, they set the building ablaze and resisted the attempts of other fire companies to extinguish the flames. The rioters split up and began spreading chaos throughout Manhattan. For both victims and participants in the ensuing events, time behaved erratically over the next four days. Mobs moved from one neighborhood to another, one street to another, at first targeting the buildings symbolizing the draft and the city's Republican elite. By the evening of the first day, antipathy toward Lincoln and the policies of his administration shifted from conscription to emancipation. Moving with great speed and ferocity, Irish mobs began targeting African American victims, viciously lynching one man and setting fire to the Colored Orphan Asylum.

Black New Yorkers could not flee without risking their lives, except with the help of sympathetic white coworkers and neighbors. Instances of such assistance included the case of a factory owner who spirited two employees concealed in boxes aboard a wagon shipment to Newark, New Jersey. In another case, an unidentified person advised his black neighbors to leave their house lights turned on, which the incendiaries understood to signify that white persons occupied the dwelling.[80] After the smoke had cleared, the abolitionist pastor Henry Highland Garnet published a card thanking "our friends and benefactors," which, among other things, mentioned "two generous young Irishmen who defended the children of the Orphan Asylum from being killed" by the mob.[81] Black residents of Flushing, Long Island, apparently recalling Garnet's 1843 call to arms, decided to take preemptive action instead of awaiting their fate. After learning "that they were to be routed out of that village and their houses burned by a mob," they appointed a committee to visit the local Roman Catholic priest. Explaining that they had always been peaceable and wished to remain so, they also made clear that they possessed weapons "for self-protection, and would not hesitate to use them." For good measure they declared their intention "to burn two of the houses of the rioters for every one of their own destroyed." "These negroes have not been molested," the report concluded. The *Anglo-African* reported favorably on the criticism that the Catholic bishops of Buffalo and Cleveland leveled at the New York rioters.[82]

The family of abolitionist William P. Powell barely survived the violence. A former seafarer originally from New York, Powell had long since left the sea, but not sailors, behind. After living in New Bedford, Massachusetts, for some years, where he and his wife operated a boarding house for seamen, they moved to Manhattan in 1839 and opened the Colored Sailor's Home. For the next twelve years the home provided an alternative to the dockside hovels that the men usually patronized. The Powells enforced the rule of sobriety and cultivated interest in reading and discussing such pressing issues of the day as abolition. They left the country following passage of the 1850 Fugitive Slave Law, but then returned to New York and their former work in 1861.[83]

In recounting their harrowing ordeal in July 1863, Powell fixed the most intense moments in time. From 2:00 P.M. to 8:00 P.M., he, his family (including a crippled teenage daughter), and several boarders were "prisoners in my own house to *king mob*, from which there was no way to escape but over the roofs of adjoining houses." At 4:00 P.M., he sent word of his plight to the superintendent of police, but to no avail. Around 8:30 P.M., the mob stormed the dwelling, just as the family escaped to the roof of an adjoining building. A neighbor, a "despised Israelite" who "Samaritan-like, took my poor helpless daughter under his protection," furnished a heavy rope by which Powell and the others descended from the roof. After hiding in a friend's cellar until 11:00 P.M., they "were taken in charge by the police, and locked up in the Station house for safety. In this dismal place, we found upwards of *seventy* men, women and children—some with broken limbs—bruised and beaten from head to foot. We stayed in this place for twenty-four hours, when the police escorted us to the New Haven boat." For Powell, his family, and the larger community of survivors and witnesses, the events remained seared in their memories for the rest of their lives. That the city's black population declined by 20 percent in the two years after the riot hints at how survivors coped with what they had endured.[84]

In the aftermath of the New York riots, Richard Cain pondered over the relationship between the secular and providential forces guiding the destiny of African Americans. In one breath he credited "time, the great revelator of the greatest events which the human mind has ever comprehended," with having "brought order out of the late confusion." Quickly checking himself, he added: "'Time' did I say? Stay! God, in the whirl of eternal revolutions, has unfolded a purpose of his divine mind, lifting the curtain of eternity that humanity may catch a glimpse of his ways, and understand that he is still the governor of the destinies of nations no less than of individuals."[85] But would the revolution move quickly enough to avert future episodes like what the urban areas experienced? And how would individual black Americans and the communities in which they resided fit into God's vision for the nation's future?

————

Emancipation took an especially fearsome about-face when persons who had become free during the war—in some cases even working for wages under the auspices of the U.S. government—fell victim to Confederate military forces that returned them to slavery. An early instance of such retrogression occurred at Edisto Island, South Carolina, soon after federal forces reestablished authority in the area in November 1861. Early in 1862, a naval officer reported on the precariousness of "the colony," which consisted of some 1,200 persons who had but a limited supply of "maize" and who were subject to gunfire from Confederate pickets. Although about fifty men with their families received passage to Port Royal to work for the government there, the remainder preferred to stay on the island, where they intended to pick the standing cotton and defend themselves with weapons furnished by the U.S. government. Following a skirmish, which rebel commanders deemed "an insurrection" fomented by the Yankees and their arms, a strong Confederate force attacked, capturing "some 80 negroes, men, women, and children." Rebel officials bound the leading men over to be tried as insurrectionists, placed the other men in irons and transported them to labor "under guard" on a nearby causeway, and dispatched the women and children to the Charleston workhouse.[86]

Such kidnappings had occurred on the Virginia Peninsula above Fort Monroe in the summer of 1861 in the midst of Confederate general John B.

Magruder's sweeps to impress black laborers.[87] And they would continue throughout the war. In the Union-held areas of Middle Tennessee and northern Alabama, federal authority at times appeared to be retreating instead of advancing. When the Confederates invaded Kentucky in August and September 1862, federal troops fell back from areas that they had controlled since their victories at Forts Henry and Donelson the previous February. Thousands of formerly enslaved people who had come to enjoy de facto freedom during the intervening months scrambled to avoid reenslavement, and not all succeeded.[88] To complete the nightmarish chain of events, when the Confederates retreated from Kentucky, hundreds of enslaved officers' servants and military laborers sought federal protection but fell into the hands of Kentucky state officials, who, instead of acknowledging their liberation under the Confiscation Acts, held them in jail under the laws of Kentucky until their owners reclaimed them.[89]

Tens of thousands of civilians took refuge from military operations, often in semiorderly retreats from vulnerable zones in advance of an impending battle. Tens of thousands of others were displaced, their homes destroyed, their livelihoods disrupted, and their communities along with the social institutions that sustained them scattered to the wind. When Confederate forces moved into Union territory, they often took African American captives. Black Pennsylvanians who encountered Lee's army in its several incursions north of the Mason and Dixon Line suffered this fate.[90] Half a continent away, formerly enslaved people experienced similar trials. As Grant's forces held Vicksburg under siege, Confederate forces capitalized on the withdrawal of federal troops from their positions west of the river. The rebels destroyed leased plantations near Goodrich's Landing, Louisiana, "setting fire to every thing as they went along." What is more, according to the commander of the U.S. Navy's Mississippi Squadron, they "carried off about 1200 negroes who were employed on the so called Government Plantations."[91] From Virginia to the Mississippi valley, black men and women within Union lines routinely fell victim to Confederate raiders who spirited them back into slavery, at times with the connivance of Union soldiers and plantation lessees.[92]

In no theater of war could federal commanders develop appropriate tactics to prevent rebel guerrillas from destroying property and reenslaving the captured laborers. Nonetheless, by 1864 in the Mississippi valley, a combination of active-duty soldiers (especially members of the U.S. Colored Troops), men serving in the invalid corps, plantation lessees, and the plantation laborers began to achieve some success. Early in the year, the general commanding the Military Division of West Mississippi instructed district commanders to be on the alert against the rumored plans by "many of the original planters" throughout the valley to "move into the interior, taking their negroes with them, for the purpose of reducing them again into a state of slavery."[93] But major operations, such as Sherman's against Meridian, removed soldiers from detached duty near the plantations, leaving them vulnerable to attack. The results followed the pattern previously established when federal forces abandoned Hampton, Virginia, in July 1861 and Edisto Island, South Carolina, in July 1862.

Taking advantage of such situations, Confederate raiders pounced with deadly effect.[94] In the case of a "devastating" raid on more than thirty government-operated plantations in Louisiana in June 1862, the rebels "drove off the animals and the young able-bodied Negroes, abused and maltreated the old and defenceless, and when possible captured the managers and treated them with severity." To compound the terror further, one group of raiders that drew the fire of a U.S. gunboat "massed the wretched, defenceless Negroes immediately in range of the shells of the Vessel" at the cost of "many lives."[95] In another raid during the summer of 1863, the terrorists burned down the plantation quarters after having scattered the occupants; months later, after the freed people had returned to the place, "quite a number are sick from exposure and diseases contracted during the summer while they were driven from their quarters," according to a federal investigator.[96] Not even the national capital proved impervious to such reverses. In the spring of 1863, fully one year after emancipation took effect in the District of Columbia, the superintendent of the main refugee camp reported kidnappings of residents while they were "out to work"; agents of their former owners were the suspected perpetrators.[97]

————

With supernatural forces aligned in favor of freedom, it remained for mortal men and women to enact their part in translating God's will and the spirit of the age into reality. After Lincoln's announcement of the preliminary Emancipation Proclamation, Henry M. Turner argued that the document "bids us rise, and for ourselves think, act, and do. We have stood still and seen the salvation of God, while we besought him with teary eyes and bleeding hearts; but the standstill day bid us adieu Sept 22, 1862." "The time has arrived in the history of the American African, when grave and solemn responsibilities stare him in the face."[98] "There will certainly be a great change in the relations of the free as well as the slave population in this country," predicted members of New York's African Civilization Society in mid-November 1863. "There will be a revolution in the North, in the opinions of men, and we will be called upon to exercise our best judgment and prudence in shaping our future course."[99] In the same vein a year later, Richard H. Cain exhorted every black

American to ask: "What is to be my status in the coming events, which this revolution will develop?"[100] "We have always been *directed by others* in all the affairs of life," Cain insisted; "they have furnished the thoughts while we have been passive instruments, acting as we were acted upon, mere *automatons*." To make freedom meaningful, "Black men must turn their eyes toward the savannas of the South, and the prairies of the West. Get hold of the land; till it; learn the handy arts; four millions are already there; there is plenty of room for more; the colored men of the South have trades; they understand all the methods of cotton and sugar planting. What is needed, is an infusion of the intellectual development of the Northern colored men and women."[101]

The *Anglo-African*'s Robert Hamilton similarly urged his fellow black Americans to take the work of emancipation into their own hands. "There is no use in our standing by marveling at the doings of Providence," he remarked after the War Department authorized the recruitment of black soldiers, "rejoicing over the noble sayings of our noble President, or expecting that emancipation is coming somehow or other—Providence has done all it can do, Abraham Lincoln has done much more than we ever dreamed he would do—it is our turn now to wheel into the ranks and shout the glad chorus of Immediate and Universal Emancipation!"[102] Benevolent associations and freedmen's relief societies, whether they operated under religious or secular auspices, had a role in shaping the outcome of the revolution. Within Northern black communities of every size, members of black churches—particularly women—formed aid societies to carry out the work of assisting the freed people.[103] They appealed to prospective donors with stories of the ordeals that freedom seekers continued to face. They recruited teachers and missionaries to work with the freed people, and they collected and shipped clothing, shoes, blankets, and other necessary supplies to designated points of distribution. They collaborated with similar societies that white missionaries and philanthropists had formed and shared the commitment to treat the refugees with "sympathy and kindness."[104]

Individual freedom seekers had to steel themselves for the eventuality that their personal revolutions might spin beyond their control, as two examples from federal operations against the Confederate supply depot of Meridian, Mississippi, in February and March 1864 demonstrated. Upon the return of the expedition to Vicksburg, some 150 miles from Meridian, an officer narrated the tale of "an old man" who was among the refugees. The observer had encountered the man warming himself by a fire of burning railroad ties and every "now and then laughing hilariously to himself." When the officer asked what was so funny, the man explained that he had worked hard for his master the entire sixty-seven years of his life, yet this night he reveled in his freedom even if it might be fleeting. "Two or three days Yankees go way, and I be slave again," he explained, "but two or three days I'se been free man, anyhow; yah! yah! yah!"[105]

Another man from Meridian drove his former master's wagon and team with his children on board assuming that his wife was among the walking refugees. Upon arriving in Vicksburg and discovering that she was not, he begged permission to return for her but the quartermaster refused owing to "the almost certain loss of the team." To resolve the dilemma, a witness explained, the man "surrendered the liberty he enjoyed for a moment" and "went back with his children to the lashes of his master, and to the love of his wife!"[106] As centuries compressed themselves into years, days became equal to lifetimes, and the whirlpool of the past could draw back into its vortex even those who had escaped.

Some found the speed, the unpredictability, and the magnitude of the change disorienting, if not downright terrifying. Shortly after Edward Pierce arrived at Port Royal early in 1862 to assume responsibility for operating the plantations under the control of Union forces, he set about asking the freed people what they thought about freedom. He marveled at the tales "of escapes, both solitary and in numbers, conducted with courage, a forecast, and a skill worthy of heroes." But some plantation residents, he noted, confounded his implicit beliefs that the victims of slavery could shed its habits quickly when the opportunity presented itself. "The white man do what he please with us," one man testified. "We are yours now, 'Massa,'" declared another. And a third claimed to care only that he "had a good master." Others acknowledged "they would like to be free, but they wanted a white man for a 'protector.'"[107] For some unknown number, freedom looked more like a forbidden country than a promised land.

Although it was impossible to determine precisely how many enslaved African Americans experienced temporary sojourns in freedom, they may have numbered in the hundreds of thousands, perhaps half again as many as the 500,000-plus who resided within Union lines in the spring of 1865. The encounters may have lasted merely for minutes or for days at a time; for many enslaved persons, interactions with Yankees recurred sporadically. Looking backward from the vantage of the 1930s, the North Carolinian Ambrose Douglass recalled that "we musta celebrated 'mancipation about twelve time." The explanation was simple: Northern soldiers on patrol would tell the slaves "we was free and we'd begin celebratin'. Before we would get through somebody else would tell us to go back to work, and we would go." In much of the Confederacy, such on-again, off-again flirtations with freedom continued until the Yankees sealed their victory in the spring and early summer of 1865.[108]

———

The sirocco of freedom affected white Confederates as well as their Yankee counterparts, prompting growing interest in emancipation. These outbursts of thought about topics normally unthinkable were no mere reactions to laws or policies adopted by the United States, such as the Emancipation Proclamation. They did, however, respond to changing military fortunes, particularly the Union's decisive victories at Gettysburg and Vicksburg on July 4, 1863. Evangelical Protestant ministers initiated one such quest for deeper understanding, and military strategists explored another. In both cases, the sojourners concluded their intellectual journeys believing that the future of the Confederate nation required granting freedom to slaves, selectively if not necessarily in mass. In that belief they remained a distinct minority.

The ministers began their exercise in discernment with the Bible. From even before the war, certain religious leaders had condemned features of Southern slavery, particularly those that appeared to violate the Ten Commandments and other basic tenets of Christianity. Chief among these was the denial of marriage to enslaved men and women. Slavery's inherent tendency to corrupt the morals of slave owners—leading them to pride, avarice, lust, and related vices—had long been another source of concern. As British missionaries to the West Indies and their abolitionist allies had learned during the 1820s, proposals to ameliorate the unchristian aspects of slavery generated a swift and severe backlash on the part of slaveholders.[109] That notwithstanding, the continuing signs of God's displeasure convinced some Protestant churchmen to consider emancipation as the only hope for regaining God's blessing and, with that, independence.[110] The implications of such reasoning posed a logical roadblock that few Confederate Christians could surpass. Large planters and the interests associated with commercial agriculture had an even more difficult time with the logic of emancipation than their conscience-stricken fellow citizens did. Even if forced to abolish slavery, they would do everything in their power to shape the new labor system into the mold of slavery. But relinquishing the old order voluntarily made no sense.[111]

Within the Union-controlled areas along the Mississippi River from Memphis to New Orleans, the officials chiefly responsible for designing and implementing the regime of compensated labor contended daily with the landowners' lingering attachment to slavery. Thomas W. Conway, the superintendent of the Bureau of Free Labor in the Department of the Gulf, could only marvel at "how intensely the Planters of this country hold the notion that *Capital* shall control *labor*." James McKaye, a commissioner with the AFIC, noted that many of the "old masters . . . scoff at the idea of freedom for the negro." Instead, "they await with impatience the withdrawal of the military authorities, and the re-establishment of the civil power of the State to be controlled and used as hitherto for the maintenance of what, to them doubtless, appears the paramount object of all civil authority, of the State itself, some form of the slave system."[112] Whether their political sympathies lay with the Confederacy or the Union, planters viewed the future through the prism of the past.

Frank F. Barclay, a Creole of color who in February 1863 conducted a survey of Louisiana plantations on behalf of General Nathaniel P. Banks, saw glimmers of hope. The landowners admittedly opposed paying wages to their workers, but he believed that they could, "by catechizing them constantly and actively," be brought around to understanding "that, not only God and humanity, but their own interest commands them to follow the dictates of the progress of the ages." For their part, the freed people that Barclay encountered were more than "willing to go to work immediately on the plantations or for the government, even without remuneration" on the condition that "they would not be whipped and separated from their families,—in fact, requesting only to be treated with humanity." To achieve recognition of their basic human rights, he reported, including compensation for their labor, they placed their trust in "the paternal Government of the United States."[113] Inasmuch as "we are living in an age of startling events," the black Washingtonian T. M. D. Ward observed, nothing was beyond belief. "The tide wave of progress touches the strand of every continent."[114] But persuading rebel slaveholders to abandon slavery and the whip for compensated labor and humane treatment would tax the persuasive powers of both clergy and government officials throughout the Confederacy. Imposing the draft and impressing enslaved laborers in defense of the nation would be child's play in comparison. Notwithstanding any number of signs of God's displeasure, Confederate leaders stood little chance of dismantling the cornerstone of the rebellion, even if independence itself hung in the balance.

Proposals to arm and train black men for service in the Confederate army demonstrated both the logical and the political limits of sacrificing slavery— even under controlled conditions—in the interest of achieving victory. Military strategists looked beyond moral regeneration for the solution to battlefield reverses, growing numbers of casualties, and the risk of demoralization in the ranks. Rebel planners matched wits with an enemy who commanded vastly superior resources, particularly in terms of manpower. Overcoming the disadvantage, some reasoned, required mobilizing the more than half a million enslaved men of military age living in the Confederate states. In early January 1864, General Patrick R. Cleburne, a division commander in the Army of Tennessee, laid just such a proposal before his superiors after much consultation among his fellow officers. The recommendation did not stop at enlistment of enslaved men into the army; instead, it envisioned freeing those who discharged their duties faithfully. Thirteen other senior army officers also affixed their names to Cleburne's letter. "Every consideration of policy and principle demand that we should set him and his whole race who side with us free," they argued. "It is a first principle with mankind that he who offers his life in defense of the State should receive from her in return his freedom and his happiness." When word of the proposal reached President Jefferson Davis, he ordered its suppression to avoid public confusion or unrest.[115]

The notion of mobilizing enslaved men as military laborers should not have encountered the ideological and political opposition that Cleburne's plan to place black men in arms faced, but all such proposals raised thorny issues that pitted slaveholders' concerns about their property rights against Confederate officials' view of the public good. A simple effort to grant the War Department greater authority to coordinate the use of enslaved laborers to support field armies brought the matter to a head. In March 1863, the Confederate Congress authorized the impressment of slaves, but the heavy-handed tactics of press gangs sparked a backlash. The following February, a new law authorized the impressment of up to 20,000 enslaved persons, with provisions to minimize the burden on individual slaveholders, but the measure failed to produce the labor force that deteriorating military conditions required.[116] By November 1864, President Davis proposed purchasing up to 40,000 persons and offering freedom as a reward for faithful service.[117] The exigencies of war convinced Confederate leaders, soldiers, and civilians alike that selective emancipation was the only way to ensure national independence and, with that, the long-term future of slavery. Most slaveholders, however, feared the plagues that might sweep the land if they lifted the lid of this Pandora's box.

After Atlanta, as military and civilian planners plotted the last stand, Davis began viewing black soldiers in a new light. In an abrupt about-face, he supported what he had earlier opposed, and Confederate secretary of state Judah P. Benjamin strongly endorsed both the enlistment of black soldiers and the promise of freedom to those who performed faithfully, prompting a vigorous debate throughout the Confederacy. Because the secessionist movement was bound with slavery from birth, die-hard proponents of Southern independence pressed their case against black enlistment. Howell Cobb, a former Speaker of the U.S. House of Representatives and secretary of the Treasury, who after a stint in the Confederate Congress assumed command of Georgia's state military forces, considered the idea preposterous. "The day you make soldiers of them is the beginning of the end of the revolution," he insisted. "If slaves make good soldiers our whole theory of slavery is wrong."[118]

Notwithstanding such opposition, a high-level consensus emerged in favor of arming slaves. When General Robert E. Lee, commander of the Army of Northern Virginia and the Confederacy's preeminent military leader, gave his blessing, the die was cast. President Davis authorized the recruitment of a black regiment in Richmond.[119] Davis remained silent regarding freedom for soldiers and their families, a key component of Cleburne's original idea. The AME *Christian Recorder* mocked the "world-wide revolution made by these arrogant rebels," whose opinion of black men had swung so quickly from "utter contempt" to "the highest adulation."[120] At the time of Lee's surrender in early April, the desperate dream of employing black men in arms to stave off defeat had advanced little beyond several companies of ill-equipped and essentially untrained men. Although popular sentiment may have begun warming to the notion of selective emancipation in the interest of independence, it was too little too late.

Still, it is remarkable that any Confederate leader, much less civilian and military officials at the highest levels, advocated in favor of arming black men. The secessionist revolution indeed had come full circle and in less than four century-like years, but only by spinning off its axis. Had Cleburne's original concept gained traction, the trade-off for freeing the soldiers and their families might have presented itself differently. Gradual emancipation—with the process extending perhaps as late as 1900, as President Lincoln himself had offered—might have appeared vastly more palatable than the immediate abolition of slavery that military defeat eventually demanded. For the principled rebels who refused to nibble at Lincoln's bait of gradual emancipation sugar-coated with federal dollars, Davis's plan was tantamount to abandoning the Confederate revolution altogether.

In stating specifically that black men would be received into the armed forces, Lincoln's Emancipation Proclamation solved the dilemma that the United States had created for itself by not enlisting them much sooner. The transformation of black men such as Gordon and Hubbard Pryor from frightened fugitives into proud soldiers wrought a social revolution, but it was one that exacted a fearful cost and generated countercurrents of its own. Like the larger revolution of which they were a part, these currents created eddies rather than simply flowing in a single direction.

A favorite argument of the opponents of enlisting black men, freeborn or enslaved, addressed the presumption of their unwillingness or inability to face the Southern chivalry on the battlefield. Formerly enslaved men proved they would fight at Milliken's Bend, Louisiana, in May 1863, when Confederate forces attacked a garrison of black soldiers amid their assault on the leased plantations in that region after other federal forces had been mobilized against Vicksburg.[121] Within months of the organization of black regiments in the North, the storied attack by the men of the Fifty-Fourth Massachusetts Volunteers against the nearly impregnable Confederate position at Fort Wagner, South Carolina, settled the matter once and for all. Within the space of less than half a year, the formerly unthinkable image of black men wearing the uniform of the U.S. Army could be seen in illustrated newspapers, in cartes de visite, and in real life. Former slaves from the South and former servants from the North had proved themselves to be not only men but heroes.

Both the army as an institution and Northern society together strained to accommodate the change and not always successfully, as the experience of the Twentieth U.S. Colored Infantry illustrates. At the same time that white New Yorkers expressed such violent opposition to being drafted into the army, their black fellow citizens clamored to enlist. Having overcome the delaying tactics of Democratic governor Horatio Seymour by appealing directly to President Lincoln for authorization, the regiment departed the city for service in Louisiana in March 1864.[122] The unit was assigned to Camp Parapet, above New Orleans, where John W. Phelps, the abolitionist general from Vermont, had earlier welcomed refugees and had begun organizing the able-bodied men as soldiers before resigning his commission in protest against General Butler's constraints.[123]

By August 1864, the steady regimen of hard work in the blazing sun had dispirited the men of the Twentieth. One of their spokesmen, a soldier named Nimrod Rowley, wrote to President Lincoln, describing their plight and asking for relief, hoping that the president would recall that his intervention allowed the regiment to be organized over the objections of the governor. "Instead of the musket It is the spad and the Whelbarrow and the Axe cutting in one of the most horable swamps in Louisiana." The work was taking a heavy toll, he explained, the regiment having lost 160 of its 1,000 men to disease in the five months since leaving New York. Like other soldiers, Rowley complained about the discriminatory pay that black soldiers received, but he particularly criticized the short rations. "We Are Nerly Deprived of All Comforts of Life," he explained, and "Hardlly have Anough Bread to Keep us From starving" and nothing but "soup meat Licqour" that "the Boys calls hot water or meat tea for Diner." He deplored being "Keept in such a state of misery Continuly." By the time the regiment was mustered out of service in October 1865, 263 had died of disease and only one from wounds sustained in combat.[124]

Other black soldiers faced the additional burden of officers who treated them with disdain, if not contempt. In June 1864, for instance, when a group of twenty men from the Forty-Ninth U.S. Colored Infantry, raised in Louisiana and stationed at Vicksburg, Mississippi, stacked their arms and refused to perform duty in protest against "the repeated ill treatment of our officers [who] were using us in the most shameful manner," the officers initiated court-martial proceedings. All the protesters were found guilty; two ringleaders were executed and the others sentenced to prison. In a petition for clemency addressed to the secretary of war early in 1865, the imprisoned men claimed ignorance of what constituted mutiny, explaining that they had tried unsuc-cessfully to have their grievances addressed and waited "untill the cruelty of those in command of us compelled us to do something." The men's petition was granted, and they were returned to duty.[125]

The Union's victory at the end of the war did not resolve the contradic-tion wherein U.S. soldiers were treated as slaves, but the demobilization of the army and the transfer of many of the recently enlisted black men to Texas (to prevent a suspected invasion by the French puppet Maximilian I) made the problem disappear from the public eye. The revolution was far from hav-ing run its course. Thomas Nast's illustration from the summer of 1865 de-picting a black soldier with his right leg amputated accompanied by the image of Columbia identified new political challenges that were beginning to arise (see figure 3.5). The caption reads: "Franchise, and Not This man?" From South Carolina, General Rufus Saxton, the military governor and overall su-perintendent of freed people, believed strongly that "the senseless prejudices and bitter contempt against their race is disappearing before their peaceful and orderly conduct under their trials and provocations, their patient hope and heroism in war." Looking to the future, he confidently predicted that the "events of four years have been disciplining the mind of the nation to prepare it to give them full recognition and ample justice."[126]

On April 11, 1865, Abraham Lincoln's public endorsement of the concept that African Americans should play a role in the political reconstruction of Louisiana likely cost him his life inasmuch as John Wilkes Booth was pres-ent in the crowd serenading the president that evening.[127] Yet it was the pres-ident's second inaugural address, delivered some five weeks earlier, that truly illustrated Lincoln's grasp of the revolution that was remaking the na-tion. Observing that both Unionists and Confederates "read the same Bible and pray to the same God" with each invoking "His aid against the other," Lincoln chose not to pass judgment that "any men should dare to ask a just God's assistance in wringing their bread from the sweat of other men's faces." Then reasoning that "this terrible war" was punishment for slavery which was "one of those offenses which, in the providence of God, must needs come, but which, having continued through His appointed time, He now wills to remove," the president echoed countless similar assessments that African American clergymen had made since Fort Sumter. "Fondly do we hope, fer-

Figure 3.5
Thomas Nast,
*Franchise. And Not
This Man?*, *Harper's
Weekly*, August 5,
1865. Courtesy of the
Library of Congress
Prints and Photo-
graphs Division,
LC-USZ62-102257.

vently do we pray, that this mighty scourge of war may speedily pass away," the president mused. "Yet, if God wills that it continue until all the wealth piled by the bondsman's two hundred and fifty years of unrequited toil shall be sunk, and until every drop of blood drawn with the lash shall be paid by another drawn with the sword, as was said three thousand years ago, so still it must be said 'the judgments of the Lord are true and righteous altogether.'"[128]

The previous July, Richard H. Cain's insightful meditation on the nature of the war reflected the thinking among observers who sought to understand the relationship among slavery, the war, and God's plan for the nation and its soon-to-be citizens of African ancestry. "We stand amazed at this cruel war which is sweeping over our land, but if we will comprehend the signs of the times, we will see the causes of this bloodshed," he explained. Looking backward, he acknowledged that "this nation has been accessory to all the crimes of the slaveholders. It has assisted in binding the fetters of the oppressed, and, while their cries have ascended to Heaven, they have stood by, and spoken no words of pity or remonstrance in behalf of the wronged slave, and now that 'judgment is laid to the line, and justice to the plummet,' they must pay an equivalent in their sons' blood as a ransom for all the sons of Afric's race, whose bones whiten the fields, and whose flesh enriches the soil of the South." Looking to the future, he predicted that "time will still unfold scenes more terrible than has been realized by this nation, unless they speedily let every slave go free, and then acknowledge the manhood of the race." Only one choice presented itself: "Give them the rights which belong to them in common with all other people in this country."[129]

"Coming events cast their shadows before them," Cain observed at the dawn of 1865. "Wise indeed are they who duly prepare to meet and perform their part in the mighty developments which are foreshadowed."[130]

PART II

Space

Wartime emancipation played out in space, but space did not serve simply as an inert platform. From well before the outbreak of hostilities, Americans had come to understand the economic and political connotations associated with geography. The Ohio River had served for years as a literal and figurative dividing line between free and slave states west of the Appalachian Mountains. The start of the war required a remapping of that terrain to accommodate the birth of the Confederate States of America. In the Union states of Delaware, Maryland, Kentucky, and Missouri, slavery remained legal and slaveholders continued to exert great influence in public affairs. Slaveholders hoped that their loyalty would guarantee the future of their prized institution under the Union's protection. In their steadfast pursuit of freedom, enslaved persons helped prepare the seedbed for antislavery political coalitions to take root, particularly in Maryland and Missouri. By early 1865, those two states had abolished slavery of their own accord.[1]

Within the Confederate States, space meant different things to different people. For Confederate soldiers it meant homes and firesides that must be defended from political and military encroachment by the Yankees. For enslaved persons, it served as the foundation of their misery but also a potential source of independence. Members of the federal armed forces viewed the South either as a miserable place to die or as territory worth dying for to preserve the nation. Once black soldiers entered the Union army, Confederate space assumed added significance as the site for staking a claim to equal citizenship, including the ballot.

Military operations had the power to affect the Southern landscape profoundly. General William T. Sherman's famous March to the Sea cut a swath across Georgia that in places was sixty miles wide, leaving such destruction behind that birds, it was said, had difficulty finding enough to eat. Then, after resting for several weeks in Savannah, Sherman and his men turned their destructive forces northward into the Carolinas to the same effect. Less dramatic but no less disruptive operations resulted in the destruction of homes and buildings (sometimes entire cities), the construction of trenches and field fortifications (many of which still stand a century and a half later), and attempts, more or less successful, to alter the natural flow of watercourses. Other changes affected the human geography, even in places where the contending forces did not draw near enough to disturb a single blade of grass. Civilians in general sought safety, often abandoning their homes in the pursuit. Enslaved persons in particular sought freedom.[2]

The war transformed space on small and subtle scales too. Plantation cabins that before the war had been the places where enslaved laborers soothed their tired bodies with sleep and their beleaguered spirits with the love of family became the sites for planning a future without slavery. Apartments and living quarters also took on new meanings. When an enslaved woman in St. Louis posted a likeness of Abraham Lincoln that she had clipped from a newspaper on the wall of her bedroom, her owner flew into a rage. "What she was doing with old Lincoln's picture," he asked, to which she replied "it was there because she liked it." She appropriated the master's space for her own ends. In the kitchens and dining rooms of virtually every slaveholding household, mistresses and enslaved cooks and housekeepers similarly contested the boundaries of acceptable behavior.[3]

Some of the most valuable agricultural land in North America served as the arena for similar contests in which proponents of the old order vied with champions of the new. Fields and meadows provided both campgrounds and battlegrounds. Away from the areas of active military operations, scenes similar to those of the big houses were enacted amid corn and cotton rows, where enslaved laborers bucked the commands of overseers (when they were present) and of mistresses and young masters (when all the adult men were absent in the army) for control over the pace of fieldwork and the larger objectives of their work. Black refugees who settled on abandoned plantations—often, but not always, with the knowledge and the approval of federal authorities—subsisted themselves from land formerly reserved for such commercially valuable but inedible crops as cotton.

Finally, on close inspection, the taken-for-granted geography of the federal occupation of rebel territory over the course of the war reveals surprising features. Specifically, most of the seceded states remained under the jurisdiction of Confederate authorities until the end. So did the civilian populations in those states, enslaved as well as free. As a result, the impact of Union-sponsored wartime experiments in compensated labor remained limited in terms of their geographical reach and the number of affected freed people. The real work of emancipation among the majority of the formerly enslaved population began only when the guns fell silent in the spring of 1865.[4]

War intensified the sensation that space was not always fixed and that, like time, it could display elastic properties. This pliability might be revealed in several ways. The first is literal, such as when armies occupied space.

When they camped for any length of time—for instance, in winter quarters—they consumed large quantities of wood for shelter and heat. In constructing fortifications and digging canals, they displaced enormous quantities of earth with little thought of returning the landscape to its original topology. Large-scale armed clashes often left battlefields as wastelands. Such changes might persist for years, even permanently.[5]

The second sense in which war uncovers the elastic property of space relates to the authority that armed forces exercise over the territory they occupy. When the power changed hands, as it did repeatedly in the Shenandoah valley of Virginia, combatants and civilians alike experienced the whipsaw effects of safe space rendered dangerous and vice versa. In cases where the combatants settled into fixed positions—for instance, during the siege operations at Vicksburg in 1863 or at Petersburg in 1864—a no-man's-land emerged where humans and animals alike transgressed at their peril. Similar danger zones also followed the fluid lines that the respective armies marked with pickets.

Finally, the innate pliability of space had special relevance for freedom seekers. Specifically, when enslaved persons encountered U.S. forces who offered protection and a passage to safety, the terrors normally associated with Confederate-controlled space disappeared. In their place appeared a protective cocoon that could hover above space and function independently of its connotations as the home of slavery. Both the blue-clad soldiers and the ground they occupied became interchangeably identified with freedom.

The three chapters in this section examine the breakdown of slavery through three aspects of space: panoramic, confined, and trembling.

Chapter 4

Panoramas

Emancipation unfolded through space, with contours that were as vast as they were varied. Enslaved people's struggles for freedom depended implicitly on the physical and human geography of the Southern states. The mountains and prairies, the rivers and forests, and the agricultural and urban landscapes defined the day-to-day lives of all Southerners. Between 1800 and 1860, cotton planters led a westward movement that exploited those features to build the most economically and politically powerful slaveholding class on the planet. Steeped in the traditions of European landholding practices, seventeenth-century English settlers in North America claimed land as property and drew lines on maps corresponding with markers on the ground to distinguish one lot from the next, one jurisdiction from the next, one colony from the next. Over time, these distinctions took on political connotations with more or less effect on the people within the boundaries of the respective polities. In February 1862, when the Confederate States of America announced itself to the world as a republic independent of the United States, it consisted of seven states; in the following four months, four more states joined. Four slave states remained within the Union.

Taken together, the Confederate States occupied more than 500,000 square miles, stretching from the Atlantic Ocean to the Rio Grande. This space incorporated mountains and forests, cultivated fields and natural pastures, freshwater as well as brackish swamps, and semiarid as well as lush prairies. To the east, the Appalachian Mountains separated waters that flowed into the Atlantic Ocean from those that flowed into the Gulf of Mexico, chiefly via the Mississippi River. The abundance of fertile soil in the region helped fuel the cotton boom that began early in the nineteenth century and still had not exhausted itself by 1860. As the architects of the plantation system expanded it westward, transportation networks designed to move bulky cotton bales to market developed apace. Yet, railroad mileage lagged significantly behind that of the North, and the network as a whole had other limitations, not least of which was the lack of a uniform track gauge. By the same token, most of the region's industrial development served local needs, relying on local raw materials and labor resources. With the outbreak of war, Confederate strategic planners had reason to wonder how to mobilize such assets in the interest of victory in the dual pursuit of achieving independence and preserving slavery. The enslaved residents of the Confederate states began a planning process of their own to determine how best to leverage the unique combination of the natural and human attributes of the South to achieve freedom and to destroy slavery.

———

The spread of cotton agriculture accounted for the distribution of the African American population across the vast territory that in 1861 became the Confederate States of America. The heaviest concentrations were in the coastal lowlands and lower piedmont regions of the states that bordered the Atlantic Ocean and the Gulf of Mexico and in the alluvial regions along the rivers of the interior, particularly the Mississippi and its tributaries. The concept of "Black Belt" neatly conflated the overlapping presence of enslaved laborers and rich soil that gave the region its distinctive character. In 1860, more than three million of the enslaved people lived and labored there, one-third of whom lived on plantations of fifty or more.

In Virginia, where African slavery first took root in the English colonies of North America, the enslaved population topped 490,000 persons, less than half of its white population of slightly more than one million, on the brink of the war. In South Carolina, however, enslaved African Americans outnumbered free white persons 402,406 to 291,300, and in Mississippi, where the black population was growing fastest, the disparity was 436,631 to 353,899. Next to Virginia, the Confederate states with the largest white populations were Tennessee with nearly 827,000 and North Carolina with nearly 630,000. Yeoman-farming households made up significant segments of the white population in the states of Georgia and Arkansas as well as Virginia, Tennessee, and North Carolina, concentrated heavily in the piedmont and mountain districts but scattered across the plantation areas as well.[1] These numbers provide a snapshot of a phenomenon that was dynamic rather than static. Migration among white Southerners reflected a pattern that predated the American Revolution, the chief feature of which was its voluntary nature, with economic opportunity (chiefly in the form of accessible land) constituting a major motive. The accompanying movement of black Southerners was involuntary and designed to achieve their exploitation, not their social advancement. The westward expansion of cotton cultivation profoundly affected the nation and not just the South. By 1860, cotton accounted for more than 60 percent of export revenues. All of Europe's manufacturing powerhouses depended so heavily on slave-grown American cotton that in 1858 South Carolina's James Henry Hammond could boast confidently to his colleagues in the U.S. Senate: "Cotton *is* king."[2]

King Cotton's retainers grafted all the modern advances in technology and communications and in business and finance onto the anachronistic system of slavery. Via railroad and telegraph lines, the merchants and factors who furnished credit and supplies incorporated even the most isolated plantations on the cotton frontier into webs of exchange that extended through local way stations to coastal seaports and thence to the commercial and industrial hubs of the North and of Europe.[3] From the Upper South states to the Gulf, various agricultural regimes and extractive industries existed as principalities on King Cotton's periphery. In the mountainous parts of Tennessee, Virginia, North Carolina, and Georgia, the comparatively few enslaved people who lived there worked in mines and lumber camps as well as on farms. In the central section of North Carolina and much of Virginia, tobacco, not cotton, was king. In Virginia's Shenandoah valley and in the counties surrounding Richmond, grains—chiefly wheat—ruled. In the Border States to the north and west, tobacco, hemp, grain, and livestock occupied the enslaved laborers. Along the southeast Atlantic coast, rice and Sea Island cotton planters amassed property and wealth on a par with their counterparts on Louisiana's sugar plantations and Mississippi's cotton plantations.

Richmond and New Orleans were the premier manufacturing centers of the Confederacy, but, like those two, Southern cities elsewhere on the seacoast and at the fall lines of rivers also supported ironworks, flour mills, cotton mills, and other industries—some powered by water, others by steam—as well as small shops that produced fine clothing, fancy carriages, and everything in between. The small commercial centers that dotted the interior provided a range of professional and artisanal services. Proprietors of these establishments proudly affirmed their determination to help ensure victory for the Confederate cause. Patriotic slaveholders everywhere parroted the official line that slaves would do their part unquestioningly. A New York newspaper correspondent in Fort Monroe, Virginia, in May 1861 reported matter-of-factly that "the slaves are beginning to catch new ideas," but hard-core rebels either did not see the evidence or did not believe what they saw.[4]

The internal slave trade that grew up alongside the westward expansion of the cotton kingdom accelerated the increasing awareness of space. Between 1790 and 1860, approximately 800,000 to 1.1 million enslaved laborers moved from east to west, one-half with their owners and the other half via the interstate trade. Richmond and New Orleans served as the regional hubs—the former the eastern collection center and the latter the western distribution center—that supplied the plantations of the Mississippi valley with laborers from the states along the Atlantic coast. This movement created a level of geographical knowledge on the part of those who were transported that belies the simple stereotype that enslaved people's spatial awareness extended scarcely beyond their home plantations.[5] For many who had endured the journey, the place names associated with the war triggered memories of people and locations from the past.

Wallace Turnage's experience illustrates the persisting effects of this upheaval into the war years. His remarkable journey began in 1860 when at age fifteen he was sold away from his mother in Virginia to an Alabama planter. Turnage traveled by train over the course of several days to Mobile and from there to Pickensville, some 200 miles to the north along the state's western border with Mississippi. In relatively short order he decided to make his way home rather than submit to the cotton plantation regime of hard work and arbitrary whippings. Over the next four years he made five attempts at freedom, although once, when accused of doing so, he insisted that his true objective was to return to Virginia, "back where I came from."[6] In the four tries that failed, he headed northward along the highways and railways of Mississippi toward Tennessee. His adventures echoed those of other refugees from slavery, including pursuit by vicious dogs, treacherous river crossings, the physical discomfort and mental anguish of hiding out during the winter months, and both the kindness and the betrayal of strangers, black and white, in every season of the year.[7]

On one occasion, a group of enslaved men on a plantation near Aberdeen, Mississippi, fed him and concealed him overnight because, as he explained, "though I was only a boy, they gloried in my spunk." A black woman who took him in for another night presented him as a long-absent son to avoid any suspicion on the part of visiting friends.[8] In one failed attempt, Turnage's luck ran out near Rienzi, Mississippi, when a man with a pack of dogs captured him and put him to work until someone answered the notice to reclaim him. The captor managed to secrete him and another man from a federal patrol that raided the neighborhood. After being reclaimed by his nominal owner, a planter named James Chalmers, Turnage and he fell into the hands of rebel pickets. Asking the planter "what good is this boy to you" if he keeps running away, the Confederates offered "to make a Target" out of him. To Turnage's relief, Chalmers intervened before they opened fire.[9]

Turnage was sold to a man in Mobile in December 1862 and had acquainted himself with the city long before federal forces gained control over Mobile Bay in the summer of 1864. Making his way to the Yankee position at Fort Powell, he recalled, "I became so impatient seeing the free country in view and I still in the slave country" that he tried floating a log across the open water. When that failed, he found a small boat in the rushes and headed toward the fort but nearly capsized as the waters became choppy. "Eight Yankees in a boat" rescued him and towed his humble craft behind "to show what a trifleing thing he came over in." Overnight he passed from slave to free man: "The next morning" he arose early and viewed "the rebels country with a thankful heart to think that I had made my escape with safety after such a long struggle; and had obtained that freedom which I desired so long." Like most successful freedom seekers, he reflected on the meaning and significance of his new life. "I Now dreaded the gun, the handcuffs and pistols no more," he reasoned, "nor the blewing of horns and the running of hounds; nor the threats of death from the rebel's authority." "I could now speak my opinion to men of all grades and colors," he boasted, "and no one to question my right to speak."[10]

As journeys such as this demonstrated, the westward expansion of the cotton plantation complex and the attendant increase in commercial activity widened everyone's horizons. Enslaved wagoners, railway porters, dockworkers, and boatmen developed detailed mental maps of the transportation networks that linked the country towns in the plantation districts with regional trading centers. Beginning in the 1830s, as private companies constructed railroads through the interior, the contractors often hired slaves from the planters and farmers whose ceded land constituted the right-of-way to clear the land, level the roadbeds, and lay the tracks. By the 1850s, the companies also hired slaves on yearly contracts, moving them to worksites farther afield and even, when owners approved, employing them on trains. Over the same period, the numbers of black men and women, enslaved as well as free, who worked on the rivers and along the waterfronts of river cities grew dramatically. By the start of the Civil War, their traditional service role as cooks and stewards to the passengers had expanded to include "deck hands and roustabouts," George Taylor Burns later recalled, as the white men who had previously held those positions either entered military service or moved from the deck into the wheelhouse as pilots, mates, and captains. Those who worked on the Mississippi River and its main tributaries, the Ohio and the Missouri, came to know the waterways, the countryside, the cities, and the people of the American heartland.[11]

In sections of the South where annual hiring was a common practice, hired slaves also learned local and regional transportation networks. The Fredericksburg, Virginia, native John Washington, for example, was "sent to Richmond, Va to be hired out" in January 1861, traveling there by train. At Christmas, he returned to his family in Fredericksburg, "having been provided with a pass and fare." In short order he "sought and obtained a home for the year of 1862 at the 'Shakespear House'" as a steward and bartender. House servants of the wealthiest planters also had opportunities to expand their geographical knowledge as they moved seasonally to summer homes in seaside resorts, in the mountains, or even in such faraway places as Newport, Rhode Island, and Saratoga Springs, New York.[12]

Expectations of freedom among politically savvy enslaved people had been growing for at least four years before Abraham Lincoln's election, since

John C. Frémont ran as the Republican Party's first presidential candidate in 1856. The widely reported insurrection scare in the Upper South in 1856 signaled the level of awareness among the enslaved. The owners of William Webb, for instance, moved him among the states of Mississippi, Tennessee, Kentucky, and Louisiana during the 1850s. At each stop, he preached a secular gospel that envisioned achieving freedom through an organization of black kingdoms in each state. "In all the States at one time," the kings would lead rebellions and "the white people would not have a chance." The kings would then usher in a regime of freedom and justice.[13] Prince Lambkin, who later served as a corporal in the First South Carolina Colored Volunteer Infantry, "had predicted the war from Frémont's time" and joined with fellow enslaved laborers in a general work stoppage on March 4, 1861, in honor of Lincoln's inauguration, "expecting their freedom to date from that day."[14] Fort Sumter announced that the time for translating dreams of abolition into reality had arrived.

————

Once the war began, great public fanfare attended the organization of military units: enlisting, outfitting, equipping, and training the men, and bidding them farewell when they departed from home. African American men and women, particularly those who worked in the households where men were preparing to depart for war, found themselves drawn into the mobilization. With the white women attentively supervising, enslaved women washed and mended clothing and prepared food for the volunteers to take. For their part, enslaved men readied the boots, shoes, sabers, saddles, and the other paraphernalia of war, and prepared horses and wagons for the trip to the predetermined gathering place.

Not through arrogance alone did Confederate apologists boast that their new republic had devised a solution to the timeless tension between those who worked and those for whom they worked—which many commentators collapsed into the shorthand terms of labor and capital. When these tensions reached the point of open conflict, the entire social order might feel the effect, as history had repeatedly demonstrated. The fires of war that flared in April 1861 would test the presumed harmony between slaveholders and their human property to limits that the philosophers and political economists hardly envisioned. At first patriotic pro-Confederate citizens perceived an ideal means to demonstrate this in practice: white men left for the front accompanied by favored and trusted servants. Louisianan Kate Stone described the highly ritualized scene in which the house servants and field hands were assembled to offer "heartfelt" wishes to her brother William, her uncle Bo, and the servant Wesley as they left for camp in Vicksburg.[15]

Yet, with the future of slavery potentially hanging in the balance, a simple "goodbye" could contain several layers of meaning. From the standpoint of the officer or soldier, "colored servants" did more than serve; they symbolized the owner's social status, upheld traditions characteristic of slave societies throughout history, and reinforced key tenets of American slaveholding ideology.[16] Owners made the case that ties of genuine affection bound owner and servant together, with both sharing danger and each looking out for the other. Personal service to a Confederate volunteer also created an understanding that the faithful fulfillment of duties obliged the master's family to protect the servant's family from the vicissitudes of war as much as possible, and this reciprocation helps explain the enduring relationships that, in many such cases, continued after the war. Enslaved people who worked in the fields felt no such bond, and the boldest began to disappear at night, many never to return. Ironically, many of those who made their way to Union lines became the servants of federal army and naval officers aiming to destroy, not strengthen, the bonds of slavery.

The Upper South states of Arkansas, Tennessee, North Carolina, and Virginia assumed new importance in the military and political geography of Confederate strategists just as the Border Slave States, particularly Maryland, Kentucky, and Missouri, did with their Northern counterparts. When rebel planners set about addressing the vulnerability that the vast northern frontier presented by virtue of its proximity to the United States, they dispatched newly organized regiments there as quickly as they could be enrolled and equipped. Almost incidentally, this movement reversed the pattern of western migration that had characterized the previous several generations—from Alabama, Mississippi, Louisiana, and Texas back toward Tennessee and Virginia.

———

All this movement sparked great interest in the military geography of the Confederacy. Notwithstanding their varying motives, persons of every description throughout the Confederate States and the United States became obsessed with the positions of armies vis-à-vis each other and the natural features of the terrain on which they operated. As volunteer units moved from the place of origin to the front, family members and friends at home and the general public craved visual depictions, especially of Virginia, which contained the Confederate capital and fronted the Union's capital and the states of Maryland, Pennsylvania, and Ohio. In the west, Tennessee was the strategic capstone shielding the states of Alabama, Mississippi, and Louisiana, the center of the prewar cotton empire.

An interest in maps accompanied this interest in Southern places. Shortly after the federal surrender of Fort Sumter, General in Chief of the U.S. Army

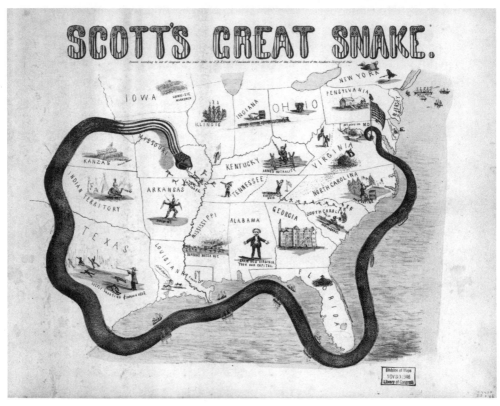

Figure 4.1 Scott's Great Snake. Courtesy of the Library of Congress Geography and Map Division, LCCN-99447020.

Winfield Scott announced his strategic plan. It had two major components: first, a naval blockade of the entire Confederate coast, which Lincoln had ordered immediately after Fort Sumter, and second, eventual military operations along the Mississippi River, which would cut the Confederacy in two. Although critics in the popular press quickly dubbed this Scott's "Anaconda Plan" because it conjured up the imagery of a snake strangling its prey (see figure 4.1), President Lincoln appreciated its conceptual simplicity. Although he, like Scott, well understood that such a vast space would likely not yield quickly to federal arms and authority, in the spring and summer of 1861 Lincoln joined the majority of Northerners in hoping for a quick deathblow rather than a gradual suffocation. Two years later, on July 4, 1863, General Ulysses S. Grant's victory at Vicksburg, Mississippi, demonstrated the underlying soundness of Scott's original vision. But at first, the popular press saw only a chance for ridicule. That notwithstanding, even crude and stylized maps provided the Northern public with a visual representation of Confederate geography.

For their part, Confederate military planners followed President Jefferson Davis's lead and reasoned that the key to victory lay in applying the lessons of the Napoleonic wars. By assuming the strategic defense, they enjoyed the military advantages derived from interior lines of communication and the political and emotional advantages associated with protecting homes and firesides. This strategy expressed confidence that the Confederate people could mobilize sufficient resources—agricultural, financial, industrial, and, most important, human—to achieve victory and, with that, independence. It also left open the possibility of assuming the strategic offense when circumstances warranted, as, for instance, General Braxton Bragg did in Kentucky from August through October 1862, and General Robert E. Lee did in Maryland in September 1862 and in Pennsylvania in June 1863.[17]

In short order, realistic maps depicting key places in the military geography of the war began appearing regularly in newspapers in both the North and the South.[18] Although advances in print technology enabled the publication of such maps, the real driving force behind their popularity was the growing interest on the part of the respective publics in visualizing the faraway places where their loved ones were risking life and limb. Major metropolitan dailies, in particular, published maps to illustrate the reports from correspondents in the field. To be sure, as a number of contemporaries noted, the war presented the occasion for a nationwide geography lesson. Civilians no less than soldiers soon memorized names of cities and towns, rivers and bays, mountains and valleys that held little, if any, significance in their lives before April 1861.[19] The fascination extended beyond the places to the residents of the Confederate states, who they were, and what they thought and did. "To thousands of people in the North, the interior of the southern states is as much as terra incognita as the interior of unexplored Africa," observed a Philadelphia newspaper in 1863. "We are learning, just now, its social features in a rapid rate." Members of the AFIC requested military maps as well as coast-survey maps of the areas where freed people had gathered in large numbers.[20]

Black Americans' interest in the political and military geography of the rebellion rivaled that of their white counterparts. Contemporary as well as later reports noted the enslaved people's interest in the news. Despite laws against teaching them to read, some enslaved people still managed to learn the art, particularly when they lived near a town or a major transportation artery such as a river or railroad. J. B. Roudanez, a free black sugar maker in Louisiana, explained to the AFIC that generally "one or more" persons on each plantation had "secretly learned to read," and they often used that knowledge to the benefit of the plantation community.[21] Roudanez himself served as a good illustration of his point that skilled literate workers carried news with them as they moved from plantation to plantation and between urban and rural settings.[22] When federal forces advanced, slaveholders began to speak in muffled voices, but enslaved people derived information about the war from other credible sources.

This dynamic applied to the Border Slave States that remained within the Union as well as to the Confederacy. In Kentucky, Elijah Marrs had responsibility for picking up the mail and the newspapers from the post office on behalf of his master, who owned "about thirty slaves" and whose plantation served as "general headquarters for the negroes" nearby. Marrs devoured the news on the return trip and then, from scraps of newsprint he picked up along the way, "would read to them for hours at a time."[23] In this way, "from mouth to ear," as the enslaved Missourian Henry Clay Bruce explained, "the news was carried from farm to farm, without the knowledge of masters."[24] Those who could write as well as read enjoyed additional advantages. To travel abroad, whether to seek freedom or to visit farms or plantations on which loved ones resided, they forged passes, confident that, as Bruce observed, illiterate white men on slave patrols "could not read writing."[25]

Freeborn African Americans in the Northern states also craved news about the war. Laura Simmes, a young woman living in Washington, described how "political excitement" had positively affected black Northerners, "increasing our knowledge of geographical localities, state boundaries, country limits, length of roads, dimensions of cities, navigable rivers, and such like things."[26] Robert Fitzgerald of Chester County, Pennsylvania, stayed abreast of developments, a relative later explained, "by reading every scrap of war news, following every skirmish and campaign, analyzing every political speech in the newspapers and keeping himself informed."[27] Before long, he and his brothers and cousins were working for the army quartermaster's department resupplying the armies fighting to capture Richmond and to control the Shenandoah valley, the breadbasket for Lee's army.

The obsession with maps signaled a growing interest in the geography of emancipation, which both white and black observers, North and South, associated with the advance of Union forces. "When have our people in the very interior of the South known so much about politics," mused the AME minister Henry M. Turner. "What geography could have ever taught them so much concerning the localities of the country as the present war has taught them?" "The election of Abraham Lincoln to the presidency," he concluded, "is worth to the nation, mentally, twenty-five years of schooling."[28] The postwar memoir that the refugee John M. Washington wrote describing his escape from slavery in Fredericksburg and his work with Union forces in Northern Virginia included his hand-drawn map depicting all the places pertinent to his narrative, with each one clearly labeled. And his account is studded with the geographical references that enabled him to negotiate the wartime terrain from Richmond to Washington and from the Shenandoah valley to the Chesapeake Bay.[29]

The military-political geography of the war ebbed and flowed with the movements of the various armies and their respective victories and defeats. More to the point, the geography of emancipation followed the footsteps of Union soldiers, particularly after the Emancipation Proclamation of January 1, 1863. As maps displaying the territory under federal control over time illustrate, the Union extended its dominion over growing expanses of Confederate territory from year to year (see figure 4.2). But the growth was far from steady and the intensity of the presence was far from uniform. As a result, for all its usefulness, such a map is also misleading in two important respects: first, its year-end snapshots freeze in time and space a process that was inherently fluid throughout the year; second, its smooth lines gloss over the irregular geography and blurred borders of federal authority at every moment, as the broad path of destruction that General Sherman's forces cut through Georgia in 1864 illustrates. Union forces set about disrupting civil society in the area through which they passed, but they had no intention of pausing to reestablish federal authority permanently. What is more, Sherman's army departed Atlanta in November and reached Savannah late in December 1864, spending at most several days in any one county and a total of less than six weeks on the entire journey. Confederate officials and citizens scarcely needed to unpack their bags at their destinations of refuge before heading home, although when they did so they found what they had left behind in shambles. Achieving military objectives, narrowly defined as the defeat of Confederate regular forces and the disruption of their lines of supply and communication, did not always coincide with the objective of disrupting slavery, even though both pursuits often involved the same people in the same operation. The terrain on which these actions occurred held no intrinsic value.

Union strategists did not intend to occupy Confederate territory for its own sake divorced from its military value, yet occupation itself took varying forms with gradations ranging from heavily armed forts to thinly manned picket lines. Accordingly, maps purporting to depict occupied territory inherently risk overstating it in terms of real estate and understating it in terms of military and political effectiveness. After adjusting for these margins of error, when the exercise is flipped upside down to determine the size of the geographical area where slavery remained largely intact into 1865, the results are sobering. Nearly all of North and South Carolina, Georgia, Florida, and Texas; most of Alabama; roughly half of Virginia and Louisiana; and smaller

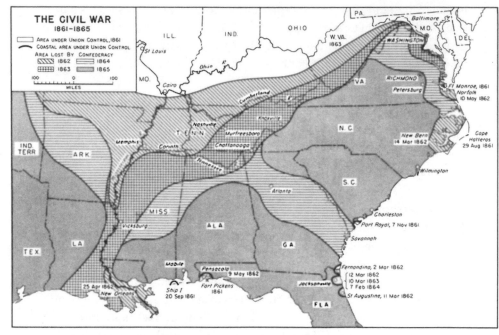

Figure 4.2 The Civil War, 1861–1865, Office of the Historian of the Army, U.S. Army. Courtesy of Wikimedia Commons.

fractions of Mississippi and Arkansas felt the influence but not the direct presence of federal armed forces. When the war ended, probably 2.6 million of the intended beneficiaries of the Emancipation Proclamation resided on the several hundred thousand square miles still under Confederate control. Those farthest removed from the terrain that the two armies contested—southwest Arkansas, for instance—lived in conditions little different from those before the war. But in areas where the mobilization drew men away to work on behalf of either Confederate or Union armed forces—southwest Georgia, for instance—the picture was more complex. Depending on the relative presence of white men to supervise field operations, work routines for women might change for the worse or the general output of the farm or plantation might decrease. Yet in either case, the absence of the working-age men also meant less reason to attempt flight.[30]

———

At the start of the war, Confederate strategists wasted little time in identifying the points of vulnerability in the respective states, with the key cities of Richmond, Charleston, and New Orleans topping the list. With the cooperation of state leaders, military engineers began reinforcing the shore batter-

140   Chapter 4

ies at key points along the Atlantic and Gulf coasts from Norfolk, Virginia, to Galveston, Texas. They also strengthened existing fortifications at such strategically important places as Memphis, Vicksburg, and Nashville, and built new ones at selected places along the Mississippi River (including Fort Pillow and Island No. 10) and its tributaries (including Fort Henry on the Tennessee River and Fort Donelson on the Cumberland River). Local authorities requisitioned laborers from nearby slaveholders to work temporarily on the fortifications. Richmond officials persuaded the central government to help foot the bill for employing free and enslaved black workers, and building and maintaining defensive works there, like nowhere else in the Confederacy, continued nearly uninterrupted for the next four years.[31] Although few recognized the impact of these actions at the time, the mobilizations began setting enslaved people in motion, cutting them loose from their customary moorings. In most cases, owners consented, even though the mobilized laborers remained beyond the owners' immediate control for the duration of their service, however temporary. During the spring and summer of 1861, work on military fortifications occupied tens of thousands of free and enslaved black men throughout the seceded states.[32]

In times of peace, no governmental authority would have dared to demand a fraction of what the Confederate States of America did, so political leaders crafted enabling legislation and procedural guidelines even as the engineers were putting men to work.[33] In the abstract, all parties understood that the needs of specific emergencies might overrule legal niceties, but for practical political reasons they also knew that the government must observe the law if it hoped to retain the allegiance of its citizens. Slaveholders generally cooperated with the drafts in the interest of the greater good, but virtually from the start impressment also provided a source of friction that embroiled owners, military officials, and civil authorities in heated conversations, if not even more heated legal disputes.

The owners often took issue with the officials over the care and treatment of their human property, particularly when the laborers became ill or injured, or they died or ran away. Interruptions to crucial agricultural operations, particularly planting and harvesting, also sparked protests. Masters appealed for relief but not always successfully. Over time, political authorities at both the state and national levels attempted to establish quotas for individual counties and to distribute the calls for laborers as equitably as possible, a practice that relieved some of the most objectionable features of the impressment system but without removing all its ills. Confederate war secretary James A. Seddon succinctly summarized the dilemma as early as January 1863. Impressment of laborers in counties close to Union lines "tends to induce their running away to the Enemy." But compensatory drafts on the "less exposed counties" that had already been tapped repeatedly risked "seriously interfering with productive operations."[34]

Such mobilizations had antebellum precedents, for instance, to maintain roads and levees. In those cases local officials issued the calls for laborers and supervised the work, and only in extreme cases did the laborers leave their home county. Calls for enslaved laborers during the war differed in several respects. First, the calls came from military authorities who neither minced words not brooked opposition. Second, requisitions often involved crossing state lines, with laborers at times traveling hundreds of miles from their homes by rail or steamboat. During the war's first weeks, for instance, the commander of Confederate forces at Norfolk, Virginia, relied on some 300 men from Tennessee to fortify the works protecting the city.[35] The rumor of their imminent departure for North Carolina to work on fortifications there prompted Frank Baker, Shepard Mallory, and James Townsend to seek the protection of General Benjamin F. Butler at Fort Monroe, which set in motion the well-known scenario that resulted in his declaring them contraband of war.[36]

Just as it had before the war, public work served as a breeding ground of political awareness among the persons mobilized. Enslaved and free men labored side by side, as did the literate with the unlettered. Amid the jokes and the banter and despite the close supervision, men found ways to discuss politics, to survey the prospects of a successful escape, and to weigh the consequences. Periodic rotations from home to worksite and back again ensured that news passed regularly in both directions. In the fall of 1863, for instance, after the men from a South Carolina plantation had been absent for a month on the fortifications in Charleston some thirty miles away, a family member reported that "the boys . . . are anxious to get home again, and are continually asking when they will get off. If you could send down another squad . . . I think it would be worthwhile." The informant added: "The Yanks continue to hammer daily. . . . Our negroes don't like it much, as the shells came too near to please their tastes."[37] Virtually every person who returned from work on the fortifications did so with a deeper understanding of the war than before. Expanded geographical knowledge represented just one piece of the new information available for future reference. Despite the shadow it cast of events yet to come, the movement of enslaved laborers was at first modest. The flurry of activity on the periphery of the Confederacy scarcely touched the heartland, which remained remarkably undisturbed. Yet the appearance of tranquility masked subsurface tensions. Even in places far removed from the Yankees, enslaved Southerners began voicing hopes of freedom, if only in secret religious gatherings or in coded prayers.[38]

Before the end of the 1861 campaign season, federal forces demonstrated how troop movements affected the geography of emancipation. Anticipating a likely assault on Port Royal, South Carolina's military leaders did as their counterparts in other vulnerable areas did: mobilized enslaved laborers from nearby plantations to reinforce the batteries at the mouth of the harbor. Facing the likelihood that the attacking force would occupy the surrounding islands and not just the tiny villages of Beaufort and Hilton Head, planters began to evacuate. They fled to their summer homes, some as near as Charleston but most to the northwest, in Columbia and the rolling hills of the state's upper piedmont, as usual, carrying their household servants, other valued slaves, and their prized possessions with them. Charlotte Forten, a freeborn black woman from Philadelphia who moved south in 1862 to serve as a teacher in the Port Royal experiment, took great delight in hearing from the freed people the accounts of masters who tried to cajole and trick heads of enslaved households into refugeeing. One owner, a freedman named Cupid informed her, "had the audacity to venture back even while the Union Troops were occupying Beaufort." The man proposed an elaborate scheme wherein Cupid would gather his family and all the furniture from the big house and meet at a designated spot. "Jus' as if I was gwine to be sich a goat," Cupid told Forten, "with a look and gesture of ineffable contempt."[39]

Between February and June 1862, Union forces reestablished federal authority in Middle and West Tennessee, southern Louisiana, the Tennessee River valley in northern Alabama, and the Mississippi River valley, except for the stretch that lay between the formidable fortresses at Vicksburg and Port Hudson, above Baton Rouge. The increasing presence of federal forces at fixed points within the Confederacy spread unrest among enslaved populations both near and far. Along the Georgia coast, for instance, planters in Liberty County complained bitterly about the disaffection. An estimated 20,000 "absconding Negroes" had already reached the enemy along the coast by the summer of 1862. Their bold forays back into the interior produced "the insecurity of the property along our borders & the demoralization of the negroes that remain, which increases with the continuance of the evil & may finally result in perfect disorganization and rebellion." Arguing that "the Negroes, constitute a part of the Body politic, *in fact*, and should be made to know their duty," one group of planters recommended "a few executions of leading transgressors among them by hanging or shooting" as the means to "dissipate the ignorance which may be supposed to possess their minds." The local Confederate commander refused to collaborate in a scheme so burdened with legal ramifications.[40]

When a group of five enslaved Floridians attempted to reach a federal fort a year later, they created a similar legal dilemma for rebel officials. The men had left their owner in Pensacola upon learning that he planned to relocate them to Alabama. Captured by Confederate forces, the men were tried and convicted by court-martial. Military authorities claimed jurisdiction because "the said slaves are inteligent beings possessing the faculties of Conveying information which would prove useful to the enemy and detrimental to the Confederate states." The owner expressed surprise to learn that the ringleader was "the most inteligent of the five," whom he had considered "a very trust worthy Servant. Not what is considered an Eye servant."[41] As unrest continued to spread among the enslaved population of the Confederate states, citizens debated with officials whether conventional legal proceedings, military tribunals, or summary execution offered the most effective deterrent to flight.

————————

Historically, war displaces civilian populations both close to and distant from the actual battlefields. The process of relocation, which in the Confederate States during the Civil War quickly came to be known as "refugeeing," could occur after much planning and packing or at the drop of a dime. Perhaps the best-known example of such refugeeing is Wilmer McLean, the retired Virginia militia officer and commodities broker who resided on a farm in Manassas, Virginia, which figured prominently in the first Battle of Bull Run in July 1861. When Union and Confederate forces reprised their engagement the following summer, he moved his family to a place that he calculated the contending armies would never find: the sleepy village of Appomattox Courthouse in the hills west of Richmond. Yet find it they did, and on April 9, 1865, Generals Lee and Grant met in McLean's parlor to sign the terms of surrender.[42] Other refugees moved serially to avoid the fate that befell McLean, who, like most refugees, relocated to a place within his home state in hopes of reversing his steps when Confederate military fortunes improved. Early in the war, numbers of his fellow Virginians took refuge in Fredericksburg, only to abandon the city in late 1862. Persons who opted for the perceived safety of the Shenandoah valley moved time and again to escape the ravages of first one army and then the other.

Even the most conservative estimate of the number of persons, black and white, enslaved and free, who left their homes for an extended period in this way must run into the hundreds of thousands. The size of the household affected how quickly and smoothly such moves could be executed even when children were not involved. The absence of the male household head created complications, particularly when the refugee party included enslaved field workers in addition to house servants. Ideally the refugees headed for a place where relatives or friends were already established, but they often had to resort to other arrangements.[43] Refugeeing divided African American families, and the physical separation of family members could wreak havoc on emotional ties. As all the world's great migrations have demonstrated, distance makes the heart grow fonder, but at the cost of fracturing personal relationships. Some partings simply could not be reversed, either because home was not what the traveler remembered—sometimes it no longer existed at all—or because the absent one became a stranger while away. Homecomings did not follow every separation, and, even when they occurred, they did not always satisfy every party's expectations.

————

Federal offensives during the early spring of 1862 vastly increased the geographical area of the armed conflict and, as a result, sparked new interest in maps. When operating in Confederate territory utterly unknown to them, federal commanders relied on enslaved persons who were familiar with the terrain to serve as their eyes and ears. In Virginia, General George McClellan bemoaned the lack of "accurate and . . . comprehensive topographical information" of the kind that only reliable maps could provide. But in the circumstances, he and his Army of the Potomac had no other choice but to rely on black residents' knowledge of the terrain and its roads.[44] Other benefits also flowed their way. A free black native of Baltimore named William Ringgold, for example, was effectively shanghaied into Confederate service in Virginia when the supply steamer on which he worked was leased to the rebels. After slipping away from the boat, Ringgold won the confidence of Alan Pinkerton, McClellan's master spy, providing valuable intelligence about the location and strength of Confederate troops.[45]

General Ormsby M. Mitchel, whose forces had taken control of the Tennessee River valley in northern Alabama, went even further than McClellan. Insisting that "the negroes are our only friends," Mitchel offered protection to "all who communicate to me valuable information."[46] Men who escaped slavery to the North recognized the potential service they could provide to federal forces operating in places with which they were familiar. Garland H. White, a native Virginian who had been the enslaved servant of Georgia senator Robert Toombs before escaping to Canada in 1859, boasted that his travels with the politician "all thro the south" had made him "well acquainted pretty much with all the Southern locality."[47]

Robert Sutton, who had escaped from the St. Mary's River region along the Florida-Georgia border, was one of untold thousands of enslaved persons who guided federal military expeditions. Sutton enlisted in the black regiment that federal authorities organized at Port Royal, South Carolina, many of whose members were refugees from Georgia and Florida.[48] In another striking example, Abraham Galloway escaped slavery in North Carolina and made his way to Fort Monroe, Virginia, where he impressed General Butler with his ability to slip in and out of Confederate lines. Butler persuaded

Galloway to accompany his expedition to New Orleans in the spring of 1862, and Galloway took part in a scouting mission to Vicksburg with a Wisconsin regiment led by Colonel Halbert E. Paine, an attorney with a strong antipathy to slavery. Captured by the rebels, Galloway regained his freedom only when federal forces captured the city in July 1863, after which he returned to North Carolina and engaged in more of the same work from his home base of New Bern.[49]

Grant's first exploratory steps during the winter of 1862–63 in what eventually became the Vicksburg campaign radically changed the military and political geography of the war and, as a result, when, where, and how the new federal policy of emancipation would manifest itself. To begin with, the mobilization of enslaved laborers reached unprecedented proportions, with perhaps as many as 80,000 on the Union side and at least that many on the Confederate side. The campaign prompted civilians by the thousands to flee from Vicksburg, from the Mississippi River valley, and from any place that ran the risk of attracting federal troops. Kate Stone, the Louisiana diarist whose family resided at Brokenburn Plantation some thirty miles upriver from Vicksburg, well captured the sense of insecurity and uncertainty that gripped the refugees. "The life we are leading now is a miserable, frightened one," she wrote in late March, the day before her family abandoned their home and began a several months' trek, first to Monroe, Louisiana, and then to Tyler, Texas, where they remained for the rest of the war. From the time that Yankees established camp at Milliken's Bend, the family had been "living in constant dread of great danger, not knowing what form it may take, and utterly helpless to protect ourselves." The present was "painful" and the future "dark" with worry over the fate of "our loved ones. We long for news from the outside world, and yet we shudder to think what evil tidings it may bring us," she lamented.[50] Upon reaching Tyler, the school-aged boys of the family soon fell out with their local classmates, who took exception to the "refugee upstarts" who had the temerity to wear "gold watch chains and black broadcloth."[51]

In April, Kate's brother Jimmy set out with a group of soldiers to return to the home plantation and retrieve "the Negroes left there." They heard that the Yankees had taken all "the furniture and movables." Their "most trusted servant" Webster, she learned, "claims the plantation as his own and is renowned as the greatest villain in the country."[52] The party faced a difficult passage owing to low water and abandoned the expedition, but May brought fairer prospects, with reports suggesting that "quite a number of Negroes have been brought out . . . recently, some from within [federal] lines."[53] Late in the month, Stone noted proudly that her brother had removed everyone from the home place except Webster, who had enlisted in the U.S. Army, and "four old

Negroes" who were left there "to protect it as far as possible."[54] The Confederate officer who accompanied Jimmy remarked favorably on the condition of the abandoned laborers at Brokenburn: "he never saw so many good things to eat: a barrel of milk, jars of delicious pinkish cream, roll after roll of creamy yellow butter, a yard alive with poultry, and hams and fresh meat just killed. The garden is stocked with vegetables, the straw-berry bed red with fruit, and then a supply of coffee, tea, flour, and such things bought from the Yankees. He says they would have been foolish Negroes to run off from a place like that." The officer's account confirmed the earlier rumors that "William and his family were occupying Mamma's room, completely furnished as we left it, and all our other possessions had been divided up among the Negroes."[55]

When planters attempted to relocate their cotton-growing operations to safer ground, they necessarily had to move field workers as well as the household staff, and take along animals, wagons, implements, and provisions. For those who had supervised such relocations to fresh cotton lands before the war, the routine must have appeared familiar. But much had also changed. When families in motion lacked the men who were absent in the army, enslaved people had greater opportunity to escape than they would have had the men been present. Kate Stone witnessed the consequences from the vantage point of a participant. On April 21, 1863, the family arrived at Delhi (outside of Monroe) and encountered a scene that "beggars description: such crowds of Negroes of all ages and sizes, wagons, mules, horses, dogs, baggage, and furniture" all thrown together. Throngs of "refugees—men, women, and children" with their belongings were all simultaneously "trying to get on the cars, all fleeing from the Yankees or worse still, the Negroes." Operations associated with the Vicksburg campaign unsettled both the permanent residents and the transient refugees. In southwestern Louisiana, federal troops liberated some 12,000 slaves, dispatching the "Sable refugees" by the "carloads" to New Orleans, where their numbers nearly overwhelmed officials responsible for feeding and sheltering them. Elsewhere in the Mississippi valley, similar forays into Confederate territory disrupted civilian life in places far removed from the river.[56]

The size and strategic significance of Grant's campaign against Vicksburg also put soldiers and sailors in motion from places far and wide. Most of the troops in the Union army's western theater of operations came from the midwestern states: Illinois, Indiana, Iowa, Ohio, Wisconsin, Michigan, and Minnesota. Although some held antislavery beliefs, most considered black people to be inherently inferior, even if they often sympathized with the slaves' plight at the hands of the rogues who had caused the rebellion. The same was true of the Union sailors in the Mississippi Squadron. Although many of them, like the soldiers, also hailed from the Midwest, the navy's chief recruiting grounds were the seaport cities of the northeast Atlantic coast, so the enlisted personnel on the western waters were considerably more diverse geographically than their counterparts in the field armies. When the large-scale recruitment of black soldiers into the U.S. Army began early in May 1863, the white volunteers accepted the idea, although often grudgingly and with lingering doubts about how well black men would fight. They did not object, however, to black men chopping down trees, building roads, and digging trenches and gun emplacements, all of which made critically important contributions to the success of Grant's operations.

At the southern end of the Mississippi River, the Union's combined naval and military operations also placed people in motion. Because of the long-standing commercial ties between New Orleans and the surrounding parishes, the city served as a beacon for freedom seekers who firmly believed that from the moment federal forces entered the city in April 1862 the government of the United States would set them free. They, too, became refugees in search of safety, but they fled toward rather than away from federal forces. They pressed the limits of federal policy during General Butler's tenure as commander of the Department of the Gulf (through mid-December 1862), and they ignored both President Lincoln's exemption of the occupied parishes from the Emancipation Proclamation and the strenuous efforts of Butler's successor, Nathaniel Banks, to have the best of both worlds, slavery and freedom. In this tightrope walk, Banks coaxed loyal planters to compensate their laborers and forsake the practices of slavery while at the same time requiring enslaved people to remain peaceably with their owners while his policies took root and began to grow. When his balance got tipsy because of the competing demands of so many constituents (loyal slaveholders; loyal shopkeepers and workingmen, white and free black; enslaved residents of the city; escaped slaves from the plantations; and the officers and enlisted men of his command), Banks righted himself by humoring the slaveholders, and particularly the large planters. True to the city's prewar history, both military and civil affairs remained tumultuous, not least owing to the relentless demands on the part of enslaved people to be free.[57]

With provost marshal guards and the city police apprehending alleged fugitives left and right and placing them in jail, New Orleans, like St. Louis, Louisville, and Baltimore, retained the prewar look and feel of a major hub of the interstate slave trade. Holding pens contained men, women, and children of all ages, incarcerated for running away, for thinking about running away, or for no reason at all. The enslaved woman Rose Herera's experience was far from unique, even to the extent of her children being removed from the city during one of her several stints behind bars.[58] In the countryside, plantation laborers simply wanted to be recognized and treated as free, but the planters clung to the old ways. As early as the fall of 1862, George H. Hanks, the military Superintendent of Negro Labor, gave shelter to "a 'family' of 205 persons" that had come "30 miles to our camp." After he had succeeded in persuading them to return, two girls arrived from the plantation and reported that "'Old Cottonbeard,' had boasted . . . how he would serve them when they returned" and, to a person, they refused to budge. "Master," one man pleaded with the federal officer, "I will go anywhere else to work, but you may shoot me before I will return to the old plantation." The planters went so far as to "try to recover their own negroes; they have even hired men to steal them from my camp," the superintendent reported.[59]

By 1864, Hanks noticed, "the negroes now begin to comprehend the fact of their freedom, and that they have a right to demand the protection of the Government." To illustrate, he described the case of a black soldier who "*demanded* his children at my hands." "I want to send them to school," the soldier explained, "my wife is not allowed to see them." When Hanks hesitated, the man explained further: "I am in your service; I wear military clothes; I have been in three battles; I was in the assault at Port Hudson; *I want those children*; they are my flesh and blood." Upon summoning the mistress and demanding that she relinquish the children, the superintendent realized that "she had bribed them to lie about their parents; but I delivered them up to the father," he explained.[60] Military service was subtly but effectively undermining the foundation of quasi slavery. In the summer of 1864, a sergeant in a black cavalry regiment visited his wife on a plantation in Lafourche Parish west of New Orleans where he proceeded to get into an altercation with the overseer. The following day all the hands did "pretty much as they pleased," according to a Treasury Department inspector who investigated.[61]

The fascinating case of Norfleet Perry illustrates how the mobilization of Confederate forces to defend Vicksburg extended hundreds of miles in every direction, straining the relationship between slaveholders and slaves, even, in some cases, between the Confederate officers and the trustworthy personal servants who had accompanied them from home to the warfront. In the spring of 1862, Norfleet Perry left Harrison County, Texas, with his owner's son, Lieutenant Theophilus Perry, to serve as a cook and body servant. The officer and the man were both recently married, and their wives, Harriet and Fannie, hoped that the two would look after each other. In one letter home, Theophilus confessed that "Norflet is of inestimable solace to me, and I do not know how I could get on without him."[62] Theophilus's family forwarded clothing, shoes, and other amenities for Norfleet on Fannie's behalf, and Harriet also wrote letters to him for her. In one dated late December 1862, Fannie expressed her undying love and wished Norfleet well. The Christmas holiday promised to bring little joy without him, she explained, but she happily conveyed a collective "Howdy" and well-wishes from "Mother, Father, Grandmama, Brothers & Sisters." Wishing that "it will not be long before you can come home," Fannie also hoped "if I never see you again . . . to meet you in Heaven."[63] Another year would pass before she saw him again—a time of anxious waiting for her but one of high adventure for him.

Early in 1863, as word of the Emancipation Proclamation spread among the servants, cooks, and teamsters who worked with the Confederate regiments in the field, Theophilus and Harriet suspected that Norfleet would "be running off with the Yankees."[64] In February 1863, as the Vicksburg campaign gained momentum, the disappearance of the colonel's cook resulted in Norfleet's reassignment to regimental headquarters. There he entered the orbit of the colonel's wife, whom Norfleet soon characterized as "too particular & hard to please" for his taste.[65] In effect, by placing Norfleet's services at the disposal of his commander, Theophilus broke the bond of trust that joined the two men in the field as well as their families at home. Feeling no sense of loyalty to the colonel and the overbearing wife who had encroached into his familiar relationship with Theophilus, Norfleet struck out for freedom with two enslaved teamsters as the regiment moved eastward toward Vicksburg. Although Theophilus hoped that Norfleet would try "to get back home," he suspected that the true destination was "the Federals."[66]

Toward the end of the year, Theophilus's father, Levin Perry, learned that Norfleet was at work at a Confederate quartermaster's depot in Bonham, Texas, 150 miles northwest of Marshall and 300 miles west of the place in Arkansas where Norfleet had last been seen. The elder Perry set out for Bonham and completed the return trip home with Norfleet in tow just before Christmas. Then the tale of Norfleet's Year of Jubilee began to unfold. Norfleet reported that he had not run away at all. Instead, while on an errand to purchase eggs, he fell into the hands of Unionist guerrillas from Kansas. These "jayhawkers" transferred him to the custody of federal forces at Helena, Arkansas, just before the battle there early in July, after which the Yankees promised him that "he would be in the next fight." Taking to his heels instead, he set his sights on Marshall, falling in with a man from Arkansas who "promised to bring him home." After realizing that the man "was carrying him in an opposite direction," Norfleet changed course again, alighting at last in Bonham. Harriet Perry "knew he would have a good tale made up," and she doubted his professions that he was "very glad to get home for no one ever tried harder than he did."[67] As a reward for his truancy, the elder Perry refused to send Norfleet back to rejoin his son in the field. Home detention proved to be a source of frustration for Norfleet but one of relief for Fanny. Like Levin Perry, she could now keep an eye on her man.[68]

Norfleet Perry's journey took him through three states and across perhaps as many as 1,000 miles, from the Confederate army, to the jayhawkers, to the Union army, then back to the Confederate quartermaster's department. His Civil War was nothing if not full of adventure, although it ended where it started, at home with his wife, Fannie. Theophilus did not fare so well. He died in the battle of Pleasant Hill, Louisiana, early in April 1864. In one of his last letters home, he still hoped that Norfleet would divulge information regarding the whereabouts of the two escaped teamsters.[69]

———

After the fall of Vicksburg, federal recruiters began a systematic sweep of plantations on both sides of the river gathering up men for army service. In responding to the drift toward social chaos, Confederate officials at times appeared to worsen rather than alleviate the troubles. General E. Kirby Smith, who commanded Confederate forces west of the Mississippi, advised General Sterling Price, who led the Confederate Army of the West, to have the planters remove all "able bodied slaves and transportation" from harm's way. A recent raid in Monroe, he explained, netted the Yankees "more than 1000 recruits, in some cases organized on the plantations and forced into the ranks." "Every sound male black left for the enemy becomes a soldier whom we have afterwards to fight," Smith concluded.[70] One viable countermeasure was to impress enslaved laborers for service as needed. "The temper of the people is now favorable for such a step," he reasoned. "There is a feeling of distrust in the loyalty of their slaves, and an anxiety to have the able boded males in the service of the Government."[71]

Planters who obeyed the evacuation orders were in for a surprise. When refugees from Louisiana crossed into Texas, they met the welcoming arms of General John Bankhead Magruder, the grand master impressment officer who had perfected the subtleties of his craft on Virginia's Peninsula during the first year of the war. In his latter-day capacity in command of the District of Texas, New Mexico, and Arkansas, Magruder viewed the mass of fleeing humanity as the answer to his prayers, and he began impressing one-fourth of the enslaved men coming out of Louisiana. The planters "complained bitterly" to General Smith about Magruder's heavy-handedness; some performed an about-face and headed home while others ignored the relocation orders, "preferring to risk the chances with the Enemy" instead. In his defense, Magruder employed the language of home to cast the planters not as refugees from the Yankees but as fugitives from their civic responsibilities.

Smith resolved the matter by forbidding Magruder to impress the slaves of migrants but also by warning the refugees that they must not "violate the spirit" of Magruder's plan "by continual moving under pretense of not being able to find a home."[72]

To resolve the Faustian dilemma that they had created for themselves by resorting to war to secure the future of slave property, refugeeing slaveholders abandoned their landed property instead. They became vagabonds, at times having to live among strangers—often social inferiors who ridiculed them and their children nonetheless—and having to move from place to place in search of an ever-fleeing sense of security. They hired their human property piecemeal to the highest bidder. They stood powerless to prevent the escape of all but their most trusted slaves. Yet on the other horn of the dilemma, those who chose not to flee before the Yankee onslaught fared little better. Those who remained on the land could retain control over it only by professing loyalty to the Union and then cooperating with federal officials who were trying to keep the land productive. The price, of course, was acknowledging the end of slavery—at least outwardly—and agreeing to pay wages or to share the proceeds of the crop in exchange for the laborers' work. Confederate forces took great delight in breaking up such operations, returning the prospective free laborers back to slavery and figuratively salting the earth rather than letting it be used to sprout freedom.[73] James McKaye, one of the three commissioners of the AFIC, found this face-to-face encounter between the past and the future—a feature of the Mississippi valley unmatched in any other theater of war—awe inspiring.[74]

In the autumn of 1864, the issue of impressment exploded once again along the Red River valley of southwestern Arkansas, when planters contemplated moving to Texas, not for fear of the Yankees but to avoid "the depredations of our own troops" on their grain crops and the fear that the government would take what the soldiers did not. General Smith urged them not to leave lest "that great granary . . . goes to waste from the absence of labor." Then he would have no choice but to withdraw Confederate forces, in which case not even Mexico could furnish "that security which you sacrifice on abandoning your homes."[75] If they succeeded in reaching the far-off-the-beaten-path places of their dreams, they could reconstitute plantation life as if the war had never begun, with enslaved people working at their appointed tasks far removed from the threat of Yankee invaders and, in some cases, even from the fear of such threats. (How they would market staple crops or even surplus grains remained to be seen.) Some such escapees succeeded in delaying emancipation—stopping time by stepping outside the course of history, at least for the moment. The involuntary black victims of such refugeeing paid multiple times over for the obstinacy of their owners, in the worst of cases, not witnessing the end of slavery until well after General E. Kirby Smith surrendered in June 1865.[76]

_____

The repercussion of military operations affected the freedom struggle long after the end of hostilities. In contested areas where the shifting Union and Confederate lines were separated by a no-man's-land, women as well as men frequently crossed back and forth, with the pickets of both belligerents often indifferent to the movement. After all, soldiers on either side did not hesitate to impress laborers when they needed the help. But otherwise, the refugees constituted a burden. For countless thousands of enslaved people, the war presented recurring cycles of motion. In the spring of 1865, whether they lived under the nominal jurisdiction of Confederate or Union authorities or somewhere in between was as much a matter of luck and timing as anything else.

The slaveholders' fears of wholesale Confederate impressment of their enslaved laborers, in the end, proved groundless. Yet over time government agencies at the national and state levels, as well as private suppliers of goods and services, began relying more and more heavily on hired slaves. By 1864, because of the impressment into military service of skilled white men who had earlier been exempted, both private and public employers began hiring skilled slaves, increasingly from distances of a day's journey or more away. Salt production illustrated the countervailing forces that such innovations mothered by necessity set loose. Salt, like other precious commodities in the Confederate war economy, became increasingly scarce—and as a result, increasingly valuable—over time. Besides the major salt-making facility at Saltville in southwestern Virginia, which federal forces destroyed in December 1864, the Confederacy also relied on works along the Atlantic and Gulf coasts. Alabama's Salt Commission oversaw several large operations along the Tombigbee River above Mobile, employing nearly 5,000 enslaved men and women hired by the year.[77] Among these were Louis and Matilda Hughes, whose master had hired them along with nearly one hundred other slaves from the plantation where they lived in Panola County, Mississippi, some 300 miles away.[78] In Florida, the operations were much smaller, with private contractors supplementing the works conducted under government auspices and all of them employing slaves hired seasonally from the plantation regions of western Florida and Southwest Georgia. It was not so much the changing amounts of seasonal daylight that affected these operations—salt makers kept their fires burning around the clock—as the length of any given season that was free from attack by U.S. vessels and their landing parties. Because of the effectiveness of naval raids against these boiling houses, enslaved men had the opportunity to escape to the U.S. Navy, yet most did not lest they risk being separated indefinitely from their families in the interior. They returned home, often to move back to the coast when the rebuilt works were back in operation.[79]

Enslaved laborers hired to such establishments worked to improve their chances.[80] At the Mobile works, Louis Hughes garnered the good graces of the superintendent (a Northerner by birth), and the two men struck up a partnership operating a tobacco concession. The Yankee purchased the tobacco, Hughes sold it to the workers, and the two men split the proceeds. "I put some agents out to sell for me," Hughes recalled, "Uncle Hudson, who took care of the horses and mules at the works; John at the hospital; William, head chopper, among the 100 men in the woods." Although the hired salt makers were subject to periodic impressment to labor on the fortifications at Mobile, the threat of a Union raid early in 1865 broke up the operation and the tobacco concession with it. The superintendent "received word that the Yankees were coming, and to send all the hands to their masters." Hughes resented having his business disrupted that way, although he appreciated having earned some money, which he anticipated putting to good use "if I gained my freedom, which I now knew was quite probable, as the Union forces were gaining ground everywhere." Although the laborers felt little sense of a personal obligation to their owners, ties to family members and neighbors often ensured that the leased laborers would return home. In that spirit, Louis and Matilda Hughes began the trek back to Panola County.[81]

––––––––

The map of the successive waves of the Union's territorial conquests during the war barely hints at the important link between military operations and emancipation in the Border States of Missouri, Kentucky, and Maryland and in the western territories. To be sure, both Missouri and Kentucky experienced a significant Confederate presence during 1861 and 1862 as did Maryland in 1862 and then again in 1863, but the most significant military operations affecting slavery in the Border States involved recruiting parties rather than pitched battles. Beginning in the summer of 1863, officials took halting steps to enlist enslaved men in the U.S. Colored Troops. Then, in October, owing to "the exigencies of the war," the War Department pulled out all the stops in Maryland, Missouri, and Tennessee, affirming that "all persons enlisted into the military service shall forever thereafter be free." Military service opened a channel to freedom and undercut the once impregnable power of slaveholders. But ironically, the removal of "the healthy, strong & able free blacks" who performed most of the labor in the rural fields and the urban workshops of Maryland, according to the antislavery judge Hugh L. Bond, placed great pressure on employers "to hire Slave labor" thereby reinforcing "the institution which no loyal man desires should be permanent" and which most hoped "the war would destroy."[82]

Although Kentucky slaveholders successfully opposed recruitment for nearly another year, they too could not escape the exigencies of war. They grew sullen over what they perceived as betrayal by the government, and they took out their frustration on the enslaved people. African American men and women in the Border States saw their hopes for freedom appear to take a step backward. What is more, they had to reconcile themselves to the surreal world in which the very same government that had declared freedom in the Confederate states and in the District of Columbia could content itself with leaving slavery undisturbed in Maryland, Missouri, and Kentucky, despite the pronounced Confederate sympathies of the slaveholders in those states.[83]

The mobilization proved effective: nearly 24,000 men enlisted from Kentucky alone and more than 8,000 each from Maryland and Missouri. These men contributed valuable reinforcements to military operations over the last eighteen months of the war, particularly in the campaigns against Petersburg and Richmond. For many of the men from Kentucky, military service looked backward in time as well as forward into the future. Their participation in the Virginia campaign brought them to places with ancestral ties. Then, after Lee's surrender, the all-black Twenty-Fifth Army Corps, composed largely of the recently organized U.S. Colored Troops units, departed for the Rio Grande border with Mexico and scattered outposts in the southwest territories, where they constituted the first wave of the nation's newest military initiative: suppressing Indian resistance to U.S. authority on the Great Plains.[84]

As the foundation of slavery in the Loyal Border States began to crumble, individuals and families took advantage of opportunities to cross into a free state. Henry Clay Bruce, for instance, left Missouri for Kansas early in 1864. He endured the regimen of life and work on tobacco plantations and in tobacco factories; he had even accepted the master's offer of monthly cash wages, board, and clothing, Bruce later recalled, "if I would remain with him on the farm." He had resisted all attempts to be dragooned into the federal army, avoiding the "Colored men [who] scoured the county in search of young men for soldiers, [and] causing me to sleep out of nights and hide from them in the daytime." By March 1864, when the lure of freedom became irresistible, he and his fiancée "decided to elope" to Kansas, crossing half the state of Missouri and then the Missouri River to safety just ahead of a pursuing posse. "Having traveled over that country so often," he later explained, "I had acquired an almost perfect knowledge of it, even of the by-paths. We avoided the main road, and made the entire trip without touching the traveled road at any point and without meeting any one." He knew that his fiancée's owner would pursue them, "but I had carefully weighed the cost before starting, had nerved myself for action," determined to fight to the death to protect "the girl I loved" who "had placed herself entirely under my care and protection."[85]

The cracks in the slave system in the Border States prompted slaveholders to take preemptive action so that their human property did not slip away. Owners in Maryland and Kentucky found ways to spirit enslaved people into Confederate territory, and their counterparts in Missouri could also opt for destinations in the west and southwest. Perhaps most ironically, as antislavery forces in Missouri slowly inched their state toward adoption of a constitutional ban on slavery, disgruntled slaveholders defied military orders and removed enslaved people to Kentucky to salvage some shred of their investment in human property. In the spring of 1863, the owner of the black teenager Mattie J. Jackson, her younger brother and sister, and their mother began to doubt his ability to keep them from fleeing his home in St. Louis. Mattie and her mother had tried on several occasions to escape, and the owner particularly resented her mother for "reading the papers and understanding political affairs." He eventually found a buyer for the "fine looking family" in the person of a steamboat captain who was confident he could remove them to Kentucky, where enslaved people still fetched "as much, or more than ever." The captain assured Mattie's mother that he would not sell her children if she promised not to run away, but he broke the bargain, spiriting the family to Louisville, where they sat for weeks in a slave pen before being sold to three separate owners.[86]

A year later, men from a regiment of Minnesota volunteers intervened to prevent a similar attempt at removing enslaved Missourians to Kentucky for sale. The soldiers stopped the train on which the victims were riding, "hurrahing for Jim Lane," the renowned champion of free-state Kansas and the first U.S. senator to represent the state in Congress.[87] The troops helped the enslaved people escape but then found themselves ensnared in the complex Unionist politics of Missouri. State military authorities arrested them and charged them with violating the articles of war. Their comrades sent accounts of the case to newspapers back home, prompting one supportive editor to insist that "every Christian man and woman at the North" would endorse their liberation, "whatever legal authorities and conservative shoulder-straps may think of it." Outraged Minnesota state legislators petitioned for clemency, and the case even came to the attention of the U.S. Senate. The men spent several months under house arrest before they were released and returned to duty with the consent of the secretary of war.[88] Emancipation on this middle ground had ramifications that radiated in every direction of the compass.

Enslaved persons who lived in the Border States had no illusions about how their lives differed from those of free persons, black or white. Although the war presented certain opportunities to resolve the contradiction by obliterating the distinction, that outcome was far from certain. And even to those who saw freedom as the only acceptable outcome, the challenge of translating hope into reality remained. Becoming free, in short, was neither simple nor straightforward. It often required a willingness to live in the overlapping space between blue and gray, without conceding acceptance of the old order and not overreaching for what presented itself as the new. Gaining freedom often required patience and flexibility, as well as the willingness to move quickly and resolutely when opportunity knocked. Throughout the war and beyond, the unsettling promises of freedom could not entirely displace the entrenched habits of slavery in the Border States, and the ground continued to shift under the feet of freedom seekers, but under the feet of their erstwhile masters too.

The service of nearly 180,000 black men in the U.S. Army dramatically affected the geography of emancipation. They came from every Union state and territory as well as every state of the Confederacy. Nearly 20,000 more served in the U.S. Navy. Despite early claims that these men would serve primarily as garrison forces, most units took part in active operations that often carried them far from the places where they enlisted and brought them face-to-face with the rebel enemy. After all, the war required the wholesale movement of men, animals, weapons, and supplies across vast expanses of territory. Freeborn men from Northern states found themselves stationed in places that stretched from Virginia through the Carolinas, Georgia, and Florida to Louisiana and Texas. Like the missionaries and teachers who came before them to these areas in 1862, black soldiers from the North often harbored stereotypical images that did not quite match what they encountered on the ground. The same was true for formerly enslaved men's encounters with Northern officers and soldiers, white and black. Operations along the South Atlantic coast, for instance, mixed black units from Massachusetts with those from South Carolina under the command of Colonel James Montgomery, a veteran of the Kansas-Missouri border wars. The vastly different worlds of their antebellum experiences came together, often changing the course of lives.

At the end of the war, memories of wartime service drew men from their original homes to the places where they had served. A number of men from the Ninety-Ninth U.S. Colored Infantry, for instance, left their native Louisiana and returned to Florida, where they had been stationed late in the war and where they had left sweethearts behind or desired to take advantage of land that opened for settlement under the Homestead Act of 1866. Men from the Fifty-Fourth and Fifty-Fifth Massachusetts Volunteers returned to South

Carolina, and men from the Twentieth U.S. Colored Infantry (recruited in New York) and the Fourteenth Rhode Island Heavy Artillery worked their way back to New Orleans.[89]

The considerable number of black men who served in the U.S. Navy—at their peak, constituting one-quarter of the entire enlisted force—meant that the geography of emancipation reached far beyond the land on which the warring armies joined battle. When Secretary of the Navy Gideon Welles authorized the wholesale enlistment of "contrabands" into naval service in September 1861, he relieved the looming manpower shortage in the rapidly growing fleet with a stroke of the pen. Welles responded to repeated inquiries from the commanders of naval vessels regarding "the large and increasing number of persons of color, commonly known as contraband, now subsisted at the navy yards and on board ships of war." He directed that "when their services can be made useful" officers should "enlist them for the naval service, under the same forms and regulations as apply to other enlistments," provided, however, that they be shipped at "no higher rating than boys, at a compensation of $10 per month and one ration a day." "They can neither be expelled from the service to which they have resorted, nor can they be maintained unemployed," Welles reasoned, "and it is not proper that they should be compelled to render necessary and regular services without a stated compensation." Besides the thousands shipped for naval service to perform the necessary and often disagreeable labor at supply bases, repair shops, and hospitals that dotted the Atlantic and Gulf coasts from Norfolk to New Orleans and extended up the Mississippi River to Cairo, the navy also employed additional thousands of black civilians—men and women alike—at those facilities.[90] In short, Secretary Welles's directive opened an avenue to freedom for tens of thousands of enslaved people.

Naval service did much more than just free persons from bondage. It carried them to places they may have heard about but scarcely dreamed of seeing. Many of the 900 Maryland men who were transferred from incomplete regiments of colored troops into the navy were assigned to the Pacific Squadron, where they patrolled the West Coast and pursued Confederate commerce raiders across thousands of square miles of open ocean. William B. Gould, who with seven other freedom seekers from Wilmington, North Carolina, sailed down the Cape Fear River in September 1862 to the federal blockading squadron offshore, promptly enlisted in the navy. Gould's subsequent duty assignments eventually carried him all along the east coast of North America and across the Atlantic to the major port cities of Europe from Ireland to Spain. In Antwerp during July 1864, for instance, he played the part of the tourist having "a fine time generaly," among other things visiting "the top of the Tower of the Cathedral by ascending six hundred and sixteen steps" and finding "every boddy very kind." The freeborn Virginian Charles B. Fisher, who like Gould served as an officer's steward on board a vessel in the European Squadron, went ashore daily while in port to purchase fresh provisions and frequently indulged in the local attractions.[91] Yet European cities presented temptation as well as amusement. "The Rebs are offering A Bounty of $300 in Gold for Men to Man thair ships in France," Gould noted. "Our men are deserting verry fast we suppose to join them."[92]

Following the occupation of Port Royal, South Carolina, in November 1861, and the establishment of the supply depot there in support of the South Atlantic Squadron, local men who enlisted in the navy or who served as contract pilots participated in actions that freed thousands of enslaved people, reversing the historical connection between water and slavery and bending the arc toward freedom instead. Yet, naval service, whether on the open seas or the inland waterways, had other perils, Charles B. Fisher explained. Sailors routinely died of shipboard accidents and disease; and, although comparatively rare, naval combat was deadly. Few sailors of any color or nationality failed to note the solemnity of the burial of a deceased shipmate at sea and to ponder over such a fate for themselves. Although all understood its necessity, few but the crustiest old salts could abandon the hope of finding their final resting place at home rather than in Davy Jones's Locker. In an especially haunting meditation on death, Fisher brooded over burial on shore in a foreign land, far removed from family members, friends, and neighbors. "And O what glory," he mused, "is it to fall upon the field of strife Far, far from your native land, with no friendly caress to soothe your suffering, and no companion near to receive your last dying feeble request; but there in a foreign land to perish unpitied, and the thorns of neglect will soon spring up and the stranger will tread upon your grave without one feeling of pity or sympathy."[93]

Becoming free required an awareness of space both as a physical reality and as a geopolitical concept. When enslaved people escaped from their owners, they sought a safe place to begin pursuing lives in freedom. That space might have been as near as the closest city, where they could disappear into the bustle with relative anonymity and with proper connections and a measure of smooth talking and good luck find shelter and employment. It might have been the nearest Union outpost—or even Confederate outpost if conditions were right—where soldiers eager for help with camp chores provided the necessary cover with little concern for the formality of free papers. For those with special determination to escape slavery altogether, the Northern states and western territories offered prospects for starting anew.[94] Others had to retrace steps across hundreds of miles, from Texas through Louisiana to

Mississippi, on an uncertain quest to find whether their former homes still existed and whether their people were anywhere to be found. The destruction of slavery occurred across a vast and varied geography, and one that, owing to the disruptive nature of the war, continued to shift right through the summer of 1865. And the geography of emancipation consisted of small spaces as well as grand ones.

Chapter 5
Confines

Like all great transformations, the contest over the future of slavery played out on small stages as well as large. These included private places, such as the kitchens and dining rooms of plantation big houses, as well as public spaces, such as the legislative chambers of the U.S. Capitol. Over the course of the war, such microenvironments hosted innumerable clashes between the partisans of the old order and the champions of the new. The victories won in these arenas could influence larger events far greater than their confined physical space might have seemed to allow, as the tale of the Confederate supply steamer *Planter* demonstrates. In the spring of 1862, Robert Small (later Smalls) and his black crewmates commandeered the vessel while the officers were absent on shore. After taking their families on board, they powered up, cast off from the dock, gave the proper signals to pass the rebel forts at the mouth of Charleston Harbor, and steamed to the Union blockading squadron lying off the coast and its incredulous officers and men. In the blink of an eye, Smalls and his mates transformed a small steamboat into a propaganda coup of international proportions. Yet it was in the even smaller, more confined spaces within the vessel that the real story began: belowdecks where the men had learned to get up steam and in the pilot house where Smalls had learned to navigate and give proper signals. From their experience in such confined spaces, the plotters knew when the tide was right, not only in the harbor but also, as Frederick Douglass had noted paraphrasing Shakespeare's Brutus, in the affairs of men.[1]

Wartime military operations had the power to transform confinement into liberation, both literally and figuratively. Earthen or masonry forts, army camps, and warships, each somewhat differently, created circumstances where enslaved men could negotiate passages to freedom. In most of these settings, smaller spaces within presented additional opportunities and constraints, as the black men impressed to work at Fort Fisher, North Carolina, just prior to the second Union attack in January 1865 learned. When shells from Union warships began falling, white Confederates took cover in bombproof shelters inside the fort but refused entry to the black laborers. Chaplain Henry M. Turner spoke afterward with these men, whose survival had depended on "the mere privilege of dodging behind the sides of the fort" instead of huddling with the rebel troops in the shelters, which the torrent of federal ordnance blew to smithereens.[2]

Federal (and for that matter, Confederate) warships represented another variety of such confined space. Contrabands were taken on board vessels to serve as cooks and stewards, preparing the meals and waiting on the tables of naval officers. They worked nearly around the clock attempting to please men who were impossible to please, and they often slept in corners of the galleys or ward rooms. The servant of Acting Paymaster William Frederick Keeler, for instance, tried mightily to satisfy the officer's high expectations regarding the shine of his shoes and the temperature of his coffee. Keeler, like many of his fellows, had a temper. When the man did not tidy the quarters properly, Keeler reported to his wife, he "blowed him up."[3] Settings like this—bounded by the walls of a fort or the hull of a ship—magnified the intensity of encounters over the boundaries between slavery and freedom and held the potential for far-reaching significance, as the experiences of Rosa Parks and the Freedom Riders demonstrated in the mid-twentieth century.[4]

––––––––––

The struggle for freedom during the war began where the antebellum struggle had left off—that is, within the context of each individual slaveholding, every one of which was a small space, regardless of its physical size. At one extreme, the holding might consist of a master and a handful of enslaved persons who lived and slept in a small cabin, ate from the same pot (figuratively if not literally), and labored together in the work of the farm. At the other extreme stood holdings of thousands of acres with hundreds of laborers and very little, if any, contact between individual enslaved people and the proprietor. Notwithstanding the fact that owners and overseers employed violence as the ultimate motivator of hard work, they also studied the physical and mental attributes of their human property, as well as their character. Doing so required getting to know each other as persons, which occurred routinely, often across generations on slaveholdings large and small. On a farm that straddled the border of the District of Columbia and Maryland, for example, three generations of the African American Thomas and Wedge families, some of whom were enslaved and others of whom were freeborn, lived and worked for years with the white family consisting of Alexander McCormick and his wife. They knew each other well.[5]

Within the space of the slaveholding, two places stand out as key arenas in the struggle for freedom. The first was the owner's home and particularly the areas where food was prepared and consumed, common sites wherein rituals of dominance and subservience have played out in hierarchical societies for millennia. Women played a disproportionately large part in the freedom struggle in these settings. Enclosed spaces devoted to satisfying such primal needs as nourishment took on increased significance over the course of the war. Kitchens and dining areas were places where the servants could gather news. "There was not a word passed that escaped our listening ears," recalled Mattie J. Jackson, the enslaved St. Louis teenager. "My mother and myself could read enough to make out the news in the papers," a skill that infuriated their master, who frequently struck them, not uncommonly drawing blood.[6] Mistresses of households often expressed surprise as well as frustration over the growing incidence of insubordination. From the perspective of the Louisiana plantation where Kate Stone resided, "the excitement in the air" accounted for the changed demeanor of the slaves.[7] The prospect of freedom excited the air.

The cruelty of his owner's wife, Louis Hughes explained, was "the main thing that made me want to be free." Close behind that was his inability to protect his own wife, Matilda, from that cruelty. One such beating left him "trembling from head to foot," he later recalled, "for I was powerless to do anything for her."[8] The beating also prompted Matilda to run away. Matilda and her mistress distrusted each other from the start. As Hughes explained, Matilda made clear that she would not submit "without resistance or protest of some kind" to the whippings that the woman administered freely to other servants. The mistress's frustration quickly blossomed into full-blown hatred. After Matilda gave birth to twins in 1859, overwork sapped her energy, and the children's health deteriorated. Faced with the prospects of a whipping, Matilda fled with the infants to Memphis. But instead of finding freedom, she was returned to her owner, who upon their return to Mississippi administered the beating that the new mother had tried to avoid. The babies died within six months of that incident. The mistress then accused Matilda of having gone "all around the neighborhood" telling "the people that I killed your babies, and almost whipped you to death." Matilda refused to relinquish her dignity despite the heavy price that her determination exacted. Although the gossip mill could not restore her lost children, it could deny ultimate victory to the mistress of the household.[9] Such struggles between the owners' quest for supremacy and the enslaved people's quest for autonomy occurred in virtually every slaveholding household during the war, even those far removed from active war zones.

Contested space spilled outside the slaveholders' dwellings, into fields and workshops, the second notable arena where enslavers and freedom seekers vied for the upper hand. When overseers entered military service, the men and boys too old or too young for military service aimed to supervise the field labor force. Absent men, women took up the work. In many places and times, the new supervisory force came close to maintaining the antebellum routines, but often with subtle and not-so-subtle changes, such as a slacking off of the inhuman prewar pace and diminishing the use of whips. The unprecedented effects of war, such as the shift from cotton to corn in the face of curtailed cotton markets and the pervasive risk of flight among the young men when federal forces approached, provided the backdrop for these struggles.[10]

Over the course of the war, slaveholders began to abdicate their responsibility for feeding and sheltering the people they claimed as property. This in turn created a peculiar refugee problem for Confederate authorities, one that they were ill equipped to resolve either ideologically or logistically and even more reluctant to admit. The institution of domestic slavery stood firmly on the assumption that masters had responsibility for feeding, clothing, and sheltering their enslaved laborers and providing medical care as well. But as Confederate authorities imposed taxes in kind, and as the forces of both belligerents appropriated livestock and provisions, local food shortages arose. In such circumstances, owners turned out their enslaved laborers with instructions to go to the Yankees or shift for themselves. Vainly hoping to suppress the growing incidence of masterless men and women, civic leaders resorted to the traditional mechanisms of incarceration, public notices of persons apprehended, and sheriffs' sales of persons whose owners failed to reclaim them. This approach proved inadequate.

Abandoned slaves included disproportionate numbers of dependent persons who were too old or too young to work and otherwise required special care. Contagious diseases, including smallpox, measles, and mumps, and gastrointestinal illnesses of every kind took a fearsome toll on such people with little prior exposure whom the circumstances of war had thrown together. Both Union and Confederate officials who undertook to manage these challenges employed the advanced theories and practices of the time—namely, those derived from the prior experience of the U.S. Army and, especially, of the U.S. Navy's system of marine hospitals, the precursor to the public health service. But the rebels put the knowledge into practice more reluctantly and tardily than their federal counterparts did.[11]

In one sense, the employment of black men and women in support of the war effort aimed to reduce the risk of flight that both owners and civil and military authorities equally dreaded. Whether they were employed by the year or impressed into service for particular projects or in specific emergencies, enslaved military laborers often lived and worked under closer observation and tighter control than they experienced at home. Over time, this employment expanded beyond digging fortifications to producing weapons, cotton and woolen textiles (and the finished goods produced therefrom), and leather products of every kind, along with wagons and caissons for the forces in the field. By 1864 government-sponsored industrial establishments—some operated directly by the staff departments of the Confederate army and others by government contractors—employed thousands of hired slaves in both skilled and unskilled capacities. These included the huge Confederate salt-works above Mobile, ammunition laboratories, clothing factories, laundries, and bakeries in cities along the fall line from Richmond, Virginia, to Montgomery, Alabama, that each employed scores to hundreds of enslaved people.

The Confederate Ordnance Department under General Josiah Gorgas became increasingly dependent on black laborers over the course of the war. The Confederacy's need for soldiers called into question the exemptions for skilled white laborers that had been permitted in the Conscription Act of 1862. Gorgas's 1864 annual report made clear that the several departments under his jurisdiction faced a challenge in meeting their production quotas owing to the growing scarcity of skilled operatives. With conscription officers drafting men directly out of the factories and workshops, production managers had no other recourse than to hire slaves. Gorgas estimated that his department directly employed 830 "negroes" during 1864, and 1,000 were employed by contractors. For 1865, he estimated the need to add 415 black men, for a total of 2,245, of whom at least 200 were to be skilled. Estimating that 3,691 white mechanics would remain in his employment as civilians, he figured that the department could meet its production target of 55,000 rifles and carbines plus the requisite amounts of gunpowder. The Confederacy would enter the final springtime of hope with nearly 40 percent of its ordnance workforce consisting of black men.[12]

The facilities in which much of this work was undertaken became grounds where hired slaves could bargain with their employers for privileges, often playing the employer against the owner to the maximum advantage possible. Persons employed by the Confederate ordnance works in Macon, Georgia, for instance, continually negotiated between their owners and their employers for privileges to control their own lives. One resulting accommodation involved the employer setting piecework quotas, which enabled laborers to earn time off, including long weekends to visit their families at home. In one instance, a hired couple arranged for their children to join them at the facility at no charge for lodging provided they shared their board.[13] Yet the new circumstances brought mixed rather than unequivocal blessings. Relocation to an urban industrial facility brought the lessees into a new environment with prospects for meeting people and experiencing life unlike anything they might have encountered on the farm or the plantation. But rather than serving as a potential springboard to freedom, such settings might serve as a deterrent, with leased laborers' attention focused on home rather than on the Yankees. Ironically, many masters hired out their laborers to reduce the likelihood that idle hands would plot escape, even while harboring grave fears that enslaved people in motion to and from the place of hire might face the irresistible temptation to flee. At times Confederate authorities themselves created the circumstances that encouraged flight to the Yankees. In late summer 1864, officials in Georgia scoured the government's workshops in various parts of the state for laborers to work on Atlanta's fortifications in advance of the Union's assault.[14] In short, even when labor in Confederate service did not clear a pathway to freedom, it frequently enabled hired men and women to establish some physical and psychological distance from their owners.

War gave rise to new varieties of small spaces that occupied a central place in the freedom struggle, one major variety of which was the so-called contraband camps that federal military authorities established in the occupied areas of the Confederacy with large populations of slaves. Camp dwellers often occupied a state of limbo between their old lives in slavery and the promise of new lives in freedom. The original impetus behind the camps was the simple recognition on the part of Union officials that self-liberated slaves sought out the Yankees because they felt safer there than anywhere else. Because the refugees associated safety not so much with specific space as with persons who might provide shelter, food, and a measure of protection, the camps at first were mobile—when the protectors moved, so did those seeking protection. From the moment federal forces entered slave territory—first the Border Slave States in April 1861 and the northern fringes of the Confederacy in May—this pattern became clear, as the ranting of such influential spokesmen of loyal slaveholders as Maryland's Charles Calvert demonstrated.[15] In the Border States, politically astute slaveholders prevented such camps from taking shape, but wily refugees found shelter inside army camps or within the relative anonymity they could find in Baltimore, Washington, Louisville, and St. Louis. When Alexandria, Virginia, and Cairo, Illinois, became important staging grounds for military and naval operations, camps took shape there as shelters for the laborers and their families, soon becoming destinations for freedom seekers, with and without the approval of authorities.

During the war's first summer, fewer than one thousand persons had taken refuge within federal lines at Fort Monroe. The following spring, as Union forces began concerted operations into Confederate territory, freedom seekers approached warships and military camps by the scores and soon the hundreds. West of the Appalachian Mountains, such settlements appeared whenever and wherever Union forces advanced: in New Orleans, Helena, and Nashville during spring 1862; and in LaGrange, Memphis, and Corinth during the ensuing summer and fall. At every town and railway junction that the forces under General Ulysses S. Grant occupied, refugees gathered. In November he placed John Eaton, the chaplain of an Ohio regiment, in charge of the camps to coordinate the provision of food and shelter while preventing the refugees from encumbering military operations. Federal officials also decided to put the refugees to work harvesting cotton to offset the cost of their support.[16]

However sensible that plan might have appeared on paper, it fell far short of solving the growing problem. Both Tennessee and the southern parishes of Louisiana won exemption from the January 1863 Emancipation Proclamation, but the number of freedom seekers who sought federal protection continued to grow, as pro-Confederate slaveholders fled the federal military advances. In and around Nashville and Memphis army quartermasters and engineers put people to work, sidestepping the issue of whether the laborers or the owners were entitled to the wages by distributing rations and recording the hours worked for settlement of pay accounts at some future date. Without earnings to provide for their families, men worked for the government employers irregularly at best. As a result, the engineers were obliged to keep thousands of men on the rolls to ensure a sufficient workforce each day. These men supplemented their government rations by working as day laborers for private employers that paid wages, and by fishing and tending garden patches. Women worked as cooks and laundresses for soldiers and private citizens. Although Military Governor (and future president) Andrew Johnson saw only the "squalrid, debased condition" of the inhabitants of the camps, viewing them as the "dross" of the enslaved population of Tennessee, other witnesses saw commendable evidence of industry and frugality.[17]

Federal commanders in other occupied areas of the Confederacy took similarly deliberate steps toward providing humanitarian assistance to black freedom seekers. At first quartermaster and commissary officers took up the work, followed by chaplains and surgeons. They registered the residents and assessed their need for special treatment, they issued rations, they employed those who were capable of working, and they ministered to the spiritual and educational needs of the residents. In the absence of unified regulations for administering the camps, superintendents enjoyed nearly unlimited authority, leaving the clear marks of their personalities and beliefs on the places and the people under their charge. They generally imposed regulations that restricted the residents' comings and goings, the company they kept, and the way they and their families comported themselves. Most superintendents also reserved the right to deny admission to refugees and to expel residents without cause. Recognizing the need for additional humanitarian resources, however, the superintendents sought and accepted the assistance of the so-called freedmen's aid associations sponsored by churches and philanthropic groups across the North.

By the spring of 1865, the number of residents at contraband camps managed under government auspices was probably close to 100,000 persons, most of whom were elderly or disabled persons or women with small children. That figure does not include the several hundred thousand persons who worked for government departments or private employers within federal lines in the Mississippi valley, tidewater Virginia, and the islands around Port Royal, South Carolina, and who had lived for a time in a refugee camp. The number of transitory residents could fluctuate, at times wildly, particularly after military operations, such as Nathaniel P. Banks's Red River Campaign and William T. Sherman's expedition to Meridian, Mississippi, during the late winter and early spring of 1864. In urban areas, some percentage of the transients found employment and shelter on their own, but federal officials assumed responsibility for most.[18] In Washington, the situations included placements in businesses and private residences on annual arrangements, seasonal work on farms, and, for those willing to relocate, situations in households in cities farther north. After its initial establishment, a camp's population of permanent residents likely grew sporadically. In short, there was no prototypical "contraband camp." Each one was a world unto itself, whose inhabitants also experienced life in the camp differently depending on their individual and family circumstances.[19]

———

Cities in the slaveholding states presented unique environments for wartime freedom seekers to pursue their dreams. At once connected with their rural hinterlands, cities also stood apart from their surroundings even before the war, in their look and feel, in the pace and variety of their economic activity, in the ethnic diversity of their white populations, and—most of all—in the range of circumstances and experiences among their black populations, slave and free. The war accentuated the differences, not least because of the role that cities played as centers of production, logistics, communication, and administration, charging virtually every Southern city with excitement. The war also magnified the antebellum tension between masters and slaves over the limits on enslaved people's autonomy in urban settings. Only in the wealthiest households did the enslaved workforce exceed a dozen, but workshops and factories often employed more, sometimes a combination of free and enslaved persons, the latter being either the property of the business owner or hired on annual contracts.

Urban space presented opportunities for slaves to meet and socialize beyond their masters' oversight and control and with a broader array of associates than were present on even the largest plantations. Indeed, in one of his several attempts at escape, Wallace Turnage reported having headed "down in the City" of Mobile "for safety being there was so many people passing and I would not be easily detected." He moved from the home of one friend to that of another, just as other freedom seekers did in cities throughout the Confederacy.[20] Not only urban masters viewed the growing independence of their slaves with concern. When rural slaveholders were required to furnish quotas of laborers to work on fortifications, they fumed over the press officers' refusal to scour the cities before squeezing them for recruits. In May 1864, for instance, a group of Alabama farmers begged for relief. "There are large numbers of negroes about our towns & cities (used for the pleasure of their owners; or idling about; a curse to the community—*consumers not producers*), that," they insisted, "might be exhausted before the agricultural labour of the country is interfered with."[21]

When the Union wrested control of New Orleans from the rebels late in April 1862, the wealthy Confederate sympathizers had already fled: eastward into Mississippi and Alabama, westward toward Arkansas and Texas, and, in some cases, southward toward Cuba, the last remaining bastion of slavery in the Caribbean. Like their counterparts to the east who had fled the Sea Islands in November 1861, they brought house servants with them and left the rest of their enslaved laborers behind to fend for themselves. But unlike the South Carolinians, nearly all of whom were dyed-in-the-wool secessionists, many of the Crescent City's residents were Unionists. Rather than flee, they stayed at home and pledged their allegiance to the stars and stripes. Among their ranks were *gens de couleur libres*, free persons of color, among whom were light-complexioned, wealthy, European-schooled physicians, planters, businessmen, and other professionals. Numbers of the shopkeepers and artisans owned slaves. Francis E. Dumas, a man of mixed European and African ancestry who had inherited a sugar plantation from his French father, reportedly owned hundreds of men, women, and children.[22]

Meanwhile, the Unionist slaveholders pursued a two-pronged approach to evade the inevitable end. Flaunting their allegiance to the United States, they first appealed to federal authorities—particularly to the local provost marshals who served as civil as well as military police—for help in keeping the enslaved people subordinate. Second, they took matters into their own hands, committing freedom seekers to the quasi-public slave pens and private jails that had served the city's bustling prewar trade in humans. Early in 1863, Mary Ann, a young woman whose master was a captain in a Confederate cavalry regiment, appealed to the Union military commander's sense of "kindness and justice even to a poor slave girl who are kept in prison as a criminal." When federal authorities occupied the city, her mistress put her "out door," telling her "to go [to] the Yankee." Unable to find work to support herself, she returned home but her mistress refused to receive her. Instead, the woman had her jailed without having committed "any offence against any one, or my mistress and master that I have faithfully served all the time."[23] In the same vein, George W. F. Johnson, a native of New Orleans who had enlisted in the U.S. Navy, appealed to the provost marshal general on behalf of his sister who suffered a miscarriage while in jail, questioning why the government was not fulfilling its promise to care for the families of men in the government's service.[24]

The case of Edith and Charley Jones and their son illuminated how wartime emancipation affected small slaveholding households in urban settings such as New Orleans. In March 1863, Edith requested the intervention of the military commander of the Department of the Gulf in mediating a dispute with her mistress that embroiled her whole family. The owner had imprisoned Charley for the previous five months and kept the couple's son "home with my ma^dame" while Edith attempted without success to earn the ten dollars per month expected for her hire. Because "times are so dull," Edith explained, she could not earn more than eight dollars, but the mistress refused to make the adjustment until "times get better"; instead, she vowed to "find a place for me in the work house or in the parish prison." Edith informed the commanding officer that she would "do whatever you a^dvised me to do anything that is just an^d right," but he chose not to respond.[25] Louisiana's exception from the Emancipation Proclamation amounted to a partial severing of the cord that bound masters and slaves. The exemption wounded slavery without killing it, thereby stunting the growth of relationships wherein individuals interacted with the world at large as free persons, responsible for their own expenses and the support of their children, collecting the value of the labor they performed in wages, and reconciling the two without the meddlesome interposition of a "ma^dame."

Federal authorities often looked the other way when self-styled loyal masters abandoned the city with their slaves. The free man of color Georges Herera appealed in vain to General Banks to stop the owner of his three small children from removing them to Cuba. The owner had incarcerated Georges's enslaved wife, Rose, and their infant baby after Rose came to blows with a relative of her mistress. With the full knowledge and cooperation of military authorities, nominally loyal slaveholders continued to enjoy the rights of mastership, jailing their "vagrant" people at will and even in some instances, as this case reveals, removing them beyond the reach of U.S. jurisdiction. Rose and Georges pursued the return of their children through military and diplomatic channels, finally succeeding in repatriating the children in 1866 but not before Georges had died.[26] Nominally loyal slaveholders in Nashville did the same, under the regime of General Lovell S. Rousseau, who routinely issued orders requiring federal forces to cooperate in the rendition of persons accused of being escaped slaves.[27]

The famous dictum that all politics is local helps to illuminate the emancipation process, as the experience of four small places, each from a different theater of the war, illustrates. The first is Fort Monroe, Virginia, the federal outpost occupying several hundred acres at the tip of the Virginia Peninsula, which remained in federal hands through secession and the entire war. The second is Port Royal and the surrounding Sea Islands off the coast of South Carolina, which federal forces occupied in November 1861. The third is Davis Bend, Mississippi, the home of Jefferson Davis and his brother Joseph, whose Hurricane and Brierfield Plantations housed more than 400 enslaved people at the start of the rebellion. And the fourth is the District of Columbia, which became an oasis of free territory owing to the congressional emancipation law of April 1862, sandwiched between the Unionist slave state of Maryland and the Confederate slave state of Virginia. Such small spaces demonstrate not only how slavery collapsed and a new order took shape on a microscopic level but also how the stories of such places illuminate aspects of emancipation that run counter to the linear, progressive narrative that a focus on law and public policy might suggest.

From early in the war, Fort Monroe and its surroundings served as a prototype of how confined space affected the options available to freedom seekers and federal policy makers alike. The stone fortress and the water-filled moat around it sat on the narrow spit of land called Old Point Comfort, where the tip of the Virginia Peninsula disappears into the waters of Chesapeake Bay. The fort had limited access by land: from the north via a narrow neck with an improved road that ran to Hampton some seven miles away, and from the west by a wooden bridge that spanned Mill Creek between the mainland and Old Point Comfort.

Once General Benjamin Butler coined the term "contraband" as a rationale for offering protection to enslaved persons whose Confederate masters employed them in support of the rebellion, freedom seekers set their bearings accordingly. But the space to accommodate the refugees was limited and their numbers grew slowly. As other Union military commanders would discover in the weeks and months to come, black refugees provided reliable sources of information regarding the strength of Confederate forces, their positioning, and sometimes even their intended operations. With intelligence provided by one such refugee from slavery, William Scott, Butler attacked Virginia state forces at Big Bethel in early June 1861, suffering a humiliating defeat in one of the earliest armed clashes of the war. After the battle, a "squad of negroes" asked a group of Yankee soldiers for directions to "the freedom fort," a characterization that clearly had entered common currency within days of Butler's decision to grant asylum.[28] Others made their way there with and without directions, swelling the number of asylum seekers to more than 900 by the end of the next month.[29]

At the beginning of July, General Butler ordered the occupation of Hampton to create a buffer protecting the fort and the federal outpost at Newport News from Confederate attack. Rebel sympathizers grabbed clothing and personal effects and fled with house servants and other selected slaves. Union troops discovered few white people in the village. The black residents occupied their customary quarters, taking custody of the scant supplies of meat and meal that had been laid up the previous fall to provision them, supplemented by the fresh produce that their gardens were beginning to yield. Officers in units under Butler's command were eager to hire servants, and the various military departments, particularly the quartermaster, wanted hands. With such concentrations of people, enterprising former slaves had ready customers for the products of their gardens, their hen houses and fishing seines, and their kitchens.[30] Close enough to the fort to enjoy the protection of its guns yet distant enough to avoid the scrutiny of its commanders, the freed people at Hampton enjoyed unprecedented control over their lives. Confederate troops and rebel sympathizers farther up the peninsula knew it and resented it.

On July 25, Butler abruptly ordered the evacuation of Hampton. Following the federal debacle at Bull Run four days earlier, the War Department had requisitioned 4,000 of Butler's men to help protect the capital, leaving him little choice but to pull back from Hampton. The departure of the soldiers prompted "a stampede of the colored population," in the words of a correspondent for the *New York Herald*. The fear of a Confederate attack and the return to slavery "lent wings to the contrabands," who grabbed what clothing, household furniture, and effects they could gather and set out over the "long and lonely road" to the wooden bridge that crossed Mill Creek to Old Point Comfort and the fort, their envisioned "haven." "Never was such an exodus seen before in this country," the reporter noted.[31] On August 17, *Harper's Weekly* reprinted much of the account accompanied by a woodcut depicting the scene (see figure 5.1). In a tribute to the unsettled state of the public mind (and the mind of the editor) regarding the status of the contrabands, the caption to the woodcut read "Stampede of Slaves from Hampton to Fortress Monroe." One small space disgorged its inhabitants onto another with no recourse for accommodating the refugees in any other way.

Figure 5.1 Stampede of Slaves from Hampton to Fortress Monroe, Harper's Weekly,
August 17, 1861. Courtesy of the Library of Congress Prints and Photographs Division,
LC-DIG-ppmsca-35556.

The reduction in the Union force at Fort Monroe and the black refugees'
evacuation of Hampton village presented Confederate general John B.
Magruder with a golden opportunity to take the offensive. A Northern newspaper that came into his hands reported that Butler intended to transform
Hampton from a defensive outpost into a staging ground for operations
against Richmond. The report also confirmed Hampton's role as a "harbor
of runaway slaves and traitors" where Butler had found useful labor for "the
many negroes in his possession," the women "attending to the clothes of the
soldiers" and the men "working on the fortifications." Realizing the town's
"extreme importance to the enemy," Magruder decided to burn it "at once,"
and on August 7 his troops applied the torch. Butler and Magruder exchanged
charges regarding ultimate responsibility for the act.[32] The Confederate terror tactic worked only for a short time. By late summer, the twice-removed
refugees began returning to Hampton, where they constructed the Grand
Contraband Camp, or Slab Town, in reference to the building materials that
had been salvaged from Magruder's fire. A number of structures in the Grand
Contraband Camp remained standing into the twentieth century, and two

of its symbolically named streets, Lincoln Street and Grant Circle, survive today. The black missionary John Oliver noted the presence of such slab towns in various locations in the tidewater region of Virginia.[33]

Not everyone viewed the fort as the last and final destination in their quest for freedom, and many found ways to use the presence of federal troops there along with the prospect of shelter and employment as a component of their strategy for independence. They might live on an abandoned plantation working a small plot of ground for vegetables, and identifying sources of protein from the fish and other creatures of the streams and rivers as well as the animals of the fields and forests. These were the independent colonists who reportedly resided at Williamsburg, having chosen to make a go of it on their own rather than settle permanently at Fort Monroe. They were the Yankee-influenced men and women rounded up during Magruder's dragnet for laborers who displayed such an uncooperative spirit when captured. A stint on the fortifications did not wear them down, nor did being returned to slavery break their spirits. They knew they could get away and find a niche in which to survive.

———

When combined military and naval forces overpowered the Confederate defenses at Port Royal, South Carolina, some fifty miles southwest of Charleston, on November 5, 1861, the resulting flight of the masters instantly gave rise to a refugee population that numbered more than 11,000 persons in the towns of Beaufort and Hilton Head and on the surrounding islands.[34] Before he left Washington, the commander of the military expedition, General Thomas W. Sherman, received from Secretary of War Simon Cameron copies of his correspondence with General Butler at Fort Monroe the summer before. To be sure, circumstances in the two settings were radically different, but what they had in common was the freed people's eagerness to leave the ways of slavery behind. Despite the stories that their owners had broadcast regarding the evil designs and practices of the Yankees, they were willing to see what the newcomers offered. In both Virginia and South Carolina, the offer included protection, shelter, food, and at least the promise of wages for work on behalf of the government. In Virginia, the work entailed labor for the quartermaster and commissary departments; in South Carolina, the government's first priority was harvesting the ripe cotton bolls bursting with the long, silky fibers of Sea Island cotton that Liverpool traders prized.[35]

In late December 1861, Treasury Secretary Salmon P. Chase called on Edward Pierce to investigate conditions among the contrabands at Port Royal, fully aware of his protégé's earlier experience at Fort Monroe. Early in February Pierce submitted his report, and soon thereafter Chase placed him in charge of an experiment to reorganize the labor system on the surrounding islands and to remake the lives of the inhabitants. Pierce recruited a band of fifty-odd men and women, mostly from New York and Boston, to manage plantations, teach in schools, and impart the economic, social, and religious values of Northern Protestantism. With implements and supplies furnished by the federal government and seed from the previous year's harvest, the freed people set about planting cotton and corn. Determined to use the inducement of wages rather than the threat of corporal punishment to spur industry, Pierce and the superintendents set about dividing fields and apportioning tasks of work to each family, much as overseers had done in the days of slavery. He wrote lengthy reports to Chase, excerpts of which appeared in the popular press. The Northerners corresponded regularly with relatives and friends and the antislavery and religious press at home, as did visitors to the area.[36]

Because the federal enclave lacked telegraph communications with the North, oceangoing vessels carried the news along with the supplies necessary to support military operations and the plantation experiment. The geographical isolation wore on the Northerners, producing a state of temporal displacement that Charles P. Ware, a recent graduate of Harvard College who served as a plantation superintendent, explained well. "Time passes fast enough here," he observed, "much faster than I expected that it would." But because each day seemed like all the others, "the great danger" was that he might lose "the run of the days altogether, & imagine it Tuesday when it is Friday." Although he could mark the change of seasons—for instance, by the shorter days of autumn—he was nonetheless disoriented by the warmer temperature than what accompanied the approach of winter in Boston. The Yankees also experienced a distinct sensation of living behind the times. "We pine for a mail," Ware observed, for letters from home, newspapers, and official government documents. Although residents of Beaufort benefited from the news that arrived with each vessel and the discussions that ensued, the information reached the surrounding islands slowly and erratically. Ware noted that "the most important" pieces of information "come out accidentally, about 3 days after a person returns from Beaufort." "That is the way always," he lamented.[37] A month after arriving at Port Royal in the fall of 1862, Charlotte Forten, the African American teacher from Philadelphia, made similar observations. "It seems so very long since we came here and yet, as they pass, the days seem short enough," she remarked. "But to look back upon the time seems very long."[38]

The disjuncture that Ware, Forten, and the other Northern adherents of clock and calendar time experienced at Port Royal did not afflict the freed people. Nor did their conversations depend on the latest news from the North.

Even if there were no important happenings to report (accidents, births and deaths, Confederate raids), there were family and community ties to maintain (information about individuals' health and about kinfolk who might have moved to Beaufort or Hilton Head to work in support of federal military or naval operations). And the medium for communication remained the spoken and not the printed or written word. The footpaths that linked plantation settlements and the waterways that flowed among the islands served in lieu of wires strung on poles that signaled modern means of communication elsewhere. Northern visitors acknowledged this grapevine telegraph, often with more frustration over what it did not do than with appreciation for what it did. Charlotte Forten observed its impact on conventional timekeeping. Having arrived at the Baptist Church one Sunday morning in November, she grew impatient because "the people came in slowly," which delayed the start of the services. "They have no way of telling the time," she noted. Only afterward, when she saw the congregants socializing, did she get a glimpse into the community-building exercise that occurred each Sunday. Though no stranger to the phenomenon in her prior experience in the North, she had not fully made peace with the apparent irreverence involved in delaying the start of worship for the sake of gossip.[39]

For their part, the freed people of Port Royal came to understand, respect, and, in some cases, care deeply for the Yankee plantation managers and teachers in their midst. They had no aversion to work, although they preferred not to work quite as long and hard as they had under the old regime. They wanted to grow corn and other provisions to feed themselves, and they continued to raise vegetables, pigs, and fowl for their own consumption as well as for trade and for sale, now also benefiting from the nearby presence of hungry sailors and soldiers. Hardly insensible to the budding market economy that the Yankees introduced in the plantation stores, they understood that the wages they earned for plantation labor—with predetermined amounts for each "task" of plowing, planting, maintaining fences and ditches, and ultimately for each pound of cotton picked—enabled the purchase of store goods. They were willing to do without the more exotic consumer items, so long as they could purchase sugar and tobacco on credit. In time they wondered aloud why they could not have land on which to build homes and subsist themselves. Most of all, they questioned why they did not receive their earned wages regularly, and why their accounts were not settled soon after the cotton crop had been harvested and sold. Tardy payment of wages characterized the Port Royal Experiment throughout the war.[40]

The activities in support of military and naval operations had as much of an impact on the free-labor experiment as did the work on the plantations. The whole strategic purpose for occupying Port Royal was to establish a supply base for the South Atlantic Blockading Squadron and a prospective launchpad for operations against Charleston. Success would require hundreds, if not thousands, of laborers to handle the food, fuel, weapons, ammunition, and spare parts. Thanks to Navy Secretary Gideon Welles's directive in September 1861 authorizing the enlistment of "contrabands" into naval service, vessel commanders whose crews were shorthanded could fill out their complements at Port Royal when there for other purposes. Skilled men and laborers worked in ship repair facilities, and men who knew the coastal waters were in demand as pilots.[41]

Unlike their counterparts on the plantations, the men who enlisted in the navy or who worked for wages in Beaufort and in Hilton Head collected their pay regularly, infusing cash into the local economy and sparking a lively trade in consumer goods. In September 1863, a young man named Esup wrote to his mother from Hilton Head, asking that she send him a peck of sour oranges by Limus's boat and that she inform his father that a good silver watch could be purchased for eight dollars in the city. By also asking "if you want me to Pick Cotton," Esup illustrated the importance of family ties between town and country that undergirded the pursuit of economic self-sufficiency under the new regime that the Northerners inaugurated.[42] Presuming to flatter Limus, William C. Gannett, one of the superintendents from Boston, noted that he possessed "the energy and *'cuteness* and big eye for his own advantage of a born New Englander." The entrepreneurial ventures of this "black Yankee" included a fourteen-acre cotton patch (cultivated by a freed family that he hired at "the rendezvous for refugees"), numerous pigs and chickens, a horse and cart, and a "large boat" in which he "makes weekly trips to Hilton Head, twenty miles distant, carrying passengers, produce and fish."[43]

In an effort to increase the security of the Union beachhead, in April 1862 General David Hunter, the recently appointed commander of the Department of the South, reprised General John C. Frémont's earlier experience in Missouri, declaring martial law and abolishing slavery. President Lincoln repudiated the order, once again signaling to the commanders of military departments that he alone would decide whether local conditions warranted action against slavery. As his emancipation plan fizzled, Hunter ignited another brushfire when he began raising a regiment of black soldiers to bolster his force and increase its operational effectiveness. But this was not a question of freeing slaves—those within Union lines were de facto free—but one of arming them as U.S. soldiers.

Hunter could have managed the organization more deftly than he did. His recruiters employed heavy-handed tactics to drag men into service, sending the laborers who were working diligently under the plantation superintendents fleeing to woods and marshes at the mere hint that strangers were about.[44] Hunter managed to feed and clothe the men from government stores, but he lacked authority to pay them. Meanwhile in Congress, Hunter's actions enabled the Conservative Kentucky representative Charles A. Wickliffe to launch a fresh attempt at embarrassing the War Department, but the general outsmarted the congressman, at least over the short run. In response to the question of whether he had enlisted a regiment of "Fugitive Slaves," Hunter replied no, but acknowledged that he had enlisted "a fine regiment of persons whose late masters are 'Fugitive Rebels'—men who everywhere fly before the appearance of the National Flag, leaving their servants behind them to shift as best they can for themselves." In the face of persistent questioning, War Secretary Stanton ordered Hunter to disband the unit early in August 1862 but soon thereafter authorized Hunter's superintendent of contrabands, General Rufus Saxton, to begin recruiting the First South Carolina Volunteers.[45]

Knowledge of the coastal waterways was a precious commodity that freed people graciously shared with their Northern guests. White residents of the region had similar knowledge, and they proved just as willing to share it, but with Confederate military commanders instead of the Yankees. The experience of Edisto Island, South Carolina, some twenty miles northeast of the Union beachhead at Port Royal, offers insight. Confederate owners had evacuated most of their laborers to the up-country at the first approach of Union gunboats. Refugees from the mainland moved into the vacuum, with their numbers growing to some 2,000 persons by the summer of 1862. In the meantime, federal officials established a military outpost on the island. The colony prospered until July 1862, when the War Department ordered General Hunter to dispatch 10,000 soldiers, nearly half of his effective troop strength, to bolster General George McClellan's forces in the Peninsula Campaign.[46] The requisition obliged Hunter to pull back, and he ordered the evacuation of the garrison and some 1,600 people from the island. "The Secesh houses" abandoned in the village on St. Helena Island were "insufficient to accommodate them all," according to one observer, and the overflow population had little choice but to "stow themselves in sheds, tents, and even in the open air." Over time, the superintendents found shelter for the "Edisto people," as they were called thereafter, in vacant quarters on the plantations where they raised "slip-potatoes and cow-pease."[47]

The following February, when the work of plowing and planting for the new agricultural year began, the Edisto Island refugees went into the fields "without the necessary number of cattle or mules, and with only their worn-out hoes." In such circumstances, the "work bids fair to be as behindhand here as it was last year," a Northern teacher noted at the time. Little wonder that they were reluctant "to start any cotton, though they work corn." "Think we'll go back to Edisto, Missy?" a youngster asked the teacher. She could offer no words of hope.[48] Against the odds, these refugees from the mainland, who were misidentified with Edisto Island, managed to establish new roots on Hilton Head Island. In late December 1864, when federal officials decided to settle some of the approximately 10,000 black refugees who had followed Sherman's army across Georgia at Hilton Head, the "Edisto people" offered encouragement to those who faced the daunting task of making their lives over, pointing to their own transformation over the previous two years. Having arrived with "noffin' at all" they now had money they had earned from growing cotton and "all the tater and hominy we can eat."[49]

After he determined that Edisto, like other abandoned islands, was by this late stage in the war safe from rebel raids, General Saxton decided to repopulate it, choosing as pioneers the persons displaced from the island more than two years earlier. One Sunday morning in mid-January, Saxton spoke at a church on St. Helena Island to explain his plan. "By telling them how he was going to send the black troops there to defend the islands," a witness to the scene, Edward Philbrick, explained, "and how they might return to their 'old homes,' etc.," Saxton hoped to gain their assent. Saxton forgot "that they were not natives of Edisto, but only refugees when there, and they were now more comfortably settled here than they were there in 1862," a lapse that "set all the Edisto people into a stew." Demoralized, "many refuse[d] to work," content to "pack up and sit still" as they awaited the relocation.[50] Similar scenes unfolded repeatedly during the spring and summer of 1865, as the original residents of the islands, whose owners had refugeed them to the upcountry, returned and found their homes occupied by strangers: the recently arrived "Georgia refugees" and the "Edisto people" who had escaped from the mainland to the island between November 1861 and June 1862.[51]

Davis Bend, Mississippi, the antebellum home of the Confederate president Jefferson Davis and his wife, Varina, and Jefferson's older brother and financial benefactor, Joseph, provided another example of a confined space that brimmed with insights into the myriad strands of the story of emancipation. The Davis brothers employed several hundred enslaved laborers on an oxbow in the Mississippi River some twenty miles below Vicksburg. Joseph had gained international notoriety before the war for having undertaken a daring social experiment at the Bend after a meeting with the Welsh industrialist and utopian socialist Robert Owen in 1825. Although hardly a blueprint for abolition, Davis's plan envisioned employing enslaved laborers cultivating cotton based on the principle of mutual interest rather than brutality. Davis introduced incentives to encourage industrious labor and established a plantation court that the laborers themselves administered. Benjamin

Montgomery, an enslaved man with great natural talent for the agricultural and mechanical arts, played a leading part. Montgomery operated a plantation store that catered to the workers, and he managed the ordering of plantation supplies on behalf of Davis. Except for the narrow neck of land connecting it to the mainland, Davis Bend was surrounded by the flowing waters of the Mississippi. It was a preeminently confined space, which, like other such bends and islands in the river, was subject to become even more confined during flood season.

In the spring and summer of 1862, after Union forces regained control over New Orleans and Memphis, and their plans to reduce Vicksburg had begun to emerge, Joseph concluded that the bend was no longer safe from the Yankees. He relocated away from the river, taking house servants and most of the field workers from both his and his brother's plantations and leaving Montgomery in charge of the bend and its remaining inhabitants. His fears of depredations by federal forces proved well founded, but he did not count on Confederate conscription officers scouring the bend in search of military laborers. Yet even as Davis attempted to remove the remaining slaves, those refugeed away from the bend earlier tried to return home because the farms he had leased contained insufficient provisions to feed them.[52]

Benjamin Montgomery remained at the bend, but with decreasing influence over the inhabitants, who helped themselves to the left-behind treasures of the big house. Continuing visits from Yankees finished the work of looting and destruction. To add insult to injury, a number of men returned from stints at work on the Vicksburg fortifications with measles, which then spread to other refugees who lacked prior exposure.[53] By the spring of 1863, as Union military and naval operations against Vicksburg intensified, Montgomery's teenage son Isaiah won the favor of Rear Admiral David D. Porter, commander of the Mississippi Squadron, who took him on as his servant. Porter also employed the elder Montgomery for a time before assisting Benjamin, his wife, and their daughters in relocating to Cincinnati. The river system of the Midwest transported them from a confined place of recurring danger to one of safety.[54]

The vagaries of war that played out on a broad geographic canvas continued creating shockwaves that ultimately affected small places. In February and March 1864, for instance, Sherman's operation against the supply depot at Meridian, Mississippi, liberated some 8,000 slaves, who returned with his troops to Vicksburg. Because of overcrowding in the camps there, federal officials moved several thousand to Davis Bend. The newcomers overwhelmed the existing community. A Treasury Department agent who surveyed the area lamented that "life and property are constantly jeopardized." A Northern missionary reported that many of the Meridian refugees resided in dilapidated structures "not fit to shelter cattle in during a storm, yet therein are our fellow creatures in all weathers subjected to disease, degradation and immorality." Colonel Samuel Thomas, superintendent of contrabands in the district of Vicksburg, distributed rations and furnished materials for building shelters. After he stationed a force of black soldiers there, the community began to thrive.

By the summer of 1864, only 3,000 of the approximately 6,000 people who had been sent there over the previous months were still under Thomas's supervision at the bend, the other 3,000 having moved to other leased plantations in the vicinity. Those capable of working entirely on their own leased two thousand acres of land, and "the enterprise," Thomas reported, "promises success."[55] A correspondent to the New York *Anglo-African* visited Davis Bend in December and marveled at its transformation. The community had become so resilient that it absorbed some 2,000 persons from the camp at Goodrich's Landing, whom government transports had rapidly evacuated in advance of a rebel raid. With a remarkable spirit of enterprise that had begun to flourish among the "contrabands," the refugees "set about to erect shelters for themselves and their little ones, and . . . in about six weeks they were as comfortably situated as the nature of the circumstances would permit." The explanation was simple: no longer a slave, "*now* he is a *freedman*, he is now at liberty to think and act for himself, and what he earns now, is his own," the reporter reasoned. "He now realizes the heaven-born right of worshipping God under his own vine and fig tree, and that his wife and little ones are no longer liable to be torn from him at the auction block."[56] "What a great, what a *mighty* change has been wrought here within the short space of four years."[57]

———

Despite its small size, the District of Columbia occupied an oversized place in the history of emancipation. Inasmuch as Congress exerted control over the affairs of the District, Republicans could legislate an end to slavery there, an ability they lacked in the states. Indeed, President Lincoln signed the bill abolishing slavery on April 16, 1862, as spring flowers were beginning to bloom in the capital, signaling to both supporters and opponents alike the coming to fruition of the abolitionist movement. Yet expectations of what emancipation entailed and the reality that residents of the capital experienced sometimes diverged. Freedom's arrival followed a crooked rather than a straight path.

As originally envisioned, the District of Columbia was a square straddling the Potomac River, whose sides measured ten miles each and whose corners aligned with the four principal directions of the compass. In 1846, the original one hundred square miles shrank to sixty-nine square miles on the retrocession of the area south and west of the river to Virginia. The District then consisted of Washington City (with its distinctive grid of streets and the well-calculated arrangement of government buildings that followed the French-born architect Pierre L'Enfant's 1791 plan for the capital city), the city of Georgetown, and Washington County, the rural area outside the two cities. Even before congressional emancipation took effect, the presence of soldiers had begun to undermine the foundation of slavery, just as it was doing in Maryland, Kentucky, and Missouri. That process produced fissures that enslaved people began to explore often with little or no fanfare. When the "model servant" Harriet F. Belt abandoned her owner William Bayley to support herself by washing for a Union soldier, she boarded at a home a mere ten blocks from her owner's residence, yet he remained unaware of her whereabouts.[58]

The chambers of the Senate and the House of Representatives of the United States constituted other small spaces whose significance has historically overleapt their walls and the Capitol building that contains them. In those rooms, the elected representatives of the American people crafted the critical pieces of national legislation affecting emancipation and engaged in some of the most far-reaching debates about the meaning of freedom in the history of the United States. To be sure, enslaved people in Washington had been struggling to be free for years, as the 1848 incident involving the seventy-seven enslaved persons who made a bid for freedom aboard Captain Daniel Drayton's schooner, *Pearl*, demonstrated. Contrary winds stalled the boat near the mouth of the Potomac River, and a posse in a commandeered steamboat overtook the sailing vessel before it could reach the open waters of Chesapeake Bay. The authorities returned the freedom seekers to their chains and imprisoned Drayton after making a public spectacle of him.[59]

Less spectacularly, the enslaved man Ignatius Tighlman made a verbal agreement in 1856 with the Sisters of the Visitation of Georgetown to purchase his family. The sisters had come to own Tighlman and his wife after a member of the order received them in the division of her father's estate. As the Tighlman family grew, eventually including six children, they straddled the line between slavery and freedom, still legally the property of the Sisters of the Visitation but also living independently and otherwise comporting themselves as though they were free. Their quest continued unfulfilled until President Lincoln signed the congressional bill abolishing slavery in the District of Columbia in April 1862.[60]

From the start of the war, Republican congressional leaders had contemplated abolition in the District. After secession and the withdrawal from Congress of most congressmen and senators from the seceded states, antislavery legislators at last had hope for success. On December 16, 1861, Henry Wilson first introduced an emancipation bill, proposing immediate emancipation with compensation in the amount of $300 per freed person on average, but the battle was just beginning. In the debating societies that constituted the bodies as a whole and their respective committees that would mark up any proposed bill, anything could happen. The pro-slavery faction from the Loyal Border States stood poised to subvert even the most modest measures affecting the peculiar institution.[61] What is more, in March, President Lincoln's message to Congress proposed federal financial assistance to any state that undertook the voluntary, gradual abolition of slavery, and Congress concurred the following month.

When the emancipation bill was reported out from committee in March, the opponents were ready to attack. Kentucky senator Garrett Davis offered an amendment to colonize all persons freed by the measure to avoid a certain "war of extermination between the races," a veritable "bloody La Vendée."[62] In the House, opponents offered amendment after amendment aiming to scuttle the bill altogether, to postpone consideration pending a referendum among the qualified electorate of the District, and to prohibit the testimony of black witnesses in any associated proceedings, with Kentucky's representative Wickliffe playing the part of obstructionist with special zeal. Representative Owen Lovejoy of Illinois reacted furiously to a suggestion that owners should receive more than what Wilson's original bill had proposed for each person emancipated, citing the case of a District slaveholder, Louis Mackall, who in June 1861 had agreed to sell to James Harod (or Harrod), a free man of color, his wife, Lena, and their daughter Rachel. As passage of the bill became more likely, Mackall reneged on the offer and removed the woman and child along with the couple's newborn baby to a slave pen in Baltimore. Characterizing Mackall as "a woman-thief, a child-thief," Lovejoy condemned the "brazen men" who "talk about robbing, because we give only three hundred dollars" in compensation to the masters.[63] Ohio's notorious copperhead Democrat Clement L. Vallandigham characterized the bill as "the beginning of a grand scheme of emancipation; and there is no calculation where that scheme is to end." Like Senator James A. Bayard Jr. of Delaware on the eve of the Senate vote, Congressman Vallandigham knew very well where it might end.[64] The Senate approved the bill on April 3, with the House following suit on April 11, but thanks to Wickliffe's special plea on behalf of his two "sickly" servants, Lincoln delayed signing it into law until April 16.[65]

By moving enslaved people out of the District in March and early April, slaveholders denied freedom to hundreds of the intended beneficiaries of the emancipation bill.[66] The brother-in-law of Elizabeth Blair Lee, a member of one of Washington's most distinguished families, moved two servants "down to the Country" after the bill passed the Senate on April 3. His action, she explained, reflected the widespread belief among Maryland owners that this was the time to send "their slaves to the Cotton states & get good prices for them" before this species of property lost all value.[67] Not to be outsmarted, enslaved people, numbering perhaps in the hundreds, took matters into their own hands and abandoned their owners before Congress and the president enacted the law. Among them was Ignatius Tighlman Jr., the teenage son of the family held by the Sisters of the Visitation of Georgetown, who departed Washington with the Army of the Potomac in March.[68]

Slightly more than four months transpired between when Henry Wilson first proposed such a measure before the Senate and when President Lincoln signed the measure into law. Over that span the cold winds and gray skies of winter gave way to the signs of spring. Perhaps ominously, Elizabeth Blair Lee awoke on April 6 to "a relapse with winter this morning." "I never saw a more backward spring," she concluded.[69] Just as winter refused to release its hold on Washington, so too did slavery maintain its grip. Given the long history of slavery in the District, these four months were short; but to persons whose fate hung in the balance, the convoluted legislative process could appear to be excruciatingly long. In fact, both of these assessments were correct. When April 17 dawned, they realized that the mere passage of the act did not usher in the millennium overnight. In the small places scattered throughout Washington, Georgetown, and Washington County, enslaved people struggled to fashion new lives that differed substantially from their experience in slavery.

The law stipulated that persons who wished compensation had ninety days in which to submit claims, that is, until July 15. Three commissioners examined the validity of each applicant's claim and determined the amount of compensation for each person freed. The commissioners forwarded the names of the persons released from service and recommended the amount of compensation to the Circuit Court. Upon its review and approval the court issued certificates of freedom to each formerly enslaved person for a nominal fee. Cases that required investigation could take weeks or longer to resolve. Meanwhile, the nominally free people remained in a slavery-like state of limbo.

Under the terms of the law, every enslaved person's freedom depended on the actions of others. First, the owner had to submit a petition for compensation to the commissioners by the stipulated deadline. Then the commissioners had to establish the validity of the claim before they would petition the Circuit Court to issue a certificate of freedom. Many slaveholders waited until the last minute; others simply did not submit a petition at all. Accordingly, days before the July 15 deadline, Congress passed a supplemental act that permitted the persons held to service to petition the commissioners directly on their own behalf.[70] Although this relieved their immediate fear that the master's inaction would stand in the way of their receiving certificates of freedom, it did not solve every problem. When the commissioners investigated petitions under the new act, owners often maneuvered to evade the law. A number of such cases continued beyond January 1, 1863, and not all were resolved in favor of the enslaved person. In short, hundreds of persons—if not more—who were entitled to freedom under the act remained unable to enjoy its most basic promise of ownership of their own persons for months, even years, after April 16, 1862.[71]

A few masters sidestepped the law, making arrangements directly with their slaves with neither party petitioning for compensation or a certificate of freedom. Elizabeth Blair Lee delighted in the discomfort that the abolitionist congressman Owen Lovejoy and his wife experienced on visiting the family's residence—directly across Lafayette Square from the White House—days after the law took effect. Her father, Francis P. Blair, was a prominent Democrat from the Jacksonian era who, despite his support for the Republican Party from its inception, could not wean himself from the service of enslaved people. He had offered them the option of continuing with his family as they had before, he explained to the Lovejoys, and only one man decided "to go *in the world* to better his condition." The visitors, Elizabeth noted gleefully in her diary, "looked amazed—said they had heard of such things but never saw them before."[72] Viewing slavery and freedom as categorical opposites, they strained to understand how the lines might blur in actual lives intertwined across generations. Emancipation in the District of Columbia was neither as simple nor as straightforward as its most fervent champions thought it would be.[73]

The experiences of three women illustrate the prolonged process that lay embedded within what even the emancipation commissioners considered to be a case of immediate emancipation. The first was Charlotte Beckett, a servant in the household of Mary Bibb, the wealthy widow of a judge who maintained a townhome in Georgetown and a farm in Montgomery County, Maryland. The second was Charlotte Brown, who hired her own time in the District, remitting monthly payments to Robert Marshal, the slaveholder from Prince George's County, Maryland, to whom she belonged. The third, Emeline Wedge, lived with her two children, her mother, and her younger sister on Alexander McCormick's farm, which lay just east of the Eastern Branch (now known as the Anacostia River), straddling the boundary line separating Washington County, D.C., from Prince George's County, Maryland. Emeline Wedge and Alexander McCormick became the chief protagonists in a dispute over how the emancipation law affected persons with one foot on slave territory and the other foot on free territory.

As Congress concluded its debate on the emancipation bill, Mary R. Bibb moved most of the servants at her Georgetown home to the farm in

Montgomery County. But two women, Charlotte Beckett and Harriet Williams, suspected Bibb's intentions and refused to relocate. Bibb spoke with Beckett and Williams, as Williams recalled, "no body else in the room but us three." Bibb did not tell them specifically that the law would free them, Williams later explained, but she said "that if the President vetoed the bill (I did not know what she meant) or allowed her anything for us she would send us right back" to Georgetown. She also threatened to have the women arrested if they left. Williams remained skeptical, but Beckett relented. Bibb arranged passage for Beckett, her four children, and their belongings "up to the country," hiring a wagon operator who, by his own account, was conducting a thriving business in exactly such relocations "just before [the] Emancipation Bill passed."[74]

After Beckett learned the particulars of the emancipation act, she felt betrayed, insisting that "she would not have gone up" had Bibb not misrepresented its intent. Seeking restitution for that wrong, Beckett gathered her children and returned to the District early in May and petitioned for certificates of freedom late in July. The commissioners quickly approved her request. Toward the end of the second month of the family's certified freedom, Mary Bibb asked the commissioners to reopen the case, which they agreed to do in mid-September. Bibb insisted that Beckett and her children were fugitive slaves rather than emancipated freed people, presenting a copy of the warrant she had sworn out for their arrest. In a split vote the commissioners ruled that Bibb had not prosecuted the warrant vigorously enough, given that the alleged fugitives had not concealed their whereabouts, and on October 1, 1862, Charlotte Beckett and her children became incontestably free.[75]

Charlotte Brown had been asserting her independence for several years before the start of the war, staying for short spells with her owner, Robert Marshal, in Prince George's County, between stints of hiring her time as a house servant in Washington. Marshal testified that he had permitted her to work in the District for the previous "2 years off & on 4 months at time"; Brown's small child stayed with Marshal during these absences. In April 1862, Brown was employed by Virginia Ann Miller, who had known her for years, "perhaps from a child."[76] After passage of the emancipation act, Marshal did not submit a claim for compensation, assuming that she remained his slave under the laws of Maryland unaffected by the law governing the District. Assisted by the abolitionist attorney George E. H. Day, Brown submitted a claim for a certificate of freedom, which the commissioners awarded on July 25. For reasons that are not fully clear, Brown petitioned again for the certificate on August 8, and the commissioners again ruled in her favor. On September 23, however, Marshal challenged the proceedings, insisting that from before enactment of the law "I had her home and ordered her to remain" there; and Marshal's son corroborated that she "went away without author-ity." After hearing additional testimony that suggested Marshal had approved of Brown's presence in the city after emancipation, the commissioners on Oc-tober 1 reaffirmed their earlier decision to award her the certificate. But throughout August and September Brown lived amid uncertainty whether her certificate of freedom was valid or whether she would have to return to her master and live under the slave code of Maryland.[77]

Even more striking than its duration, Brown's case is notable for the in-sight it provides into the lives of enslaved people whose suburban masters hired their services to persons in the city. Brown exercised a considerable degree of personal control over her movements between Prince George's County and the District of Columbia. As Miller explained, Brown "used to go home sometimes twice sometimes once a month to see her child gener-ally of a Saturday night & return Monday or Tuesday." She did not always keep her master or Miller aware of her comings and goings. One weekend she left Miller's "on Saturday evening and returned on Sunday saying she started home and was stopped" at the Eastern Branch bridge only a stone's throw from Maryland "by an officer who told her she was free." Brown's fellow ser-vants reinforced the same message. Miller overheard a conversation in the kitchen in which they told her "you are free, and she said I know I am." De-spite Marshal's insistence that Brown was a fugitive, a neighbor in the city explained that "she did not act like a runaway" but instead moved openly about the streets. In one final act of defiance before striking out entirely on her own, Brown had a testy exchange with Miller, laughing and saying "she would have to live where her wages could be paid to her." "Well you will have to live somewhere else," Miller shot back. "I hired you of Mr Marshal and must pay him."[78]

Emeline Wedge and her younger sister initiated one of the last cases that the emancipation commissioners heard and surely its most intriguing. Al-though Wedge—like her two small children (Martha Ann Elizabeth and George Washington), her sister (Alice Thomas), and her mother (Mary Thomas)—belonged to Alexander McCormick, she was married to a free black man. Emeline's husband, George Wedge, had lived in McCormick's household for more than six years before taking up residence with his par-ents less than a mile away. George Wedge continued to work for McCormick, hauling and marketing farm produce. Until shortly before the emancipation bill became law, the women and children lived in the home that McCormick and his wife shared with their enslaved and hired laborers, black and white. McCormick's farmhouse, stable, outbuildings, and pens for hogs and cattle were in Washington County, some 100 to 150 yards inside the District line. McCormick hoped to evade the law by throwing up a hastily constructed

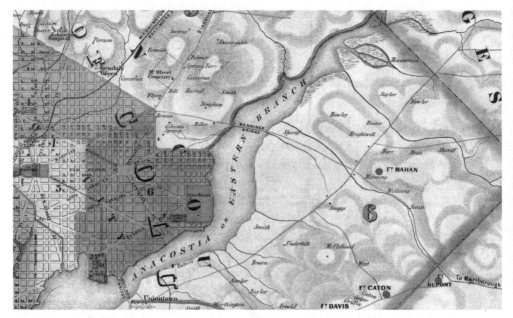

Figure 5.2 From E. G. Arnold, *Topographical Map of the Original District of Columbia and Environs Showing the Fortifications around the City of Washington.* The farm of Alexander McCormick (spelled Macommick on the map) lies in the upper-right corner, just east of where the Eastern Branch crosses the District Line. Courtesy of the Library of Congress Geography and Map Division, LCCN-88690604.

dwelling—witnesses later described it as a "quarter"—about 100 yards on the Maryland side of the line and ordered the woman and children to move there (see figure 5.2). Emeline, her children, and Alice Thomas did reluctantly, but Mary Thomas refused.

Moving the women and children to Maryland was the first step in McCormick's plot. The second and trickier step involved confining their labor strictly to the Maryland side. He devised elaborate schemes, such as employing a free black woman to unpen the cattle from their enclosure in Washington County and walk them to the border, where Emeline and Alice took over, leading them to the pasture in Maryland. At the end of the day, they reversed the steps. In spite of McCormick's threats, the women found it necessary to cross the line, for instance, when a stray cow left the meadow and headed back toward the pen. On occasion, Emeline and Alice played McCormick's rule to their advantage. Once, for example, they informed a hired laborer that they could not help him tend the hogs because their master forbade them to cross into the District. Some tasks required McCormick to bend his own rules. During the bean season of early summer, Emeline and Alice joined their mother and McCormick's wife at the kitchen table of the farmhouse and shelled what they had picked, just as they had in prior years. George Wedge normally picked up the produce and carried it to market, but on one occasion when he overlooked a basket, Emeline and Alice brought it to the Wedge home.

By midsummer, the charade began to wear thin. Having refused to move to the quarter in the spring, Mary Thomas took advantage of the provisions of the supplemental law and petitioned for a certificate of freedom on her own behalf on July 26. The commissioners heard and approved her case the same day, uncontested by McCormick.[79] Sometime during the summer George Wedge's mother took ill, and he asked McCormick's permission for Emeline and Alice to care for her overnight, and McCormick consented. For the rest of the summer and throughout the fall, the young women would arrive each evening, "sometimes before candlelight sometimes just after sunset," and then leave in the morning "when it was light." During most of that time the children remained with their grandfather Wedge.[80] On several occasions, Mc-Cormick's wife also kept vigil, once having brought a "mustard plaster" to relieve the pain from what eventually proved to be a fatal illness. After her mother-in-law died, Emeline ignored repeated entreaties "to bring [the] children home" to the McCormick's farm.[81]

Early in September, Emeline and Alice submitted petitions for certificates of freedom and the commissioners held a hearing. McCormick snubbed the summons to appear because "he believed the law to be unconstitutional and he was willing to bide his time" until it was voided. Witnesses—including Mc-Cormick's neighbors—testified that the two women had worked in the District after as well as before April 16. The commissioners ruled in their favor the same day. In mid-December, McCormick underwent a change of heart and decided to challenge the decision, and the commissioners agreed to re-open the case. With fresh determination to assert his rights, he participated fully in the second round of proceedings, testifying and cross-examining the other witnesses in an attempt to establish that Emeline, Alice, and the children neither lived nor worked in the District. On December 30, 1862, the commissioners rendered a decision, dismissing McCormick's claim. The makeshift quarter he constructed on the Maryland side of the line, they concluded, "could scarcely be said to be inhabitable." What is more, McCormick himself had directed the women to carry "vegetables from the farm" to George Wedge for him to take to market. The ruling affirmed that the petitioners were "entitled to their freedom." Holding fast to the conviction that the women were "his Slaves" who had "absconded from the State of Maryland," McCormick disputed "the effect & correctness" of the ruling, but in vain.[82]

Had the commissioners accepted McCormick's version of the facts, Emeline, her children, and her sister would have been remanded to his custody under Maryland's slave code. From April 16 until December 30, the fear of such an outcome must have haunted them through the daily chores of a full agricultural year. Clearly, their ingenuity and persistence helped achieve the freedom that the law promised. The routine patterns of work on the farm and the entwined lives of the people who performed it contributed to that outcome, sometimes inadvertently. Ultimately, the extended illness and death of George Wedge's mother helped give the lie to McCormick's version of affairs, thereby bolstering the case for freedom of her daughter-in-law and grandchildren. In the end, McCormick could not sustain the fiction that slavery and freedom could follow the surveyor's invisible line through his property any more than he could alter the routine, daily interactions that entangled him and his wife with three generations of the Wedge and Thomas families, free and enslaved. Old habits undermined his effort to thwart the dawn of a new day for Emeline, Alice, and the children.[83]

The imperfectly executed emancipation in the District of Columbia reverberated through time and space. In the summer of 1863, when Colonel William Birney first began recruiting black soldiers in the state of Maryland, he learned that some unknown number of men, women, and children who were "entitled to their freedom in the District of Columbia and persons claimed as slaves by rebels or rebel sympathizers" were being held in slave pens in Baltimore. Birney liberated the captives, enlisting the men into military service. The women and children, according to a report in the *Christian Recorder,* "found comfortable homes among the friends in the city."[84] When Birney and his men visited Camlin's Slave Pen, the inmates they liberated included Lena Harrod and Rachel Harrod, whom Congressman Owen Lovejoy had referenced in the House debate over the emancipation bill in April 1862. Birney's roster did not list Lena's infant, who presumably died at some point during the intervening fifteen months.[85]

––––––––

The confined space of a Union military hospital produced one of the most searing indictments of slavery and emancipation's promise for the future of the entire Civil War era. Spotswood Rice left his home in Glasgow, Missouri, during the winter of 1863–64 to enlist in the Sixty-Seventh U.S. Colored Infantry at Benton Barracks, St. Louis, the rendezvous point for the three black regiments being raised in the state. He was a literate tobacco roller and manager of his owner's farm. In September 1864, Rice was recuperating from rheumatism contracted the previous spring. The extended stay offered him the opportunity to write to his two enslaved daughters, Mary and Corra, and to the woman who claimed Mary as her property.[86] To be sure, the letters are remarkable for the love he communicated to his children and the hatred he harbored toward Mary's enslaver. But without his hospitalization and the particular circumstances that the hospital setting presented, he might never have penned them at all.

Rice addressed his daughter's owner familiarly as "Kittey diggs" without the customary "Miss" and declared her to be his enemy, a transgression that before the war likely would have prompted a severe whipping, if not worse. He upbraided her for not permitting his daughter to join him and the rest of their family in St. Louis. He boasted that he and an army of U.S. soldiers by his side would free his daughter and "exacute vengencens on them that holds my Child." After reminding her that he had once offered to buy his daughter, he now advised that she "hold on to hear as long as you can" but remember that "the longor you keep my Child from me the longor you will have to burn in hell and the qwicer youll get their." "This whole Government gives chear to me," he concluded, "and you cannot help your self." Rice's view of the war and its consequences was apocalyptic, and he was fully prepared to play the role of avenging angel. To his daughters, Rice spoke tenderly, affirming his intention to rescue them. He condemned "Your Miss Kaitty" for accusing him of trying to steal Mary, and he advised that "You tell her from me that She is the frist Christian that I ever hard say that aman could Steal his own child especially out of human bondage."[87]

Rice was among the lucky black recruits from Missouri. He, unlike scores of his comrades, survived the diseases that beset the men after they left their homes for the enlistment rendezvous. He was doubly lucky in that his hospitalization prevented him from being deployed to Louisiana in June 1864. Posted at Morganza, some fifty miles above Baton Rouge, the Missourians faced the Mississippi River to the east and dense swamps to the west. By October, 488 of the original 1,035 men in Rice's regiment had died of disease, and an additional 53 had been discharged, most for medical reasons. The men in the two other regiments fared just as poorly owing to their compromised health when they left Missouri and the relentless labor to which they were assigned in Louisiana's unhealthy environment.[88]

The raw power of Rice's words disguises the obvious influence that the confined space of Benton Barracks Hospital had on his view of the world undergoing revolutionary change. At Kitty Diggs's home, where Mary Rice lived and worked, he had experienced the emotional pain of pleading for the release of his child, only to be flatly rejected. In the confines of the post office in Glasgow, Missouri, where Diggs's brother, the postmaster, knew not just the names and addresses of the residents but also the handwriting of regular correspondents, he could spy at a glance that Rice's letter to his sister spelled trouble. He forwarded it to military authorities for action. But most of all, for Rice's plot to reach the advanced stage that it did almost required

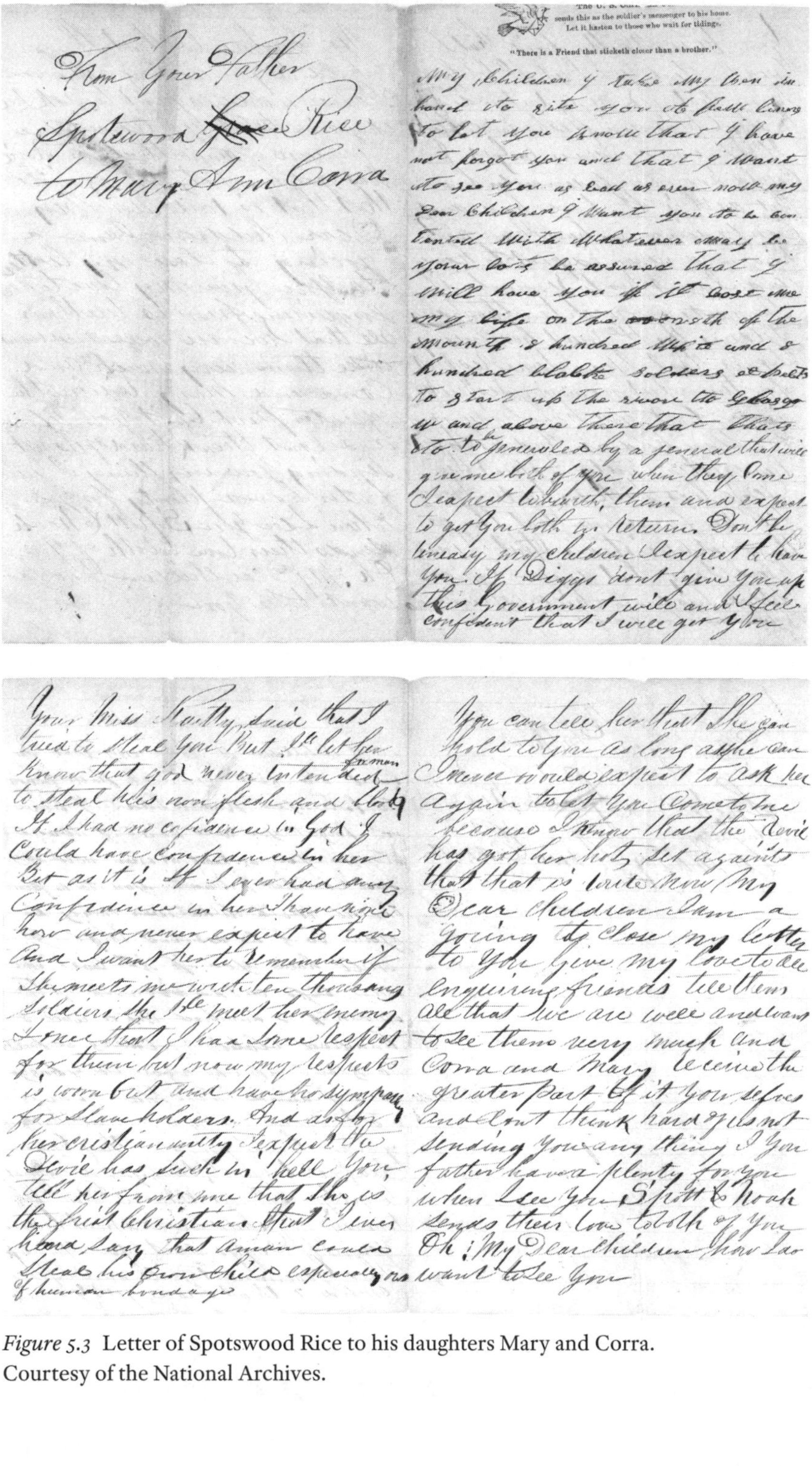

From Your Father
Spotswood ~~Rice~~ Rice
to Mary Am Corra

The U. S. ... sends this as the soldier's messenger to his home. Let it hasten to those who wait for tidings.

"There is a Friend that sticketh closer than a brother."

My Children I take my pen in hand to rite you a few lines to let you know that I have not forgot you and that I want to see you as bad as ever now my Dear Children I want you to be contented with whatever may be your lots be assured that I will have you if it cost me my life on the 28th of the mounth 8 hundred White and 8 hundred black solders expects to start up the rivore to Glasgow and above there thats to be jeined by a regiment that will give me both of you when they Come I expect to be with them and expect to get you both in return. Dont be uneasy my children I expect to have you. If Diggs dont give you up this Government will and I feel confident that I will get you

Your Miss Kaitty said that I tried to steal you But I'll let her know that god never intended for man to steal his own flesh and blood. If I had no cofidence in God I could have confidence in her But as it is If I ever had any Confidence in her I have none now and never expect to have And I want her to remember if she meets me with ten thousand soldiers she will meet her enemy I once thought that I had some respect for them but now my respects is worn out and have no sympathy for Slaveholders. And as for her cristianantty I expect the Devil has such in hell You tell her from me that she is the frist Christian that I ever hard say that aman could steal his own child especially out of human bondage

You can tell her that She can hold to you as long as she can I never would expect to ask her again to let you come to me because I know that the devil has got her hot set againsts that that is write now My Dear children I am a going to close my letter to you Give my love to all enquiring friends tell them all that we are well and want to see them very much and Corra and Mary receive the greater part of it you sefves and dont think hard of us not sending you any thing I you father have a plenty for you when I see you Spott & Noah sends their love to both of you Oh! My Dear children how I do want to see you

Figure 5.3 Letter of Spotswood Rice to his daughters Mary and Corra. Courtesy of the National Archives.

the enabling environment of a military hospital such as Benton Barracks. Relieved from the normal duties of a soldier, Rice had ample time at his disposal. But time alone was not enough, even for a man who had already mastered the arts of spelling and writing. The letter to Kitty Diggs was on plain stationery and entirely in Rice's handwriting, but the one to his daughters bore the letterhead of the U.S. Christian Commission, and more than four-fifths of it is written in a different handwriting, likely that of a hospital attendant employed by the commission. Apparently taking the pen from Rice midsentence, at the point where he neared exhaustion, the scribe wrote the rest of the letter in the words he dictated (see figure 5.3).

In time, Rice and his children were reunited. He became an ordained minister in the AME Church after the war, serving the small black communities in Kansas, Colorado, Wyoming, and New Mexico.[89] Remarkably, Rice's daughter Mary recounted her memories of slavery to an interviewer with the Works Progress Administration in 1937. At the time she was living in St. Louis County, Missouri. She proudly referenced her father's military service as well as that of her husband, her brother, and her son (the lattermost of whom was stationed in the Philippines at the time). "I love army men," she concluded. "I love a man who will fight for his rights, and any person that wants to be something."[90] The confined space of a Civil War military hospital provided a window into the mind and heart of one such freedom fighter, her father, Spotswood Rice.

Chapter 6

Tremors and Whirlpools

War tends to exaggerate what human societies have known from at least the time of the agricultural revolution—namely, that physical space reflects what the people who possess it choose to make of it. In modern Western societies, where land and other features of the natural environment are considered property, owners may dispose of it as they please. Even in peacetime, disputes over the possession and use of land often assume political connotations, but in war, control over physical space serves as one of the markers of the relative strength of the disputants. At the end of a war, the victor may take complete control over the territory of the vanquished, and stalemates that result in negotiated settlements generally include the disposition of land. War often renders space unstable, subjecting it to the immediate goals of the party that occupies it. Both by accident and by design, military operations alter space. Although Civil War armies did not go so far as salting the earth, as the Roman conquerors of Carthage reportedly did, they wrought permanent changes to the earth's surface.[1]

———

After the attack on Fort Sumter, Union military strategists moved quickly to defend the national capital. Legend has it that the first blood shed in defense of the Union belonged to a black man named Nicholas Biddle. Biddle was born into slavery in Delaware in the 1790s and he escaped to Pennsylvania during the 1830s, settling in Pottsville. Having befriended members of the local militia companies, he planned to accompany them to Washington to defend the nation's capital after Fort Sumter. Denied permission to enlist, Biddle volunteered as the servant of an officer in one of the units. On April 18, 1861, while changing trains in Baltimore, the Pennsylvanians encountered an angry mob of Confederate sympathizers and he suffered a laceration to his head. The wound was not debilitating, and Biddle remained with the company for the rest of its three-month term of service. By 1864, he had gained notoriety for his experience at Baltimore. By then, none could deny the central role that black Americans occupied in the momentous events that Nicholas Biddle's bandaged head had portended at the outset of the war.[2]

On April 19, 1861, as Massachusetts troops passed through Baltimore, mobs again attacked, this time with far bloodier results: four soldiers and twelve civilians lay dead and scores of others injured.[3] Some 200 of the city's "*most respectable people of color"* offered to help restore peace, but authorities demurred. The incidents gave Northerners a clear view into the divided loyalties in the Border States and raised new concerns about the fate of Lincoln's government if rebel sympathizers gained full control over Maryland. Accordingly, as a brigade of Massachusetts militiamen rushed to Washington, their commander, General Benjamin F. Butler, a prominent Democratic politician, decided to bypass Baltimore in favor of Annapolis, Maryland's capital, as an alternate rail route to Washington. On April 23, in his first official act, Butler offered his services to Governor Thomas H. Hicks "in suppressing, most promptly and effectively, any insurrection," such as the one reportedly being planned by the "negro population of this neighborhood." He wished to reassure both political leaders and "all classes of persons that the forces under my command are not here in any way to interfere with, or countenance any interference with, the laws of the State," by which, of course, he meant the laws of slavery.[4]

Upon learning of Butler's offer, Massachusetts governor John A. Andrew took exception to the use of the state's troops for that purpose. "The matter of servile insurrection among the community in arms against the Federal Union," the governor insisted, "is no longer to be regarded by our troops in a political, but solely in a military point of view." Thus, it represented "one of the inherent weaknesses of the enemy" that should be exploited, not neutralized. In reply, Butler explained that after offering "to put down a white mob" in Baltimore he could hardly permit "a black one any preference in the breach of the laws." Elaborating, Butler made clear that he abhorred slave insurrection, citing Saint-Domingue as an example of what might result. He even declared that he would make common cause with Confederate forces if necessary to suppress a slave rebellion.[5]

Military and civil authorities soon realized that Maryland's enslaved people had no desire to foment insurrection and thereby risk provoking the wrath of the men they hoped might set them free. With Maryland's political geography destabilized by secession and by the arrival of soldiers from the abolitionist hotbed of Massachusetts, freedom seekers did not have to wait long or look far for sympathizers. But they soon learned that breaking the chains of slavery was not only a risky business but also a messy one. Escape often involved multiple attempts, some of which ended voluntarily and others of which resulted in capture, in either case with consequences that might include death.[6] What is more, flight was too dangerous to try on the spur of the moment without providing for loved ones and formulating contingency plans. Success often involved being able to blend in with rather than stand out from the world. It also required an ability to suspend time, enduring hardship for days or months on end and knowing that the consequences of actions often manifested themselves slowly. Most enslaved persons had already learned these lessons.

Notwithstanding General Butler's affirmation of his true intentions, the mere presence of Massachusetts troops in Maryland upset the traditional balance of power among masters, slaves, and state and local authorities. As Union soldiers moved toward Washington—with New Englanders and New Yorkers approaching from the northeast, midwesterners from the northwest, and Pennsylvanians from both directions—and as they established camps in and around Washington, they represented a mobile authority that could potentially be used against masters and could create a state of quasi freedom independent of the constraints of slavery. Almost overnight, military units turned into a magnetic force attracting those who would be free. New England troops showed an early dislike for slaveholders and the dirty work they expected of the soldiers. So did men from the northern sections of Ohio, Indiana, and Illinois who were in the vanguard of troops sent to defend the capital. Slaves who would be free set their bearings accordingly.

———————

In the early days of the war, freedom seekers hoped that putting both distance and countervailing authority between themselves and their owners would constitute the all-important first step in achieving their goal. In doing so, they created spaces where the laws of war allowed for a suspension of slaveholders' prerogatives without doing away with them. Army camps—just like ships on the sea—were self-contained entities that existed outside conventional space and time while at the same time functioning within the real world. Although individual fugitive slaves could not fully control these novel spaces, they quickly realized that neither could their masters.

The first units that arrived to defend Washington consisted largely of ninety-day militiamen with little experience and varying degrees of discipline. Over time, officers and men learned each other's habits and the appropriate ways of interacting both with each other and with various civilian constituencies. They did this within the semiporous boundaries of military camps. Although a combination of regulation and custom prescribed their physical layout and specified the exact times for performing certain activities, the inhabitants could also exert a certain amount of discretion. The pattern of interactions between the volunteer regiments and the civilian population of Maryland quickly demonstrated that although officers might be inclined to give respectful hearings to persons in search of alleged fugitives, enlisted men gave cover to the freedom seekers and hurled insults, if not objects, in the direction of owners and their agents. In short, the soldiers reset the boundaries of the camps.

Confident that the federal troops and the government they represented would grant shelter and protection, refugees from Maryland and Virginia began making their way to Washington. Fugitives from Virginia ran the gauntlet even before they reached the Long Bridge across the Potomac River into the city. They contended with hunger, exposure to the elements, and rivers obstructing their paths, often with irate owners and Confederate soldiers in hot pursuit. One group of refugees told a shocked African American minister of even having to abandon small children "to facilitate their flight."[7] In July 1861, the military governor of Washington instructed a justice of the peace to consider the newcomers from Virginia "as Contrabands," protect them, and put them to work. Military authorities in Alexandria also offered protection and employment.[8] Fugitives from the loyal state of Maryland, in contrast, faced a very different reception.

In late June, for instance, several Ohio regiments were accused of "practising a little of the abolition system of protecting the runaway" when agents of a Montgomery County slaveholder came away from the camps empty-handed. The soldiers were "so violent," one owner confessed, "that he would rather lose his negro than *risk his life* by going among them again."[9] Because comparatively few Northern soldiers thoroughly believed in "the abolition system," fugitives who did nothing more than appeal to the presumed antislavery sentiments of the soldiers took a huge risk, but it was one that they were willing to take. Soldiers offered shelter and protection to the fugitives, often with the full or tacit approval of their company officers. Yet the owners of accused runaways also continued to enjoy success when they requested relief from regimental and brigade commanders.[10]

The fugitives achieved a real breakthrough when they realized that providing service for their hosts might extend their stay. In the summer of 1861, Charles B. Calvert, a Maryland congressman from one of the state's leading families, complained to the secretary of war that his constituents were having problems "retaining their Slaves at home, in consequence of the tempting offers made to them by some of the volunteer regiments."[11] As the problem grew rapidly worse, Calvert demanded that the commander of the Military District of Washington order "the immediate arrest of all Slaves now found in any Camps either in Maryland or Virginia and their confinement in Some place of Safety until their owners can reclaim them."[12] The city jailer in Washington willingly complied. When the guards at the bridge across the Eastern Branch could not be persuaded to look the other way, freedom seekers simply made their way across the river's shallows farther upstream and entered the District from the north.

Not beholden to the established political, economic, and social elites, the Northerners believed that the national emergency gave them a claim to the services of the slaves that overrode that of the owners. They quickly opened unofficial lines of communication with the enslaved that bypassed the slave-holders and the military brass alike. George E. Stephens, a freeborn black man whose family had fled Southampton County, Virginia, following Nat Turner's 1831 rebellion, served as cook and servant to an officer in a volunteer unit from Pennsylvania. While camped in Maryland during the early months of the war, Stephens helped provide shelter to freedom seekers, advised them about how best to gain admission into Union lines, and in one case found employment with the regiment for a man whose owner had been particularly abusive. Although Stephens deplored the bitterness of feelings that many soldiers harbored toward the suffering slaves, he took "great pleasure" in witnessing how they challenged slave catchers and helped spirit freedom seekers to safety.[13] Thanks to the soldiers, the critical dynamic at the center of the master-slave relationship began to unravel.

Black citizens of Washington took up the cause of defending alleged fugitives, and through the fall of 1861 and into the winter of 1861–62 kept daily vigil at the Circuit Court, haranguing owners who sought court orders to apprehend alleged runaways and occasionally freeing captives. In early December the secretary of state reminded military and civil officials that the Confiscation Act required them to protect fugitives who had been employed in Confederate service, and instructed them to stop arresting persons merely "upon the presumption, arising from color, that they are fugitives from service or labor."[14] Indeed, the incarceration of suspected runaways in the city jail, which the secretary of the interior had likened to "the black-hole of Calcutta," prompted widespread coverage in the press and, in turn, a national outcry. In mid-December, men and women from a Pennsylvania town begged Congress to act, claiming that the inmates were being denied "the comforts of life, to which every prisoner in a civilized land is entitled." "They are ragged & almost naked," the petitioners reported, "hungry, have no fire, & not even a pillow, on which to lay their heads, & are filthy & being devoured by vermin." A congressional investigation confirmed the allegations, including dreadful overcrowding, the use of cruel punishments, the incarceration of slaves for "safe-keeping" and of free black persons on flimsy charges, and a racketeering scheme whereby jailors, military officers, and slave catchers divided the fees for apprehending freedom seekers.[15] The stench of these practices reached President Lincoln himself.[16]

————

In these circumstances, freedom seekers experienced space not strictly as fixed and firm but also as shifting and malleable. The case of the freedom seeker John Boston reveals strong symbolic associations as well. During the fall of 1861, Boston left his wife, Elizabeth, and other family members behind in Anne Arundel County, Maryland, and found shelter with a volunteer regiment from New York. On January 12, 1862, he wrote to his wife that "this Day i can Adres you thank god as a free man." Having escaped "the Slavers Lash," he proudly announced that he was "With a very nice man and have All that hart Can Wish." Boston noted cryptically that he had "had a little truble in giting away" but quickly added that "as the lord led the Children of Isrel to the land of Canon So he led me to a land Whare freedom Will rain in spite Of earth and hell." He longed to see his wife and commended her for choosing "the Wise plan Of Serving the lord," which likely glosses over what must have been a heart-wrenching conversation about whether she should accompany him or remain behind with their child Daniel and "Father and Mother," to whom he wished to convey his love.[17]

Like most men and women who escaped the house of bondage, Boston framed the account of his deliverance in time and space, but with a special twist. First, as to place: the land to which the Lord had led him, "Whare freedom Will rain in spite Of earth and hell," was the Confederate state of Virginia, whose capital and chief city, Richmond, served as the seat of government of the upstart nation dedicated to perpetual slavery. It was the space occupied by the Fourteenth Regiment at any given time. While the regiment was at rest, its camp was clearly defined, with a fixed perimeter secured by armed guards—temporary, perhaps, but real nonetheless. As the regiment moved, Boston continued to enjoy its protection despite having abandoned the fixed space of the camp. The "land" to which Boston referred was metaphorical more so than actual. As to time: John Boston's clock operated on providential time. Looking backward, he likened his own escape to that of the ancient Israelites who fled Egyptian slavery to the Promised Land. Looking forward, he hoped to meet his wife again on earth but contented himself in knowing that, if not, they would reunite in "heven Whare Jesas ranes." The quest for freedom compressed providential time and conventional time together and overrode the distinctions between Union and Confederate territory and, for that matter, between earth and heaven.[18]

As federal forces advanced from the Union's Border Slave States into the adjacent Confederate states, similar scenes played out but with the slaveholders unable to claim loyalty as grounds for returning their escaped slaves. Faced with growing numbers of freedom seekers, federal commanders such as Henry Halleck in the Department of the West, William T. Sherman in the Department of the Cumberland, and George B. McClellan, first in the Army of the Ohio and then the Army of the Potomac, issued orders prohibiting their entry into military lines. But congressional legislation that banned members of the armed forces from returning alleged fugitives created openings for officers and soldiers who wanted to undermine slavery or simply to gain some relief from annoying camp chores.[19] For their part, the refugees associated even greater possibilities with the Union soldiers and the space they occupied, beyond food, shelter, and protection from their masters.

The enslaved man William H. Robinson imagined a promised land, in both figurative and literal senses of the term. As he assisted Union soldiers in liberating enslaved people near Greenville, Tennessee, in the fall of 1863, he hesitated. "I was inviting [them] to liberty," he pondered, "yet I had not a shelter in all the world to put my head save the canopy of Heaven. But I had heard of a country where all men were free, and like Bunyan's Pilgrim I had started to make it my home."[20] Like John Boston, Robinson spoke figuratively. The country he described could not have been Tennessee, which, as he knew, was exempt from the Emancipation Proclamation. He had no idea where the army was heading next. Robinson's freedom, like that of Boston and tens of thousands of other freedom seekers, existed within the aura created by the armed forces of the United States.

Perhaps ironically, the Confederate mobilization also transformed the social landscape of slavery. Although political as well as military leaders repeatedly insisted that slaveholders' rights to their human property were sacrosanct, officers and soldiers had other objectives, often the self-serving one of relief from onerous camp chores. In the places and at the times that the slave regime grew unstable, soldiers ignored the formality of free papers and passes before putting black people to work, much as their Yankee counterparts did.

The Confederate mobilization of black industrial workers further illustrates the process. From early in the war, the government had hired enslaved men and women in the production of arms, ammunition, clothing, leather goods, and other articles of war. The facilities were located in the inland cities and towns: Richmond and Petersburg, Virginia; Raleigh, Durham, Charlotte, and Greensboro, North Carolina; Columbia, South Carolina; Augusta, Macon, and Columbus, Georgia; and Selma and Montgomery, Alabama. At first, most of these laborers were unskilled, but by 1864, as exemptions for skilled workers under the 1862 Conscription Act came to an end, the number of black artisans in the government shops began to grow. Although the officers in charge of these operations often advertised far and wide to fill their needs, they relied primarily on local markets in hired slaves.[21] The circuits that connected production facilities with nearby villages and plantations carried information about the war as well as people.

Employing hired slaves in Confederate industry stretched the parameters of traditional slave hiring in new directions. The facilities made important contributions to the larger war effort. Both the owners of the hired slaves and the hired slaves themselves came to understand this urgency, and each learned to exploit the associated vulnerability somewhat differently. Enslaved workers could ally with their masters to bargain for various privileges, such as specific arrangements regarding shelter, food, and clothing, or the privilege to work overtime for pay, or to visit home on holidays or weekends. Conversely, they could ally with the hiring authority to permit family members to visit the installation or, in some cases, to take up residence there. In short, these unprecedented circumstances created by the war introduced the prospect that a new external authority could insert itself into the traditional bilateral relationship between master and slave. And the facilities themselves—like army camps and other such artifacts of the war—created pliable spaces where enslaved people could begin to explore new ways of thinking and behaving that looked beyond slavery.[22]

———

Water occupied a central place, both literally and figuratively, in the history of emancipation during the Civil War. Of course, water has been associated symbolically with human passages from ancient times to the present. Crossing the Jordan River marked the start of the ancient Israelites' ascent as a people. Christian baptism washes away original sin and initiates the participant into the faith. Long before the Middle Passage added a shuddering new framework of meaning, water figured prominently in African beliefs and practices, as it continues to do in African and African-diasporic cultures.[23] In the antebellum United States, crossing the Ohio River symbolized the passage to freedom in perhaps the most celebrated novel of the nineteenth century, Harriet Beecher Stowe's *Uncle Tom's Cabin*. For the thousands of real-life freedom seekers after whom Eliza was modeled, the passage was more than fictional.

Water set the boundary of the Confederacy along its northern, eastern, and southern perimeters, and the Mississippi River flowed north to south through its middle. In every coastal Confederate state from Texas to Virginia, one or more major rivers connected the interior to the sea. Although military strategists on both sides understood the importance of defeating the opponent's armies, collaboration between military and naval forces figured in the operational plans of both the United States and the Confederate States. When Union naval forces gained control over the Mississippi after the victories at Vicksburg and Port Hudson in July 1863, the balance of power in the North American heartland tipped decisively against the Confederacy. As Winfield Scott's much maligned Anaconda Plan had predicted, this left the rebellion more vulnerable than at any time earlier. The Union blockade of the coast interdicted most international trade through the port cities of Wilmington,

Charleston, Savannah, Mobile, and Galveston. As a result, the Confederacy became ever more dependent on the production of essential war goods at home, thereby diverting valuable resources—including human resources—from other uses.

Just as federal strategists exploited the rivers of the Confederacy in the pursuit of victory, enslaved people took advantage of inland waterways in the pursuit of freedom. The two initiatives quickly converged. In August 1861, Thomas T. Craven, commander of the Potomac Flotilla, reported to the secretary of the navy that "four colored men" had rowed "a small skiff" to his ship bearing valuable intelligence. Two of the men had been "employed helping to build batteries," the guns for which were "on their way from Richmond and are daily expected." In customary fashion, Craven sent the men to the Washington Navy Yard.[24] This was but one of the many such reports that prompted Navy Secretary Gideon Welles to encourage the captains of naval vessels to enlist able-bodied "contraband" men into service.[25]

From Welles's perspective, like that of his counterpart Simon Cameron in the War Department, the government was obliged to protect the fugitives but not to support them in idleness. But whereas enlisting black men into the army appeared to violate the whites-only provisions of the 1792 Militia Acts (as well as, some argued, the tenets of civilized warfare), black men's service in the navy carried no such stigma. In time, water provided the route to freedom for some 8,000 slave-born men of the roughly 18,000 men of African ancestry who served in the navy during the war.[26] The watery routes to freedom included the blue waters of the Atlantic Ocean, Chesapeake Bay, the Sounds of North Carolina, Tampa Bay, Mobile Bay, and the Gulf of Mexico. They also included the brown waters of rivers in the seceded states that bore such names as Rappahannock, James, Mississippi, Tennessee, Cumberland, and Red, where Union gunboats operated.

From December 1860 through May 1861, as the states that eventually formed the Confederacy left the Union one by one, their African American residents found themselves in the unenviable position wherein their owners expected loyalty to the Confederacy while their own political sensibilities aligned with the Union. For those who lived close to an interior river or the coast, water sometimes marked the border between the Union and the Confederacy, but one that could be readily transgressed. It was not coincidental that on the morning of March 12, 1861, one week after President Abraham Lincoln's inaugural address had referenced "the safeguards of liberty," four enslaved men commandeered a boat and made their way to Fort Pickens, a federal installation on a barrier island in Pensacola Bay, Florida. In reporting the incident, the commander of the fort noted that the men came "entertaining the idea that we were placed here to protect them and their freedom." "I did what I could to teach them the contrary," he added; in fact, that afternoon he carried them across the bay and "delivered them to the city marshal to be returned to their owners." Undeterred, four more men arrived at the fort that evening; they too were returned to the city the next morning.[27]

As human societies had learned long before the nineteenth century, waterways could serve apparently opposite goals: as channels for joining people and places together and as barriers for keeping them apart. These functional roles could change over time and even operate simultaneously, as prewar commercial activity along the Atlantic and Gulf coasts and the great inland waterways of North America demonstrated. The Ohio River, the line of demarcation between the free and the slave states, also served as a key route for carrying Northern grains and manufactured goods into the South. And the coastal trade that brought Southern cotton and sugar to the Northeast also carried enslaved people from Baltimore, Alexandria, and Richmond to New Orleans for sale to the plantations that raised those products. The increasing volume of trade drew black men and women into maritime work as deckhands and firemen, as cooks and servants, and even as engineers and pilots. Enslaved persons were often bound to the vessel on which they worked, either owned by or leased to the boat's owner or its captain.[28]

From early in the war, black sailors and boatmen learned how the waterborne trade in goods that supported the Confederacy ensnared them in a quandary that pitted their livelihoods and their own political sensibilities against those of their owners and employers. The Union's Potomac Flotilla routinely arrested black men engaged in smuggling goods and people between Maryland and Virginia and from Chesapeake Bay up the Rappahannock River. Enslaved men living in both states were pressed into this business, rowing when and where their owners directed. The line separating their prewar working lives from what they now did may have appeared faint, but it was real. Illicit trade was a punishable offense, and lives hung in the balance when federal forces pursued suspected smugglers.[29]

The Confederate government also took to leasing boats with their crews outright, at times even impressing them into service. African American pilots who knew the waters of the south Atlantic coast and the Gulf of Mexico were also lured into Confederate service, not always willingly. When Robert Small (later Smalls) testified before the AFIC, he disingenuously described himself as "a rigger and Stevedore and not a regular pilot for Charleston harbor." Flag Officer Samuel F. Du Pont, who commanded the South Atlantic Squadron when Smalls and his shipmates performed the "bold feat" of capturing the Confederate supply steamer *Planter*, described him as a man "superior to any who have yet come into the lines." Like other U.S. naval officers, Du Pont valued Smalls's experience on "the inland waters with which he appears to be very familiar" and with which the unfamiliar ventured only at their peril.[30] The Confederates had their own version of just such a hero in the person of Moses Dallas, pilot of the CSS *Savannah*, who suffered a mortal gunshot wound participating in the capture of the USS *Water Witch*.[31] Hundreds of other knowledgeable black watermen guided vessels for the respective belligerents in the coastal waters from Chesapeake Bay to Galveston Bay and along the inland rivers.[32]

Like seafarers in every age and place, free men could fare as poorly as enslaved men did when the owner of the vessel opted for illicit trade. In the spring of 1861, William Ringgold, a free Marylander, worked as a steward on a steamboat out of Baltimore that plied the waters of the Chesapeake and its tributaries. At the start of the war, the boat and its crew were pressed into Confederate service to transport soldiers and enslaved laborers along Virginia's York River in support of Confederate military operations. Only in November did he and two of his fellow crewmen succeed in making their way back to Baltimore.[33] In August 1861, when a federal gunboat overhauled the schooner *Reliance* out of Baltimore, William Posey, a free black man who had "sailed in her for several years," testified that the master of the vessel was "a rank secessionist" who used the vessel to carry contraband goods from Baltimore to Virginia.[34]

The experience of William E. Johnson, a freeborn native of Virginia, mirrored Ringgold's but with a curious twist. When Johnson was a youth, his family had moved successively from one town to the next along the Ohio River until the 1850s, when they settled in Iowa. Johnson knew that the Mississippi River and its tributaries furnished employment for those who could navigate the hazards of steamboats and the hardscrabble people who worked on and around them. New Orleans presented special risks. Louisiana (like other slave states along the Gulf and south Atlantic coasts) required black sailors to carry papers that certified their free status or face incarceration and possible enslavement. Lacking such documents from his native state, Johnson obtained a counterfeit version from the clerk of a Catholic Church in New Orleans who sold copies of the baptismal certificates of freeborn babies who had died in infancy. At the start of the war, Johnson was employed on a steamboat out of St. Louis whose owner leased it along with the services of the crew to the Confederacy. Johnson bided his time until he found an opportunity to escape with a white shipmate. Commandeering a small boat, this real-life version of Huck and Jim set out for New Orleans several hundred miles downriver. Notwithstanding several close calls, the two arrived at their destination, where

Johnson enlisted in the U.S. Navy, reporting his name as Edward Cendyrlin, as it appeared on the baptismal certificate.[35]

Freedom seekers who had access to boats continued to use the rivers of the Confederacy as escape routes as the federal presence on those waters increased.[36] General Samuel R. Curtis, who commanded U.S. forces at Helena, Arkansas, conveyed formerly enslaved people on government transport vessels to freedom at Cairo, Illinois. Among the beneficiaries were those who had belonged to Confederate general Gideon J. Pillow.[37] Military and naval authorities used water as a medium for transporting large numbers of refugees out of the war zone. One such instance was in the Red River Campaign in Louisiana during June 1864, when USS *Lafayette* towed a coal barge with some 600 persons, "both great and small," to safety, as the captain's steward told the tale.[38]

A Confederate raid on Hutchinson Island, South Carolina, in June 1862 illustrates the role that water played in enabling communities of freed people to begin supporting themselves while at the same time facilitating quick access to friend and foe alike. After the removal of federal pickets early in the month, a force of some 300 Confederates, led by a black guide who was formerly employed by the U.S. Army and who knew of the recent troop withdrawal to support operations in Virginia, moved from plantation to plantation searching for the "d—d Yankees," burning dwellings, stealing property, and shooting those who resisted. Navy lieutenant W. T. Truxtun, commander of the U.S. sloop-of-war *Dale* in St. Helena Sound, responded to the alarm that a rebel force had commenced "killing all the negroes."[39]

Knowing that the narrow, shallow, and winding waterways of Big River Creek that led to the scene were impassible for the ship, Truxtun proceeded upstream aboard its tender (a sailboat) accompanied by five small boats propelled by oarsmen. After first encountering "a canoe containing three negroes" who furnished some details of what awaited them, the sailors were then "constantly met by canoes with two or three negroes in them, panic stricken . . . while white flags were to be seen flying from every inhabited point around which were clustered groups of frightened refugees." At one landing they encountered "over one hundred souls, mostly women and children in the utmost distress." After posting a picket guard, the boats began ferrying the refugees, some of whom had been shot or clubbed by the rebels, to safety. Upon returning to transport the remainder, the boatmen witnessed a scene of "the utmost confusion," with people "dashing wildly into the marshes and screaming, 'the Secesh are coming back.'"[40]

Truxtun was incredulous at the rebels' "extreme barbarity to negroes, most of whom were living on the plantation where they had been born, peacefully tilling the ground for their support, which their masters by deserting had denied them, and who were not even remotely connected with the hated Yankee." Despite the officer's warning of potential danger, the freed people had "the most perfect faith in the protection of the ship," even though it was "ten or twelve miles away." In the end, about seventy of the island's inhabitants accepted Truxtun's offer of transportation to Hilton Head, but more than thirty of the original number "insisted on remaining" on the island "because it was their home," he explained.[41] The attraction of home coupled with the expectation of federal protection—even at an unsafe distance—could outweigh the danger of Confederate marauders. But in such circumstances, home could hardly be considered safe and secure.

––––––––

Boats signaled the advent of freedom in a figurative as well as a literal sense. In 1862, poet John Greenleaf Whittier penned what became the wildly popular "Song of the Negro Boatmen," his homage to the men who rowed the boats that moved people and goods from island to island in the waters around Port Royal and the nearby Sea Islands. Its opening passage cited the transformation that freedom entailed:

> Oh, praise an' tanks! De Lord he come
> To set de people free;
> An' massa tink it day ob doom;
> An'we ob jubilee.[42]

The boatmen and their songs had long attracted the attention of visitors to the region. When Charlotte Forten arrived at Port Royal to take up her post as a schoolteacher, she planned to have the oarsmen sing the words to Whittier's poem. On one trip to Beaufort to shop for bread, she expressed her disappointment that the boatmen did not sing. "I thought *everybody* sang down here. Certainly every boat crew *ought*."[43]

Not every attempt to escape by water resulted in freedom, as several incidents involving men at Fort Monroe who attempted to rescue their families during the summer of 1864 illustrated. In the first episode, a number of men employed at Fort Monroe and Hampton Hospital persuaded General Edward A. Wild to permit them to undertake an expedition to Smithfield, some twenty miles away by water on the southern shore of the James River. Accompanied by an escort of soldiers, they gathered their families into the boats but "became delayed by the numbers of women and children anxious to follow, whom they packed in extra boats, picked up there, and towed along."

An alarm sounded and a well-armed irregular force intercepted them before they could reach open water, and they "rowed over to the opposite bank and scattered over the marshes." The soldiers barely escaped to tell the tale, but the black liberators and their families did not.[44]

The second incident involved men who had escaped from Surry County, Virginia, nearly thirty miles farther up the James River beyond Smithfield. They received permission to use four government boats to undertake a mission to free their families. With several white accomplices, they proceeded along a creek to their home neighborhood when a band of Confederate regulars discovered and captured them. Arguing that the party had crossed the river "for the purpose of plunder," a rebel officer reported that "18 negroes were killed, wounded, and captured" and that "two white men"—presumed to be their accomplices—"were afterward found dead." The officers justified the decision by the squad leader to administer "lynch parole" to the captives in light of the distance from camp and the presence of Union troops nearby. "This summary treatment has had a very good effect," the officer concluded, in rendering the "villainous negroes . . . pretty shy how and where they land."[45]

Happy endings to such escapes often required a combination of good timing and good luck. Early in December 1861, Lieutenant S. L. Phelps, who commanded USS *Conestoga* on the Cumberland River in Tennessee, dispatched a small boat to rescue a man who had signaled the ship for help from the shore. The man was being "chased by blood hounds in full cry after him" and "by rebel cavalry" intent on "seizing him and taking him to Dover to work upon the fortifications." In January 1863, Confederate forces seized five supply vessels anchored in the Cumberland River, capturing wounded federal officers and soldiers who were on board and destroying the boats and their contents. "The negro crews," according to an account from the scene, "were stripped of their clothing, tied to trees, cow-hided and left to starve on shore."[46]

———

The experience of African American men in the U.S. Navy illustrates the corrosive effect that water had on slavery during the Civil War. Life aboard naval vessels consisted largely of mind-numbing tedium punctuated by the excitement that accompanied a chase. Just as in the days of Admiral Horatio Nelson, the cry of "Sail, Ho!" set hearts beating furiously, and, as the vessels closed, men took their places at their assigned battle stations in anticipation of putting their hours of training into practice: manning great guns; carrying powder and shot from the magazine to the gun deck; and wielding cutlasses to repel boarders, buckets and hoses to douse flames, or axes to cut away splintered spars and tangled rigging. Charles B. Fisher, a freeborn African American steward from Alexandria, Virginia, who served aboard USS *Kearsarge* during the legendary battle with CSS *Alabama* off Cherbourg, France, in June 1864, described the excitement that attended the summons to general quarters. "No man is down hearted," he reported on the day before the engagement. "All the boys are in high glee. Some dancing. Some singing their Saturday songs and some spinning cuffers as usual."[47]

Men who served on vessels of the blockading squadrons experienced similar excitement pursuing blockade runners. When incoming vessels ran aground, men were eager to join the parties that manned small boats to capture what crewmen they could and destroy the vessels. Neither routine shipboard life nor civilian life presented such occasions for men to release pent-up fury in quite the way that destroying blockade runners did. But the work was also dangerous. Confederate troops often captured men who were stranded when adverse winds and tides created breakers that the crews of the small boats could not overpower. Rebel sharpshooters also preyed on the sailors as they moved about the wrecked vessels and then headed back to their ships. John Robert Bond, an English-born seaman of mixed African and Irish parentage who enlisted in the U.S. Navy in 1862, suffered a debilitating gunshot wound to his shoulder in one such incident. After recovering for nearly four months (including a final stint at the naval hospital in Portsmouth, Virginia, where he met the formerly enslaved woman who eventually became his wife), he received a disability discharge.[48]

Because naval vessels operated in the medium of water, constant motion caused by waves, currents, and breezes defined the wartime experience of sailors. Their perspective on emancipation was unique as a result. They served in a hidebound institution whose rigid hierarchy closely approximated that of the antebellum plantation. Indeed, when reformers finally succeeded in abolishing flogging in the naval service in 1850 they made their case in part on the inhumanity of treating free men like slaves. Career naval officers were, as a class, social conservatives, and they had little sympathy for slaves or for abolitionists who wished to destabilize the domestic relations of the South and, by extension, the peace of the nation. That notwithstanding, the secretary of the navy, Gideon Welles, favored abolition, and he quietly but consistently advised the commanders of vessels operating in hostile waters to receive refugees, to enlist into naval service those whose labor was needed, and to transport the rest to places of safety.[49] Black sailors helped advance the work of liberation materially, as the sailor George W. Reed, who served in the Potomac Flotilla, explained. In letters to the *Anglo-African* and the *Christian Recorder*, Reed noted the black sailors' enthusiastic participation in landing parties. "At first there was a little prejudice against our colored men going on shore, but it soon died away." Their bravery and efficiency in liberating persons "from the horrible pit of bondage" and skirmishing with Confederate home guards made believers of their once-skeptical shipmates.[50]

Black men in the naval service could, at times, experience opportunities to develop new skills, to travel to foreign lands and meet fascinating people, and to prepare themselves for civilian life as a free person after the war. Following his September 1862 escape with seven other men from Wilmington, North Carolina, William B. Gould enlisted in the U.S. Navy, and over the next three years he visited all the major coastal cities between North Carolina and Nova Scotia, the Madeira Islands, and the seaports of Spain, Portugal, France, the Netherlands, England, and Ireland. He kept a diary that meticulously recorded how naval service transformed his life. Gould had worked as a skilled carpenter and plasterer in Wilmington and had learned how to read and write before his escape. While serving aboard USS *Cambridge* on blockading duty off the coast of North Carolina, he occasionally "heard from my people" courtesy of refugees from the city. It also appears that some mail made its way from Wilmington to the fleet via New Bern.[51]

Gould's naval experience was exceptional for formerly enslaved men, largely because he and his comrades from Wilmington enlisted directly on board a ship on blockading duty off the coast. The ships on which he served, USS *Cambridge* and USS *Niagara*, were oceangoing gunboats that both officers and sailors alike considered among the elite ships of the service. Their crews were more experienced than those of other vessels in the blockading fleets, with a comparably larger proportion of men from the seaport cities of the northeastern United States who had had prewar nautical experience and a comparably smaller proportion of men of African ancestry. After a prolonged stint in a naval hospital caused by a bout with the measles, Gould pined "to be afloat [once] more." "There is nothing like the whistling wind and the danceing Bark on the Bounding Billow bearing its precious treasure to the shores of some distant clime," he rhapsodized.[52]

Thanks to the intervention of a naval surgeon whose good graces Gould enjoyed, in October 1863 he shipped aboard USS *Niagara* at the start of a cruise to Europe in pursuit of Confederate privateers. Rated as assistant steward for the ship's officers, Gould was at their beck and call in the wardroom, serving them their meals and coffee, and otherwise ministering to their needs at all hours of the day and night. In exchange for such dubious privileges, stewards enjoyed benefits unavailable to their crewmates. When in port, for instance, they typically went ashore daily to purchase fresh food for the officers' mess.[53] William B. Gould's experience, though arguably unusual, was not unique. A skilled artisan, he enjoyed a measure of respect among the officers and the crewmen with whom he served. That notwithstanding, he could not entirely shed the opprobrium attached to the term "contraband" that the navy labeled him and other men who had escaped from slavery throughout the war, even long after it had fallen out of public use.[54] A formerly enslaved man such as he was a curiosity in that he rose to a station that freeborn, experienced, and literate black men might hope to occupy—but one still lower in the naval pecking order than those to which their white shipmates had access.[55]

For the thousands of the formerly enslaved "contrabands" who lacked basic literacy and whose sole prewar experience had been as a plantation or farm laborer, naval service held little opportunity to advance their skills or otherwise prepare for a future in freedom. Instead, their role in the naval service was to perform manual labor. They made up a disproportionate share of the crews of supply ships and coaling schooners that serviced the various squadrons. At Port Royal, South Carolina, the supply base of the South Atlantic Blockading Squadron, they constituted nearly the entire crew assigned to USS *Vermont* (see figure 6.1), a veritable floating warehouse, where they loaded and unloaded crates and barrels of stores, spare parts, weapons, and ammunition for the fleet. Although most of these men had escaped from slavery in South Carolina, Georgia, and Florida, they took full advantage of the opportunities that freedom presented to them, and some learned to read and write. Besides the vital service they performed supplying the ships of the squadron, they also volunteered for missions into the interior to liberate slaves. All the while they picked the brains of any Northerner they encountered who would engage them in conversation.[56] Black sailors and seamen played an especially important role in the transfer of information about the war and what the future might hold. Water brought Northern people and Yankee culture, replete with such consumer goods as Northern newspapers, to the backwaters that antebellum planters had deliberately shielded from such influences. This Northern anointing changed the formerly enslaved people, in some respects permanently.

In the spring of 1864, the War Department and the Navy Department agreed to the transfer of some 800 men from partially filled regiments of U.S. Colored Troops into the navy. The moniker "contrabands" followed them throughout the rest of their service. So did the prejudices that their white shipmates associated with men who had previously been enslaved, as the several hundred men who were assigned to vessels in the Pacific Squadron learned. On USS *St. Mary*, for instance, during the evening dogwatches when men would gather on deck to relax, a rowdy group of white sailors customarily threw gun chocks—the triangular wooden blocks used to prevent guns from rolling—at any black shipmate who dared venture from below. A "serious riot" nearly ensued when the black men threatened retaliation, but the

Figure 6.1 Contrabands aboard U.S. Ship Vermont, *Port Royal, South Carolina.*
Gilman Collection, Gift of The Howard Gilman Foundation, 2005. Courtesy of the
Metropolitan Museum of Art (https://www.metmuseum.org).

captain summoned the guard with muskets loaded to restore order.[57] Thousands of miles from Maryland in the Pacific Ocean, the sailors confronted racial animosity every bit as hateful as what they had experienced at home, but with one major difference. The ship at sea offered them few places to hide and absolutely no way to escape.

A fire on the gunboat *Glide* in the Mississippi Squadron in early February 1863 illuminated the pervasive suppositions of inferiority that followed formerly enslaved sailors wherever they went. At the time, the crew consisted of "8 white men and 30 negro contrabands," and the vessel was undergoing repairs at Cairo, Illinois. The night in question was "a cold one," and a group of black sailors had made a fire in the ash pan near the boilers below decks. Flames somehow worked their way into the hold below, and all efforts to extinguish the blaze proved ineffective. "The cause of the fire is undoubtedly traceable to the character of her crew," concluded the two naval officers who investigated the case, most of whom were "contrabands, sensitive to the cold and reckless of the consequences of building a fire anywhere." The investigators exonerated the officer of the watch, "a young and inexperienced master's mate," and did "not find any want of vigilance or the usual precaution against fire" on the part of the white seamen insofar as "they could not keep the other guard and at the same time watch the lights and the negroes below."[58]

Figure 6.2 Deck of the Gunboat *Hunchback*. Courtesy of the National Archives.

Yet for all the supposed ignorance of the contrabands, the navy found them too useful in the hot, humid, and feverish environment of the Mississippi valley to do without. In July 1863, David D. Porter, commanding officer of the Mississippi Squadron, ordered the masters of vessels under his command to make greater use of contrabands "for the efficiency of the vessels" in light of "the increasing sickness" among white sailors, who "can not stand the southern sun." Accordingly, he stipulated that boats' crews should consist "altogether" of black men and that they should perform every other duty "requiring exposure to the sun," with due precaution taken. Shortages of white crewmen would justify employing black men "to defend the vessels." He emphasized that "none but the best class of negroes should be taken into the service," and that "when qualified" they might "be promoted to second-class firemen, coal heavers, landsmen, ordinary seamen, but not to petty officers." As to their responsibilities aboard vessels, Porter conceded that "they can be stationed at guns when vacancies exist, to pass shot and powder, handle handspikes, at train-tackles and side-tackles, pumps, and fire buckets." But "in all cases," he ordered, "they must be kept distinct from the rest of the crew," even to the extent of being "exercised separately at great guns and small arms." In a gratuitous aside, Porter noted that "great attention will be necessary as respects the cleanliness of the blacks, as they are not naturally clean in their persons."[59]

Six months earlier the crew of Porter's flagship, USS *Blackhawk*, pressed the campaign for good hygiene to the extreme. In a ritual ostensibly designed to bathe contraband recruits who had reached the ship covered in muck—but one that also carried strong overtones of hazing into the naval service—they doused the men with fire hoses. After enduring this initiation in December 1862, Robert Scott died of pneumonia several weeks later.[60] With the liberating potential of water all around them, the U.S. Navy's contrabands struggled mightily but for the most part unsuccessfully to escape the negative associations of their enslaved past. In the nominally integrated naval service, new regulations grafted onto past practices combined to segregate black men and, for many, to make their time in service akin to the slavery from which they had escaped (see figure 6.2).

———

However strong one's passion to be free, fleeing from slavery always presented dangers. When Yankee forces occupied a fixed position with established picket lines, the challenge, as Louis Hughes discovered on two occasions, was to reach it unmolested. But Union soldiers on patrol often bypassed even the most pitiable freedom seekers except when under express orders to assist. In November 1863, the abolitionist commander of the so-called African Brigade in coastal North Carolina wished to avoid all possibility of misunderstanding. General Edward A. Wild pointedly instructed the soldiers about to embark on a "recruiting expedition" to protect "all Africans, including men, women, and children." Permit them to take "their masters' property with them" as well as "axes, scythes, &c., for their defence and horses and wagons for the transportation of their baggage." "When you return," he explained, "march slowly, so as to allow the fugitives to keep up with you."[61]

The following month, Wild led an operation to South Mills and Elizabeth City, North Carolina, which among other things liberated some 2,500 black refugees along with "their baggage, horses, and carts." This count was an estimate, he explained, inasmuch as "their exact numbers" were "impossible to count, as they were constantly coming and going." He was particularly disappointed in the small number of "able-bodied negroes" but reasoned that they "have had ample opportunities for escape heretofore, or have been run over into Dixie."[62] Wild recommended to his superiors that the Union's perimeter be advanced deeper into Confederate territory, which would deny rebel guerrillas the "neutral ground," bring under federal jurisdiction an area of "exceedingly productive tracts," and "attract . . . great numbers of blacks from the region beyond."[63] Wild's observations about the refugees' back-and-forth movements suggest that leaving slavery behind did not involve a simple one-way journey from Confederate to Union lines and from bondage to freedom. Captain Horace James, the superintendent of Negro affairs in the Department of North Carolina, similarly noted that refugees routinely came and went owing to circumstances that neither they nor the federal authorities could control. "The fact is that nothing can be relied on in this District, except the certainty of change," he explained. "What with confederate troops, guerillas, small pox and yellow fever, the negroes (and poor whites as well) have been tossed upon a sea of troubles."[64]

Particularly noteworthy was the Confederate capture of the Union-occupied town of Plymouth, North Carolina, in April 1864, which resulted in the precipitous decline in the number of black refugees in the town from nearly 900 to fewer than 100. With considerable understatement, James concluded that "it was a hard day for the poor negroes." Although "many of the women and children" were evacuated before federal forces surrendered, the captured black soldiers and government employees were "treated with shocking barbarity," either murdered or "remanded back to slavery in the interior."[65] Plymouth, like Warrenton, Virginia, and other such cities that changed hands repeatedly, symbolized the ambiguities inherent in emancipation on the ground. Under Union control, the residents could hope to start new lives in freedom, even when that meant relocation to a safer place, such as Roanoke Island, and the disruptions associated with such a move.[66] Falling into Confederate hands often meant a geographical and existential journey back into slavery—except for black soldiers, whose journey often ended abruptly in death.

Captain James's metaphor of a "sea of troubles" nicely captures the challenges that enslaved people faced in attempting to reach the shores of freedom. It also helps explain why many chose to remain moored to the dock of slavery until they viewed the passage as safe enough to risk the venture. In September 1864, the Northern-born African American sailor George W. Reed struggled to comprehend such inexplicable behavior. On a mission up the Rappahannock River in Virginia, for the purpose of "getting a Union man's family away to go North," the party met "an old colored" man who was carrying "some bacon and hams" to the home of the family the sailors aimed to rescue. Although the encounter "created a great deal of laughter" among his shipmates, that was not the end of their disbelief. A force of rebels opened fire after the sailors reached the farmhouse, forcing them to retreat back to the river. They "succeeded in bringing off the family," he reported, "but had to abandon all the furniture and farming utensils." He was "sorry to say that the colored people belonging to the family refused to come," for reasons he could not understand.[67]

Perhaps even more perplexing to anyone who did not witness it were the cases in which armed combatants agreed to suspend the normal conventions of warfare and to transgress the forbidden no-man's-land that lay between the lines. The correspondent Thomas Morris Chester noted a number of occasions when the "Smoked Yankees" in the Union trenches and the "grayback" Johnnies in the Confederate trenches called makeshift truces to exchange food, tobacco, and newspapers.[68] In January 1865, the rebels put on a "thrilling" display of "cordiality," permitting black soldiers to gather corn from a patch close to their lines that "in their haste" they had failed to harvest the previous fall, a gesture that the Yankees reciprocated. Foraging parties from both sides even met in the field together. "On one of these occasions," Chester reported, "a hog suddenly appeared" and blue- and gray-clad men "joined in the chase with much animation, and upon the best of terms." At last a rebel fired a shot that missed the hog but nearly struck one of the black soldiers. "Halloo, Johnny! what do you mean?" the federal asked. "'I am not shooting at you,' replied grayback, 'but at that other hog.'" Ignoring the insult, the Yankees found the explanation "satisfactory," Chester explained, and they let the rebels have the hog, "the Johnnies being the hungriest."[69] Soldiers often followed rules of their own making, whether civilians understood them or not.

The notion of pliable space helps explain the reports—both at the time and subsequently—of black Confederates. To be sure, Confederate officials did not attempt to organize black men as soldiers until days before the surrender, long beyond the point where even limited numbers of such units might have offered a lifeline to General Robert E. Lee's depleted forces. But the fact remains that the Confederacy, like other slave societies, retained the option to mobilize enslaved men under arms from the start of the contest. That government officials did so sparingly does not negate the fact that they could. Testimony of men such as the Virginian John Parker, who narrated an account of service with a Confederate artillery battery at the first Battle of Bull Run, is instructive. Over the preceding several months, Parker and other enslaved men had been impressed to work on fortifications at Winchester, Fredericksburg, and Richmond when the call came to report for duty at Manassas. He arrived two days before the battle, one of four black men assigned to a battery. The newcomers had barely learned what was expected of them when the fighting commenced. After the battle, the officers directed them to go home; Parker headed for the Yankees instead, after making arrangements for his wife to join him.[70]

Such behavior hardly counts as Confederate patriotism. Nor does that of any of the enslaved servants, cooks, teamsters, and laborers that accompanied every rebel unit—in larger numbers at each successive level of organization from the company to the corps—and who may have discharged weapons in the direction of the Yankees. In the terror of the battlefield and the fog of war, they followed their instincts to survive. "The balls from the Yankee guns fell thick all around," Parker later recalled. He added: "I felt bad all the time, and thought every minute my time would come; I felt so excited that I hardly knew what I was about, and felt worse than dead." Both during and after such engagements, the men were torn: "We wish[ed] to our hearts that the Yankees would whip" the Confederates, he added. But short of that outcome, they bided their time, performing their expected tasks and praying that they never encountered the Yankees on the battlefield—the war's preeminent unstable space—again.[71]

For hundreds of thousands—indeed, several millions—of enslaved men and women, the uncertainty of their future continued until the end of the war. Modern research into the psychology of risk aversion helps explain why persons would choose not to abandon the known world of home for the unknown one that offered hopes of freedom but without guarantees. Slaveholders went to great lengths to dissuade flight to the Yankees, casting them as devils who would sell the refugees to Cuba; as Captain Charles B. Wilder, the superintendent of contrabands at Fort Monroe, testified, the stories gave people pause. That notwithstanding, as far as 200 miles in the interior, freedom seekers formulated schemes to reach federal lines at Fort Monroe, many of which succeeded. Men typically came in advance of their families to survey a route and to be sure that the slaveholders' tales about the Yankees were not true, according to Superintendent Wilder. Then they worked and saved in preparation for the return home for their families, at times borrowing money from federal soldiers to finance their trips. Although not every journey ended happily, the men insisted that they were not afraid. Even if recaptured, they informed Wilder, "we can get away again." What is more, the erosion of the slaveholders' authority created openings for communities of refugee squatters to arise. "There are hundreds of negroes at Williamsburg with their families working for nothing," Wilder reported, reasoning that if they were not going to be paid for their work at the fort, "they had rather stay where they are." Superintendents Vincent Colyer in New Bern, North Carolina, and B. F. Lee at Hilton Head, South Carolina, witnessed—and, indeed, encouraged—similar audacity.[72]

Even when federal officials attempted to assist the freedom seekers, their own bumbling miscalculations or the exigencies of military operations led freed people to question whether they had done the right thing in leaving home. John Oliver, an African American missionary affiliated with the American Missionary Association, described events in November 1862 in eastern Virginia in which military authorities decided to relocate the contrabands who had taken refuge in Newport News to Craney Island, at the mouth of the James River. Although the ostensible reason for the relocation was to teach them to become "self sustaining," the tiny spit of land had few resources to support them. What is more, the regiments charged with supervising the relocation consisted of "wild Irish gards" from New York who treated the people roughly. Rather than submit to this abuse, some forty or fifty men left for the interior "saying good by union I never will come within your lines again."[73]

Several months earlier, "two colored scouts" in North Carolina had a similar experience, spending more than a week behind Confederate lines, "without blankets, without food, except such as they could get by chance; with nothing, in fact, but a few shillings and a good revolver in their breast." They returned to New Bern "full of information that they had risked their lives to obtain," only to discover that the newly appointed military governor, Edward Stanly, opposed offering government protection to black refugees. In fact, Stanly had gone even further, in one notorious case ordering the return of a young woman to her nominally loyal owner. The case created an uproar, with members of the African American community soon persuading federal military authorities to reverse the governor's action. But the scouts had heard and seen enough. Before spending a single night with the federals, they assembled a party of twenty persons who headed back into Confederate territory, confident of finding "the same kind of protection" that the Yankees offered.[74] They did not cringe at the prospect of a whipping at home or even death if they fell into Confederate hands. Their knowledge of the terrain and how to survive in it created a sense of confidence—even invincibility—that emboldened them to wave good-bye to their self-styled Yankee friends.

Abraham Galloway and dozens of other African American spies and guides moved regularly between New Bern, the federal army's base in eastern North Carolina, and the Confederate interior, capitalizing on the "general spirit of insubordination" among the enslaved people that a correspondent to a New York newspaper reported at the time, and escorting men, women, and children out of slavery.[75] Harriet Tubman, the Maryland native who liberated herself and hundreds of other enslaved people before the war, similarly worked with a cadre of local spies in the Department of the South to gather military intelligence and other information useful to Union forces. In June 1863, she accompanied Colonel James Montgomery and the soldiers of his Second South Carolina Colored Volunteers on a raid up the Combahee River that freed more than 700 slaves.[76] Samuel Ballton, who had escaped to Union lines at Fredericksburg, described the technique he used to return home for his wife. After crossing into "the rebel country," he "put on a bold face and told the rebs that he had been captured by the Yankees, but had escaped

and was going back to his 'old massa.' Many, many, 'good niggers' were bestowed on him when he told that story," he later recalled.[77]

Even when they managed to evade the Confederates, the freedom seekers at times encountered federals who offered cold shoulders rather than open
arms. In Norfolk, Virginia, the members of the Ninety-Ninth New York Volunteers reportedly ran a thriving business robbing the refugees and, on occasion, returning them to their owners for a fee. Not far away in Suffolk,
members of the same regiment reportedly collected between twenty and fifty
dollars for each rendition.[78] In the context of pro-Union politics in the South,
where federal officials hoped to draw out prospective loyalists, both military
and civilian representatives of the government in Washington often curried
the favor of slaveholders regardless of the consequences for the slaves. In
North Carolina, Virginia, Tennessee, and Louisiana—at least part of the latter three of which enjoyed exemptions from the Emancipation Proclamation—
enslaved people had good reason to pause over their masters' accounts of
what fate awaited if they cast their lot with the Yankees. This uncertainty continued long after federal policy offered protection and employment to the
refugees from slavery.

————

From the Atlantic Ocean to the Rio Grande, the war created unprecedented
circumstances wherein the authority of the slaveholders was subject to challenge by not just one but two competing governments, both of which could
resort to armed force at their discretion. Enslaved people faced unique opportunities to play their own interests against those of the masters, the Confederate States and the United States, and assorted other third parties. As a
planter in the Mississippi Delta north of Vicksburg reported to the Confederate secretary of war in November 1863, if Confederate authorities attempted
to relocate slaves to places of safety, the removal of "the very first lot" would
set loose "a stampede of all the balance, who would take every mule with them
to the Yankees." He cited the case of a man whom rebel soldiers had visited
twice. The first time they removed the laborers until the danger had passed;
the second time word of the planned removal arrived before the soldiers did,
with the result that "all the men laid out for over a week and many were scared
off entirely to the Yankees." While insisting that his laborers "have made up
their minds to stay at home and wait the issue of events if they are permitted
to do so," he begged the secretary to leave such decisions to the owners. The
Confederate government and its slaveholding citizens came to diametrically
different conclusions regarding the best way to keep the valuable resource of
black men out of the hands of the Yankees. What public officials viewed as
the cure often struck slaveholders as the worst possible variant of the disease.[79]

Like their counterparts in other states, Virginia's slaveholders distrusted the government's approach to preventing the escape of their human property. In January 1864, a special committee of the Virginia legislature informed the Confederate secretary of war that planters opposed the mandatory employment of able-bodied men on public works projects such as fortifications or their forced relocation deeper into the interior. Such a plan "would be attended with very serious mischiefs," the lawmakers warned, for two reasons. First, most young men had already reached federal lines "forcibly or voluntarily," and "the few remaining are retained, generally, by strong local, or family, attachments." Before submitting to a "military raiding party . . . they would fly to the woods, or to the enemy, soon to be followed by their families," to the great detriment of "the loyal whites (chiefly females and children)." Second, slaveholders in the interior will object to bringing among their slaves "those who had become imbued by the enemy with ideas and habits, but little consistent with the obedience and subordination proper to their condition, and necessary to the peace and safety of the whites."[80]

Owners who hoped to avoid the further dissolution of their authority by hiring enslaved people as cooks, servants, and laundresses to Confederate military forces often met disappointment. Over time, Confederate officers and soldiers alike ignored the strict obligation to employ only black persons who produced free papers or proof of their owner's authorization to work. In their desire for relief from onerous camp chores, for which they offered food and shelter with few additional questions asked, they contributed to what the slaveholders viewed as the growing demoralization among black people. Ironically, harboring fugitives mimicked one of the Yankees' most detested practices. Something about military camps enabled—even encouraged—suspending the conventions of slave society. This experience had wide-ranging implications for the men and women in such spaces, where not all the normal rules applied.

In a word, the war upset the delicate balance in the traditional relationship among masters, slaves, the persons and institutions of civil society, and, ultimately, the state. Slaveholders no longer stood as gatekeepers between the people they claimed as property and the outside world. Over time, the circumstances of war compromised slaveholders' authority, often through official government decree and the unofficial actions of soldiers and civilians alike. All the while, enslaved people sought and found openings to subvert the old order and to interact with individuals and institutions as though they were the masters of their own destiny. Often the owners were the first to recognize the change within their own households, on their own farms and plantations, and in their own neighborhoods. The ground beneath domestic slavery trembled as never before.[81]

In their search to dissolve the master-slave relationship, enslaved people leveraged employment relationships with civilians as well as the Confederate government to weaken the bonds. The enslaved man John M. Washington of Fredericksburg, Virginia, worked with a different employer every year, often making his own arrangements and remitting payments to his owner. At the beginning of 1861, his owner sent him to Richmond under the care of an agent to find work. Washington traveled "with a great many of old Friends" who instilled in him the hope that "it was a good place to make money for myself." He found employment at an "Eating Saloon."[82] After the war began, he "Eagerly watched" the newspapers "for tidings of the war" and he knew "that slaves was daily making their Escape into the union lines."[83]

Returning home to Fredericksburg at Christmastime 1861, he defied the will of his owner and refused to return to Richmond. He made employment arrangements for 1862 at a hotel in Fredericksburg and soon after the New Year married his fiancée. As federal forces approached the city that spring, the proprietors planned to move Washington to North Carolina, "out of the reach of the Yankees." On Good Friday an alarm reporting that the Yankees were approaching set off "hurried words and hasty foot steps." The owners joined in the retreat, leaving the premises in Washington's charge with money sufficient to pay off all the employees. Washington did so, treating everyone to drinks in the barroom, toasting the Yankees' health, and advising his co-workers to flee. Washington and two traveling companions reached the Rappahannock River, where they signaled to Union pickets on the other side to dispatch a boat. After making the crossing, Washington won "their good opinions right away," having "stuffed [his] pockets with rebel newspapers." When the soldiers learned that his master was in the Confederate navy, they informed him that he was free.[84]

The aide-de-camp to General Rufus King hired Washington to manage the mess for the general and his staff. When the federal forces crossed the river into Fredericksburg, they brought Washington as their guide. After spending several days in the city, during which "Hundreds of colord people obtained passes and free transportation to Washington and the North, And made their Escape to the *Free States*," the army left for the Shenandoah valley. As federal forces moved through the valley, "hundreds of colord men, women, and children followed us closely on foot," Washington later recalled. "Poor mothers with their Babys at their breasts, Fathers with a few cloths in Bundles or larger children accompanying them followed close in the foot steps of the soilders, Seeming to think this would be their surrist way to freedom." From there they were transported by rail to Washington. When Union troops were on the move, the highways presented quite a scene: "the roads was packed Crowded and Jammed with Calvary, Artillary, infintry wagons,

Contrabands, refugees and Cattle." Like the teamsters and laborers who tended the supply train, he took no shelter for granted, even when that meant sleeping "in an ammunition wagon" on "Boxes of Bumb-Shells."[85]

Although authorities in Fredericksburg had issued a reward of $300 "for [his] head," Washington obtained a pass from the federal commander to return to the city. He found his wife and "Remained at home about one week Enjoying my freedom with friends and acquaintances." He had "intended now to stay at home and make a living and after a while, perhaps, to go north some where" with his wife. But she had become ill, and when Union forces evacuated Falmouth at the end of August, "friends advised me to leave at the earliest opportunity for the sake of safety." He crossed the bridge that the army had constructed across the Rappahannock, after which "I hastened to the Top of the Hill at the East end of the Bridge and looked back at the town that had given me birth with a sad heart and full eyes thought of some of the joys I had felt within its limits." Turning his back on the city at last, he "thought of my poor young wife, who could not fly with me."[86]

Nearly two years later, as Union General George G. Meade's Army of the Potomac moved southeast from Fredericksburg in an attempt to outflank Lee's Army of Northern Virginia, Commissary Sergeant John C. Brock, a Philadelphia native who served with the Forty-Third U.S. Colored Infantry, marveled at the "fine state of cultivation" and the "large crops of corn" intended to feed the Confederate army. "The rebels," Brock reported, had taken "most of their slaves and driven them South," advising those left behind "to take care of themselves as best they could" and filling their ears with "frightful tales about the Yankees" before departing. "As soon as we came along," he added, "fathers, mothers, and their little children, picked up their bundles and marched along with us, carrying them on their heads."[87] Like John Boston, they associated freedom not with the land—even land brimming with the food that might nourish them—but with the federal soldiers, especially the colored troops. Brock and his comrades knew better: the military operations in which they were then engaged did not readily accommodate a train of refugees. Within a matter of weeks they would be busy day and night digging trenches before Petersburg. Accordingly, they guided the freedom seekers, some 500 in all at this time, to the army's supply base at White House Landing on the Pamunkey River for transportation to Washington.[88]

––––––––

In his passage out of slavery, the Tennessean George Knox trod slippery ground nearly every step of the way. Knox belonged to a man who had hired him out for wages since he was a youth. In the process he learned shoemaking as well as a variety of routines associated with farming, tanning hides, and sawing and milling lumber.[89] His owner joined a volunteer regiment during the first wave of enlistments, served for one year, and then returned home, where he became a schoolteacher, with an exemption from future service under the April 1862 Conscription Act. During the man's absence, Knox occupied himself making shoes for Confederate soldiers. In the charged political atmosphere created by the war, Knox also learned the new signals emanating from the voices and the body language of the slaveholders. He observed how their mood varied with the war news. When Confederate forces appeared to have the advantage, "you could hear them yell and order the slaves around"; but when the North gained the upper hand, they "were as kind as could be." As he made his rounds delivering shoes, he played along—at least to outward appearances—bemoaning "how bad it was that the Yankees had whipped us again" while "secretly rejoicing at the success of the Union army." "I had to show my sympathy for the south," he explained, "in order that they would not mistrust me."[90]

The revised Confederate Conscription Act of September 1862 revoked the earlier exemptions for crucial occupations, and in March 1863 Knox's owner decided that rather than await the inevitable call-up he would reenlist and take Knox with him "for safe keeping."[91] Once in the field, Knox moved about at his own discretion, even to the point of befriending two black men who were captured in company with a group of Union soldiers. "Of course the rebels were very rough to these fellows," Knox explained, because they were trying to escape slavery. "To save themselves from being severely punished," the black captives "declared they had been taken away from the rebels against their wishes." But to Knox they explained that the Yankees had treated them well and even favored "giving us our freedom." When the two men finally succeeded in escaping, their captors became furious. Unsure of his own chances to follow their lead, Knox bided his time, hoping that a Union assault might result in his capture. "I reasoned this way," he explained: "if I were captured and taken away by the Yankees, and not satisfied, I could come back and the rebels would have nothing against me."[92] Indeed, as Samuel Ballton discovered, they would welcome him back with open arms and pats on the head.

Fully aware that his owner was keeping him with the army for safekeeping, Knox requested permission to go home. Perhaps to his surprise, the man responded with a qualified yes, the qualification being that he might leave when Confederate military fortunes appeared heading toward victory. Knox then took his leave without notice. Upon reaching home he observed that "everybody had gone from the country except the women and children," and he "felt almost that the day of jubilee had come."[93] Soon after he found work on a farm, the Yankees arrived with "a great band of slaves following them." Knox decided to join the procession, and he went to town, where he discovered "many of my acquaintances ready to go too." The enslaved freedom seekers gathered at a designated meeting place and formulated a plan to go, but a young lady "for whom I had the greatest regard" pleaded with him to stay and he agreed.[94] Even an unmarried young man such as Knox could not always act alone regarding the dangerous business of seeking freedom.

In May 1863, Knox's owner came home and insisted that he return to the army to avoid the possibility that "the Union army would come and take me and he would lose me." "From that moment," Knox made up his mind "to run away."[95] He assembled a small circle of coconspirators to assist in executing the plan. He brought his younger brother into the fold through "a colored girl" whom he trusted. He arranged to stay in a hideaway beneath the cabin of a friend's wife, "a considerate soul," until the proper season to escape arrived. That time came when his owner had passed the word through a third party to his brother that Knox had better return to the army. Instead, the two brothers along with two other men set out for the federal post at Murfreesboro, some twenty-five miles away. After a nightlong journey through territory where Confederate "bushwhackers" were numerous and where "all the dogs were loose and all the people up," they reached the Union pickets.[96] But their journey to freedom was not yet over.

As they passed from one ring of pickets to the next, each successive encounter with the guards produced a fresh chance of being shot. Having at last been admitted to the camp of an Indiana regiment, the four men were put to work sweeping the stables. Then the hazing began, with the soldiers resorting to the same means of intimidation that slaveholders routinely employed. Knox "overheard a couple of Yankees saying, 'There is a big fellow up there . . . that we could get $2,000 for in Cuba,'" and another man stood menacingly over the sweepers "with a great long wagon whip." Knox "afterwards found out that that whip was all for mischief," but not before confessing to his brother that "this is hell."[97]

Once the men endured this initiation, their new hosts put them to work, Knox as a teamster. When one after the other became "homesick," Knox combined words of encouragement with reminders that returning home would result in a certain whipping. When his brother died after a brief illness, Knox's "heart was filled with grief," heavy with the knowledge that people back home "would blame me for taking him away to his death."[98] Knox took part in the federal operations against Chattanooga, and when Union forces entered the city, he advised a group of black women in the town, "You had better stay with your mistress until the war is over," because life with the army was nothing but "hard times." One woman recounted a conversation with her mistress in which she announced her intention not "to milk any more cows" because "the Yankees have come and I am free now." The women would hear nothing of

Knox's cautions, insisting instead that "the year of jubilee had come and there was no more milking of the cows."[99] The "new man" Knox met the "new women" of Chattanooga, for whom their owners' definitions of home no longer rang true. In time Knox became the servant of an officer. Accompanying the unit home on a furlough in the spring of 1864, he decided to remain there. He defied the warnings that some of the white soldiers issued to the effect that they "would kill the first 'nigger' they saw on Indiana soil." Knox eventually became one of the leading citizens of the state, a mainstay in the state Republican Party, a successful businessman, and the publisher of the *Indianapolis Freeman*, which reached African American communities across the nation.[100]

Like George Knox, William Robinson attended his master in the Confederate army. When the owner was killed during operations in East Tennessee in the fall of 1863, Robinson "remained as a cook for the company." He was among the fifty-odd cooks whom federal forces captured as the Confederates retreated. After enduring a ritualized hazing in which his liberators put him through mock military drills, he began cooking for Generals Ambrose Burnside and George H. Thomas.[101] When the army passed through Greenville, Tennessee, Robinson recounted bringing the news of freedom to his mother and a man he referred to as "Uncle Isaac." Isaac maintained the "great house" and farm of his owners, who had refugeed to safety but then decided to "come back and forth, sometimes staying weeks at a time."[102] When the people from the farm had gathered, Robinson "made a short speech . . . telling them to hitch their ox and mule carts, and load up their things and go to the Yankees." Although initially stricken by "considerable fear," they soon accepted the assurances of the soldiers and before long "the yard was fairly lined with wagons, carts and every conceivable beast of burden." Heading toward Knoxville, "we had four or five hundred men, women and children in this great march from a land of servitude to a land of liberty."[103] Like John Boston earlier, Robinson learned that Union forces had the power to transform the very ground beneath the feet of freedom seekers.

———

On April 17, 1865, a week after Robert E. Lee surrendered to Ulysses S. Grant at Appomattox, Virginia, several hundred miles to the south in North Carolina, Reverend Henry McNeal Turner, chaplain of the First U.S. Colored Infantry, witnessed a curious scene. The regiment, which was organized in Washington, D.C., during the spring and summer of 1863, had participated in the second attack on Fort Fisher, North Carolina, in January 1865. In the intervening several months, the First had performed occupation duty at various places including Wilmington, one of the last Confederate strongholds on the South Atlantic coast. As General William T. Sherman and his army of westerners moved toward the state capital at Raleigh, other federal troops moved out of Wilmington to join them. In these final military operations in the eastern theater of the war, the federals did not disguise their intention to free any and all slaves they encountered, but they also made emphatically clear that their operational goals were military, not humanitarian. Still, desperate refugees—growing numbers of whom were starving white Carolinians—took their last chance and followed the blue-coated swarm.

Turner's unit stopped at Warsaw, North Carolina, where large crowds of refugees, some white but most black, quickly gathered. Turner and other commentators who witnessed such scenes elsewhere in eastern North Carolina around this time noted the haggard condition of the refugees and the desperation in their eyes as they begged for food and protection. When Turner's regiment received orders to proceed to Raleigh, "the colored people became wonderfully excited," he reported. Although many were too tired to walk, "vast numbers" proceeded to straggle along behind the soldiers—improbably going deeper into Confederate-held territory rather than heading toward Wilmington where he had advised them to go.[104]

The refugees of the spring of 1865 who sought the protection of Union armies experienced time and space through the same lenses that John Boston had in the fall of 1861 and George Knox and William Robinson had in the summer and fall of 1863. Far from fixed and precisely definable, the land of freedom, like freedom itself, possessed the property of motion. It could appear in unlikely places such as Virginia and Tennessee, and it could quiver like a summer's mirage in likely places such as Pennsylvania and Indiana. Freedom became associated with people, not with space or, even less, an exact place. When Chaplain Turner advised the refugees at Warsaw to seek safety in Wilmington, his words fell on unreceptive ears. Heading south toward Wilmington while the Union army headed north appeared fraught with danger, including the risk of death or reenslavement. The blue-clad army constituted not just the symbol of freedom but freedom itself, and the Promised Land of liberty consisted of everywhere Yankee soldiers could be spied with the naked eye.[105]

PART III

Home

At times of social upheaval, individuals and communities seek stability. The term "home" resonated with meaning amid the turbulent seas of the Civil War and the storms set loose by emancipation. In its most common usage, home signified a dwelling, a place of shelter and repose, and the site where families socialize successive generations into the ways of the world. Home also connoted a neighborhood composed of people who interacted regularly in common space and who knew each other by sight if not always by name. Home in these two senses of dwelling place and neighborhood could generate deep emotional attachments, particularly over time. Persons separated from home—for instance, women through marriage, families through migration from East to West, and enslaved persons through sale—might find it difficult to reconstruct the old sense of comfort and belonging in their new settings, pining for the faces and places left behind. For many, home also served to describe the large, impersonal yet very real "imagined communities" represented by such abstract geopolitical entities as states and nations.[1] Most mid-nineteenth-century Americans employed the term "home" in all these senses, literally and figuratively, past and present. The war stretched the traditional definitions of the term "home" in unforeseen ways, but economic and social change had begun to exert pressure over the preceding half century, as the experience of the domestic household—the basic definition of home—illustrates.

In the North, the growth of commerce, the rise of factory production, and the revolutions in transportation and communication had promoted a spirit of individualism that weakened the traditional family. While some sought firm footing in religion, sparking waves of evangelical revivalism, and others in politics, initiating campaigns to broaden the elective franchise, those perceived solutions served to exacerbate the underlying problem rather than resolve it. Social conservatives denounced the leveling of class distinctions and other markers of what they considered proper order as a threat to civilization itself. They blamed a host of "isms," including abolitionism and feminism, for the declining authority of domestic institutions. Southern slaveholders took special pride in their model of the patriarchal household, which they saw as a bulwark against the atomizing forces that wracked the North. The slave master's "family, white and black" was the foundation of all other interpersonal relationships and the key to social stability. The inability of the political system to harmonize these varying interests gave rise to yearnings for radical change, even to the point of dissolving the Union created in the wake of the Revolution.[2] Once the war began, rebel leaders extolled the slaveholding household as the cornerstone of the Confederacy; after little more than a year of fighting, federal leaders declared war on slavery as a way to topple the superstructure that it supported.

Enslaved Southerners had for years pressed against the physical and psychological constraints imposed by the slaveholding patriarchy, among the most glaring incongruities of which included treating adults as though they were children and buying and selling persons as though they were cattle. The outbreak of war created opportunities for freedom seekers to slip the chains of slavery, and they watched somewhat incredulously at first as representatives of both governments—first the Confederates and then the Yankees—assumed the stance of a powerful third party in the sacred space that patriarchs had considered their unrivaled domain. Enslaved people imagined new possibilities with the breakup of the patriarchal household. Independent African American households could become the cornerstone of freedom.

This exercise coincided with what various African American observers sarcastically described as a case of "negro mania on the brain."[3] Government officials, representatives of charitable and benevolent organizations, and assorted shapers of public opinion framed the challenge the nation faced as the enslaved people's war for freedom merged with the Union's war against slavery in terms of "what is to be done with the Negroes?" From modest beginnings with regard to providing food and shelter to persons who sought refuge at Fort Monroe, the issue took on more complex dimensions that ultimately extended to the rights and privileges of citizenship. Over time, officials devised numerous plans to answer the question, even flirting with such fanciful notions as colonizing freed people outside the United States. During 1864, interest grew in congressional proposals to create a bureau of emancipation to help oversee the transition from slavery to freedom. Supporters and detractors of the concept debated the propriety of the government's exercise of a "paternal discipline" over the novice freed people, but they rarely bothered to consult with "the Negroes."

As a result, the expectations and goals of the planners diverged from those of the presumed beneficiaries. The common language of home fell short of spanning the different assumptions and expectations of the various sides. African Americans in the Northern states entered eagerly into the national debate, using what access to public space prior years of agitation had cleared for the antislavery cause. Freed people, who had no comparable openings, nonetheless found ways to express their views to the Northern soldiers, missionaries, teachers, relief workers, and newspaper reporters in their midst. They shared an understanding that emancipation would ring hollow without strong government protection for African American families to function as all free families did, as the source of shelter and subsistence, the fundamental building block of neighborhoods, and the crucial link between individuals and institutions that together composed society. In that sense, emancipation had as much to do with black people throughout the nation and as it did with freed people in the former slave states.

The next three chapters examine emancipation through the prism of "home" in both its theoretical and its practical meanings. The first explores the topic from the vantage of "what to do with the Negroes," the conceptual shorthand that white Northerners used to frame the myriad social and political challenges that the end of slavery presented. The second examines Southern freed people's efforts to build new lives, filling the void left by the collapse of slavery. The third treats Northern free black people's struggles to achieve equality, erasing the stigma that slavery had consigned to all persons of African ancestry in the United States. In a sense, all Americans searched for new meanings of home to account for the end of slavery. Two things remained to be seen. First, could Americans of European ancestry— Northern as well as Southern—envision a nation free from the invidious distinctions based on the legacy of African slavery? Second, would Americans of African ancestry—Northern as well as Southern—succeed in achieving their dreams of freedom, civic and political equality, and the chance to partake in the other benefits that derived from being citizens of the United States?

Chapter 7

Our Home and Country

The Civil War was about citizenship as much as it was about slavery. For the partisans of secession, the government of the United States ceased to embody the ideal of representative government when the election of Abraham Lincoln in November 1860 appeared to jeopardize the property rights of slaveholding citizens. For the partisans of the Union, secession threatened the integrity of the nation created by the Founders, the only sure bulwark for preserving the rights of all citizens. But thanks to the principle of federalism enshrined in the U.S. Constitution, citizenship came in many guises and under multiple auspices, with the states exerting much greater impact on the day-to-day meaning of citizenship than the national government did. This was especially true regarding the citizenship rights of persons whose ancestors did not all hail from Europe and of women of every racial group and nationality. Persons so marginalized had protested their unequal treatment for decades, and, as the war to suppress the rebellion became a war against slavery, African Americans saw an opportunity to challenge the white public's acceptance of such discrimination as part of the natural order of things.

As federal policy makers focused more and more intently on undermining slavery to weaken the rebellion, the institutional foundation that underlay race-based discrimination would feel the effects. The statecraft of race—discussions and debates over public policies that pertained to African-descended persons as a racial group—soon came to preoccupy both policy makers and ordinary citizens everywhere. At stake was the nature of the relationship between individuals and the bodies politic that the respective states and the nation represented. At stake, too, was the nature of the polities to which citizens felt that they belonged, in which they experienced a sense of home.

In June 1864, after the action on the part of the Unionist Louisiana State Convention to abolish slavery, an African American soldier stationed in New Orleans reported with delight that the streets teemed with persons celebrating "a great epoch in the history of their race." Not only had a convention "composed of slaveholders" voted to abolish slavery, but "the friends of freedom are sanguine of success" that similar action would follow regarding the right of suffrage. "Under God, this will yet be a pleasant land for the colored man to dwell in, the declarations of the colonizationists to the contrary, notwithstanding," he concluded. "This is our home and country."[1]

The repatriation of a black abolitionist from England in 1854 provided a preview into the semantic and political significance of the terms "home" and "country." Among the crowd that welcomed William Wells Brown back to Boston was Wendell Phillips, the noted abolitionist. When a man such as Brown returned to the United States, Phillips asked rhetorically, to what did he return? "Not to what he can call his 'country,'" he answered. "The white man comes 'home'" to a country where he had a stake in the future of liberty and "where his manhood was recognized," but "the black man comes home to no liberty but the liberty of suffering [and to] struggle in fetters for the welfare of his race." Indeed, the Supreme Court's key ruling in the 1857 decision against Dred Scott's claim to freedom was the inadmissibility of his petition on the grounds that persons of African ancestry were not citizens.[2]

An earlier rumination by George Washington Parke Custis, the step-grandson of George Washington, adds insight. Custis spoke before the fourteenth annual meeting of the American Colonization Society (ACS) in 1831 to counter what he foresaw as "a mighty appeal . . . being made for Africa" on the part of the emerging abolitionist movement. Repeating Thomas Jefferson's discredited charge that "our ancient Rulers" foisted the trade in captive Africans on unwilling subjects, Custis blasted those who "in the overflowings of their philanthropy, advocate amalgamation of the two classes" by freeing "the coloured class" and permitting them to "remain among us as denizens of the Empire." "What right," he demanded to know, "have the children of Africa to an homestead in the white man's country?" He proposed a different future, one in which "the regenerated African [would] rise to empire . . . returning 'redeemed and disenthralled,' from their long captivity in the New World" to reside "under the shade of their native palms."[3] Like white nationalists from the time of Thomas Jefferson to the present, Custis envisioned a future in which European-descended people alone would reap the benefit of North America's wealth and exert uncontested political power. From its founding in 1816, the ACS had championed such notions. Early in 1848, in the aftermath of its annual meeting, the society counseled slaveholders regarding the advantages of Liberian colonization. "We are satisfied that in this country [the Negro] never can enjoy a permanent home; can never rise above his present depressed condition," the statement asserted. "He may stay here for years and years yet to come. But the day must come, sooner or later, when he must depart."[4]

African Americans had an ambiguous relationship with the ACS, for the most part steadfastly opposing the organization's mission and message but at times conceding that the climate of racial hostility in the United States—for which slavery was only the most flagrant example—might warrant pursuing freedom and full citizenship on distant shores. One of the most steadfast opponents of colonization was the prominent abolitionist Henry Highland Garnet, whose family had escaped from slavery when he was a youth and whose 1843 remarks to the National Convention of Colored Citizens advising enslaved people to "let your motto be resistance" had electrified black Americans. Five years later, his speech before the Female Benevolent Society of Troy, New York, titled "The Past and the Present Condition, and the Destiny, of the Colored Race" staked out the anticolonizationist position unequivocally and forcefully. He remained optimistic about the progress of the race despite slavery's entrenched strength. He viewed the nation's recent "triumphs" over Mexico as "defeats in disguise." The imminent acquisition of a vast new territory would convey an intriguing mixture of people, including white "ultra Abolitionists" and "liberty-loving brethren" with dark complexions. Convinced that *this western world is destined to be filled with a mixed race*, he rejected the "utopian plan" of colonizing all the victims of the Atlantic trade back "to the shores of Africa." No people "in this wide earth" is "so poor as to be without a home and a country," he insisted. "America is my home, my country, and I have no other."[5]

———

In April 1861, emancipation was the farthest thing from President Abraham Lincoln's mind. Yet, as he searched for the words that would describe the outbreak of war in terms of national unity, he understood as well as anyone the link between secession and the future of slavery. The potential backlash from the Loyal Border States—as well as other places scattered throughout the other Union states—against any measure threatening property in humans was real. Notwithstanding such political constraints, abolitionists and antislavery members of the Republican Party viewed Fort Sumter as a godsend, the pretext for preemptive executive action. They cited the argument that John Quincy Adams had laid before his congressional colleagues in April 1842. War, the former chief executive argued, "whether servile, civil or foreign," justified any sitting president "to order the universal emancipation of the slaves." Staunch opponents of slavery such as Lewis Tappan urged Lincoln to follow his predecessor's advice if he truly intended to save the Union.[6]

Lincoln balked, insisting—though not completely accurately—that the states, not the national government, had jurisdiction over slavery and other such "domestic institutions." But bigger issues were at stake. Liberating enslaved people without compensation to the owners might lead owners of other kinds of property to question the government's commitment to protecting their rights. On the positive side, abolishing slavery would align the United States with the progressive sentiment of the age, and prospectively reduce the chances that Great Britain or France might grant diplomatic recognition to the Confederacy. Antislavery opinion had "been spreading and swelling into action throughout the civilized world," the final report of the AFIC noted in May 1864, "till not a nation in Europe, Christian or Mohammedan, Spain alone excepted" had failed to outlaw slavery.[7] The United States was on the wrong side of history.

The spirit of the age, of course, said nothing about the social and political consequences of emancipation. "To have set men at liberty is not all," the French official Augustin Cochin noted in his 1862 survey of emancipation in the Caribbean territories of the European powers, "it is necessary to place them in society."[8] The implications began with the affected individuals—formerly enslaved persons and former enslavers—and radiated outward from that starting point. Although one informed observer later characterized the challenge as attempting to "ensure [the] good" of the freed people "with [the] least social disturbance," emancipation was nothing if not a huge social disturbance.[9] It required policy makers and ordinary citizens to redefine the social compact between individual and government throughout the nation and not just in the states where slavery held legal standing in April 1861. The ensuing change would reverberate into the wider world.

The peculiar exercise of simultaneously facing and averting the prospect of abolition recurred in cycles beginning in the late eighteenth century. By the start of the rebellion, a sizable, growing, and readily available literature offered insightful commentary on state-sponsored emancipations from the 1790s onward. Moreover, journalists reported on the emancipations that were playing out in real time, such as in Russia, where Tsar Alexander II decreed an end to serfdom in 1861, and in various locations in the Caribbean and South America, most notably Cuba and Brazil, where abolitionist movements were gaining momentum.[10]

Two emancipations were of special interest. The first was Saint-Domingue, France's "Jewel of the Antilles," where a protracted struggle that began in 1791 amid the French Revolution culminated in the creation of Haiti as an independent nation in 1804. The second was the British West Indies, where a parliamentary act of 1833 abolished slavery effective August 1, 1834, which would be followed by a mandatory apprenticeship period of up to six years. This system of quasi slavery satisfied no one, and the legislative bodies in all the colonies lifted the requirement and announced complete emancipation in 1838, if not earlier. Each example offered contradictory evidence of what might unfold if the United States were to abolish slavery. In the eyes of most Europeans and European Americans, Saint-Domingue stood as a symbol of revolutionary excess, where resentment against the slaveholders' notorious cruelty exploded in torrents of bloodshed. And even in the British West Indies, where slavery ended without comparable violence, the variety of experiences from one colony to the next fairly guaranteed that the friends and foes of emancipation would fight over the lessons learned.[11]

Just as the war began, William G. Sewell, a member of the editorial staff of the *New York Times*, published *The Ordeal of Free Labor in the British West Indies*, a book-length compilation of published accounts of his visits to the British Caribbean over the previous several years. From statistical data on agricultural production in the various colonies before and after emancipation, Sewell disputed the planters' contention that free labor destroyed the West Indian plantation system. Into his broad strokes regarding the overall impact of emancipation, he textured finer ones describing the diversity of experiences. "Emancipation was an isolated experiment in each of the different colonies," he explained, and, as a result, "precedents and rules of action for one" generally did not apply to the others. Whereas several colonies adjusted quickly to the end of slavery, others—Jamaica in particular—experienced a long, drawn-out contest wherein the advocates of "slave labor" battled the partisans of "free labor" to a state of "exhaustion" all around. Freedom, he insisted, "unshackled . . . the commerce, the industry, and the intelligence of the islands, and laid the foundation of permanent prosperity." "I came to the West Indies imbued with the American idea that African freedom had been a curse to every branch of agricultural and commercial industry," he concluded. "I shall leave these islands overwhelmed with a very opposite conviction."[12]

Sewell faulted the critics of emancipation for harping constantly on "an ethnological issue"—that is, the unfounded claim of African inferiority, which he considered entirely irrelevant to the political economy of emancipation. The formerly enslaved people could hardly be faulted for not demonstrating "the cardinal virtues of civilization" at the moment of freedom. But with education and "the dominion of an enlightened government," he concluded, "they will become still more elevated in the scale of civilization." After two decades, he credited "the West Indian Creole" with having "made a good fight." When "divested of such foreign incumbrances" as the presumed defects in African character, emancipation "is simply a land question, with which race and color have nothing whatever to do."[13]

Commentators from a wide spectrum of opinion praised Sewell's work. A notice in the *New York Times* credited him with performing "a lasting service to mankind" for which public opinion on both sides of the Atlantic should be grateful. The work demonstrated that "emancipation in the Antilles has not proven a failure" and that abolition "was a measure founded in wisdom as well as in justice; neither a Quixotic nor Utopian scheme, but the development of a policy that will inure to the commercial prosperity of its possessions."[14] Both the *Anglo-African* and the *Christian Recorder* commented favorably, the latter reprinting an opinion from the *National Anti-Slavery Standard*. "Emancipation has not been wholly successful, because the experiment has not been wholly tried," the observer reported, "but the success is none the less emphatic and decided."[15]

Conservatives tended to reject Sewell's optimism. "If our republic is to be perpetuated, this negro question has got to be met," the *New York World* asserted. Far from the opening statement of a case for racial reconciliation and collaboration, the editorial raised a warning about an impending demographic nightmare. With census data suggesting that the enslaved population doubled every thirty years, persons currently alive would see the day when the figure reached thirty million, "a number equal to its entire white and black population at the present time," a weight that "no rational being can believe that our free institutions could carry." Certain that "a convulsion of some sort would inevitably ensue," the editorialist nonetheless stopped short of predicting what form it would take.[16] But something had to be done to avert catastrophe.

During the succeeding months, Sewell's study inspired various investigations into the prospective impact of emancipation on staple-crop production in the slave states. The Boston cotton manufacturer Edward Atkinson, for instance, believed implicitly that free labor held the key to the future of the cotton economy. While conceding that "the law of competition is inexorable," he saw in Texas a place where white yeoman farmers and wage-earning freed people would rewrite the books regarding productivity. The "sound principles of political economy," he concluded, dictated that "free labor upon cotton is an absolute necessity, to enable this country to maintain its hold upon the cotton markets of Europe." As an added bonus, emancipation offered a "summary process for disposing of the negro question."[17]

African American commentators contributed significantly to this debate in another important way, insisting that policy makers take into account the emancipations that various Northern states enacted after the Revolution and into the nineteenth century. These examples furnished both positive and negative lessons. Black observers insisted that for reasons specific to the various colonies (later states) during the war for independence, black men and women had become free, often gaining citizenship rights in the process. In addition to the New England states and New York, where enslaved persons constituted a comparatively small proportion of the population, states with much higher proportions of slaves, such as North Carolina, permitted manumission and even the selected enfranchisement of African-descended men. While it is true that many white New Englanders forgot this story as a way of erasing their region's past ties to slavery, residents of New York and New Jersey had no such luxury. In the Empire State, slavery did not officially end until July 4, 1827, a year after the famous abolitionist Sojourner Truth, born Isabella Baumfree, escaped from a Dutch owner in Ulster County, New York. At the start of the Civil War, many adult New Yorkers recalled the celebrations that accompanied the end of slavery. As for New Jersey, the emancipation law did not take effect until April 18, 1846, and even then it mandated that all children born in the state thereafter were free but enslaved adults would remain apprenticed to their former owners for the rest of their lives. The 1860 federal census report indicated the presence within the state's borders of eighteen "Colored apprentices for life."[18]

For African American Northerners, these emancipations furnished object lessons in how quickly the tide of revolutionary zeal could ebb, leaving hopes of economic, social, and political betterment high and dry. But they also drew positive lessons, the most important of which involved the connection between the abolition of slavery in the New England states and the military and naval service of black men—many of whom were enslaved—in the forces of the American patriots. Black Bostonians pressed the point even further, claiming Crispus Attucks, a free black seaman who died at the Boston Massacre in March 1775, as the first martyr in the cause of American independence. In several of the states the revolutionary momentum did not dissipate before officials granted voting rights to black men. Having fought for independence, the "colored patriots" claimed the new nation as their rightful home and sought to participate in its civic culture as equals with all other members of the state and national families. "The love we bear our native land, our respect and veneration for the institutions and government of our country, are so many cords which bind us to our home, the soil of our birth," declared a resolution passed at an antiemigration mass meeting in New York in 1839. "Wet by the tears and fertilized by the blood of our ancestors," the statement continued, and "placing our trust in the Lord of Hosts, we will tell the white Americans, that their country shall be our country, we will be governed by the same laws and worship at the same altar, where they live we will live, where they die there will we be buried, and our graves shall remain as monuments of our suffering and triumph, or of our failure and their disgrace."[19]

Policy makers at both the national and local levels largely ignored the opinions of black leaders. Instead, they assumed that they knew what was in the best interest of their respective constituencies, black residents included. In fact, abolitionists and other white proponents of African American legal and political equality at times appeared little different from opponents of emancipation and impartial citizenship in their suppositions about the decision-making process regarding issues that affected the public good. Yet the vagaries of war created openings that both enslaved persons and free people of color devised ways to exploit. Government officials found themselves responding to the political pressures generated by the segment of the population that the Supreme Court had emphatically labeled noncitizens in 1857.

————

Despite official claims that the war was about national unity rather than slavery, events at the federal enclave of Fortress Monroe, Virginia, proved otherwise, and the question of "what is to be done with the Negroes" arose in bold relief. In late May 1861, shortly after assuming command of the Union army's new Department of Virginia headquartered there, General Benjamin F. Butler had an epiphany. Mere weeks after offering to suppress a rumored slave insurrection in loyal Maryland, he grasped the political value of a vastly different response to slave unrest in a disloyal state. By refusing a slaveholder's demand for the rendition of three men who had sought federal protection, Butler presented his superiors in Washington with a public relations coup. Though falling short of fully disposing of the Negro question, granting shelter constituted an important first step. Wartime events and the circumstances that federal commanders soon encountered in the toeholds they gained in Confederate territory called for additional ones.

Federal officials quickly realized that the able-bodied refugees could perform labor. What they did not at first understand, however, was its transformational impact, not just in terms of relieving soldiers and sailors from exhausting labor. Work fundamentally altered the relationship between the government and the refugees from one involving a benefactor and beneficiaries to one involving an employer and employees. Employment implied the legal equality of the contracting parties, supplanting the implicit social hierarchy associated with almsgiving. But given the power that the government wielded—including, of course, its armed forces—and the stigma attached to formerly enslaved persons, the standing of the two parties was anything but equal. The underlying tension revealed itself first in the persistent neglect on the part of government employers to settle payroll accounts in a timely manner. This practice reflected the widespread popular assumption that the formerly enslaved people held no valid claims on the government that delivered them from bondage. If anything, by this line of reasoning, the freed people were indebted to the government for the priceless gift of freedom.

Even before General Butler departed Fortress Monroe in August, some hints of the awkwardness of this new relationship had begun to emerge.

Almost as soon as he decided to employ able-bodied persons, he planned to tax their earnings in support of those who could not work. To his superiors in Washington, he vowed to keep "a strict and accurate account" of each man's earnings and deductions. "The worth of the services and the cost of the expenditures" were to be "determined by a board of survey, hereafter to be detailed," he reported, based on a standard wage of ten dollars per month. Secretary of War Simon Cameron approved, and before the end of the summer Congress had passed the Confiscation Act authorizing such employment.[20] It appears that Butler never established the board of survey to determine the particulars and many of the laborers never received their pay.

Private Edward L. Pierce was a soldier in one of the ninety-day volunteer regiments from Massachusetts under Butler's command. Pierce's unassuming rank hardly reflected his Ivy League credentials (bachelor's degree from Brown and law degree from Harvard) or his close personal ties with Senator Charles Sumner and Treasury Secretary Salmon P. Chase. Early in July, when Butler ordered the occupation of Hampton to build a buffer against Confederate attack, he placed Pierce in charge of recruiting black laborers and supervising their work even though the ninety-day men's enlistments were about to expire. With little time to waste, Pierce assured the sixty-odd men he recruited that they would be treated "like human beings," but, with regard to compensation, the best he could do was promise future payment, noting each man's name, his owner's name, and the number of days worked. In the meantime, he issued a soldier's ration to each man daily plus half a ration for each dependent. To Pierce's delight, the men quickly proved to be diligent workers, accomplishing more than equal numbers of soldiers and finishing "the nicer parts—the facings and dressings—better."[21]

Pierce did not stop there. Seeing an opportunity to draw larger lessons that might help shape future policy, he began gathering information with an eye toward entering the rapidly heating national debate over the war's implications for the enslaved population. To understand the freed people's "feelings, desires, aspirations, capacities, and habits of life," he occupied his "leisure time in conversations with the contrabands, both at their work and in their shanties."[22] Like other observers of enslaved and recently liberated people throughout the Americas, Pierce wished to gauge their fitness for freedom, a term that had gained popular currency on both sides of the Atlantic during British West Indian emancipation. In the end Pierce concluded that the experiment in free labor would succeed if the freed people were given a fair chance. Ominously, when his regiment departed for the North, he had made little progress toward getting the men paid. Given the vibrancy of slave hiring in the Chesapeake tidewater before the war, the workers well understood the value of their labor. Private Pierce's much ballyhooed system of compensated labor appeared strange indeed when its champion could not deliver the promised wages.[23]

The November 1861 issue of the *Atlantic Monthly* contained the results of Pierce's investigation, which he titled "The Contrabands at Fortress Monroe." To policy makers, philanthropists, and the Northern reading public, Pierce addressed issues relevant to the freed people in legal, political, and historical terms. He demonstrated that the war had destabilized slavery and, in the process, called into question the federal government's traditional practice of protecting the property rights of the masters rather than the human rights of the enslaved. The article also revealed the ideological assumptions and cultural values of middle-class Protestant Northerners who hoped that the war would destroy slavery. Military victory constituted the foundation of the process. But even short of final triumph, where Union forces regained dominion, the work of constructing the framework for a new social order could begin. That work involved preparing formerly enslaved persons to assume the responsibilities of free men and women as hardworking contributors to the greater good and, potentially, as citizens of the republic.[24]

The freed people understood "perfectly," he explained with evident approval, that "although the object of the war was not to emancipate them, yet that might be its result."[25] On that assumption, these protocitizens would have to learn their individual rights and responsibilities as well as their duties to family, community, and nation. Their industry, their awareness of their abstract rights, and their desire to learn to read spoke well of their fitness for freedom with only one caveat. "The first generation," he explained, "might be unfitted for the active duties and responsibilities of citizenship, but this difficulty, under generous provisions for education, would not pass to the next."[26] Unable to shed the cultural biases in which his past had thoroughly steeped him, Pierce nonetheless drew insightful lessons from a tiny spit of land at the tip of Virginia's Peninsula. He identified key challenges that the freed people faced and that the nation, in turn, would be obliged to address during the months and years ahead.

Military officials tried in vain to evade the appearance of hypocrisy, as their failure to pay the men for their work contradicted the words that extolled the virtues of compensated labor. In the process the freed people learned to distrust their nominal liberators. This pattern did not simply reflect well-meaning missteps in the early phase of a great experiment in philanthropy—it recurred again and again in other Union-occupied areas of the Confederacy. And conditions did not improve at Fort Monroe. Six months after Pierce's departure, a witness reported that little had changed with regard to payments. "A very large proportion" of the more than 600 men working at the fort, he explained, "have been paid nothing or next to nothing." The same was true at Craney Island, across Hampton Roads from the fort, according to another witness. There, most of the 750 women who worked were in fact *"slaves"* to the hospitals at Newport News and Hampton, "doing all of the dirty work" without pay for more than five months.[27] The Boston philanthropist LeBaron Russell, who represented the Boston Educational Commission, reported in mid-December 1862 that the various military departments owed more than $33,000 in unpaid wages to persons who had supported the army's operations at Fort Monroe.[28] Most of those accounts were settled only years later, if at all.

————

Once federal authorities agreed that military commanders should provide shelter and other material assistance to freedom seekers who sought their protection, they faced the related challenge of how to do so at the least expense to the government. They could easily justify furnishing rations to persons who worked, even clothing, blankets, and tenting from surplus supplies, but caring for the nonworking dependents of laborers as well as the new arrivals within federal lines continued to present problems. Following in Butler's footsteps, the career officer who succeeded him in command of the Department of Virginia, General John A. Wool, promulgated orders during the fall of 1861 stipulating that "all able-bodied colored persons" who were not employed as servants were to "be immediately put to work, in either the engineer's or quartermaster's departments" at ten dollars per month plus a ration for men, with lesser amounts for women, boys, and "sickly or infirm negro men." The quartermaster allowed the men a nominal allowance of two dollars per month "for their own use," minus deductions for clothing drawn from government stores, and held the remainder of each man's earnings "for the support of the women and children, and those that are unable to work."[29]

By early in the New Year, Lewis C. Lockwood, a missionary associated with the American Missionary Association, labeled the practice "Contrabandism" and characterized it as "another name for one of the worst forms of practical oppression—government slavery." "By what constitutional right does government treat these persons as slaves," Lockwood fumed, "and by what military right does government become a great practical slaveholder?" Quoting from General Wool's own estimate, the reverend reported that quartermasters had skimmed off thousands of dollars from the fund by reducing the daily ration.[30] In response to the criticism, Wool created a three-person investigating commission, which completed its work in March 1862.[31] The commissioners touted laissez-faire economic principles as the key to solving the problem posed by the "contrabands" (a term they used interchangeably with "vagrants"). Laborers' wages should "be determined by individual skill, industry, and ability, and regulated by supply and demand," and the workers should collect all their earnings "for their own use and enjoyment." Government aid, the commissioners argued, sapped "the energies of an individual or a people" and created the false hope "that the Herculean arm of the nation" would come to the rescue. Citing the laudable work of philanthropic associations from the North, they saw no need "for any governmental charity." The extent of government intervention, in their view, should consist of the appointment of "a man of elevated moral character, high social position and intelligence" to serve as superintendent. This man would inculcate "honesty, industry, temperance, economy, patience, and obedience to all rightful authority, leaving out of the question their social and political rights," which, the commissioners believed, "belong[ed] more properly to the government." Within days of receiving the report, Wool appointed the Boston abolitionist Charles B. Wilder as superintendent of contrabands.[32]

While not entirely unsympathetic to the government's multiple roles of protector, employer, and mentor, the commissioners concluded that the model of a uniform wage coupled with a tax to support the dependents failed on every count: it frustrated the industry of the laborers; it generated insufficient funds to support the dependents; and it lacked scalability to larger numbers and transportability to other places. The key to the model's limited success, they argued, lay in the fact that "the demands for government labor at this post is limited." But with "almost no limit to the demands on its charity," as Union armies advanced, "the system is . . . incapable of expansion, and cannot, from its very expensiveness to government, be carried on with a much larger number."[33] At this comparatively early stage of the war, strategists fell far short of reconciling the novel circumstances with conventional liberal economic orthodoxy. So, the practice of employing the able-bodied at stipulated wages with mandatory deductions to support dependent persons persisted despite its imperfections.

The model of charging a "contraband tax" to support dependent freed people proved to be especially contentious at the logistical operations in and around Washington, D.C., and Alexandria, Virginia. "I have heard the colored people complain often of this policy," the superintendent of a camp not far from the White House reported, not least because the tax was deducted regardless of the man's monthly wage or the amount of time he might have lost to sickness.[34] According to the chief quartermaster of the Department of Washington, teamsters "lodge with their trains, and are furnished with mess kits to cook their food," and laborers live together in quarters with "their food prepared in public mess houses." But because the teamsters received their pay quarterly at best, their families appeared little different from the thousands of other refugees who sought government shelter and subsistence. The practice affected free black men and formerly enslaved men, and the former protested loudly.[35]

Shortly after "The Contrabands at Fortress Monroe" hit the newsstands, Pierce relinquished his role as expert commentator and assumed that of key participant in the experiment that was beginning to unfold on the Sea Islands surrounding Port Royal. Under the auspices of the U.S. Treasury Department, Northern businessmen, missionaries, and teachers planned to construct a model whereby the freed people would work for wages raising market staples on the plantations where they had formerly been enslaved. In the process, the Yankees would dispense lessons in assuming personal responsibility for one's actions, rising above the enforced degradation of slavery, and making the necessary preparations for eventual citizenship. This bold plan had some hope for success only by virtue of the fact that the former plantation owners had fled from the region, that Sea Island cotton occupied a privileged place in international markets, and that federal forces protected the islands. Pierce's former employer and mentor, Treasury Secretary Salmon P. Chase, considered him to be the ideal leader of this experiment, not least of all because of his prior experience at Fort Monroe and Hampton.

As earlier, Pierce observed the private lives as well as the work habits of the native Sea Islanders. He could hardly have found a field of study farther removed from Fortress Monroe. In a series of long letters, which were soon published, Pierce outlined for Chase a model for reconstructing the plantation system of the Deep South.[36] In his early encounters with the people, Pierce strove to contrast their new responsibilities in freedom with their old ones in slavery. Late in January he visited a Baptist church, where he first read several "passages of Scripture" and then "pressed on them their practical duties." "If they did not behave well now and respect our agents and appear willing to work," he explained, "Mr. Lincoln would give up trying to do anything for them." Such an outcome would leave "their children and grandchildren a hundred years hence . . . worse off than they had been." Pierce employed Lincoln's name because it was "more likely to impress them than the abstract idea of government."[37] Pierce viewed the work as an "opportunity . . . to make of them, partly in this generation, and fully in the next, a happy, industrious, law-abiding, free and Christian people."[38]

As he pondered how to organize the plantations, Pierce criticized the proposal that some had put forward to lease the abandoned plantations "and the people upon them." In one such proposal, a Dutch immigrant to Iowa addressed Congress shortly after the capture of Port Royal on the theme of *"What must we do with the slaves?"* In answering the question, the petitioner proposed leasing abandoned lands for a number of years, with the lessees being able to "use the labor or service of persons that have belonged to the owners of said estates for the same number of years." The laborers would work under "a rule of apprenticeship" that stipulated their wages, a portion of which were "to be retained by competent authority." For their part, lessees were obliged to furnish schools and to promote family stability. At the end of the apprenticeship, the laborers were "at liberty to select a place of permanent residence outside of the United States" (their transportation costs to be paid from their withheld wages) or "to bind themselves voluntarely in servitude to any other man."[39] Based on "the History of British East India, and of all communities where a superior race has attempted to build up speedy fortunes on the labor of an inferior race occupying another region," Pierce considered apprenticeship and variants of serfdom as worse than slavery.[40] Believing that the nation had the "duty to deal with the negro question in the light of existing facts, and not upon abstractions," a resident of Indiana also endorsed "a wise and humane system of apprenticeship," but one that would settle the freed people among "the thinking, working moral people of the north" instead of the South; but the proposal gained little, if any, traction.[41]

Like other official strategists of emancipation, Pierce looked to draw larger lessons from the myriad practical problems that arose day to day. The "system of administration" best designed to "advance the civilization of the age," he argued, was wage labor under the direction of Northern plantation superintendents, who would exert a necessary yet temporary "paternal discipline." And there was more: "As fast as the laborers show themselves fitted for all the privileges of citizens, they should be dismissed from the system and allowed to follow any employment they please and where they please." More than simply a labor regime, narrowly defined, Pierce touted its ability to prepare the freed people "for the full privileges of citizens," relying "upon their better nature and the motives which come from it—the love of wages, of offspring, and of family, the desire for happiness and the obligations of religion." If these motivators failed, the superintendents must not resort to the lash "but to the milder and more effective punishments of deprivation of privileges, isolation from family and society, the workhouse, or even the prison."[42]

"In the end," Pierce firmly believed, cotton cultivation in South Carolina would "be carried on more scientifically and cheaply than before, the plow taking very much the place of the hoe, and other implements being introduced to facilitate industry and increase the productive power of the soil."[43]

Remarkably, following a stay of merely three months, Pierce somehow foresaw "industrial results" that would "put at rest the often reiterated assumption that this territory and its products can only be cultivated by slaves."[44] Over the following months and years, Pierce's concept of "paternal discipline" resurfaced wherever Union military forces reestablished authority over Confederate territory where sizable black populations resided or sought refuge. But in the nature of paternalism, each variant differed from the others.

The pattern of discovery repeated itself in each succeeding advance of Union forces into the Confederacy. Timing constituted a constant challenge. In Pierce's case, his arrival at Port Royal in mid-January 1862 left him and the other plantation superintendents at a distinct disadvantage. By the time they could assemble the necessary tools and seeds, "the negroes had commenced putting corn and potatoes into their own patches" but had prepared no land for cotton, being "strongly indisposed" to its cultivation. Pierce worked hard "to convince them that labor on cotton was honorable, remunerative and necessary to enable them to buy clothing and the fitting comforts they desired." Ominously, he noted that the work of plowing and planting that normally commenced early in February did not begin until late in March, correctly predicting the adverse impact on the fall harvest. Similar delays at the start of the agricultural year plagued other federal experiments in cultivating cotton with compensated laborers for the rest of the war.[45]

As he prepared to exit Port Royal early in June, Pierce claimed more than a partial victory, informing Secretary Chase that "a social problem, which has vexed the wisest, approaches a solution. The capacity of a race and the possibility of lifting it to civilization without danger and disorder even without throwing away the present generation as refuse, is being determined, and thus the way is preparing by which the peace to follow this war shall be made perpetual."[46] Were it not for the fact that Pierce had casually referenced discarding the present generation as incapable of exercising the responsibilities of citizenship, the metaphor might be considered a figure of speech rather than a blueprint for policy, but a disturbingly large number of his contemporaries employed generational references to the same effect. The superintendent of Craney Island, Virginia, for instance, declared that "a new generation will have to grow up to be freemen." In the meantime, cultivating the soil "under suitable guardianship" away from disruptive influences represented "their only chance." If in twenty years they are not self-sustaining and self-governing, "we will then admit that it takes a longer time to get rid of the curse of slavery than we supposed, and the system is a great deal worse than we ever thought it to be."[47] The architects of emancipation wrestled with competing notions of whether success required freedom's early shoots to benefit from a protective hothouse atmosphere or to be sown broadcast in the wild where they would have to vie for the necessary sunlight, moisture, and nutrients against all other living things.

Such flights of fancy consumed most white Northerners who came south to work among the freed people in the wake of successful military operations. They hoped that in a matter of years, at most, they would undo the habits of lifetimes, and the formerly enslaved people would quickly learn the habits of industrious workers, frugal managers of their earnings in the interest of enlightened consumption, mirrors of Yankee cultural values, and citizens in the making. In a second article in the *Atlantic Monthly*, published in September 1863 and titled "The Freedmen at Port Royal," Pierce recapitulated his 1862 experience and offered additional reflections based on a return visit to South Carolina in the spring of 1863. His optimism remained strong, viewing the changing terminology he used to describe formerly enslaved people—"contrabands" at Fort Monroe and "freedmen" at Port Royal—as "milestones in our progress." He confidently predicted that both of these terms would give way to "the better and more comprehensive designation of citizens."[48]

In effect, Pierce reengaged the antebellum debates about whether the United States of America could accommodate persons of African ancestry in an economic, social, and political role in which they were free rather than enslaved. In the resolution he foresaw, the nation recognized the freed people not as resident aliens but as citizens with the full complement of rights that every other member of the civic family enjoyed. This concept contained broadly theoretical and narrowly practical implications laden with ambiguity, as his return visit to the islands in the spring of 1863 revealed. Pierce toured a school on St. Helena's Island, where he applauded the students' command over the poet John Greenleaf Whittier's new song, composed especially for them. The closing stanza is especially instructive:

> For none in all the world before
> Were ever glad as we,—
> We're free on Carolina's shore,
> We're all at home and free.[49]

Whittier's verse exposed one of the central dilemmas that ending slavery presented to the nation. On the one hand, the concept of freedom—especially as the antithesis of slavery—held liberating possibilities, the full extent of which produced uninhibited joy. On the other hand, the concept of home associated with this freedom held no comparable reach, spatially or metaphorically, owing to its specific association with coastal South Carolina. A

Figure 7.1 Timothy O'Sullivan, *Fugitive African Americans Fording the Rappahannock* (August 1862). Courtesy of the Library of Congress Prints and Photographs Division, LC-DIG-cwpb-00218.

figurative glass dome limited the heights to which the bird of freedom might fly.

———

In the spring of 1862, the advance of Union forces into Louisiana, Arkansas, and Tennessee in the western theater and toward Richmond on Virginia's Peninsula in the East brought military forces face-to-face with enslaved freedom seekers on a scale unknown during the war's first year (see figures 7.1 and 7.2). Prospects for a dramatic growth in the refugee population prompted philanthropists and alarmists alike to wonder anew "WHAT SHALL WE DO WITH FOUR MILLIONS OF SLAVES?"[50]

Two important new initiatives in Washington signaled a significant shift in policy regarding the black refugees, away from alleviating their immediate needs and toward providing for their long-term future. The congressional bill to end slavery in the District of Columbia, first introduced in December 1861, was one; Lincoln's message to Congress in March, urging federal support to states that would "adopt gradual abolishment of slavery," was the other.[51] Despite assorted differences—the emancipation measure, for

Figure 7.2 Theodor Kaufmann, *On to Liberty*. Gift of Erving and Joyce Wolf, in memory of Diane R. Wolf, 1982. Courtesy of the Metropolitan Museum of Art (https://www.metmuseum.org).

instance, explicitly referenced colonizing the freed people, whereas the president's message did not—both envisioned monetary compensation for slaveholders. But more to the point, they sought to address the challenges that would inevitably follow the end of slavery, and not just provide for the material wants of wartime refugees. Persons from every background and in every section of the United States understood the gist of the change and began speculating about possible consequences.

The tensions that had begun to sprout in the controlled experiment on the Sea Islands fully bloomed on the open prairies of the Midwest. In the southernmost regions of Ohio, Indiana, and Illinois along the Ohio River, fears of an influx of free black persons had shaped local politics for years.[52] Now, as talk of adopting policies to do away with slavery not only in the Confederate States but also in the Loyal Border States filled the air, the specter of wholesale migration of freed people northward loomed larger. Political arsonists tossed the explosive term "amalgamation" into the public arena to reignite longstanding fears of race mixing, to which the Ohio legislature had reacted in 1861 by banning interracial marriage. Midway through 1862, Democratic congressman Samuel S. Cox asked his congressional colleagues and his home-state constituents: "Is Ohio to Be Africanized?" "If you permit the dominant and subjugated races to remain upon the same soil, and grant them any approach to social and political equality," Cox insisted, "amalgamation, more or less, is inevitable," from which "brutality, cowardice, and crime" would inexorably flow.[53]

B. Gratz Brown, a Republican senator from Missouri, denounced amalgamation as a hoax, as "the ghost in grave-clothes that walks to terrify and affright," but the fearmongers took no notice.[54] Black leaders worried that federal officials would abandon emancipation before fully embracing it. A correspondent to the *Christian Recorder* summarily refuted the charges that emancipated slaves would overrun the North "as the frogs did Egypt in the days of Moses" or that "they will refuse to work, and will engage in robbery and murder, to obtain the means of living." In a similar vein, the editor of the *Recorder* denounced insinuations that even if emancipation did not produce "a mixing of the races" a race war would ensue.[55]

Yet in the states of the old Northwest territory, fear often triumphed over reason. The respective state legislatures aimed to take preemptive action, adding new teeth to antebellum laws restricting the settlement of black people within their borders. In March 1862, the editor of the Philadelphia *Ledger* suggested that the assortment of such bills then under consideration reflected "the silent workings of the law of races." If by this "law of races," a correspondent to the *Christian Recorder* wondered, the editorialist meant that legislative bodies would respond negatively to growing black populations until "the negroes are expelled from the land," then he took exception. Such a day would arrive only "if the civilized world was going backward," a thought too horrible to concede. "The world is silently, but certainly, marching onward to a higher and nobler destiny." Slavery, which had "stayed the progress of . . . civilization," was moving toward extinction, the letter writer claimed.[56]

Lincoln's message to Congress did little to soothe the anxiety. "*What shall be the future condition of the colored race in this land?*" wondered the Reverend William Aikman, a Presbyterian pastor from Wilmington, Delaware. Like such black commentators as the Reverend Henry McNeal Turner, Aikman believed that Lincoln's proposed compensated emancipation "marked an era in the history of the world" that will "be looked back upon in all future time as one of the grand events of this century."[57] Aikman also viewed the question he posed as "over-mastering all others for many years to come," having "already pushed itself into the foremost place." An African American "Observer" of recent congressional debates wrote to the *Christian Recorder* in a similar vein. With the topic of slavery intruding into every piece of congressional business, he theorized that "the only way to get rid of the debate on slavery is,—to abolish slavery itself."[58] The "pangs which are the birth-throes of a nation," Aikman explained, portended "a mighty change, perhaps the greatest ever seen in the world before."[59] What Lincoln later described as a new birth of freedom had occupied observers of national events long before November 1863, when he delivered the Gettysburg Address.

Aikman did not hesitate to acknowledge emancipation as a fixed fact. And, like growing numbers of his contemporaries, he dismissed the various "opinions, theories, or prejudices" that suggested the former slaves' "inferiority" or their "inability to support themselves." Colonization was utterly impracticable: as "a matter-of-fact calculation in ships and money and time," the notion of removing four million people "with a yearly increase of sixty thousand" constituted "a wild dream."[60] But he puzzled over their social and political integration into the nation and whether they could "ever on this continent abide on terms of social equality." "*Is this country to be the ultimate home of this people?*" he asked. "No," he answered. The "great laws" of commerce ensure that they will return to Africa, their original home, and "bring with them the arts and practices of civilized and Christian life." In the process, God's purpose behind the African Americans' sojourn in the United States would be fulfilled. Here was the hoary specter of the ACS recostumed in the garb of liberal political economy and divine providence.[61]

Not just political outliers feared the unrestricted movement of emancipated freed people. George Boutwell, a native of Boston, a former governor of Massachusetts, and the nation's first commissioner of internal revenue, proposed that "the states of South Carolina, Georgia, and Florida should be dedicated to the black race, and all along the gulf stream, if necessary." Though Boutwell's plan was superficially similar to the plan that General William T. Sherman announced in his Special Field Order No. 15 in January 1865, which reserved the coastal areas of those states for the exclusive settlement of black persons, Boutwell had an ulterior motive that, if anything, outweighed his strong belief in the propriety of freeing the slaves. Establishing the three states as free territory would attract freedom seekers from across the Confederacy, which would dissuade them from migrating to the North. What is more, he believed "that the mild power of persuasion should be used to get the intelligent colored people from the north to emigrate there and establish a nationality." The spirit of racial exclusionism was not confined to the "butternut" regions of the Midwest and to the constituents of Samuel Cox and the copperhead Democrats. It embraced New England and the antislavery Republicans who supported George Boutwell. While ostensibly promising that African Americans might enjoy full economic, social, and political equality in the designated states, such proposals also made clear the obstacles that black citizens would face in achieving full acceptance into the American family.[62]

———

Debates over African Americans' future in the republic took on new urgency after Lincoln issued the preliminary Emancipation Proclamation in late September. Soon thereafter, a group of prominent Bostonians formed the Emancipation League to help shape the ensuing national debate. With a view toward "what is to be the *status* of the negro after the Rebellion is suppressed," they aimed to understand "the capacities of the colored men of the South" to "take their place in society, as a laboring class, with a fair prospect of self-support and progress." One of the founders of the league, Samuel Gridley Howe, the renowned physician, philanthropist, and antislavery activist who was one of the "Secret Six" funders of John Brown's 1859 raid on Harper's Ferry, insisted that "we must collect facts and use them as ammunition." At his urging, the league appointed a committee (which included Howe) to investigate conditions among the formerly enslaved people in places under federal control: Washington, D.C., and its immediate Virginia suburbs, Fort Monroe and vicinity, and Port Royal.

The fact gatherers sent questionnaires to superintendents of contrabands seeking information about the numbers of freed people under governmental jurisdiction; their "dispositions" toward work, education, religion, and their former owners; and their treatment at the hands of federal military personnel.[63] Despite some surprises, the respondents generally confirmed what the questioners had already suspected: the freed people were industrious and eager to overcome the forced ignorance of their past, but they were naive in religious terms and lax in moral terms. The black refugees displayed little vindictiveness toward their former owners and remarkable equanimity in the face of ill treatment by their nominal liberators. They had little desire to relocate to the North, preferring instead "to remain on the soil where they were born," except to avoid reenslavement.[64]

With facts in hand, members of the league petitioned Congress to act. Building on Aikman's metaphor of rebirth, they observed that the war had created "a crisis—'a nation born in a day,'" in which both political leaders and citizens must assume responsibility "to preside at the birth of a race." Yet they feared "that the great experiment of the reconstruction of southern society on the basis of free labor may fail solely through neglect or mal-administration." They decried the "irregularity and injustice in the government of these persons," with "one rule prevailing in Port Royal, another at New Orleans, a third in Kentucky, and a fourth in Washington." "The want of a well-defined policy on the part of the government" often crippled efforts to alleviate their needs.[65] What is more, such decentralization obstructed the development of a national strategy for reconstructing Southern society in the aftermath of slavery.

As an alternative to Washington's neglect, the league held up the examples of England, France, Russia, Denmark, and Holland, which in "similar emergencies" had created fact-finding commissions "to guide the actions" of policy makers. The petitioners insisted that the emancipated people held legitimate claims against the nation for "justice" and "fair play"—that is, "to a fair trial or the experiment of their capacity for self-support and progress." If the experiment were to fail, "we shall be held responsible to God and to posterity." Stabilizing "the great source of wealth in a large part of our country—the laboring population," while at the same time recognizing that the laborers are "human beings" "and members of a race whom we have long and cruelly oppressed," required a systematic approach directed from the highest levels of government. Nothing less than a federal bureau would suffice. "Without some such system for the speedy organization," the government's new policy of emancipation "will prove either fruitless or only a proclamation of anarchy." But when properly designed, implemented, and managed, "emancipation is prosperity."[66]

Two influential antislavery politicians from Massachusetts, Senator Charles Sumner and Governor John A. Andrew, also argued for better planning, as did abolitionists outside government circles. J. Miller McKim, the respected Presbyterian minister and abolitionist from Philadelphia, pressed Secretary of War Edwin M. Stanton to create a government commission along the lines that the Emancipation League had recommended. In mid-March 1863, Stanton called on three prominent men to form the American Freedmen's Inquiry Commission (AFIC). The three were social reformers with legitimate antislavery credentials but without the standing in the abolitionist movement that Sumner might have desired. Robert Dale Owen, who chaired the commission, was the Scottish-born son of the founder of the utopian community of New Harmony, Indiana. As an adult, Owen advocated feminism, abolitionism, and spiritualism, and under the Democratic Party banner he won a seat first in the Indiana state legislature and then in the U.S. House of Representatives before becoming U.S. minister to the Kingdom of the Two Sicilies. A firm believer in "the Divine economy" and the "progressive spirit of Christian civilization," Owen had written a series of public letters in 1862, one each to the secretary of the treasury, to the secretary of war, and to President Lincoln. While he opposed taking "revolutionary short-cuts out of a difficulty," he insisted that there was no alternative to "general emancipation" with compensation to owners.[67] Chiding officials that "administrative capacity in public affairs is not our strong point," he observed that developing such capacity would be necessary not only to win the war but also to save "our entire governmental experiment."[68] Leaders of modern states required both a rational policy-making apparatus and efficient managerial practices to meet contemporary challenges.

The second commissioner was Samuel Gridley Howe, stalwart member of the Emancipation League of Boston. Howe championed information gathering but also dabbled in questionable racial theorizing, influenced to a great extent by his friendship with Louis Agassiz, the renowned Harvard University geologist and biologist. Agassiz was one of the chief proponents of polygenesis, which held that the presumed races of humankind were in fact separately created species, a theory that endeared him to proslavery apologists. Both Howe and Agassiz were part of the "Saturday Club" of influential Bostonians that had begun meeting regularly before the war and whose members included Senator Sumner, Governor Andrew, and the writers John Greenleaf Whittier and James Russell Lowell, among others.[69]

The third commissioner, James McKaye, began his career somewhat inauspiciously as a schoolmaster at a quasi-military academy and later pursued business and the law, becoming president of the American Telegraph Company by the eve of the Civil War. Through a combination of Whig politics and journalism, he immersed himself in the antislavery cause and used his home in Buffalo, New York, as a safe house on the Underground Railroad. Friends and strangers alike addressed him as "Colonel" for his many years of service as an officer in the New York state militia.[70] McKaye chided national leaders for attempting "to conquer a peace" while neglecting the enemy's vulnerable point, slavery, and thus effectively serving as "the keeper . . . of four millions of his subjects, for his sole benefit and support."[71] Slavery threatened the nation's future as well as the current war effort. "In the ethical evolutions of our national history, a second great era presents itself," he argued late in 1862. "Slavery by its own act has outlawed itself," he insisted, and the United States should complete the work. A thoroughgoing policy of emancipation would affirm "our common humanity" and contribute to "national regeneration and glory."[72]

In his charge to the commissioners, Secretary Stanton stated the challenge posed by "the great and constantly increasing colored population" for which U.S. military forces had become responsible. He instructed them to gather "authentic and accurate information" and to recommend "such practical measures" that would place the freed people "in a state of self-support and self-defense, with the least possible disturbance to the great industrial interest of the country," and would enable them to contribute most effectively to the war effort. The secretary gave the commissioners broad leeway to devise a plan of action for achieving that goal. In mid-March, Stanton met with

Commissioners Owen and McKaye, who in turn arranged to brief their absent colleague about what had transpired. In advance of that meeting, Howe outlined an approach that involved "Enquiry" and "Recommendations" focusing on three subsets of persons: the refugees already within U.S. lines, persons "in slavery who can be induced to come out & join us," and the black population generally. Paraphrasing Stanton's charge, Howe subtly changed it to devising "measures to ensure their good with [the] least social disturbance."[73]

From April to early June, the commissioners went about their initial inquiries, largely following the still-fresh footprints that Howe and the Emancipation League had left behind. At the end of June, they published a preliminary report, a key component of which involved establishing baseline assessments of the freed people's aptitude for assimilating fully into the civic culture of their communities and the nation. The commissioners took special interest in determining the black refugees' willingness to support themselves through industrious labor, to spend their earnings wisely, and to educate themselves and their children. They also wished to know the state of their moral development, particularly with regard to marital fidelity and parental responsibility, their religious sensibilities, and their willingness to aid the Union cause as soldiers or military laborers.[74]

Commissioners Owen and Howe, who visited Washington and the accessible areas around Fort Monroe and in eastern North Carolina, drew generally positive conclusions about the freed people in those districts, praising their loyalty to the government and their willingness to work.[75] In South Carolina, however, Commissioner McKaye encountered sharply different conditions, which prompted an epiphany similar to Edward Pierce's a year earlier. "The system of negro slavery" around Port Royal, McKaye concluded, had developed "with the least modification from contact with external civilization." Family life suffered as "the maternal relation was often as little respected as the marital," and the net result was a marked "deterioration of the race." Notwithstanding the colonel's sobering findings, the commissioners concluded that the freed people of South Carolina might "in a comparatively brief period, be in a measure reformed by judicious management" and two other motivators. The first was "the payment of wages for work done"; the second was "military training," the font of "self-respect and self-reliance." "The negro has a strong sense of the obligation of law and of the stringency of any duty legally imposed upon him," they explained. "The law, in the shape of military rule, takes for him the place of his master," but with one major improvement, namely, "he submits to it heartily and cheerfully, without any sense of degradation."[76]

In their preliminary report, the commissioners advocated the creation of a "Bureau of Emancipation," an idea that—thanks in part to the work of the

Emancipation League of Boston—had been growing in popularity over the previous several months. The AFIC proposed "a plan of provisional organization for the improvement, protection and employment of refugee freedmen." It consisted of a system of "superintendencies," with a superintendent-general of freedmen providing overall direction, assisted by department superintendents (one to each state) and resident superintendents and assistants (approximately one per each 3,000–5,000 freed people). Each residency would offer hospital services and "enlightened instruction, educational and religious." Where the ordinary courts were not in session, provost judges would hear cases, aiming to teach "the important lesson that the obedience which, as slaves, they paid to the will of a master, must now be rendered . . . to established law—care being taken not to encourage them to be litigious."[77] Their operational guidelines followed the logic of their conceptual framework wherein the abstract law would replace the personal master.

Like Pierce and other emissaries of Northern culture, the commissioners assumed a paternalistic stance toward "the African race." Describing the presumed beneficiaries of the recommendations as persons "of genial nature, alive to gratitude, open to impressions of kindness, and . . . readily influenced," they recommended against treating the freed people "with weak and injurious indulgence," lest they act like "children of preference, fostered by charity, dependent for a living on government or on benevolent associations." Instead, circumstances called for a combination of "mild firmness" and "even-handed justice." "In their new character of freedmen," they must understand that "self-reliance and self-support are demanded."[78] Turning attention to the broader challenges that emancipation posed, Owen, Howe, and McKaye sought to dispel the dual fears of mass migration northward and racial amalgamation that Congressman Cox and other such nativists were fomenting. "The local attachments of the negro," they asserted confidently, were "eminently strong." What is more, the "genial climate" of the Southern states would prove so attractive that "half the free negro population" of the North would soon cross "the Mason and Dixon's line to join the emancipated freedmen of the South." Correctly perceiving that "the chief object of ambition among the refugees is to own property, especially to possess land," the commissioners nonetheless stopped short of recommending how to translate that aspiration into reality.[79]

––––––

The preliminary report made little impression on Secretary Stanton. It did, however, attract considerable attention both in Washington and in the field. Members of Congress who had begun drafting measures to create the bureau of emancipation cited it, and Chaplain John Eaton, superintendent of contrabands in General Ulysses S. Grant's Department of the Tennessee, indicated that Grant and Adjutant General Lorenzo Thomas had "pronounced it a 'very sensible and useful Report.'" The eminent Congregational minister Charles B. Boynton, who served as the corresponding secretary for the Western Freedmen's Aid Commission in Cincinnati, took the matter further. Believing that the commissioners had authority to appoint superintendents, Boynton noted that the work in the West had virtually come to a halt, "convinced that we can do nothing effectually for the increasing thousands of suffering ones, until some such plan as you set forth in your Report is adopted in this field." Based on the reliable estimate of "officers of high rank" that the number of refugees in the department might eventually rise to "half a million" persons, he hoped that the commissioners would appoint someone soon, hopefully a person "in whom the Christian public of the West already have confidence."[80]

Without Stanton's support, however, the concept of superintendencies could not advance beyond the arrangements that military authorities in the field had already adopted to suit their circumstances. By the spring of 1863, the commanders of all the army's administrative departments along the eastern seaboard from Virginia to South Carolina and along the Mississippi River from Tennessee to Louisiana had appointed superintendents of freedmen. Most were either chaplains in volunteer regiments or staff officers in the quartermaster's department, and most exercised responsibilities broadly similar to what the AFIC proposed.[81] When Eaton traveled to Washington in July 1863 to explain his work to Lincoln, the president instructed him to meet with the AFIC. Eaton spoke at length with the commissioners and left with them a detailed report. "After carefully considering the facts set forth, and questioning me personally," he later recalled, "they concluded that our experience in the Valley was a very valuable contribution to solving the problem of how the freedmen should be treated." Because the commissioners "had nothing essentially new to suggest" by way of practical recommendations, Eaton took pride in knowing "that men of sound judgment, and training in humanitarian work, should find themselves in sympathy, from the theoretic standpoint, with the measures" he had adopted.[82] In retrospect Eaton credited the commissioners with "preparing the way for the formation of the Freedmen's Bureau," but Stanton's aloofness would hardly have predicted that outcome. Early in the summer of 1863, Owen, Howe, and McKaye still hoped to make the case for creating "some central point of control which should insure united and uniform effort."[83]

The respect that the commissioners showed to Eaton and the high regard they expressed for his work casts into bold relief their comparative indifference to the testimony of African American participants in the struggle to end slavery and construct a new society in its place. To be sure, the commissioners' desire to gather statements from black witnesses of varying geographical regions and backgrounds was laudable but by no means unique given the rapidly changing status of freed people before the law. (The District of Columbia's emancipation law, for instance, obliged the panel charged with its implementation to accept the testimony of witnesses without regard to color.) Yet the motives of the AFIC commissioners were not entirely clear. The largest number of black informants consisted of the Afro-Canadians that Samuel Gridley Howe interviewed to prove his theories about race mixing and the future prospects of African-descended people in the Northern latitudes. Next highest in number came the persons that Howe and Owen interviewed in Missouri, Tennessee, and Kentucky, including several who were still legally enslaved.[84] The commissioners did not consult the numerous national black leaders (or the local ones who emerged in response to the challenges and opportunities posed by the war), many of whom had themselves been enslaved and had highly developed visions for the future of African Americans in the United States. In fact, Owen, Howe, and McKaye ignored the suggestion of James N. Gloucester, the noted New York minister and abolitionist, who in July 1863 proposed that they create "a sub committee, or a General Superintendency, of three inteligent, well informed Colored Men" as advisors. "For you must be aware Gentlemen," Gloucester explained, "that it is not so much the present position of these freedmen, as their ultimate state in the American republick, that makes it to the republick, a question of such immense importance."[85] It appears, then, that the commissioners relied on African American testimony less to inform their conclusions than to furnish anecdotes for their reports. As a result, the persons with the greatest stake in the struggles for freedom and equal citizenship had, at best, limited influence on the AFIC's work.[86]

Although the preliminary report proclaimed the freedmen's "duty to fight for their own freedom," it also described that obligation as a general one that devolved on all oppressed people who aspired to be free. In the specific context of the mid-nineteenth-century United States, other implications followed from black men's military service, specifically the chance to "ensure for their race, from the present generation in this country, common respect and decent treatment in their social relations with whites." "Only by proving their manhood as soldiers," the commissioners pointedly observed, only through "a baptism of blood—can they bring about such a change in public opinion." That notwithstanding, in the preliminary report the commissioners equivocated. They appeared to envision military labor as the key contribution freedmen could make to the war effort. Properly organized into labor battalions—"with badges around their hat, labelled 'United States service'" and "marched regularly to and from work," they argued, such a force might release 100,000 white soldiers from ancillary duties.[87] The commissioners did not address whether military laborers stood equal to soldiers in proving their manhood and demonstrating their fitness for citizenship and the vote.

———

Within weeks of the release of the AFIC's preliminary report, the victories at Gettysburg and Vicksburg injected new hope into the Union war effort on the part of soldiers and civilians alike. The news also strengthened the case for emancipation, which, in turn, prompted Samuel Gridley Howe to begin a fresh round of fact gathering in the form of printed questionnaires. In a short-form version, modeled after the Emancipation League's inquiry, he asked public officials in various Northern cities to compare black and mulatto residents with each other and with white residents regarding their health, their intelligence, and their industry. He particularly sought confirmation of his theory that mulattoes were weaker and less prolific than either of the unmixed races. More generally, however, he wished to know whether the persons of African ancestry were "valuable members of the community or not."[88] Howe directed a long-form questionnaire to superintendents of freed people in the Union-controlled areas of the Confederacy. Besides general information about the black residents, he also sought insight into slavery's effects on family values, religious sensibilities, habits of obedience, and traits that would promote self-support and property accumulation. He wished to know whether their "local attachments" overrode any desire to migrate north. In short, were they "fit to take their place in society with a fair prospect of self-support and progress," or did they need "preparatory training and guardianship."[89]

Howe's general fascination with the racial traits of pure blacks and mulattoes had recently reached new heights thanks to an exchange of letters with his friend Louis Agassiz. Howe sought advice regarding the "political, physiological, and ethnological principles" that impinged on the vast subject of emancipation, so that appropriate policies might be adopted that were consistent with "the natural laws of increase and their modification by existing causes." The question that "occupies me most now" was whether "the African race" would persist or "be absorbed, diluted, and finally effaced by the white race." Closely related was whether "the general practical amalgamation fostered by slavery" would become more prevalent after emancipation.[90] Agassiz responded dutifully, acknowledging Howe's "influence in the councils of the nation upon this most important subject."[91]

Howe surely knew that his questions about amalgamation would elicit a pointed response, and Agassiz, who termed race mixing "most repugnant to my feelings," indeed "unnatural," did not disappoint. He confirmed Howe's suppositions about the "sickly physique" and "impaired fecundity" of mulattoes and hoped that "sound policy" would "put every possible obstacle to the crossing of the races, and the increase of half-breeds." If, on the other hand, "the ideas now generally prevalent about amalgamation" were to gain "a practical influence" over "the affairs of the nation," he concluded, "the progress of civilization" itself might be threatened.[92] While admitting that he "rejoice[d] in the prospects of universal emancipation," Agassiz did not view "equality" in monolithic terms. "Legal equality," he argued, "should be the common boon of humanity," but "social equality" was not "a necessary complement of legal equality." Nor was political equality, which held the potential to promote "conflicting interests, before we have ascertained what may be the practical working of universal freedom and legal equality for two races, so different as the whites and negroes, living under one government."[93]

Howe's letters to Agassiz contain a jumble of racial and political theories sprinkled with what he took for granted as natural "laws." He blasted slavery "as a disturbing force in the development of our national character," which had "produced monstrous deformities of a bodily as well as moral nature" that "impaired the purity and lowered the quality of the national blood." Slavery enabled masters to cultivate licentious habits, from which a sizable mixed-race population resulted. Many of the "vigorous black race" and the "feeble mulatto breed," Howe lamented, "have drifted northward, right in the teeth of thermal laws, to find homes where they would never live by natural election."[94] Howe believed that emancipation would give "fair play" to the natural laws, with the net result that "the colored population will disappear from the Northern and Middle States . . . before the more vigorous and prolific white race." "It will be the duty of the statesman," he concluded, "to favor, by wise measures, the operation of these laws and the purification and elevation of the national blood."[95]

Fixing his gaze more narrowly on the South than his friend did, Agassiz was convinced that emancipation would enable the "unmixed negroes" to prosper there. He went even further to suggest "that the negro race must be considered as permanently settled upon this continent, no less firmly than the white race, and that it is our duty to look upon them as co-tenants in the possession of this part of the world."[96] In Agassiz's view, cotenancy presumed legal equality but neither social nor political equality. In the South, he concluded, where the black population outnumbered the white, political equality would be especially risky. In their search for a formula to minimize adverse consequences, Howe and the commissioners refused to paint themselves into the same logical corner that Agassiz occupied. For them, granting the vote to freedmen offered the only hope of avoiding long-term federal oversight.[97]

———

On December 1, 1863, representatives of the freedmen's relief societies of Boston, New York, Philadelphia, and Cincinnati met with President Lincoln to press the case for a bureau of emancipation. Their rationale neatly summarized the growing Northern consensus about divine intervention in the war against slavery. For generations the nation had managed to avoid its certain reckoning with "civil war and social revolution," which slavery invariably "calls down . . . upon its own domain." "But God took that question out of the hands of man; away from prudential, economic, or human calculations, and made it simply a fact and a necessity." "The national instincts of self-preservation," they reasoned, "have precipitated general, if not universal, emancipation upon us a century in advance of merely human arrangements or hopes." At Lincoln's urging, the philanthropists petitioned Congress, and before the end of the month the Massachusetts Republican Thomas D. Eliot introduced a measure proposing to create such a bureau.[98] At the same time, the first inklings of a constitutional amendment outlawing slavery appeared from the pen of the Ohio congressman James M. Ashley. Robert Hamilton's New Year's editorial in the *Anglo-African* praised the idea of such a bureau that would be "capable of organizing the freedom of 'three millions and a half of fellow-creatures, fellow-countrymen and citizens!'" For Hamilton and other African American observers, the overarching political question of their future place in the American republic had already been decided in favor of freedom, citizenship, and equality. What remained to be seen were the specific ways in which the envisioned constitutional amendment and bureau of emancipation would advance those goals.[99]

A handful of congressional Republicans, led by Senator Henry Wilson of Massachusetts and Representative Eliot, had shown interest in creating the bureau as early as the previous January, hard on the heels of the Emancipation Proclamation, and each had introduced a bill to that effect. Referred to committee, both measures quietly and quickly died. But in January 1864, when Eliot's revised bill reached the floor of the House, proponents did not hesitate in pressing hard for passage. Eliot led the charge, urging his colleagues to take responsibility for these "children of the Government." Predictably, Democrats rose in opposition.[100] New York congressman James Brooks objected to the proposed agency's scope, labeling it "vast in its territory, vast in its objects, vast in its purposes, vast in its intentions." He noted sarcastically that the bill could not have been Eliot's work, for it showed no signs of "the practical mind of Massachusetts." Instead, he concluded, it "must have come from some of the freedmen's commissioners—perhaps from Robert Dale Owen; for the bill is Socialistic, Fourieristic, Owenistic, erotic." The Ohioan George H. Pendleton condemned emancipation in toto, arguing that the more than half a million freedmen under federal jurisdiction "long for the repose and quiet of their old homes, and the care of their masters" inasmuch as "the promised boon" of freedom had "proven itself to be a life of torture, ending only in certain and speedy death."[101]

Despite such attempts at sabotage, on March 1, 1864, the House passed the measure but only by the narrow margin of two votes. When the Senate took up the bill the next day, attention turned quickly to the administrative home for the proposed agency. Whereas the House located it in the War Department, Senator Charles Sumner, who chaired the Select Committee on Slavery, favored the Treasury Department. Sumner's version of the bill won the Senate's approval late in June, but the House refused to take up the proposed substitute and deferred the matter until the next session of Congress.[102] For another six months, the clock stood still—once again—on an important legislative component of the Union's piecemeal and slowly evolving emancipation policy. Meanwhile, the growing number of army recruits satisfied expectations that the enslaved must fight for their freedom. What remained to be decided was their role in determining the future of the nation after the restoration of peace.

―――――――

As the 1864 military campaign season got under way, with Sherman setting his sights on Atlanta and Grant and Meade on Richmond, the AFIC commissioners worked on their final report. Oddly, although not entirely surprisingly, the three commissioners went their separate ways, each man pursuing further specialized study. Chairman Owen investigated the demographics of the transatlantic trade in captured Africans from the fifteenth to the nineteenth centuries and of their descendant communities in the Americas. He also pored over documents and treatises to build an unassailable legal justification for the president's Emancipation Proclamation. Howe wrote up what he had learned from "the experience of the colored people in Canada" as it informed "the future condition" of their counterparts in the United States.[103] Finally, James McKaye headed for New Orleans to gain insight into the monumental struggle over the new labor system to replace slavery that federal authorities had introduced in the Mississippi valley.

In mid-May, fourteen months after being empaneled, the AFIC submitted its final report to Secretary Stanton. Long, sprawling, and even at times self-contradictory, the document bore fresh witness to the unresolved tensions of the nation's emancipation policy.[104] Absent was the immediacy of the preliminary report, which arose largely from the commissioners' recently completed fact-finding forays into the field. Instead, the final report contained detailed, often ponderous arguments, having little to do with Stanton's original charge. The first of its three chapters, which made up more than half of the document, presented the results of Owen's months of study. With meticulous detail, he estimated the overall numbers of African captives and the chief points of embarkation in the Americas. One of its major conclusions— one corroborated by recent scholarship—was the large discrepancy in the reproductive rates of the African-descended populations in North America (where the population experienced net growth) as opposed to everywhere else (where the population failed to grow by natural increase). Yet, despite its intrinsic value as a pioneering work of scholarship, Owen's findings appear to have had negligible influence on Lincoln or Stanton and the emancipation policy they pursued.[105]

In the report's second—and next longest—chapter, Owen crafted an elaborate legal argument in defense of emancipation. Lincoln, he argued, had no choice but to respond when the secessionists attacked Fort Sumter to prevent the dissolution of "the great American Union" into another example of the "petty discordant sovereignties . . . found in more southern portions of our hemisphere." And emancipation offered "the only practicable road to domestic tranquility," the "progress of civilization and humanity," and "the national honor."[106] "The crime which we are now expiating in blood must be atoned for . . . by thrusting out from among us the wrong of the age." As to the decree of emancipation itself, the Constitution did not prohibit seizing "incorporeal things" such as "legal claim[s] to the labor of another," which (unlike the terms "slave" and "slavery") the nation's founding document recognized. Owen's logic may have impressed jurists, but it gained little popular support. In the early summer of 1864, the Northern public looked not to legal scholars but to Grant, Sherman, and Meade to deliver the knockout blow to the Confederacy, which would make justifying emancipation moot.[107]

The third and last chapter of the AFIC final report, "The Future in the United States of the African Race," made up barely 10 percent of the document. Its brevity notwithstanding, the discussion addressed three critical policy areas that remained explosive through Reconstruction and beyond: (1) the responsibility of the federal government to oversee "the stormy transition from slavery to freedom," (2) the nature of citizenship and the determination of who had legitimate claims to its rights and privileges, and (3) the ability of local communities and the broader civic culture to accept African Americans as equal contributors to the public good and beneficiaries of the nation's bounties. The commissioners also advocated strongly for employing black men as soldiers but insisted that they not be treated as "stepchildren":

"No discrimination should be made either as to wages or in any other respect, between the white and the colored soldier."[108]

Perhaps surprisingly, the final report said nothing about the superintendencies that had figured so largely in the preliminary version. The commissioners clearly puzzled over the level of federal assistance that was "necessary or desirable" and concluded "there is as much danger in doing too much as in doing too little."[109] Knowledgeable government experts were of mixed opinion. General James Wadsworth, for example, who was the former military governor of Washington then serving as a War Department special examiner in the Mississippi valley, advocated for "a system of guardianship" to last no more than five years.[110] Major George L. Stearns, chief recruiter of black troops in Tennessee, believed simply "that the less gov't interference we can have the better."[111] Given the mixed testimony, the commissioners pulled their punches. They conceded the need for "a freedman's bureau," but with only lukewarm conviction: they referenced it only once, using lowercase letters. What is more, they quickly added that "the freedman should be treated . . . as any other free man," subject to "the natural laws of supply and demand." "All aid given to these people," Owen, Howe, and McKaye argued, "should be regarded as a temporary necessity," and "all supervision over them should be provisional only, and advisory in its character."[112]

The commissioners believed that the new relationship between the government and its citizens rested on two pillars. The first was the responsible freedman who headed his own household. Drawing from the laudable "display of manhood in negro soldiers," they argued that "the negro, in his new condition as freedman," represented "a changed being."[113] In his supplementary report, Howe elaborated. "The manner in which twenty thousand are taking care of themselves in Canada" answered the question of "what shall be done with the negroes." His logical progression was simple, from the individual freedman, through the family, to the community: they "earn a living, and gather property; they marry and respect women; they build churches, and send their children to schools; they improve in manners and morals."[114] The second pillar of the commissioners' envisioned relationship between the government and its black citizens was equal civil and political rights, which they believed (prematurely as it turned out) would be guaranteed in the proposed constitutional amendment outlawing slavery. "Secured in equal rights," the commissioners argued, "the enfranchised negro" will prove to be "as capable of taking care of himself and his family as any other portion of our people."[115]

When the commissioners addressed the communities in which the freedmen and their families would reside, their model succumbed to the influence of Howe's racial theorizing. They accepted his notions about "thermal lines" and about the presumed inferiority of the mixed race "in physical power and in health to the pure race, black or white." If these natural laws failed to "denude the North of its negro population," they reasoned, "the personal prejudice against negroes," which was "stronger in the Northern than in the Southern States," would deliver the coup de grace. A North denuded of black inhabitants would present a clear field for persons of European ancestry to regenerate the national blood and thereby ensure the future prosperity of the nation. The interactions between black and white persons in the South would help dull "the edge of national prejudice and weaken the feeling which regards [the Negroes] as a separate and alien race."[116] Again, Howe's supplemental report elaborated. In the South "the negroes will imitate the best traits of white civilization, and will improve rapidly." Their "industry and thrift" would "forward the industrial interests of the country, without the fearful demoralization heretofore caused by their oppression and debasement."[117]

Notwithstanding the hints of foreboding in these predictions, the commissioners remained cautiously optimistic. "Offer the freedmen," they concluded, "temporary aid and counsel until they become a little accustomed to their new sphere of life; secure to them, by law, their just rights of person and property; relieve them, by a fair and equal administration of justice, from the depressing influence of disgraceful prejudice; above all, guard them against the virtual restoration of slavery in any form, under any pretext, and then let them take care of themselves." This constituted a remarkably tall order of contingencies on which the success of emancipation would depend, especially from men as worldly wise as Owen, Howe, and McKaye. Yet the three also seemed content to let "future harmony" evolve out of small acts of kindness toward those who, having just emerged from bondage, were "weak and dependent."[118] Emancipation is prosperity.

The reports that Commissioners Howe and McKaye each submitted as supplements to the commission's joint work highlight the persistent contradictions in the government's effort to guide the formation of emancipation policy. Howe's *Refugees from Slavery in Canada West* aimed to demonstrate that abolishing slavery would not jeopardize Northern communities or threaten the nation with ruin. Yet Howe succumbed to the danger that William Sewell had cautioned about regarding attempts to assess the results of emancipation in the British West Indies. Howe "dragged into the argument," to use Sewell's terminology, "an ethnological issue, quite foreign to the case," finding evidence in Canada to support spurious theories of racial degeneration that he believed would also affect the free black population of the Northern United States.[119] Curiously, Howe held Sewell's *Ordeal of Free Labor* in high regard. In detailed comments he made on the text, Howe praised Sewell's appreciation for the unique characteristics of the various colonies in terms of their history, their climate and resources, the "habits and customs" of each island's people, "their industry, their commerce and their government."[120] Yet his obsession with racial theorizing got the better of him, and in the end his *Refugees from Slavery* presented troubling evidence of the breadth and depth of public prejudice that the egalitarian vision for the future would have to overcome.

James McKaye's supplement exuded pessimism rather than the qualified optimism of the commission's joint document. Without a thought to racial theorizing, McKaye focused instead on understanding the day-to-day dynamics of revolutionary social change. Titling his work *The Mastership and Its Fruits: The Emancipated Slave Face to Face with His Old Master*, McKaye aimed to convey the immediacy and the intensity of the transition from slavery to freedom on the cotton and sugar plantations of the Mississippi valley. There a contest raged between the entrenched advocates of the old order and the champions of change, a sometimes quarrelsome coalition of Northern officials, missionaries, philanthropists, and entrepreneurs, and Southern freed people. From ample testimony he learned how strongly former slaveholders believed they would turn back the hands of time once the Yankees conceded the folly of their ways and returned to the North. McKaye saw only one way to avoid this dark vision for the future: "the ultimate division of the great plantations, into moderate sized farms, to be held and cultivated by the labor of their owners." "No such thing as free, democratic society can exist in any country where all the lands are owned by one class of men and are cultivated by another," McKaye insisted.[121]

In the end, the AFIC preliminary and final reports contributed significantly to national discussions over emancipation policy. The two documents, along with Howe's supplementary study focusing on the black communities of Canada West, concluded that legal equality and manhood suffrage held the key to black Americans' success in freedom. McKaye's hope to break up the large plantations appeared in a watered-down version in the March 1865 act establishing the Bureau of Refugees, Freedmen, and Abandoned Lands. The law gave the bureau control over confiscated and abandoned lands and authorized the commissioner to distribute the land to "loyal refugees and freedmen" in parcels of "not more than forty acres," which could be either rented or purchased based on the estimated value of each parcel in 1860.[122] But the act stopped far short of "the ultimate division of the great plantations" that McKaye had proposed and the freed people expected in return for their years of unpaid labor and for their loyalty to the Union during the war.

————

Unlike the Freedmen's Bureau Act, the main object of which was to develop and then monitor the ground rules of freedom in the former slave states, the proposed amendment to the U.S. Constitution focused on the reverse side of that exercise, namely, outlawing slavery. Although Republican leaders had employed the language of the Northwest Ordinance of 1797, which banned slavery or involuntary servitude except as punishment for crime, certain lawmakers hoped to achieve a broader declaration of what freedom entailed in the draft constitutional amendment.[123] In December 1863, early in the first session of the Thirty-Eighth Congress, Ohio representative James M. Ashley's resolution proposing to abolish slavery sparked fierce debate between supporters and opponents of the measure. At the center of the controversy was a concept favored by Senator Charles Sumner and Representative Thaddeus Stevens, and referenced in the AFIC's final report. It featured joining to the prohibition against slavery an affirmation of every person's equal standing before the law, but the draft containing that wording died in committee. In April 1864, the Senate approved a measure that incorporated the language of the Northwest Ordinance, which the House rejected, at the same time deferring the matter to the next session of Congress.[124] In his annual message to Congress in December, shortly after his reelection, President Lincoln urged the House to reconsider the Senate's version and then commenced an intense lobbying campaign. On the last day of January 1865, the House approved the joint resolution, thereby moving it for ratification to the states, where it was beholden to the same complex of legislative calendars, rules, personalities, and partisan considerations that had characterized the debate in Congress.[125]

After more than ten months of such proceedings, on December 6, 1865, Georgia's legislature voted to approve, marking the twenty-seventh and deciding "aye" necessary to meet the constitutional requirement of consent by three-quarters of the states; and on December 18, 1865, Secretary of State William H. Seward announced that the Thirteenth Amendment prohibiting slavery was the law of the land.[126] This was the event that Charles Wesley commemorated on that mid-December day at Howard University in 1940. But the amendment fell far short of what the freed people expected of the nation's official announcement that slavery had come to an end. After all, it said only what was not to be, which they already knew, not what was to be, which they desperately wanted to know.

Chapter 8

The Blessings of a Home

In late March 1864, Henry Clay Bruce and his fiancée executed a bold escape from their owners in central Missouri to Leavenworth, Kansas. Bruce had been managing a farm, acting as an intermediary between his owner and his fellow enslaved laborers. At the start of the year, the owner had offered him "a free pass" to travel about at will as well as "fifteen dollars per month, with board and clothing," and Bruce accepted despite grave misgivings. Commencing the dash for freedom, the couple knew that her owner would be in hot pursuit. After crossing the Missouri River safely into Kansas, "I then felt myself a free man," he recalled—a "new man." The couple headed straight for the minister of the AME Church in Leavenworth, "who united us in marriage in his parlor."[1] Becoming a legitimate family was of the highest priority for the new man and the new woman, followed closely by making a home for themselves befitting their new status.

Tens of thousands of freedom seekers undertook the journey from slavery to freedom, undergoing the transformation from persons dependent on their owners into new men and women. They did so in steps, some small and others large, some of their own volition and others forced by circumstances over which they had no control. Severing the physical and mental ties with owners always came first. For some it was the easiest step, but for others it was the hardest. When members of the AFIC visited Louisville, Robert Dale Owen met two enslaved women who hired their own time, sheltering and boarding themselves. Although both were well on their way toward independence, neither could escape the ties that bound them to "home"—that is, the dwellings of their owners, where their children still resided but where "nothing short of compulsion would cause either of them to return." Like countless other freedom seekers, the two women faced the Faustian dilemma that pitted their ability to act like free persons—however, constrained by the fact that they were still enslaved—against the welfare of their families. They were suspended between slavery and freedom.[2]

In 1863, Thomas Nast, the noted illustrator of *Harper's Magazine*, employed the popular before-and-after visual device to illustrate how emancipation exchanged the prewar horrors of slavery (including the sadistic abuse of enslaved people by means of branding irons and whips, the separation of families through sale, and the pursuit of freedom seekers with dogs) for the postwar promises of freedom (including compensated labor, schools, and

Figure 8.1 Thomas Nast, *Emancipation*. Courtesy of the Library of Congress
Prints and Photographs Division, LC-DIG-pga-03898.

churches under the aegis of the national flag) (see figure 8.1). By portraying
slavery's negative impact on families, Nast created an effective foil for the ide-
alized family occupying the cabin he depicted in the centerpiece. The pater-
familias is surrounded by his wife and his children as well as an elderly woman,
presumably his mother or mother-in-law. Warm from the radiated heat of a
Union stove, he sits in an upholstered chair surrounded by three children
while his wife cooks. In the background are two young adults, a man and a
woman, who appear to be examining material, perhaps for a wedding dress.
From above, the goddess Columbia symbolically blesses the new domestic
ideal that was to supplant the battered slave family in the new era of freedom.[3]

This image, like the others Nast would subsequently create, drew on popular sentiment and helped shape public opinion regarding the place of African Americans in the war effort and in a reconstructed United States of
America. Despite the damaging legacy of slavery, the African Americans Nast
portrayed shared the same values that European Americans held dear. They
deserved sympathy and assistance. With protection ensured for their homes
and firesides, the progressive influence of compensated labor, public education, and organized Christianity would transform brutalized slaves into up-

standing and productive citizens of the new republic. As of January 1863, the vision of emancipation's transformative power stopped short of manhood suffrage, but by 1865 Nast's images suggested that the sacrifices African American soldiers endured in defending the nation constituted a legitimate claim for the vote.

———

"Home" is one of the most commonly used English words. Like its counterparts in other languages, it has multiple meanings. In its literal sense, it refers to a residence or a place of origin. In its figurative senses, it suggests belonging to an identifiable community, whether small scale such as a neighborhood, or larger scale such as a people or a nation. Estrangement from home—whether voluntarily or involuntarily—can have profound negative connotations, the ultimate of which—homelessness—suggests a state of extreme alienation. In the mid-nineteenth-century United States, the term "home" and its close correlate "family" took on special meaning: in the slave states, the heads of slaveholding households owned unrelated persons as property. From a legal standpoint, the enslaved persons were entirely subordinate to their owners.

Emancipation forced on adult freed people the dual challenge of establishing their own personhood—a sense of a personal identity as well as the associated habits of thought and action—and strengthening their families, the chief building block of community and nation. To be sure, military and naval service went a long way toward accomplishing this transformation among the men who served. This process began when the federal government intruded into the master-slave relationship. As Ellen Roberts, a black Kentuckian, explained in the course of presenting regimental colors to the 107th U.S. Colored Infantry in the fall of 1864, enlistment changed former slaves into men who could now "call their wives and children their own."[4] Roberts's notion of possession was the opposite of the kind that slaveholders had formerly enjoyed. It implied the black head of household would fill the roles of protector and provider that the master had formerly occupied and serve as the intermediary between the family and the larger world.

For individuals and communities of African descent, the war undermined every definition of home derived from the model of the slaveholding household. Navigating the postslavery world required devising proper substitutes. But where should that work begin—did it depend on individual self-improvement, for instance, by learning to read and write? Or was it a matter of establishing independent households, as the Bruces did, symbolized by a dwelling but also including wage employment and participation in the larger civic culture? Or did economic independence constitute the necessary starting point, in which case freed people needed to purchase land to farm or acquire marketable skills with which to conduct independent businesses? And was recognized membership in the body politic—that is, full citizenship, including manhood suffrage—a necessary prerequisite for achieving these other goals or the reward for having done so?

Slavery bestowed an ambiguous legacy on all these efforts, and especially on those designed to guarantee that the United States constituted the proper "homeland" for people of African descent. When several black soldiers referred to themselves as "the Grandsons of Mother Africa Never to Flinch from Duty,"[5] they affirmed their patriotism to the Union through a preexisting African identity. Robert Hamilton, editor of the New York *Anglo-African*, envisioned a "Black Nationality" as a natural parallel to the many nationalist political movements of the time. The secular spirit that shaped human events required such a development "for the purpose of lifting the race to the level of civilization, and enabling it to contribute its share to the progress of the age."[6] Here the circle closed, with nationality, community, home, and family feeding into each other in a continuous cycle. Realizing the true goal of full belonging required simultaneous attention to all levels of awareness and engagement, from the individual to the national.[7]

The teenaged Virginian John Quincy Adams accompanied one of the sons of his mistress into the army at the start of the war but within a matter of months returned home to Winchester after becoming ill. Adams's family had been instructed "to take care of old mistress and young misses," and they did, "protect[ing] them many times from outrages that would have been committed upon them." Despite the ill treatment they continued to receive, "father told us that we must be good to them, work for them in the day-time and take care of them at night." When Union operations in the area created an opportunity to escape, however, the family took it. Adams later learned "that when old mistress got up in the morning, [and] found all the negroes gone," she figured that "the devil had got into them." She managed to send word promising that "if we would come back they would set us all free." Reasoning that "this was my time," Adams, with the other members of his family, settled in Harrisburg rather than return to Winchester.[8]

For other native Virginians who had been separated from their families during the cotton boom of the second quarter of the nineteenth century, home connoted a place far away in space and time. Hawkins Wilson, whose involuntary journey ended in Galveston, Texas, hoped that emancipation would enable him to reestablish ties with the people he last saw more than twenty years earlier. In May 1867, he sought the help of Freedmen's Bureau officials in Virginia to locate ten family members he identified by name along with their residences and the names of their owners that he recalled from his youth. He enclosed a letter to his sister that recounted childhood incidents to refresh her memory and described key events in his own life over the intervening years, including his marriage to a "very intelligent and lady-like woman" who was originally from Georgia. "Your advice to me to meet you in Heaven has never passed from my mind," he wrote, but now he hoped to be able to "drop in upon you some day like a thief in the night," erasing both the miles and the years that stood between them.[9] Wilson's dreamed-of reunion did not take place: the bureau agent in the referenced locality could not locate a single member of his family. Yet thinking and talking about loved ones and places far away enabled the persons who flowed through the interregional trade to rise above their victimization and retain a sense of their own humanity. Emancipation offered the chance, but not the guarantee, of reversing the steps, of returning home.[10]

––––––––––

When Henry Clay Bruce and his new bride began to establish a household, they faced formidable challenges. Assisted by friends in Leavenworth, Bruce soon found employment, but he remained vexed. Having "never been trained in the school of economy, where I could learn the art of self-support," he nonetheless had "to make my own bargains for whatever necessaries we needed, and to provide for a rainy day, all of which experiences were new to me." Although a man of twenty-eight years, he felt "almost as helpless as a child" in that he "had not learned the art of spending my earnings to the best advantage" or of providing for all of life's necessities. To escape high rents, Bruce and his wife soon attempted to purchase a home. They paid two-thirds of the asking price before discovering that the seller owned the dwelling but not the lot on which it stood and that the landowner demanded rent. Bruce concluded from the experience that white men in Kansas and the other free states were not as truthful in dealing with black men as were slaveholders in Missouri.[11] This was the "herculean task" that freed people everywhere faced after the war. "These freedmen must be educated," exhorted the editor of the *Christian Recorder*, "they must be instructed how to take care of, and act for themselves. Hitherto their masters have acted and done for them, but now that they are free they must be taught how to be free."[12]

Another Missourian, the teenaged Mattie J. Jackson, negotiated the challenges posed by the turmoil of the Civil War with a close eye to the impact on her family. From before her birth, Jackson's parents had struggled against slavery. Her father managed, with her mother's help, to escape to Chicago when Mattie was a child. Her mother remarried and then assisted in the escape of her second husband, who settled first in Canada and later in Lawrence, Massachusetts. When the war began, both Mattie and her mother displayed a sense of independence that their owners resented. Mattie's mother spent a month in a slave pen after the mistress discovered a picture of Abraham Lincoln in her room. Notwithstanding the ever-present threat of such punishment, the enslaved people of the household delighted in how news of Union victories affected the owners. "The days of sadness for mistress were days of joy for us," Mattie recalled. "We shouted and laughed to the top of our voices."[13]

By the dawn of 1863, as talk of freedom filled the air, Mattie was less inclined to do her chores as thoroughly and rapidly as before, for which she was condemned as "saucy" and beaten. Following one such altercation, Mattie fled to the protection of the St. Louis arsenal, the headquarters of federal troops in the city, spattered in blood from a blow to her head. Authorities there placed her in a boarding house for her safety, but in nominally loyal Missouri, where the Emancipation Proclamation did not apply, her owner promptly redeemed her from custody for nothing more than a promise of good behavior. Like thousands of similarly situated freedom seekers in the Loyal Border States, Mattie discovered that representatives of the national government were more beholden to loyal slaveholders than to the loyal persons held as slaves.[14]

Mattie's owner then jailed her in one of the city's numerous slave pens (the likes of which also dotted the main streets of Louisville and Baltimore, notwithstanding the presence of federal troops nearby), where she languished for three months before an acquaintance informed the authorities, who fined the owner but again returned her to his custody. Several months later a steamboat captain purchased the "fine looking family," hoping to capitalize on slaveholders' growing fear of emancipation. Slaves bought at bargain-basement prices in Missouri could be sold for "as much, or more than ever" in Kentucky. He assured Mattie's mother that, in exchange for her pledge not to run away, he would not sell them. The deal meant that the family would remain among their neighbors and friends in St. Louis. Or so they thought.[15]

In March, the captain spirited the family out of St. Louis to Louisville, where they remained for weeks in another slave pen before being sold to three separate owners. Then followed six months of backbreaking labor during which Mattie worked as a house servant and befriended a network of "colored people" who offered her access to much more than religious fellowship and emotional support—a link to the underground railroad. With their assistance she crossed the Ohio River into Indiana, soon making her way to Indianapolis, where she remained for the rest of the war. After setting her feet on free soil, she sighed with relief that "now this constant fear and restless yearning was over. It appeared as though I had emerged into a new world."[16] Mattie J. Jackson had transformed herself into a new woman.

During the summer of 1865, Mattie's mother and half brother also escaped slavery. They reunited with Mattie in Indianapolis and then proceeded home to St. Louis. When Mattie and her mother encountered their former owners, they took some satisfaction in seeing how the tables had turned.[17] The "old mistress" was obliged to trudge to market, "with a large basket on her arm." Other previously unthinkable events had come to pass, including employment of an Irish cook, which the old master had sworn that he would never do. In a word, the former owner and his family "were on an equality with the black man," as Mattie observed. She worked for several months as a servant before moving with her half brother to Lawrence, Massachusetts, to live with his father (her mother's second husband). Mattie's mother married a former free man of color to whom she had been engaged when the captain kidnapped the family out of Missouri. In the supportive environment of a new home and a new extended family, Mattie learned to read and write and, aided by her stepfather's wife, published the account of her ordeal. By exploding the slave-holding household, wartime emancipation forced changes—some welcome, others unwelcome—on both former owners and formerly enslaved persons.[18]

The military mobilization opened new pathways to the North for those who considered freedom incompatible with the homes and neighborhoods of their antebellum masters. Out of an abundance of caution, many a freedom seeker negotiated those routes with an eye toward reversing course if the odds against success appeared insuperable. The Tennessean George Knox, for instance, had been forced into Confederate service before he escaped and found shelter and employment with the Union army. He and several companions accompanied an Indiana regiment home on furlough, but then faced a major choice as the unit prepared to return to Tennessee. Despite the discrimination they frequently endured north of the Ohio River, Knox—alone among his comrades—decided to stay. He reasoned that leaving would be tantamount to going "out of heaven into hell." But "the colored boys" who had come north with him "said they were in a strange land and they were going back South as they wanted to go home."[19]

For many, escape to the Yankees was not a single life-or-death dash for freedom as much as a series of reconnaissance missions and trials, with movements back and forth. That refugees from the Virginia Peninsula applied this tactic in May 1861, at the very start of hostilities, suggests its origins in antebellum freedom struggles. The war presented opportunities for enslaved people along the entire face of battle between Union and Confederate forces, but now with places of refuge much closer than before. Between November 1862 and June 1863, thirteen persons, a number of whom were related, managed to slip away from a Unionist owner in Clarksville, Tennessee, according to the post commander at Fort Henry, and serially "found their way into our lines." In one encounter with Union troops, Iowa volunteers invited a man who was searching for his wife to "wade in" with them where his safety would be ensured.[20]

The freedman Archer Alexander, who escaped bondage in rural Missouri and took refuge in St. Louis with William Greenleaf Eliot, the prominent Unitarian minister, educator, and official in the Western Sanitary Commission, kept in touch with his enslaved wife, Louisa, and eventually secured her escape with the assistance of "Germans who lived in the neighborhood."[21] The couple made a new home in a cottage that Eliot rented to them, although this idyllic arrangement did not last long. About a year after the war ended, by Eliot's account, Louisa "became anxious to visit her old home 'to get her things;' that is, her bed and clothes, and little matters of furniture." While there, she took ill suddenly and died. A year later, Alexander remarried and "moved to his own hired house, feeling," Eliot observed, "that it was one more step of freedom."[22]

Notwithstanding the manifest dangers of attempting escape in a large group, that was one way to keep the core of a family intact. In perhaps the most famous example, Robert Small (later Smalls) and his fellow enslaved crewmates on the Confederate supply steamer *Planter* freed themselves and their loved ones by commandeering the vessel and steaming it past the defenses protecting Charleston Harbor to the Union blockading fleet offshore.[23] In another case, the men, women, and children from several plantations near Jefferson City, Missouri, attempted to flee captivity on a raft during the summer of 1863. The leader of the group, a rail-splitter and Baptist preacher named Robert Thomas Hickman, had been threatened with a whipping for visiting his wife on another plantation. He and a number of other men built the craft and launched it into the Missouri River, where they were overtaken by a transport steamer whose sympathetic captain agreed to tow the party to Fort Snelling, Minnesota. The group settled in St. Paul and built a thriving community centered on Hickman's church.[24]

———

The federal campaign against Vicksburg gave fresh exposure to the nexus between home and family and the disruptive social impact that military operations had on both. As he toured the refugee camps in the Department of the Tennessee in the spring and summer of 1863, the abolitionist Levi Coffin witnessed firsthand war's devastating effects on plantations and their communities. On the road to Corinth, which ran partly through rebel territory with Union pickets every few miles along the way, "the desolation wrought by the war was visible on every side." "Fences were gone," he observed, "houses burned, and plantations deserted; everything seemed to be going to destruction. Two large armies had passed over the land, leaving ruin in their track." As a result, "nothing remained for the poor slaves to live upon," and the persons who had been abandoned by their owners—"the women and children, and the aged and feeble"—were rapidly approaching starvation. "Our soldiers frequently shared their rations with them, but could do little to alleviate the sudden and general distress."[25] And hunger was only one of their worries. Through entire sections of immensely productive cotton country, the military forces of both belligerents disrupted plantation operations, burning buildings and harvested crops, trampling fields, scattering the residents, and paralyzing with fear those who had remained at home. In such circumstances, the residents could hardly be expected to provide for their future, yet, against the odds, many did.

In April 1863, Chaplain John Eaton, the general superintendent of contrabands for the Department of the Tennessee, prepared a detailed report on his efforts on behalf of the freed people for the AFIC, which he dutifully forwarded through his commanding officer, General Ulysses S. Grant. Eaton estimated that more than 22,000 persons had passed through the various camps. "Some of these," he added, "in various ways have gone back to slavery—others found Northern homes." Some 5,000 who had taken refuge at Cairo had "chiefly gone North," he reported.[26] As later generations of migrants from Southern farms and plantations to Northern cities discovered, despite the assistance provided by networks of family members and neighbors from home, seeking housing, employment, and a sense of belonging in a strange place exacted a heavy toll. And the welcome was not always warm. The *Christian Recorder*'s Washington correspondent Thomas H. C. Hinton warned the young ladies of the city to "look out" for the young men from "the rice swamps, the sugar-cane-brakes, the tobacco plantations and the cotton fields" whom the war had brought to the capital area. They "are after you, who have been always free," he advised, hinting at illicit desires that blended color, status, and sex.[27]

Eaton described how factors over which the refugees had little or no control could affect their health and well-being in their new surroundings. Shortages of physicians and medicines, for instance, left the refugees particularly vulnerable to pneumonia, measles, and unnamed "common diseases," presumably fevers and intestinal ailments.[28] The federal soldiers assigned to guard the refugees often proved to be as dangerous to life and limb as the microbes. In Grand Junction, Tennessee, for instance, home to slightly more than 1,700 souls, "the freedmen suffered robbery and all manner of violence dictated by the passion of the abandoned among the soldiery," and in Providence, Louisiana, the nearly 2,400 refugees endured "great evils" by virtue of their camp's proximity to the "town and troops."[29] This problem, of course, was not confined to any particular theater of the war. The residents of one plantation on St. Helena Island, South Carolina, for instance, "were not as interesting and pleasant" as their neighbors, Charlotte Forten observed. Their "bad reputation" derived from "their near vicinity to Land's End and the soldiers there," which "has not tended to improve them."[30]

Freedwomen employed at washing and ironing were especially vulnerable to unwanted sexual advances. In one notorious case, officers of a black regiment stationed at Fort Jackson, Louisiana, nearly touched off a riot after taking liberties with the wives of several men.[31] Richard H. Cain, an AME minister in Brooklyn, admonished Northern black men to take up two interrelated duties during "the present great revolution." The first was "to sustain the Government," the source of "protection in person and property." The second was to volunteer their services as missionaries and teachers among the freed people because "the white men from the North are doing more to degrade the character of those people, than the system of slavery has heretofore." The professed liberators who claimed "to relieve them from bondage" and "lift them above bestiality" instead debased the freed people by unleashing their "ungovernable and licentious passions." Even while reiterating the maxim that "revolutions do not go backwards," Cain also emphasized the need for concerted effort to keep this particular revolution moving in the proper direction.[32]

———

Even in the midst of contested areas, planters whose loyalties lay with the Confederacy often managed to maintain sufficient control over the enslaved population to create the impression of antebellum normalcy—at least until Yankee forces appeared. In the spring of 1863, the abolitionist Levi Coffin encountered an elderly woman at the refugee camp in La Grange, Tennessee, who told a fascinating tale. She was among a group of thirty persons recently escorted to the camp by a federal patrol that had freed them from a wealthy rebel sympathizer. The woman estimated her age at seventy-five or eighty but explained that "dey tole me I was twenty-one and made me do de work of a gal." She had been milking cows when the Yankee troopers arrived in the yard. Her heart leaped for joy when the officer in charge instructed the people to get their belongings and prepare for the trip "out of slavery." After carrying the bucket of milk to the kitchen, she returned to the yard "and tole de captain how dey had used us and how dey had 'bused us, all right before massa's face and he dasn't cheep." To Coffin and the camp superintendent she explained that "dis is all de work of de Lord," to whom she had prayed for years, asking that "He would send deliverance to us poor slaves, and my faith never failed me dat He would hear my prayer, and dat I would live to be free." Among the liberated were a number of her children and grandchildren.[33]

By describing to Coffin the confrontation with her former owner, the woman began the process of creating a freedom narrative that she and her children and grandchildren could turn to as the moment that their new lives began and that described their transformation into new men, new women, new children. Survivors such as Kate Drumgoold's brother—who claimed with tongue in cheek to have walked on water during his escape—told their stories with fresh embellishments in each retelling. Although some published their tales in newspapers or, less frequently, in books, most relied simply on the spoken word. Even as the journey to freedom unfolded, storytelling served important purposes. It helped maintain an awareness of where the family or neighbors (and even strangers) had come from and what they experienced in transit, an important early step toward stabilizing the family and reconstructing the community in freedom.[34] For all their psychic value in helping persons in the vortex of revolution cope with the strains that they endured, the stories also had great practical value as a means of communicating important information among persons separated from each other because of the exigencies of war. Hence George Knox's concern that his brother's death might blemish his reputation back home.

An abiding faith enabled families to bide their time until opportunities to achieve freedom arrived, preferably in the guise of the U.S. Army. With the protection of the soldiers, men, women, and children gathered their belongings into farm wagons drawn by any available beast of burden. After reaching Union lines, the refugees encountered officers who assigned them to the nearest refugee camp with available accommodations. Displaced persons of today joined those of yesterday and the day before. As newcomers entered, others departed: to plantations, to army units, to hospitals, or to graveyards. In militarily contested areas, those who left stood mixed chances of returning, but in places close to federal outposts, a semblance of order replaced the chaos, particularly when the owners abandoned the plantations, leaving behind "the original hands that have worked the plantations they are on, for years." In one "tier of 34 plantations" along the Mississippi River near Natchez, for instance, Colonel Samuel Thomas, superintendent of freedmen at Vicksburg, praised the overall spirit of industry and contentment, which he attributed to the fact that "they have the little community commonly known as 'fellow servants' all together," as they were before the war.[35]

Despite the challenges, individuals and families found ways to overcome the destructive tendencies set loose by the war. The case of an "old man" named Josua Culverson, left behind when his owner fled to Texas with all the hearty young workers early in 1863, illustrates how abandoned and uprooted freed people maintained the integrity of family ties and re-created the substance of home with a vision for a productive future. Culverson persuaded federal authorities to lease him 150 acres of cotton land on his former owner's plantation near Vicksburg and to "take some of his relations from the Contraband Camp to his home." "I Know he has the means to support them," a witness who spoke of his "Honesty and Industry" testified.[36] By mid-1864, seventy families of freed people cultivated cotton lands on their own account at nearby Davis Bend. Still others did so on abandoned lands elsewhere in the Vicksburg district and in other federally supervised regions along the river.[37] With a chance to reap freedom's richest rewards through independent farming, the lessees nonetheless lived on a bubble that, thanks to the vagaries of war and weather, was constantly at risk of popping. Though far from a certain cure, the presence of family helped reduce the risks.

Inasmuch as work, like family, created social bonds among the people who were engaged in common productive activity, the workplace supplemented the home as a site for defining the new contours of freedom and connecting individuals to the wider world of community and nation. In most of the facilities that supported army and naval operations, the workforce consisted mostly of men, who often messed and bunked with their fellow laborers apart from their families.[38] At work and at rest, they developed the social habits of free men, establishing the seedbed on which a class of compensated free laborers could take root and grow. Most women employed by the government worked in such traditional occupations as cooking and washing and ironing. Over time, they also assumed the role of nurses ministering to the sick and wounded soldiers, especially the U.S. Colored Troops. Susie King Taylor, whose husband served in one of the black regiments organized on the Sea Islands of South Carolina, served in all those capacities.[39] As had been true before the war and after, performing traditional domestic chores allowed mothers to care for their children while they worked and to build the web that served as the female caregivers' collective safety net.[40] On government-supervised plantations or plantations sold or leased to Northern investors, men and women worked together, if not necessarily side by side, in every task. In those settings, the emerging work culture displayed links to the past more so than a glimpse into the future. The one major difference, of course, was that laborers worked on the promise of wages and not out of fear of the bullwhip.[41]

Working with the engineer, quartermaster, and commissary departments that supported the federal armed forces offered many refugees the opportunity to escape from field labor. Much of that work, such as digging fortifications, handling military stores, driving mule teams, cooking, and washing, was exhausting. Yet persons with skills might enjoy higher wages than what their unskilled counterparts earned, and less strenuous workloads to boot. In short, working for government departments or subsidiary contractors presented options. Laborers could leave one employer for another in search of higher wages, better working conditions, proximity to home, or other advantages. Regardless of the setting, however, the employed refugees faced the common threat of employers who delayed payments or skimped on the amount due. In Union-occupied areas as far flung as Tennessee, Louisiana, Port Royal, and Washington, D.C., and its suburbs, the pattern was the same.

Such drawbacks notwithstanding, military camps also provided amenities, such as access to Northern consumer goods courtesy of post sutlers. But perhaps the most important benefit was access to the schools sponsored by army chaplains or Northern philanthropic associations. Although families often relied on their children's earnings from paid employment or scavenging, where schools were available they had the option of preparing the succeeding generation for participation in the economy and civic society with the benefit of one of the fundamental tools of citizenship in the American republic, namely, literacy. Children who could read and write would serve as a valuable asset in advancing the home-building project from the level of the household and the family to those of the community and the nation.

———

On the farms and plantations that remained under Confederate jurisdiction, the war also profoundly affected every traditional sense of the term "home." Oddly, even as wartime circumstances proved capable of eroding customary relationships of authority and deference, they could also reinforce ties of interdependence as families, white and black, pooled resources in the face of adversity. What is more, the Confederate government's need to mobilize enslaved people in support of the cause created additional turmoil in plantation households, presenting the possibility that both Union and Confederate authorities might figuratively cross the threshold into the domain of the patriarch. And against the encroachment of the former, slaveholders often summoned the latter, as the planters in Liberty County, Georgia, had demonstrated during the summer of 1862. Invoking the notion that the enslaved residents of the Confederacy "constitute a part of the Body politic," they petitioned the local military commander to execute "Negroes *taken in the act of absconding*." Through such examples, the slaves would "be made to know their duty . . . [to] their owners & the Government."[42]

As rebel officials shifted their attention back and forth between restless (if not rebellious) slaves and federal forces, they found new value in an old tactic as a way to address both challenges simultaneously: impressment. Notwithstanding the fact that impressed laborers generally served for only short stints—usually not more than a month—and that authorities in Richmond and on the local scene gave at least nominal surety for their safe return, the vagaries of war regularly intervened. Accidents occurred; federal attacks materialized without warning; people went missing. In such government-sponsored labor settings as transportation depots, coal and nitrate mines, armories and arsenals, cotton factories, brickworks, and saltworks, men and women worked on annual contracts that ran from New Year's Day to Christmas. Per the custom of the region, the agreements permitted hired persons to visit their families during the holiday and often at other negotiated times during the year. For families thus separated, even short absences seemed like an eternity, yet the prospect of reuniting with loved ones generally proved to be enough of an incentive to keep the laborers dutifully at work.[43]

Confederate partisans could never bring themselves to admit their own complicity in one of the greatest sources of domestic instability, namely, refugeeing. Removing healthy men to the interior and abandoning the rest of the enslaved people to survive on their own disrupted black families, but planters justified the tactic in terms of depriving federal forces of prospective army recruits and, at times, of saddling the Yankees with dependent women and children. Grant's Vicksburg campaign between December 1862 and July 1863 intensified this dynamic, which had first revealed itself in federal operations in West Tennessee and northern Mississippi over the preceding several months. At the approach of federal forces, slaveholders abandoned their home plantations for places of safety deeper in Confederate territory. East of the river they headed for Alabama and Georgia, and west of the river they steered for Texas, and the movement continued after Grant's army occupied the city. "Visburg is gone and as a consequence Mississippi is gone and in the opinion of allmost every one here the Confederacy is gone," lamented one rebel partisan in late July 1863. "On every road leading from the western Country there is a constant stream of negroes running into Ala & Georgia & the Carolinas," who, if left unchecked, "will destroy all the food in those states like an army of locusts." Echoing the thoughts of foresighted slaveholders at the start of the war, this man proposed conscripting into the army "every able bodied *Negro* man from the age of sixteen to fifty" as the only viable alternative to certain ruin.[44] Of course, only a fraction of slaveholders agreed that arming black men, even under close supervision, offered a solution to any problem.

Enslavers and their overseers relied instead on various combinations of incentives, threats, and examples of deadly force to maintain discipline. They portrayed the Yankees as demons who would sell captured slaves to Cuba rather than grant them freedom. They resorted next to hiding their human property in hard-to-find places to avoid Yankee patrols. Planters devised drills for evading federal forces by hiding in woods and canebrakes and for protecting valuable possessions, which ranged from jewelry, gold and silver kitchenware, and other household effects to work animals, tools, and provisions. This technique worked to avoid gray-clad impressment officers as well as to escape blue-clad liberators. Amid persistent rumors of planned insurrection, planters around Natchez, Mississippi, unleashed a reign of terror over the first two years of the war that resulted in scores, if not hundreds, of deaths. The killings came to an end only in July 1863, after federal forces occupied the city.[45]

Refugeeing fell far short of solving the rebels' challenge of either preserving the value of human property or disrupting federal operations. When planters betrayed the telltale signs that they were contemplating such a move, the "fear of being driven South" and its associated imponderables prompted flight to the federals. When the traumatized remnants of such shattered families and communities arrived at contraband camps, they, the existing residents, and camp officials sought to establish a measure of stability by addressing essential needs, particularly food, shelter, clothing, and blankets. From such a foundation, they hoped in time to restitch remnants of families into sustainable communities. The opportunity to be free, and as John Eaton observed, to "make their own money and protect their families," kept the flicker of hope alive through the storms that howled around them.[46]

To be sure, Yankees' ineptitude and greed threatened the experiment of raising cotton with free labor, but to nowhere near the extent that Confederate raiders did. From the summer of 1863 onward, both regular and irregular rebel forces attacked plantations, murdering and reenslaving freed people, capturing livestock, and burning and otherwise destroying buildings, farm implements, and growing crops. Persons who managed to escape the raids either squatted in the ruins or made their way back to the nearest federal outpost, which in turn served as the stepping stone to the nearest contraband camp, where officials ministered to their gunshot wounds, broken bones, cuts and bruises of every kind, and the effects of sickness and exposure suffered along the way. Neither salve nor the kind words of strangers could assuage such trauma. In the war zone, preserving families, much less building communities, posed challenges equal to that faced by Sisyphus, whose punishment for offending Zeus was having to push a boulder up a mountain endlessly, repeating the cycle each time it rolled back down. But, through it all, most freed people looked with gratitude to the Union's armed forces and the representatives of Northern benevolent associations for their work in destroying slavery and creating a seedbed for freedom. The formerly enslaved people's encounters with the Yankees, both amicable and contentious, offered valuable lessons in citizenship. Those experiences, in turn, deepened their allegiance to the national government.

––––––––

Despite those challenges and in defiance of the odds, a civic spirit often developed at the contraband camps.[47] The camps around Memphis illustrate this process. At first, the nominal refugees consisted of city residents whose masters had fled before Union forces took control, and, in fact, they required little, if any, material assistance from the federal forces. But when freedom seekers from rural farms and plantations relocated there—in many cases after their owners had fled with the healthy young men—federal officials could not long ignore the resulting demand for shelter and food. When men who escaped from their fugitive masters headed there to reunite with their families, owners pursued them with special ferocity, vowing, as one contemporary explained, that they "had rather shoot them down than let them go free."[48] By the spring of 1863, nearly 1,400 persons lived in the contraband camps, and 2,500 lived "about town," according to Chaplain Eaton. Camp Holly Springs was located approximately two and a half miles below Memphis, within easy walking distance of the city and even closer to Fort Pickering, whose great guns commanded the river. Its initial residents were evacuees from the camp at Holly Springs, which Confederates uprooted in December 1862.[49]

When James Yeatman of the Western Sanitary Commission visited the camp the following fall, he was favorably impressed. Its "clean and airy" dwellings consisted of "four rows of good log huts . . . with small plots for gardens in front. The streets and alleys were all clean and well swept, having good drainage and excellent police arrangements." The residents, who numbered nearly 100 men in the Invalid Corps (army enlistees who were physically unable to serve in the field but who were nonetheless fit for guard duty and other light service) and roughly 300 women and an equal number of children "were generally well clothed, and were cheerful and contented." The camp also boasted a school with "a full corps of teachers."[50] Husbands of the residents generally lived at the fort; they were men who enlisted in the two regiments of Tennessee Heavy Artillery (African Descent), which were organized in the summer of 1863.

Shiloh, which Eaton described as "a little village of their own building," was located closer to the city and adjacent to Fort Pickering. In his April 1863 report on the state of the camps, Eaton noted that the engineer's rolls carried the names of some 2,000 men who lived with their families at Shiloh and "about the city," yet only 400, on average, presented themselves for work each day. He concluded that they preferred vagrancy and crime to steady employment on behalf of the government, which explained to his satisfaction why the village, which once had "a guard of their own, preachers of their own, and a school," was in a state of decline. In short, for want of proper "management," Shiloh had become "a den of thieves." By Eaton's lights, the inhabitants appeared increasingly indifferent to such fundamental tenets of free society as "the Christian family" and "the innate love of possession, on which is based the acquisition of wealth, and all the relations of property." The role of Union management of contraband affairs, then, required both addressing "their great necessities" of a material nature and instilling within them "those principles, which alone can render them the constituents of any proper society."[51] Curiously, when Yeatman visited Camp Shiloh in the fall of 1863, he found its 600 residents to be "mostly, if not entirely, self-supporting" and needing "no aid," owing largely to the earnings of the men and women employed at the fort.[52]

Despite his posturing, Eaton knew there was more to the story of the engineer's laborers than idleness and thievery. "Many soldiers and some officers manifest only bitterness and contempt," he observed, which resulted "in the violence and abuse of these helpless people, in addition to the injuries heaped upon them by the vicious & disloyal of the community." And he noted how men detailed to work for various military departments had sometimes been "most grossly abused—as, for instance, worked all day in water, drenched, nearly frozen, and then driven to tents for shelter, to sheds for sleep, without covering, and almost without fire and food," an incident so shocking that both Eaton and the camp superintendent, Chaplain A. Severance Fiske, referenced it in the reports they submitted to the AFIC. In the circumstances, the workmen died "by scores," and "the services of a large number" of others "have been stolen outright," Eaton reported.[53] Like many of the Northerners who ministered to the needs of the freed people, Eaton fluctuated between compassion and frustration as he compared what he witnessed on the ground with his preconceptions about African-descended people. Yet he needed no racialized theory of "'Kin' attachment" to explain why women and children followed their husbands and fathers to Union-held positions where they would likely encounter "neglect [and] abuse." By his own admission, "the men labor best when near their kin, lodging with their families, or seeing them weekly unbothered by concerns about their safety."[54]

Civil War refugee camps in contested areas of the Confederacy, like their twenty-first-century counterparts in war zones throughout the world, alternately fostered and undermined the development of stable communities. At their worst, the camps succeeded in concentrating dependent persons in small spaces where they became vulnerable to inadequate food, shelter, and medical care and to the depredations of military personnel and civilians alike. But what refugees viewed as activity necessary to their survival, federal authorities often considered subversive to good order. At Vicksburg, for instance, the post commander treated soldiers' wives as "Common place women of the town."[55] From the spring of 1864 into the spring of 1865, military authorities in Memphis tried to break up the camps of "Temporary huts" that hundreds of "negro women" occupied on the outskirts of the city. The occupants were "for the most part, idle, lazy vagrants" who carried off rations and tools to support their "households" and exercised "a very pernicious influence over the colored soldiers of this post," reported the commander of a regiment of men raised in Tennessee, echoing the views of John Eaton rather than those of James Yeatman.[56]

The camp at Davis Bend, Mississippi, however, enjoyed advantages that enabled it to achieve an enviable level of stability. Its inaccessibility by water after federal gunboats began patrolling the river was the first advantage. And three companies of soldiers secured the narrow neck where the bend joined the mainland. Second, the community retained a core group of the prewar residents. Finally, the high political visibility of the place prompted federal officials, ranging from Admiral David D. Porter, commander of the Mississippi Squadron, to Colonel Samuel Thomas, superintendent of freedmen in the District of Vicksburg, to pay special attention. The influx of several thousand refugees from federal military operations bent but did not break the community-building process.[57]

When federal officials decided to relocate camps or smaller groups of their residents, the recuperating networks of families and communities endured additional stress. Although some commanders routinely factored the needs of dependent freed people into their operational planning, others did not. What is more, orders from federal superiors could be as effective as surprise rebel attacks in undermining the best-laid plans, as the November 1862 relocation of refugees from Newport News to Craney Island, Virginia, illustrated. When an infusion of fresh troops at Newport News required the use of the barracks where displaced persons had been living, military authorities prodded them like cattle onto transport vessels for the voyage across Hampton Roads. In a symbolic gesture of independence and defiance, a number of the men headed back into Confederate territory rather than be subjected to such abuse.[58] Their protest did little to help their families endure their ordeal, and it did not shame federal officials into considering the adverse impact of their decisions on the intended recipients.

The residents of the camp established at Roanoke Island, North Carolina, faced similar challenges that persisted through the rest of the war.[59] The island presented itself as an ideal location for such a settlement, except that its scarcity of natural resources and susceptibility to coastal storms accounted for why it was uninhabited save for the parties of fishermen who camped there in season. The healthy young men enlisted in the army after receiving assurances from camp superintendents that their families would receive government rations and be protected from depredation. The recruits then left for Virginia, only to learn later that the officials had reneged on both promises. Following a mass meeting in March 1865, the "Colored men of this Island" wrote to President Lincoln. The "head men" in charge of the colony, they explained, "have done every thing to us that our masters have done except by and Sell us and now they are Trying to Starve the woman & children to death." But no one appeared to have taken note. Several months later, after the fighting ceased, the soldiers protested the suffering their families still endured. Having "served in the US Army faithfully and don our duty to our Country," they faulted camp superintendents who not only neglected to provide the promised rations but also permitted white soldiers to "steal our chickens [and] rob our gardens."[60]

—————

Government-leased plantations, whether in the Mississippi valley or along the Eastern Seaboard, proved to be a particularly challenging environment for freed people to organize stable households that could serve as the foundation stones of independent lives. First, the regulations often worked to the disadvantage of formerly enslaved people who had sufficient experience to farm on their own but lacked the necessary capital. Second, in their single-minded pursuit of profits, a number of lessees treated the freed people little better than slaves. In the worst cases, they barely disguised their hostility toward the Union and compensated labor, ignoring their contractual obligations to provide shelter, rations, and stipulated wages or shares of the crop. Although Northern missionaries and teachers took deliberate steps to remedy some of slavery's intellectual and cultural legacies, more than philanthropy inspired the work. Freed people on the Union-occupied islands of South Carolina drew a direct connection between some lessees' obsession with the price of Sea Island cotton on international exchanges and their penchant for settling payroll accounts slowly and quibbling over each laborer's earnings.[61]

In the western theater, mutual distrust, which often bordered on outright contempt, characterized the relationship between army and Treasury Department officials. As a result, when the agencies traded jurisdiction over leased plantations at the start of each year, hardship invariably followed. Most notably, delays in promulgating regulations caused delays in plowing and planting. Seedling plants sprang from the ground later than usual, thereby increasing their vulnerability to environmental hazards, such as the heavy rains followed by an infestation of army worms that plagued much of the Mississippi valley during the spring and summer of 1864. In these circumstances, life on the government-sponsored plantations resembled an exercise in survival more than an experiment in compensated labor. Meanwhile, the representatives of the respective agencies worked at cross-purposes to each other and to the freed people.[62]

————

In the eastern refugee camps, residents and officials, with the assistance of local leaders and Northern philanthropists, worked deliberately to build communities grounded in the Christian family and the home wherein its members dwelled. Settlements in and around the District of Columbia had a unique attribute: proximity to the seat of the national government. This made them the special object of official interest, which, in turn, drew the attention of the local and national press and visitors from around the world. From the moment federal troops crossed the Potomac River into northern Virginia in May 1861, military operations pushed wave after wave of displaced persons toward the capital area. From the start of the spring 1862 campaign through the end of the war, virtually every wagon, railroad car, and steamboat returning from the front carried freedom seekers.[63] Upon reaching the capital, officials spirited them to whichever camp had available space. Even apart from the necessary confusion that attended these relocations, families were in for an additional shock when they arrived in the camps.

Early in the spring of 1862, to accommodate the influx of black refugees, military officials in Washington authorized the use of Camp Barker, a collection of barracks and stables where a cavalry company had resided, as a shelter. The impetus behind organizing the camp came in part from the growing embarrassment created by Duff Green's Row, a lockup within a stone's throw of the Capitol building. Although intended to serve as a more humane alternative to the Old Capitol Prison, where a congressional investigation uncovered evidence of a number of corrupt practices, including masters' use of the facility as a holding pen to prevent their slaves from escaping, Duff Green's Row reproduced many of the evils it was intended to cure.[64] Federal authorities also hoped that Camp Barker would house the families of men employed in government departments and shops in the capital area. But what they failed to account for sufficiently was the pressure that the influx of newcomers to the city would place on the facility. As employed men found shelter for their families, their wives and children left the camps. Yet the number of newcomers always exceeded the available space. The camp superintendent, Reverend Danforth B. Nichols, reported that "we have had as many as 26 [persons] in one cabin" measuring ten feet by twelve.[65]

The Reverend Nichols was a Methodist minister affiliated with the AMA. Like his counterparts at similar camps in other areas under control of Union military forces, he established rules for the camp and punished transgressors in ways that many inhabitants likened to slavery. Lucy Ellen Johnson's encounter with him illustrated the tensions that might develop between overweening officials and formerly enslaved people who wished to be accorded the respect due to free adults. Johnson had escaped from Fredericksburg at the time of the Union attack in December 1862, then made her way to Washington and got married. She and her husband had worked for various employers, military and civilian, and rented "a shanty on the riverbank" near the Long Bridge, where, she explained "we had lived peaceably until disturbed by soldiers." After her husband found work at the government corral in Alexandria, he arranged with Superintendent Nichols for Lucy Ellen to move to Camp Barker rather than risk further molestation at the shanty.[66]

She moved into the camp while recuperating from an illness that had rendered her temporarily unable to work. She attempted to draw rations of "a bed tick, a blanket, a pair of shoes and a dress" but was denied after Nichols learned that her husband earned twenty-five dollars per month. The exchange became testier and Nichols grew impatient. When the superintendent insisted that she pay board, she retorted that "if I have to *pay* my board," Nichols should have "explained it to my husband when he asked to bring me into camp." The reverend summoned the guards, who suspended her by the thumbs for approximately half an hour and then ordered her to leave the camp. Her father tried to intervene, even to the point of confronting a soldier who held a fixed bayonet, but the abuse continued. As in days of yore, he could do little but watch his daughter's pain and humiliation helplessly.[67] Another occupant of the camp, a formerly enslaved man from Maryland whom Nichols had employed as a cook, witnessed other similar incidents. Speaking "from my heart before the Lord," the man reported, "the conduct of Mr Nichols was worse than the general treatment of slave owners."[68] In the contraband camps, residents often learned that asserting themselves might produce results similar to what they had experienced in slavery.

By the spring of 1863, despite the limitations of space, the camp in Washington housed approximately 600 persons and, according to Superintendent Nichols, had temporarily sheltered nearly 5,000 in the nine months since it opened. Residents of Camp Barker, like their counterparts in other refugee camps, faced overcrowding and disease. While "out to work," residents were susceptible to being kidnapped by slave catchers or strong-armed into accepting employment with nominally loyal (but actually pro-Confederate) Marylanders and Virginians who connived with military authorities for farm hands, Superintendent Nichols informed the members of the AFIC. One slaveholder received permission to retrieve from the camp three children who, he claimed, "had run away." A woman who confronted her former master as he was trying to lure her daughters into leaving begged Nichols to take a "butche[r] Knife" to the rascal.[69]

To ease the endemic overcrowding, Nichols and the chief quartermaster of the Department of Washington, Lieutenant Colonel Elias M. Greene, lobbied to build a spacious new camp for the refugees, which opened in the summer of 1863.[70] Freedman's Village, as it was named, occupied a portion of the Arlington Estate, the prewar home of Robert E. Lee and Mary Anna Custis Lee, which lay across the Potomac River from the White House (see figures 8.2 and 8.3). The site had numerous natural advantages including abundant sources of fresh water and timber, arable land, and proximity to the markets and other amenities of Washington City. What is more, it possessed unrivaled political cachet. The village was intended to serve as both a showcase of governmental and private philanthropy and a case study in transforming refugees into citizens. Government officials, newspaper reporters, and a wide array of visitors from across the United States and Europe visited to bear witness. With fifty-odd duplex houses of solid wood construction neatly arrayed along both sides of a curved drive, the village also housed a school, a chapel, a hospital, a home for the indigent, and various workshops where men and women learned useful trades. Sojourner Truth was doing "all I can in the way of instructing the people in habits of industry and economy," she informed President Lincoln in December 1864. "Many of them are entirely ignorant of house keeping."[71] Arable land adjacent to the village enabled residents to grow vegetables for their own tables and for sale. Several churches served their spiritual needs. In a word, it was an environment custom-designed to support families and to foster a sense of community within eyesight of the nation's capital.

Despite Nichols's skill as a planner, not all of the intended beneficiaries of the experimental village appreciated his heavy-handed administrative style. Specifically, they faulted both Nichols and his counterpart, Albert Gladwin, superintendent of the refugee camp in Alexandria, with imposing restrictions and administering discipline for alleged infractions that closely mimicked the treatment they had endured in slavery. Indeed, Gladwin employed his magistrate's powers to imprison freed people in the city slave pen, on one occasion reportedly confining two "young girls" there for a ten-day "time out" and then neglecting "to release them" at the expiration of the term.[72] "The large proportion" of the camp residents in Washington who were being "urged to go" to Freedman's Village refused to do so, according to one witness, "because they would not be under Nichols." An elderly female veteran of Camp Barker testified to his poor treatment of the residents. She, too,

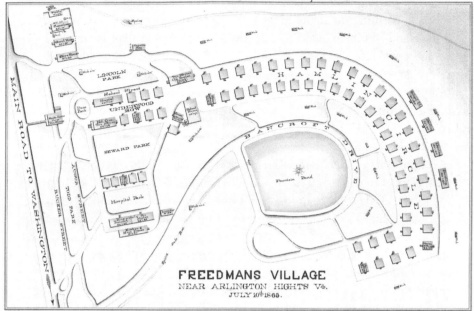

Figure 8.2 Freedman's Village, near Arlington Heights, Virginia, July 10, 1865. Courtesy of the National Archives.

Figure 8.3 Freedman's Village, Arlington, Virginia. Courtesy of the Library of Congress Prints and Photographs Division, LC-DIG-ppmsca-34829.

stayed behind in the city, but with decidedly mixed feelings. Her numerous children, old and young, whom she reported as "doing right smart" for themselves in Washington, opposed her relocation, but she clung to the belief that if she could "get them together in a little house we would all be better off than we are now." Thomas H. C. Hinton, the Washington correspondent to the *Christian Recorder*, characterized Nichols as "a perfect tyrant," who in early June 1864 "drove some half a dozen poor superannuated souls, men and women" from the camp. "They were all over town, begging people for something to eat."[73]

Notwithstanding such misgivings, families in need of shelter filled the cabins of the village. Nichols issued regulations that prescribed proper behavior with respect to work ("all the able-bodied men and women will be required to labor each day, either on the farms or in one of the mechanical shops"), school (all children under fourteen years of age must attend, with truants subject to arrest by the guard, who will "take the delinquent to school"), and structures ("the buildings and other public property must be kept in good order"). Minor offenses would be punishable by the reduction of the "ration of sugar" for five days or the denial of passes to leave the camp; more serious offenses would be adjudicated by "a commission" consisting of camp officials who might proscribe such punishment as "deprivation of privileges, fine, or imprisonment in [the] guard-house." Those who had "voluntarily left" the camps "for service outside" would not be permitted to return unless the superintendent determined that they had been treated cruelly or were subject to be defrauded of their earnings.[74]

Although such arrangements intended to promote habits of industry, frugality, domestic economy, and morality, overzealous superintendents such as Nichols left the freed people little room to fulfill the needs and goals to which they aspired. To be sure, the refugees remained grateful to the government for shelter and rations and to the relief associations for clothing and other amenities, but they resented the constraints and punishments, which often appeared arbitrary, and the condescending tone, which was offensive. When, for instance, AFIC members quizzed Superintendent Nichols about the impact of long-term residence at the camp, he described a "demoralizing" effect: "the longer they stay there the worse they become; the more vicious in their habits, and the less inclined to work."[75] The residents viewed the matter differently. The Reverend Robert Laws, pastor of a local Baptist church, rose to influence among the camp's residents challenging the administrative practices of the superintendents, beginning with Nichols. Laws remained a champion of the freed people at Freedman's Village for years after the war.[76]

Freedman's Village, like most other refugee camps, demonstrated the important role that churches and schools played in the community-building process among freed people. Such institutions linked local groups into larger networks of like-minded persons engaged in the work of moral uplift and self-improvement. These could have more or less explicit affiliations with specific Protestant missionary associations or denominations, such as the AMA or the AME Church. Although the dynamics of community-building differed in time and place, the early sequence followed a similar pattern, with the missionaries and teachers making their appearance only after U.S. forces established firm footing on the ground, as the AMA's John Oliver demonstrated at Norfolk and the AME Church's James Lynch did at Port Royal. Besides serving as emissaries of Northern culture—black and white—the missionaries also filled an important advocacy role. They communicated among and between leaders of the communities and civil and military officials, and they wrote letters to the black and abolitionist press. They traveled throughout the North raising funds and collecting donations, thereby establishing important ties between the Southern freed people and networks of supporters in the free states. But, as the experiences of Harriet Jacobs and Julia Wilbur at the Washington-area camps suggested, one of their chief responsibilities was keeping imperious camp superintendents from destroying the freed people's dignity and self-respect.[77]

Missionaries affiliated with the AME Church and the AME Zion Church played an especially important role in this process. As Henry M. Turner observed in a September 1864 letter to the bishops of both affiliations, the recent victories in Virginia and elsewhere placed Union forces in cities that presented good opportunities for missionary work. Deep within the Confederacy, the urban black congregations were largely affiliated with the Methodist Episcopal Church, South, and he sensed that the impending end of slavery might also result in a decrease in the level of white oversight over black congregations. Turner correctly predicted a wave of struggles for autonomy across the South in the months following the end of the war, and he urged leaders of the two major black denominations to be prepared to offer the right hand of fellowship.[78]

———

Owing to their relatively high levels of population density and opportunities for employment, cities helped families, neighbors, and the various social institutions that buffered their interactions with the broader world to offset the disintegrating forces set loose by the war. Such a dynamic characterized cities everywhere in the South, but differently depending on a range of political and military constraints. In the cities of the Confederacy that remained relatively unscathed by war until the fall of 1864 or later—most notably Richmond; Wilmington, North Carolina; Charleston; and Savannah—churches and their leaders took on greater importance than ever before as a place for balancing the quest for freedom with protecting the integrity of families and shielding the most vulnerable members of the community. As Secretary of War Stanton and General Sherman learned from their conversation with the Savannah ministers in January 1865, black churches served their congregants in particularly significant ways in such cities, ministering to their spiritual needs and bolstering their confidence that relief from slavery was close at hand.[79]

In Union-controlled areas, a key consideration was whether the Emancipation Proclamation applied. In New Bern, North Carolina, the group of political activists associated with Abraham Galloway criticized federal authorities freely in the interest of the freed people. Although they collaborated with federal forces, they also established links with like-minded African American leaders and communities in the Confederate states (in Confederate-controlled areas as well as Union-controlled areas) and in the North (in the Border Slave States as well as the free states).[80] In the cities within areas exempted from the Emancipation Proclamation, such as New Orleans, Nashville, and Memphis, local leaders and missionaries had to balance the competing demands of two masters, as the anonymous "Colored man" in New Orleans had described it: a rebel master and a Union master.

Memphis presented opportunities for as well as challenges to the formation of a viable community of freed people. The public celebration of the second anniversary of the Emancipation Proclamation illustrated what inspired the community and what it valued. The key feature of the commemoration was a public parade. Following the grand marshal and the band were the teachers and pupils of the colored schools. Then, in the fashion of such events from long before the birth of the republic, came representatives of the various trades demonstrating their crafts, beginning with the printers who distributed fresh copies of Lincoln's proclamation. Fraternal and benevolent societies, including the Sons and Daughters of Ham, marched next, and then the people at large. Participants carried banners that proudly revealed the community's loyalty to the national government and awareness of the heroes and events of the war. With the words "Liberty or Death," they pronounced 1863 as "The Year of Jubilee," dedicating themselves to achieving the goals of "Liberty, Education, and the Right of Suffrage." The procession ended at the Pleasure Gardens, where the celebrants feasted amid the obligatory speeches from military officials extolling the virtues of responsibility and hard work.[81] Similar events occurred to mark the anniversary of emancipation in cities large and small, in both the North and the Union-occupied sections of the Confederacy.[82]

———————

By opening the army to black men, the Emancipation Proclamation signaled a new relationship between freed people and the national government that black residents of the Confederate states immediately grasped. Some freedom seekers saw military service as a way both to free themselves and their families and then to build a firm foundation for a new life. The North Carolina native William Henry Singleton, for example, escaped from service to a Confederate officer after federal forces occupied New Bern in 1862. He "commenced to recruit a regiment of colored men . . . and I drilled them with cornstalks for guns," and eventually became a sergeant in the Thirty-Fifth U.S. Colored Infantry.[83] After several trips back and forth between Union and Confederate lines and a stint working as a teamster in support of the rebel army, Samuel Hall escaped slavery and enlisted in the U.S. Army. In the style that Spotswood Rice envisioned, Hall made his way home accompanied by a number of other black soldiers with the intention of freeing his family. After ignoring his owner's plea that he remain and his comrades' advice that he "beat the man's brains out," Hall gathered his wife and children as well as a wagon, mule team, and provisions for their journey first into Union lines and then north to freedom.[84] Sergeant Joseph J. Harris, who was stationed in Florida, was poorly situated to free his family near Bayou Sara, Louisiana, but he had a plan. Late in 1863, he wrote to General Daniel Ullmann, commander of a brigade of black soldiers near his home, requesting help with a small matter that he estimated would not involve "mor then three or four Hours trubel." His parents, his brother's wife, his sister, and their children and grandchildren were living with a woman who refused to free them and let the children attend school. Harris warned Ullmann to ignore any objections his relatives might raise to leaving "becaus their Misstes have led them to beleive there is no liven in the Lines of the Yankees."[85] The incident revealed that Harris's family had misgivings about abandoning their known world for his, which in their view circled a different sun.

Political theorists and recruiters also came to realize that families provided the link between prospective black recruits and the nation. If the government needed the service of the men, some provision needed to be made for their wives and children. Most observers reasoned that a monthly wage that was slightly above what unskilled laborers earned in civilian labor markets plus enlistment bounties would suffice. The thinking was wrong on two counts. First, whereas white soldiers earned $13.00 plus a $3.50 clothing allowance per month, War Department officials decided that black soldiers were subject to the salary cap of $10.00 per month less $3.00 for clothing referenced in the 1862 Militia Act. Second, despite the limitations imposed by that law, skilled "contrabands" in such places as Port Royal no less than in metropolitan areas like Washington could earn $25.00 or more as civilian employees in the quartermaster's, the commissary's, or the engineer's departments. Hence a decision to enlist had real monetary implications for the men and their families.[86]

William J. Brown was a freeborn company sergeant in the Third U.S. Colored Heavy Artillery, which was originally organized as the First Tennessee Heavy Artillery (African Descent), most of whose men were formerly enslaved Tennesseans. Brown protested the multiple hardships that unequal pay caused his men. As "the first to sign my name," Brown felt responsible to "the many Anxious and disappointed men of this *Reg.*" who followed his lead into military service and who never had their "Just Rights." Many "have Families to support" with "no other means" than their wages as soldiers. They drew small consolation from hearing "the white privates tell us we Should get the same pay as they do" but only pain from knowing that they "toil[ed] day and night" for seven dollars per month performing "the very Labour" for which contrabands earned ten dollars. Addressing the secretary of war, Brown wished to know whether they might "Expect in the final settlement to get our full Rights as was promiced us" at the time of enlistment.[87]

Formerly enslaved soldiers and their families in South Carolina faced continuing difficulties in coming to a common understanding with military officials regarding the mutual responsibilities between the government and its new citizens. In November 1863, when men in the Third South Carolina Colored Volunteers protested the inequity of their reduced pay by stacking their arms and refusing to perform further duty, their regimental commander charged them with mutiny. Sergeant William Walker, a senior noncommissioned officer, was tried, convicted, and executed for his role in the disturbance, which did not resolve the pay dispute. Neither did it alleviate the suffering of their wives and children. In fact, General Rufus Saxton, superintendent of contrabands in the Department of the South, rebuffed the appeal submitted by sympathetic officers on behalf of the men's families. Saxton believed that soldiers' dependents could not possibly qualify for government assistance to the "destitute" because the men received "seven dollars a month, besides rations and clothing for themselves." "A habit of dependence upon the Government for food and clothing," he argued, "ought to be discouraged among the freedmen, even at the risk of some suffering." The liberal political theorists of emancipation believed that simply removing the slaveholder from the web of relationships that linked individuals to their families and from there to the social and political institutions of free society sufficed. Incidental suffering was to be expected.[88]

Northern plantation superintendents came to understand the importance of family as the building block of community and nation. Despite Lincoln's reversal of David Hunter's emancipation order in May 1862, officials at Port Royal knew that the future lay with free labor. Yet they also recognized the importance of retaining certain prewar practices. Providing access to garden plots, for instance, would enable families to raise vegetables and even cotton for home use or sale. Organizing fieldwork by the task, with assignments varying according to the nature of the work and the sex and (to some extent) the age of the laborer, would enable family members to assist each other in completing their daily tasks in the plantation crop and then work together in the garden. A revolutionary force, the newcomers believed, would take the place of the lash. It was "the dime," whose motive power Frederick A. Eustis, a Massachusetts man who had inherited a plantation on an island in the Union-controlled area, described as "the great civilizer." But the freed people stubbornly resisted having the Yankees' notion of civilization shoved down their throats on terms they found unpalatable.[89]

Northerners learned some lessons only slowly, if at all. When, for instance, plantation superintendents failed to deliver on promises of pay and other amenities, they faced the unexpectedly stern judgment of the laborers. In March 1862, William C. Gannett observed the pervasive resentment that resulted when the newcomers failed to distribute clothing, salt, and tobacco as the former owners had done "in stated quantities at stated times." If the new superintendents simply followed the old rules, the laborers "would be contented and would work well." But even neophytes to the cash economy felt the hardships that the nonpayment of wages caused; after all, as Gannett observed, "promises to pay . . . for the last three months have n't kept them warm." Two months later, superintendent Edward S. Philbrick marveled that the people worked at all. Failure to deliver promised wages, he well knew, "would not have gotten an acre planted by Irish laborers."[90]

Apparently of the opinion that military orders provided all the convincing that the freed people would require to do as the self-styled liberators instructed, General Hunter developed a bold but simple plan to mobilize "all able-bodied volunteers of proper age and fitness" to serve as soldiers. He envisioned that the recruits would eventually form several regiments, thereby replenishing the Northern volunteer units grown thin by disease and thereby maintaining an effective deterrent to Confederate military operations.[91] But almost immediately coercion replaced voluntarism, and military authorities issued orders requiring all able-bodied men of military age to report to Hilton

Head for enlistment. The special agent of the Treasury Department charged with supervising plantation labor wrote to Hunter, explaining the detrimental effect of the dragnet. "The corn, vegetables, and cotton" now required cultivation, he explained, and the withdrawal of two-thirds of the able-bodied would leave "only women and children, and old or sickly men, to cultivate the crops." This would have an "injurious influence upon the sensitive minds and feelings of those who remain, greatly diminishing the results of their labor." What is more, it would also affect the men. "They are ignorant, suspicious, and sensitive," Superintendent Pierce explained. "They have not acquired such confidence in us;—they have not so far recovered the manhood which two centuries of bondage have rooted out;—they do not, as yet . . . realize that they have a country to fight for." He suggested that "their indisposition to become soldiers" will only pass away over time as the Northerners earned their trust.[92] When recruiters moved from plantation to plantation, the able-bodied men fled to the woods. When overtaken by the recruiting parties and marched away, both they and their families tearfully assumed that this might be their final parting. One plantation superintendent noted icily that many "sighed . . . for the 'old fetters,' as being better than the new liberty."[93]

The resentment against Hunter's impressment lingered, curtailing voluntary enlistments. As the plantation superintendent Charles P. Ware explained in the fall of 1862, recruiting was "slow work" because the men combined the specific fears recalled from the spring (that is, "of cruel treatment" and "of non payment") with general fears about military service (that is, "of being shot" and "about leaving home"). Echoing Edward Pierce's previous observation about their ill-formed "notion of nationality, of the importance of showing themselves men," he properly linked their distrust "of all promises" to their poor treatment in the spring.[94] After all, men with dependents had good cause for objecting to forced conscription into the army—namely, securing the well-being and safety of their families, the building blocks of every nation. Despite past failures to make impressment work, military commanders resorted time and again to the tactic. In May 1863, they dispatched recruiters to the plantations again, and the men headed back into the swamps as they had the year before. The foreman on one plantation, a man named Primus, spoke so passionately against the draft that the soldiers carried him away to prevent him from turning other men against military service; and when officers refused to discharge him after he became ill, he deserted and returned home. In another incident at the same time, black recruiters exchanged gunfire with two men whom they chased into a marsh before capturing and hauling them into camp. The men later admitted to having fired "to scare away the soldiers" and thereby avoid impressment. All the men "who were drafted have been deserting," one Gideonite reported. Their objective, like that of Primus, was to "come home."[95]

In contrast, men from the lumber camps of Florida, who, having reached federal forces, were shipped to Hilton Head and recruited into the army, took a much different approach to military service. For them, wearing the blue uniform and participating in raids on their old communities offered the opportunity to free loved ones and acquaintances and to inflict damage on their former exploiters. Robert Sutton was a prime example. After enlisting, the former lumberman led federal raiding parties through the rivers and swamps of his home state.[96] These incidents revealed the complex process of nation building that secession and war had set loose. As Edward Pierce reasoned, freed people identified more readily with the name of Abraham Lincoln than with the abstract concept of the United States. But, most of all, they read the faces and the words and the actions of the Union's local representatives for signs of what loyalty to the nation actually meant. One of the first and truest tests was the level of respect that plantation superintendents and army officers showed for the freedmen and their families.

———

Enslaved people in the states of Maryland, Kentucky, and Missouri, who from January 1863 had lived in a time warp owing to the exemption of the Border States from the Emancipation Proclamation, faced long odds against establishing valid claims to freedom. With slavery still legal there, the federal government deferred to the authority of the slaveholders, which left enslaved people with no firm recourse to a third party that might intervene on their behalf. But by the summer of 1863, as the federal government began enlisting black men into military service—first in Maryland, then in Missouri, and only months later in Kentucky—that dynamic began to change. Federal authorities stepped between the enslaver and the enslaved, thereby empowering those who had been powerless. To be sure, men viewed enlistment as a way to not only help defeat the rebellion but also gain their own freedom and perhaps that of their families. But they had little interest in leaving loved ones vulnerable to the wrath of the owners in the process. For their part, women as well as men maneuvered for advantage. Missouri senator J. B. Henderson estimated in January 1863 that perhaps 20,000 enslaved persons had left the state since 1860, with the result that the border counties abutting Kansas and Iowa "have been deprived of almost their entire slave populations." The ranks of such freedom seekers increased dramatically in the months that followed.[97]

The Confederate army's forays into the Border States—Missouri and Kentucky in 1861 and 1862, and Maryland in 1862 and 1863—had exposed the fragility of home and family and nation for the enslaved residents of those states. In each of these incursions, rebel forces took pains to take black civilians—both enslaved and free—as prisoners. Rebel forces in Kentucky impressed slaves to work on Fort Donelson, a major defensive point on the Cumberland River, the likely federal invasion route to Nashville. As if to add insult to injury, when Confederate generals Braxton Bragg and E. Kirby Smith retreated from their abortive invasion of Kentucky in the fall of 1862, they abandoned laborers and servants whom they had earlier impressed from Tennessee and Kentucky. Still other enslaved people managed to escape the rebels, "hoping to find protection among the Union party." But Kentucky officials, rather than considering them as "forever free" under the terms of the Confiscation Acts, instead confined them as runaway slaves, posting newspaper notices inviting the owners to claim their missing property, and auctioning off to the highest bidders those who remained unclaimed.[98]

The periodic raids of Confederate forces in Maryland, including attacks on Rockville and Silver Spring just north of Washington, and the wholesale movement of Robert E. Lee's Army of Northern Virginia in the operations that led up to the battles of Antietam in September 1862 and Gettysburg in July 1863, repeated what happened in Kentucky earlier. When the rebels crossed the Potomac River back into Virginia following Gettysburg, they took an estimated several hundred to more than two thousand black people, many of whom had been free for years, if not their entire lives. The plunderers destroyed the ironworks of Thaddeus Stevens, taking "into slavery," as the Republican congressional stalwart later reported, "a colored widow with four children." Early in December 1865—just before ratification of the Thirteenth Amendment—Stevens sought assistance from the Freedmen's Bureau to provide transportation for their return, the children from Richmond and the mother, Jane Tyler, from Savannah.[99]

Separation from loved ones exacerbated the uncertainties that were an inevitable by-product of the war. Every community had stories about the bad consequences that families suffered after their men departed. In a letter to her soldier husband written shortly after Christmas 1863, the enslaved Missourian Martha Glover informed him that her owners "abuse me because you went," quarreling with her and beating her. She refused to attend a party to which she was invited, noting that she was "in too much trouble to want to go to parties." As to encouraging other men to enlist, "You ought not to left me in the fix I am in & all these little helpless children to take care of." "You need not tell me to beg any more married men to go," she concluded. "I see too much trouble to try to get any more into trouble too."[100] A Kentucky soldier, George Winlock, reminisced years later that whenever the men heard about the troubles afflicting their families at home, "we would all be sad." They could take some consolation from their commanding officer's assurances that "everything is all right at home, Boys," yet the miles that separated them from home provided fresh fuel for their worries.[101]

"What a glorious age is this we live in!" marveled a black resident of St. Louis early in 1864, "unparalleled in the history of the world. Who can point out, in sacred or profane history," he wondered, "where an oppressed people, like we have been in the United States, were raised to such eminence in this short civil war?" This was a fulfillment of the prophecy that "a nation shall be born in a day," as the advance of Union armies marching under the banner of emancipation destroyed the much-vaunted "corner stone of the Confederacy."[102] "Let us awake, arise, and make due preparation," the AME minister Frisby J. Cooper addressed his "fellow citizens" at a celebration of the first anniversary of the Emancipation Proclamation in Wilmington, Delaware. Echoing Spotswood Rice and the increasingly common refrain among black people across the nation, Cooper argued that as a result of emancipation, "we assume a new relationship in this government."[103] Striking a less triumphalist tone, John Randolph of Washington, D.C., noted that achieving the "capabilities of our race" presented both obstacles and opportunities. "Taking all things in consideration, we feel encouraged, although our case is a critical one, indeed." If the cause of freedom were to stumble short of victory, "our last state will be worse than the first." He took sufficient inspiration from "our friends at the North, and the heroic deeds of colored men on the battle field" to prove "to the world that we are deserving the rights and titles of citizens—a people worthy to be free —worthy to be respected."[104]

———

Over the course of 1864, emancipationist political movements made headway in the Loyal Border States of Maryland and Missouri and in the former Confederate states of Louisiana and Tennessee. In fact, when the House of Representatives approved the draft language for the Thirteenth Amendment at the end of January 1865, slavery held legal status only in Delaware (where the enslaved population numbered perhaps several hundred and the institution had nearly expired) and Kentucky (where some 65,000 persons remained in chains).[105] Thomas James, a formerly enslaved man from New York who had managed to escape to Canada while a teenager and then returned to become an abolitionist and an AME minister, was a participant-observer in the demise of slavery in Kentucky. While operating under the auspices of the AMA, James received quasi-military powers from the federal authorities to recruit soldiers, break up the attempts to remove enslaved people from the state for sale, and liberate persons from the slave pens and jails where their masters had hidden them. "Rebel bushwhackers" made innumerable threats and several attempts on his life. A savage attack by a pro-Confederate blacksmith left his arm "partially paralyzed and almost useless" thereafter.[106] At the refugee camps, he witnessed sickness and death, heard accounts of separation of family members, and collected evidence of physical abuse, adding up to an atmosphere of "gloom" that "will never fade from my recollection."[107] He witnessed, in short, the circumstances that carried away from Camp Nelson the family of Private Joseph Miller, one by one.

Early in 1864, Massachusetts senator Henry Wilson introduced into the Senate a bill to promote enlistments, one section of which stated that the recruit as well as "his mother, wife, and children" would be "for ever free."[108] For the next year, conservative members of Congress, led chiefly by men from the Border Slave States, adamantly opposed the measure, at first suggesting on narrow grounds that it would be unenforceable because the laws of the states do not recognize the marriage and paternity of enslaved people but then broadening their objections to accommodate their fear that passage would mean the end of slavery. To counter that logic, Wilson and his legislative allies cited the vulnerability to sale and other kinds of abuse that the soldiers' families suffered after the men left home.[109] When the measure finally became law in March 1865, hundreds of men enlisted to take advantage of its provision to free their families, which, as they sadly came to realize, cut in several directions. To be sure, the enlistees' loved ones gained freedom, but often at a price, particularly when the new units were dispatched first to Virginia for the final campaign against Richmond and then to Texas to secure the border with Mexico. From such a distance the men were powerless to act as protectors. Many had delayed enlisting for more than a year precisely out of concern for the safety of their families, only to have their worst fears materialize during the final days of the war and over the succeeding months.[110]

In May of 1865, General John M. Palmer, the antislavery commander of the Department of Kentucky, issued orders permitting black Kentuckians to travel in search of employment—even to the free states north of the Ohio River—without the approval of their nominal owners. With Palmer's blessing, Thomas James intervened repeatedly to protect enslaved Kentuckians from the wrath of their owners. In an impromptu speech to black residents of Louisville on July 4, 1865, Palmer advised them: "My countrymen, you are *substantially* free." James recalled that "for our amusement" Palmer also read several letters that anonymous irate Kentuckians had written to him.[111] The slaveholders found neither the general's words nor his actions amusing, and they tightened the screws on the persons still under their dominion. A delegation of black Kentuckians traveled to Washington in late June to lay before President Andrew Johnson their case for a continuation of martial law in light of "the terrible uncertainty of their future." They feared for the worst in the event that the former "civil authorities" regained control over the state government. Such an outcome would undo the good work of General Palmer, "under whose Protection we have allmost learned to Realise the Blessings of a Home under the Safeguard and Sanction of law."[112]

———

Freed people understood that the transition from slavery to freedom would require devising new social relationships. Age-old institutions, like the family, would take a new form with new responsibilities. Other institutions, which either did not exist in slavery or existed in stunted form, such as churches and fraternal and benevolent associations, would take on a new appearance and gain new importance. With family, these relationships served as the bones, ligaments, and muscles that made up local neighborhoods and communities. Ultimately, freed people would participate in civil and political culture of American society, reaching the pinnacle in the imagined community that was the nation.

Because of the ambiguity associated with the historical relationship between persons of African ancestry and the government of the United States, most enslaved people viewed the motives and actions of the agents of that government with caution. To be sure, they hoped that Lincoln's soldiers would bring liberty. But they also wondered if that government would ever recognize their inherent equality and remove the barriers to full and equal citizenship with persons of European ancestry and the stigmas associated with enslavement. Free black people who lived in the Northern states gave the fullest expression to the concept of a "Black Nationality" as a goal that embodied independence and as an ideology for achieving it. Robert Hamilton, editor of the New York *Anglo-African*, saw such nationality as a natural by-product of the nineteenth century. The secular spirit that shaped human events required such a development "for the purpose of lifting the race to the level of civilization, and enabling it to contribute its share to the progress of the age."[113] For many, the concept represented an ideal of economic and political power that later generations would describe as self-determination, an antidote to the alienation from the tarnished ideals and discriminatory practices of the American republic. Wherever Northerners and formerly enslaved Southerners interacted—in military and naval service, in contraband camps and the various experiments in compensated labor, and in the schools and churches established in Union-occupied areas of the Confederacy—they exchanged ideas about freedom and citizenship, which went a long way toward enriching concepts of nationhood and peoplehood on all sides.

Undergirding this process was the concept of home—its faces, its sounds, its aromas, its warmth—that freedom seekers in the Confederate States and Loyal Border States felt acutely. Indeed, so deeply was this understanding embedded in everyone's sense of a properly ordered world that observers from every background and of every description used the term uncritically, each person presuming that his or her understanding of "home" accorded precisely with everyone else's. Such a presumption was faulty. For some, the old neighborhood—perhaps the home place itself, when shed of the trappings and habits of slavery—best captured that ideal. For others, the freedom that could never be realized there might be achievable by returning to Maryland or Virginia, the partially known places of youthful memories, both pleasant and painful. For still others, the war transformed these places and their inhabitants, destroying the former and making refugees of the latter. In those circumstances, some felt the age-old pull of the storied lands beneath the North Star, Canada, or one of the free states above the Ohio River and the Mason and Dixon Line. If those prospects were too remote geographically and conceptually, then anywhere within sight of the U.S. flag flying over a federal outpost sufficed. A Kentuckian who successfully escaped slavery observed that the war had transformed the political geography of freedom seeking: the daunting prewar trek of 500 miles had been reduced to fewer than 20 miles. "*Camp Nelson* is now *our* Canada," he proclaimed.[114]

Regardless of the site for pursuing freedom, it had to offer the joys of home, as Nast's illustration suggested, in a literal sense as the key to prosperity for free families and in the figurative sense of the foundation stone of the free institutions that together made up the republic. The concept of a "Black Nationality" served as a motivating spirit to advance the processes of home- and community-building and African Americans' long-stifled claims to full inclusion in the American democratic experiment. In its antebellum form, the emigrationist variant of this nationalist spirit had staked out the position that the full enjoyment of freedom had to be much more than the absence of slavery. Governments had responsibility for ensuring that every person living within their jurisdictions had access to the economic, civic, political, and social rights every other person enjoyed, without distinction of color or previous condition—in short, for enabling their citizens to experience the joy of feeling at home in every sense of the word. The question remained: Would emancipation fulfill this promise?

Chapter 9

The Home of the Brave

In September 1863, when Robert Hamilton of the New York *Anglo-African* criticized the lack of "settled principles" and a "settled organization" to guide the process of emancipation, he also cautioned against another potential pitfall: "gradual emancipation." This was "the process which the blacks have been undergoing in the so-called free States for the last fifty years" and which was, in fact, little more than "a mockery of freedom." Because Northern "free blacks (so called) . . . know more on these subjects than all the world," he urged them to take up the responsibility of "forming organizations and spreading the doctrines of IMMEDIATE EMANCIPATION with affranchisement."[1] With the ballot, black men could participate in shaping public policy and not just be commentators and outside agitators for political change. From the inside, they hoped, they would shape the second emancipation more effectively than their forbears could influence the first.

By linking the franchise to freedom, Hamilton proposed to avoid the earlier experience of black men in New York, Connecticut, Pennsylvania, Virginia, and North Carolina. Each of these states granted "citizenship to the extent of voting at the polls to black men for their soldierly deeds in the Revolutionary war, and then gradually took back the well-earned right."[2] Hamilton might well have continued enumerating the other manifestations of second-class citizenship in the Northern states. From the 1830s through the Civil War, for instance, virtually every state and national convention of black citizens spoke as forcefully against the discriminatory laws and practices that adversely affected their communities as they did against slavery.[3] Delegates to the National Emigration Convention in 1854 faulted black Northerners for accepting these invidious "political distinctions," which constituted "our greatest social curses" and which, "more than any thing else," tended "to divide our interests and make us indifferent to each others' welfare."[4]

Because free black people considered racial discrimination a legacy of slavery, they viewed the fight against second-class citizenship as an integral part of emancipation. Yet, the operational strategies against the two enemies had to differ: whereas the United States arrayed its entire might against the Confederacy, the chief bastion of slavery, the nation as well as its constituent states upheld race-based discrimination in law and in practice. In the most hallowed spirit of federalism, the states imposed restrictions, some more or less offensive or burdensome to black residents than others, which reflected their respective histories and the economic, demographic, and cultural forces that shaped their politics.[5] What is more, the process was inherently fluid, alternately relaxing and tightening the restrictions in response to broader social and political considerations. Whereas white residents of New England viewed their states as liberal bastions of equality, even going so far as to fantasize a past devoid of slavery and hence any possible lingering prejudice, their counterparts in New York and New Jersey, could hardly forget the slave past that had ended barely a generation before secession.[6]

In the states carved from the Northwest Territory, slaves remained a presence—notwithstanding the Northwest Ordinance—beyond the midpoint of the nineteenth century. As the Dred Scott case demonstrated, the routine changes in personnel at military installations throughout the region ensured the ongoing presence of enslaved servants who often accompanied the officers. Southerners who visited the Northern states on business and pleasure traveled with enslaved men and women. Commercial centers such as New York and Philadelphia routinely hosted them, as did such summer resorts as Newport, Rhode Island, and Saratoga Springs, New York, in season. European-descended settlers employed enslaved (and semienslaved) laborers in the western territories, a practice that continued even after the war ended and the Thirteenth Amendment ostensibly outlawed such practices.[7]

From the start of the war, black commentators in the North insisted that for emancipation to have meaning, black Americans must enjoy all the fruits of citizenship, including unrestricted manhood suffrage, nondiscriminatory access to schools and other such public amenities, and the opportunity to improve themselves economically as other citizens did. What remained unresolved, however, was the level of public support for doing so and the willingness of elected officials to tread such uncharted terrain. In the states that had seceded, the federal government might require emancipation as a precondition for reentering the Union—a precedent established when West Virginia was admitted to the Union as a new state. But through the end of the war, the states regulated their electoral institutions just as they did their domestic institutions. As a result, even as Northern black leaders attempted to create a single movement in pursuit of emancipation and full citizenship, the magnitude of the envisioned social change, coupled with the political realities inherent in the federal system, guaranteed that the fragmentation of goals and means of achieving them would pose an obstacle to success.

———

To achieve this dual victory, the national movement had long since committed to engaging the political system on terms of its own assumptions, beliefs, and practices. As a result, black communities, large and small, throughout the free states had achieved a high level of civic awareness and organizational experience. Despite periodic flirtations with thoughts of overseas migration, most African American residents of the Northern states believed that the United States represented the most promising future home. By showing a strong desire to help crush the rebellion and save the Union, black Northerners hoped to strengthen the claims to equal citizenship, an end to racial discrimination, and access to economic opportunity, for which they and their parents had struggled for generations. The responsibilities of citizenship required political awareness, which in turn was best developed and maintained by gathering political information and subjecting it to discussion and debate. The black and abolitionist press provided the raw material, which black communities consumed and recycled for reconsumption in forums that ranged from supper tables to church gatherings and from worksites to public lecture halls. Black Northerners held deep respect for the nation's economic and political institutions as beacons of hope for the entire world, notwithstanding their flaws.[8]

The prospect of ending slavery in the South profoundly affected black Northerners. By practicing the key Christian virtues of frugality, piety, loyalty, and hard work, their households would serve as civic nurseries. Having demanded of the government "equal rights, the elective franchise, and rights of citizens," a resident of Indianapolis noted, "all intelligent people" agree "that, at this time, all of our efforts should be put forth by way of moral and mental improvements, in order that we be prepared for our new status." "Those who are informed," the observer suggested, must "urg[e] on those who are more tardy and not yet awakened to the great work that lies before them, to be up and doing, by cultivating their intellectual faculties and preparing to be freemen and help sustain a free and Republican Government."[9]

Whereas the war drew legions of women into charitable activities, the fight against slavery added components of civic and political activism to that work but with confining as well as liberating results. Northern middle-class assumptions about the proper behavior of the sexes imposed certain restraints, but larger cultural changes were beginning to destabilize the status quo. As earlier, black and white women assumed conventional roles, collecting and distributing clothing, blankets, and shoes and volunteering as schoolteachers, but wartime circumstances created new opportunities. Elizabeth Keckly, for instance, who was Mary Todd Lincoln's dressmaker and confidant, helped establish the Freedmen's Aid Society in Washington. Within the White House, she was well positioned to keep the Lincolns apprised of the relief work and to solicit a donation or two in support of the cause. The famed abolitionist orator Sojourner Truth taught domestic economy to the female residents of Freedman's Village in Arlington, Virginia, but also wrote letters to abolitionist newspapers and even met with President Lincoln regarding her work. Formerly enslaved women, such as Truth and Harriet Jacobs, as well as freeborn white women, such as Julia Wilbur and Josephine Griffing, did more than provide direct services to the needy; they assumed management responsibilities in the relief enterprise and filled important intermediary roles among donors, shippers, and directors of charitable organizations and government officials. As the wave of civic activism within churches and community groups continued to crest, with public speakers and newspaper editors extolling the work, fresh volunteers redoubled the relief efforts at home and replenished the ranks of direct-service providers in the Union-controlled regions of the Confederacy.[10]

Stable homes and families would serve as the building blocks of the post-slavery world, and women's role in nurturing future citizens rivaled that of the men. Yet long-standing conventions of women's place being in the home did not always yield readily to the new dispensation. When the AME minister Henry M. Turner encouraged young women to participate in the lyceum that he organized at Israel Bethel Church in Washington, for instance, they responded slowly, despite their active involvement in the Sabbath-school association. In late summer 1863, when Agnes E. Burke delivered a lecture titled "On Matrimony" before the gentlemen, a reporter noted that she was the first and only female member of the lyceum.[11]

Christian churches hosted much of this activism on the part of women and men alike, facilitating the interconnected struggles against slavery and racial discrimination through their organizational networks. The AME Church was particularly effective, given its presence in the major cities of the Northeast from Washington to Brooklyn, and with congregations affiliated with the other major denominations figuring more or less prominently in the various cities. Other Christian denominations also took new approaches to fulfilling the needs of their communities in the changed circumstances created by the war. In Washington, D.C., for instance, the Colored Catholic Benevolent Society successfully petitioned Congress for an act of incorporation in June 1864, which, among other things, permitted this "body politic and corporate" to hold real estate. For members and—when the officers "shall deem it expedient"—the families of members, the society would help provide "for the care and comfort" of those who were "sick, disabled, or dependent" and "for the decent internment" of those who passed away.[12] And members of the Fifteenth Street Presbyterian Church, who included many of Washington's free black elite, began venturing into the choppy waters of political debates over slavery and black citizenship. They formed the Social, Civil, and Statistical Association, akin to the group of the same name that William Still and other black activists in Pennsylvania had organized in 1860 for the purpose of conducting research, sponsoring public programs, and challenging discriminatory treatment.[13] Veterans of the antebellum abolitionist and state convention movements often contributed their leadership experience to these new initiatives.

The African Civilization Society (ACS) in New York occupied a somewhat ambiguous place in the growing constellation of advocacy groups. Having entered the field of freedmen's aid in 1863, the ACS early in 1864 opened a school in Washington over the spirited objections of such abolitionist stalwarts as George T. Downing and Charles Lenox Remond, who accused Richard H. Cain, chief spokesman of the venture, as "the tool of Colonizationists."[14] The organization's pro-emigration past hung like a rain cloud over its fledgling work on behalf of the freed people. Founded in 1858 with an eye toward supporting interest in Haitian emigration, the ACS enjoyed considerable public attention because of its leaders' close ties to Robert Hamilton and the New York *Anglo-African*. At the time, James Redpath, the English-born abolitionist and journalist, was leading an intense lobbying campaign on behalf of Haitian emigration. Leaders of the ACS joined forces with Redpath to promote Haiti as a possible destination for achieving the dreams of freedom, self-sufficiency, and political equality that had remained so long out of reach in the United States. As late as April 1861, the interest in Haiti was so strong that Frederick Douglass had planned to journey there but abruptly canceled his plans following the Confederate attack on Fort Sumter.[15]

A national black emigration convention in 1854, at which Martin R. Delany and Theodore J. Holley were influential participants, produced a stunning declaration, captioned as a "Report on the Political Destiny of the Colored Race, on the American Continent," which described the West Indies and Central and South America as "the Western Continent," where "colored persons" must forever be "the *ruling element*." "A fixed fact in the zodiac of the political heavens," the authors reasoned, was "that the blacks and colored people are the stars which must ever most conspicuously twinkle in the firmament of this division of the Western Hemisphere."[16]

Thanks largely to this interest in emigration to Africa, Haiti, and Central America over the preceding several years, African Americans in the Northern states did not reflexively dismiss its new manifestations after the war began. Accordingly, in the spring of 1862 when President Lincoln proposed federally supported colonization as an incentive for slave states to adopt gradual emancipation, he benefited from several pockets of supporters willing to listen. Lincoln's strong pitch garnered special interest in Washington, thanks in part to the colonization provisions included in the April 1862 act abolishing slavery in the District of Columbia and in part to a meeting he held with a small group of black ministers in August. Although the president invited them to take their time in developing a response to his overture, the clergymen faced opposition from their congregations, based as much on the manner in which they were selected for the audience as on the substance of the message they planned to deliver. The committee never reported back to the president.[17]

Interest in migration to Liberia or to Central America and the Caribbean on the part of individuals and groups continued to flicker during the war in particular circumstances. In April 1862, for instance, "a young colored man" who had abandoned New Orleans for Monrovia several years before the war explained why he left. "I wanted liberty, for which my Maker created me," Balus Watkins asserted. "Although I was a free resident of New Orleans, yet I could not enjoy liberty there, and I became tired and sick of the privation against which I had to contend, and I determined to leave my native land and seek for freedom in some other."[18] Around the same time, Joseph E. Williams, the peripatetic advocate of emigration, submitted a petition to Congress bearing the names of approximately sixty men who spoke "for themselves, their relatives, and friends." They requested the government's assistance to migrate to Central America because "we could not be a people here." The wording of the petition—apparently the work of Williams—captured the conflicting thoughts and emotions that black Americans harbored toward emigration during the Civil War era. Liberia was "too distant from the land of our birth," the petitioners argued, and the disappointment that the recent Haitian emigrants—including Williams himself—had experienced soured them to the prospects of building new lives in "Hayti, or either of the Africo-West India Islands."[19] Among the signers was Henry M. Turner.

To win the favorable consideration of Congress, Williams and the other petitioners employed the well-worn tool of deference. "Slavery, if it must be borne," they argued, "is more endurable under a race we have long been taught to look up to and regard as superior, than under one originating in Africa, degraded by abject slavery under Spanish and French greed, and still further brutalized by unrestrained and licentious liberty." "Aid us to get there—protect us for a short while, and we will prove ourselves worthy and grateful." They would cultivate "in the free spirit of liberty" the "cotton, sugar, and tobacco" that they had grown as slaves and "aid in bringing to you that great commerce of the Pacific, which will still further increase the wealth and power" of the United States.[20]

In this spirit, they reiterated themes with respect to African Americans' prospective missionary and commercial work in Africa that aligned well with the statements of other proponents of emigration whose ranks ranged from the missionary and educator Alexander Crummell to the Presbyterian clergyman William Aikman.[21] "Though colored, and debarred from rights of citizenship," the petitioners insisted, "our hearts, none the less, cling to the land of our birth." Stopping short of declaring this to be "our country," they referred instead to "this great country" or, more tellingly, "your country." Nonetheless, making permanent the freedom of the "so long oppressed colored race" required that they have access to a place "in which they may seek and secure, by their own industry, that mental and physical development which will allow them an honorable position in the families of God's great world."[22] The petitioners offered the key for unlocking the meaning of emancipation in the North—not the stifling gradual emancipation that was the legacy of the Revolution, but the ennobling freedom possessed by fully vested citizens of a modern republic in a progressive age.

The stirring vision the petitioners expressed did no more than President Lincoln's advocacy had done to create mass interest in favor of emigration, despite black Northerners' strong support for extending diplomatic recognition to Haiti and Liberia. The appearance of two Liberian gentlemen in Washington to lobby in favor of establishing formal relations prompted a foe of emigration to explain the case against "an entirely African nationality," a concept, he argued, that "should not belong to this age." "Our destiny on this continent," he insisted, "is inseparably joined to the now dominant race, our hopes are all bound up in the future of this, our country." Quickly checking himself by adding "we have little incentive to say, 'our country,'" he refused to concede, as Joseph Williams had, that the nation and its future belonged solely to the white race. From the dawn of the colonization debate in the early days of the republic, African Americans alternately expressed hope and despair over the prospects for achieving a true home in the United States.[23]

By the fall of 1862, the fires of emigration began to fizzle and only sparks remained. Even before Lincoln issued the preliminary Emancipation Proclamation late in September, a resident of Galena, Illinois, argued that the prevailing antiblack prejudice in his part of the state stopped well short of what "politicians would have us believe." Although some black residents considered leaving if a backlash against emancipation materialized, "the people" as a whole were "unfavorable toward emigration at present. They seem to prefer holding the matter under advisement, until the war is over."[24] The nation's new commitment to emancipation effectively quashed the search for a homeland outside the United States for the rest of the war. Confident that freedom and citizenship were in the offing, black communities contented themselves to wait and see, sincerely hoping that President Lincoln would not betray their trust or his own word.

———

Talk of emancipation accelerated the hope that black men would finally get the opportunity to fight for freedom. President Lincoln's several calls for troops to defend the Union offered an ideal opportunity to act. Yet authorities in both Washington and the respective states rebuffed every such offer of service. Even at this stage of the war, many white Northerners considered the possibility that free black men—not to mention slaves—might be permitted to fight disturbing, if not terrifying, although public opinion was beginning to change. By the summer of 1862, Illinois governor Richard Yates was willing to take the risk. After all, he reasoned, the Confederates "arm negroes and merciless savages in their behalf," so the Union must abandon its "conservative policy" and strike at "the vital part of the Rebellion." "Summon to the standard of the Republic all willing to fight. . . . Let loyalty, and that alone, be the dividing line between the nation and its foes."[25]

As early as the first Battle of Bull Run in July 1861, Union soldiers encountered black men in arms serving with the rebel units. The widely circulated testimony of one such man, John Parker, who subsequently escaped to Union lines, bore personal witness to the accuracy of the claims. The following month, a federal officer who investigated the Confederates' burning of Hampton, Virginia, cited reports to the effect that one of the participating gun batteries was "manned in part by negroes."[26] Yet large segments of the white public remained cool to the idea of arming black men. James McKaye, an active foe of slavery, a veteran militia commander in New York, and a future member of the AFIC, voiced a mixed strain of the popular misgivings. He believed that military service would enable the "colored men of the South" to gain "the needed discipline and necessary preparation for the possession of freedom" as well as "their own redemption." If the nation's leaders would pledge "to organize and guide them in the ways of civilized warfare," he insisted, theirs was the "road to freedom, and ours to national regeneration and glory." But if not, they will "grow into an irrepressible mass of barbarism, by and by to burst into a wild and all-devouring conflagration."[27]

Federal officials knew of the past service of black men during the American Revolution because the governors and congressional representatives of the New England states referenced it repeatedly, as did such national and local black leaders as Frederick Douglass, John S. Rock, and Henry M. Turner. Massachusetts claimed Crispus Attucks, an African American who lost his life in the Boston Massacre in March 1770. In the eyes of many, he was the first casualty of the American Revolution, a hero to future generations of black schoolchildren, and an inspiration to adults engaged in the cause of freedom. (When black men in Albany, Ohio, formed a militia company at the start of the Civil War, they named it the Attucks Guards in his honor.[28]) After the Declaration of Independence and the start of the war with England, Massachusetts, Connecticut, and Rhode Island raised black regiments, and men of African descent from every colony north of Maryland served in Washington's

Continental Army. An awareness of that service helped tilt public opinion against slavery in the New England states during and after the Revolution.[29] South of Maryland, free men of color participated in militia companies in the colonies along the Gulf coast during the days of French and Spanish rule. During the War of 1812, at the culminating Battle of New Orleans in January 1815, the free black companies of the city played such a pivotal role that General Andrew Jackson commended both their bravery and the value of their contribution to defeating the British.

After the United States became independent, organized a permanent government, and began to create a body of law and administrative procedures, a consensus quickly emerged whereby militia service was the responsibility and the prerogative of white men.[30] That notwithstanding, a few men of African ancestry either passed for white or persuaded local officials to look the other way, allowing them to participate in musters or tolerating their presence on the parade grounds on muster days, sometimes imitating and sometimes mocking the evolutions of the militiamen. As Nicholas Biddle of Pottsville, Pennsylvania, demonstrated, keeping company with militiamen might open the door to participation, even if as an officer's servant instead of a man in arms.

When Lincoln called for ninety-day volunteers following Fort Sumter, many of these militia regiments entered federal service, and when they took to the field, the black men who had passed into the ranks or who served as supernumeraries generally accompanied them without fanfare. As national black leaders campaigned to convince the War Department and state authorities to enlist men of African ancestry, hundreds, if not thousands, slipped quietly into the white volunteer units.[31] H. Ford Douglas, who had become an abolitionist lecturer in the Midwest during the 1850s after he escaped slavery, enlisted in the Ninety-Fifth Illinois Volunteer Infantry with the full knowledge of his superior officers and comrades in the ranks. A black man named James Reeder fought with a Rhode Island artillery battery in the first Battle of Bull Run, having insisted that he wear the uniform of a U.S. volunteer instead of a servant's livery. And Edwin Belcher, the son of a white planter from South Carolina and an enslaved mother, whose father had sent the family to live in Philadelphia before the war, enlisted in the Seventy-Third Pennsylvania Volunteers when the unit was organized in the summer of 1861. Belcher served throughout the war, taking part in a number of battles, including Gettysburg and Missionary Ridge, and rising to the rank of captain by early 1865.[32]

As the combatants emerged from winter hibernation amid the first signs of spring in 1862, black men across the North reopened their campaign to join the fight. From Pittsburgh, Pennsylvania, Rufus Sibb Jones, the captain of the Fort Pitt Cadets, promised to furnish 200 men, "able-bodied and of un-questionable loyalty to the United States of America," to garrison Southern forts. The "Hannibal Guards" in New York City were also ready for action. The noted African American abolitionist and attorney John S. Rock was tour-ing the Northern states arguing that black soldiers would acquit themselves well if "guaranteed the recognition of their manhood," and Henry Highland Garnet himself reiterated his earlier call for armed struggle.[33]

Advocates of black military service invoked the imagery of manhood with striking consistency throughout the war. Such imagery, of course, was not unique to African Americans. Anglo-American recruits wished to fulfill the responsibility that state and national militia acts imposed on white men. Men with ancestral roots in other parts of Europe or in Africa viewed volunteer-ing as a way to overturn suspicions of inferiority based on color or national origins and thereby gain membership in that fraternity. For black men in par-ticular, a war against slavery offered a chance to free the persons of African ancestry who were unjustly held in bondage and to destroy the slave power. Honorable service, they believed, would lead to full citizenship, including suf-frage. Donning the blue uniform would affirm their role as protectors and defenders of their families and communities. Finally, military service to the nation in its time of need offered free black men in the North the promise of new leverage in the patron-client relationships that often constrained their interactions with neighbors or employers. African American men, both free-born and formerly enslaved, stood to gain much by establishing the kind of direct relationship to the federal government that bearing arms in its defense would entail. So they offered their services, even if warily.

Men who had fled to Canada during the 1850s to escape slavery and its long enforcement arm began sensing the winds of change in federal policy and offering their services. From Canada West, the Reverend Garland H. White, who had been the body servant of Georgia senator Robert Toombs before es-caping north, informed the secretary of war that the refugees wished to re-turn "to serve as soldiers in the southern parts during the summer season or longer if required." Professing their "love for the north & the government at large," they prayed that the Union's triumph would "overthrow . . . the insti-tution of slavery which is the cause of all our trouble" and offered to do their part to achieve that result.[34] As was true for the prior year, all such represen-tations met only cold silence or a curt "No!" But besides the men of African ancestry who had slipped into white volunteer units, thousands of others ac-companied them as servants, cooks, and teamsters. Robert Fitzgerald and his brothers and cousins from eastern Pennsylvania, like hundreds of other like-minded black patriots, made their way to Perryville, Maryland, to work as civilian employees of the army quartermaster's department. Before long, they were working on the wagon trains that supplied the armies in the field in Virginia.[35]

From early in the war, naval service beckoned to young black men who lived in the seaport cities from Baltimore, Maryland, to Portland, Maine, and to the Canadian Maritime Provinces as well. With the decline in commercial shipping owing to the Union's blockade of the Confederate seacoast, men who made their living at sea were looking for berths, and men who worked on the docks often followed the path of their coworkers, family members, friends, and neighbors to naval recruiting offices. Naval service, however, did not generally appeal to men who had no prior experience with ships and the sea or the wharves of the major seaports.[36] African American leaders shared the broader society's characterization of seafaring as a lowly profession. Although Frederick Douglass had worn sailor's clothing as a disguise when he escaped from slavery, later priding himself in being able to speak "sailor's talk like an 'old salt'" and rhapsodizing about the imagery of freedom created by white-sailed ships on Chesapeake Bay, by 1861 the docks of Baltimore, their people, and their ways had receded deep into his memory.[37] By mid-1864, black sailors constituted approximately 25 percent of the navy's enlisted force, contributing materially to the Union's naval superiority. Yet black leaders hardly gave this service its proper due, particularly in the war against slavery. Instead, they considered enlistment in the army as the key to saving the Union and destroying slavery. What is more, only by facing Confederate soldiers across a field of battle and refusing to flinch from the roar of the cannon and the fear of death would black men demonstrate their true manhood and their fitness for full citizenship.

As McClellan's Peninsula Campaign stalled, public sentiment in favor of employing black men systematically in support of the war effort grew, as evidenced by the Second Confiscation Act and the Militia Act that Congress approved in the summer of 1862. In the same spirit, Senator James H. Lane of Kansas began organizing a black regiment, whose members consisted largely of formerly enslaved men from Missouri. He uniformed, equipped, sheltered, and fed the unit from conventional military stores, but because he had not fully informed Washington officials of his true intentions, the War Department refused to pay the volunteers. Only in the spring of 1863, after watching their families endure months of privation, did the men receive their first pay.[38] Unaware of Lane's spat with the War Department, black leaders in other states looked to Kansas as a possible passageway into military service. The governors of several New England states, particularly John A. Andrew in Massachusetts and William Sprague in Rhode Island, also expressed support for organizing units of black volunteers. Governor Horatio Seymour of New York, like his Pennsylvania counterpart Andrew G. Curtin, showed no sympathy for black enlistment. In the face of such indifference, the editor of the *Christian Recorder* advised black Pennsylvanians to "stay in their own State, and let the whites battle away at their pleasure. The good Lord will make all things right."[39]

Lane's regiment offered fascinating insight into the war's larger implications in the West, where, at the time of Fort Sumter, tensions had barely died down from the violent border warfare of the 1850s following passage of the Kansas-Nebraska Act. Lane's recruiters correctly assumed that black Missourians would serve willingly. When the unit began participating in military operations in the fall of 1862, the soldiers routinely liberated enslaved people in western Missouri and Arkansas, transporting them back to Leavenworth in the empty supply wagons. In engaging with Confederate forces, they sometimes encountered Cherokee and Choctaw units, which, on several occasions, killed or scalped their black captives. Lane's regiment, in turn, assisted enslaved men who had escaped from the Indian nations in reaching Kansas, some of whom enlisted and returned to the field. In the end, the Civil War on the western frontier did much more than disrupt slavery in the Union state of Missouri, in the Confederate state of Arkansas, and among the sovereign tribes in the Indian Territory. It exposed conflicting conceptions of sovereignty and property among the various Indian and European cultures, as well as layers of domestic institutions with subtle gradients between slavery and freedom and not the stark contrasts—the black and white—with which most Easterners (North and South) conceptualized emancipation.[40] The differences grew even more pronounced after the war.

Lincoln's final Emancipation Proclamation cleared the lingering doubts about the need for black soldiers and their potential effectiveness. Some black leaders mistrusted the motives behind this belated call to arms. "Before they take any hasty steps," warned the editor of the *Christian Recorder*, recruits should determine whether they will "have all the rights and privileges of other citizens in every state of the Union, and receive as much compensation for their services as any other soldier according to their rank in the army."[41] Northern officials took varying stances, based on a combination of circumstances that included their personal views and those of key constituencies, their political party affiliation, and the racial demographics of the respective states. Governor Andrew assured both prospective enlistees and the recruiters they retained to fill the ranks that the men would receive "the same pay, rations, and family aid" that white volunteers did, according to a report from New Bedford in February 1863. Other Republican governors did the same. Thanks to stalemates and reverses on the battlefield, "the public mind has greatly changed" over the first two years of war, and the white soldiers who had threatened to abandon the cause "if the black man were armed and made equal to them" relinquished their opposition instead. "Our country's salvation depends upon you," dead soldiers called from the grave. Therefore, "in the name of God come, and help our surviving comrades, that our land may be 'The land of the free, and the home of the brave.'"[42]

Early in March 1863, Frederick Douglass issued his famous call, "Men of Color, to Arms!," in which he encouraged black men throughout the North to enlist in the Massachusetts regiments. "I am authorized to assure you," he announced on behalf of Governor Andrew, "that you will receive the same wages, the same rations, the same equipments, the same protection, the same treatment and the same bounty secured to white soldiers." Black soldiers promised to tip the scales in favor of Northern victory, ensuring both the defeat of the Confederacy and the abolition of slavery. Douglass insisted that "one gallant rush from the North" would liberate the slaves: "The day dawns— the morning star is bright upon the horizon!" "The chance is now given to you to end in a day the bondage of centuries," he exhorted, "and to rise in one bound from social degradation to the plane of common equality with all other varieties of men." The suffering of the past would be erased and the promise of the future secured in this one transformative, revolutionary moment.[43]

African-descended communities throughout the North sprang to action in answer to the call. In Cincinnati, Columbus, Indianapolis, Detroit, Chicago, and the other cities of the heartland, community leaders made contact with organizers working on behalf of the New England regiments. Chicago's John Jones, who for years had advocated to repeal the state's hated Black Laws, took up the work of enlisting men. The abolitionist Mary Ann Shad Cary collaborated with Martin R. Delany and with various state officials in Connecticut and Rhode Island to recruit men for the black regiments they were forming.[44] W. H. Gibson had been emancipated in Maryland in 1847 on the condition that he leave and never return. He settled in Indianapolis. When Massachusetts began enlisting for the second regiment of black volunteers, he crossed the Ohio River expecting to reap a rich harvest. His work "excited the disloyal conservatives of Kentucky," whose complaints resulted in his being summoned before military authorities. Advised that the state "was not ready for such a movement, and that colored people would be better off in their present condition, as no quarters would be given them in the army," he departed. Some one hundred recruits followed.[45]

Enlisting in a volunteer regiment from another state highlighted the ambiguous relationship that existed between Northern black communities and their respective state governments and the national government. Local officials emphasized state pride in organizing volunteer units but relegated black men to the sidelines. Only by claiming allegiance to the larger national cause, which superseded their states of residence, could national and local black leaders hope to realize their goals. By doing so, however, they ventured into uncharted territory, particularly after the federal draft took effect in the summer of 1863. Although the advocates of enlistment pinned their hopes on believing that military service would open the door to citizenship rights, no one knew for sure what that might entail, given that state officials determined who was a citizen and what rights and privileges citizens enjoyed.

————

As they prepared to depart for the front, the Massachusetts soldiers' expectations of glory soared to new heights. Through the successful lobbying of Governor Andrew and the regiment's commander Colonel Robert Gould Shaw, the unit was assigned to the Department of the South, where the first of several attempts to attack Charleston by land was about to be launched. By acquitting themselves well at James Island on July 16, 1863, the unit won respect and the dubious honor of leading the suicidal attack against Fort Wagner scheduled for July 18. "From a purely military stand-point, the assault upon Fort Wagner was a failure," concluded George Washington Williams, a veteran and one of the early chroniclers of the black military experience. Yet from the jaws of defeat the officers and men of the Fifty-Fourth Massachusetts snatched a huge moral victory. They gave the lie to their detractors, transforming the regiment into heroes and dispelling doubts about Northern black men's martial ability, bravery, and loyalty to the government.[46]

Confident in their heroic stature among friends of liberty throughout the North, the Massachusetts men could scarcely believe the news that they would not receive the same pay as their white counterparts. They decided to take a principled stand, insisting that if the government would not respect them as men and honor its promises to them, they would refuse to accept the inferior pay. This episode rightly takes its place among the great civil rights struggles of the Civil War era, but the soldiers' protest extracted a fearsome toll on their families at home, particularly when the men spurned the offer of Governor Andrew to make up the shortfall with state funds. Several other regiments that were organized in 1863—including the Third U.S. Colored Infantry, which was recruited in Philadelphia—also refused to accept the seven dollars offered by the paymaster. The South Carolina Volunteers took the same stance as their Northern comrades. According to Colonel Thomas Wentworth Higginson, commander of the First Regiment, the men received the promised pay of thirteen dollars for five months before their paymaster "was compelled by express orders to reduce it" to the lower rate. Having on an earlier payday resigned themselves to receiving ten dollars per month in cash, they drew the line when three dollars was withheld for clothing. A soldier in the regiment reported that a few men with extenuating circumstances grudgingly accepted the seven dollars, but the rest of the men "could not see it" and took nothing.[47]

A freeborn seaman from New Bedford, Massachusetts, who had enlisted in the Fifty-Fourth Massachusetts Volunteers offered a stunning commentary on the policy's adverse effects on the soldiers and their families and its damaging impact on the credibility of the government that had accepted the men into service. Corporal James Henry Gooding pored over the relevant laws and regulations to understand the justification for treating Northern black men differently from Northern white men. He found the answer in the Confiscation Act, which applied to men who were considered property capable of being confiscated, that is, slaves. Free black men, in contrast, "were not enlisted under any 'contraband' act" and therefore should not be subjected to its provisions. While conceding that the service of the contrabands was "undoubtedly worth much to the Nation," their special circumstances "as slaves freed by military necessity" dictated that the government act in the capacity of "their temporary Guardian." Northern men had "the advantage of *thinking*, and acting for ourselves" and, accordingly, wished to have "their service . . . fairly appreciated, by paying them as american SOLDIERS, not as menial hierlings."[48]

Gooding was sensitive not just to the affronts to the dignity of the soldiers but also to the impact of the practice on their families. "Black men You may well know, are poor," Gooding reminded the president, and "three dollars per month, for a year, will suply their needy Wives, and little ones, with fuel."[49] Other soldiers added evidence from their own experience. Several men in the Twentieth U.S. Colored Infantry also wrote to Lincoln describing the hardships their loved ones endured as a result of the decision to reduce black soldiers' pay. After being organized in New York City in the spring of 1864, the unit departed for New Orleans, where it served for the rest of the war. One of the correspondents reported that he had been enslaved in Maryland for twenty-five years before escaping to the North. Insisting that they "came out to be true union soldiers the Grandsons of Mother Africa Never to Flinch from Duty," they were painfully aware of their families' plight yet powerless to assist. One whose wife asked that he send money to support their three children lamented "i have No way of getting Eney money to send to her Because i cant Get my Pay. And it gos very hard with me to think my family should be At home A suffering [when I] have money earnt and cant not get it."[50]

In black communities throughout the North, the government's policy of unequal pay caused divisions, with some leaders arguing that it must not deter enlistments and others insisting that the government must show them respect. A Philadelphia correspondent to the *Christian Recorder* hoped "that no one will be deterred from taking up arms from this consideration." The editor of the *Recorder*, who had previously urged caution, now took a "bold stand for our soldiers" and advocated for equal rights. The editor also assured readers that Major George L. Stearns, a former associate of John Brown's and now a recruiter for the state of Massachusetts, "and all of these men who believe in a just God, will never stop until colored men have the same wages and the same bounty as our white fellow citizens."[51] These promises of a speedy resolution only deepened the frustration for those who put aside their pride in the interest of the greater good and trusted that justice would prevail.

Families of soldiers in the Northern states also wondered why they had to suffer the brunt of the government's broken promises. After all, while their soldier husbands and fathers refused to accept the inferior pay, the men still received rations daily and clothing as needed. Women-headed households relied on their traditional networks of kinfolk, neighbors, and friends, pooling resources as necessary to provide for themselves and their children. They took in boarders and laundry and engaged in petty trade to earn cash. When all else failed, they sought help from relief agencies, benevolent associations, and church congregations. Just before Christmas 1863, the wives of four unpaid soldiers from Brooklyn approached the directors of the Freedman's Friend Society only to be turned away on the grounds that the funds being raised were earmarked for the contrabands of the South. A witness wondered why a portion could not be directed to the benefit of soldiers' families who are "shivering with cold, without the necessities of life." In view of precisely such needs, the Freedmen's Aid Association of Washington changed its name to Freedmen's and Soldiers' Aid Association in December 1863 and began offering assistance to the needy families of soldiers.[52]

During the fall of 1864, the protest against accepting inferior pay generated a backlash among formerly enslaved soldiers. They resented the invidious distinctions based on the accidents of birth and circumstances that Corporal Gooding and his Massachusetts comrades had drawn. They also questioned the motives of the black Yankees in pressing the matter of pay so relentlessly. That October, two sergeants of the Seventy-Eighth U.S. Colored Infantry, a regiment of formerly enslaved men from Louisiana that was on garrison duty at Port Hudson, charged the Northern freeborn soldiers with placing higher priority on their stinted pay than on the well-being of their families or the destruction of slavery. A sergeant in a Pennsylvania regiment disputed the charges, arguing that most Northern men had been "earning more at home than we do in the army," and that they fought "for liberty, and to assist in putting down this rebellion" just as their Southern comrades did. Another freeborn Northerner stationed in Louisiana also took issue with the men of the Seventy-Eighth for disparaging "the heroes of South Carolina, (colored), who have proved themselves as men, of some spirit and dignity, as well as bravery" and hoped "that there will be more union among the colored troops than there has been" because "we have been disunited long enough."[53]

Having committed to the protest, the soldiers aimed to maintain it, in some cases ignoring the advice of their officers to give up the fight. An anonymous correspondent to the *Christian Recorder* reported that when the paymaster arrived at the camp of the Thirty-Second U.S. Colored Infantry, raised in Philadelphia during the spring of 1864, the officers advised the men to accept the lower amount. After the men refused the repeated entreaties, the officers began treating them "like dogs," bucking and gagging them, marching them back and forth with full knapsacks, and forcing them to stand in the South Carolina sun for hours on end, even after men began falling out from sunstroke. The writer upbraided Sergeant-Major George W. Clemens, "one of your Philadelphia sports," for accepting the inferior pay after "bragging to the men" that he would never do so.[54]

Soldiers appealed "to the leaders of this great Republic to know the reason why they hesitate to give us our God-given rights" and why they appeared to be "keeping us behind the times."[55] The delay in resolving the matter resulted largely from the obstructionist tactics of congressmen and senators from the Loyal Border States, not from any lack of determination on the part of War Department officials or congressional Republicans to reverse a practice that Representative Thaddeus Stevens of Pennsylvania described as "abhorrent to the feelings of the age." Senator Henry Wilson introduced a measure to equalize the pay of all soldiers regardless of color or previous condition early in February 1864 but faced opposition from the start, particularly over "that portion which makes it retrospective." Senator Willard Saulsbury of Delaware, a persistent foe of emancipation, ranted sarcastically that "the advancement of civilization and Christianity and refinement," which he accused the Republicans of promoting, did not require "perfect equality" between black and white soldiers.[56] Only after several more months of wrangling did the two bodies agree to a provision of the military appropriations bill, enacted in June 1864, stipulating that "persons of color" in the army "shall receive the same uniform, clothing, arms, equipments, camp equipage, rations, medical and hospital attendance, pay and emoluments . . . as other soldiers of the regular or volunteer forces of the United States of like arm of the service." The protesting soldiers and their families had endured a practical eternity of anxiety, fear, and self-doubt that tarnished their hopes of what the new relationship to the civic polity might actually entail.[57]

————

On the Northern homefront, black community leaders saw the mobilization of black soldiers as an opportunity to reenergize struggles against the various forms of racial discrimination that were among the legacies of slavery that gradual emancipation did not erase. In urban areas, segregated streetcars represented a particularly offensive practice, but one with remarkably shallow roots given that public streetcars dated from midcentury rather than in the hoary past. Although the cars were horse-drawn, the systems employed the latest technology. In July 1864, the congressionally approved charter for the Metropolitan Railroad Company in the District of Columbia stipulated that the company "place first-class cars on said railways, with all the modern improvements for the convenience and comfort of passengers."[58] Nominally in deference to the sensibilities of white patrons, street railway companies in every major metropolitan area, from Boston and New York, through Pittsburgh, Cleveland, and Chicago, to San Francisco, banned black passengers outright or, at best, permitted them to ride on outdoor platforms at the front or the rear of the cars. Platform passengers encountered the noise and dirt of the streets and, worse yet, inclement weather, which nullified one of the chief benefits of this modern mode of transportation. In New York City, the black community protested vigorously against exclusion and prosecuted several successful lawsuits with the result that, by the eve of the Civil War, most of the streetcar companies admitted black passengers without distinction, although the prominent Sixth Avenue line did not.[59]

In Philadelphia, the first street railway appeared in 1858 and more than twenty followed in rapid succession. Most lines prohibited black riders altogether, but several permitted "colored" passengers to ride on the front platform with the driver. As early as 1859, African American activists such as William Still, of Underground Railroad fame, had protested against the blatant discrimination. The protests continued into the war years, led by the Social, Civil, and Statistical Association (SCSA) of the Colored People of Pennsylvania. One winter day, Still subjected himself to the indignity of riding on the platform in the interest of arriving timely at his place of business. Although "already thoroughly chilled with the cold," he found the platform to be "utterly intolerable" when snow began to fall, forcing him to exit the car and walk the rest of the way.[60] In early March 1862, "a highly respected and intelligent colored lady" flouted the prohibition and managed to gain admission into a car "in the midst of a violent storm of wind and rain" only to be subsequently ejected. The editor of the *Christian Recorder* described the incident as an "Outrage."[61]

The growing sense of public embarrassment over such incidents created a climate for change. In May 1863, a black woman "with a child in one arm and a basket in the other" hailed a car and asked the conductor if she might ride, and the conductor did what was previously unthinkable. He asked the passengers if they had any objection, and "one unanimous no, rang through the car." Then he "very politely helped her" on board.[62] In this instance, the "City of Brotherly Love" lived up to its reputation.[63] But the "outrages" against black citizens continued, including the case of a black minister who died as a result of falling from the platform of a car.[64] By the summer of 1863, the policies began undermining the military mobilization. Men from a black militia company that Philadelphians had organized and that had volunteered its services to help repel Robert E. Lee's invasion of their home state in late June were delayed in leaving the city due to the refusal of the streetcars to carry them to the railway station. Similarly, when recruits in the black regiments being organized at Camp William Penn on the outskirts of the city could not get access to the cars, they risked punishment for returning to duty late. The policy of exclusion prevented the wives and mothers of convalescent black soldiers from visiting their hospitalized loved ones, and when the local press called attention to this injustice the managers of the streetcar companies simply looked the other way.[65] Not even nationally recognized military heroes were immune to discrimination. In January 1865, Robert Smalls, commanding officer of the *Planter*, which was undergoing repairs at the Philadelphia Navy Yard, was denied a seat in a streetcar.[66]

By the summer of 1864, women and men filled public meeting halls calling for an end to segregation in the cars and noting that other major cities of the North had done away with the practice. At one such gathering, a speaker sought an explanation for the seemingly endless delays particularly in light of the fact that "the social system of the South has been literally revolutionized in three years." The AME minister Jonathan Gibbs insisted that the protesters stop begging for change and demand it.[67] In December, the SCSA submitted another petition bearing hundreds of signatures, including those of pastors of leading white Protestant churches in the city, requesting that the streetcar companies "rescind the rules indiscriminately excluding colored passengers from the inside of the cars."[68]

As a result of this agitation, one line began operating separate cars in late 1864, but the others refused to modify their policies. The presidents of the other lines conducted a straw poll in January 1865 in which white riders were asked whether they favored lifting the restrictions, and a majority opposed any change. A month later the Fifth and Sixth Street Passenger Railway Company announced its intention to open the cars to black passengers.[69] A black Philadelphian who was serving in the trenches before Richmond described this as "another progressive stride, which redounds to the credit of the Quaker City, and her liberal minded citizens." But the liberalism clearly had not yet progressed to the point of granting black people access to all the streetcar lines much less "the full rights of citizenship."[70] As earlier, the managers of the other lines refused to budge.

Black leaders devised a strategy of pursuing a legislative remedy and began lobbying Republicans in the state capital of Harrisburg. Two years later, in March 1867, as Congress was wresting control over Reconstruction from President Andrew Johnson, lawmakers passed a measure prohibiting the streetcar companies from discriminating on account of color. An elated, but nonetheless subdued, state senator observed that "the same bill, which finally became a law in matter and substance, was six years old, and the principle contained in the bill is a matter as old as Adam."[71] Amid the lightning-fast changes associated with emancipation, integrating public conveyances was remarkably difficult to accomplish. The democratic process proved to be a slow and cumbersome means of promoting social change with a view toward erasing the legacies of slavery. As a result, expatriates such as Charlotte Forten could not avoid mixed feelings about the city. While she retained strong emotional ties with her family who resided there, she faulted "old abominable P[hiladelphia]" for its discriminatory ways.[72] Although slavery had not existed in the Northern states for years, the residue of second-class citizenship remained as the unfished business of gradual emancipation. Discriminatory practices constrained the actions of black residents throughout the region, stunting the growth of a sense of fully belonging to the local community, a critical element in belonging to the nation as a whole.

Once emancipation entered the nation's vocabulary, African American citizens in cities throughout the North escalated pressure against segregation, often with the support of local abolitionists or prominent white clergymen. In San Francisco, Charlotte L. Brown and her father, James Brown, achieved notable success in a lawsuit that held a streetcar company liable for damages following her forcible ejection from a streetcar in April 1863. Soon thereafter, she and her father were ejected from another car and they sued the company. In October 1864, a district court judge issued a precedent-setting ruling that the streetcar companies were common carriers that could not arbitrarily deny access to the services they provided to a portion of the public.[73] Over the period during which Brown pursued legal action, streetcar lines in New York, Boston, and Pittsburgh rescinded their exclusionary policies.

In Washington, the agitation against segregated streetcars followed a similar course, but with several twists. For one thing, the controversy played out in the nation's capital, seat of the federal government and host to visitors from around the nation and the world. Moreover, the increasingly activist Republican-controlled Congress, which enjoyed full legislative authority over the District and, incidentally, issued charters to the street railways, began paying attention. In the summer of 1863, as the First U.S. Colored Infantry was being organized in the city, groups of recruits bulldozed their way onto the cars whenever they pleased in utter defiance of the white passengers and conductors. "You might just as well declare war against them," observed one Washingtonian, "as to declare that they can't ride there because they are colored."[74]

Individual black persons, even those in uniform, did not fare so well. An especially notorious case involved the surgeon Major Alexander T. Augusta. On a rainy morning in February 1864, Augusta attempted to board a streetcar to expedite his arrival at a military court hearing in which he was to serve as a witness. The conductor refused him a seat and, following Augusta's protest, ejected him from the platform. Augusta made his way on foot, arriving late and spattered in mud. "Though very inconvenient for the doctor," a correspondent to the *Anglo-African* observed, the incident "may turn out to be a great good for our people, as both the military and congressional authorities have taken the matter in hand."[75] Indeed, Massachusetts senator Charles Sumner had for the previous year been employing the congressional chartering authority as the means to prohibit discrimination on Washington's streetcars. Between March 1863 and March 1865, Republican lawmakers inserted wording into the charters prohibiting denial of access "on account of color."[76] Notwithstanding these changes, conductors and white passengers continued to eject black passengers from the cars. Sojourner Truth tussled with fellow passengers, conductors, and police on several occasions when they tried removing her.[77]

Individually and collectively these incidents indicated that the struggle to establish civic equality, though intimately related to the struggle against slavery, was also very different and would likely take longer than the duration of the war to achieve. After all, here the enemy was not an armed insurrection whose leaders aimed to create a sovereign nation. This enemy resided in the laws, policies, and practices of the United States and the various state governments, in the actions of corporate bodies and private citizens, and, most of all, in the minds and hearts of men and women. It was not simply that old habits die hard. The habits reflecting the new state of personal relationships, predicated on equality before the law rather than racial hierarchy, had to be built from the ground up in many cases. A veteran black abolitionist commented insightfully on Philadelphia Quakers' unwillingness to accept black children into their schools. "Whatever they do for us savors of pity," remarked Samuel Ringgold Ward, "and is done at arm's length."[78] When the nominal friends of freedom and equality acted this way, their enemies felt little compunction to occupy higher moral ground.

The story of segregated public streetcars demonstrates the malleable nature of Northern white prejudice during the Civil War era. Although the racial stereotypes and the associated fears supporting segregation had deep roots, their application extended only as far back as the introduction of the new technology, which was measured in years, not decades. Nonetheless, proponents of equal access faced formidable challenges that operated entirely independent of—indeed, almost impervious to—the success of Union arms and the Confederacy's fading fortunes. The wartime struggles over integrated public transportation in the North indicated that the structures of inequality and the habits they fostered did not ultimately depend on slavery for their legitimacy. Unbound from slavery, they could withstand its death. Such an outcome portended a long and contentious future for the emancipation process even after the defeat of the rebellion.

————

As many as 80,000 persons may have made their way to the Midwest from the slave states of the Mississippi valley over the course of the war.[79] Freedom seekers in the Upper South regions of the Confederacy relied on military authorities to reach the North, as the experiences of David Haywood, Sam Washington, and the other enslaved people from Confederate general Gideon Pillow's Arkansas plantation demonstrated. Through the assistance of Union general Samuel R. Curtis, they gained steamboat passage to Cairo, Illinois, and became part of the growing community of freedom seekers there.[80] In the Shenandoah valley of Virginia, the father of John Quincy Adams along with the rest of his family fled enslavement in Winchester, Virginia, in June 1862, courtesy of Union general John Geary, who issued them a pass to Pennsylvania.[81]

The Tennessean George Knox escaped from his owner and the Confederate army during the summer of 1863 and found refuge with a regiment of Indiana volunteers. After accompanying the unit home on furlough, Knox decided to remain in the Hoosier State. Over the next several decades, he established himself as perhaps the most prominent black citizen of the state. Time and again he encountered incidents wherein white Indianans questioned the right of any black person to reside in the state. As he later recalled, he often found it necessary to fight fire with fire, alerting ruffians to the fact "that the first man who touched me would be a dead man." The incessant prejudice took a toll. "As soon as my nerves began to quiet somewhat and I became more composed," following a threat to his life or livelihood, "someone would whisper in my ear, 'they are preparing to mob you to-night,' and then all would assume gloominess once more."[82]

Like Henry Clay Bruce, George Knox portrayed himself as master of his own destiny, but he also revealed—perhaps unwittingly—the extent to which he relied on family, friends, and acquaintances in the quest to become a new man. After once delaying his flight to the Yankees at the request of a woman, Knox later changed his mind. Upon his departure, his brother and several other friends and acquaintances accompanied him. Though physically separated from home, he remained emotionally attached, worrying, for instance, what effect his brother's death would have on his own reputation. In both Confederate and Union service, he relied on the friendship and trust of other black cooks, servants, and teamsters. And before deciding to stay in Indiana, he consulted with his bunk-mate and the other black men who had accompanied the regiment north. Then and in subsequent years, he relied on black employees, neighbors, and acquaintances, both in his immediate neighborhood and elsewhere in the state, to ensure his safety and success. Marrying the daughter of an established and influential black farmer helped cement his own standing in the community as a person whom his neighbors could rely on and trust.[83]

Knox's struggle to escape the shadows of slavery continued for decades after the war ended. Family and friends, who reinforced their personal relationships through such social institutions as workplaces, churches, fraternal organizations, and—in the end—political action under the banner of the Republican Party, enabled him to endure these tribulations. He made a home for himself and his family, yet he continued to feel ill at ease even as the black community applauded his accomplishments. His eventual participation in the imaged civic communities of Indiana and of the United States, as exemplified in his prominence in local, state, and national Republican Party politics, could not quite overcome the lingering feeling that he was not fully at home in those white-majority polities. The rights of citizenship, even manhood suffrage, were not the panacea for which wartime advocates—black no less than white—had prayed. Still, access to the processes whereby public policy was made and administered in any form—as a voter, an elector, or a public officeholder—gave cause for hope, a hope that was unthinkable in Knox's Tennessee youth.

Northern black leaders took a multipronged approach to achieving economic self-sufficiency, a hallmark of an independent citizenry with strong stakes in both the local community and the nation. To address the general needs of the freeborn residents of the North as well as the freed people of the former slave states, they insisted on working-people's rights, particularly to adequate wages regularly paid, an ideal that government agencies and their subcontractors often observed in the breach. Advocates of black workers called out discriminatory hiring practices that consigned black working men to the lowest rungs of the occupational hierarchy and black women to service positions in private homes. As long as Northern philanthropic organizations remained active in the former slaveholding states (which a number did even beyond the effective expiration of the congressional mandate of the Freedmen's Bureau in 1872), freed people had at least some access to information about better wages elsewhere and to programs that provided instruction in trades or occupations for which there was more demand and at higher wages than what ordinary laborers and household servants earned. Some opportunities for occupational diversification and advancement occurred during the war years as a result of the mobilization, but the return of peace brought the return of the prewar patterns, which changed slowly at best despite the emergence of a union movement among African American tradesmen under the leadership of Isaac Myers in Baltimore.[84]

For years, William Still had advocated in favor of black men and women operating grocery stores, millinery shops, and other such businesses. Independent establishments provided an escape from the racially restricted labor markets of the large cities, essential services to black communities, and places where "our young men and women . . . might learn trades and business." Still practiced what he preached, even before the war undertaking successful ventures dealing in real estate, stoves, and coal, and, after the recruitment of black soldiers began, opening a sutler's post at Camp William Penn, the rendezvous and training point for U.S. Colored Troops in Philadelphia. A visitor to the camp in the fall of 1864 reported that Still, with a "corps of assistants," operated "quite a neat and tasteful little place," transacting "business in his own peculiar and energetic style."[85]

––––––––

Black residents of the North, like their counterparts in the South, realized that the full enjoyment of citizenship in the republic required removing the legal proscriptions—some constitutional and other statutory—in various states that barred black persons from enjoying certain rights and responsibilities that other citizens possessed. Chief among these were the various exclusionary provisions and "Black Laws" that dated from colonial or territorial days. Pennsylvania, for instance, required separate, segregated schools when the number of black pupils in a district numbered twenty or more. Like all the other free states, even progressive Massachusetts carried a constitutional provision that mirrored federal guidelines restricting militia service to white men. The states created from the Northwest Territory went much further, restricting black residents from offering testimony in legal proceedings and from serving on juries, and, in the worst cases, even from residing in the state. Ohio, which had relaxed some of the restrictions of its Black Laws in 1849—particularly by abolishing the requirement of annual bond that dated from the first decade of the century—stopped well short of granting full and equal citizenship to persons of African ancestry. Reflecting the fresh fears of "amalgamation" that the war set loose, the legislature prohibited interracial marriage in 1861. Several states, including Maine, Rhode Island, Indiana, and

Michigan, which had not previously outlawed interracial marriages, enacted such measures after the war.[86]

Indiana, Illinois, Michigan, Iowa, and Oregon required black residents to post annual bond to ensure their good behavior, and Indiana, Illinois, and Iowa prohibited free black emigrants from other states to settle within their borders.[87] These laws were enforced erratically, but one particularly egregious case late in December 1862, when the nation stood poised to receive the Emancipation Proclamation, demonstrated their potential for stifling the African American freedom struggle. A free black man named Nelson had entered Illinois and was arrested, jailed, convicted, and fined fifty dollars for breaking the law. Unable to pay, he was sold as an indentured servant until he could settle the debt. Supporters entered a suit on his behalf, and in February 1865 the state supreme court abolished the ban on black immigration. The ruling, however, stopped short of removing the prohibitions against black people's testimony or service on juries, which the petition on Nelson's behalf had also raised.[88]

As had been the case regarding such matters in prior years, Massachusetts served as a bellwether for progressive constitutional and legal developments of this kind. Early in 1864, thanks largely to the splendid record of service that the state's black volunteer regiments had achieved, legislators struck the word "white" from the state's militia act. This cleared the way for the formation of militia companies, one of which, the Shaw Guards, was named in honor of Colonel Robert Gould Shaw of the Fifty-Fourth Massachusetts Volunteers, who died in the attack on Fort Wagner. Activists also mounted a successful campaign to remove the designation "Colored" from tax and voting records. Charles W. Slack, the longtime abolitionist editor of the *Boston Commonwealth*, urged his fellow city councilmen to respond to the "spirit of the time" and cease using the demeaning label, which they did. Beginning in 1866, black men from Boston competed successfully for seats in the state legislature.[89]

As a result of these progressive changes, Boston and its suburbs attracted thousands of black veterans, not all of whom had lived in the state when the war began. Navy veterans John Robert Bond, who was born free in Liverpool, England, of African and Irish parentage, and William B. Gould, who had escaped from slavery in North Carolina in 1862, settled there.[90] Gould made his home in Dedham, where he fathered a large family, whom he supported from his earnings as a master plasterer. Like his former comrades, he took active part in the Grand Army of the Republic (GAR), serving for many years as the local post commander and participating regularly in public holidays and funeral services. Ever mindful of his North Carolina roots, Gould found his permanent home in Massachusetts.[91] Another navy veteran and a Boston native, James H. Wolff, rose to the command of the GAR's Department of Massachusetts by the turn of the twentieth century, a distinction that no other man of African descent in any other state enjoyed.[92]

————————

In October 1863, black leaders in Kansas saw an opportunity to revive the tradition of the antebellum state conventions as a vehicle for advancing the cause of full citizenship. This time was different, though, with the nation at war and nearly 2,000 men having enlisted in the state to serve in the two black regiments organized by Senator James Lane. In making a fresh case for the elective franchise, they observed that the custom was not new but, in fact, had been present from the founding of the nation. Denial of the vote to men on account of color was a relatively recent invention, they argued, dating from only the 1830s, when North Carolina and Tennessee imposed the ban. Not coincidentally, this was precisely the same period in which the profits from slave-grown agricultural products blinded Americans in the North as well as the South to the evils of the system and to the accompanying denial of natural rights to all black people, free as well as enslaved. "But in the providence of God," the leaders asserted, "the injustice of nations, as of individuals, brings its punishment." From the ashes, a new order would emerge. "In the progress of this war, destructive of so many prejudices and fruitful of so many new ideas," the nation would find it "as necessary to make the black man a voter, as it was to make him a soldier." In the latter capacity, he helped "to RESTORE the Union." In the former he would help "to PRESERVE it."[93] "Take counsel of your courage, and conquer your prejudices," they urged their white fellow citizens. "Anticipate the fruition of time, and grant us today, what you will certainly grant us in a few years at most."[94]

A preview of that approach played out in the Indian Territory in 1865 and 1866. U.S. officials used the Confederate defeat and emancipation as leverage against the Cherokee, Creek, Seminole, Choctaw, and Chickasaw nations, which had been relocated there in the infamous Trail of Tears during the 1830s and 1840s. The commissioners who negotiated the new treaties insisted that the nations emancipate their slaves and grant the freed people citizenship rights. Although the Cherokees adopted emancipation before the treaty would have required them to do so, they were no more willing to grant citizenship to the freed people than were the other tribes. With the Civil War having divided the Indian nations much as it did the Loyal Border States, small wonder that bitter divisions over U.S.-imposed emancipation wracked them too in the years after the treaties were adopted.[95] With those agreements as guides, Indian commissioners throughout the western territories attempted to persuade other Native nations to free their captives, forsake their nomadic ways, and permit settlers of European ancestry to establish homesteads on what had previously been considered common land. On October 5, 1877, mere miles from the Canadian border in Montana Territory, the last Indian war against the U.S. government came to an end. Then and there Chief Joseph and the Nez Perce surrendered to forces commanded by General Oliver O. Howard, former commissioner of the Freedmen's Bureau and president of Howard University. Three years earlier, Howard "gladly" left Washington for Portland, Oregon, to assume command over the Department of the Columbia, relieved that the military court of inquiry investigating his stewardship of funds during his tenure as commissioner of the Freedmen's Bureau completely exonerated him.[96]

In a further irony, black soldiers served with the Regular Army units that fought the Plains Indians, even as they and their families were struggling to find remunerative employment and to enjoy the rights of freed people at home. Black recruits from Kentucky who had enlisted late in the war (including those who did so following the March 1865 congressional resolution that freed the families of soldiers) constituted a significant presence in the original units that later came to be known as the Buffalo Soldiers.[97] They found themselves in very strange circumstances, indeed, nearly powerless to assist their families by virtue of their distance from home. In July 1866, a group of men in the 116th U.S. Colored Infantry, which had been organized at Camp Nelson the year before, wrote to President Andrew Johnson. Citing a rumor that they would not get their promised enlistment bounties, the men asked how they could be expected to live if the government "should turn out the men of our standing barehanded." "We are a nation that was poor and had nothing when we came to the service," the men explained, "we had neather house nor money no place to put our familys. now these poor nation of colour have spent the best part of his days in slavery. now then what must we do. must we turn to steal to get a start?"[98]

Black communities in other Northern states also hoped to use military service as the entry point to a fuller sense of belonging in their respective states and the nation. In Michigan, proponents of a color-blind suffrage convened on December 31, 1863, to devise a strategy for achieving equality. Although an unexpected blizzard prevented the planned keynote speaker, H. Ford Douglas, from attending, the delegates proceeded with the work at hand, claiming full citizenship rights "as native born Americans" and urging political leaders in their home state and in the "other nominally free States of the North . . . to repeal all laws and parts of laws and constitutions, making distinctions on account of color." A follow-up meeting at the end of January resolved to petition the legislature to repeal the provision in the state constitution "which debars us from the right of elective franchise in this State on account of COLOR."[99]

Such grassroots initiatives on behalf of equal rights led to a call to resuscitate the national convention movement, the most recent gathering of which had taken place at Philadelphia in the fall of 1855. Organizers laid plans to meet in Syracuse, New York, in October 1864. From before the opening session, the delegates and the constituencies they represented shared the common understanding that this was a momentous occasion. With the upcoming presidential election reemphasizing the importance of voting in the routine work of the republic, the time was right to make a case for full citizenship. The participation of nearly 200,000 African American men in the armed forces could only strengthen the earlier appeals to justice, to the nation's democratic ideals, and to the past precedents of a number of states.

During the summer of 1864, as black leaders across the North and in the Union-controlled portions of the Confederacy began to plan for the October gathering, a fascinating exchange between two prominent black leaders, Henry Highland Garnet and Richard H. Cain, illustrated the multiple meanings of the term "home" and its relevance to the destruction of slavery and the demand for full citizenship. Garnet disputed Cain's insistence that local communities select representatives to ensure the "calm and mature deliberation and interchange of views by the thinking minds of all sections of the republic." "With us there should be no East, West, North nor South." Garnet argued in reply: "The truth is, that we have scarcely a home, and certainly but few rights anywhere in this our native land."[100]

Cain responded with a comprehensive view that situated the struggle for freedom and equal rights within the global context of "human progress" in which millions of citizens of Italy, Hungary, and Germany as well as the United States, who "have been baptized in the spirit of liberty," were then engaged. In imagery that gained greater currency with each passing day, he faulted the nation for having been "accessory to all the crimes of the slaveholders" and for not having pitied "the wronged slave." Anticipating an image that Lincoln would employ to such stunning effect in his second inaugural address, Cain argued that Northerners "must pay an equivalent in their sons' blood as a ransom for all the sons of Afric's race, whose bones whiten the fields, and whose flesh enriches the soil of the South." Expiation required letting "every slave go free" and acknowledging "the manhood of the race." "The duty of the hour is clear," he concluded. Black people must "move out of the old routine, and take a stride forward." "First, just now, as a people, we want homes more than any thing else. We want to be owners of lands, houses and stocks" even "*more than political rights*!"[101] It remained to be seen how the organizers would manage the competing expectations of different constituent groups.

In black communities throughout the Northern states, residents held public meetings to choose delegates.[102] The *Christian Recorder* proposed four goals: promoting unity; determining the "will of our people" regarding whether "to remain in the land of their birth"; developing action plans to achieve full political and civil rights in each state and in the nation; and encouraging the development of "a business-doing class" with investments in merchandising, transportation, and international trade.[103]

The language of time suffused the proceedings of the convention, beginning with Frederick Douglass's opening remarks on accepting the nomination to be the permanent president. He noted the common desire "to show that . . . like all other progressive races of men, we are resolved to advance in the scale of knowledge, worth, and civilization, and claim our rights as men among men." One after the other, the speakers invoked similar words. "My very soul leaps onward a full century," Paschal Beverly Randolph, a delegate from New York, rhapsodized, "and its vision falls on fertile fields, with no slave-driver there, no hearts crushed by fierce oppression, no more heads bowed down." "Though we are unfortunately situated," declared John S. Rock, "I am not discouraged. Our cause is flying onward with the swiftness of Mercury. Every day seems almost to be an era in the history of our country."[104]

Over the four days that they met, the delegates focused more on political rights and moral and educational uplift than on African Americans' economic future. Unsurprisingly, their resolutions and statement of grievances, titled the "Declaration of Wrongs and Rights," largely addressed the goals and aspirations of Northern free people rather than Southern freed people. Asserting that the "unquestioned patriotism and loyalty of the colored men of the United States . . . vindicate our manhood," and affirming their belief in "the fundamental principles of this Government, the force of acknowledged American ideas, the Christian spirit of the age, and the justice of our cause," the resolutions prayed that the nation will "grant us our full measure of citizenship." The delegates declared that any attempt "to reconstruct the Union with slavery" would constitute a betrayal "to be resisted by the whole moral power of the civilized world." To the freedmen of the South, they extended "the right hand of fellowship," wishing "our warmest sympathy, and our deep concern for their welfare, prosperity, and happiness" and exhorting them "to shape their course toward frugality, the accumulation of property, and, above all, to leave untried no amount of effort and self-denial to acquire knowledge, and to secure a vigorous moral and religious growth."[105]

The imagery of home and nationality also framed key points of the declaration. "As a branch of the human family," the delegates argued, "we have for long ages been deeply and cruelly wronged by people whose might constituted their right." But the events of the war had made clear that the spirit of divine justice as well as the spirit of the enlightened age now intervened. The United States was paying the price for standing in the way of "self-enlightenment and personal and national elevation" and for deeming its black residents "incapable of self-government." "As a people," they argued, "we have been denied the ownership of our bodies, our wives, houses, children, and the products of our own labor." Firesides have been "desolated" in the course of being subjected "to wrongs deeper and darker than the earth ever witnessed in the case of any other people."[106]

The declaration faulted the nation for having delayed so long in addressing the critical issues of freedom and equality. Notwithstanding the commitment to emancipation, the delegates feared it would degenerate into complacency once the war appeared to be won. With that, the hope for immediate and radical improvement in the status of black people throughout the nation would evaporate. When black men pressed for the opportunity to serve, political leaders temporized; then, having denied the black soldiers equal pay, government officials waited "until public opinion demanded it," and even then moved "tardily." "We have fought and conquered," but black men "have been denied the laurels of victory." "As natives of American soil" they claimed that "the right to remain upon it" was theirs by birth. The loyal service of "our fathers and our brothers" should have guaranteed "the full enjoyment of enfranchised manhood, and its dignities." They claimed "our fair share of the public domain" and recommended "to colored men from all sections of the country to settle, as far as they can, on the public lands."[107] Their birthright stake in the nation was literal as well as figurative. "Emerging as we are from the long night of gloom and sorrow," they concluded, "we are entitled to, and claim, the sympathy and aid of the entire Christian world"; and, echoing the Declaration of Independence, "we invoke the considerate aid of mankind in this crisis of our history, and in this hour of sacrifice, suffering, and trial."[108] Such phrases as "the long night of gloom," "the crisis of our history," and "this hour of sacrifice" employed images that they hoped would resonate with their white fellow citizens. They wished to break free of the perpetual uncertainty resulting from second-class citizenship, the particular forms of which fluttered one way and then another with the changing political winds.

The convention adjourned into the National Equal Rights League, a national organization "with auxiliaries and subordinate associations in the different states." "The objects of this League," its constitution announced, were "to encourage sound morality, education, temperance, frugality, industry, and promote every thing that pertains to a well-ordered and dignified life;

to obtain by appeals to the minds and consciences of the American people, or by legal process when possible, a recognition of the rights of the colored people of the nation as American citizens."[109] Upon their return home, the delegates busied themselves reporting to their constituents and organizing state-level affiliates of the National Equal Rights League.[110] In Bridgeport, Connecticut, for instance, they endorsed the measures intended to aid the families of "the noble heroes" of the armed forces, and particularly the widows and children of those "who have laid down their lives for the cause of liberty, justice and their country." For the freed people, they applauded the efforts undertaken to promote "industry, temperance, civil and religious liberty, and universal education."[111] The afterglow of the national convention created a source of light that illuminated activities in local black communities across the United States and the areas where federal armed forces had reestablished the national authority. Indeed, African American women in Pennsylvania formed a network of locally based affiliates that advocated for black women's suffrage. The public statements that emanated from these meetings consti-tuted a counterdialogue to the one in which white politicians and newspa-per editors, ministers, and ordinary citizens pondered over "what shall be done with the Negroes."[112]

––––––––

Despite the strong emphasis that the National Equal Rights League placed on manhood suffrage, as of the spring of 1865, black men could vote without restriction only in the New England states of Maine, New Hampshire, Ver-mont, Massachusetts, and Rhode Island, and upon meeting property quali-fications in Connecticut and New York. Beginning in 1842, Ohio permitted men of mixed African and European ancestry to vote if their color and fea-tures suggested the preponderance of European ancestry, but in 1859 a new law closed the loophole by essentially requiring that such a person be able to pass for white.[113] The states of Iowa and Minnesota granted black men suf-frage in 1868, on the grounds that their wartime service under arms deserved to be rewarded. The small number of prospective black voters in the two states suggested that, even if they voted in a racial block, they would have little ability to sway the outcome of an election, which surely factored into the out-come as well (see figure 9.1).[114] But the other midwestern states, including Ohio, Indiana, Illinois, and Michigan, each of which had been credited with 1,000–5,000 black soldiers, presented a very different picture. Each time Republican leaders tried to pass legislation granting the vote, they encoun-tered intense Democratic opposition, which in several cases cost them con-trol over their respective state governments as well as passage of the equal suffrage bill.[115]

Figure 9.1
A. R. Waud, *The First Vote*. Courtesy of the Library of Congress Prints and Photographs Division, LC-DIG-ppmsca-31598.

When the New England Convention of Colored Citizens met in Boston on December 1, 1865, its members had the perspective of more than six months since the end of the war to assess the progress that had been made to date and to chart a direction for the future. Respecting the condition of black residents in the Northern states, they chided the legislatures of Connecticut, Wisconsin, and Minnesota for "refusing to allow colored citizens the right to vote for their rulers" on the terms and conditions that their white fellow citizens did, and they urged Congress to prohibit states from enacting laws that discriminated on the basis of skin color. In the former Confederacy, freed people faced far more urgent concerns, including violence at the hands of former owners under sanction of "the cruel and oppressive laws which have been enacted by the provisional legislatures of the Southern States." The delegates urged Congress to empower the Freedmen's Bureau to offer meaningful protection against the obvious plan "to forcibly drive the negroes from the country"—the very nation that they helped build and that they recently defended with their blood.[116]

In Pennsylvania, New Jersey, and New York, the advocates of unrestricted black manhood suffrage faced similar obstacles to those faced by their counterparts in other Northern states. Speaking in March 1865 before the SCSA of Pennsylvania, Republican congressman William D. Kelley insisted that slavery alone did not cause the war; rather, the nation's failure to observe "a fundamental law of God . . . the law of human equality" also played an important part. He held up the example of Massachusetts, where black men voted and served on juries "and there is no trouble or revolution there."[117] In New York, Republican supporters of removing the property requirement that had limited black voting for decades looked for an appropriate legislative strategy. Early in 1869, as Congress debated the proposed Fifteenth Amendment to the U.S. Constitution, which prohibited states from denying the vote to any man on the basis of color, Republican supporters chose to delay submitting the matter to the electorate until after the legislature approved the amendment. In April 1869, six weeks after the congressional joint resolution moved the proposed amendment to the states, New York's legislature voted in favor, but the gambit backfired. In the following fall elections, voters soundly rejected the suffrage measure and ousted the Republicans. When the Democrats assumed control in January 1870, the legislature took the unusual step of rescinding the Republican body's approval of the amendment only to turn around and give it their own assent two months later.[118]

Black New Yorkers stood awestruck at how quickly their political fortunes could whipsaw between bright prospects for the future and dark reminders of the past. This chronicle illustrated the disruptive effect that popular opinion and party politics could exert on realizing the fruits of freedom piecemeal. In the circumstances, many wondered when, if ever, the emancipation process would run its full course. Gradualism redux raised new doubts whether citizens of European descent would ever accept persons of African descent on terms of full equality and whether the United States could ever serve as a true home.

———

As the war drew to a close, the topic of emigration sparked but did not catch fire. In Canandaigua, New York, for instance, a large crowd attended a lecture by their fellow townsman Henry W. Johnson on the topic of "what is to become of the colored population?" While the newspaper account of the meeting did not cover the substance of his talk, one of the resolutions of thanks that the meeting adopted indicated that he was about to depart for "the native home of his race."[119] So the large and enthusiastic crowd apparently had gathered to bid farewell to their neighbor and friend but not to accompany him on the journey to the motherland.

Despite the infighting at the Syracuse national convention in October 1864 over the role of the ACS in helping to chart the future of the race, the leaders of the ACS were busy remodeling its image, aiming to move beyond its roots in the Haitian emigration movement of the late 1850s. The society's success in employing teachers and managing schools for the benefit of the freed people in Washington, D.C., paid dividends in this campaign. That notwithstanding, Richard Cain found himself repeating over and over to his fellow delegates "that the object of the African Civilization Society is not to colonize the colored people." The prominent Rhode Island caterer and abolitionist George T. Downing challenged Cain's depiction of the society, labeling it "the child of prejudice" whose "originators assert that the colored man cannot be elevated in the United States; that black men must be 'massed to themselves,' and have a grand fight for a 'Negro nationality,' before they can be respected!" Other critics reaffirmed that the struggle for equality must be fought and won in the United States, not in Africa.[120]

But times changed, and with the North's victory appearing more certain with each passing day, old proponents of emigration began to view the prospects of achieving full and equal citizenship in the United States preferable to the chances of doing so anywhere else. Early in 1865, Cain sensed that "the great question of the right of the black men of this nation to the ballot box must be settled soon." Without it, the nation's "great march of human development, and universal freedom" would be delayed. "The genius of the age," he insisted, "demands it." What is more, "the progress of civilization, the future greatness of the republic, and the perpetuity of the Union" all required "that the millions of faithful, patient children, descendants of Africa, be incorporated into the brotherhood of the nation." As long as a single "white man remains in it . . . we intend to stay and enjoy all the luxury and pleasures of this lovely climate and beautiful country."[121] The United States, not Liberia or Haiti, was home, but gone was his earlier concern about building an economic foundation for the home to survive and prosper.

From North Carolina, Chaplain Henry M. Turner reported that the topic of colonization was then "very much spoken of, and very thoroughly canvassed by some of the army petit maitres." Presuming that "there is a large sum of money in the treasury, for emigration purposes" that "sharpers" were trying to lay hands on, he encouraged "the thinking part of our race, to look that bull in the eye." "As soon as this rebellion is over," he predicted, "it will be the chief topic in every legislative department, from Congress down to town councils." While demurring from entering "any political arena, pro or con," he advised "the colored politicians north" to study the topic thoroughly and be prepared to address "historical, ethnological, or philosophical arguments."[122] He clearly had read between the lines of the reports issued by the AFIC. Indeed, the Northern legislatures that added new strength to the old exclusionary laws pandered to exactly such apprehensions. Even as Radical Republicans began seriously considering federal legislation to guarantee the civil rights of citizens, the project reflected the fundamental inability of legislative bodies to reach consensus over what rights and privileges every citizen enjoyed by natural right. That challenge long outlasted the Civil War era.

———————

Yet hope sprang eternal, or so it appeared. As General Sherman's forces made their way toward Atlanta in the spring of 1864, the likelihood of victory quickened the hearts of every partisan of the Union. James Smallwood, a Philadelphia native and recent graduate of the Institute for Colored Youth, delivered a lecture titled "Progress of Liberty," an overview of how the concept migrated in ancient times from Egypt to Greece and then to Rome, from where it spread to Europe and beyond in modern times. He identified a "spirit of '64," which "soars higher aloft than that of '76" and which affirms that "there is no master, no slave, no particular race; but 'One humanity, one law, one love from all and for all.'" This "spirit of '64," he predicted confidently, "will go to Liberia and Sierra Leone, to fortify those outposts of freedom. It will penetrate the interior of that vast Africa, to drive back the wretches from their cruel pursuit of men, women, and little children, and restore Africa to her former splendor, her former greatness. It will go into Asia, to awaken questions dormant for ages."[123] Smallwood's musings posed the question of whether men and women of African descent would enjoy a full measure of liberty in the land of their birth, but neither Sherman's victory nor Lincoln's reelection nor Lee's surrender answered it conclusively.

Epilogue

Illusions of Emancipation

The Civil War ended slavery but stopped short of ridding the nation of its legacy. The collapse of the Confederate government took with it the legal, political, and social infrastructure that had long supported the South's "peculiar institution." As the end drew near, enslaved persons who remained at home maneuvered for advantage in full expectation that Union victory would end their suffering. Yet they remained cautious, if not downright apprehensive. Sunrise on April 10, 1865, the day after Lee surrendered, did not usher in the Day of Jubilee in all of Virginia, much less in the other states of the Confederacy. In Texas, Confederate regulars did not lay down their weapons for another two months.[1]

After the last rebels gave up the fight, fled west, or left the country, Union forces set about rooting out the last pockets of slavery. As earlier, freedom arrived in bursts. Federal soldiers carried news of the war's outcome from major cities to small towns and beyond.[2] Agents of the War Department's Freedmen's Bureau came next, soon followed by the representatives of Northern religious, educational, and charitable organizations. Black men and women joined in this work, to which the freed people responded enthusiastically. "It is now that a nation is just born," noted Benjamin M. Bond, a member of the Fifty-Fourth Massachusetts Infantry, from the coast of South Carolina in June 1865, echoing a familiar refrain. "A country has just emerged from a slough of despondency, and now looks forward to the glorious future with delight." "The power of pure democracy, and the popularity of equal rights, through the instrumentality of God's providence," he proclaimed, "has overthrown the power of despotism, and has destroyed the ignominious rule of the demagogues, and has established a republican form of government that will give honor to our nation, and wealth and prosperity to its citizens."[3] As early as September 1863, Robert Hamilton, the editor of the New York *Anglo-African*, foresaw the magnitude of the challenge. Abolition was not the same as emancipation, he observed. Whereas the former demanded "aggressive, destructive, might," the latter required "gifts of construction."[4] The real work of emancipation—the constructing—had barely begun.

The collapse of the Confederacy meant much more than just the end of slavery; it also signaled the supremacy of Northern industrial capitalism over

Southern plantation agrarianism. Thenceforth, a single standard guided the relationship between capital and labor, one that recognized the equality before the law of employers and employees and the obligation of the former to compensate the latter for services performed. Thanks to the Thirteenth Amendment, this new understanding applied not only to the former slave states but also to the western territories and to any future territory that the United States might acquire.[5] Until well into the twentieth century, however, the states of the former Confederacy struggled to break out of the economic and political subordination to the industrial North that followed from the defeat of their rebellion.

The end of slavery reverberated far and wide. It jolted credit markets in the United States and Europe, thereby affecting the course of economic development. Besides liquidating some $4 billion worth of capital that had formerly been invested in human beings, emancipation also brought to an end the mechanism whereby wealth emerged from the wombs of enslaved women and then grew in value as the child advanced in age. The Confederate defeat undermined the last two remaining planter classes in the Americas—in Cuba and Brazil—and slavery ended there during the 1880s. Yet conceding control over the reunited country to the war's Northern victors did not prevent Southern elites from reasserting economic and political influence regionally, with ultimately fateful consequences not only for the freed people and poor whites of the region but also for the entire nation.[6]

The ensuing changes brought risks as well as rewards to the laborers, who, once freed from slavery, were entitled to compensation for their work, but, as Henry Clay Bruce learned, also responsible for supporting themselves and their families. By removing barriers that had prevented enslaved persons from participating in the market economy as wage earners, independent proprietors, investors, and savers in their own right, emancipation left the freed people directly vulnerable to the ebbs and flows of large economic forces, without the buffering effect—however minimal—that slaveholders had formerly provided. Any lingering doubts of this impact fell by the wayside following the Panic of 1873, and particularly when the Freedmen's Savings and Trust Company failed.[7]

As freed people searched for their footing on the new landscape, a racist coalition of white elites and plain people rallied under the banner of Conservatism and the Democratic Party. The conservatives resisted Republican attempts to redefine the relationship of the federal government to the states and the citizens thereof, throwing their weight behind President Andrew Johnson in his increasingly acrimonious disagreements with Congress regarding Reconstruction policy. The stakes were high inasmuch as the Thirteenth Amendment effectively invalidated the three-fifths clause of the

Constitution, whereby the slave states had benefited by counting three-fifths of the enslaved persons for purposes of determining congressional representation. Now, with the entire black population being tallied, former Confederates stood to reap a political windfall. Congressional Republicans countered with the Reconstruction Acts of 1867, which granted suffrage to black men in the states undergoing reconstruction. The Civil Rights Act of 1866 had already guaranteed the citizenship of native-born persons regardless of race or previous condition and asserted that such citizens of every color enjoyed all the legal rights of white citizens.[8] With suffrage came the right to serve in public office and to participate in public affairs, rights that the Fifteenth Amendment granted to all men regardless of color or previous condition in 1870.[9] But between 1867 and 1870, black men living in the tier of Northern states extending between New Jersey and Pennsylvania in the East and Minnesota and Wisconsin in the Midwest watched in frustration as one state legislature after another refused to grant them voting privileges. They looked with envy at the freedmen in the former Confederate States, who both voted and occupied elected offices.

The Radical Republicans' legislative agenda intended to prevent the former Confederate States from reentering the Union under the control of the same proslavery interests that had orchestrated secession and war. At once an outgrowth of the wartime strategy of emancipation, the postwar initiative also benefited from the service of nearly 200,000 African American soldiers and sailors and the ensuing groundswell of public opinion that had arisen in favor of granting the vote to black men in the rebel states. Northern leaders of the antebellum colored convention movement lent support. The National Equal Rights Convention of October 1864 had led to the formation of pro-suffrage Equal Rights Leagues in black communities throughout the North and in Union-occupied areas of the Confederacy. That momentum, in turn, gave new life to the state convention movement, beginning in Louisiana in January 1865 and continuing in all the other Southern states and several Northern ones through the fall.[10] These gatherings went to great lengths to strike a balance, however precarious, among the views of the various constituencies—formerly enslaved versus freeborn, Northern versus Southern, urban versus rural, light complexioned versus dark, and entrepreneurs and artisans versus unskilled laborers. They viewed the Civil Rights Act and the Reconstruction Acts as the national government's proper recognition of their loyalty during the war and after.

————

Although the national impact of emancipation often revealed itself slowly and subtly, the end of slavery caused sudden and unmistakable effects on the persons who had been bound together in the master-slave relationship. The implications reached from the affected households into their surrounding communities, continuing to distort perceptions of time and place, and transforming prior understandings of the meaning of home as well.

Time started over with Lee's surrender, appropriately in early springtime, when plant life emerges from its winter dormancy, bringing hope that shines as brightly as the sun. Rural people went to work instinctively planting food crops and vegetables but disdaining commercial crops at first. Former masters lacked real leverage to prompt industry, but they hoped that Union authorities would come to their assistance, which they did, to some extent at least. As he explained in his annual report to the secretary of war in December 1865, Freedmen's Bureau commissioner Oliver O. Howard not only promoted the use of contracts to formalize the employment relationship between landowners and laborers but also favored the use of the law to oblige the contracting parties to abide by the agreements. Having found "the plantation negroes inclined to leave their homes, and go to the cities, villages, and military posts, with no good prospect of work or support," Howard favored "a system like the ordinary intelligence office"—a mid-nineteenth-century term for an employment office—to help them find "good places." In the face of "authentic complaints of idleness, for which no remedy seemed to exist," the commissioner "directed that the vagrant laws of the respective States, so far as they applied to whites, be extended to freedmen," excepting any use of corporal punishment.[11]

Under the Bureau's aegis, written contracts succeeded in giving shape to the initial attempts of landowners without laborers and laborers without land to enter binding agreements whereby the latter would work in exchange for wages or a share of the crop, payable after the harvest. The landowners would furnish shelter and rations until settlement day; they soon discovered that contracts enabled them to leverage time—the workday, the workweek, the agricultural season—to gain a measure of control over the laborers themselves. When laborers were absent or tardy or otherwise inattentive to their contracted responsibilities, employers docked wages and stinted on rations. The most unscrupulous landowners went even further, dismissing persons altogether for contrived infractions or for no infraction at all.[12] Such actions added fresh evidence to the freed people's mistrust of the contracting process.

When the fall legislative sessions opened in the former Confederate states, employers insisted that antebellum vagrancy laws be strengthened and enforced. The draconian nature of a number of these Black Codes betrayed the underlying intent to continue slavery under a different guise.[13] Through the legal device of apprenticeship, former owners in several states hoped to retain the services of nominally orphaned children and young adults until the age of maturity. In Maryland and North Carolina the practice became widespread, causing a public outcry. In other former slave states, apprenticeship spawned innumerable petitions from freed people to the Freedmen's Bureau requesting that the agreements be invalidated, chiefly because former slaveholders had misrepresented to the courts that the prospective apprentices were orphans. Edwin Belcher, a light-complexioned man of mixed parentage who had risen to the rank of captain in a Pennsylvania volunteer regiment during the war and served afterward as a bureau agent in Georgia, described the practice as a "new slavery." Officials largely ignored his warnings, and former owners continued to reach backward in time for tools to shape their vision of the future. Yet, despite its attractiveness to individual landholders in certain circumstances, apprenticeship could hardly serve as a foundation for the new labor system.[14]

From the beginning of the formal contracting process, disagreements arose over a range of issues wherein landowners took for granted certain assumptions that freed people rejected outright. One notable example involved the performance of routine maintenance work not directly associated with producing the market staples. Another involved the hours and pace of work and the deportment of laborers during both after-work hours and on weekends. Laborers arrived in the field late, left early, and used plantation mules and wagons without permission to visit friends and neighbors. Freed people expected additional pay or other contractual consideration for repairing fences, felling trees, and maintaining buildings. Landowners rejected discretionary comings and goings and the unauthorized use of animals and equipment. They demanded that their hired laborers perform maintenance work without additional compensation.[15]

As the midsummer laying-by season arrived, the time when commercial crops were tall enough not to require constant weeding, large planters and small farmers alike began discharging employees, confident that they could hire sufficient day laborers to take off their crops at harvest time. In exchange for that risk, they reaped the reward of the back wages of the persons discharged and the obligation to furnish shelter and rations for the rest of the year. The small likelihood of federal intervention against such breaches of contract emboldened landowners both to reject the new requirements of free labor and to shed traditional obligations. By fair means and foul, cotton growers in the Southern states managed to realize a near sevenfold increase in the cotton crop between 1864 and 1865, from 299,000 bales to 2,094,000 bales.[16]

———

The North's victory expanded the geographical reach and other spatial implications of emancipation in unexpected ways. One element of this expansion was strictly geographical. Beyond the former Confederate States and the Loyal Border States, the impact of abolition radiated through the Northern states and the unorganized western territories. North of the Ohio River, emancipation raised concerns not only about a possible influx of formerly enslaved laborers who might compete with current residents for jobs but also about extending citizenship rights—particularly the vote—to black residents new and old. For black Northerners, the end of the war demonstrated the link between slavery and citizenship to which they had been drawing attention for years.[17]

Although the mass movement of freed people northward that many had feared during the war never materialized, the local movements that Commissioner Howard had decried were more than figments of the imagination. When the guns fell silent, people began to move about, but freed people were not the only persons in motion. Veterans of the armed forces of both belligerents headed home. Servants and laborers who accompanied the armies did the same, either returning to their places of origin or accompanying discharged service members to theirs, as Wallace Turnage did. At the same time, the hundreds of thousands of black men and women who had been involuntarily refugeed to the Confederate interior sought to reunite with their families. Still others took to the public highways involuntarily, as a result of being driven from their homes.[18] An incident early in December 1865 illustrates the unforeseen consequences that might result. "Refugees from the 'up country,'" a Freedmen's Bureau official in South Carolina reported, had been "driven away without money or produce by planters who had solemnly promised them a share of the crop." The persons forced into vagabondage headed straight for Edisto Island, which during the war had served as a destination for refugees from the interior and continued to be a focus of attention as part of the reserve that General William T. Sherman's Special Field Order 15 had created in South Carolina, Georgia, and Florida for the exclusive settlement of freed people the previous January. They arrived in the midst of the crisis produced when President Johnson ordered Commissioner Howard to restore the land to its prewar owners.[19] Despite the inherent risks, formerly enslaved persons moved in search of relatives or to return to old home places; they moved to nearby cities to escape the labor regime of the plantations; they moved to reunite families. They moved down the road or across the region just because they could.

The development of new agricultural frontiers and new extractive industries also helped fuel this mobility. Bureau officials provided transportation to enable persons to travel to states where labor was in demand as well as to reunite destitute families. Commissioner Oliver O. Howard himself entertained requests from prospective employers soliciting government transportation.

One such supplicant was none other than Nathan Bedford Forrest, the former slave trader and Confederate general implicated in the Fort Pillow massacre and future leader of the Ku Klux Klan. In 1866 Forrest was developing plantations on the Arkansas side of the Mississippi River and wanted "1000 able bodied Negro laborers" to construct a railroad linking the region to Memphis.[20]

Cities and towns also served as destinations of choice for persons who sought a change of scenery and circumstances from the prewar days. Urban economies furnished employment opportunities, although day labor was typically irregular. Refugees from the plantations might find shelter and more with relatives and friends who had scouted ahead. The most concerted efforts on the part of federal officials fell well short of steering migrants away from the cities. As a result, black urban populations grew, often dramatically. In Washington, D.C., for instance, the number of black residents increased from roughly 5,000 in 1860 to an estimated 30,000 by the end of the war. The majority of the newcomers were refugees from surrounding slave states. Many, according to Julia A. Wilbur, the Washington agent for the Rochester Ladies' Antislavery Society, had no intention of returning to their prewar homes. "The colored people," she observed, "know as well as we do that they are not safe in many parts of Maryland and Virginia," obliterating the wartime distinctions between the former Union state and the former Confederate state.[21] Refugees to the cities often had difficulty finding employment, although persons with marketable skills and those whom Wilbur described as having "aspirations to become something more than mere servants and laborers for others" fared better than those who lacked such traits.[22] In fact, many of the newcomers maintained contact with their families in the countryside, returning home when family needs dictated, much as later generations of migrants from the Southern countryside would do.[23]

Men and women living in urban areas constituted a reserve labor force for surrounding farms and plantations, especially during periods of peak demand, such as the harvest. From early in the postwar period, towns in plantation districts became gathering places for field laborers, who stopped work at noon on Saturdays, with or without contractual authorization, to socialize. Such movements back and forth enabled freed people to become acquainted with the whereabouts of Freedmen's Bureau offices and perhaps even the attending officials (see figure E.1). They grew accustomed to taking their grievances there, asserting to employers, neighbors, travelers on the highway, and residents of and visitors to the town the independence that emancipation conveyed. Like other small spaces, the offices of the bureau provided a point of entry into the larger arenas where public policy regarding the contours of the new social order was developed, debated, and adjudicated.

Figure E.1 Office for Freedmen, Beaufort, South Carolina. Phot. Nov. 1864.
Courtesy of the National Archives.

When an agent of the bureau could not grant relief, the next stop might be an attorney's office, and then a courthouse. The small spaces to which freed people gained access as citizens promised to continue the transformation of their lives that wartime emancipation began.

Of course, freed people's interest in small spaces burned most intently around the prospect that the government would make homesteads available on reasonable terms from the land that had been abandoned or confiscated during the war. Indeed, the Treasury Department had conducted tax sales of such properties on the Sea Islands in 1863 and 1864, although most of the land fell into the hands of investors instead of freed people. Interest spiked again in January 1865 following General Sherman's order, but the long-term validity of the "possessory titles" that he referenced was questionable from the start. The Freedmen's Bureau Act of March 1865 granted the commissioner authority "to set apart, for the use of loyal refugees and freedmen" such parcels for a term of three years at which time they could purchase the plot they had improved. Forty acres available to each family promised to go a long way toward achieving the revolutionary transformation in the relations between the laborers and the soil and between the laborers and the antebellum landowners that would have given fresh meaning to the biblical prophecies of a promised land.[24] At every opportunity, freed people had voiced this dream to federal officials during the war. In June 1863, the South Carolina freedman Harry McMillan explained the universal desire for small plots of land to the AFIC, and in January 1865, Garrison Frazier reiterated that position during the famous conversation that he and other black ministers from Savannah, Georgia, had with War Secretary Edwin M. Stanton and General Sherman.[25]

———

Given the unlikelihood that the federal government would distribute land to the freed people, the default option whereby they would provide for their own shelter, food, clothing, and the other amenities of life became compensated labor. To be sure, they knew how to work, but they often chose when and for whom to work based on considerations that did not always align perfectly with those of their employers or Freedmen's Bureau agents. To the extent that federal officials traced such independent-mindedness to an employer's ill treatment, they were inclined to intervene. But when they realized that not every instance of truancy could be traced to such a cause, some reverted to stereotypes that cast persons of African descent as inherently lazy. Others assumed that persons born into slavery could never shed the habit of malingering that the institution had fostered, and that the Northerners would have to await the arrival of generations born after the war for any hope of seeing the rise of Yankee virtue in the South. Such theorizing often drew on faulty conceptual models of compensated labor as a timeless ideal rather than a social practice that was comparatively new in human history and that changed over time. The critics of the freed people's habits rarely paused to note the variable forms that "free labor" took north of the Mason and Dixon Line and the Ohio River, or the evolving nature of the concept and its various manifestations. As a result, they came only slowly and reluctantly to understand that the transition from slavery to compensated labor would proceed in fits and starts rather than in an orderly progression, even with the benefit of an antislavery constitutional amendment. Postwar emancipation, like its wartime counterpart, involved steps forward and backward, victories and defeats. Centuries could not be compressed into years indefinitely.

In mid-1867, Julia Wilbur described this widening gap between expectation and reality. In her attempts to find employment for the freedwomen in Washington, she turned increasingly to the middle-class households of Northern cities. She soon discovered, however, that women who had worked only in the fields, with "no idea of housework," stood little chance of success in such circumstances. "Some of these can get work in Washington and vicinity, where the Southern slip-shod way of doing work is tolerated or submitted to as a necessity, but Northern people would not have them." Prospective employers often wished for the impossible: a "neat, tidy, honest, strong woman; one who is good natured, and kind to children, can do general housework, and is good looking." Half-amused and half-exasperated, Wilbur declared that "the millennium has not yet come. There was nothing in Slavery to form such characters, and all the domestic virtues and Christian graces will not come of a few years of freedom."[26]

But whereas the Northerners hoped to instill principles of economic individualism, formerly enslaved people insisted on providing for the common good, the foundation of individual prosperity. Downplaying the emerging individualist ideology, they took pains to safeguard the collective interests. Late in 1865, a Northern visitor to St. Catherine's Island, Georgia, described how its residents aimed to safeguard their future together. The community in question owed its existence to Sherman's field order. Tunis G. Campbell, a black New Jersey native, served as intermediary between the Freedmen's Bureau and its 356 members. His son, Tunis G. Campbell Jr., assisted in the work. According to one witness, during the summer of 1865 all the residents were "dependent," but by the end of the year all but eleven were "self-supporting." The island's legislative body held its first session early in November, passing bills to collect revenue to support the general government and schools, to regulate fishing and oystering, and to protect crops from cattle, horses, and hogs that roamed at large. Lawmakers reached consensus around these contentious issues, offering a model—albeit a short-lived one—for resolving differences between landowners and propertyless laborers.[27]

In one of the last letters he penned from Port Royal before returning to Boston early in 1865, Edward S. Philbrick, one of the pioneers of the experiment that began three years earlier, also harbored second thoughts. He described a strained conversation with the laborers on a certain plantation who were dissatisfied with the amount of their end-of-year settlements, in light of the rent he charged for corn land and what he paid them for "yellow-cotton," the inferior-grade product of their small patches. But "then came the talk about next year," which continued for more than half an hour in a steady rain as the freed people insisted that they be paid one dollar per task, the quarter-acre sections of plantation fields that had been the standard day's work from long before the Civil War.[28]

An impartial observer might well have marveled at how well the freed people responded to what Philbrick himself had earlier described as appeals to their *human nature* by making readily available "articles which they never had in abundance before." "To multiply their simple wants" was to "motivate industry." As the freedman Esup's letter to his mother had demonstrated, former slaves knew the value of both their labor and the consumer goods they desired. They also understood that a dollar had more purchasing power than a dime—William Eustis's "great civilizer." But the freed people's demonstration of what they had learned moved Philbrick to frustration, not admiration. Having resorted to "the usual amount of reasoning," among other things, "enlarging upon the future uncertainty of prices of cotton, &c.," he reluctantly conceded that he had "made little or no impression on them." When at last he broke off the discussion, "the choir of hands" sang out "'A dollar a task!' 'A dollar a task!'"[29]

Like Philbrick, other emissaries of the new order of compensated labor often found themselves squirming over how quickly the freed people learned its basic lessons and then wielded that knowledge to their own advantage. On Edisto Island, South Carolina, in October 1865, for instance, a series of meetings occurred that demonstrated clearly to the freed people what they could hope to expect from the government of the United States. Through their spokesmen, Henry Bram, Ishmael Moultrie, and Yates Sampson, the island's residents explained their expectations for the future to Commissioner Howard, who was present, and to President Andrew Johnson in Washington, the two federal officials in whose hands their fate rested. They pleaded not to be subjected to a new order defined by the architects of the old one. "We Have property in Horses, cattle, carriages, & articles of furniture, but we are landless and Homeless," they explained. "From the Homes we Have live In In the past we can only do one of three things Step Into the public *road or the sea* or remain on them working as in former time and subject to [the land owners'] will as then."[30]

From his Boston home, Edward Philbrick followed reports of events on Edisto Island closely. To a fellow Gideonite, he observed that Commissioner Howard had a "tough job" in trying to see "if he can reconcile the claims of the negroes on Edisto and other islands with those of the former owners." Observing that "the tide of emigration southward" suffered because "the South is still intolerant of Yankees," Philbrick reiterated the assumption that not only abstract Northern principles but also actual Northern entrepreneurs were necessary to bring compensated labor into full bloom. "The rabble and the young men are still clinging to the hope that they are going to have their own way about managing the *nigger*" just "as soon as they get rid of the United States forces." Then the former Confederates would remove the kid gloves. Philbrick also waxed philosophical, momentarily forgetting the echoes of "A dollar a task!" ringing in his ears. Doubting "that the present generation of negroes will work as they were formerly obliged to," he reasoned that "the race will not produce so much cotton" as they did before the war. "The change is too great a one to be made in a day." "It will take many years to make an economical and thrifty man out of a freedman," he concluded, "and about as long to make a sensible and just employer out of a former slaveholder."[31]

Like the entrepreneurs, teachers, and missionaries who had ventured south to Port Royal, Philbrick believed at the outset that building a system of compensated labor on the ruins of slavery was the work of, at most, several years. But as a result of his experience, he found the need to adjust the timeline while not abandoning the hope of eventual success. Neither he nor other champions of Northern ways foresaw the long future that lay ahead. Nor would they have been willing to admit how their sense of cultural and moral superiority—and, often, their selfishness and greed—contributed to the process.[32]

———

To be sure, freed people sought access to land as a just remedy for years of unrequited toil. But for purposes of building homes and a future, they hoped for more than what white settlers had rejected or the marginally productive tracts in Florida that lawmakers periodically considered for distribution. In April 1863, for instance, a black resident of Massachusetts dismissed a proposed petition requesting Congress "to grant the state of Florida to the colored race as a home." "The whole South has been enriched by the blood of our race, we have cultivated it, and made its inhabitants wealthy," he insisted, and "by right it belongs to us." Yet home consisted of much more than territory—it also had to convey citizenship. In the Bay State, "we enjoy nearly all our rights as citizens," he added, "more than in any other state." Against that standard, Florida had nothing to offer.[33]

A year later, the AME minister (and later distinguished bishop) Jabez P. Campbell further developed the concept of an unpaid debt the nation owed to African-descended people. He faulted "our own colored lecturers" for not adequately pressing "the black man's bill of claims against this nation for his labour performed during the past two hundred and forty-five years." The particulars included "free soil, free speech, free men, and no slaves; equal pay, equal bounty, equal rights, equal privileges, and equal suffrage with the white man, under the constitution and laws of the government of these United States, without any distinction whatever on account of color." Black leaders needed to "urge the claim, until the bill is paid." A year earlier, as President Lincoln pitched the idea of colonization to black pastors in Washington, the Reverend Henry M. Turner explained their cool reception to the president's offer. "I suppose no colored man in the nation would have any objection to going any where," Turner quipped, "if this government pay them for their two hundred and forty years' work."[34]

In the fall of 1865, Jourdon Anderson, who had fled during the war with his family from "the dear old home" in Tennessee and settled in Dayton, Ohio, wrote to his former owner, Colonel P. H. Anderson. Responding to the colonel's offer of a "good chance," Anderson wished to know the details. What wages did he propose? Did "a comfortable home" await his family? Would neighbors address his wife, Mandy, as "Mrs. Anderson," as those in Dayton did? Would their children have access to schools? Would young white men respect his daughters? Finally, as a test of the former owner's "sincerity" and as a way "to make us forgive and forget old scores," Jourdon and Mandy Anderson asked for their unpaid wages, with interest, totaling more than $11,000. "Surely there will be a day of reckoning for those who defraud the laborer of his hire," Anderson added.[35] Mattie J. Jackson reasoned similarly but took matters into her own hands before escaping to freedom. Inasmuch as "the laborer was worthy of his hire," she later explained, "I thought my wages should come from my master's pocket." Accordingly, she helped herself to twenty-five dollars to defray the expenses of her journey of freedom from Kentucky to Indiana. "After I was safe and had learned to write," she reported, "I sent him a nice letter, thanking him for the kindness his pocket bestowed to me in time of need."[36]

Though neither the first nor the most elaborate claims for reparations, the statements of Jourdon Anderson and Mattie J. Jackson make clear that emancipation left a debt unpaid. Nearly 250 years of exploitation was not erased simply by declaring all enslaved persons free, outlawing slavery, and granting them full ownership of their own bodies. After all, the "precious boon of freedom" that countless petitions referenced was a fundamental human birthright and not a substitute for unpaid labor over lifetimes. It remained to be seen whose claims would prevail as the architects of Reconstruction debated the appropriate government action to redress the balance not only with declarations or even certificates of freedom but also with tangible forms of restitution.[37]

––––––––

Over the course of its short life, the Bureau of Refugees, Freedmen and Abandoned Lands represented the national government's concerted effort to bring the kind of order to federal emancipation policy that the Emancipation League of Boston had found wanting in the fall of 1862. Although much maligned at the time and since, the Freedmen's Bureau stands as a monument to the aims of uplifting the freed people and assisting their incorporation into free society.[38] The pioneering work that wartime freedom seekers had done in escaping from slavery and forcing federal authorities to address their status paid dividends. But the ballooning number of beneficiaries of federal emancipation—from roughly 500,000 persons in Union-controlled areas during the spring of 1865 to more than three million stretching from Delaware to Texas several months later—placed unprecedented strain on administrative resources, material and human alike.

The bureau addressed three major challenges that Republican Party leaders, the nation, and—in particular—the freed people faced. The first was stabilizing Southern agriculture, the great industrial interest that Secretary Stanton had identified in his charge to the AFIC. This involved providing food, temporary shelter, and medical attention to needy white refugees as well as freed people and supervising the process whereby landowners and laborers agreed to contracts in which the latter were compensated for their work in either wages or a share of harvested crops.[39] The bureau's second goal was to support education and, in doing so, to repudiate one of slavery's most objectionable legacies. Bureau officials worked closely with parents and community leaders and with representatives of Northern religious and benevolent associations to identify suitable structures to use as schools (constructing them when necessary) and to supply them with teachers and books. The bureau also sponsored high schools in the larger cities and towns, and several colleges and universities.[40] Besides providing a foundation for the development of Christian virtue, economic independence, and civic responsibility, bureau-sponsored schools enabled parents to remove their children from working in fields and households—at least while schools were in session. In the process, the schools served the important role of an intermediate social institution between the household and society at large. Bureau-sponsored schools taught parents as well as pupils invaluable lessons in republican citizenship.[41]

The bureau's third, and in some ways most daunting, goal was to substitute the rule of law for the arbitrary will of the slaveholder, thereby advancing the process of integrating the freed people—and, it was hoped, their former enslavers—into the civic culture of the reunited nation. During the first two postwar years, agents of the bureau served as justices of the peace when and where local judicial processes did not function, and when courts were reestablished they advocated on behalf of the freed people (see figure E.2). Following passage of the Reconstruction Acts in March 1867, bureau personnel also assisted freedmen in exercising the new citizenship responsibilities: forming political organizations and organizing electoral campaigns, voting, and serving in public office. As formerly enslaved persons became active participants in the political process, vigilante violence increased dramatically in the attempt to intimidate them from asserting themselves both as workers and as citizens. Bureau agents hoped to curb such attacks but with only mixed results until Congress authorized the use of federal force to suppress the Ku Klux Klan and other violent groups in 1870.[42]

Figure E.2 A. R. Waud, *The Freedmen's Bureau*. Courtesy of the Library of Congress Prints and Photographs Division, LC-USZ62-105555.

Indeed, in some areas, the violence did not represent a break from practice as much as the end of a temporary lull. A black soldier working as a clerk for Freedmen's Bureau assistant commissioner Colonel Samuel Thomas in Vicksburg, Mississippi, insightfully assessed conditions in the state at the end of 1865. Calvin Holly was a thirty-eight-year-old native of LaGrange County, Tennessee, when he enlisted in an artillery regiment of the U.S. Colored Troops in February 1865. Just before year's end, Holly wrote to General Howard. As if to confirm the validity of the warnings James McKaye had issued in *The Mastership and Its Fruits*, Holly explained that the freed people were "in a great many ways being outraged beyound humanity" at the hands of the former rebels, who robbed them, shot them, turned them out of their homes, and drove them off "in the cold to frieze and starve to death." "The safety of this country," he insisted, required "giving the Colered man all the rights of a white man . . . and let him know that their is power enough in the arm of the Government to give Justice, to all her loyal citizens." The former rebels, however, aimed to "spoil the whole thing," and "they are doing all they can to prevent free labor, and reasstablish a kind of secondary slavery." Holly denounced as "a lie" the rumors "accusing the colered peple of an insorection," but he warned that without federal intervention "there will be trouble in *Miss.* before spring."[43]

General Oliver Otis Howard, the agency's only commissioner, bore a stellar reputation for virtuous habits and gentlemanly demeanor in addition to his impressive military record (he lost his right arm in the Battle of Fair Oaks, Virginia, in June 1862 but returned to active duty and eventually became a trusted subordinate of General William T. Sherman, commanding the Right Wing of his army that marched across Georgia in late 1864). When he assumed leadership of the bureau, Howard learned from Secretary of War Edwin M. Stanton "that it was Mr. Lincoln's request before he died" that Howard lead the agency.[44] He did not flaunt his accomplishments or curry special favors; but he believed passionately in the mission of the bureau and worked tirelessly to help it succeed. In 1870 New York Democratic congressman Fernando Wood, a longtime foe of emancipation, charged Howard with numerous counts of fraud and misappropriation of government funds in connection with both the Freedmen's Bureau and Howard University. An investigation by the House Committee on Education and Labor exonerated Howard, with the report proclaiming that "no thirteen millions of dollars was ever more wisely spent." To the rhetorical question, "Has the Bureau been a success?" the investigators replied exuberantly, "The world can point to nothing like it in all the history of emancipation."[45]

———

When Mississippi Democrats employed wholesale fraud, intimidation, and violence to capture the election in 1875, they signaled what lay ahead for the three states of Louisiana, South Carolina, and Florida, which Republicans still controlled. Following the presidential election of 1876, congressional Republicans brokered a deal whereby they claimed the presidency in exchange for conceding those three states to Democratic control, signaling the end of Reconstruction in the South. The withdrawal of federal troops from the region merely formalized what had already become evident: the freed people and the assorted coalitions of native whites and migrants from the North that had gathered under the Republican banner would have to fend for themselves.

With the restoration of what even Republican leaders casually referred to as "home rule," white conservatives in the former Confederate states set about undoing what the Freedmen's Bureau, Republican-controlled state legislatures, and national laws had done since war's end to suppress the vestiges of slavery and to offer the freed people a modicum of protection of their economic, civil, and political rights. In the name of good government, the white supremacists curtailed access to the ballot box, first by intimidation and violence and later through such schemes as poll taxes and literacy tests. Longing to turn back the hands of time, the self-styled "redeemers" aimed to recreate a version of the paternal relationship of slavery days, but one that treated the lives and the nominal legal and political rights of the freed people with contempt. While conceding that humans were no longer property, some kept challenging the federal government's preemptory abolition of property rights in enslaved persons into the twentieth century.[46] The "home" envisioned in this variant of home rule afforded no place to African Americans except as resident drudges.

Under the guise of efficiency and economy, post-restoration state legislatures took steps to ensure that property owners wielded political control over government and society. Most went even further, adopting new measures to curtail freed people's access to independent subsistence that, among other things, included fence laws, which outlawed the free-ranging of cattle, hogs, and other animals on which landless people depended, and fishing and hunting laws, which limited freed people's independent access to nature's bounty. But, unlike the black lawmakers on St. Catherine's Island who sought to balance competing interests, the old guard of landed wealth, which had joined forces with the emerging business elites in what W. E. B. Du Bois later aptly characterized as a "counter-revolution of property" and continued the work of reducing the freed people to slave-like economic, political, and social subjugation.[47]

The piecemeal erosion of citizenship rights that accompanied the overthrow of Republican state governments had a real impact on black Southerners' overall sense of security and their confidence in truly belonging to their surrounding civic communities. Frustration surfaced repeatedly. By the mid-1870s, a Colonization Council had taken root in Louisiana, the emissaries of which traversed the state drumming up support for Liberian emigration. During the spring of 1875, black leaders from throughout Tennessee gathered at an emigration convention to consider the prospect of moving west, and a delegation visited Kansas to scout the feasibility of forming a settlement. A year later, some 1,500 to 2,000 persons from Middle Tennessee planned to make the move. The Nashville *American* sarcastically dismissed the migrants' claims that they could not find work in Tennessee and faulted them for succumbing "to the illusion" that "a bag of gold await[ed] them at the end of a rainbow." Sarcasm aside, the editor could not deny the sentiment that had emerged from the freed people's political meetings, namely, that because "they could have no voice in the politics of Tennessee" they hoped to relocate westward "where they could have the entire control of affairs." By 1879–80, black Tennesseans constituted an integral part of the so-called Exoduster movement to Kansas, one of its two most influential leaders, Benjamin Singleton, being a native of the state. The other, Henry Adams, was a stalwart member of Louisiana's Colonization Council.[48]

As the nineteenth century drew to a close and conditions throughout the South deteriorated, with lynching on the rise and the systematic separation of the races codified in the former Border States as well as the Confederate states, the fight to keep the promise of Reconstruction alive continued. Champions of racial equality who had come of age during the Civil War, such as the white Ohio native turned North Carolina carpetbagger Albion Winegar Tourgée, joined forces with up-and-coming black leaders, such as Ida B. Wells, in denouncing these practices and the associated abandonment of the nation's founding principles. Henry McNeal Turner, by then an influential AME bishop, similarly blasted national leaders for tolerating the flagrant disregard for the lives and civil rights of black citizens. When legitimate demands for justice failed to convince Washington officials of the need for action, he looked farther afield than Kansas for relief, becoming the nation's leading advocate of emigration to Africa. Liberia beckoned as a place where black men and women could pursue economic independence and political autonomy without constantly fearing for their lives. In short, it offered the prospect of a home as well as a nation. Early in the twentieth century, the Jamaican-born Marcus Garvey took up the mantle of black nationalism, and the movement experienced a new lease on life.[49]

———

Their best efforts notwithstanding, Radical Republicans of the Civil War era failed to guarantee basic citizenship rights for the freed people, much less to address the structural economic and social conditions that reproduced oppression and poverty instead of civic equality and the chance for economic improvement. To be sure, the official actions that took the form of proclamations, laws, and constitutional amendments addressed specific issues often with the net result of amelioration. Yet they proved unequal to the challenge of developing an achievable vision and implementing it into meaningful social policy. In hindsight, Henry Wilson's *History of the Antislavery Measures* marks so many miles to an often-imprecise destination. Looking forward instead of backward, the road was shrouded in fog, and even the staunchest advocates of freedom and equality often appeared to take political expediency as their only guiding light. To be sure, emancipation enabled individuals to enjoy personal freedom that was categorically denied during slavery—to move about at will; to marry, make contracts, and enter into other legal proceedings; to own dwellings, land, and other valuable property; and to be compensated for their labor. But for most, the reality fell short of the expectations.

In different neighborhoods and communities throughout the nation, African Americans celebrated January 1, 1863, or June 19, 1865, or some other appropriate date to memorialize emancipation. Most of these events took place annually, others on special anniversary dates, such as the centennial of Lincoln's birth in 1909 and the seventy-fifth anniversary of the Thirteenth Amendment in 1940. The commemorations aimed to recapture and keep alive the hopes of freedom that wartime emancipation had made possible but that postwar developments had stifled. And for the family members, the friends, and even the practical strangers who participated, the celebrations offered the opportunity to commit themselves anew to the quest for freedom and justice no matter how long and difficult the journey. Such gatherings also kept extended families anchored to a place and in the process wove webs that over time extended from the Carolinas to New York, from Tennessee, Alabama, and Mississippi to Chicago, and from Arkansas, Louisiana, and Texas to Los Angeles.

More than 150 years after the Civil War, the Promised Land still appears to be an elusive destination. Obstacles overcome earlier in the journey come back to life obstructing the road ahead. Yet the quest for a home beckons—a literal place in which to dwell in peace and a figurative community wherein all members share the benefits equally. "The eternal laws of progress still mark the onward march of events," noted the AME minister Richard H. Cain in the spring of 1866, following the congressional override of President Johnson's veto of the Civil Rights Act and its firm declarations of birthright citizenship and of every citizen's right to the protection of the law. "Amid the revolutions, which have, and are passing over this land, the Negro still holds a central position," he stated unequivocally, "and the decrees of Heaven direct his certain and full recognition in the mighty march of civilization."[50]

As wartime emancipation makes clear, the human struggle for freedom and equality lends itself to illusions. Time may move erratically; space may shift; and the sense of belonging to social networks that all humans crave—family, neighborhood, community, polity—may prove ephemeral. Revolutions may go backward. Yet, as Miguel de Cervantes's immortal fictional character Don Quixote learned from his adventures, illusions that disguise the cruelty and injustice of the world as it is also provide glimpses into a future that may be.[51] Ever subject to shatter against hard reality, illusions also inspire hope.

Acknowledgments

This book has been in the making longer than I wish to admit: it germinated during the late 1970s, then went largely into hibernation between 1998 and 2013, and finally sprang back to life in 2014. Its origin story lies in the wonder-filled years that I spent with the Freedom and Southern Society Project at the University of Maryland, College Park, between 1977 and 1984. During that time I benefited from working with Ira Berlin, Barbara J. Fields, Thavolia Glymph, Steven Hahn, Steven F. Miller, Leslie S. Rowland, and Julie Saville, coediting the first four volumes of *Freedom: A Documentary History of Emancipation, 1861–1867*. For much of that period we labored under the watchful eyes of Sara Dunlap Jackson and Armstead L. Robinson, whose knowledge of the Civil War military records at the National Archives that pertained to emancipation was unrivaled. It is impossible to describe the intellectual rewards that I reaped from that association, which continue to pay dividends right up to the present. I am proud to be able to count them among my colleagues and friends. I also benefited from the intellectual company of other scholars who worked on the project for stints of varying lengths of time. They include Garrine P. Laney, Gail P. Thomas, Wayne K. Durrell, Lawrence McDonnell, Michael K. Honey, and Leslie A. Schwalm, as well as the other editors who worked on future volumes after my departure, particularly René Hayden, Anthony E. Kaye, Kate Masur, Susan E. O'Donovan, John C. Rodrigue, and Stephen A. West.

The fifteen-year hiatus resulted from my having accepted administrative positions at Howard University first as associate dean of the Graduate School and then as an associate provost. I continued to benefit from intellectual interactions with colleagues, including those from disciplines other than history, many of which enriched my appreciation for how much we have in common. I am particularly grateful for the university's generous support of my leave from all academic responsibilities during 2014 and much of 2015, which enabled me to complete the research and produce a first draft of the manuscript. I am grateful to Provost Kurt L. Schmoke, who first suggested the possibility of such leave, and to his successors in the Office of the Provost, Wayne A. I. Frederick, now president of the university, and Anthony K. Wutoh, who have been unfailing in their support for this project. Donald Bell, who served as vice president for presidential initiatives under former president Sidney Ribeau, also deserves thanks for his role in crafting the program that enabled the leave. My colleagues in the Provost's Office, particularly Regina Y. Drake, LaRue Barkwell, Vancito Wallace, Chieh Hsiung Chang, Shelese Smith, Deborah Elliott, Yolanda Rogers, and Joyce Stewart, assisted me in countless ways large and small and covered for me when my mind wandered from the twenty-first century back to the nineteenth. Jonathan Ajose accommodated me with a comfortable place to work.

I wish also to express enduring thanks to the archivists and librarians who facilitated my research. At the National Archives, I am especially grateful to Sara Jackson,

Michael Musick, and Rebecca Livingston. At Howard University's Founders Library and the Moorland-Spingarn Research Center, Ishmael Childs, Joellen ElBashir, Alliah Humber, Ida B. Jones, Richard Jenkins, and April Juniper provided valuable assistance. Howard Dodson, the former director of university libraries, was particularly generous in furnishing a microfilm reading machine, an increasingly arcane piece of equipment in the age of the internet but one not quite ready for the dustbin of history. Adele Logan Alexander, Gwendolyn N. Everett, Whitney Stewart, Chris Myers Asch, and Jane Freundel Levy steered me to material that I would have otherwise missed. Thanks also to Gwendolyn Everett and Scott W. Baker of the Howard University Gallery of Art for the image of Edmonia Lewis's *Forever Free*.

I am grateful to former students and colleagues who have shared generously of their time and expertise. They include Adele Logan Alexander, Roger A. Davidson, Barbara P. Josiah, Jeffrey R. Kerr-Ritchie, and Edna Greene Medford. For insights into the black sailors' experience, I am particularly grateful to Adele Alexander and William B. Gould IV, who brought their Civil War–era progenitors back to life, and to Roger Davidson, Homer Fleetwood II, Joy P. Jackson, Barbara Josiah, Lisa Y. King, Learie B. Luke, Sharon Pierre-Luke, Craig A. Schiffert, Michael A. Southwood, James Peckham Stephens, Robert T. Vinson, Bennie Visher III, and Yohuru R. Williams, who assisted ably in the research. Special thanks are due to Edna Medford for inviting me to participate in the Abraham Lincoln bicentennial conference at Howard University in 2009 and to Leslie Rowland and Matthew Mason for the opportunity to take part in the tribute to Ira Berlin at the University of Maryland College Park in 2015. At both of these events I received valuable feedback on my ideas regarding time and space.

Ana Lucia Araujo kindly hosted my presentation of a draft of chapter 3 at a 2016 meeting of the Howard University Seminar on Slavery, Memory, and the African Diaspora, where I benefited from the engagement with colleagues, students, and guests. Among the lattermost was Daniel Rood, who was in Washington on a fellowship at the time. Rael A. Sternhell offered insightful comments on an early version of arguments that now appear in chapter 3 and chapter 4; Adele Alexander and Edna Medford provided close readings and useful suggestions on the entire manuscript at a critical stage; and Gary W. Gallagher and Kate Masur read the work on behalf of the press. My arguments are stronger and clearer thanks to their input.

Gary Gallagher and T. Michael Parrish have been model editors for the Littlefield History of the Civil War Era, and I am especially thankful for the patience they have shown to me over the years. Mark Simpson-Vos, the current editorial director of the University of North Carolina Press, as well as former editor in chief David Perry offered as much moral support as technical assistance, for which I am grateful. Others at the press also merit thanks for their belief in the merits of this project and their diligence to bringing it to fruition; they include associate editor Jessica Newman, marketing director Dino A. Battista, project manager Iris Oakes, acquisitions manager Cate Hodorowicz, cover designer Courtney Leigh Baker, and all of their associates. The keen editorial eyes of Michelle Witkowski and Liz Schueler, of Westchester Publishing Services, saved me from stylistic miscues and incomplete documentation. Their unfailing grace and professionalism is the fulfillment of every author's dream. Special thanks to Matthew White for preparing the index.

Last but not least, I gratefully thank my family for enduring my preoccupation with this project over the years. My two daughters not only have grown to adulthood while it gestated but also have had children of their own (in Rachel's case, a daughter, Hannah, and a granddaughter, Hayden; in Megan's case, three sons, Joey, Jacob, and Matty, and a daughter, Emily). All are a source of boundless delight and inspiration. My wife, Patricia, has been both my mainstay and my best friend for the past half century, and I look forward to being able to say that for many more years to come. I just hope that I have been a worthy recipient of her love and that I have repaid in equal measure all that she has given to me.

Notes

List of Abbreviations

AFIC	American Freedmen's Inquiry Commission
AFIC Records, Harvard	United States American Freedmen's Inquiry Commission Records, 1862–64, Harvard University
DocSouth	Documenting the American South, North American Slave Narratives, University of North Carolina, Chapel Hill
Freedom: Black Military Experience	*Freedom: A Documentary History of Emancipation*, ser. 2, 1982.
Freedom: Destruction of Slavery	*Freedom: A Documentary History of Emancipation*, ser. 1, vol. 1, 1985.
Freedom: Land and Labor, 1865	*Freedom: A Documentary History of Emancipation*, ser. 3, vol. 1, 2008.
Freedom: Land and Labor, 1866	*Freedom: A Documentary History of Emancipation*, ser. 3, vol. 2, 2013.
Freedom: Wartime Genesis, Lower South	*Freedom: A Documentary History of Emancipation*, ser. 1, vol. 3, 1990.
Freedom: Wartime Genesis, Upper South	*Freedom: A Documentary History of Emancipation*, ser. 1, vol. 2, 1993.
FSSP	Freedmen and Southern Society Project, University of Maryland, College Park
LC	Library of Congress
MSRC-HU	Moorland-Spingarn Research Collection, Howard University
National Archives	National Archives and Records Administration, Washington, D.C.
Official Records	United States. United States War Department. *The War of the Rebellion*, 1880–1901.
Official Records, Navy	United States. United States Department of the Navy. Naval War Records Office. *Official Records of the Union and Confederate Navies in the War of the Rebellion*, 1894–1922.
RG	Record Group

Introduction

1. See Dyson, *Founding of Howard University*, 11–13; claim of John A. Smith, filed May 29, 1862, http://civilwardc.org/texts/petitions/cww.00549.html; *Emancipation in the District of Columbia*, 38th Cong., 1st Sess. (1864), H. Exec. Doc. No. 42, serial 1189, at 48. Smith coincidentally served as clerk of the U.S. Circuit Court of the District of Columbia, which registered the freedom of the persons who were emancipated.

2. *Inaugural Ceremonies of the Freedmen's Memorial Monument to Abraham Lincoln*. Savage, *Standing Soldiers, Kneeling Slaves*, 52–122, provides a comprehensive examination of the imagery of emancipation.

3. Wesley, *Thirteenth Amendment*, 6–7.

4. Eliot, *Story of Archer Alexander*, 11, 88. With Alexander's visage on the memorial "as correct as that of Mr. Lincoln himself," Eliot concluded that "the ideal group is thus converted into the literal truth of history without losing its artistic conception or effect" (14).

5. Buick, *Child of the Fire*, 50–67, on *Forever Free*, and especially 60–61 regarding its suggestions about the black family. Cf. Boime, *Art of Exclusion*, 163–67.

6. *Inaugural Ceremonies of the Freedmen's Memorial Monument to Abraham Lincoln*, 3, 11, 27; Quarles, *Lincoln and the Negro*, 3–14; Medford, *Lincoln and Emancipation*, 105–6. During the 1850s, Langston achieved national notoriety as an abolitionist activist and attorney. After the war, he relocated from Ohio to Washington, where he served as dean of the Howard University school of law and, for a time, as acting president of the institution. See Logan, *Howard University*, 73–80.

7. *Inaugural Ceremonies of the Freedmen's Memorial Monument to Abraham Lincoln*, 10, 19.

8. *Inaugural Ceremonies of the Freedmen's Memorial Monument to Abraham Lincoln*, 20.

9. *Inaugural Ceremonies of the Freedmen's Memorial Monument to Abraham Lincoln*, 22, 23.

10. *Inaugural Ceremonies of the Freedmen's Memorial Monument to Abraham Lincoln*, 23; Wesley, *Thirteenth Amendment*, 6; the quotation derived from Douglass's speech "West India Emancipation," delivered August 1, 1880, which is published in Douglass, *Life and Times*, 601–18, quotation at 608. See also American Freedman's Union Commission, *Results of Emancipation*, 5. More generally, see Quarles, *Negro in the Civil War*; and Quarles, *Lincoln and the Negro*.

11. Wesley, *Thirteenth Amendment*, 5–6.

12. Blight, *Race and Reunion*, 347–54; Hahn, *Nation without Borders*, 485–97.

13. Wilson, *History of the Antislavery Measures*, 147.

14. "A Call to Action," *Christian Recorder*, Oct. 4, 1862, 157. Note that while many black observers were willing to praise Lincoln for issuing the Emancipation Proclamation, some faulted him for doing so "as a 'war measure' for the salvation of the country" rather than as a matter of justice to the enslaved. See "Emancipation Proclamation," *Christian Recorder*, Mar. 14, 1863, 42. Every study of Lincoln treats emancipation, but for especially insightful observations, see Quarles, *Lincoln and the Negro*, 125–52; Franklin, *Emancipation Proclamation*; Peterson, *Lincoln in American*

Memory; McPherson, *Battle Cry of Freedom*; Guelzo, *Lincoln's Emancipation Proclamation*; Wilson, *Lincoln's Sword*, 105–42; Holzer, Medford, and Williams, *Emancipation Proclamation*; Masur, *Lincoln's Hundred Days*; Foner, *Fiery Trial*; Medford, *Lincoln and Emancipation*.

15. Garnet, *Memorial Discourse*; "The World Moves," *Christian Recorder*, Feb. 18, 1865, 26.

16. Butler, *Autobiography and Personal Reminiscences of Major-General Benj. F. Butler*, 256–64, quotation at 260.

17. Sherman to John A. Spooner, July 30, 1864, in *Freedom: Black Military Experience*, 111.

18. Henderson, *Speech of Hon. J. B. Henderson, of Mo., on the Confiscation of Property*, 14.

19. General Orders, No. 7, Headquarters Ullman's Brigade, June 10, 1863, in *Freedom: Black Military Experience*, 413–14. See also Fields, "Who Freed the Slaves?"

20. AFIC, "Final Report," 91. Secretary of War Edwin M. Stanton created the AFIC early in 1863 to study the conditions of the freed people in Union-occupied areas and offer recommendations to the Lincoln administration regarding emancipation policy.

21. See General Orders, No. 116, Department of the Gulf, Dec. 24, 1862, in *Freedom: Destruction of Slavery*, 236–38.

22. Washington, "Memorys of the Past," in Blight, *Slave No More*, 186.

23. Washington, 237; *Anglo-African*, Jan. 28, 1865.

24. *National Celebration of Union Victories*, 67.

25. Botts to Fry, Jan. 22, 1864, Abraham Lincoln Papers, LC.

26. The full title of Du Bois's work is *Black Reconstruction in America: An Essay toward a History of the Part Which Black Folk Played in the Attempt to Reconstruct Democracy in America, 1860–1880*. For his case regarding the impact of the general strike and black military service, see 55–127. Woodson's works include *The Education of the Negro Prior to 1861* (1915), *A Century of Negro Migration* (1918), *The Negro in Our History* (1922), *The Mind of the Negro as Reflected in Letters Written during the Crisis: 1800–1860* (1926), and (with Charles H. Wesley) *The Story of the Negro Retold* (1935). Taylor's monographs studied Reconstruction in three former Confederate States: *The Negro in the Reconstruction of Virginia* (1926); *The Negro in South Carolina during the Reconstruction* (1924); and *The Negro in Tennessee, 1865–1880* (1941). See also Dunning, *Reconstruction: Political and Economic* (1907); Burgess, *Reconstruction and the Constitution, 1866–1876* (1902). Wesley's other books include *Negro Labor in the United States* (1927) and *The Collapse of the Confederacy* (1937). Incidentally, Du Bois credited Edmund Ruffin—the proslavery ideologue from Virginia whom he described as "white-haired and mad"—with freeing the slaves by pulling the lanyard of the first gun fired at Fort Sumter. *Black Reconstruction*, 55.

27. Franklin, *From Slavery to Freedom*.

28. Quarles, *Negro in the Civil War*, 42–182; Quarles, *Lincoln and the Negro*, esp. 25–52; Franklin, *Emancipation Proclamation*; Peterson, *Lincoln in American Memory*, 348–58, 371–72. Historians of European ancestry, inspired at least in part by the Civil Rights Movement, also contributed revisionist interpretations of the period; see especially Wiley, *Southern Negroes*; Cornish, *Sable Arm*; McPherson, *Negro's Civil*

War; Williamson, *After Slavery*. Scholars such as Herbert Aptheker, Kenneth M. Stampp, and C. Vann Woodward offered antiracist interpretations of slavery and the post-Reconstruction period that challenged the prevailing wisdom about those eras. See especially Aptheker, *American Negro Slave Revolts*; Stampp, *Peculiar Institution*; and Woodward, *Origins of the New South*. During the 1970s, influential revisionist works also included Blassingame, *Slave Community*; Rawick, *From Sundown to Sunup*; Genovese, *Roll, Jordan, Roll*; Gutman, *Black Family in Slavery and Freedom*; and Litwack, *Been in the Storm So Long*.

29. Franklin, *From Slavery to Freedom*, 3rd ed., xii.

30. See *Freedom: Black Military Experience*, xi, xx–xxii, for a summary of the origins of the FSSP. Between 1977 and 1984, I had the pleasure of collaborating with Ira Berlin and Leslie S. Rowland, as well as Barbara J. Fields, Thavolia Glymph, and Steven Hahn, who worked as editors with the FSSP on stints of varying duration. From 1984, when I left for Howard University, through 1993, I continued to collaborate on the volumes in the Civil War series, during which time Steven F. Miller and Julie Saville had also joined the project as editors.

31. *Freedom: A Documentary History of Emancipation, 1861–1867* is divided into series containing one or more volumes. The series numbers, subtitles, and editors of each are as follows: ser. 1, vol. 1, *The Destruction of Slavery* (1985), Berlin, Fields, Glymph, Reidy, and Rowland, eds.; ser. 1, vol. 2, *The Wartime Genesis of Free Labor: The Upper South* (1993), Berlin, Miller, Reidy, and Rowland, eds.; ser. 1, vol. 3, *The Wartime Genesis of Free Labor: The Lower South* (1990), Berlin, Glymph, Miller, Reidy, Rowland, and Saville, eds.; ser. 2, *The Black Military Experience* (1982), Berlin, Reidy, and Rowland, eds.; ser. 3, vol. 1, *Land and Labor, 1865* (2008), Hahn, Miller, O'Donovan, Rodrigue, and Rowland, eds.; and ser. 3, vol. 2, *Land and Labor, 1866–1867* (2013), Hayden, Kaye, Masur, Miller, O'Donovan, Rowland, and West, eds. Related and derivative publications include Berlin, Fields, Miller, Reidy, and Rowland, eds., *Free at Last* (1992); Berlin, Fields, Miller, Reidy, and Rowland, *Slaves No More* (1992); Berlin and Rowland, eds., *Families and Freedom* (1997); Berlin, Reidy, and Rowland, eds., *Freedom's Soldiers* (1998).

32. Fields, "Who Freed the Slaves?"; McPherson, "Who Freed the Slaves?"; Berlin, "Who Freed the Slaves?"; Richards, *Who Freed the Slaves?*; Williams, *I Freed Myself*. Du Bois laid the foundation for this debate by suggesting that enslaved Southerners engaged in a "general strike" against the Confederacy. *Black Reconstruction*, 55–83. Recent elaborations of the concept include Hahn, *Political Worlds*, 55–114; and Roediger, *Seizing Freedom*, 1–65. Although the terms "general strike" and "slave rebellion" offer insight—in no small measure due to their shock value—they also risk oversimplifying the complex challenges that enslaved people faced in the quest to survive and achieve freedom.

33. On contingency, see McPherson, *Battle Cry of Freedom*, 857–58; Ayers, *In the Presence of Mine Enemies*, xix–xx, 275–76; Gallagher, *Union War*, 88–92. Blight's *Race and Reunion* remains the indispensable starting point with respect to Civil War memory.

34. For examples of works by scholars of varying backgrounds who reach differing conclusions, see Davis, *Problem of Slavery in the Age of Emancipation*; Oakes, *Freedom National*; Rael, *Eighty-Eight Years*; and Edwards, *Legal History of the Civil*

War and Reconstruction. Scholars of Lincoln keep finding creative new avenues to explore, as Douglas Wilson and Louis Masur demonstrate with each new work; two other recent studies of the sixteenth president bear special mention: Foner, *Fiery Trial*; and Medford, *Lincoln and Emancipation.*

35. Fields, *Slavery and Freedom on the Middle Ground*; Saville, *Work of Reconstruction*; Kaye, *Joining Places*; O'Donovan, *Becoming Free*; Rodrigue, *Reconstruction in the Cane Fields*; Schwalm, *"A Hard Fight for We"*; Masur, *Example for All the Land*; Kantrowitz, *More Than Freedom.* In the best tradition of Charles Wesley and Armstead L. Robinson, Levine, *Confederate Emancipation* and *Fall of the House of Dixie*, and McCurry, *Confederate Reckoning*, provide important insights into dynamics within the Confederacy. Especially influential are Berlin, *The Long Emancipation*; Hahn, *Nation under Our Feet*; Hahn, *Political Worlds of Slavery and Freedom*; and Glymph, *Out of the House of Bondage.*

36. Fine recent accounts of black soldiers include Ash, *Firebrand of Liberty*; Edgerton, *Thunder at the Gates*; Reid, *African Canadians in Union Blue*; Samito, *Becoming American under Fire*; and Spurgeon, *Soldiers in the Army of Freedom.* The collection of essays on the Fifty-Fourth Massachusetts Volunteer Infantry assembled by Blatt, Brown, and Yacovone in *Hope and Glory* constitutes the gold standard for such works. For a comparative international perspective that spans centuries and continents, see Brown and Morgan, *Arming Slaves.* On the navy, see Ramold, *Slaves, Sailors, Citizens.*

37. Of special note are Holt, *Problem of Freedom*; Scott, *Degrees of Freedom*; Blackburn, *American Crucible*; Scott and Hébrard, *Freedom Papers*; Rothman, *Beyond Freedom's Reach*; Kerr-Ritchie, *Rites of August First*; and Sinha, *Slave's Cause.*

38. Representative works include Ayers, *In the Presence of Mine Enemies*; Ayers, *Thin Light of Freedom*; Phillips, *Rivers Ran Backward*; Brooks, *Captives and Cousins*; Smith, *Freedom's Frontier*; Krauthamer, *Black Slaves, Indian Masters*; and Hahn, *Nation without Borders.*

39. On print culture, see Fahs, *Imagined Civil War*, esp. 150–94; Hager, *Word by Word*; Gardner, *Black Print Unbound*; Gallagher, *Union War*, esp. 93–118; on the imagery of emancipation, Willis and Krauthamer, *Envisioning Emancipation*, is the indispensable starting point; on iconic events, see, for example, Varon, *Appomattox*; and Hodes, *Mourning Lincoln.*

40. Faust, *This Republic of Suffering*; Humphreys, *Intensely Human*; Wells, *Civil War Time*; Sternhell, *Routes of War*; Nelson, *Ruin Nation*; Williams, *They Left Great Marks on Me*; Levy, *Freaks of Fortune.* Although I applaud Jim Downs's effort in *Sick from Freedom* to question conventional assumptions concerning the government's response to the public health crisis that the war and emancipation precipitated among the freed people, I stop short of accepting all the pessimistic conclusions that he draws. See also his essay "Emancipating the Evidence," about working with the records of the Freedmen's Bureau.

41. Berry, *Weirding the War*; Blight and Downs, *Beyond Freedom.* Similarly thought provoking are Link and Broomall, *Rethinking American Emancipation*; and Downs and Masur, *The World the Civil War Made.*

42. See especially Fox-Genovese and Genovese, *Mind of the Master Class*; Johnson, *River of Dark Dreams*; Baptist, *The Half Has Never Been Told*; and Glymph, *Out of the House of Bondage.*

43. A future volume of *Freedom* will explore this topic thoroughly in the context of family and community, but preliminary interpretive insights, as well as representative documents from the records of the National Archives, appear in Berlin and Rowland, *Families and Freedom*.

44. See especially Berlin, *Slaves without Masters*. Davis, *Problem of Slavery in the Age of Emancipation*, stresses the intertwined nature of the free black and the enslaved experiences in a chapter he titles "Free Blacks as the Key to Slave Emancipation" (193–225).

45. Du Bois, *Black Reconstruction*, 580–636. See, for example, LeFloria, *Chained in Silence*; de Jong, *You Can't Eat Freedom*; Sugrue, *Origins of the Urban Crisis*; Alexander, *The New Jim Crow*; and, more generally, Berlin, *Making of African America*, esp. chap. 4.

46. See, for instance, *Freedom: Black Military Experience*, xxiii–xxviii.

47. Franklin titles his analysis of the impact of the Civil Rights Act of 1964, the Voting Rights Act of 1965, and other landmark pieces of federal legislation enacted during Lyndon B. Johnson's presidency as "The Illusion of Equality." Franklin, *From Slavery to Freedom*, 3rd ed., 635–45.

48. United States, *Statutes at Large*, 13:774–75.

Part I

1. Crosby, *Measure of Reality*, 78–79, dates the earliest mechanical clocks to the thirteenth century. For twenty-first-century timekeeping advances, see Hinkley et al., "An Atomic Clock with 10^{-18} Instability."

2. In the 1890s, the New York Standard Watch Company developed a fascinating promotional brochure titled "The Story of My First Watch," which featured the reflections of leading public figures on receiving their first watch. Unlike other contributors, Frederick Douglass explained that he had neither the means nor the opportunity to own a first watch until after he escaped to freedom as a young man. Thereafter, he explained, "no article in my ownership has been more serviceable to me" for purposes of maintaining the "punctuality" on which "my successive life has depended." "The Story of My First Watch," folder 75, box 28-4, Frederick Douglass Collection, MSRC-HU.

3. See Bartlett's *Familiar Quotations* for the varying usages in English. See also Aveni, *Empires of Time*; Cippolo, *Clocks and Culture*; Landes, *Revolution in Time*; and Crosby, *Measure of Reality*. Recent studies, such as Ogle, "Whose Time Is It?," examine the tensions between European colonial administrators, businessmen, and missionaries and various colonial subject populations, focusing on the clashes between standardized time and local time and between concepts of time as a commodity that needed to be employed responsibly—that is, consistently with Christian European values—and traditional notions. As the following chapters illustrate, aspects of that dynamic were at work in areas of the Union-occupied Confederacy. That notwithstanding, Northern representatives of the federal government—including military and government officials and the civilians who hoped to plant the seeds of a viable free-labor economy complete with other trappings of Yankee culture—quickly came to realize that the freed people were fully conversant with clock time and its creative as

well as restrictive possibilities. When Northern employers neglected to pay wages at the agreed-on times, they often fretted over the resulting absenteeism. From the laborers' perspective, however, if time was money, then time would have to be expended where its value could be realized. See also Bartky, *Selling the True Time*; Bartky, *One Time Fits All*; McCrossen, *Marking Modern Times*; Smith, *Mastered by the Clock*; Smith, "Counting Clocks, Owning Time;" Smith, "Old South Time;" and Wells, *Civil War Time*.

4. The popular works by the neuroscientist David Eagleman offer an accessible introduction into how the human brain keeps time. See, for example, Eagleman, *Incognito*; and Eagleman, *Brain*. See also Burdick, *Why Time Flies*; Garfield, *Timekeepers*; Gleick, *Time Travel*.

Chapter 1

1. Scholarship on emancipation during the Civil War era from Du Bois's *Black Reconstruction* to Oakes's *Freedom National* has for the most part employed official actions of the U.S. government, including presidential proclamations, congressional laws, and the directives of administrative and military officials to mark the course of emancipation. Litwack's *Been in the Storm So Long* placed a fresh focus on the experience of the enslaved, which the work of the FSSP (Berlin et al., *Freedom*) advanced further. Blight's *Race and Reunion* added the perspective of how subsequent generations selectively remembered and forgot the lessons of the war. Intriguing recent treatments of distortions produced by the war include Berry's edited collection, *Weirding the War*; Nelson, *Ruin Nation*; and Wells, *Civil War Time*.

2. See especially, for the United States, Zilversmit, *First Emancipation*, and Melish, *Disowning Slavery*; and for the West Indies, Dubois, *Colony of Citizens*; and, particularly, Ferrer, *Freedom's Mirror*, for the intertwined histories of Saint-Domingue and Cuba during the revolutionary period. For overall context, Williams, *Capitalism and Slavery*, James, *Black Jacobins*, Davis, *Problem of Slavery in the Age of Revolution*, and Blackburn, *Overthrow of Colonial Slavery*, remain indispensable. Doyle, *American Civil Wars*, offers valuable insights into the relationship between the U.S. Civil War and contemporary struggles over representative government and the future of slavery in Europe and the Americas.

3. See Davis, *Problem of Slavery in the Age of Revolution*; Davis, *Inhuman Bondage*; Davis, *Problem of Slavery in the Age of Emancipation*; Blackburn, *Making of New World Slavery*; Blackburn, *Overthrow of Colonial Slavery*; Tomich, *Through the Prism of Slavery*; Tomich, *Politics of the Second Slavery*; Drescher, *Abolition*; Johnson, *River of Dark Dreams*; Beckert, *Empire of Cotton*.

4. Medford, *Lincoln and Emancipation*, 61–73, esp. 68–69.

5. First Lieutenant Joseph Nichols of the Nineteenth Maine Volunteer Infantry, who, before the enemy in Virginia, expressed the opinion that the proclamation "was inexpedient and unconstitutional, and, in consequence, could not honorably serve under it," was dishonorably discharged. See General Orders, No. 29, Feb. 4, 1863, in United States War Department, *General Orders of the War Department Embracing the Years 1861, 1862, & 1863*, 2:15–16. Second Lieutenant George D. Wiseburn of the 133rd New York Volunteer Infantry was similarly dismissed for having disparaged the proclamation,

claiming that its provision to receive "all colored persons of good condition . . . into the armed service" made "the negro my equal." General Orders, No. 377, Nov. 21, 1863, in United States War Department, *General Orders of the War Department Embracing the Years 1861, 1862 81863*, 2:645–46. More generally, see Phillips, *Rivers Ran Backward*, 207–35, 248–51, 254–56; Ayers, *Thin Light of Freedom*, 34–40.

6. Cox, *Emancipation and Its Results—Is Ohio to Be Africanized?*, 7.

7. Entries for Dec. 27 and Dec. 30, 1862, Strong, *Diary*, 282, 284, quoted in Wilson, *Lincoln's Sword*, 138.

8. Aptheker, *Documentary History*, 1:476–77.

9. Washington *Evening Star*, Jan. 1, 1863, 2 (second edition), accessed Mar. 20, 2018, http://chroniclingamerica.loc.gov/lccn/sn83045462/1863-01-01/ed-1/seq-2/; Franklin, *Emancipation Proclamation*, 93; Leech, *Reveille in Washington*, 249; Washington, *They Knew Lincoln*, 90–91; "The Watch Meeting," *Pacific Appeal*, Jan. 3, 1863, 2. The quotations from the man who anticipated celebrating freedom at midnight spelled "the" as "de" and "first" as "fust."

10. "Camden Correspondence," *Christian Recorder*, Jan. 10, 1863, 6.

11. *Evening Star*, Jan. 1, 1863, 2, accessed Mar. 12, 2018, http://chroniclingamerica .loc.gov/lccn/sn83045462/1863-01-01/ed-1/seq-2/.

12. Franklin, *Emancipation Proclamation*, 94–95, describes the sequence of events succinctly. See also Guelzo, *Lincoln's Emancipation Proclamation*, chap. 4, esp. 181–86.

13. Notices in the *Evening Star*, Dec. 31, 1862, 2, advised officers of the army and the navy when the president would receive them.

14. Turner, *Negro in Slavery, War and Peace*, reprinted in McPherson, *Negro's Civil War*, 50. Turner recorded similar sentiments at the time; see "Washington Correspondence," *Christian Recorder*, Jan. 10, 1863, 5. Contrast this with his description of President Lincoln's March 1862 message to Congress regarding compensated gradual emancipation, which he described as "one of the most ingenious subterfuges, to pacify the humane and philanthropic hearts of the country, that was ever produced." See "Turner on the President's Message," *Christian Recorder*, Mar. 22, 1862, 46.

15. Douglass, *Life and Times*, 429–30; Aptheker, *Documentary History*, 1:476–77; *Inaugural Ceremonies of the Freedmen's Memorial Monument to Abraham Lincoln*, 21–22. See also Goodheart, *1861*, 218–21. The *Christian Recorder*, Nov. 2, 1861, 171, noted the start of direct telegraphic communication between San Francisco and the East beginning October 25. The full text of the proclamation reached the West Coast by January 3, appearing in the *Daily Alta California* (San Francisco) on January 4, 1863, p. 1 (see the California Digital Newspaper Collection, accessed Feb. 2, 2017, https://cdnc.ucr.edu/cgi-bin/cdnc?a=d&d=DAC18630104.2.8&e=————————-en——20——1——txt-txIN————————1).

16. "Preliminary Emancipation Proclamation," Sept. 22, 1862, in Basler, Pratt, and Dunlap, *Collected Works*, 5:434; "Emancipation Proclamation," Jan. 1, 1863, in Basler, Pratt, and Dunlap, *Collected Works*, 6:29–30; Franklin, *Emancipation Proclamation*; Guelzo, *Lincoln's Emancipation Proclamation*; Wilson, *Lincoln's Sword*; Masur, *Lincoln's Hundred Days*. In March 1862, six months before the preliminary Emancipation Proclamation, Congress authorized a new article of war prohibiting

members of the armed forces from returning black refugees to persons who claimed to be their masters.

17. "Preliminary Emancipation Proclamation," Sept. 22, 1862, in Basler, Pratt, and Dunlap, *Collected Works*, 5:434.

18. Entry for Jan. 1, 1863, in Billington, *Journal of Charlotte Forten*, 171–72.

19. Entry for Jan. 1, 1863, in Billington, *Journal of Charlotte Forten*, 171–72; Higginson, *Army Life in a Black Regiment*, 58–61. See also Franklin, *Emancipation Proclamation*, 118. Toward the end of the proceedings a false rumor spread like wildfire through the assembly that General John C. Frémont had been named general in chief of the army, which both Higginson and Forten promptly discounted as "picket news." Higginson, *Army Life in a Black Regiment*, 61; Billington, *Journal of Charlotte Forten*, 173.

20. Higginson, *Army Life in a Black Regiment*, 60; Billington, *Journal of Charlotte Forten*, 172–73, 175; Rose, *Rehearsal for Reconstruction*, 195–98.

21. In General Orders, No. 1, dated January 2, 1863, the adjutant general of the army, on behalf of the secretary of war, distributed Lincoln's Proclamation. See United States War Department, *General Orders of the War Department Embracing the Years 1861, 1862, & 1863*, 2:1–2. Because Port Royal lacked telegraphic communication with the North, official copies of documents often took a week or longer to reach the headquarters of the Department of the South from Washington via Fort Monroe by sea. Unofficial copies of what appeared in the major metropolitan daily newspapers generally arrived more quickly via commercial steamships as well as army and navy vessels plying between various Northern seaports and Port Royal. On an expedition into Florida that departed Beaufort on January 23, 1863, Thomas Wentworth Higginson reported having received copies of "the President's Proclamation, then just issued," from Massachusetts governor John A. Andrew. Higginson, *Army Life in a Black Regiment*, 64, 71. William B. Gould, an African American sailor aboard USS *Cambridge* off the coast of North Carolina, noted in his diary that an official copy reached the ship March 8, 1863. Gould, *Diary of a Contraband*, 137.

22. Plans for the celebration at Hampton are noted in "Domestic Items," *Christian Recorder*, Jan. 3, 1863, 3. See also Engs, *Freedom's First Generation*, 28. See *Anglo-African*, issues for Jan. 10 and Jan. 17, 1863, for numerous accounts of celebrations of emancipation in cities throughout the North and the Union-occupied regions of the South.

23. John Oliver to Brother Jocelyn, Jan. 14, 1863, in Ripley et al., *Black Abolitionist Papers*, 5:173. An unidentified document compiled by the AFIC confirms Oliver's account, noting that the exemption "produced considerable revulsion of feeling" among certain military officials, including the general commanding the city, no less than the freed people. "Memoranda Made during Expedition to Fortress Monroe, May 1863," Series I, item 177, AFIC Records, Harvard University.

24. See *Freedom: Destruction of Slavery*, 187–243, for details of how slavery unraveled in the thirteen exempt parishes during the eight months preceding the Emancipation Proclamation.

25. See General Orders, No. 116, Department of the Gulf, Dec. 24, 1862, in *Freedom: Destruction of Slavery*, 236–38, quotations at 236 and 237.

26. General Orders, No. 116, Department of the Gulf, Dec. 24, 1862, in *Freedom: Destruction of Slavery*, 236.

27. General Orders, No. 116, Department of the Gulf, Dec. 24, 1862, in *Freedom: Destruction of Slavery*, 236. For Banks's orders regulating labor, see the excerpt from General Orders, No. 12, Headquarters, Department of the Gulf, Jan. 29, 1863, in *Freedom: Wartime Genesis, Lower South*, 414–16; and Circular of the U.S. Sequestration Commission, Feb. 6, 1863, in *Freedom: Wartime Genesis, Lower South*, 419–21.

28. The full text of Banks's General Orders, No. 12, Jan. 29, 1863, includes Lincoln's Emancipation Proclamation. See *Official Records*, ser. 1, vol. 15:666–69.

29. John W. Horner to W. R. Rowley, Feb. 27, 1864, in *Freedom: Destruction of Slavery*, 318–19. See also *Report of the Commissioners of Investigation of Colored Refugees*, 38th Cong., 2d Sess. (1865), S. Exec. Doc. No. 28, at 11.

30. N. B. Lucas to Jno. H. Cochrane, Nov. 10, 1865, in *Freedom: Destruction of Slavery*, 310–11.

31. Lincoln to A. G. Hodges, Apr. 4, 1864, in Basler, Pratt, and Dunlap, *Collected Works*, 7:282.

32. Peter Kolchin characterized emancipation in the United States as "'post-planned' rather than 'pre-planned'" in the sense that it largely "followed rather than preceded emancipation itself." Kolchin, "Emancipation in Comparative Perspective," 15. At no time from the founding of the nation through the Civil War did the legislative process enable a comprehensive, preplanned emancipation. Indeed, the framers designed the process precisely to prevent such an outcome, and, but for secession and war, it is likely that slavery would have survived into the twentieth century.

33. In both congresses, the Senate met in special sessions during the month of March following the biennial elections: the Thirty-Seventh Congress in March 1861 and the Thirty-Eighth Congress in March 1863. The Thirty-Seventh Congress met in three regular sessions. The first session gathered at President Lincoln's behest on July 4, 1861, and met through August 6, 1861; the second session met from December 2, 1861, to July 17, 1862; and the third session met from December 1, 1862, to March 3, 1863. The Thirty-Eighth Congress was more typical of prewar Congresses. It met in two sessions, the first session from December 7, 1863, through July 4, 1864, and the second session from December 5, 1864, through March 3, 1865. State legislatures operated similarly, but often with a single session in which the body conducted all its business.

34. Masur, *Example for All the Land*, 91–97. Henry M. Turner began attending congressional debates soon after moving to Washington in the spring of 1862.

35. Wilson, *History of the Antislavery Measures, 1864*. As both contemporary and later commentators have noted, the record of accomplishments of these two bodies was remarkable. What is more, several key pieces of legislation regarding slavery drew extended—not to mention heated—debate, being approved and forwarded to the president for signature only on the last day of the session. In the Thirty-Seventh Congress, the First Confiscation Act fit this description, winning approval only on the last day of the first session; the same is true of the Second Confiscation Act and the Militia Act, which were also passed on the last day of the second session. In the Thirty-Eighth Congress, the president signed the Freedmen's Bureau Bill and the joint resolution declaring the enslaved wives and children of black soldiers free on the last day of its second session, March 3, 1865. See Bogue, *Earnest Men*; Curry, *Blueprint for Modern America*; Bensel, *Yankee Leviathan*.

36. Wilson, *History of the Antislavery Measures, 1864,* v–vi. Chief among the actions whose histories Wilson narrated were the First and Second Confiscation Acts (August 1861 and July 1862); the joint resolution prohibiting the return of fugitive slaves (March 1862); the act abolishing slavery in the District of Columbia (April 1862); the president's offer of aid to any state that would abolish slavery voluntarily (March 1862, endorsed by Congress in April); the prohibition against slavery in the territories (June 1862); the proposed wording for the constitutional amendment abolishing slavery (which the Senate approved in April 1864 and the House approved in January 1865); the repeal of the Fugitive Slave Law (June 1864); the military appropriations bill that equalized the pay of black soldiers with that of their white counterparts (June 1864); the resolution freeing the families of black soldiers (March 1865); and the Freedmen's Bureau Act (March 1865). Wilson published an updated edition in 1865, which reprinted the first edition with updates regarding the Freedmen's Bureau Act and the Thirteenth Amendment, whose legislative histories continued into 1865. The usefulness of such time lines of key events in the emancipation process is revealed by the inclusion of one in the War Department's *Official Records.* See *Official Records,* ser. 2, vol. 1:749–50. See also Richards, *Who Freed the Slaves?,* appendix A; and "Chronology of Emancipation during the Civil War," Freedmen and Southern Society Project, accessed Mar. 1, 2018, http://www.freedmen.umd.edu/chronol.htm.

37. One source attributed the use of "contraband" in Butler's sense to the chief quartermaster at the fort, Captain Greer Tallmadge, who had served in the army since his graduation from West Point in 1848. In reporting Tallmadge's death in October 1862, Tenney, *Military and Naval History of the Rebellion,* 740, noted: "The 'contraband' idea put in practice by Gen. Butler, originated with him." On the term "contraband," see Masur, "Rare Phenomenon of Philological Vegetation." On wartime confiscation generally, see Witt, *Lincoln's Code.*

38. While I do not disagree with James Oakes's assessment of the importance of Secretary Cameron's August 8, 1861, approval of Butler's decision to offer military protection and material aid to the families of the working men he employed, his view runs the risk of adding that date to the already crowded field of official milestones in the history of emancipation. As I argue throughout this book, understanding emancipation as a linear succession of official actions obscures more than it illuminates. Oakes, *Freedom National,* 106–44. Cameron's letter to Butler appears in *Official Records,* ser. 2, vol. 1:761–62; the secretary was responding to Butler's letter of July 30, 1861, for which see [Peterson & Brothers], *Life and Public Services of Major-General Butler,* 58–61.

39. Cong. Globe, 37th Cong., 1st Sess. 32 (1861).

40. Cong. Globe, 37th Cong., 1st Sess. 120 (1861).

41. Cong. Globe, 37th Cong., 1st Sess. 218 (1861).

42. Witt, *Lincoln's Code,* 70–72.

43. Cong. Globe, 37th Cong., 1st Sess. 218–19 (1861).

44. Cong. Globe, 37th Cong., 1st Sess. 191 (1861).

45. Cong. Globe, 37th Cong., 1st Sess. 219 (1861).

46. Cong. Globe, 37th Cong., 1st Sess. 219 (1861).

47. Cong. Globe, 37th Cong., 1st Sess. 409 (1861).

48. Cong. Globe, 37th Cong., 1st Sess. 410 (1861).

49. Cong. Globe, 37th Cong., 1st Sess. 412 (1861).

50. Cong. Globe, 37th Cong., 1st Sess. 414 (1861).

51. Cong. Globe, 37th Cong., 1st Sess. 427 (1861).

52. Cong. Globe, 37th Cong., 1st Sess. 434 (1861); United States, *Statutes at Large*, 12:319.

53. "District of Columbia," *Christian Recorder*, Dec. 14, 1861, 194.

54. Brasher, *Peninsula Campaign and the Necessity of Emancipation*, argues convincingly that military intelligence furnished by enslaved people helped federal policy makers understand the value of antislavery legislation. See, for instance, 117–18, 151–56, 178–79.

55. United States, *Statutes at Large*, 12:589–92 (Confiscation Act), 597–600 (Militia Act). The new Confiscation Act declared treason a capital crime that merited forfeiture of all property, including slaves. It also declared the property of specified Confederate officials and officeholders—including their slaves—subject to confiscation. Slaves of any owner who gave "aid or comfort" to the rebellion who came under the control of the United States would be "deemed captives of war" and declared "forever free of their servitude, and not again held as slaves." The act also reiterated the provisions of the March article of war prohibiting members of the armed forces "to decide on the validity of the claim of any person to the service or labor of any other person, or surrender up any such person to the claimant." The act authorized the president "to employ as many persons of African descent as he may deem necessary and proper for the suppression of this rebellion" and granted him the discretion to "organize and use them in such manner as he may judge best for the public welfare." Finally, in deference to President Lincoln's obsession with colonization, the act also provided "for the transportation, colonization, and settlement, in some tropical country beyond the limits of the United States" such persons freed by the act "as may be willing to emigrate."

56. Siddali, *From Property to Person*, 245–47, 249–50.

57. James H. Gooding to Abraham Lincoln, Sept. 28, 1863, in *Freedom: Black Military Experience*, 386. See also Masur, "Rare Phenomenon of Philological Vegetation"; Reidy, "Black Men in Navy Blue," 156–57; Valuska, *African American in the Union Navy*; Ramold, *Slaves, Sailors, Citizens*; Bennett, *Union Jacks*; McPherson, *War on the Waters*; Tomblin, *Bluejackets and Contrabands*.

58. Good recent overviews of these matters may be found in the following works: for Canada West, in Reid, *African Canadians in Union Blue*, 11–36; for New England, in Kantrowitz, *More Than Freedom*, 13–262; and, for the midwestern United States, in Phillips, *Rivers Ran Backward*, 15–77. For an intriguing contemporary perspective on Canada, about which more will be said below, see Howe, *Refugees from Slavery*.

59. See especially Rael, *Black Identity and Black Protest*; and Gardner, *Black Print Unbound*.

60. On freedom narratives generally, see Andrews, *To Tell a Free Story*; Gates, *Classic Slave Narratives*; Lovejoy, "'Freedom Narratives,'" 91–107. On Douglass, see especially his *Narrative* (1845) and *My Bondage and My Freedom* (1855); Foner, *Life and Writings of Frederick Douglass*; and Blassingame et al., *Frederick Douglass Papers*. Essential secondary accounts of Douglass include Martin, *Mind of Frederick Douglass*; Blight, *Frederick Douglass' Civil War*; Stauffer, *Giants*; and Oakes, *The Radical and the Republican*.

61. In August 1861, Turner encouraged the AME Church to take interest in the "untrodden fields of Africa, and Hayti, in which we may one day ramble." "Letter from Baltimore," *Christian Recorder*, Aug. 31, 1861, 134. Although he opposed forced emigration, he applauded Liberian emigrants' pursuit of "freedom and independence" and even credited the American Colonization Society with enabling "many poor oppressed slaves" to escape "the ignominious chains of slavery." Freedom, he concluded, was "preferable to slavery, though it be achieved at the risk of hell itself." *Christian Recorder*, Dec. 14, 1861, 194. On Turner's pastoral work in Baltimore, see *Christian Recorder*, Aug. 10, 1861, 122.

62. "Letter from Hayti," *Christian Recorder*, Apr. 13, 1861, 54. The *Anglo-African* was closely affiliated with the African Civilization Society, which the Reverend Henry Highland Garnet and others founded in Brooklyn in 1858 to promote interest in and emigration to Africa and various locations in the Americas, including Haiti. On the *Recorder* during this period, see Gardner, *Black Print Unbound*, esp. 40–50.

63. "Letter from Washington," *Christian Recorder*, May 4, 1861, 66.

64. "War! War!! War!!!," editorial, *Christian Recorder*, Apr. 20, 1861, 58.

65. For examples of his initial standoffish editorials, see *Christian Recorder*, Apr. 13, 1861, 51; Apr. 20, 1861, 58; Apr. 27, 1861, 62. Although he published correspondence that represented a broad range of opinions on national affairs, Weaver commented infrequently and, when he did so, with a skeptical view of the government's intentions regarding slavery. Only in late March 1862, after Lincoln's message to Congress proposing to encourage the states to adopt gradual abolition, did the editor begin to soften, noting "this is the first time that we have said anything about the matter" and promising more in the future. See "Emancipation and Its Opposition," *Christian Recorder*, Mar. 29, 1862, 50. See also Gardner, *Black Print Unbound*, esp. 41–52, 61–73.

66. Marrs, *Life and History*, 17.

67. Ben. R. Johnson to the Editor, *Christian Recorder*, Jan. 16, 1864, 9. Also see Redkey, *Grand Army of Black Men*, 277.

68. "Army Correspondence. By Chaplain Turner," *Christian Recorder*, Dec. 17, 1864, 201.

69. T. W. Sherman to L. Thomas, Dec. 15, 1861, in *Official Records*, ser. 1, vol. 6:205; "Letter from Rev. H. M. Turner," *Christian Recorder*, Nov. 30, 1861, 186.

70. *New York Tribune*, Mar. 7, 1862, 4; Mar. 8, 1862, 4.

71. "Turner on the President's Message," *Christian Recorder*, Mar. 22, 1862, 46.

72. Letter from Cerebus, *Christian Recorder*, Aug. 9, 1862, 125; for similar observations, see *Harper's Magazine*, Dec. 12, 1863, 796.

73. "Letter from Washington," *Christian Recorder*, July 5 and 19, 1862, 105, 113.

74. "Washington Correspondence," *Christian Recorder*, Aug. 30, 1862, 137–38; unattributed commentary on President Lincoln's meeting with black ministers, Sept. 20, 1862, 149. See Masur, *Example for All the Land*, 13–16; and Masur, "African American Delegation to Abraham Lincoln."

75. Wilson, *History of the Antislavery Measures*, 66; Elizabeth Blair Lee to Phil [her husband], Apr. 18, 1862, in Laas, *Wartime Washington*, 131, quotes Lovejoy. Elizabeth Blair Lee was the sister of Frank and Montgomery Blair.

76. Wilson, *History of the Antislavery Measures*, 43–44, 47, 54, 55.

77. "Sketches from Washington," *Christian Recorder*, Apr. 26, 1862, 65. Slaveholders' "vaulting ambition" killed slavery in Washington, noted the *Recorder's* editor. Emancipation would have been unthinkable had they "submitted quietly to lawful authority." "Freedom in the National Capital," editorial, *Christian Recorder*, Apr. 26, 1862, 65.

78. "Washington Correspondence" and "A Call to Action," *Christian Recorder*, Oct. 4, 1862, 157. Following Turner's call to action, Jabez P. Campbell, an AME minister in Philadelphia and, like Turner, later a distinguished bishop in the church, reported the results of a survey of Washington's contraband camps that he conducted along with J. T. Costin, a prominent local leader. *Christian Recorder*, Nov. 1, 1862, 173. In November, Turner reaffirmed his confidence in the president, predicting that "Abraham Lincoln will yet write his name upon the pages of History, so indelibly, that time's indefatigable cycles shall never be able to efface it." "Washington Correspondence," *Christian Recorder*, Nov. 22, 1862, 186.

79. "Special Correspondence," *Christian Recorder*, Oct. 18, 1862, 166. Although signed "Africanus," the letter displays Turner's effusive style in every sentence.

80. "Our Washington Correspondent," *Christian Recorder*, Nov. 1, 1862, 174.

81. "The Plagues of this Country," *Christian Recorder*, July 12, 1862, 109.

82. McWhiney and Jamieson, *Attack and Die*, 3–24; Rable, *Fredericksburg! Fredericksburg!*, 218–36; and, more generally, Hess, *Civil War Infantry Tactics*.

83. "Washington Correspondence," *Christian Recorder*, Dec. 27, 1862, 205. Similarly conflicting reports had followed the first Battle at Bull Run (see "Victory and Defeat," *Christian Recorder*, Aug. 3, 1861, 118) and, indeed, every major action of the war. Turner returned again and again to this theme of reversals as part of God's plan, aimed both to cleanse the nation and to prompt its citizens to "rely upon him and the resources of our own actions" to ensure freedom to the slaves. See "Washington Correspondence," *Christian Recorder*, Jan. 24, 1863, 13.

84. H. M. Turner to E. M. Stanton, Aug. 24, 1863, and S. P. Chase and O. Lovejoy to E. M. Stanton, Sept. 4, 1863, filed with T-18 1863, Letters Received, ser. 360, Colored Troops Division, Records of the Adjutant General's Office, RG 94, National Archives [FSSP file No. B-44]. Turner had also written to Stanton on August 1, 1863, asking if the secretary "would greatly relieve me, by informing me ONCE FOR ALL whether it is the intention of the government to have colored chaplains or not." Filed with T-18 1863, Letters Received, ser. 360, Colored Troops Division, Records of the Adjutant General's Office, RG 94, National Archives.

85. See Levy, *Freaks of Fortune*; Faust, *This Republic of Suffering*; Skocpol, *Protecting Soldiers and Mothers*.

86. General Orders, No. 100, War Department, Adjutant General's Office, Apr. 24, 1863, "Instructions for the Government of Armies of the United States in the Field," in *Official Records*, ser. 3, vol. 3:148–64. As early as August 1862, Confederate authorities declared persons engaged in arming slaves for military service against their masters as felons, subject to execution upon capture by Confederate forces. (See General Orders, No. 60, Adjutant and Inspector General's Office, Aug. 21, 1862, in *Official Records*, ser. 2, vol. 4:857.) In mid-November 1862, President Jefferson Davis approved the execution of a black Union soldier who was one of six men taken by Confederate forces "with arms in hand against their masters and wearing the abolition uniform." Secretary of War James A. Seddon communicated the president's approval "that the

negro be executed as an example." (H. W. Mercer to Brigadier General Jordan, Nov. 14, 1862, with endorsement by J.A.S., in *Official Records*, ser. 2, vol. 4:945–46.) Before the end of the year, in the context of declaring that Union general Benjamin F. Butler "be no longer considered or treated simply as a public enemy of the Confederate States of America but as an outlaw and common enemy of mankind" for committing "hostilities" in his administration of affairs in Louisiana that bear "no resemblance to such warfare as is alone permissible by the rules of international law or the usages of civilization" but instead consists of "repeated atrocities and outrages," which, among other things, have excited "the African slaves ... to insurrection" and to "servile war—a war in its nature far exceeding in horrors the most merciless atrocities of the savages," Davis ordered that black captives be turned over to "the executive authorities of the respective States to which they belong" for disposition under relevant state laws. (General Orders, No. 111, Adjutant and Inspector General's Office, Dec. 24, 1862, in *Official Records*, ser. 2, vol. 5:795–97.) On May 1, 1863, the Confederate Congress passed a joint resolution requiring the transfer of black prisoners to state authorities. (Joint Resolution of the Confederate Congress, May 1, 1863, in *Official Records*, ser. 2, vol. 5:940–41.) For a thorough treatment of these conventions and their broader influence, see Witt, *Lincoln's Code*.

87. General Orders, No. 252, War Department, Adjutant General's Office, July 31, 1863, in *Freedom: Black Military Experience*, 583.

88. Hannah Johnson to Hon. Mr. Lincoln, July 31, 1863, in *Freedom: Black Military Experience*, 582. In November 1862, Attorney General Edward Bates responded to an inquiry by Secretary of the Treasury Salmon P. Chase regarding the citizenship of a freeborn African American ship's captain. Bates declared that a free man of color, "if born in the United States ... is a citizen of the United States." See *Opinion of Attorney General Bates on Citizenship*, 26–27. Bates pointedly offered no opinion on the citizenship of persons born as slaves. *Opinion of Attorney General Bates on Citizenship*, 14. Black Northerners quickly seized on his opinion as the basis for assaulting discriminatory laws in the various Northern states. See *Proceedings of the National Convention of Colored Men ... 1864*, 15; "National Equal Rights League," *Christian Recorder*, Dec. 10, 1864, 198.

89. Notwithstanding the Confederate congressional resolution requiring black prisoners to be remanded to state authorities, military officers continued to dispose of the prisoners as they saw fit, selling them into slavery, retaining them to work as laborers, and even summarily executing them, as the notorious massacre at Fort Pillow, Tennessee, in April 1864 illustrated. See Elias Shull to G. G. Adam, Aug. 14, 1864, in *Freedom: Black Military Experience*, 592–93, for the case of two men from the Fifty-Ninth U.S. Colored Infantry who were captured by Confederate cavalry, then sold into slavery in Mississippi, and not released until late July 1865. In the summer of 1864, General Benjamin Butler created a stir over the use of captured black soldiers in building Confederate fortifications, subjecting them to federal fire. Butler retaliated by placing Confederate prisoners at work on the Dutch Gap Canal below Richmond, where they, too, became subject to hostile fire. The Confederate secretary of war instructed General Robert E. Lee to appeal to his counterpart, General Ulysses S. Grant, to overrule Butler's use of Confederate prisoners in this way. See James A. Seddon to R. E. Lee, Oct. 15, 1864, in *Official Records*, ser. 2, vol. 7:990–91. For additional treatment of

this incident, see *Official Records*, ser. 2, vol. 7:1010–12, 1015–16, 1018–19, 1029–30; and *Freedom: Black Military Experience*, 590–91.

90. United States, *Statutes at Large*, 12:597–600.

91. Wilson, *History of the Antislavery Measures*, 293–312, charts the convoluted debates between January and June 1864 over equalizing black soldiers' pay with that of their white comrades, as first the members of the Senate and then those of the House sparred over the terms and conditions of the equalization and whether retroactive adjustments would be made. Despite the resolution of the matter in law as of June, military paymasters moved at a leisurely pace in making their rounds. The paymaster did not find his way to the Fifty-Fourth Massachusetts Infantry until September 30. See "From Folly Island," *Christian Recorder*, Nov. 12, 1864, 181. See also *Freedom: Black Military Experience*, 369–405; and Redkey, *Grand Army of Black Men*, 229–48, for a sampling of black soldiers' opinions.

92. "Washington Correspondence," *Christian Recorder*, Feb. 14, 1863, 25.

93. General Lorenzo Thomas, adjutant general of the army, laid out the rationale for this plan to the secretary of war on April 1, 1863, after visiting the contraband camp at Cairo, Illinois. Thomas to Edwin M. Stanton, April 1, 1863, in *Freedom: Black Military Experience*, 487–89; see also "The Arming of Negroes," in "Domestic Items," *Christian Recorder*, Apr. 25, 1863, 63.

94. See James C. Beecher to Edward A. Wild, Sept. 13, 1863, in *Freedom: Black Military Experience*, 493–94; Th. J. Morgan to R. D. Mussey, Dec. 6, 1863, in *Freedom: Black Military Experience*, 499–500. Good treatments of this complex subject include Glatthaar, *Forged in Battle*; Wilson, *Campfires of Freedom*; and Samito, *Becoming American under Fire*.

95. See Hollandsworth, *Louisiana Native Guards*, 48–69; Ochs, *Black Patriot and a White Priest*, 132–64; Thompson, *Exiles at Home*, 210–14; Joshi and Reidy, "To Come Forward and Aid," 326–28; Berry, "Negro Troops in Blue and Gray," 165–70; Everett, "Ben Butler and the Louisiana Native Guards," 202–4. The daily press of New Orleans followed the organization of the free black population with great interest, quoting their resolutions to stand ready "together with the other inhabitants of this city, against any enemy who may come and disturb its tranquility" and noting that a mass meeting resulted in the 1,500 men of "the Creole free colored population down town" who "had taken the war question into consideration, and determined to offer their services to Gov. Moore, for home defence." *New Orleans Daily Crescent*, Apr. 22, 27, 1861. See also *New Orleans Daily Picayune*, Apr. 21, 28, 1861; and the *New Orleans Daily True Delta*, Apr. 23, 27, and May 2, 1861; *New York Times*, Nov. 5, 1862.

96. J. Lofficial et al. to Lieutenant Col. Parker, [Nov. 1863], in *Freedom: Black Military Experience*, 159–61.

97. N. P. Banks to L. Thomas, Feb. 12, 1863, in *Freedom: Black Military Experience*, 316.

98. General Orders, No. 40, Headquarters, Department of the Gulf, May 1, 1863, in "Negro in the Military Service," Records of the Adjutant General's Office, RG 94, National Archives. Louisiana was ultimately credited with more than 24,000 black soldiers, nearly 4,000 more than Tennessee and more than 6,000 more than Mississippi, the other two Confederate states with the largest total of black enlistments. See *Freedom: Black Military Experience*, 12.

99. "The Colored Soldiers of Louisiana," *Anglo-African*, July 25, 1863; R. H. Isabelle to Wickham Hoffman, Mar. 1, 1863, in *Freedom: Black Military Experience*, 323. Early in June, Isabelle informed the commander of a black brigade that more than 1,000 "free colored citizens" of New Orleans were prepared to offer their service, asking only that they have "the privilage of selecting their own lines officers or for you to select from our own race such persons as you might find qualified." Isabelle to Brig. Genl. Ullman, June 12, 1863, in *Freedom: Black Military Experience*, 330.

100. See J. B. McPherson et al. to Abraham Lincoln, February 1864, in *Freedom: Black Military Experience*, 356–58. The brigade in question was commanded by General William Birney, the son of abolitionist James G. Birney and an ardent recruiter of black troops. The previous summer, white ruffians who objected to seeing a black man in a U.S. Army officer's uniform assaulted Augusta on a train in Baltimore. Augusta's first-person account of the incident, "The Late Outrage upon Surgeon Augusta, in Baltimore," appeared in the *Christian Recorder*, May 30, 1863, 89. John V. DeGrasse, a Boston native who served with the Thirty-Fifth U.S. Colored Infantry in Wild's African Brigade, was similarly attacked by a group of U.S. naval officers at Plymouth, North Carolina. See Cecelski, *Fire of Freedom*, 90–93; Kantrowitz, *More Than Freedom*, 300–303. And officers in the Fifty-Fourth Massachusetts Volunteers successfully opposed the promotion of the Massachusetts physician Theodore J. Becker from the rank of hospital steward to surgeon. See "Folly Island Correspondence," *Christian Recorder*, Sept. 24, 1864, 153.

101. Emilio, *History of the Fifty-Fourth Regiment*, 194, 268. Two other sergeants in the Fifty-Fourth, Peter Vogelsang and Frank M. Welch, were commissioned and mustered in as officers—despite more backpedaling by the War Department—in May 1865. Sergeants George E. Stephens and Albert D. Thompson were commissioned, but the War Department refused to muster them, so they remained officially noncommissioned officers when the regiment was disbanded. Emilio, 315.

102. J. A. Garfield to E. M. Stanton, Mar. 28, 1865, enclosing John M. Langston to E. M. Stanton, Mar. 20, 1865, in *Freedom: Black Military Experience*, 346–47. When a War Department official replied in mid-May, he simply stated that "recruiting has ceased, and there is no vacancy to which you can be appointed." C. W. Foster to John M. Langston, May 17, 1865, in *Freedom: Black Military Experience*, 347.

103. George E. Smith to Gen. Wise, Jan. 4, 1864, with endorsements (including that of Gen. Edwd. A. Wild, Jan. 14, 1864), case number 3516, Records of General Courts-Martial and Courts of Inquiry of the Navy Department, 1799–1867 (Microfilm Publication M273, roll 122), Records of the Office of the Judge Advocate General (Navy), RG 125, National Archives. Stray punctuation in the original is removed from the quotation.

104. Wm. D. Mayo to Abrham Lincon, Oct. 7, 1864, in *Freedom: Black Military Experience*, 452–54.

105. Testimony of A. G. Bennett in the court-martial case of William Walker, Jan. 11, 1864, in *Freedom: Black Military Experience*, 391–92; statement of William Walker in his court-martial case, Jan. 12, 1864, in *Freedom: Black Military Experience*, 392–93; General Orders, No. 8, H.Q. Dist. of Florida, Feb. 28, 1864, in *Freedom: Black Military Experience*, 394.

106. "Washington Correspondence," *Christian Recorder*, June 13, 1863, 97. By the time the regiment was ready to take the field, the officer corps included men like Cap-

tain James J. Ferree, who in the estimation of J. W. Forney, publisher of the Washington *Daily Chronicle*, had shed his prior "political prejudice against the colored race . . . since the opening of this grand drama" and had reached "the conclusion that if liberty is to be secured to us, permanent and practical liberty, it must be by the aid of the colored races upon this continent." "Washington Correspondence," *Christian Recorder*, Aug. 22, 1863, 137 [misnumbered 133].

107. Jamison, *Autobiography and Work*, 28–31.

Chapter 2

1. "Spring Work," *Christian Recorder*, Apr. 19, 1862, 61.

2. Sternhell, "Bodies in Motion," 15–41.

3. Charlie Aarons, LC, *Born in Slavery*, Alabama Narratives, 1:3. Aarons accompanied his master's son into Confederate service as "his body guard."

4. Ball, *Fifty Years in Chains*, 387–465. See also Troutman, "Grapevine in the Slave Market," 214–15.

5. Ball, *Fifty Years in Chains*, 382.

6. Ball, 387–88.

7. Ball, 392–93, 398–99, 408–9, 416–17, 425–26.

8. Ball, 420.

9. Ball, 426–43.

10. Ball, 441–42.

11. Ball, 443–44.

12. Ball, 450–51, 454, 456, 458.

13. Ball, 447–50, 452, 453.

14. Ball, 464. Ball did not date his return precisely; this date is an approximation based on internal evidence in his narrative. After being captured and returned to slavery in Georgia, Ball engineered another escape, but this time by ship from Savannah rather than overland. On the second journey, he relied on the help of others to achieve his goal.

15. Hughes, *Thirty Years a Slave*, 188.

16. Hughes, 80–90.

17. Hughes, 90–94.

18. Hughes, 125. Kate Stone recounted "the scene of excitement" when a transport stopped at the landing of her mother's plantation and "women, children, and all the servants" headed madly for shelter in a cornfield after having gathered the valuables. Entry for June 25, 1862, in Anderson, *Brokenburn*, 122–23.

19. Hughes, *Thirty Years a Slave*, 131.

20. Hughes, 132.

21. Hughes, 133–36.

22. Hughes, 139–46, quotations at 141, 143, 146. The refugee Gordon, who fled across some forty miles of hostile territory from his owner's plantation on the Atchafalaya River to federal forces at Baton Rouge, "rubbed his body freely" with onions to avoid detection by the hounds he knew would be pursuing him. See *Harper's Weekly*, July 4, 1863, 429. For additional discussion of Gordon's escape, see chapter 3.

23. Hughes, *Thirty Years a Slave*, 172, 175–87, exchange between Matilda's sister and the mistress quoted at 182–83; Medford, *Lincoln and Emancipation*, 76.

24. Tennessee, *Acts and Resolutions*, 1861, 49–50.

25. On this phenomenon generally, see Jordan, *Black Confederates and Afro-Yankees*; Barrow, Segars, and Rosenburg, *Forgotten Confederates*; Rollins, *Black Southerners in Gray*; and Segars and Barrow, *Black Southerners in Confederate Armies*. A number of former Confederate states made pension benefits available to former body servants in the early twentieth century. See Hollandsworth, "Looking for Bob," 295–324. For an account of Marlboro Jones, whose ambrotype image in a Confederate uniform has become one of the centerpieces of the present-day debate over "black Confederates," see MacKethan, "Reading Marlboro Jones," 165–75.

26. Entry for May 26, 1861, in Anderson, *Brokenburn*, 17–18. Uncle Bo "would not take a man for himself," saying that "a private has no business with a body servant"; but Stone noted that "if he changes his mind, a boy can be sent to him at any time." Both William and Uncle Bo served the entire war in Virginia and survived. Two younger brothers of hers, Coleman and Walter, each of whom enlisted separately in 1862, served in Mississippi and died during the war. See also Glymph, *Out of the House of Bondage*, 101–2.

27. Aleckson, *Before the War, and after the Union*, 86–87, quotation at 87.

28. C. C. Washburn to Maj. Gen. Curtis, Aug. 22, 1862, in *Freedom: Wartime Genesis, Lower South*, 660. Army regulations provided for servants to commissioned officers in prescribed numbers according to rank, ranging from one for lieutenants and captains to four for major generals and lieutenant generals. Although not prohibited from employing servants, enlisted men did so at their own expense. See *Revised United States Army Regulations of 1861*, 544–45.

29. Jno. M. Gregory to James A. Seddon, Mar. 7, 1863, in *Freedom: Destruction of Slavery*, 750.

30. These included Richmond, Norfolk, Hatteras Point, Wilmington, Charleston, Port Royal, Savannah, Fernandina, Jacksonville, St. Augustine, Tampa Bay, Pensacola, Mobile, New Orleans, Galveston, Port Hudson, Vicksburg, Memphis, and Nashville. In the spring of 1863, a knowledgeable Virginian estimated that as many as 40,000 men were at work in Confederate camps in that state. Gregory to Seddon, Mar. 7, 1863, in *Freedom: Destruction of Slavery*, 750.

31. Winters, *Civil War in Louisiana*, 34–35, 103–67; Brewer, *Confederate Negro*, 6–14.

32. Jamison, *Autobiography and Work*, 40–41, quotation at 41. Jamison recalled being forced to work on the breastworks in northern Alabama when he was barely a teenager. He "was put to carrying water" when the overseer realized that he "was not strong enough to roll a wheelbarrow up the steep inclined plane."

33. C. B. Cosby to Col. Crump, July 28, 1861, in *Official Records*, ser. 1, vol. 2:1007; J. Bankhead Magruder to S. Cooper, Sept. 20, 1861, enclosing copy of J. Bankhead Magruder's proclamation, Sept. 7, 1861, in *Official Records*, ser. 1, vol. 4:654. See also Brasher, *Peninsula Campaign and the Necessity of Emancipation*, chap. 2 and esp. 29–31; Martinez, *Confederate Slave Impressment*, chap. 1; Brewer, *Confederate Negro*, chaps. 1, 6.

34. C.R.B. to the Gentlemen of Yorktown, July 4, 1861, enclosed in J. Bankhead Magruder to George Deas, July 7, 1861, in *Official Records*, ser. 1, vol. 2:966.

35. Butler to Cameron, July 30, 1861, in [Peterson & Brothers], *Life and Public Services of Major-General Butler*, 59; Magruder to Sir, Aug. 2, 1861, in *Official Records*, ser. 1, vol. 4:570; Ro. Johnston to Cosby, July 27, 1861, *Official Records*, ser. 1, vol. 2:1004; Magruder to Deas, Aug. 9, 1861, in *Official Records*, ser. 1, vol. 2:570–73.

36. John Tyler and Hill Carter to the Secretary of War, Aug. 26, 1861, in *Official Records*, ser. 1, vol. 4:636; L. C. Walker to J. B. Magruder, Aug. 28, 1861, in *Freedom: Destruction of Slavery*, 686–88.

37. See, for instance, L. C. Walker to J. B. Magruder, Aug. 28, 1861, in *Freedom: Destruction of Slavery*, 686–88.

38. Pierce, "Contrabands at Fortress Monroe," 632–34.

39. Sherman to L. Thomas, Dec. 15, 1861, in *Official Records*, ser. 1, vol. 6:205. Before the expedition, War Secretary Cameron sent Sherman copies of his letters of May 30 and August 8 to General Butler at Fort Monroe regarding the disposition of refugees from slavery. "Avail yourself of the services of any persons whether fugitives from labor or not who may offer them to the National Government," Cameron advised Sherman, and assure loyal masters that Congress would resolve the matter of compensation. Employ them in "such services as they may be fitted," with the exception only of bearing arms. The secretary concluded that this solution "will best secure the substantial rights of loyal masters and the benefits to the United States of the services of all disposed to support the Government." Just as important, it avoided "all interference with the social systems or local institutions." Cameron to Sherman, Oct. 14, 1861, in *Official Records*, ser. 2, vol. 1:773. This was the report that prompted Henry M. Turner's criticism of Sherman's callous misrepresentation of the freed people.

40. Reidy, "States of Dependence and Independence," 47. On the Confederate debate over exempting overseers from the draft, see Robinson, *Bitter Fruits of Bondage*, esp. 178–88. For an excellent recent overview of Confederate agriculture, see Hurt, *Agriculture and the Confederacy*; note especially his treatment of Confederate cotton policy, which involved such considerations as the disposition of cotton planters' property (including whether to burn it); the management of enslaved laborers; the civilian and military demand for cotton goods; and cotton as an object of commercial intercourse with the Yankees and as a factor in international finance and diplomacy. After their clear emergence in 1862, these issues remained volatile for the rest of the war (93–99).

41. See, for example, *Southern Cultivator* 20 (July–Aug. 1862): 132. See also Reidy, *From Slavery to Agrarian Capitalism*, 113–18; Gray, *History of Agriculture*, 2:912; Robinson, *Bitter Fruits of Bondage*, 121–28; Hurt, *Agriculture and the Confederacy*, 117–20. Although Du Bois used the term "general strike" to describe enslaved Southerners' demonstration of support for the Union's armed forces, he also notes that "it was a strike on a wide basis against the conditions of work." *Black Reconstruction*, 67.

42. Entry for Jan. 22, 1862, in Anderson, *Brokenburn*, 83. Five months later she noted that the "fortifications at Vicksburg . . . are going up rapidly." Entry for May 11, 1862, in Anderson, 105.

43. Wilson, *History of the Antislavery Measures, 1864*, 28. The subject arose in the course of debate over the joint resolution prohibiting members of the armed forces to assist in the rendition of suspected fugitive slaves.

44. "A Bill [An Act] for the enlistment of cooks in the Army," passed April 21, 1862, in *Official Records*, ser. 4, vol. 1:1079–80. The Confederate Congress created the rendezvous depots for the slaves unlawfully employed on October 13, 1862; the Office of the Adjutant and Inspector General issued General Order 25 to enforce it on March 6, 1863. *Official Records*, ser. 2, vol. 5:844–45.

45. "Circular" distributed by the National Freedmen's Relief Association, *Christian Recorder*, May 24, 1862, 81.

46. Stewart Van Vliet to R. B. Marcy, Aug. 2, 1862, *Official Records*, ser. 1, vol. 11, pt. 1:156–61. Two years later Henry M. Turner, chaplain of the First U.S. Colored Troops then stationed at Harrison's Landing, faulted McClellan for having abandoned "government property" worth in excess of $2 million during the retreat. See "Army Correspondence," *Christian Recorder*, Sept. 24, 1864, 154.

47. Recent scholars estimate McClellan's force to have been in excess of 120,000. See, for example, Weigley, *Great Civil War*, 123. On the Peninsula Campaign more generally, See Weigley, 122–34; and McPherson, *Battle Cry of Freedom*, 423–89.

48. Pearson, *Letters from Port Royal*, 171; E.S.P. [Edward S. Philbrick] to Dear Charles, May 1, 1863, and [C. P. Ware] to Dear Sister, Mar. 10, 1863, Series A: Correspondence, box 109-1, Charles Pickard Ware Papers, MSRC-HU.

49. Jamison, *Autobiography and Work*, 40–41.

50. Testimony of Robert Houston before the American Freedmen's Inquiry Commission, June 6, 1873, in *Freedom: Wartime Genesis, Lower South*, 737–39.

51. T. Williams to R. S. Davis, July 4, 1862, in *Official Records*, ser. 1, vol. 15:26–30; Williams to Davis, July 6, 1862, in *Official Records*, ser. 1, vol. 15:31.

52. Entry for June 29, 1862, in Anderson, *Brokenburn*, 125.

53. Selim E. Woodworth to D. D. Porter, July 1, 1862, in *Freedom: Wartime Genesis, Lower South*, 655–58, quotations at 656–58. For Welles's instructions of September 25, 1861, and April 30, 1862, regarding the enlistment of contrabands as boys, the lowest naval rating, see *Official Records, Navy*, ser. 1, vol. 4:692, and ser. 1, vol. 23:80–81.

54. "Prof. [Richard T.] Greener Lauds General Howard . . . ," undated clipping [probably c. 1906] from the *Chicago Conservator*, folder 117, box 53-3, Oliver Otis Howard Papers, MSRC-HU. For Eaton's account of the early days of addressing the needs of the refugees, see *Grant, Lincoln, and the Freedmen*, 18–45. Also see endorsement of J. S. G. Morton, Nov. 13, 1863, on E. C. Brott to A. A. Genl., Oct. 14, 1863, in *Freedom: Wartime Genesis, Upper South*, 408–10; *Report of the Commissioners of Investigation of Colored Refugees*, 38th Cong., 2d Sess. (1865), S. Exec. Doc. No. 28, esp. 1–20.

55. Rodrigue, *Reconstruction in the Cane Fields*; Messner, *Freedmen and the Ideology of Free Labor*; Ripley, *Slaves and Freedmen*; Roland, *Louisiana Sugar Plantations*. On the Magnolia Plantation incident, see Litwack, *Been in the Storm So Long*, 145, 148–49 (quotation of the owner at 148). Phelps eventually resigned his commission in protest against orders to curb his antislavery zeal. See J. W. Phelps to R. S. Davis, June 16, 1862, in *Freedom: Destruction of Slavery*, 210–16; Phelps to Davis, July 30, 1862, and Phelps to B. F. Butler, Aug. 2, 1862, in *Freedom: Black Military Experience*, 62–65.

56. Statement of Stephen Jordon, in Albert, *House of Bondage*, 114–16. Jordon spent the rest of the war in Texas, returning to New Orleans only after the return of peace.

57. Glatthaar, *Partners in Command*, 163–90, treats the collaboration among Generals Grant and Sherman and Flag Officer Porter in the combined operations against Vicksburg.

58. *Freedom: Wartime Genesis, Upper South*, 408–10. See also Cimprich, *Slavery's End in Tennessee*, esp. chaps. 2, 3, 7, and 8; Ash, *When the Yankees Came*, 149–69.

59. Chas. A. Dana to E. M. Stanton, Apr. 2, 1863, in *Official Records*, ser. 1, vol. 24, pt. 1:70.

60. Frederick E. Prime and C. B. Comstock to T. S. Bowers, Nov. 29, 1863, in *Official Records*, ser. 1, vol. 24, pt. 2:177. The engineers paid the men ten dollars per month "in accordance with law." See also S. R. Tresilian to James H. Wilson, June 1, 1863, in *Official Records*, ser. 1, vol. 24, pt. 2:203–6.

61. P. J. Osterhaus to John A. Rawlins, June 12, 1863, in *Official Records*, ser. 1, vol. 24, pt. 2:222. For black soldiers' experience as military laborers generally, see *Freedom: Black Military Experience*, 483–516.

62. "Prof. [Richard T.] Greener Lauds General Howard . . . ," undated clipping [probably c. 1906] from the *Chicago Conservator*, folder 117, box 53-3, Oliver Otis Howard Papers, MSRC-HU. Greener gave special credit to the woodchoppers who supplied fuel for the gunboats and the transport fleet. "In these woodyards alone," he reported, "3,000 negro men and women were employed—the men as choppers, haulers, the women in loading and unloading the wood on arrival."

63. S. A. Hurlbut to the President of the U. States, Mar. 27, 1863, in *Freedom: Destruction of Slavery*, 304–6.

64. Endorsement by Edwin M. Stanton, Apr. 16, 1863, on Hurlbut to the President of the U. States, Mar. 27, 1863, in *Freedom: Destruction of Slavery*, 306.

65. Sherman to John A. Rawlins, Jan. 3, 1863, in *Official Records*, ser. 1, vol. 17, pt. 1:607.

66. Samuel H. Lockett to R. W. Memminger, July 26, 1863, and F. M. Cockrell to Memminger, Aug. 1, 1863, in *Official Records*, ser. 1, vol. 24, pt. 2:332, 416.

67. John A. Logan to Colonel Rawlins, July 7, 1863; U. S. Grant to J. B. McPherson, July 7, 1863; Jas. B. McPherson to Lieutenant-General Pemberton, July 7, 1863, in *Official Records*, ser. 1, vol. 24, pt. 3:483–84. In Stier's later recollections of this time, he resented that the "Yankees tuck us by starvation." He also faulted his captors for having placed him in jail until he agreed "to take up arms wid de Nawth." He eventually relented and, by his account, remained in the U.S. Army until 1866, "all the time hopin' that I could slip off an' work my way back home." Testimony of Isaac Stier, LC, *Born in Slavery*, Mississippi Narratives, 9:146–48. See also Glymph, *Out of the House of Bondage*, 101.

68. *Message of the President . . . in Relation to the Freedmen*, 38th Cong., 1st Sess. (1863), S. Exec. Doc. No. 1, serial 1176, 1.

69. *Message of the President . . . in Relation to the Freedmen*, 2. The "gentlemen representing the Freedman's Aid Societies of Boston, New York, Philadelphia, and Cincinnati," who communicated with the president on December 1, 1863, estimated that recent military operations in East Tennessee "had probably, loosed fifty thousand freedmen." The gentlemen likely exaggerated, but at the same time representatives of the Ladies Contraband Society of St. Louis estimated that "at least 100,000" refugees lived at various points along the Mississippi River between St. Louis and Vicksburg, emphasizing that most were the wives and children of soldiers and that

they "were in a suffering condition." Testimony of Ladies Contraband Society before the American Freedmen's Inquiry Commission, [Dec. 2, 1863], in *Freedom: Wartime Genesis, Upper South*, 582.

70. "Our Failures and Their Causes," *Christian Recorder*, Feb. 27, 1864, 33.

71. "Brooklyn Correspondence," *Christian Recorder*, Nov. 26, 1864, 190. Before the election, Cain had berated his black fellow citizens for their apathy regarding the contest, given that the nation was "in the midst of a great revolution—a revolution bearing immediately on their disinthrallment and redemption." "Brooklyn Correspondence," *Christian Recorder*, Sept. 24, 1864, 154. Sherman is quoted in Weigley, *Great Civil War*, 390, from his *Memoirs*, 2:152. See also Glatthaar, *March to the Sea and Beyond*; Rubin, *Through the Heart of Dixie*.

72. "Where a million of people find subsistence," Sherman informed Grant, "my army won't starve." Sherman to Grant, Sept. 20, 1864, in *Official Records*, ser. 1, vol. 39, pt. 2:412.

73. Glatthaar, *March to the Sea and Beyond*, 62–63.

74. Glatthaar, 54–55, 58–59, 64; Drago, "Sherman's March through Georgia," 369–70; and Mohr, *On the Threshold of Freedom*, 94.

75. The estimate of 10,000 comes from Glatthaar, *March to the Sea and Beyond*, 54. On the Yankees' seizure of enslaved people's property, see testimony of Charles Jess, [Mar. 12, 1872], Samuel Elliot, [July 17, 1873], and Nancy Johnson, [Mar. 22, 1873], before the Southern Claims Commission, in *Freedom: Destruction of Slavery*, 143–54; and Penningroth, *Claims of Kinfolk*, 70–76. The Southern Claims Commission was established by Congress in 1871 to provide restitution for Unionists in the former Confederate States whose property had been appropriated by federal forces during the war. Only a fraction of the claims were fully settled.

76. Newspaper clipping captioned "The Freedmen in Georgia," [Feb. 13, 1865], in *Freedom: Wartime Genesis, Lower South*, 331–37.

77. Special Field Orders, No. 15, Jan. 16, 1865, in *Freedom: Wartime Genesis, Lower South*, 338–40.

78. See, for instance, J. Townsend to D. E. Sickles, Jan. 5, 1866, and E. A. Kozlay to M. N. Rice, Jan. 8, 1866, in *Freedom: Land and Labor, 1865*, 490–93. References to the "Georgia refugees" appear in Pearson, *Letters from Port Royal*, 293–96, 306–8, 314.

79. Blackett, *Thomas Morris Chester*, 219–87, quotations at 277–78.

80. McPherson, *Ordeal by Fire*, 471. A knowledgeable engineering officer explained that the pioneer corps attached to each of the seven divisions in the Right Wing of Sherman's army consisted of one hundred white soldiers and seventy black pioneers. O. M. Poe to Sir [Chief Engineer, Military Division of the Mississippi], Dec. 26, 1864, in *Official Records*, ser. 1, vol. 49:59.

81. "Army Correspondence by Chaplain Turner," *Christian Recorder*, Apr. 15, 1865, 57. Mary Boykin Chesnut described them as "destroyers." Entry for May 2, 1865, Chesnut, *Diary from Dixie*, 384.

82. Excerpt of O. O. Howard's remarks to the American Missionary Association in Hartford, Connecticut, *American Missionary* 13, no. 7 (July 1869): 155, which reports the substance of Howard's speech to the American Missionary Association, folder 83, box 53-2, Oliver Otis Howard Papers, MSRC-HU. Glatthaar, *March to the Sea and Beyond*, 54, estimated the number of black refugees from the Carolinas at 7,000.

83. Entry for April 13, 1861, Chesnut, *Diary from Dixie*, 38. See also Litwack, *Been in the Storm So Long*, 4. Litwack also notes the presence of "a 'wait and see' attitude" among slaves who were reluctant "to commit themselves irretrievably to either side" due to the fluctuating military situation (20).

84. Statement of "A Colored man and one of the union Colored friends," [Sept.? 1863], in *Freedom: Black Military Experience*, 153–56.

85. Statement of "A Colored man and one of the union Colored friends."

86. Hughes, *Thirty Years a Slave*, 123, 125–27.

87. Hall, *Samuel Hall, 47 Years a Slave*, 22.

88. Entry for Mar. 24, 1863, in Anderson, *Brokenburn*, 185.

89. Testimony of C. B. Wilder before the American Freedmen's Inquiry Commission, May 9, 1863, in *Freedom: Destruction of Slavery*, 89.

90. James, *Annual Report, 1864*, 3–4.

91. John Eaton Jr. to Jno. A. Rawlins, Apr. 29, 1863, in *Freedom: Wartime Genesis of Free Labor, Lower South*, 684–98, quotations at 686.

92. The three states together accounted for nearly 41,000 black enlistees in the Union Army: Maryland, 8,718; Missouri, 8,344; and Kentucky, 23,703. These figures represented a remarkable percentage of the black men of military age counted in the 1860 federal census: 28 percent in Maryland, 39 percent in Missouri, and a stunning 57 percent in Kentucky. The Border State of Delaware accounted for 954 recruits (25 percent of the military-age men). See *Freedom: Black Military Experience*, 12. The War Department's concession to loyal owners was to pay them the enlistment bounty that otherwise would go to the recruit in lieu of compensation for the value of their property that became free at the moment of enlistment.

93. Wilson, *History of the Antislavery Measures*, 306.

94. Martha to My Dear Husband, Dec. 30, 1863, in *Freedom: Black Military Experience*, 244. See also Burke, *On Slavery's Border*, 268–307.

95. See David Branson to R. B. Irwin, July 7, 1864, with endorsements; and Daniel Ullmann to C. T. Christensen, Oct. 29, 1864, with enclosed tables, in *Freedom: Black Military Experience*, 504–5, 513–14. Steiner, *Medical History of a Civil War Regiment*, provides a sobering account of one of these regiments, the Sixty-Fifth U.S. Colored Infantry. By the time of its discharge, the unit had lost 749 of its men to death from disease (68 percent of its original strength of 1,104) and not a single man to wounds from combat. This was far and away the highest rate of mortality from disease among all Civil War regiments.

96. Bruner, *A Slave's Adventures toward Freedom*, 42–43.

97. Affidavit of Joseph Miller, Nov. 26, 1864, in *Freedom: Black Military Experience*, 269–71.

98. Taylor, "How a Cold Snap in Kentucky Led to Freedom for Thousands," 191–214; Sears, *Camp Nelson, Kentucky*, 135–36, 220–21; Downs, *Sick from Freedom*, 18–21; Manning, *Troubled Refuge*, 147–48.

99. See Saml. R. Curtis to H. W. Halleck, July 31, 1862, in *Official Records*, ser. 1, vol. 13:525. For the wording of the certificates, see General Orders, No. 35, Department of the Missouri, Dec. 24, 1862, in *Freedom: Destruction of Slavery*, 443. Similarly worded passes that permitted the freedmen and their families to pass through federal lines invited trouble rather than protection when they encountered Confederates. See Spe-

cial Orders, No. 1250, Army of the Southwest, Aug. 15, 1862, in *Freedom: Destruction of Slavery*, 292.

100. Gallagher, *Shenandoah Valley Campaign of 1862*, and *Shenandoah Valley Campaign of 1864*; Ayers, *In the Presence of Mine Enemies*, 254–76, and *Thin Light of Freedom*, 244–54. For accounts of this experience from the standpoint of two formerly enslaved men, see Adams, *Narrative of the Life of John Quincy Adams*, 35–37; Washington, "Memorys of the Past," in Blight, *A Slave No More*, 197–212.

101. Ash's *When the Yankees Came*, 76–107, provides a useful schematic framework for understanding the spatial dimensions of the Union army's presence in Tennessee.

102. See especially Rose, *Rehearsal for Reconstruction*; Williamson, *After Slavery*; Saville, *Work of Reconstruction*; Schwalm, "*Hard Fight for We.*"

103. Brasher, *Peninsula Campaign and the Necessity of Emancipation*, esp. 82–85, 92–95.

104. Jamison, *Autobiography and Work*, 28–29. See also testimony of Jasper Battle, LC, *Born in Slavery*, Georgia Narratives, 4, pt. 1: 67; Burton, *Memories of Childhood's Slavery Days*, 9; Rudd and Bond, *The Life of Scott Bond*, 18, 21.

105. Wadley Clemens, LC, *Born in Slavery*, Alabama Narratives, 1:79.

106. Cheney Cross, LC, *Born in Slavery*, Alabama Narratives, 1:99–100.

107. Emilio, *Brave Black Regiment*, 40–44; "Colored Troops, No. 2," *Christian Recorder*, July 11, 1863, 113.

108. *Freedom: Wartime Genesis, Lower South*, 647–48; Samuel Thomas to John Eaton Jr., Mar. 14, 1864, in *Freedom: Wartime Genesis, Lower South*, 812. Jefferson had left the area to assume the presidency of the Confederacy early in 1861. Joseph remained until the spring of 1862, fleeing to the interior after the federal occupation of New Orleans signaled the coming of the Yankees.

109. A. McFarland to Wm. P. Mellen, Mar. 11, 1864, in *Freedom: Wartime Genesis, Lower South*, 795. For an insightful study of an area—namely, southwest Arkansas, which remained largely outside the influence of Union forces until the summer of 1865—see Poe, "Contours of Emancipation," esp. 126–30.

110. General Order No. 3, Headquarters, District of Texas, June 19, 1865, in *Official Records*, ser. 1, vol. 48, pt. 2:929. "This involves an absolute equality of personal rights and rights of property between former masters and slaves," Granger further explained, "and the connection heretofore existing between them becomes that between employer and hired labor." For an insightful general treatment of emancipation celebrations, see Wiggins, *O Freedom!*

111. "Letter from the 39th Regiment U.S.C.T.," *Christian Recorder*, Apr. 1, 1865, 49; see also "Letter from Wilmington," *Christian Recorder*, Mar. 18, 1865, 41.

112. Clement, *Memoirs of Samuel Spottford Clement*, 9–10.

113. Diary entries of May 4, May 18, and July 4, 1865, Chesnut, *Diary from Dixie*, 385, 390, 403.

114. Quoted in Ward, *Slaves' War*, 178–79.

Chapter 3

1. "Colored Troops. No. 2," *Christian Recorder*, July 11, 1863, 113. See also Weiss, "The Horrors of San Domingo," which appeared in serial form in the June, August,

September 1862, and March 1863 issues of the *Atlantic Monthly*. On the impact of the Haitian Revolution in Haiti, see Dubois, *Colony of Citizens*; and in Cuba, Ferrer, *Freedom's Mirror*. More generally, see Davis, *Problem of Slavery in the Age of Revolution*; Blackburn, *Overthrow of Colonial Slavery*; Blackburn, "Haiti, Slavery, and the Age of the Democratic Revolution"; and Genovese, *From Rebellion to Revolution*.

2. "Nature of Struggle agitating Europe," July 20, 1853, Collection of lectures, addresses, articles, by O. O. Howard and others, item 29, folder 84, box 53-2, Oliver Otis Howard Papers, MSRC-HU. Four years earlier, while still at Bowdoin, he explored the same theme in his essay "Are the Countries of Europe Prepared for a Republican Form of Government?" On July 4, 1853, Howard delivered an address to the cadets at the academy in which he urged them to take seriously the mantle of responsibility that was theirs, but at the same time encouraging the "Young Gentlemen" to "rise above" the "strong sectional feelings." Items 26 and 30 in folder 84, box 53-2, Oliver Otis Howard Papers, MSRC-HU. See also Fleche, *Revolution of 1861*, 5, 10, 73, 78, 153–54.

3. "Hope and Despair in These Cowardly Times," Apr. 28, 1861, in Blassingame et al., *Frederick Douglass Papers*, 3:428.

4. Thomas, *Confederacy as a Revolutionary Experience*, 23–42; Fleche, *Revolution of 1861*, esp. chaps. 2, 4, and 6; Freehling, *Road to Disunion*.

5. Fox-Genovese and Genovese, *Mind of the Master Class*.

6. For a good recent overview, see Doyle, *Cause of All Nations*.

7. The California State Convention of Colored Men in October 1865 noted that "the results of the late unfortunate and unsuccessful revolutions of Poland and Hungary to free these countries from the tyranny of Russia and Austria, cause regret and commiseration to every friend of human liberty." Foner and Walker, *Proceedings*, 2:195.

8. Basler, Pratt, and Dunlap, *Collected Works*, 5:48–49; "Policy for Suppressing the Insurrection," *Christian Recorder*, Dec. 14, 1861, 196. For a succinct treatment of Lincoln and emancipation that strikes a nice balance between the contributions of African American actors in the process and those of Lincoln and Congress, see Medford, *Lincoln and Emancipation*. See also Foner, *Fiery Trial*.

9. McClellan to Lincoln, July 7, 1862, Abraham Lincoln Papers, LC, accessed Mar. 20, 2018, https://www.loc.gov/item/mal1685900/.

10. *Anglo-African*, Apr. 20, 1861; McPherson, *Negro's Civil War*, 18.

11. *Douglass' Monthly*, June 1861, reprinted in Blassingame et al., *Frederick Douglass Papers*, 3:428–35; Yacovone, *Freedom's Journey*, 20. Other abolitionists besides Douglass turned the slaveholders' metaphor regarding revolutions back on them. In mid-February 1861, as the Provisional Confederate States Congress was at work in Montgomery, Alabama, Wendell Phillips also observed that "revolutions never go backward." Bartlett, *Familiar Quotations*, 641.

12. Ripley et al., *Black Abolitionist Papers*, 5:61.

13. Testimony of B. F. Butler before the American Freedmen's Inquiry Commission, [May 1, 1863], in *Freedom: Wartime Genesis, Lower South*, 446.

14. Brown, *Immediate Abolition of Slavery*. Brown captioned the speech "Revolutions Never Go Backward." The phrase continued to inspire black Republicans during the unsettling times of Reconstruction. See Harper, *End of Days*, 60.

15. Reprinted under the caption "Negroes in the Halls of Congress," in *Liberator*, Jan. 6, 1865, 1. Masur, *Example for all the Land*, 91–100, succinctly treats the signifi-

cance of black people's gaining access to such "high places" as the White House and the Capitol.

16. Higginson, *Army Life in a Black Regiment*, 47. Rose titled the last chapter of *Rehearsal for Reconstruction* "Revolutions May Go Backward . . ." after Higginson's remark, 378–408.

17. *Record of Action of the Convention held at Poughkeepsie, N.Y., July 15th and 16th, 1863*, 6; Ripley et al., *Black Abolitionist Papers*, 5:225. The black reporter who was a wartime correspondent for the *Philadelphia Press*, Thomas Morris Chester, later employed the term "car of progress" to describe emancipation in Louisiana. Blackett, *Thomas Morris Chester*, 67–68. See also "The Law of Agitation," *Christian Recorder*, Jan. 10, 1863, 5, which noted that "Light and darkness, heaven and hell, are irreconcilable antagonisms that moral chemistry cannot commingle. There is no affinity between liberty and slavery"; and "Our Colored Regiment," *Christian Recorder*, Apr. 18, 1863, 57, to the effect that "the principles involved in the present war for and against the Union, are, Freedom *vs*. Slavery, Right *vs*. Wrong, Light *vs*. Darkness, Truth *vs*. Error, and the immutability of God, against the subtlety and unholy ambition of the Devil . . . we believe that there can be no neutrals in such a contest, but that all must be participants on one side or the other in the common conflict."

18. Sumner, *Indemnity for the Past and Security for the Future*, 16.

19. "Washington Correspondence," *Christian Recorder*, Aug. 22, 1863, 137, describes the presentation of the flag. The Contraband Relief Association, in which Elizabeth Keckly, who served as a seamstress and confidant to Mary Todd Lincoln, figured prominently, commissioned the flag, which was executed by the noted designer of such flags, David Bustill Bowser of Philadelphia. Bowser also made flags for the Third, Sixth, Twelfth, Twenty-Fourth, Forty-Fifth, and 127th U.S. Colored Infantry regiments. See "Photographs Flags by David Bowser," folder 112, box 127-5, ser. D (David Bustill Bowser), Bustill-Bowser-Asbury Family Collection Papers, MSRC-HU. "Our Colored Regiment," *Christian Recorder*, Apr. 18, 1863, 63, also portrays the war in dichotomous terms.

20. Sarah Emery et al. to the Honorable Senate and House of Representatives in Congress Assembled, Dec. 14, 1861, in *Freedom: Destruction of Slavery*, 176. Writing from Vicksburg in early 1864, Union general William T. Sherman traced the origins of the rebellion to secessionists' fears about the future safety of their slave property, "a species of property in opposition to the growing sentiment of the whole civilized world." Sherman to R. M. Sawyer, Jan. 31, 1864, in *Official Records*, ser. 1, vol. 32, pt. 2:280.

21. "Washington Correspondence," *Christian Recorder*, Mar. 14, 1863, 41; "Correspondence," *Christian Recorder*, Sept. 17, 1864, 149; "Progress and Faith," editorial, *Anglo-African*, May 4, 1861; "Brooklyn Correspondence," *Christian Recorder*, Sept. 3, 1864, 142.

22. "Frederick Douglass on the Crisis," *Douglass' Monthly*, June 1861, 473; Goodheart, *1861*, 317. For a succinct treatment of the role of providential reasoning in wartime emancipation, see Newman, "Grammar of Emancipation," 18–22.

23. "Fremont's Proclamation," *Christian Recorder*, Sept. 14, 1861, 144. Henry M. Turner employed the same terminology, opening one of his weekly installments of "Washington Correspondence" with the observation "We are moving on here as fast as the current of events can drift us along." *Christian Recorder*, Aug. 2, 1862, 121.

24. Lincoln to A. G. Hodges, Apr. 4, 1864, in Basler, Pratt, and Dunlap, *Collected Works*, 7:282.

25. Brown, *Immediate Abolition of Slavery*, 6. "W.P.G.," a correspondent to Garrison's *Liberator*, had earlier employed the imagery of "We Are the Revolution" to denounce the critics of General Ambrose Burnside's attempt to silence the anti-Republican rantings of the copperhead Democrat Clement Vallandigham and the Chicago *Times*. *Liberator*, June 12, 1863, 2.

26. Entry for Jan. 1, 1860, in Billington, *Journal of Charlotte L. Forten*, 129. Later in the same entry she marveled at how "the wealth of the ages can be ours" through books. "That we can live, not in this century, this corner of the world, alone, but in every century, and every age, and every clime!" The soldiers at the Dutch Gap Canal are described in "Negro Soldiers in the Dutch Gap Canal," *Anglo-African*, Dec. 31, 1864.

27. "Departure of 'The Seventh' from New York," *Christian Recorder*, Apr. 27, 1861, 61. Emphasis in original.

28. "Serfdom and Slavery," *Christian Recorder*, Sept. 24, 1864, 153.

29. Higginson, *Army Life in a Black Regiment*, 97, 102–3. On Higginson's romanticism, see Kytle, *Romantic Reformers*, 206–52; and Howard N. Meyer's introduction to the reissue of *Army Life in a Black Regiment* (New York: W. W. Norton, 1984), 9–25.

30. Higginson, *Army Life in a Black Regiment*, 83, 200, 114. In June 1863, Colonel Montgomery led the federal expedition to Darien, Georgia, commanding men from the Fifty-Fourth Massachusetts Volunteers as well as men from his own regiment. His order to sack and burn the town drew national notoriety after the place was reduced to ashes. For a positive contemporary account of the raid, see "Colored Troops, No. 2," *Christian Recorder*, July 11, 1863, 113. On hard war, see especially Grimsley, *Hard Hand of War*. See also chapter 2.

31. "Brooklyn Correspondence," *Christian Recorder*, Nov. 7, 1863, 178. Writing as "Junius," Cain also cheered the recent defeat of Spanish troops by "two thousand Dominicans" at Puerto Plata, Santo Domingo, as "just retribution" for Spanish perfidy. "These scenes of oppression will have an end when mankind shall learn righteousness," he concluded.

32. "Drafts of a Bill for Compensated Emancipation in Delaware," Nov. 26, 1861, in Basler, Pratt, and Dunlap, *Collected Works*, 5:29–30. The two drafts of the bill differed mainly regarding their effective dates. In one version, slavery would end on January 1, 1867, with portions of the enslaved population becoming free each year between enactment of the law and the end date of slavery. In the other version, which Lincoln favored, all persons born after enactment of the law would be free, and everyone enslaved at that time would become free at age thirty-five until January 1, 1893, when all remaining enslaved persons would become free. In both versions, the state was authorized to establish a system of apprenticeship until the age of majority for all minors born to unfree mothers. "Drafts of a Bill for Compensated Emancipation in Delaware," Nov. 26, 1861, in Basler, Pratt, and Dunlap, *Collected Works*, 5:30.

33. "Annual Message to Congress," Dec. 3, 1861, 5:35–53, quotation at 48.

34. "Message to Congress," Mar. 6, 1862, in Basler, Pratt, and Dunlap, *Collected Works*, 5:144–46, quotation at 144.

35. *New York Tribune*, Mar. 7, 1862, 4 (two editorials), and Mar. 8, 1862, 4.

36. McPherson, *Negro's Civil War*, 43.

37. "The Proclamation," reprinted in *Christian Recorder*, Oct. 18, 1862, 167. In February 1865, the *Recorder's* editorial captioned "The World Moves" noted the recent address of the prominent clergyman Henry Highland Garnet before Congress. *Christian Recorder*, Feb. 18, 1865, 26. In mid-April 1865, as Northern cities sponsored victory parades to commemorate the Confederate surrender, the exclusion of black participants from an event in Columbus, Ohio, prompted one observer to note that "the world does move, sometimes in a right, sometimes in a wrong direction. When will it move right?" "From our Indiana Corresponding Editor," *Christian Recorder*, Apr. 29, 1865, 65.

38. O. M. Mitchel to Geo. S. Coe, Sept. 28, 1862, in *Freedom: Wartime Genesis, Lower South*, 212–18, quotations at 215 and 217. Richard Hofstadter's famous description of the Emancipation Proclamation as a document with "all the moral grandeur of a bill of lading" combines this impression of emancipation's grandeur with Karl Marx's charge that "all Lincoln's Acts appear like the mean pettifogging conditions which one lawyer puts to his opposing lawyer." See Hofstadter, *American Political Tradition*, 132; Karl Marx to Frederick Engels, Oct. 29, 1862, in Marx and Engels, *Civil War in the United States*, 258. The term "the world moves" or "the world moves on" was common currency during the war. See the editorial "Treason and Copperheadism Overthrown! The Union Saved" in the Cumberland (Md.) *Civilian and Telegraph*, Nov. 17, 1864, 2 (LC, Chronicling America).

39. "From a Soldier in the Army of the Potomac," reprinted in *Civilian and Telegraph*, Feb. 7, 1863, 24.

40. Owen, *Wrong of Slavery*, 125.

41. "Annual Message to Congress," Dec. 1, 1862, in Basler, Pratt, and Dunlap, *Collected Works*, 5:530. For Lincoln's original proposal of compensated emancipation, see "Message to Congress," Mar. 6, 1862, in Basler, Pratt, and Dunlap, *Collected Works*, 5:144–46; for his estimate of the costs and benefits, see Lincoln to James A. McDougall, Mar. 14, 1862, in Basler, Pratt, and Dunlap, *Collected Works*, 5:160–61.

42. Douglas to Dear Sir [Ralph Roberts], Jan. 11, 1863, in Ripley et al., *Black Abolitionist Papers*, 5:169–70. Three days earlier Douglas had written to Frederick Douglass from Colliersville, Tennessee, jubilant that "The slaves are *free!*" and confident that "This war will educate Mr. Lincoln out of his idea of the deportation of the Negro, quite as fast as it has some of his other proslavery ideas with respect to employing them as soldiers." He closed by encouraging Douglass to "finish the crowning work of your life. Go to work at once and raise a Regiment and offer your services to the Government." Douglas to Douglass, Jan. 8, 1863, in Ripley et al., *Black Abolitionist Papers*, 5:166–67.

43. W. T. Sherman to John A. Spooner, July 30, 1864, and R. D. Mussey to [Charles W. Foster?], Aug. 2, 1864, in *Freedom: Black Military Experience*, 110–11.

44. "Letter from Trenton," *Christian Recorder*, Dec. 31, 1864, 209.

45. "Doings of Congress," *Christian Recorder*, Jan. 14, 1865, 6.

46. Ball, *Fifty Years in Chains*, 411, 413, 414.

47. "Journal of Wallace Turnage," in Blight, *Slave No More*, 254.

48. Chesnut, *Diary from Dixie*, 31. For two decades, historians have examined slavery and wartime emancipation through the present-day perspective of posttraumatic

stress, but that approach has not yielded the interpretive dividends that some early practitioners might have predicted. See Dean, *Shook All Over Hell*. More recently, scholars have begun to explore the notion of risk in history. For a pioneering example, see Levy, *Freaks of Fortune*. It remains to be seen how readily such an approach might be applied to other dimensions of human behavior that involve risk, such as a family's decision to flee from slavery and seek the protection of U.S. soldiers.

49. Testimony of Octave Johnson, Feb.[?] 1864, in *Freedom: The Destruction of Slavery*, 217.

50. Jackson, *Story of Mattie J. Jackson*, 9–31, esp. 16, 31.

51. Woodcut images of Gordon appeared in *Harper's Weekly*, July 4, 1863, 429. The original photograph is attributed to Wm. D. McPherson and his assistant, Mr. Oliver, of New Orleans; a carte-de-visite copy bears the mark of Matthew Brady's studio. A photograph captioned "Overseer Artayou Carrier whipped me . . . ," is in Photographic Prints of the John Taylor Album, RG 165, Records of the War Department General and Special Staffs, 1860–1952, National Archives, accessed Mar. 20, 2018, http://research.archives.gov/description/533232. The caption on this copy identifies him as Peter, not Gordon.

52. "The 'Peculiar Institution' Illustrated," *Liberator*, June 12, 1863, 3; "The Scourged Back" (reprinted from the *Independent*), *Liberator*, June 19, 1863, 1 (quotation). See also Abruzzo, *Polemical Pain*, 200–205. The surgeon of the First Alabama, Volunteers, African Descent, similarly noted the marks of whipping and other kinds of physical abuse on the men he examined for military service; see "Barbarity of Slavery," *Anglo-African*, June 27, 1863.

53. See Erina Duganne, "Black Civil War Portraiture in Context," The Mirror of Race, accessed Sept. 9, 2015, http://mirrorofrace.org/blackcivilwar/; Coddington, *African American Faces of the Civil War*, 123–28; and the blog posting by Alice Fahs, plus replies, at "Picturing U.S. History," accessed Sept. 7, 2015, http://picturinghistory.gc.cuny.edu/?p=942. See also Nelson, *Ruin Nation*, 173–74; and Boime, *Art of Exclusion*, 73, 75–76, 115–16 (thanks to Gwendolyn Everett for calling Boime's work to my attention).

54. *Douglass' Monthly*, Aug. 1863, 852. The Rev. Dr. A. L. Stone, a former chaplain in a regiment from Massachusetts that was stationed in New Bern, North Carolina, resorted to the caricature in describing the transformation of "Sambo" from "a squalid, thievish-looking being" into a soldier. Hawkins, *Lunsford Lane*, 248–49.

55. The Metropolitan Museum in New York holds a copy of the photograph reproduced here: http://www.metmuseum.org/art/collection/search/283194 (accessed Mar. 20, 2018). In January 1864, *Harper's Weekly* published an engraving of the group, accompanied by an article describing the fund-raising campaign and offering a description and brief biography of each of the eight subjects. "White and Colored Slaves," *Harper's Weekly*, Jan. 30, 1864, 69, 71. The following summer, a military commission found Hanks guilty of corruption, and he left the service. See *Freedom: Wartime Genesis, Lower South*, 370.

56. For the account of the commanding officer of the Forty-Fourth U.S. Colored Infantry describing the Confederates' mistreatment of the captives, which included stealing their shoes, returning men to slavery, and summarily shooting those who re-

fused to cooperate, see L. Johnson to R. D. Mussey, Oct. 17, 1864, in *Official Records*, ser. 1, vol. 39, pt. 1:717–21, esp. 720–21.

57. Quoted in Coddington, *African American Faces of the Civil War*, 128.

58. Ward, *Slaves' War*, 93.

59. Browning, *Diary*, 2:541. Browning met with Lincoln on Monday, April 14. See Medford, *Lincoln and Emancipation*, 51; Richards, *Who Freed the Slaves?*, 59.

60. Elizabeth Blair Lee's estimate that "about two thousand" enslaved persons were removed from the city at this time appears inflated. Laas, *Wartime Washington*, 130–31, quotation at 130. The bill contained a provision that stipulated evasion of the law by removing its intended beneficiaries from the District was a felony punishable by up to ten years in prison. Kidnapping of freed people continued after April 16, but it does not appear that anyone was ever prosecuted under this provision of the law, despite the fact that officials as well as ordinary citizens, white and black, knew of its occurrence. An enslaved woman, Emily Johnson, was removed from the city two days after the bill took effect. A woman who lived next door and for whom Johnson did washing testified that "after all other servants were free" her owner sent her to Frederick County, Maryland. The commissioners not only took no action against him but also chose not to recommend issuance of the certificate of freedom for which she applied in early January 1863. See Testimony of Margaret Stackpole, Jan. 5, 1863, claim of Emily Johnson, filed Jan. 5, 1862, accessed Mar. 8, 2018, http://civilwardc.org/texts /petitions/cww.00990.html; *Emancipation in the District of Columbia*, 38th Cong., 1st Sess. (1864), H. Exec. Doc. No. 42, serial 1189, at 73.

61. Petition in the claim of Teresa Ann Seffell et al., claim 1085, filed Oct. 7, 1862, accessed Mar. 8, 2018, http://civilwardc.org/texts/petitions/cww.01085.html; *Emancipation in the District of Columbia*, 74. The family—minus the father—returned to the city in September 1862 and became free. See also Winkle, "Mining the Compensated Emancipation Petitions."

62. See, for instance, "The Rights of Colored Men and Women," *Christian Recorder*, Jan. 7, 1865, 1; unsigned letter from Hillsboro, Ohio, *Christian Recorder*, May 16, 1863, 77. See also "Speech of John S. Rock, Esq.," *Christian Recorder*, Feb. 22, 1862, 31; Gasparin, *Uprising of a Great People*, chap. 9.

63. "Dr. Thompson on the Rebellion," reprinted in *Christian Recorder*, Feb. 22, 1862, 30.

64. Hon. B. B. Munford, "The Vindication of the South," reprinted from the *Richmond Times*, Oct. 22, 1899, in *Southern Historical Society Papers* 27 (1899): 78.

65. Rable, *God's Almost Chosen People*. For insights into Frederick Douglass's providential view of the war, see Blight, *Frederick Douglass' Civil War*, 101–21.

66. *Christian Recorder*, Jan. 18, 1862, 11.

67. "Federal Writers' Project: Slave Narrative Project, Vol. 1, Alabama, Aarons-Young," 307, *Born in Slavery: Slave Narratives from the Federal Writers' Project, 1936 to 1938*, Library of Congress. Accessed July 19, 2018, https://www.loc.gov/item/mesn010/.

68. Drumgoold, *A Slave Girl's Story*, 33–34.

69. "Journal of Wallace Turnage," in Blight, *A Slave No More*, 251.

70. "Sketches from Washington," *Christian Recorder*, Apr. 26, 1862, 65. A conference of the African Methodist Episcopal Zion Church that met in Philadelphia in

mid-May noted that "the present national difficulties" were helping to advance "the great interests of justice, humanity, and the Christian religion," to secure "the existence, prosperity, and future glory of the nation," and "to inaugurate a policy looking to the ultimate and inevitable extinction" of slavery. These human events occurred within "the order of an all-wise and inscrutable Providence." "The A. M. E. Zion Conference," *Christian Recorder*, May 17, 1862, 78. Days after signing the emancipation bill, President Lincoln met with AME bishop Daniel Alexander Payne, one of the leading black clergymen in the nation at the time. Payne reportedly assured Lincoln that he "had the prayers of the colored people," and Lincoln, in turn, expressed "his reliance on Divine Providence." "Letter from Washington," *Christian Recorder*, Apr. 26, 1862, 66.

71. Wild to Robert S. Davis, May 12, 1864, in *Freedom: Destruction of Slavery*, 95–97, quotations at 97. Wild was subsequently court-martialed and found guilty, but the departmental commander overturned the conviction. See also Casstevens, *Edward A. Wild and the African Brigade*, 159–60.

72. White recounts the meeting in his "Letter from Richmond," *Christian Recorder*, Apr. 22, 1865, 62. See also Miller, "Garland H. White," 201–18; Hager, *Word by Word*, 184–85. Toombs also served briefly as the Confederate secretary of state and then as a general in the Confederate army and the Georgia state militia. When he returned to civilian life in March 1863, he became a staunch critic of President Jefferson Davis and his policies.

73. Gasparin, *Uprising of a Great People*, 257–58. See also Kolchin, "Emancipation in Comparative Perspective," esp. 7–35; Blackburn, *American Crucible*.

74. "A Great Event. Russia Emancipates Her Serfs," *Douglass' Monthly*, May 1861, 459–60; "Russia and America," *Christian Recorder*, Feb. 22, 1862, 29.

75. The pseudonymous San Franciscan Cosmopolite offered an extended comparison between Russia and the United States in "Serfdom and Slavery," *Christian Recorder*, Sept. 24, 1864, 153. Church gatherings celebrated "the advancement of the principles of liberty and equality" that the world's great emancipations signaled, as abolitionists throughout the world lauded the accomplishments. "Abolition of Slavery in Brazil," *Christian Recorder*, July 27, 1864, 117; "The Genesee Conference—Concluded," *Christian Recorder*, Oct. 4, 1862, 157 (quotation); "Annual Conference, Southern District, A. M. E. Zion Connexions in America," *Christian Recorder*, May 2, 1863, 69. Missouri senator B. Gratz Brown also compared conditions in the slaveholding states to those of Russia and Mexico. Without ignoring the importance of Russia's grant of freedom to the serfs, he speculated on the future of the tillers of the soil if the large landholders continued to control the land "in mortmain." "Deprived of homes, yet granted liberties, what can you hope but three million freedmen will fall under disorderly conditions if you open no avenue to permanent and prosperous settlement?" Brown asked. "The policy of small freeholds must be initiated to enable freedom to maintain itself." *Immediate Abolition of Slavery*, 9.

76. AFIC, "Final Report," 369. Robert Dale Owen, chair and lead author of the commission, reproduced the report virtually verbatim in his *The Wrong of Slavery and the Right of Emancipation*. For this reference, see p. 195.

77. Speech by Frederick Douglass delivered in National Hall, Market Street, on Jan. 14, 1862, *Christian Recorder*, Jan. 18, 1862, 11. Douglass's contemporaries frequently cited Shakespeare's metaphor of rising and sinking tides to similar effect; see,

for instance, "Things Here and There—A Voice from the South-West," *Christian Recorder*, Feb. 27, 1864, 33. Douglass returned to the theme in his famous speech of March 1863, "Men of Color, To Arms!," *Douglass' Monthly*, Mar. 21, 1863, 1.

78. "Our Duty in the Crisis," *Christian Recorder*, May 7, 1864, 73.

79. Quarles, *Negro in the Civil War*, 237–38. Regarding Detroit, see Tenney, *Thrilling Narrative from the Lips of the Sufferers*. The *Christian Recorder*'s local correspondents reported these incidents in 1862 as well as 1863—see "War Mobs," editorial, Aug. 9, 1862, 126; "Brutal Barbarism," Aug. 16, 1862, 129; letter from Aleph, Sept. 20, 1862, 149 (Cincinnati, Hamilton, and Rochester, Ohio; and Albany, Indiana); "Mob Law in Detroit," editorial, Mar. 14, 1863, 42; letter from Lancaster, June 20, 1863, 102 (Washington, D.C.).

80. Several weeks after the carnage, Richard H. Cain, minister of an AME church in Brooklyn and a regular correspondent to the *Christian Recorder*, noted the toll that the riot had taken in terms of churches destroyed and black families left homeless, while also deploring the role of the Irish police in refusing to protect black citizens. "Brooklyn Correspondence," *Christian Recorder*, Aug. 1, 1863, 126. See also "The Late Riots," *Anglo-African*, July 25, 1863, for the account of the factory owner. Schecter, *Devil's Own Work*, 161, 169, reports other cases in which white residents protected their black neighbors. See also Cook, *Armies of the Streets*; Bernstein, *New York City Draft Riots*; Harris, *In the Shadow of Slavery*; Foner, *Reconstruction*.

81. "The Colored People of New York to Their Friends," *Anglo-African*, July 25, 1863.

82. "The Late Riots," *Anglo-African*, July 25, 1863 (the incident in Flushing); "Roman Catholic Sentiment," *Anglo-African*, Aug. 1, 1863 (the bishops). The latter issue also reprinted from the *Catholic Telegraph* "Thoughts for the White Laborer," the message of which was that as long as slavery existed in the South, "you cannot hope to be respected there, because if you are poor your honesty will not protect you from the sneer of the master and the laughter of the slave."

83. Harris, *In the Shadow of Slavery*, 238–39; Newmark, "Face to Face with History," 22–25. A grown son, William P. Powell Jr., who had studied medicine during the family's sojourn in England, served as a contract surgeon and, for a time, as supervising surgeon at the Contraband Hospital in Washington.

84. Wm. P. Powell to Friend Garrison, July 18, 1863, *Liberator*, July 24, 1863, 118. See also Ripley et al., *Black Abolitionist Papers*, 5: 229–32; and Yacovone, *Freedom's Journey*, 73–74. Cook, *Armies of the Streets*, 175, estimates that the black population of New York declined by more than 20 percent between 1860 and 1865, from 12,581 to 9,943 persons.

85. "Brooklyn Correspondence," *Christian Recorder*, Aug. 29, 1863, 138.

86. Danl. Ammen to Saml. F. Du Pont, Jan. 21, 1862, in *Official Records, Navy*, ser. 1, vol. 12:516–17; Confederate accounts of the "January 22–25, 1862 Expedition to Edisto Island, S.C.," in *Official Records*, ser. 1, vol. 6:77–82.

87. Benj. F. Butler to Simon Cameron, July 30, 1861, in [Peterson and Brothers], *Life and Public Services of Major-General Butler*, 59; John B. Magruder to Sir, Aug. 2, 1861, in *Official Records*, ser. 1, vol. 4:570; Ro. Johnston to Cosby, July 27, 1861, in *Official Records*, ser. 1, vol. 2:1004; Magruder to Deas, Aug. 9, 1861, in *Official Records*, ser. 1, vol. 2:570–73. Magruder also impressed black laborers in the spring and summer of 1862 to thwart Union general George B. McClellan's Peninsula Campaign.

88. *Freedom: Destruction of Slavery*, 557–64, 566–79, 591–93.

89. E. Smith to W. H. Seward, Jan. 6, 1863, in *Freedom: Destruction of Slavery*, 565. For good measure, the Irish mayor of Cincinnati impressed black men to work on the fortifications below Covington, using the Irish police to go house to house rounding them up. See "Editorial Correspondence," *Christian Recorder*, Sept. 20, 1862, 150. Some 300 men were shanghaied this way. The incident forced the provost marshal to supersede the authority of the mayor and police to stop "their cruelty toward colored people." Also see Taylor, *Frontiers of Freedom*, chap. 9. In Alexandria, Virginia, contrabands were impressed to work on fortifications in the summer of 1863, when fears abounded that Lee's army might attack the capital. "Washington Correspondence," *Christian Recorder*, June 13, 1863, 97. As Confederate forces moved into Pennsylvania in June, authorities in Baltimore began to impress black men for such work, but the black community countered that move by volunteering, hoping to demonstrate their willingness to defend the city "when she was threatened . . . by the enemies of the American government." See "From Baltimore," *Christian Recorder*, July 4, 1863, 109. The future Medal of Honor recipient Christian A. Fleetwood, who preferred to avoid the impressment dragnet, described his adventures to his father. See Fleetwood to Dear Pap, June 23, 1863, Christian A. Fleetwood Papers in Carter G. Woodson Papers (roll 6), LC.

90. See Ayers, *In the Presence of Mine Enemies*, 323, 396–98, 405–7; and Ayers, *Thin Light of Freedom*, 45–49. Sears, *Gettysburg*, 110–12, estimates that Confederate forces kidnapped several hundred African Americans from Pennsylvania.

91. David D. Porter to Gideon Welles, July 2, 1863, in *Freedom: Wartime Genesis, Lower South*, 712.

92. Testimony of C. B. Wilder, May 9, 1863, in *Freedom: Destruction of Slavery*, 90. Without mentioning Wilder by name, the *Preliminary Report* of the AFIC described the practice whereby soldiers at Suffolk, Virginia, returned refugees for a fee, to which Wilder had referred in his testimony. AFIC, *Preliminary Report*, 18. See also "Report of the Committee on the Judiciary on the Case of William Yokum," 38th Cong., 1st Sess. (1864), H. Rep. No. 118, serial 1207; and testimony of Morris McComb, Dec. 31, 1863, proceedings of general court-martial in the case of William Yokum, in *Freedom: Wartime Genesis, Upper South*, 654–57. Yokum was tried by a military commission and found guilty of delivering a contraband named Morris McComb to an agent representing McComb's master in exchange for a fifty dollar fee. Samuel Sawyer et al. to Maj. Gen. Curtis, Dec. 20, 1862, in *Freedom: Wartime Genesis, Lower South*, 675–76; James Bryan to E. M. Stanton, July 27, 1863, in *Freedom: Wartime Genesis, Lower South*, 715–17; and David D. Porter to L. Thomas, Oct. 21, 1863, in *Freedom: Wartime Genesis, Lower South*, 746–49, all documented similar abuses elsewhere in the Mississippi valley. See also Rothman, *Beyond Freedom's Reach*, 164–68.

93. M. D. Landon to Wm. P. Mellen, May 12, 1864, in *Freedom: Wartime Genesis, Lower South*, 828–29. Landon, a Northern lessee, described the self-defense measures made possible by the collaboration among military authorities, plantation lessees, and plantation laborers. "Fort Landon" on the plantation he leased was "*iron clad*, with 36 stand of arms and one cannon." The Superintendent of Negro Labor in the Department of the Gulf applauded the work of some thirty-odd plantation laborers in repelling rebel attacks on leased plantations in mid-June 1863. See *Freedom: Wartime*

Genesis, Lower South, 459; General Orders, No. 82, Military Division of West Mississippi, Jan. 31, 1864, in *Official Records*, ser. 1, vol. 41, pt. 4:828.

94. See David D. Porter to Gideon Welles, July 2, 1863, in *Freedom: Wartime Genesis, Lower South*, 712–13; L. Thomas to E. M. Stanton, Oct. 15, 1863, in *Freedom: Wartime Genesis, Lower South*, 739–41.

95. Geo. H. Hanks to N. P. Banks, July 12, 1863, in *Freedom: Wartime Genesis, Lower South*, 458–59.

96. Julian P. Bryant to Captain, Oct. 10, 1863, in *Freedom: Wartime Genesis, Lower South*, 734. "Almost nothing has been done to raise the negro to a higher level, or to convince him that our Government is in earnest in its declarations that he is a free man with all a freeman's rights and privileges," Bryant observed. "In this District during the past summer, he has been in a far more servile and pitiable condition than when a slave under his master." Bryant to Captain, 729.

97. Testimony of D. B. Nichols before the American Freedmen's Inquiry Commission, [Apr.? 1863], in *Freedom: Wartime Genesis, Upper South*, 292–93.

98. "A Call to Action," *Christian Recorder*, Oct. 4, 1862, 157.

99. "The African Civilization Society," *Christian Recorder*, Nov. 14, 1863, 182.

100. "Brooklyn Correspondence," *Christian Recorder*, Oct. 17, 1863, 165.

101. "The Rights of Colored Men and Women," *Christian Recorder*, Jan. 7, 1865, 1.

102. Editorial in *Anglo-African*, Sept. 26, 1863, quoted in Ripley et al., *Black Abolitionist Papers*, 5:59.

103. See, for instance, Keckley, *Behind the Scenes*; "Societies in Washington, D.C., for the Benefit of Contrabands," editorial, *Christian Recorder*, Nov. 1, 1862, 174; "Washington Correspondence," *Christian Recorder*, Aug. 22, 1863, 133.

104. "Circular," National Freedmen's Relief Association, *Christian Recorder*, May 24, 1862, 81. For detailed accounts of the work of Julia Wilbur and Harriet Jacobs in ministering to the needs of the freed people in Alexandria, Virginia, see "Diaries of Julia Wilbur, March 1860 to July 1866" (Originals at Haverford College, Quaker and Special Collections, Transcriptions by Volunteers at Alexandria Archaeology), accessed Feb. 8, 2018, https://www.alexandriava.gov/uploadedFiles/historic/info /civilwar/JuliaWilburDiary1860to1866.pdf; and Yellin et al., *Harriet Jacobs Family Papers*, vol. 2.

105. "Condition of the Negroes Who Came into Vicksburg with Sherman's Army, as Described by Mr. N. M. Mann, Agent of the Western Sanitary Commission," [March 1864], accessed Apr. 7, 2015, http://library.duke.edu/digitalcollections /sizes/broadsides_bdsms21226/. Samuel Spottford Clement recounted a similar scene from Virginia. See Clement, *Memoirs of Samuel Spottford Clement*, 9–10, and chapter 2.

106. "Condition of the Negroes Who Came into Vicksburg with Sherman's Army."

107. Pierce to Chase, Feb. 3, 1862, in *Freedom: Wartime Genesis, Lower South*, 137.

108. The FSSP's editors calculated that 474,000 formerly enslaved persons worked directly under federal auspices at war's end. *Freedom: Wartime Genesis, Lower South*, 77–80. As I noted in the Introduction, adding military laborers and persons freed by state action to that count boosts the total to 1.1 million freed people in April 1865. Gerteis, *From Contraband to Freedman*, 193–94, estimated that one million overall lived

within Union lines in the spring of 1865, 240,000 of whom (not counting soldiers) worked under federal supervision. However, the figure of one million included an estimated 770,000 persons in the counties of the Mississippi Valley under Union control north of those under the jurisdiction of the Department of the Gulf, which was headquartered in New Orleans. This high estimate counts all of the enslaved persons that U.S. census takers attributed to those counties in 1860, a large (but ultimately unknowable) number of whom had died, had fled from, or had been refugeed away from the river during the war. More generally, see Litwack, *Been in the Storm So Long*; and, for a succinct recent treatment of the importance of physical mobility in the formerly enslaved people's postwar assertion of freedom, Sternhell, *Routes of War*, esp. 167–79; and Sternhell, "Bodies in Motion," esp. 16–23. Douglass's account is quoted from the Library of Congress Folk History of Slavery collection in Downs, "Force, Freedom, and the Making of Emancipation," 61.

109. Holt, *Problem of Freedom*.

110. Beringer et al., *Why the South Lost*, 366–67; Noll, *Civil War as a Theological Crisis*, 51–94; Rable, *God's Almost Chosen People*, 147–65, 280–86.

111. Beringer et al., *Why the South Lost*, 366–67; Rable, *God's Almost Chosen People*, 280–86; Genovese, *Consuming Fire*, 105.

112. Thomas W. Conway to B. F. Flanders, Nov. 22, 1864, in *Freedom: Wartime Genesis, Lower South*, 559–60; McKaye, *Mastership and Its Fruits*, 21–22.

113. Frank P. Barclay to Nathaniel P. Banks, Feb. 22, 1863, in *Freedom: Wartime Genesis, Lower South*, 426–28. Barclay's reference to the "paternal Government" comes from his report to General Banks of March 5, 1863, in *Freedom: Wartime Genesis, Lower South*, 428.

114. "Letter from Washington," *Christian Recorder*, June 4, 1864, 90.

115. P. R. Cleburne et al. to the Commanding General, the Corps, Division, Brigade, and Regimental Commanders of the Army of the Tennessee, [Jan. 2, 1864], in *Official Records*, ser. 1, vol. 52, pt. 2:586–92, quoted at 590. See also Levine, *Confederate Emancipation*, 2; Rubin, *Shattered Nation*, 102–11; Durden, *Gray and the Black*, 53–67; McCurry, *Confederate Reckoning*, 325–37. Davis passed word down the chain of command to suppress "the memorial" and to refrain from "all discussion and controversy respecting or growing out of it." Durden, *Gray and the Black*, 67.

116. Two acts passed in February 1864, one on the 16th and the other on the 17th, addressed impressment, one revising the act of March 26, 1863, to permit exemptions on farms and plantations that raised grain, and the other specifying the limit of 20,000 men. Confederate States of America, *Public Laws of the Confederate States* 192–93, 235–36.

117. In March 1864, the adjutant and inspector general distributed the act of Congress, approved February 17, 1864, that authorized the impressment of up to 20,000 slaves and stipulated the conditions of their employment. The order fixed the maximum term of service at twelve months. General Orders, No. 32, Adjutant and Inspector General's Office, Mar. 11, 1864, in *Official Records*, ser. 4, vol. 3:207–9; Jefferson Davis, Message to the Senate and House of Representatives of the Confederate States of America, Nov. 7, 1864, in *Official Records*, ser. 4, vol. 3:790–800, esp. 797–99. Davis expressed unequivocal "dissent from those who advise a general levy and arming of the slaves for the duty of soldiers," although within a matter of weeks his

opposition softened. See also Brewer, *Confederate Negro*, 6–12; Spraggins, "Mobilization of Negro Labor," 170, 175–79, 192–93; Robinson, *Bitter Fruits of Bondage*, 106–9; Reidy, *From Slavery to Agrarian Capitalism*, 119–27; and, especially, Martinez, *Confederate Slave Impressment*.

118. Howell Cobb to J. A. Seddon, Jan. 8, 1865, "Documents; Georgia and the Confederacy, 1865," *AHR* 1, no. 1 (Oct. 1895): 97. "The moment you resort to negro soldiers," Cobb added, "your white soldiers will be lost to you." See also Levine, *Confederate Emancipation*, 1–5, which quotes Cleburne at 2. Cleburne suffered a mortal wound in November 1864 at the battle of Franklin, Tennessee, just as President Davis began reconsidering the proposal to arm slaves. See Durden, *Gray and the Black*, esp. 53–63 on Cleburne; McCurry, *Confederate Reckoning*, 325–37; Robinson, *Bitter Fruits of Bondage*, 274–83; Thomas, *Confederacy as a Revolutionary Experience*, 129–32; Wesley, *Collapse of the Confederacy*, 83–91; and Wesley, "The Employment of Negroes as Soldiers," 239–53.

119. For General Orders, No. 14, Adjutant and Inspector General's Office, Richmond, Va., Mar. 23, 1865, which distributed the text of "An Act to Increase the Military Force of the Confederate States," approved Mar. 13, 1865, and prescribed how the act would be implemented, see *Official Records*, ser. 4, vol. 3:1161–62.

120. "Rebel Adulation of the Black Man," *Christian Recorder*, Mar. 18, 1865, 42.

121. See Emilio, *Brave Black Regiment*; Cornish, *Sable Arm*; Quarles, *Negro in the Civil War*, esp. 214–32; Trudeau, *Like Men of War*; Dobak, *Freedom by the Sword*. In October 1862, seven months before Milliken's Bend, the First Kansas Colored Volunteers, organized by Senator James Lane and composed mostly of men who had escaped slavery in Missouri, fought Confederate forces to a draw. See Spurgeon, *Soldiers in the Army of Freedom*, 97.

122. See *First Organization of Colored Troops in the State of New York*. A number of the prominent white New Yorkers who joined forces with the black proponents of enlistment to outmaneuver Governor Horatio Seymour were also instrumental in providing relief to the black community following the riots. When the regiment left for the warfront, a correspondent for the *Christian Recorder* noted the undercurrent of ill will that Irish New Yorkers still expressed toward the regiment and black residents of the city, despite the prominent role their countryman Henry O'Rielly had played in raising the regiment. "Our Washington Correspondent in New York City," *Christian Recorder*, Mar. 12, 1864, 41.

123. J. W. Phelps to R. S. Davis, June 16, 1862, in *Freedom: Destruction of Slavery*, 210–16; J. W. Phelps to R. S. Davis, July 30, 1862, and J. W. Phelps to B. F. Butler, Aug. 2, 1862, in *Freedom: Black Military Experience*, 62–65.

124. Anonymous to "My Dear Friend and x Pre," August 1864, in *Freedom: Black Military Experience*, 501–2. Rowley's letter was filed with another in the same handwriting attributed to him in the correspondence of the War Department's Bureau of Colored Troops. The mortality figures come from the New York State Military Museum and Veterans Research Center, New York State Division of Military and Naval Affairs, accessed Mar. 8, 2018, http://dmna.ny.gov/historic/reghist/civil/other/coloredTroops/coloredTroopsMain.htm.

125. Price Warefield et al. to E. M. Stanton, Feb. 20, 1865, in *Freedom: Black Military Experience*, 459–60.

126. R. Saxton to Edwin M. Stanton, Dec. 30, 1864, in *Freedom: Wartime Genesis, Lower South*, 330. The illustration in Baptist, *Half Has Never Been Told*, 405, is unusual for its depiction of the transformation from slave to soldier not in two panels but in twelve, the last of which shows Columbia by the man's side following his death in battle.

127. Last Public Address, Apr. 11, 1865, in Basler, Pratt, and Dunlap, *Collected Works*, 7:399–405, esp. 403–4. A year earlier, Lincoln had recommended to Louisiana's Unionist governor Michael Hahn that the upcoming constitutional convention might consider granting suffrage to "some of the colored people . . . as, for instance, the very intelligent, and especially those who have fought gallantly in our ranks." Lincoln to Hahn, Mar. 13, 1864, in Basler, Pratt, and Dunlap, *Collected Works*, 7:243.

128. Second Inaugural Address, Mar. 4, 1865, in Basler, Pratt, and Dunlap, *Collected Works*, 7:332–33. By this stage of the contest, others of Lincoln's contemporaries expressed similar sentiments though arguably not as eloquently as he. See, for instance, the preliminary and final reports of the AFIC, written by Robert Dale Owen. "If, then, emancipation be the price of national unity and of peace, and if a people, to be emancipated, must draw the sword in their own cause," he argued, so be it. AFIC, *Preliminary Report*, 38–39. "God is offering to us an opportunity of atoning, in some measure, to the African for our former complicity in his wrongs," he also argued. "For our sake as well as for his, let it not be lost." Owen, *Wrong of Slavery*, 225.

129. "Brooklyn Correspondence," *Christian Recorder*, July 30, 1864, 122.

130. "The Rights of Colored Men and Women," *Christian Recorder*, Jan. 7, 1865, 1.

Part II

1. See especially Essah, *House Divided*; Wagandt, *Mighty Revolution*; Fields, *Slavery and Freedom on the Middle Ground*; Parrish, *Turbulent Partnership*; Arenson, *Great Heart of the Republic*; Burke, *On Slavery's Border*; Astor, *Rebels on the Border*; and Phillips, *Rivers Ran Backward*.

2. Sternhell, *Routes of War*, esp. 94–107; and Sternhell, "Bodies in Motion," 15–41.

3. Jackson, *Story of Mattie J. Jackson*, 11. For context, see Glymph, *Out of the House of Bondage*.

4. See especially *Freedom: Wartime Genesis, Upper South*, 1–82; *Freedom: Land and Labor, 1865*, 1–70.

5. Nelson, *Ruin Nation*, 10–159; and Nelson, "The Pleasures of Civil War Ruins," 36–53.

Chapter 4

1. Kennedy, *Population of the United States in 1860*, 592–95; McPherson, *Ordeal by Fire*, 150–51.

2. Commentators on the phenomenon have properly noted that the more than one million persons who were relocated from east to west in the decades before the Civil War represent more than twice the number of enslaved Africans who were transported to North America via transatlantic trade. See Troutman, "Grapevine in the Slave Market," 205. For a pioneering treatment of the cultural transformation within African American communities that accompanied the migration, see Gutman, *Black*

Family in Slavery and Freedom, esp. pt. 1. For Hammond's boast, see Hammond, *Selections from the Letters and Speeches*, 317, which Beckert, *Empire of Cotton*, 242–45, succinctly contextualizes.

3. Woodman, *King Cotton and His Retainers*; Beckert, *Empire of Cotton*, chaps. 5 and 6; Baptist, *Half Has Never Been Told*, 352–53; Schermerhorn, *Business of Slavery*.

4. "Our Fort Monroe Correspondent," *New York Herald*, May 29, 1861, 1.

5. Pritchett, "Quantitative Estimates of the United States Interregional Slave Trade," 467–68. Of the vast literature on the interregional human trade, see especially Bancroft, *Slave-Trading*; Fogel and Engerman, *Time on the Cross*; Tadman, *Speculators and Slaves*; Johnson, *Soul by Soul*; Berlin, *Making of African America*; Deyle, *Carry Me Back*; and Schermerhorn, *Business of Slavery*. See also Baptist, *Half Has Never Been Told*, 170–71.

6. "Journal of Wallace Turnage," in Blight, *Slave No More*, 245.

7. "Journal of Wallace Turnage," 214–58. On such movement generally, see Sternhell, "Bodies in Motion," esp. 16–23.

8. "Journal of Wallace Turnage," in Blight, ed., *Slave No More*, 231–32.

9. "Journal of Wallace Turnage," 243–45.

10. "Journal of Wallace Turnage," 253, 255–57.

11. Narrative of George Taylor Burns, in Rawick et al., *American Slave*, suppl. ser. 1, vol. 5, Indiana and Ohio Narratives, 29–30, quotation at 29. More generally, see Buchanan, *Black Life on the Mississippi*, esp. 53–80.

12. Washington, "Memorys of the Past," in Blight, *Slave No More*, 185–87.

13. Webb, *History of William Webb*, 13–30, quotation at 18. Other rebels against slavery, including David Walker and Nat Turner, mixed secular messages with religious ones.

14. Higginson, *Army Life in a Black Regiment*, 23.

15. Entries for May 25 and May 26, 1861, in Anderson, *Brokenburn*, 16–18, quotation at 18.

16. Brown and Morgan, *Arming Slaves*.

17. Dawson, "Jefferson Davis and the Confederacy's 'Offensive-Defensive' Strategy," 591–607; Beringer et al., *Why the South Lost*, 47.

18. Bosse, *Civil War Newspaper Maps*; Andrews, *North Reports the Civil War*.

19. See Bosse, *Civil War Newspaper Maps*.

20. The comment from the Philadelphia *Dial*, reprinted in the *National Anti-Slavery Standard*, is quoted in Frankel, "Predicament of Racial Knowledge," 57. On the AFIC's interest in maps, see J. C. Woodruff to Robt. Dale Owen, July 26, 1863, and J. E. Hilgard to Hon. R. D. Owen, July 27, 1863, James Morrison MacKaye Papers, LC. Woodruff was a member of the staff of the army's chief engineer, and Hilgard was the assistant to the chief of the Coast Survey Office.

21. Testimony of J. B. Roudanez before the American Freedmen's Inquiry Commission, Feb. 9, 1864, in *Freedom: Wartime Genesis, Lower South*, 524–25.

22. Kaye, *Joining Places*, 153–207.

23. Marrs, *Life and History*, 9, 17.

24. Bruce, *New Man*, 100.

25. Bruce, 96. Cf. Faulkner, *The Mansion*, 50, where the fictional Mink Snopes tells the warden of Parchman Penitentiary, where he was being held: "I can read reading, but I can't read writing good."

26. "From Washington," *Christian Recorder*, Nov. 7, 1863, 178.

27. Murray, *Proud Shoes*, 116.

28. "Republican Form of Government. By Rev. H. M. Turner," *Christian Recorder*, Oct. 3, 1863, 157.

29. Reproduced in Blight, *Slave No More*, between 162 and 163.

30. Poe, "Contours of Emancipation," esp. 125–26; O'Donovan, *Becoming Free*, esp. 70–109.

31. Hess, *Field Armies and Fortifications*, 42, 113, 131, 171–72.

32. Cimprich, *Slavery's End in Tennessee*, 14–16, briefly treats the mobilization of slaves and freemen in Tennessee during the first year of the war, particularly the impressment of slaves under orders by Confederate generals Gideon J. Pillow and Leonidas Polk to strengthen the fortifications along the Tennessee and Cumberland Rivers. See also Robinson, *Bitter Fruits of Bondage*, 104–12, on the importance of impressed black laborers, enslaved and free, on the forts of "the Upper South frontier," which consisted of "a rough triangle centered in [Nashville,] Tennessee with an apex in central Kentucky and a baseline across the middle of Georgia, Alabama, and Mississippi" and which "protected the Northern gateway to 'The Heartland of the Confederacy,'" the "South's most highly concentrated aggregation of mineral, agricultural, and industrial production; its geographic core; and the transportation lifelines of the Confederacy." Robinson, 104.

33. Nelson, "Confederate Slave Impressment Legislation," 392–410.

34. Martinez, *Confederate Slave Impressment*, 18–131, quotation at 68.

35. *New York Herald*, May 30, 1861.

36. Butler to Scott, May 24, 1861, in *Official Records*, ser. 1, vol. 2:649–50; Pierce, "Contrabands at Fortress Monroe," 627; *New York Herald*, May 29, 1861, 1 (the dispatch was dated May 25). The three men belonged to Colonel Charles King Mallory, a prominent attorney, political figure, state militia commander, and distinguished resident of Hampton. In Pierce's account, the three took advantage "of the terror prevailing among the white inhabitants" around the secession balloting on May 23 and "escaped from their master, skulked during the afternoon, and in the night came to our pickets." Pierce reported that, following Butler's decision to grant them asylum, he put them to work assisting masons who were "constructing a new bakehouse within the fort." Neither Butler nor Pierce made any mention of the men having already worked on Confederate fortifications or of their having reached the fort any other way than by approaching the pickets guarding the bridge linking Point Comfort's causeway to the mainland. Several secondary accounts of the events suggest that the three men fled by boat from the Confederate works under construction at Sewell's Point, across Hampton Roads from Fort Monroe. See Goodheart, *1861*, 297–99; Witt, *Lincoln's Code*, 202. Butler's original report of the incident to General Scott on May 24 (with an addendum on May 25) said nothing to the effect that Baker, Mallory, and Townsend had worked at Sewell's Point. In a follow-up report to General Scott several days later, Butler reported that twelve men had reached Fort Monroe in search of protection after fleeing the batteries at Sewell's Point. See Butler to Lt. Gen. Scott, May 27, 1861, in *Official Records*, ser. 1, vol. 2:52–54, quotation at 53. The first mention Butler made of Baker, Mallory, and Townsend having labored there came in 1892 when he published his recollections of the war. Butler, *Autobiography and Personal Remi-*

niscences, 256–57. In his later retelling, Butler also reported that the three men had come to the fort because Mallory was "making preparation to take all his negroes to Florida" and they did not want "to go away from home." Butler, 256.

37. Quoted in Ball, *Slaves in the Family*, 336. At the time, a family member noted: "Our time of trial is at hand and I do not see what we are to do for our poor Negroes. They will have to take to the Woods when the [Federal] Boats go up the river." Ball, 340–41.

38. Statement of Garrison Frazier, Clipping from the New-York *Daily Tribune*, [Feb. 13, 1865], in *Freedom: Wartime Genesis, Lower South*, 335; statement of Charlotte Brooks in Albert, *House of Bondage*, 55–56; Lane, *Autobiography of Bishop Isaac Lane*, 50–51.

39. Billington, *Journal of Charlotte L. Forten*, 161. General David Hunter coined the term "Fugitive Rebels" to describe the slaveholders who abandoned the coast for the upcountry. See [David Hunter] to Edwin M. Stanton, June 23, 1862, in *Freedom: Black Military Experience*, 51.

40. R. Q. Mallard et al. to Brigadier General Mercer, [Aug. 1, 1862], in *Freedom: Destruction of Slavery*, 795–98, quotations at 797.

41. Proceedings of a general court-martial in the case of George, Robert, Stephen, Peter, & William, Apr. 6–8, 1863, in *Freedom: Destruction of Slavery*, 785–88. The procedural irregularities arising from the fact that the accused were civilians warranted submission to the secretary of war for review, and the record does not indicate clearly if the prescribed execution of the two ringleaders ever occurred.

42. Varon, *Appomattox*, 53, wryly describes McLean as "a man with an exceedingly unlikely story."

43. See Massey, *Refugee Life*, 68–94; Sternhell, *Routes of War*, 140–51.

44. Geo. B. McClellan to Lorenzo Thomas, Aug. 4, 1862, in *Official Records*, ser. 1, vol. 11, pt. 1:8; Brasher, *Peninsula Campaign and the Necessity of Emancipation*.

45. On Ringgold, see Brasher, *Peninsula Campaign and the Necessity of Emancipation*, 72–73, 87–89. More generally, see Tomblin, *Bluejackets and Contrabands*; and King, "Wounds That Bind."

46. O. M. Mitchel to E. M. Stanton, May 4, 1862, in *Official Records*, ser. 1, vol. 10, pt. 2:162.

47. Garland H. White to E. M. Stanton, May 1, 1862, in *Freedom: Black Military Experience*, 82–83; see also Hager, *Word by Word*, 197; Miller, "Garland H. White," 201–18. Ahead of his time, White offered to raise a regiment to protect "the southern forts during the sickly season," but his proposal quickly made its way to the War Department's equivalent of the dead-letter office. White eventually served as chaplain in the Twenty-Eighth U.S. Colored Infantry, a unit that he helped recruit in Indiana. See White to Stanton, May 1, 1862, in *Freedom: Black Military Experience*, 83.

48. Higginson, *Army Life in a Black Regiment*, 62–132, esp. 62–63, 70–71, 77, 82–83 regarding Corporal Robert Sutton.

49. Cecelski, *Fire of Freedom*, 51–57, 62.

50. Entry for Mar. 24, 1863, in Anderson, *Brokenburn*, 185.

51. Entries for Oct. 29 and 30, 1863, in Anderson, 249–51, quotations at 250 and 249.

52. Entry for Apr. 21, 1863, in Anderson, 192–93.

53. Entries for May 10 and 22, 1863, in Anderson, 207–9.

54. Entry for May 22, 1863, in Anderson, 208–9.

55. Entry for May 22, 1863, in Anderson, 210.

56. See endnote to Geo. H. Hanks to N. P. Banks, July 12, 1863, in *Freedom: Wartime Genesis, Lower South*, 459.

57. For a lively and insightful account of the tumultuous early history of the Crescent City, see Powell, *Accidental City.*

58. Rothman, *Beyond Freedom's Reach*, 106–14.

59. Testimony of Col. Geo. H. Hanks before the American Freedmen's Inquiry Commission, Feb. 6, 1864, in *Freedom: Wartime Genesis, Lower South*, 518.

60. Testimony of Col. Geo. H. Hanks before the American Freedmen's Inquiry Commission, 519.

61. George T. Converse to S. W. Cozzens, June 16, 1864, in *Freedom: Wartime Genesis, Lower South*, 536–37.

62. Johansson, *Widows by the Thousand*, 1–2, 19. Unlike other members of his family, Theophilus often spelled Norfleet with one "e" instead of two.

63. Campbell and Pickens, "My Dear Husband," 363.

64. Johansson, *Widows by the Thousand*, 94, 105.

65. Johansson, 94, 105.

66. Johansson, 109.

67. Johansson, 184.

68. The historian who has most thoroughly explored the complex interpersonal dynamics between slaveholders and enslaved persons is Eugene D. Genovese. See especially *Roll, Jordan, Roll*, 70–87, 327–65.

69. Johansson, *Widows by the Thousand*, 205; Campbell and Pickens, "My Dear Husband," 362–63. Harriet Person Perry left Texas after the war, returning with her two children to her family's home in North Carolina.

70. E. Kirby Smith to Maj. Genl. Price, Sept. 4, 1863, in *Freedom: Destruction of Slavery*, 772.

71. E. Kirby Smith to J. B. Magruder, Sept. 5, 1863, in *Freedom: Destruction of Slavery*, 804.

72. E. Surget to S. S. Anderson, Sept. 29, 1863, with endorsement by J. B. Magruder, Oct. 9, 1863, in *Freedom: Destruction of Slavery*, 773–74.

73. N. B. Lucas to Jno. H. Cochrane, Nov. 10, 1865; affidavit of Mackey Woods, Dec. 12, 1865, in *Freedom: Destruction of Slavery*, 310–11, 327; affidavit of Joseph Abernathy and Hustin Abernathy, June 19, 1865; William French to Clinton B. Fisk, Aug. 8, 1865, in *Freedom: Wartime Genesis, Upper South*, 467–73. Freedmen who hoped to lease land often encountered plantation superintendents who confiscated their animals and provisions. See, for instance, testimony of Harvy Pendicord, Oct. 14, 1874; testimony of Alfred Scruggs, July 31, 1872; testimony of Squire Newman, Jan. 17, 1877; testimony of Benjamin Haynes, May 14, 1875; and testimony of Charles Bunch, May 12, 1873, in *Freedom: Wartime Genesis, Upper South*, 387–89, 447–48, 452–56.

74. McKaye, *Mastership and Its Fruits.*

75. [E. Kirby Smith] to R. C. Cummings et al., Nov. 23, 1864, in *Freedom: Destruction of Slavery*, 780–81.

76. Poe, "Contours of Emancipation," 109–30.

77. See "Using Primary Sources in the Classroom: Civil War Unit," Alabama Department of Archives and History, accessed Mar. 8, 2018, http://www.archives.alabama.gov/teacher/civilwar/civ1.html, for documents regarding the saltworks, which in July 1864, became the subject of debate over whether to impress men to work on the fortifications at Mobile; see F. S. Blount to Charles E. Sherman, July 11, 1864, Alabama Salt Commission, General correspondence, SG5979, folder 25, Alabama Department of Archives and History, Montgomery, Alabama, accessed Feb. 12, 2018, http://www.archives.alabama.gov/teacher/civilwar/lesson1/2.html; Lonn, *Salt as a Factor in the Confederacy*; Vandiver, *Plowshares into Swords*.

78. Hughes and his wife remained at the Mobile saltworks until early 1865, when the threat of a federal raid prompted their recall to Panola County. See Hughes, *Thirty Years a Slave*, 160–68.

79. See Lonn, "Extent and Importance of Federal Naval Raids on Salt-Making in Florida," 167–84; Lonn, *Salt as a Factor in the Confederacy*, esp. 172–73; O'Donovan, *Becoming Free in the Cotton South*, 91–92, 98; Rivers, *Rebels and Runaways*, 149–50.

80. For related opportunities in Macon, Georgia, see Reidy, *From Slavery to Agrarian Capitalism*, 113–33.

81. Hughes, *Thirty Years a Slave*, 165–68, quotations at 167 and 168.

82. War Department, General Orders, No. 329, Oct. 3, 1863, in *Official Records*, ser. 3, vol. 3:860–61. In November, General John M. Schofield, commander of the Department of the Missouri, issued supplemental orders affecting recruitment in Missouri. See Department of the Missouri, General Orders, No. 135, Nov. 14, 1863, in *Official Records*, ser. 3, vol. 3:1034–36; Hugh L. Bond to E. M. Stanton, Aug. 15, 1863, in *Freedom: Black Military Experience*, 200–203, quotation at 200.

83. On Maryland, see Wagandt, *Mighty Revolution*; Fields, *Slavery and Freedom on the Middle Ground*; Fuke, *Imperfect Equality*. On Missouri, see Parrish, *Turbulent Partnership*; Astor, *Rebels on the Border*. On Kentucky, see Howard, *Black Liberation in Kentucky*.

84. Taylor, *In Search of the Racial Frontier*, especially chaps. 2 and 3.

85. Bruce, *New Man*, 107–9.

86. Jackson, *Story of Mattie J. Jackson*, 14–23. Generally, see Burke, *On Slavery's Border*, 268–307, and esp. 287–89; Astor, *Rebels on the Border*, 104–20.

87. E. B. Brown to O. D. Greene, Jan. 26, 1864, *Information Relating to the Arrest and Imprisonment*, 38th Cong., 1st Sess. (1864), S. Exec. Doc. No. 24, at 7.

88. Undated statement of "Volunteer," E. B. Brown to E. H. E. Jameson et al., Dec. 7, 1863, and H. J. Fisher to B. Gratz Brown, Dec. 16, 1863, *Information Relating to the Arrest and Imprisonment*, 3–6. See also *Freedom: Destruction of Slavery*, 467–69; Lundstrom, *One Drop in a Sea of Blue*, chaps. 3 and 4.

89. Deposition of Charles F. Brown, July 16, 1895, case of Robert Devins, Invalid Certificate No. 1,068,449, RG 15, Records of the Veterans Administration, National Archives. Brown enlisted in the Twentieth U.S. Colored Infantry in New York in December 1863 and settled in Gretna, Louisiana, after discharge late in 1865. He knew Devins, who served in the Ninety-Ninth U.S. Colored Infantry, during and after the war. Joseph Campbell, a native of Louisiana who served as a private in the Ninety-Ninth U.S. Colored Infantry, remained in Leon County, Florida, after his muster out

of service, and married the native Floridian Josephine Ellis several years after the war. See Joseph Campbell, Declaration for Pension, Aug. 24, 1907, case of Joseph Campbell, Widow's Certificate No. 839,938, RG 15, Records of the Veterans Administration, National Archives.

90. Gideon Welles to Thomas T. Craven, Sept. 25, 1861, in *Official Records, Navy*, ser. 1, vol. 4:692. Welles reiterated these guidelines in April 1862. *Official Records, Navy*, ser. 1, vol. 23:80–81. For the fascinating story of the eleven black women who were shipped into naval service as nurses and hospital attendants, see King, "In Search of Women of African Descent," 302–9.

91. Entry for July 21, 1864, Gould, *Diary of a Contraband*, 15–17, 202; Sluby and Wormley, *Diary of Charles B. Fisher*, 8 (entry for Mar. 12, 1862), 18 (entry for Sept. 9, 1862), 70 (entry for Apr. 1, 1864), and 78 (entry for May 7, 1864).

92. Entry for July 23, 1864, Gould, *Diary of a Contraband*, 203.

93. Entry for Jan. 25, 1863, Sluby and Wormley, *Diary of Charles B. Fisher*, 30–31; for similar sentiments, see Fisher's notation for Aug. 19, 1863, Sluby and Wormley, 46–47.

94. Johnson, "Out of Egypt"; Schwalm, "Overrun with Free Negroes"; Schwalm, *Emancipation's Diaspora*.

Chapter 5

1. "Men of Color, To Arms!," *Douglass' Monthly*, March 1863, 801; *Julius Caesar*, act 4, sc. 3, 218–24.

2. "Army Correspondence by Chaplain Turner," *Christian Recorder*, Feb. 18, 1865, 25.

3. Daly, *Aboard the USS Monitor: 1862*, 24.

4. Kelley, "We Are Not What We Seem," 102–10.

5. See the claim of Emeline Wedge et al., filed Sept. 8, 1862, "Records of the Board of Commissioners for the Emancipation of Slaves," RG 217, Records of the United States General Accounting Office, National Archives; an online transcript of this petition is part of the petitions series of the Civil War Washington Project at the University of Nebraska-Lincoln: http://civilwardc.org/texts/petitions/cww.00984.html (accessed Mar. 8, 2018), hereafter cited as "Claim of Emeline Wedge et al." For a partial transcript of the testimony in this case, see Reidy, "Winding Path to Freedom," 18–22. See also Winkle, "Emancipation in the District of Columbia"; and Winkle, "Mining the Compenated Emancipation Petitions."

6. Jackson, *Life of Mattie J. Jackson*, 10–13, quotation at 10.

7. Quoted in Glymph, *Out of the House of Bondage*, 100. Like Fox-Genovese's *Within the Plantation Household*, Glymph's work brims with insights into the power struggles that occurred in such confined settings.

8. Hughes, *Thirty Years a Slave*, 79, 99.

9. Hughes, 95–100. On the significance of rumors in the struggle for freedom, see especially Hahn, "'Extravagant Expectations' of Freedom"; and Hahn, *Nation under Our Feet*, chap. 3.

10. See McCurry, *Confederate Reckoning*, 218–309; Robinson, *Bitter Fruits of Bondage*, 104–88; *Freedom: Destruction of Slavery*, 663–818.

11. See Downs, *Sick from Freedom*, 18–41; Long, *Doctoring Freedom*, esp. 44–89.

12. See J. Gorgas to J. C. Breckinridge, Feb. 9, 1865, enclosing three reports—note esp. No. 3: J. Gorgas to J. A. Seddon, Feb. 2, 1865, captioned "Report of Operations (White and Slave) Made," *Southern Historical Society Papers*, no. 2 (July 1876): 58–62.

13. Reidy, *From Slavery to Agrarian Capitalism*, 120–28.

14. Reidy, 130–31.

15. Chas. B. Calvert to Genl. Mansfield, July 17 and 27, 1861, in *Freedom: Destruction of Slavery*, 169–71.

16. Eaton, *Grant, Lincoln, and the Freedmen*, chaps. 3–5.

17. Testimony of Gov. Andrew Johnson before the American Freedmen's Inquiry Commission, Nov. 23, 1863, in *Freedom: Wartime Genesis, Upper South*, 411–14, quotation at 412. For less pessimistic insights into the freed people's ability to support themselves, see *Report of the Commissioners of Investigation of Colored Refugees in Kentucky, Tennessee, and Alabama*, 38th Cong., 2d Sess. (1865), S. Exec. Doc. No. 28. Johnson believed that once the masters came to understand "that they ought to . . . give them employment and pay them for their work," then "the whole question is settled." *Freedom: Wartime Genesis, Upper South*, 412.

18. Testimony of Lucy Smith, [Jan.? 1864], in *Freedom: Wartime Genesis, Upper South*, 331–32.

19. The literature on Civil War contraband camps continues to grow. See Walker, "Corinth"; Click, *Time Full of Trial*; Glymph, "This Species of Property"; Manning, "Working for Citizenship" and *Troubled Refuge*; Sears, *Camp Nelson, Kentucky*. See also the valuable work by Abigail Cooper of the University of Pennsylvania: "'Lord, until I Reach My Home'" and "Interactive Map of Contraband Camps," accessed Feb. 13, 2018, http://repository.upenn.edu/hist_digital/1/.

20. "Journal of Wallace Turnage," in Blight, *Slave No More*, 248. Mattie Jackson's mother similarly took shelter in St. Louis among friends, one of whom later betrayed her. Jackson, *Story of Mattie J. Jackson*, 14.

21. Wm. N. Harris et al. to Jefferson Davis, May 6, 1864, in *Freedom: Destruction of Slavery*, 756–58, quotation at 758.

22. Blassingame, *Black New Orleans*, 79–105. General Benjamin Butler installed Dumas as major in the Second Louisiana Native Guard regiment that he organized during the summer of 1862. "He had more capability as Major, than I had as Major-General," Butler later explained, "if knowledge of affairs, and every thing that goes to make up a man, is any test." Testimony of B. F. Butler before the American Freedmen's Inquiry Commission, [May 1, 1863], *Freedom: Black Military Experience*, 314.

23. Mary Ann to N. Banks, Jan. 8, 1863, in *Freedom: Destruction of Slavery*, 239–40.

24. [George W. F. Johnson] to Genarl Franch, Jan. 7, 1863, in *Freedom: Wartime Genesis, Lower South*, 407–8.

25. Edith Jones to Major General Banks, Mar. 4, 1863, in *Freedom: Wartime Genesis, Lower South*, 429.

26. Rothman, *Beyond Freedom's Reach*, explores the case of Georges and Rose Herera and their children; for the text of Georges's letter to General Nathaniel P. Banks, the commander of the Gulf, in January 1862, see 109. More generally, see Blassingame, *Black New Orleans*.

27. *Freedom: Wartime Genesis, Upper South*, 380–81; and Lovell H. Rousseau to W. D. Whipple, Jan. 30, 1864, in *Freedom: Wartime Genesis, Upper South*, 429–31.

28. Pierce, "Contrabands at Fortress Monroe," 628. On the Battle of Big Bethel, see Goodheart, *1861*, 336–37; Quarstein, *Big Bethel*.

29. Butler to Cameron, July 30, 1861, in [Peterson and Brothers], *Life and Public Services of Major-General Butler*, 58–62; "Important from Fortress Monroe," *New York Herald*, July 29, 1861, 1.

30. Pierce, "Contrabands at Fortress Monroe," 632. *Africans in Fort Monroe Military District*, 37th Cong., 2d Sess. (1862), II. Excc. Doc. No. 85, serial 1135, at 10, notes that "service in the navy is decidedly popular" among the refugees. "The navy rates them as boys; they get $10 a month, and are entitled to all the privileges of ships' crews, and besides, have absolute control of the earnings of their own labor."

31. *New York Herald*, July 29, 1861, 1; July 30, 1861, 2. The dispatches were dated July 26 and 27.

32. Magruder to George Deas, Aug. 9, 1861, in *Official Records*, ser. 1, vol. 2:570–73, quotation at 571; Butler to Scott, Aug. 8, 1861, in *Official Records*, ser. 1, vol. 2:567–68, quotation at 568. In the same letter that chronicled the burning of Hampton, Magruder requested funds to pay for the laborers he had hired "as a great many of them are free negroes, who have families, who must starve if they are not paid." Colonel J. W. Phelps, commander of the Vermont regiment that had made an early reconnaissance to Hampton on May 23, reported that 9,000 Confederates took part in the assault, "among which was the Richmond Howitzer Battery, manned by negroes." J. W. Phelps to Charles C. Churchill, Aug. 11, 1861, in *Official Records*, ser. 1, vol. 2:569.

33. See Testimony of F. W. Bird before the American Freedmen's Inquiry Commission, Dec. 24, 1863, in *Freedom: Wartime Genesis, Upper South*, 178–79. Bird also reported that federal authorities had recently opened a steam sawmill a short distance away from the camp, with the boards being "furnished to the freedmen for their cabins." Testimony of F. W. Bird, 179. Surviving photographs from the period indicate wooden boards as the building material of choice for most of the structures. See "Hampton, Virginia, Slab-town," Library of Congress, accessed May 9, 2016, http://www.loc.gov/pictures/item/cwp2003006010/PP/. John Oliver's comments appear in "Norfolk Correspondence," *Christian Recorder*, Oct. 1, 1864, 157. See also Nelson, *Ruin Nation*, 19–29.

34. In June 1862, the Treasury Department's superintendent of plantations estimated that 9,050 persons lived and worked on plantations under his general supervision. An additional 2,000 persons were in the vicinity of the army camps at Beaufort, Hilton Head, Bay Point, and Otter Island. Edward L. Pierce to Salmon P. Chase, June 2, 1862, in *Freedom: Wartime Genesis, Lower South*, 191–93.

35. T. W. Sherman to L. Thomas, Dec. 15, 1861, in *Official Records*, ser. 1, vol. 6:205.

36. Edward L. Pierce to Salmon P. Chase, Feb. 3, Mar. 2, and June 2, 1862, in *Freedom: Wartime Genesis, Lower South*, 124–51, 155–62, 190–208; Pierce, *Freedmen of Port Royal, South-Carolina*; Pierce, "Freedmen at Port Royal," 291–315. See also Botume, *First Days amongst the Contrabands*; Higginson, *Army Life in a Black Regiment*; Pearson, *Letters from Port Royal*; Billington, *Journal of Charlotte L. Forten*. The classic secondary account is Rose, *Rehearsal for Reconstruction*, especially 32–103, on the early days.

37. Charles P. Ware to Sister [Emma Ware], July 30, 1862 (first quotation on time passing fast enough here), and Oct. 9, 1862 (other quotations), folders 52 and 54, box 109-1, Charles Pickard Ware Papers, MSRC-HU.

38. Entry for Nov. 30, 1862, in Billington, *Journal of Charlotte L. Forten*, 158.

39. Entry for Nov. 2, 1862, in Billington, *Journal of Charlotte L. Forten*, 147.

40. See, for example, Pearson, *Letters from Port Royal*, 111–14; Rose, *Rehearsal for Reconstruction*, 297–313. Although tardy remittances from governmental agents and overseas marketers often resulted in such delays, superintendents also withheld payments from laborers as an incentive to industry. The object, Edward Philbrick explained to Charles Ware, was "to reward obedience to law, by omitting payment to the ugly ones." E. S. Philbrick to Charles [Ware], Aug. 24, 1864, folder 32, box 109-1, Charles Pickard Ware Papers, MSRC-HU.

41. Reidy, "Black Men in Navy Blue," 158; Tomblin, *Bluejackets and Contrabands*, 7–30, 134–279; Ramold, *Slaves, Sailors, Citizens*; Valuska, *African American in the Union Navy*; King, "Wounds That Bind"; Davidson, "Question of Loyalty."

42. Esup to Dear Mother, Sept. 25, 1863, box 109-2, folder 79, Charles Pickard Ware Papers, MSRC-HU.

43. Quoted in Pearson, *Letters from Port Royal*, 37–38n.

44. *Freedom: Black Military Experience*, 37–41, 46–60; *Freedom: Wartime Genesis, Lower South*, 97–100; Pearson, *Letters from Port Royal*, 38–43. See also Rose, *Rehearsal for Reconstruction*, 144–49, 187–90.

45. Hunter to Stanton, June 23, 1862, in *Freedom: Black Military Experience*, 50–53, quotation at 51. More generally, see *Freedom: Black Military Experience*, 46–61.

46. Stanton to Hunter, July 3, 1862, in *Official Records*, ser. 1, vol. 11, pt. 3:290–91; Hunter to Horatio G. Wright, July 11, 1862, in *Official Records*, ser. 1, vol. 14:363–64. Hunter had reported his aggregate troop strength present for the month of June at 21,630 men, half of whom were concentrated at James Island, South Carolina, and the remainder scattered at outposts between Port Royal and Key West. *Official Records*, ser. 1, vol. 14:362. To counterbalance the loss, Hunter asked permission to enlist "all loyal men to be found in my department," a subtle repetition of the earlier requests for authorization to recruit black soldiers that he had made since April. Hunter to Stanton, July 11, 1862, in *Official Records*, ser. 1, vol. 14:363.

47. C. P. Ware to Dear Sister [Emma Ware], July 15 and 20, 1862, folder 51, box 109-1, Charles Pickard Ware Papers, MSRC-HU; Pearson, *Letters from Port Royal*, 71–73. A correspondent's report captioned "The Trial of Free Labor," which originally appeared in the *Lutheran and Missionary*, noted the evacuation of Edisto Island as one of the several unforeseen events that set back the experiment in compensated labor at Port Royal. See *Christian Recorder*, Oct. 11, 1862, 162. See also Rose, *Rehearsal for Reconstruction*, 182–83. Hawkins, *Lunsford Lane*, 304, recorded that "seventeen journeymen carpenters, all colored men" under the direction of a freedman were entirely responsible for building homes to shelter the Edisto refugees on Port Royal Island.

48. Pearson, *Letters from Port Royal*, 150–51. This delay reprised that of the previous spring, when the plowing commenced in late March instead of at the beginning of February, with crops suffering as a result. See Pierce to Chase, June 2, 1862, in *Freedom: Wartime Genesis, Lower South*, 196–97.

49. Pearson, *Letters from Port Royal*, 150–51, 294.

50. Pearson, 306–7. For additional comments on this episode, see the letter fragment from Charles P. Ware to his sister Emma, [Jan. 1865], in "Charles P. Ware to Emma Ware, Undated" folder 50, box 109-1, Charles Pickard War Papers, MSRC-HU. On the Sherman Reserve more generally, see Schwalm, *"Hard Fight for We"*; Saville, *Work of Reconstruction*, 72–101; Oubre, *Forty Acres and a Mule*, 47–71; Foner, *Reconstruction*, 70–72; and *Freedom: Land and Labor, 1865*, 392–493.

51. The experience of the freed people of Edisto Island won instant notoriety in the fall of 1865 when they resisted President Andrew Johnson's restoration of land to the prewar owners. Their petitions to the president and to General Oliver O. Howard, commissioner of the Freedmen's Bureau, spoke eloquently of how their inability to access land would hamstring their quest for freedom, likely to the point of "being driven out Homeless upon the road" with no other choice but to accept wage employment from *"your* late and thier *all time enemies."* See Henry Bram, Ishmael Moultrie, and Yates Sampson to O. O. Howard, [Oct. 20 or 21, 1865] and to the President of These United States, Oct. 28, 1865, in *Freedom: Land and Labor, 1865*, 440–44, quotations at 440; Howard's reply appears on 441–42.

52. Hermann, *Pursuit of a Dream*, chap. 2.

53. Hermann, chap. 2.

54. David D. Porter to L. Thomas, Oct. 21, 1863, enclosing Ben Montgomery to My Dear son, Oct. 14, 1863, in *Freedom: Wartime Genesis, Lower South*, 746–49.

55. A. McFarland to Wm. P. Mellen, Mar. 11, 1864, in *Freedom: Wartime Genesis, Lower South*, 795 (quotation); Henry Rowntree to Esteemed Friends, Apr. 14, 1864, in *Freedom: Wartime Genesis, Lower South*, 822 (quotation); Samuel Thomas to John Eaton Jr., Mar. 14, 1864, and Samuel Thomas to L. Thomas, June 15, 1864, in *Freedom: Wartime Genesis, Lower South*, 812, 837 (quotation). For additional details, see *Freedom: Wartime Genesis, Lower South*, 647–48.

56. "Six Months in Dixie—No. IV. The Contrabands," *Anglo-African*, Dec. 24, 1864.

57. "Six Months in Dixie—No. III. The Bend," *Anglo-African*, Dec. 10, 1864.

58. Testimony of Patrick Selvey, Charles P. Bayley, and William Bayley, claim of Harriet F. Belt, filed Aug. 16, 1862, "Records of the Board of Commissioners for the Emancipation of Slaves," RG 217, Records of the United States General Accounting Office, National Archives; an online transcript of this petition is part of the petitions series of the Civil War Washington Project at the University of Nebraska-Lincoln: http://civilwardc.org/texts/petitions/cww.01008.html (accessed Mar. 8, 2018).

59. Pacheco, *The Pearl*. See also Drayton, *Personal Memoir*, esp. 26–35.

60. Claim of the Sisters of the Visitation of Georgetown, D.C., filed June 2, 1862, "Records of the Board of Commissioners for the Emancipation of Slaves," RG 217, Records of the United States General Accounting Office, National Archives; an online transcript of this petition is part of the petitions series of the Civil War Washington Project at the University of Nebraska-Lincoln: http://civilwardc.org/texts/petitions /cww.00569.html (accessed Mar. 8, 2018), hereafter cited as "Claim of the Sisters of the Visitation of Georgetown, D.C."; *Emancipation in the District of Columbia*, 38th Cong., 1st Sess. (1864), H. Exec. Doc. No. 42, serial 1189, at 49. See also Corrigan, "'It's a Family Affair,'" 163–65; U.S. Census Returns, 1860, Free Inhabitants of the 4th Ward, Georgetown, District of Columbia, June 26, 1860, 188, RG 29, Records of the

Bureau of the Census, National Archives (Ancestry.com, accessed Jan. 10, 2015). In 1870 the family still resided in Georgetown, where Ignatius worked as a "Common laborer," two grown daughters, Mary and Jane, were employed as "Domestic Servants," and Ignatius Jr. was employed as a "Clk in Store." U.S. Census Returns, 1870, Inhabitants of Georgetown, District of Columbia, June 13, 1870, 47.

61. Wilson, *History of the Antislavery Measures*, 38–78.

62. Wilson, 43–45, quotations at 43 and 45.

63. Cong. Globe, 37th Cong., 2d Sess., 1646 (Apr. 11, 1862); Wilson, *History of the Antislavery Measures*, 75.

64. Cong. Globe, 37th Cong., 2d Sess., 1646–49 (Apr. 11, 1862); Wilson, *History of the Antislavery Measures*, 38–78. Vallandigham's remarks appear in Cong. Globe at 1647, and in Wilson, *History of the Antislavery Measures*, at 76.

65. Wilson, 65, 77.

66. Affidavit of Grandison Briscoe, Feb. 6, 1864, in *Freedom: Destruction of Slavery*, 365. Briscoe sought relief for his wife and his mother, whose masters had whipped and imprisoned them.

67. Elizabeth Blair Lee to Phil [her husband], Apr. 4, 1862, in Laas, *Wartime Washington*, 122. See also Lee to Phil, Mar. 25, 1862, in Laas, 117. Based on the advice of B. M. Campbell of Baltimore, "an experienced dealer in slaves," and other such expert witnesses, the commissioners charged with administering the act concluded that "slaves, in fact, cannot be said to have had a current saleable value since the commencement of the war," owing largely to "the disturbed state of the country." *Emancipation in the District of Columbia*, 2.

68. "Claim of Sisters of the Visitation of Georgetown, D.C."

69. Lee to Phil, Apr. 6, 1862, in Laas, *Wartime Washington*, 125.

70. United States, *Statutes at Large*, 12:539.

71. One intriguing case involved James Payton, a Unionist who had left Fredericksburg and taken refuge in Washington accompanied by an enslaved servant, Charles Henry Lemor, a sixteen-year-old youth. By submitting an emancipation petition on Lemor's behalf to the Circuit Court in mid-October 1863, Payton raised—but did not answer—the intriguing question of why they felt the need to take this step at this time. After all, most Unionists had fled Fredericksburg when Union and Confederate forces battled there in December 1862. See petition of James Payton, Oct. 13, 1863, Emancipation Papers, series 33, Slavery Records, U.S. Circuit Court for the District of Columbia (Microfilm Publication M433, roll 3), RG 21, Records of the District Courts of the United States, National Archives.

72. Elizabeth Blair Lee to Phil, Apr. 18, 1862, in Laas, *Wartime Washington*, 130.

73. Blair submitted a successful compensation claim for two enslaved girls, one aged thirteen and the other eight. Claim of Francis P. Blair, filed May 27, 1862, "Records of the Board of Commissioners for the Emancipation of Slaves," RG 217, Records of the United States General Accounting Office, National Archives; an online transcript of this petition is part of the petitions series of the Civil War Washington Project at the University of Nebraska-Lincoln: http://civilwardc.org/texts/petitions/cww.00483 .html (accessed Mar. 8, 2018). The commissioners awarded him $475.60. *Emancipation in the District of Columbia*, 44.

74. Testimony of Benjamin Cooley, Sept. 20, 1862, claim of Charlotte Beckett and her children, filed July 29, 1862, "Records of the Board of Commissioners for the Emancipation of Slaves," RG 217, Records of the United States General Accounting Office, National Archives; an online transcript of this petition is part of the petitions series of Civil War Washington, University of Nebraska-Lincoln: http://civilwardc.org/texts/petitions/cww.00967.html (accessed Mar. 8, 2018), hereafter cited as "Claim of Charlotte Beckett and her children"; Emancipation in the District of Columbia, 76. According to the emancipation act, the three-person commission made its decisions on the principle of majority rule. Bibb had submitted a timely claim for compensation for Harriet Williams and received $372.30. Claim of Mary Rebecca Bibb, submitted June 28, 1862, "Records of the Board of Commissioners for the Emancipation of Slaves," RG 217, Records of the United States General Accounting Office, National Archives; an online transcript of this petition is part of the petitions series of Civil War Washington Project at the University of Nebraska-Lincoln: http://civilwardc.org/texts/petitions/cww.00792.html (accessed Mar. 8, 2018), hereafter cited as "Claim of Mary Rebecca Bibb"; Emancipation in the District of Columbia, 62.

75. Testimony of Jane E. Dennis, Sept. 29, 1862, "Claim of Charlotte Beckett and her children"; Emancipation in the District of Columbia, 76. "Claim of Mary Rebecca Bibb"; Emancipation in the District of Columbia, 62.

76. Testimony in the claim of Charlotte Brown, filed July 25, 1862, "Records of the Board of Commissioners for the Emancipation of Slaves," RG 217, Records of the United States General Accounting Office, National Archives; an online transcript of this petition is part of the petitions series of the Civil War Washington Project at the University of Nebraska-Lincoln: http://civilwardc.org/texts/petitions/cww.00993.html (accessed Mar. 8, 2018), hereafter cited as "Claim of Charlotte Brown."

77. Testimony of Harriet Lent, Sept. 23, 1862; George R. W. Marshall, Sept. 23, 1862; Susan Marshall, Sept. 23, 1862; George W. Halton, Sept. 25, 1862; George W. Miller, Sept. 29, 1862; and deposition of Virginia Ann Miller, Oct. 1, 1862, in "Claim of Charlotte Brown"; Emancipation in the District of Columbia, 72.

78. Deposition of Virginia Ann Miller, Oct. 1, 1862, in "Claim of Charlotte Brown."

79. Testimony of David Cole, claim of Mary Thomas, filed July 26, 1862, "Records of the Board of Commissioners for the Emancipation of Slaves," RG 217, Records of the United States General Accounting Office, National Archives; an online transcript of this petition is part of the petitions series of the Civil War Washington Project at the University of Nebraska-Lincoln: http://civilwardc.org/texts/petitions/cww.01057.html (accessed Mar. 8, 2018).

80. Testimony of George Wedge, Dec. 30, 1862, and William Edge, Dec. 30, 1862, "Claim of Emeline Wedge et al."

81. Testimony of James Fowler, Dec. 22, 1862; of George Wedge, Dec. 30, 1862; and of Emeline Wedge, Dec. 30, 1862, "Claim of Emeline Wedge et al." Former mistresses at times ministered to formerly enslaved people even after the war. See testimony of Rachel Cruze, in Rawick et al., American Slave, suppl. ser. 1, vol. 5, Indiana and Ohio Narratives, 308.

82. Testimony of Alexander McCormick, Dec. 11, 1862, and of George Wedge, Dec. 30, 1862; Alex. McCormick to the Honorable Commissioners, Dec. 30, 1862, "Claim of Emeline Wedge et al."; Emancipation in the District of Columbia, 11.

83. As a coda to this story, the 1870 population census for the District of Columbia lists the family of George and Emily Wedge with three children, Martha (age fourteen), Mary A. (age five), and Emeline (age three). Also living in the household was Mary A. Thomas. 1870 Population Census, Ward 7, Washington, D.C., 319, RG 29, Records of the Bureau of the Census, National Archives (Ancestry.com, accessed Mar. 14, 2018). Today U.S. Route 50 crosses the Anacostia River at the District Line where McCormick's farm formerly stood.

84. A. W. W. to the editor, *Christian Recorder*, Oct. 10, 1863, 161.

85. William Birney to Wm. H. Chesbrough, July 27, 1863, in *Freedom: Black Military Experience*, 198–99. See also Fields, *Slavery and Freedom on the Middle Ground*, 122–28; Wagandt, *Mighty Revolution*; Wagandt, "Army versus Maryland Slavery"; Blassingame, "Recruitment of Negro Troops in Maryland."

86. Spotswood Rice to My Children, Sept. 3, 1864, and Spotswood Rice to Kittey Diggs, Sept. 3, 1864, enclosed in F. W. Diggs to Genl. Rosecrans, Sept. 10, 1864, in *Freedom: Black Military Experience*, 689–91.

87. Rice to My Children, Sept. 3, 1864, and Rice to Diggs, Sept. 3, 1864, in *Freedom: Black Military Experience*, 689–90. Diggs's brother was the postmaster and he intercepted the letters and forwarded them to the commander of the Department of Missouri with the request that "the scoundrel" Rice be removed from the state. He explained that Rice's daughter, who was owned by his sister, had been hired out, but when "she went to see the person that hired her . . . they refused" to let her go. Professing to be a loyal Union man who realized from the start of the war that "slave property . . . was defunct never to be resusitated," he reported that six of his slaves had already enlisted and he informed the rest "when they wished to go just say so" and he would write them passes. Postmaster Diggs claimed Rice's other daughter, Corra, as his property. F. W. Diggs to Genl. Rosecrans, Sept. 10, 1864, in *Freedom: Black Military Experience*, 691. See also Burke, *On Slavery's Border*, 268–70.

88. See chapter 2, n. 95.

89. See documents in his pension file: Spotswood Rice, 67th U.S. Colored Infantry, Widow's Certificate 659775 (Eliza Rice), RG 15, Records of the Veterans Administration, National Archives.

90. Interview with Mary Bell, Aug. 19, 1937, in Rawick et al., *American Slave*, ser. 2, vol. 11, Arkansas Narratives Part 7, and Missouri Narratives, 31. Thanks to Adele Logan Alexander for calling this item to my attention.

Chapter 6

1. Nelson, *Ruin Nation*, offers imaginative insights into the war's destructive effects.

2. John David Hoptak, "Nick Biddle: A Forgotten Hero of the Civil War," *Pennsylvanian Heritage* (Spring 2010), accessed Aug. 26, 2017, http://www.phmc.state.pa.us /portal/communities/pa-heritage/nick-biddle-forgotten-hero-civil-war.html. See also Quarles, *Negro in the Civil War*, 24–26.

3. "April 19th, 1861. A Record of the Events in Baltimore, Md., on that Day," 251–69.

4. The reference to Baltimore's respectable people of color appears in "Letter from Washington," *Christian Recorder*, May 4, 1861, 66. B. F. Butler to Thos. H. Hicks,

Apr. 23, 1861, in *Official Records*, ser. 1, vol. 2:593. Governor Hicks replied the same day, thanking Butler but declining his offer on the grounds that "the citizens of the county are fully able to suppress any insurrection of our slave population." *Official Records*, ser. 1, vol. 2:594.

5. John A. Andrew to B. F. Butler, Apr. 25, 1861, and Butler to Andrew, May 9, 1861, in Butler, *Private and Official Correspondence*, 1:37–38, 39–41. Andrew replied on May 13 faulting Butler for publishing their exchange without his knowledge (79–80).

6. In August 1861, Samuel Cox of Charles County, Maryland, whipped his slave Jack Scroggins to death "for having escaped to the Federal lines, whence he was recaptured." [Charles H. Howard] to John P. C. Shanks, [Nov. 20,] 1867, in *Freedom: Destruction of Slavery*, 347–48, quotation at 348.

7. "From Washington," *Christian Recorder*, Sept. 13, 1862, 146.

8. J. K. F. Mansfield to Justice Dunne, July 4, 1861, in *Freedom: Destruction of Slavery*, 167.

9. E. D. Townsend to Brigadier Genl. McDowell, July 9, 1861, in *Freedom: Destruction of Slavery*, 343–47, quotations at 346.

10. In August 1861, Maryland newspapers printed (and reprinted) a report describing an incident in which a master had succeeded in appealing to the commander of a Connecticut regiment for the rendition of his male slave. "Such a course," the report concluded, "is calculated to disarm enemies and create friends for the General Government." See the *Frederick Herald of Freedom and Torch Light*, Aug. 21, 1861, reprinting the account from the *Boonsboro' Odd Fellow*, accessed Mar. 8, 2018, http://www .crossroadsofwar.org/research/newspapers/?id=2189. Both Boonsboro and Frederick lie in the Appalachian foothills some fifty miles north of Washington where old Indian trails leading northeast into Pennsylvania and southwest into Virginia intersected with the east-west routes linking Baltimore with the Ohio River and points west.

11. Chas. B. Calvert to Simon Cameron, July 8, 1861, in *Freedom: Destruction of Slavery*, 347.

12. Chas. B. Calvert to Genl. Mansfield, July 17, 1861, in *Freedom: Destruction of Slavery*, 169–71.

13. See his reports from Southern Maryland during October and November 1861, in Yacovone, *Voice of Thunder*, 131–44, quotation at 144.

14. W. R. Montgomery to Simon Cameron, Sept. 9, 1861; affidavit of Thomas Martin, Oct. 25, 1861; [James A. Handie] to J. Hooker, Dec. 1, 1861; and William H. Seward to George B. McClellan, Dec. 4, 1861, in *Freedom: Destruction of Slavery*, 172–75; Masur, *Example for All the Land*, 28–29.

15. Green, *Washington: Village and Capital*, 252–53, 273–74; Sarah Emery et al. to the Honorable Senate and House of Representatives in Congress Assembled, Dec. 14, 1861, in *Freedom: Destruction of Slavery*, 176; *Condition and Management of the Jail in the City of Washington*, 37th Cong., 2d Sess. (1862), S. Rep. No. 60, serial 1125, at 2–3, 6, 10, 12–13, 19, 25–27, 35–36, 39–41. *Frank Leslie's Illustrated Newspaper*, Dec. 28, 1861, 88–89, offered striking images of conditions in the jail; also see Masur, *Example for All the Land*, 23–24.

16. Thos. A. Davies to Col. Miles, July 14, 1861, with Miles's endorsement, in *Official Records*, ser. 2, vol. 1:759–60, quotation at 760. For representative samples of the communications and orders regarding the ban of fugitive slaves within military camps in

the area of Washington, Maryland, and northern Virginia, see Schuyler Hamilton to Brig. Gen. McDowell, July 16, 1861; E. D. Townsend to Gen. Mansfield, [July 17, 1861]; and General Orders, No. 3, Department of Washington, July 17, 1861, in *Official Records*, ser. 2, vol. 1:760.

17. Boston to Elizabeth Boston, Jan. 12, 1862, in *Freedom: Destruction of Slavery*, 357–58. Boston took refuge with the Fourteenth New York Volunteer Militia, which had been recruited in Brooklyn at the start of the war. It is likely that Boston joined the regiment in Anne Arundel County, Maryland, in April or May 1861 near his home, which was along the route of the Annapolis and Elkridge Railroad, one leg of the alternate route to Washington that Northern troops took following the anti-Union riots in Baltimore in mid-April.

18. *Freedom: Destruction of Slavery*, 357; Harper, *End of Days*, 2–5; Noll, *Civil War as a Theological Crisis*, 64–74. More generally, see Raboteau, *Slave Religion*; Walker, *Rock in a Weary Land*; and Genovese, *Roll, Jordan, Roll*, esp. 159–284. Thanks in part to the routine forced separations resulting from the interstate trade, references to reunions in heaven were a staple of communications among nineteenth-century African Americans. See Keckley, *Behind the Scenes*, 27, which reprints a letter from her father to her mother in 1833; see also the copy of Amos Yorke to Vincent Colyer, Aug. 27, 1862, James Morrison MacKaye Papers, LC.

19. *Official Records*, ser. 2, vol. 1:764–66, 775–77; United States, *Statutes at Large*, 12:354.

20. Robinson, *From Log Cabin to the Pulpit*, 103.

21. Brewer, *Confederate Negro*, chaps. 2–5, provides a valuable overview of this practice.

22. Brewer, chaps. 2–5; Reidy, *From Slavery to Agrarian Capitalism*, chap. 5.

23. Langston Hughes, "The Negro Speaks of Rivers," in *The Weary Blues*, 33. Harding, *There Is a River*, suggests the importance of water in the African experience in the Americas, as do works such as Gilroy, *Black Atlantic*; Berlin, *Many Thousands Gone*; and Genovese, *Roll, Jordan, Roll*.

24. Thos. T. Craven to Gideon Welles, Aug. 30, 1861, in *Official Records, Navy*, ser. 1, vol. 4:645.

25. Welles to Craven, Sept. 25, 1861, in *Official Records, Navy*, ser. 1, vol. 4:692.

26. This estimate derives from the data collected as part of the African American Civil War Sailors Project, jointly sponsored by the National Park Service, the Naval Historical Center, and Howard University. Naval records did not record a man's status as enslaved or free, but they did note the birthplace of approximately 17,000 of the roughly 18,000 men presumably of African ancestry who served. Some 7,800 of them were born in states that joined the Confederacy. Assuming that no more than 500 of the men from Confederate states had been born free and that no fewer than 1,000 of the nearly 3,000 men who enlisted in the Loyal Border States (chiefly Maryland) had been born enslaved yields a total of 8,300 men. See Reidy, "Black Men in Navy Blue," 156–57.

27. A. J. Slemmer to L. Thomas, Mar. 18, 1861, in *Official Records*, ser. 2, vol. 1:750.

28. See Buchanan, *Black Life on the Mississippi*; Cecelski, *Waterman's Song*; testimony of George Taylor Burns, in Rawick et al., *American Slave*, suppl. ser. 1, vol. 5, Indiana and Ohio Narratives, 27–31.

29. Vessels of the Potomac Flotilla routinely picked up black boatmen on suspicion of illicit trading with Confederates. See *Official Records, Navy*, ser. 1, vol. 4:640, and vol. 5:59, 83, 105, 113, 131–32, 135, 144, 152, 158, 210–11.

30. Testimony of Robert Small before the American Freedmen's Inquiry Commission, 1863, in Blassingame, *Slave Testimony*, 373; S. F. Du Pont to Gideon Welles, May 14, 1862, in *Freedom: Destruction of Slavery*, 122–23, quotations at 123. After speaking with Smalls's wife, Hannah, the abolitionist J. Miller McKim attested to "the courage evinced in this transaction by the whole party" and in particular "the cool, strategic skill of its leaders." M'Kim, *Freedmen of South Carolina*, 19–20. Despite a popular misconception, Smalls did not command *Planter* while the vessel was in naval service, although he did serve as pilot on that vessel as well as a number of other naval vessels in the waters of the South Carolina coast. In December 1863, however, when the boat was attached to the army quartermaster's department and operating in Folly Island Creek, enemy fire prompted the captain to desert the pilothouse, whereupon Smalls "took command of the boat, and carried her safely out of the reach of the guns." General Quincy A. Gillmore, commander of the Department of the South, thereupon named Smalls *Planter*'s captain. See the congressional report *Authorizing the President to Place Robert Smalls on the Retired List of the Navy*, 47th Cong., 2d sess. (1883), H. Rep. 1887, 1–3, quotation at 3. This report also indicates that when Smalls served on *Planter* in Confederate service, he was "virtually the pilot of the boat, although he was only called a wheelman, because at that time no colored man could have, in fact, been made a pilot" (1).

31. Melton, *Best Station*, 54, 221, 317–32. See also Maurice Melton, "Casualties of War: Two Georgia Coast Pilots and the Capture of the U.S.S. Water Witch," Savannah Squadron, accessed Feb. 14, 2018, http://savannahsquadron.com/ships/water -witch, for an abbreviated account of Dallas's life and death. A Moses Dallas also served in the United States Navy, but, despite the claim of Mohr, *On the Threshold of Freedom*, 289–90, it is unlikely that he is the same man as the Confederate pilot.

32. Consolidated Correspondence File: Pilots, RG 45, Naval Records Collection of the Office of Naval Records and Library, National Archives.

33. Brasher, *Peninsula Campaign and the Necessity of Emancipation*, 27, 72–73.

34. Thos. T. Craven to Gideon Welles, Aug. 30 1861, in *Official Records, Navy*, ser. 1, vol. 4:639–40.

35. Pension record of William E. Johnson (alias Edward Cendyrlin), Invalid Certificate No. 41808, RG 15, Records of the Veterans Administration, National Archives. More generally, see Buchanan, *Black Life on the Mississippi*.

36. For good overviews of black maritime life during slavery, see Cecelski, *Waterman's Song*; and Buchanan, *Black Life on the Mississippi*.

37. Testimony of David Haywood and of Sam Washington, June 27, 1863, in *Freedom: Wartime Genesis, Lower South*, 661–64. In the summer of 1862, General Pillow had accused U.S. forces under Curtis's command of taking "all my negroes, men woman and children some 400 in number," many of whom had made their way to Memphis, where some were "suffering for food" and some eighty-five were reportedly sequestered "in a cotton warehouse or negro mart." See Gid. J. Pillow to Saml. P. Walker, Aug. 2, 1862, in *Freedom: Destruction of Slavery*, 285–86, quotations at 285.

38. Reidy, "Black Men in Navy Blue," 159.

39. W. T. Truxtun to S. F. Du Pont, June 13, 1862, in *Freedom: Destruction of Slavery*, 125–27, quotations at 126 and 125.

40. Truxtun to Du Pont, June 13, 1862, 125–26.

41. Truxtun to Du Pont, June 13, 1862, 127. The Confederate commander who led the attack reported that the crops included "some 250 acres corn, 25 acres potatoes and 10 acres peanuts" in addition to cotton. R. J. Jeffords to E. H. Barnwell, June 14, 1862, in *Freedom: Destruction of Slavery*, 128.

42. Child, *Freedmen's Book*, 257–58, quotation at 257.

43. Entry for Oct. 28, 1862, and Jan. 31, 1863, in Billington, *Journal of Charlotte L. Forten*, 144–45, 179–80.

44. Edwd. A. Wild to G. F. Shepley, Sept. 1, 1864, in *Freedom: Destruction of Slavery*, 98–99.

45. James F. Milligan to S. Cooper, Jan. 1, 1865, in *Official Records*, ser. 1, vol. 42, pt. 1:867–70.

46. S. L. Phelps to A. H. Foote, Dec. 10, 1861, in *Official Records, Navy*, ser. 1, vol. 22:457; "Fallen among Thieves," *Christian Recorder*, Jan. 24, 1863, 16.

47. Entry for June 18, 1864, in Sluby and Wormley, *Diary of Charles B. Fisher*, 83.

48. Alexander, *Homelands and Waterways*, 69–89.

49. Gideon Welles to Thomas T. Craven, Sept. 25, 1861, in *Official Records, Navy*, ser. 1, vol. 4:692; Welles to C. H. Davis, Apr. 30, 1862, in *Official Records, Navy*, ser. 1, vol. 23:80–81.

50. Redkey, *Grand Army of Black Men*, 272–76, quotations at 272.

51. Gould, *Diary of a Contraband*, 104–274. For notations about news regarding his "people," see Gould, 105, 111.

52. Gould, 143.

53. Gould, 144, 146; entry for Mar. 12, 1862, in Sluby and Wormley, *Diary of Charles B. Fisher*, 8.

54. On the etymology of the word "contraband," see Masur, "Rare Phenomenon of Philological Vegetation."

55. See Reidy, "Black Men in Navy Blue," 158–62.

56. Letter from Ben. R. Johnson, *Christian Recorder*, Jan. 16, 1864, 9. The captain of USS *Vermont* cited the importance of the contrabands' work supplying the fleet. [William Reynolds] to Admiral, Dec. 9 [1863], in *Freedom: Wartime Genesis, Lower South*, 275–76. King, "'They Called Us Bluejackets,'" notes their service on expeditions into the interior and in naval brigades to support army operations.

57. "A Personal Reminiscence by Edward W. Hammond, Boatswain, U.S. Navy, of an Incident on board the U.S. Ship St. Mary's in Valparaiso Harbor 1865," Apr. 5, 1894, in folder "1865: NJ—Attempt by crew members to run the USS St. Mary into the mole," file NJ—Discipline and Minor Delinquencies, Subject File, RG 45, Naval Records Collection of the Office of Naval Records and Library, National Archives; Reidy, "Black Men in Navy Blue," 159–60.

58. T. Pattison, S. L. Phelps, Wm. D. Faulkner to A. M. Pennock, Feb. 28, 1863, in *Official Records, Navy*, ser. 1, vol. 24:309–10.

59. General Order, No. 76, U.S. Mississippi Squadron, July 23, 1863, in *Official Records, Navy*, ser. 1, vol. 25:327–28.

60. Death certificate of Robert Scott, date of death: Jan. 2, 1863, vol. 9, p. 121, Death Certificates and Reports of Medical Surveys, RG 52, Records of the Bureau of Medicine and Surgery, National Archives.

61. Hiram W. Allen to A. G. Draper, Nov. 17, 1863, in *Freedom: Destruction of Slavery*, 92–93. Allen was Wild's adjutant, and Draper commanded the Second North Carolina Colored Volunteers, which was later designated the Thirty-Sixth U.S. Colored Infantry.

62. Edward A. Wild to George H. Johnston, Jan. 1864, in *Official Records*, ser. 1, vol. 29, pt. 2:911–17.

63. Wild to Johnston, Jan. 1864, 914–15.

64. James, *Annual Report, 1864*, 3–4.

65. James, 34–35. Orderly Sergeant Samuel Johnson of the Second U.S. Colored Cavalry managed to escape the barbarity by donning civilian clothing in advance of the surrender. After being put to work helping to raise the Union vessels that had been sunk in the battle, he was sent to Richmond and then later employed as a servant to a Confederate army officer before managing to escape to Union lines. He reported that "all the negroes found in blue uniform or with any outward marks of a Union soldier upon him was killed" and testified to having witnessed their execution by various means on the day of the battle and the one following. Affidavit of Samuel Johnson, July 11, 1864, in *Freedom: Black Military Experience*, 588–89.

66. Click, *Time Full of Trial*, 94–95, 128–29. See also Horace James to J. G. Foster, Sept. 5, 1863, in *Freedom: Wartime Genesis, Upper South*, 161–63.

67. Reed's letter to the editor of the *Christian Recorder* is reproduced in Redkey, *Grand Army of Black Men*, 275–76.

68. Blackett, *Thomas Morris Chester*, 116. At times the black troops rebuffed the entreaties of Confederates to trade tobacco for food. Blackett, 122–23. Chester's references to the rebels' use of the term "Smoked Yankees" in regard to the U.S. Colored Troops appear in Blackett, 202 and 261.

69. Blackett, 228–29.

70. "A Contraband's Story," *Douglass' Monthly*, March 1862, 617.

71. "A Contraband's Story," 617. More generally, see Jordan, *Black Confederates and Afro-Yankees*, esp. 216–31.

72. Testimony of C. B. Wilder before the American Freedmen's Inquiry Commission, May 9, 1863, in *Freedom: Wartime Genesis, Upper South*, 88–90. See copy of order by Brig. Gen. Foster, Apr. 24, 1862, James Morrison MacKaye Papers, LC, which obliged regimental commanders to honor passes that Colyer issued to freed people authorizing them to move in and out of Union lines; see also the testimony of B. K. Lee Jr. before the American Freedmen's Inquiry Commission, [June 1863], in *Freedom: Wartime Genesis, Lower South*, 113. The growing historical literature on the assessment and mitigation of risk—for instance, Knowles's *Disaster Experts*, and Levy's *Freaks of Fortune*—offers intriguing interpretive avenues into what freedom seekers experienced as they sought to transform dreams of freedom into reality. For additional insights into risk taking from the standpoint of social and organizational psychology, see Trimpop, *Psychology of Risk Taking Behavior*.

73. John Oliver to [Simeon S. Jocelyn], Nov. 25, 1862, in Ripley et al., *Black Abolitionist Papers*, 5:161.

74. "Mr. Colyer and the Negro Schools at Newbern," *Christian Recorder*, June 21, 1862, 98; Cecelski, *Fire of Freedom*, 74–76. Colyer, a New York Quaker, was an artist and philanthropist. After the war he championed federal support for Indian schools.

75. Cecelski, esp. 58–82. The correspondent is quoted at 61.

76. See Larson, *Bound for the Promised Land*, 203–28, esp. 209–17, regarding Tubman's activities as a spy.

77. Testimony of Samuel Ballton, in Blassingame, *Slave Testimony*, 546. Later in the war, Ballton traveled to Boston, where he enlisted in the Fifth Massachusetts Colored Cavalry.

78. John Oliver to Brother Jocelyn, Jan. 14, 1863, in Ripley et al., *Black Abolitionist Papers*, 5:173; testimony of C. B. Wilder before the American Freedmen's Inquiry Commission, May 9, 1863, in *Freedom: Wartime Genesis, Upper South*, 90.

79. Jon'a Pearce to J. A. Seddon, Nov. 3, 1863, in *Freedom: Destruction of Slavery*, 775–76.

80. Wyndham Robertson to James A. Seddon, Jan. 13, 1864, in *Freedom: Destruction of Slavery*, 778–79; McCurry, *Confederate Reckoning*, 299–300.

81. McCurry, esp. chaps. 6 and 7.

82. Washington, "Memorys of the Past," in Blight, *Slave No More*, 185.

83. Washington, 186.

84. Washington, quotations at 188, 190, 193, 196.

85. Washington, 196–206, quotations at 202, 205, 206. Washington often inserted periods as punctuation marks at the end of phrases, which here have been silently changed to commas. See also Murray, *Proud Shoes*, 117–23, for an evocative portrait of the experience of African American employees of the quartermaster department during the Civil War that is based on her grandfather Robert Fitzgerald's wartime service as a teamster (he subsequently also served in the navy and the army).

86. Washington, quotations at 208, 209, 210. Washington eventually reunited with his wife and other family members in Washington, D.C. Blight, *Slave No More*, 52–54.

87. "Soldier's Letter," *Christian Recorder*, June 25, 1864, 101 (Brock's letter is dated May 26, 1864).

88. "Our Army Correspondence," *Christian Recorder*, Aug. 6, 1864, 126; "Letter from Hanover, Va.," *Christian Recorder*, June 18, 1864, 98.

89. Knox, *Slave and Freeman*, 43–46.

90. Knox, 49–50.

91. Knox, 50–51. Because the owner was not an officer, he was not authorized to employ a servant; but he got around the technicality by having Knox assigned to serve his captain on the tacit understanding that Knox would perform camp chores for his owner as well.

92. Knox, 51–52.

93. Knox, 51–52.

94. Knox, 51–53, quotation at 53.

95. Knox, 53.

96. Knox, 53–56.

97. Knox, 53–58.

98. Knox, 57–58, quotations at 58.

99. Knox, 60–61.

100. Knox, 69.

101. Robinson, *From Log Cabin to the Pulpit*, 96–101, quotation at 98.

102. Robinson, 102–3, quotation at 103.

103. Robinson, quotations at 103–4, 104, and 105.

104. "Army Correspondence," *Christian Recorder*, May 6, 1865, 69. Turner's letter is dated April 17, 1865. For earlier reports from Turner on the refugees, see "Army Correspondence by Chaplain Turner," *Christian Recorder*, Apr. 15, 1865, 57; and "Army Correspondence," *Christian Recorder*, Mar. 4, 1864, 33.

105. More than 8,000 refugees followed Sherman's army to Fayetteville, North Carolina, "two-thirds of whom were negroes," according to General Oliver Otis Howard, who commanded the right wing of Sherman's army. (See the excerpt from Howard's 1869 remarks to the American Missionary Association in Hartford, Connecticut, folder 83, box 53-2, Oliver Otis Howard Papers, MSRC-HU.) The remaining one-third consisted of white refugees from the Carolinas. A smattering of black refugees from Georgia continued to follow the army after it left Savannah at the beginning of February, but most of the estimated 10,000 former slaves from up-country Georgia remained on the reservation that Sherman's Special Field Order, No. 15, established along the coast for their settlement. General William T. Sherman's Special Field Order, No. 15, Jan. 16. 1865, is published in *Freedom: Wartime Genesis, Lower South*, 338–40.

Part III

1. Anderson, *Imagined Communities*.

2. For two recent overviews, see Howe, *What Hath God Wrought*; and Hahn, *Nation without Borders*, esp. 79–113.

3. "Cairo Correspondence," *Christian Recorder*, Apr. 22, 1865, 61. For an earlier expression of a similar sentiment, see "Speech of John S. Rock, Esq.," *Christian Recorder*, Feb. 22, 1862, 31.

Chapter 7

1. "A Letter from a Soldier in New Orleans," *Christian Recorder*, July 16, 1864, 113.

2. Nell, *Colored Patriots*, 326. See also Kantrowitz, *More Than Freedom*.

3. [Society for Colonizing the Free People of Colour of the United States], *Fourteenth Annual Report*, xxi; see also Logan, "Some New Interpretations of the Colonization Movement," 330.

4. "Things Which Every Emigrant to Liberia Ought to Know," Appendix, in [American Colonization Society], *Thirty-First Annual Report*, 40, 41. For brief overviews of Jefferson's thinking about slavery and colonization (and that of his white contemporaries), see Sinha, *Slave's Cause*, 87–91; Fredrickson, *Black Image*, chap. 1; and Boles, *Jefferson*, 177–82, 504–5. More extended treatments may be found in Jordan, *White over Black*, chap. 12; and Kendi, *Stamped from the Beginning*, 79–158.

5. Garnet, *Past and Present Condition*, 21, 25–26. For his 1843 address to the National Convention of Colored Citizens, see Ripley et al., *Black Abolitionist Papers*, 3: 403–11.

6. Tappan, *Immediate Emancipation*, 2.

7. The best recent survey of the international context is Doyle, *Cause of All Nations.* AFIC, "Final Report," 90.

8. Cochin, *Results of Emancipation,* 342.

9. Samuel Gridley Howe's penciled notations on Robert Dale Owen and James McKaye to Howe, Mar. 19, 1863, Series I, Item 76, AFIC Records, Harvard.

10. Contemporaries of various political and religious persuasions commented extensively on Russian abolition. For a sampling, see "Russia and America," *Christian Recorder,* Feb. 22, 1862, 29 (reprinted from *Lutheran and Missionary*); "Annual Conference, Southern District, A. M. E. Zion Connexions in America," *Christian Recorder,* May 2, 1863, 69; "Abolition of Slavery in Brazil," *Christian Recorder,* June 23, 1864, 117; Mitchell, *Letter on the Relation of the White and African Races in the United States,* 6–7.

11. See especially Holt, *Problem of Freedom*; Dubois, *Avengers of the New World*; Scott, *Slave Emancipation in Cuba*; and Ferrer, *Freedom's Mirror.*

12. Sewell, *Ordeal of Free Labor,* 311, 177. See also A Cotton Manufacturer [Atkinson], *Cheap Cotton by Free Labor,* 4–6; and Goodloe, *Emancipation and the War,* 11–12.

13. Sewell, *Ordeal of Free Labor,* 317–22.

14. *New York Times,* Mar. 30, 1861.

15. "Free Labor in the West Indies," *Christian Recorder,* June 29, 1861, 97; "West India Emancipation. The Commercial Aspects of Freedom. The Whole Case Well Stated," *Anglo-African,* Apr. 27, 1861. The *Anglo-African* reprinted a review from the New York *Evening Post* that praised Sewell for giving hope that "men are now living who will see the end of negro slavery on this continent. To those who are privileged to aid in this great deliverance, the results of West Indian Emancipation may give a stronger faith; while the errors we may now discern in the *manner* of that measure, will serve as a beacon to guide our own experiment to a surer, speedier, and better fulfilment." A week later, the *Anglo* published another favorable commentary on *Ordeal of Free Labor*; see "West India Emancipation," editorial, *Anglo-African,* May 4, 1861. Cochin, *Results of Emancipation,* surveyed emancipation in the Caribbean basin, drawing conclusions remarkably similar to Sewell's regarding both the British possessions and those of France, Denmark, Sweden, and Holland. From the 1830s, African Americans had commemorated August 1 of each year to mark the anniversary of West Indian Emancipation as both a milestone in the global antislavery struggle and a model for the United States to emulate. See Kerr-Ritchie, *Rites of August First.*

16. The editor of the *Christian Recorder* approvingly reprinted the editorial under the title "The Necessity of the Hour," *Christian Recorder,* May 24, 1862, 81.

17. A Cotton Manufacturer [Atkinson], *Cheap Cotton by Free Labor,* quotations at 25, 49, 4, and 6.

18. Kennedy, *Population of the United States in 1860,* 594–95. For a concise recent overview of this "Long Northern Emancipation," see Sinha, *Slave's Cause,* 65–85. Between 1776 and 1784, Pennsylvania and the New England states abolished slavery either outright or over a period of years; the institution remained legal, however, in Rhode Island and Connecticut until the 1840s and in New Hampshire until the 1850s. See also Berlin, *Long Emancipation,* esp. 1–46; and Rael, *Eighty-Eight Years,* 1–235.

19. Nell, *Colored Patriots*, 378–81, quotations at 392. Nell chronicled the effort on the part of black men in Massachusetts during the 1850s to remove the state constitution's prohibition against their serving in the state militia and decried the unevenness with which officials issued passports to black Americans who wished to travel abroad. Nell, 101–18, 326. "Arming the Slaves," *Anglo-African*, Mar. 23, 1861. See also Kantrowitz, *More Than Freedom*; Melish, *Disowning Slavery*; and Zilversmit, *First Emancipation*.

20. Butler to [Winfield] Scott, May 27, 1861, in *Official Records*, ser. 1, vol. 2:52–54, quotation at 53; see also Cameron to Butler, May 30, 1861, in *Official Records*, ser. 2, vol. 1:754–55; Butler to Cameron, July 30, 1861, in Butler, *Private and Official Correspondence*, 1:185–88; and Cameron to Butler, Aug. 8, 1861, in *Official Records*, ser. 2, vol. 1:761–62; Pierce, "Contrabands at Fortress Monroe," 629–30. Oakes, *Freedom National*, chap. 4, sees this exchange, and particularly Cameron's letter of August 8, as the foundation of federal emancipation policy. See also Siddali, *From Property to Person*, 51–54. In mid-October, when a combined army-navy operation undertook the capture of Port Royal, South Carolina, Cameron forwarded copies of his earlier correspondence with Butler to General Thomas W. Sherman, commander of the military force, for his information. "Avail yourself of the services of any persons whether fugitives from labor or not" in any capacity for which "they may be fitted" except bearing arms, he instructed, assuring loyal masters that Congress would compensate them for their losses. The secretary concluded that this approach would "best secure the substantial rights of loyal masters" and assure the government access to needed services, while at the same time avoiding "all interference with the social systems or local institutions." Cameron to Sherman, Oct. 14, 1861, in *Official Records*, ser. 2, vol. 1:773.

21. Pierce, "Contrabands at Fortress Monroe," 632–35. The abolitionist Lewis Tappan, who became actively involved in affairs concerning the contrabands under the auspices of the American Missionary Association, also insisted that kind treatment accompany the promise of wages to the formerly enslaved workers. See De Boer, "Role of Afro-Americans," 222. Like other participants in this experiment, a man named Suthey Parker, who began work in June 1861, was still seeking payment of his wages months after the war had ended. See Affidavit of Suthey Parker, Sept. 2, 1865, in *Freedom: Wartime Genesis, Upper South*, 110–11. More generally, see "Negroes: Employment," Consolidated Correspondence File, ser. 225, RG 92, Records of the Office of the Quartermaster General, National Archives.

22. Pierce, "Contrabands at Fortress Monroe," 635–36, 630–31. Federal troops first entered Hampton on May 28, but because nearly all the white inhabitants had fled, they felt no need to occupy the village. Soldiers on picket duty returned "intermittently" through the month of June. The permanent outpost established a forward defensive position against Confederate attacks on either Fortress Monroe or Newport News. Pierce, 630.

23. Pierce, 632–38.

24. Pierce, "Contrabands at Fortress Monroe," 626–40. Although Pierce did not reference William Sewell's *Ordeal of Free Labor* in assessing the fitness for freedom of the enslaved people of the Confederate States, he favorably cited the opinions of the Unitarian theologian William Ellery Channing. "As a race," Pierce observed, the contrabands "may be less vigorous and thrifty than the Saxon, but they are more docile, and affectionate, fulfilling the theory which Channing held in relation to them" (640).

In an 1841 pamphlet describing "a short residence among the negroes in the West Indies," Channing defended the emancipated slaves and refuted charges of their "peculiar incapacity of moral elevation." "The European race have manifested more courage, enterprise, invention; but in the dispositions which Christianity particularly honours, how inferior are they to the African!" he argued. "The African carries within him much more than we the germs of a meek, long-suffering, loving virtue." Channing, *Emancipation*, 21–22, 32–34, quotations at 33–34.

25. Pierce, "Contrabands at Fortress Monroe," 638.

26. Pierce, 639.

27. Statement of C. B. Wilder, Dec. 30, 1862; and of O. Brown, Dec. 31, 1862, Emancipation League of Boston, *Facts concerning the Freedmen*, 5–6.

28. Copy of LeBaron Russell to E. M. Stanton, Dec. 13, 1862, Series I, Item 90, AFIC Records, Harvard. Russell expressed feelings of "mortification" and "surprise" at having "never received the slightest notice from the Secretary of War" that his report was received, much less whether he had "performed [his] mission acceptably or not." See Russell to J. McKaye, Apr. 28, 1863; Russell to Edwin M. Santon, Jan. 2, 1863; Russell to P. H. Watson, Jan. 30 and Feb. 20, 1863; and Russell to John M. Tucker, Nov. 23, 1862, James Morrison MacKaye Papers, LC.

29. Special Orders, No. 72, Department of Virginia, Oct. 14, 1861; General Orders, No. 34, Department of Virginia, Nov. 1, 1861; *Africans in Fort Monroe Military District*, 37th Cong., 2d Sess. (1862), H. Exec. Doc. No. 85, serial 1135, at 2. See also *Freedom: Wartime Genesis, Upper South*, 111–12. The second order stipulated that "any unusual amount of labor" was eligible for "extra pay" to be given directly to the men for their own use, while at the same time authorizing deductions for absenteeism.

30. Lewis C. Lockwood to Hon. Senator Wilson, Jan. 29, 1862, in *Freedom: Wartime Genesis, Upper South*, 112–14, quotations at 112 and 113. The chief quartermaster, Captain Greer Tallmadge, the son of former New York senator N. P. Tallmadge, died at Fort Monroe on Oct. 11, 1862. See General Orders, No. 181, War Department, Adjutant General's Office, Nov. 1, 1862, in United States War Department, *General Orders*, 1: 445. Wool ordered the removal from office and arrest of a quartermaster sergeant identified only by the surname of Smith. See *Africans in Fort Monroe Military District*, 4–6; *Freedom: Wartime Genesis, Upper South*, 119.

31. *Africans in Fort Monroe Military District*, 3.

32. Cram, Cannon, and Jones to Wool, Mar. 20, 1862, in *Africans in Fort Monroe Military District*, 3–13, quotations at 4, 11, and 12. A slightly different version, transcribed from a manuscript copy of the report, appears in *Freedom: Wartime Genesis, Upper South*, 114–20. The wartime superintendents of contrabands played a critically important role as mediators between high-level government officials and representatives of nongovernmental charitable institutions and the freed people. In that capacity, they daily resolved the most pressing needs of the refugees, often under considerable duress and with little thanks. In addition to Wilder, other superintendents of freed people included Danforth B. Nichols in Washington; Orlando Brown in Virginia; Horace James and Vincent Colyer in North Carolina; Rufus Saxton in South Carolina; George H. Hanks and Thomas Conway in Louisiana; and John Eaton in Mississippi and Tennessee. Several women served in similar capacities, although the government declined to acknowledge that fact with official appointments. Notable

among these were Josephine Griffing in Washington and Julia Wilbur and Harriet Jacobs in Alexandria, Virginia. Several of the men later served with the Freedmen's Bureau, including Brown, Saxton, Conway, and Thomas.

33. Cram, Cannon, and Jones to Wool, Mar. 20, 1862, 11.

34. Testimony of D. B. Nichols before the American Freedmen's Inquiry Commission, [Apr.? 1864], in *Freedom: Wartime Genesis, Upper South*, 288.

35. Elias M. Greene to Chas. Thomas, Dec. 17, 1863, in *Freedom: Wartime Genesis, Upper South*, 315. Superintendent Nichols reported their irregular pay in his AFIC testimony. Testimony of D. B. Nichols, in *Freedom: Wartime Genesis, Upper South*, 288.

36. Pierce to Chase, Feb. 3, Mar. 2 and 14, and June 2, 1862, in *Freedom: Wartime Genesis, Lower South*, 124–53, 155–66, 190–208. The letters appeared in the *Rebellion Record* in 1863, and they were reprinted in pamphlet form as Pierce, *Freedmen of Port Royal*, 302–23. See Rose, *Rehearsal for Reconstruction*, esp. 21–36.

37. Pierce to Chase, Feb. 3, 1862, in *Freedom: Wartime Genesis, Lower South*, 131–32. Pierce described a visit to a school for black children in which he employed a similar technique of "dialogue" to determine how well they understood their obligations to work and to spend their earnings wisely, to include supporting their ministers and teachers in addition to purchasing necessities. "Freedmen at Port Royal," 306–7.

38. Pierce to Chase, Feb. 3, 1862, in *Freedom: Wartime Genesis, Lower South*, 142. Recall his slightly different reflections on the prospects for intergenerational change based on his interactions with freed people in Virginia a year earlier: "The first generation might be unfitted for the active duties and responsibilities of citizenship," he wrote, "but this difficulty, under generous provisions for education, would not pass to the next." "Contrabands at Fortress Monroe," 639.

39. Henry P. Scholte to the Honorable Senate and House of Representatives of the United States, Nov. 30, 1861, Broadside, Duke University Digital Collections, accessed Mar. 17, 2017, http://library.duke.edu/digitalcollections/sizes/broadsides _bdsia10410/. The word "voluntarely" is misspelled in the original.

40. Pierce to Chase, Feb. 3, 1862, in *Freedom: Wartime Genesis, Lower South*, 142.

41. T. A. Goodwin to Robert Dale Owen, May 1, 1863, James Morrison MacKaye Papers, LC.

42. *Freedom: Wartime Genesis, Lower South*, 142–43.

43. *Freedom: Wartime Genesis, Lower South*, 145.

44. Pierce to Chase, June 2, 1862, in *Freedom: Wartime Genesis, Lower South*, 208. For a companion piece to Pierce's recommendations, see A Cotton Manufacturer [Atkinson], *Cheap Cotton by Free Labor*. Edward Atkinson, a Boston cotton manufacturing agent and one of the earliest recruits to the Port Royal experiment, subsequently figured prominently—and often controversially—in the reorganization of the Sea Island cotton plantation regime. See Rose, *Rehearsal for Reconstruction*, esp. chaps. 2, 5, 7, and 8.

45. Pierce to Chase, June 2, 1862, in *Freedom: Wartime Genesis, Lower South*, 195–96.

46. Pierce to Chase, June 2, 1862, 208.

47. Statement of O. Brown, Dec. 31, 1862, in Emancipation League of Boston, *Facts concerning the Freedmen*, 7.

48. Pierce, "Freedmen at Port Royal," 291–315, quotation at 292. See also the fascinating commentary on Pierce's observations about Port Royal in Hawkins, *Lunsford Lane*,

292–305, which concluded that "whether our military necessities require a proclamation of emancipation or not, no human power can turn back the revolution begun" (305).

49. Pierce, "Freedmen at Port Royal," 304.

50. Stone, *Emancipation*, 10–11, quotation at 10.

51. Message to Congress, Mar. 6, 1862, in Basler, Pratt, and Dunlap, *Collected Works*, 5:144–45.

52. See especially Taylor, *Frontiers of Freedom*, 161, 176–77; Phillips, *Rivers Ran Backward*, 72–77.

53. Cox, *Emancipation and Its Results—Is Ohio to Be Africanized?*, 9.

54. Brown, *Immediate Abolition of Slavery*, 12; Howe, *Refugees from Slavery*.

55. "What Would Be the Effect of the Emancipation of the Slaves!," *Christian Recorder*, Jan. 4, 1862, 1; "Emancipation and Its Opposition," editorial, *Christian Recorder*, Mar. 29, 1862, 50.

56. "The Colored People and the State Legislatures," *Christian Recorder*, Mar. 29, 1862, 50. Racial theorists such as Josiah Nott had posited the extinction of what he (and others) labeled "inferior" races as one such law. See Fredrickson, *Black Image*, 78–82, esp. 79. For general context, see Phillips, *Rivers Ran Backward*, 211–35, esp. 223–25 for Illinois.

57. Aikman, *Future of the Colored Race in America*, 8. Aikman's work originally appeared in the *Presbyterian Quarterly* of July 1862.

58. "Sketches from Washington," *Christian Recorder*, Apr. 5, 1862, 53. See also "Turner on the President's Message," *Christian Recorder*, Mar. 22, 1862, 46.

59. Aikman, *Future of the Colored Race in America*, 3, 11.

60. Aikman, 14. The *Christian Recorder*, Sept. 13, 1862, 145, reprinted a long extract from Aikman's treatise.

61. Aikman, *Future of the Colored Race in America*, 17, 33, 35.

62. "Washington Correspondence," *Christian Recorder*, Aug. 16, 1862, 130. See also Voegeli, "Rejected Alternative," 775; and, more generally, Voegeli, *Free but Not Equal*; Melish, *Disowning Slavery*; and Phillips, *Rivers Ran Backward*. Boutwell became one of the Radical Republicans' foremost advocates of "the full and equal rights of the colored people of the South," to include voting and holding elective office, during Reconstruction, yet he did not quite abandon his preference that the freed people remain in the South. See, for example, "Equality of the Negro" (May 31, 1866), Boutwell, *Speeches and Papers*, 468–76, quotation at 469.

63. Emancipation League of Boston, *Facts concerning the Freedmen*, 3; S. G. Howe to F. W. Bird, Sept. 17, 1862, quoted in McPherson, *Struggle for Equality*, 180–81.

64. Emancipation League of Boston, *Facts concerning the Freedmen*, 11. For the rest of the war, commentators on conditions among the "colored Refugees," as LeBaron Russell, the secretary of the Boston Educational Commission, termed them, gauged their status against this template of assumptions first compiled by the Boston Emancipation League. See a copy of Russell's extended and sympathetic report on conditions at federal positions at the mouth of Chesapeake Bay (from Fortress Monroe to Norfolk) to the secretary of war late in 1863. Russell to Stanton, Dec. 25, 1863, Series I, Item 91, AFIC Records, Harvard.

65. *Memorial of the Emancipation League of Boston, Massachusetts*, 37th Cong., 3d Sess. (1862), S. Misc. Doc. No. 10, serial 1150, at 2. Among the signatories were S. E.

Sewall, president of the Emancipation League, and George L. Stearns, Samuel Gridley Howe, and Edward Atkinson, members of the Executive Committee. See also Frankel, "Predicament of Racial Knowledge," 45. Frankel, "Predicament of Racial Knowledge," 45. The notion of "a nation born in a day" had deep roots in Southern black Christianity; see Harper, *End of Days*, 18–44.

66. *Memorial of the Emancipation League of Boston, Massachusetts*, 1–2. See McPherson, *Struggle for Equality*, 188–91, on the role of abolitionists in lobbying for creation of such a bureau; also see Bentley, *Freedmen's Bureau*, 36–43. For insights derived from the congressional debates, see Wilson, *History of the Antislavery Measures*, 328–33, 405–16.

67. Owen, *Policy of Emancipation*, 10, 39, 12–13. For a sympathetic biography of Owen that views him through the prisms of journalist, lawmaker, diplomat, pamphleteer, and mystic, see Pancoast and Lincoln, *Incorrigible Idealist*.

68. Owen, *Policy of Emancipation*, 37.

69. See Schwartz, *Samuel Gridley Howe*. On his friendship with Agassiz, see Agassiz, *Louis Agassiz*, 2: 546–47, 591–617; and Richards, *Letters and Journals of Samuel Gridley Howe*, 2:505–6. Also useful are Fredrickson, *Black Image*, 160–64 and, more generally, chaps. 4–6; Irmscher, *Louis Agassiz*, 245–51, 255–62; Frankel, *States of Inquiry*, 204–33; Furrow, "Samuel Gridley Howe," 352–53; Fields and Fields, *Racecraft*, 207–8; and Gould, *Mismeasure of Man*, 74–82. Howe's racial views mix curiously with his support for John Brown and especially with his membership (along with Thomas Wentworth Higginson, Theodore Parker, Franklin B. Sanborn, Gerrit Smith, and George L. Stearns) in the so-called Secret Six, who bankrolled Brown's raid on Harper's Ferry in October 1859.

70. For a brief account of the commissioners and their work on the AFIC, see McPherson, *Struggle for Equality*, 182–88.

71. McKaye, *Of the Birth and Death of Nations*, 27.

72. McKaye, 27, 30–31.

73. Edwin M. Stanton to Robert Dale Owen, James McKaye, and Samuel G. Howe, Mar. 16, 1863, in *Official Records*, ser. 3, vol. 3:73–74, quotations at 73; Robert Dale Owen and James McKaye to S. G. Howe, Mar. 19, 1863 (on which Howe penciled his notations), Series I, Item 76, AFIC Records, Harvard. See Sumner to Howe, Apr. 29, 1863, James Morrison MacKaye Papers, LC; and Sumner to S. G. Howe, Aug. 21, 1863, Series I, Item 107, AFIC Records, Harvard. See also Escott, "*What Shall We Do with the Negro?*," esp. 73–93.

74. AFIC, *Preliminary Report*, 3–4. The preliminary report was also printed in *Official Records*, ser. 3, vol. 3:430–54. See also Furrow, "Samuel Gridley Howe," 348–49.

75. AFIC, *Preliminary Report*, 3–7.

76. AFIC, 9–12.

77. AFIC, 27–31.

78. AFIC, 33. See also McPherson, *Struggle for Equality*, 178–81.

79. AFIC, *Preliminary Report*, 14.

80. Furrow, "Samuel Gridley Howe," 367–68; J. Eaton Jr. to Robert Dale Owen, Aug. 27, 1863, Series I, Item 37, AFIC Records, Harvard; Boynton to American Freedmen's Aid Commission, Sept. 15, 1863, Series I, Item 17, AFIC Records, Harvard.

81. *Freedom: Wartime Genesis, Lower South*, 1–83, esp. 31–32; Gerteis, *From Contraband to Freedman.*

82. Eaton, *Grant, Lincoln, and the Freedmen*, 92–93, quotation at 93. For a sizeable extract from the report, see excerpt of John Eaton Jr. to Jno. A. Rawlins, Apr. 29, 1863, in *Freedom: Wartime Genesis, Lower South*, 684–97; for the full report see Eaton to Rawlins, Apr. 29, 1863, filed with O-328 1863, Letters Received, ser. 12, RG 94, Records of the Adjutant General, 1780s–1917, National Archives.

83. Eaton, 93. See especially Frankel, "Predicament of Racial Knowledge."

84. The commissioners took it as a matter of pride that they sought out the testimony of black witnesses. A Northern newspaper reported the great interest that the commissioners had shown in a case that a provost judge in eastern Virginia settled in 1862. It involved a freedman who had been authorized by the superintendent of contrabands to cultivate land on the farm that his owner had abandoned in the summer of 1861. The owner returned after the harvest and demanded the crop, and the freedman laid the matter before federal authorities. After the provost judge ordered the litigants to split the harvest, Commissioners Owen and Howe viewed it as "the first oath and testimony of a slave." "New Law and Justice in Virginia," *Anglo-African*, Feb. 6, 1864 (reprinted from the *Springfield Republican*).

85. Gloucester to Robert Dale Owen, James Mackaye and Dr. Howe, July 1863, Series I, Item 41, AFIC Records, Harvard, electronic version accessed Mar. 28, 2016, http://iiif.lib.harvard.edu/manifests/view/drs:42905839$1i. The commissioners responded to Gloucester by sending a copy of their preliminary report, to which Gloucester promptly replied that he and an associate, William J. Wilson, a noted champion of impartial suffrage and educator of black children in New York, "can best serve the cause of the Commission—the Freedmen and the Country in the Office of Resident Superintendent." See James N. Gloucester to the American Freedmen Enquiry Commission, Sept. 2, 1863, and William J. Wilson to the American Freedmens Inquiry Commission, Sept. 1, 1863, James Morrison MacKaye Papers, LC. See also J. D. Colors to R. D. Owen, Aug. 11, 1863, James Morrison MacKaye Papers, LC.

86. Blassingame, *Slave Testimony*, 369–444, reprints the testimonies of nearly fifty formerly enslaved persons that the AFIC interviewed. For the questions, see Blassingame, 370–71. Furrow, "Samuel Gridley Howe," makes the same point somewhat differently.

87. AFIC, *Preliminary Report*, 20, 14, 16. See also McPherson, *Struggle for Equality*, 178–81. Although the final tally remains conjectural, it is likely that considerably more than 100,000 black men and women provided such support service, taking into account the cooks, servants, and laundry workers employed by military officers and enlisted men, as well as the teamsters, pioneers, and general laborers who supported naval and military operations. Some unknown multiple of that number labored on behalf of Confederate forces. In recognizing that armed service would almost certainly create a strong claim for citizenship, the commissioners echoed a theme that abolitionists generally—and such black abolitionists as Frederick Douglass particularly—had foreseen from the first shot.

88. See Samuel G. Howe to Dear Sir, Sept. 15, 1863, with responses from George E. Palmer, [undated], Series I, Item 77, AFIC Records, Harvard. Howe also communicated

with directors of institutions for the insane in the Northern states, inquiring particularly about their black inmates, and with revenue officials, asking the amount of taxes black residents paid. See Series II, items 127–57, and Series I, Item 112, AFIC Records, Harvard.

89. See Robert Dale Owen, James McKaye, and Samuel G. Howe to Dear Sir, [undated] 1863, with responses from D. R. Anthony, Aug. 30, 1863, Series I, Item 5, AFIC Records, Harvard .

90. Howe to Agassiz, Aug. 3, 1863, in Agassiz, *Louis Agassiz*, 2: 592–93.

91. Agassiz to Howe, Aug. 10, 1863, in Agassiz, *Louis Agassiz*, 2: 602.

92. Agassiz to Howe, Aug. 9, 1863, 2: 599. The fear regarding the progress of civilization appears in Agassiz to Howe, Aug. 10, 1863, 2: 600–601.

93. Agassiz to Howe, Aug. 10, 1863, 2: 604. For broader context, see Richardson, *Death of Reconstruction*, 122–55; Stanley, "Instead of Waiting for the Thirteenth Amendment"; and Stanley, "Slave Emancipation and the Revolutionizing of Human Rights."

94. Howe to Agassiz, Aug. 18, 1863, in Agassiz, *Louis Agassiz*, 2: 614–15.

95. Howe to Agassiz, Aug. 18, 1863, 2: 612, 614–15.

96. Agassiz to Howe, Aug. 9, 1863, in Agassiz, *Louis Agassiz*, 2: 598.

97. Agassiz to Howe, Aug. 10, 1863, 2: 605.

98. *Message of the President of the United States Communicating a Letter Addressed to Him from a Committee of Gentlemen*, 38th Cong., 1st Sess. (1863), S. Exec. Doc. No. 1, serial 1176, at 1–2. See also McPherson, *Struggle for Equality*, 188–89.

99. "The New Year," editorial, *Anglo-African*, Jan. 2, 1864.

100. Wilson, *History of the Antislavery Measures*, 328–29; McPherson, *Struggle for Equality*, 188–90; Du Bois, *Black Reconstruction*, 226–30.

101. Wilson, *History of the Antislavery Measures*, 330–33.

102. Wilson, 333–36.

103. Howe, *Refugees from Slavery*, 5–6; Furrow, "Samuel Gridley Howe," 352–62.

104. Although Stanton forwarded both the preliminary and the final reports to Congress at the end of June (see *Report of the Secretary of War Communicating . . . a Copy of the Preliminary Report, and Also of the Final Report of the American Freedmen's Inquiry Commission*, 38th Cong., 1st sess. (1864), S. Exec. Doc. No. 53,), the final report—unlike the preliminary one—was not published separately. With only minor changes, however, Owen published the final report under his own name and the title *The Wrong of Slavery and the Right of Emancipation and the Future of the African Race in the United States*. Howe and McKaye each published a supplementary report: Howe's was titled *The Refugees from Slavery in Canada West: Report to the Freedmen's Inquiry Commission*, and McKaye's *The Mastership and Its Fruits: The Emancipated Slave Face to Face with His Old Master*.

105. Owen's work represents an underappreciated contribution to the historical scholarship on the trade. His conclusions regarding the number of victims is closer to the estimate of Du Bois's *Suppression of the African Slave Trade* than to that of the revisionist scholarship initiated by Philip Curtin's *Atlantic Slave Trade: A Census* and the ongoing work of David Eltis and colleagues in the Trans-Atlantic Slave Trade Database Project, http://www.slavevoyages.org/assessment/estimates (accessed July 10, 2017). Like more recent commentators, Owen drew attention to the remarkable growth of the African-descended population in North America (from roughly 0.5

million persons imported to 4.5 million descendants in 1860) versus the shocking decline elsewhere in the Americas (from more than 15 million persons that he estimated were transported to fewer than 12 million descendants in 1860).

106. AFIC, "Final Report," 84, 89–90.

107. AFIC, 72, 81.

108. AFIC, 108–9, quotations at 109.

109. AFIC, 109.

110. Testimony of Gen. [Jas. S.] Wadsworth before the American Freedmen's Inquiry Commission, [Jan.? 1864,] in *Freedom: Wartime Genesis, Lower South*, 497–98. A month earlier, Wadsworth had completed a tour of the lower Mississippi valley and submitted to the War Department a valuable report on conditions among the freed people in their several capacities as soldiers, residents of contraband camps, and laborers on leased plantations. See excerpts in Jas. S. Wadsworth to the Adjutant General U.S. Army, Dec. 16, 1863, in *Freedom: Wartime Genesis, Lower South*, 757–62.

111. Testimony of Maj. Geo. L. Stearns before the American Freedmen's Inquiry Commission, [Nov. 23, 1863,] in *Freedom: Wartime Genesis, Lower South*, 416. Tennessee's military governor Andrew Johnson endorsed Stearns's view based on his firm belief that wage labor was developing on its own in Tennessee without any intervention on the part of federal authorities. See Testimony of Gov. Andrew Johnson before the American Freedmen's Inquiry Commission, Nov. 23, 1863, in *Freedom: Wartime Genesis, Lower South*, 412–13.

112. AFIC, "Final Report," 381–82. Curiously, McKaye considered the proposal to establish "some uniform system of supervision and guardianship for the emancipated population" during "their transition from slavery to freedom" as one of the commission's three key recommendations (the other two being "personal freedom" and "civil and political rights"). *Mastership and Its Fruits*, 38, 34.

113. AFIC, "Final Report," 99.

114. Howe, *Refugees from Slavery*, iii–iv, 103–4.

115. AFIC, "Final Report," 99–100.

116. AFIC, 102–3.

117. Howe, *Refugees from Slavery*, iii–iv, 103–4.

118. AFIC, "Final Report," 109–10.

119. Sewell, *Ordeal of Free Labor*, 317.

120. See Howe's abstract of Sewell's "The Ordeal of Free Labor in the British West Indies," Series III, Item 164, AFIC Records, Harvard. See Bn. P. Hunt to American Freedmen's Inquiry Commission, May 27, 1863, James Morrison MacKaye Papers, LC, which references having forwarded a box containing fifty-seven volumes to "aid you in the investigations with which you are occupied." Hunt viewed Jamaica as an especially apt comparative model.

121. McKaye, *Mastership and Its Fruits*, 36–37.

122. United States, *Statutes at Large*, 13:507–9.

123. Besides the D.C. emancipation bill, which became law on April 16, 1862, President Lincoln's draft proposals, dating from late November 1861, which offered federal bonds to the state of Delaware in exchange for its agreement to abolish slavery over time, also contained such wording. Drafts of a Bill for Compensated Emancipation in Delaware, [Nov. 26? 1861], in Basler, Pratt, and Dunlap, *Collected Works*, 5:29–30;

Vorenberg, *Final Freedom*, offers a definitive account of how the antislavery amendment became part of the U.S. Constitution.

124. Wilson, *History of the Antislavery Measures*, 249–72.

125. Wilson, 377–94; Annual Message to Congress, Dec. 6, 1864, in Basler, Pratt, and Dunlap, *Collected Works*, 8:149.

126. Delaware, Kentucky, and New Jersey considered and rejected the amendment during February and March 1865 only to approve it subsequently—New Jersey in 1866, Delaware in 1901, and Kentucky in 1976. On December 5, 1865, Mississippi's legislature passed up the opportunity to be the decisive twenty-seventh state needed for ratification by rejecting the measure. The state's legislature did not approve the Thirteenth Amendment until 1995.

Chapter 8

1. Bruce, *New Man*, 107–9.

2. Owen, *Wrong of Slavery*, 124; AFIC, *Preliminary Report*, 14.

3. See Nelson, *Ruin Nation*, 78–97, for additional insight into the material and symbolic significance of slave cabins during the Civil War.

4. "From Louisville, Ky.," *Christian Recorder*, Nov. 26, 1864, 189.

5. George Rodgers, Thomas Sipple, and Samuel Sampson to Mr. President, Aug. 1864, in *Freedom: Black Military Experience*, 681. The letter is in the handwriting of the men's comrade Nimrod Rowley, a native New Yorker, who attested to the authenticity of their words.

6. "Wanted! A Nation!," editorial, *Anglo-African*, May 11, 1861.

7. For a fascinating recent treatment of the visual images of black people in the early nineteenth-century North and of the clues the images reveal about the place of free African Americans in their communities and in the nation, see Cobb, *Picture Freedom*. I am grateful to Whitney Stewart for calling this work to my attention.

8. Adams, *Narrative of the Life of John Quincy Adams*, 34–36.

9. Hawkins Wilson to Chief of the Freedmen's Bureau at Richmond, May 11, 1867, enclosing Hawkins Wilson to Sister Jane, [May 11, 1867], in Berlin and Rowland, *Families and Freedom*, 17–20.

10. Because Wilson's letter to his sister remained in the files of the Freedmen's Bureau, it is likely that they did not reestablish contact. See Williams, *Help Me to Find My People*, esp. 140–68; and Litwack, *Been in the Storm So Long*, 229–39, for succinct treatments of this important component of the emancipation process. For a more extended discussion, see Gutman, *Black Family in Slavery and Freedom*, 363–431.

11. Bruce, *New Man*, 112–15. Employers frequently used similar metaphors likening the freed people's readiness to support themselves to that of a child; see, for instance, Eliot, *Story of Archer Alexander*, 84.

12. "Libby, Andersonville," editorial, *Christian Recorder*, Apr. 15, 1865, 58.

13. Jackson, *Story of Mattie J. Jackson*, 10–11.

14. Jackson, 12–13. For intriguing insights into the contested meaning of loyalty during the Civil War, see Mathisen, *Loyal Republic*, esp. 87–117.

15. Jackson, 14–16. Generally, see Burke, *On Slavery's Border*, 268–307; Astor, *Rebels on the Border*, 104–20.

16. Jackson, *Story of Mattie J. Jackson*, 18–23.

17. Jackson, 25–28. Although Mattie heard that her sister had also escaped to a free state, the family did not succeed in locating her and reuniting.

18. Jackson, 28–30.

19. Knox, *Slave and Freeman*, 75. Before escaping from Confederate service, Knox took steps to ensure that he had options.

20. William P. Lyon to Wm. M. Michael, July 3, 1863, in *Freedom: Wartime Genesis, Upper South*, 394–96, quotation at 395.

21. Eliot, *Story of Archer Alexander*, 78–81, quotation at 78.

22. Eliot, 83.

23. Family members of several of the men lived on plantations on the Union-occupied islands surrounding Port Royal, and the men successfully petitioned federal authorities to permit their relocation to Beaufort. See Pearson, *Letters from Port Royal*, 45–47.

24. Testimony of Robert Thomas Hickman, in Rawick et al., *American Slave*, suppl. ser. 1, vol. 2, Arkansas, Colorado, Minnesota, Missouri, and Oregon Narratives, 108–11. Hickman became pastor of the Pilgrim Baptist Church in St. Paul.

25. Coffin, *Reminiscences*, 635–36.

26. John Eaton Jr. to Jno. A. Rawlins, Apr. 29, 1863, in *Freedom: Wartime Genesis, Lower South*, 684–98, quotations at 686. Lieutenant Colonel Rawlins was General Grant's assistant adjutant general.

27. "Washington Correspondence," *Christian Recorder*, Apr. 30, 1864, 69.

28. See Downs, *Sick from Freedom*, 40, 47; Long, *Doctoring Freedom*, 44–69.

29. Eaton to Rawlins, Apr. 29, 1863, in *Freedom: Wartime Genesis, Lower South*, 689–90.

30. Entry for May 14, 1864, in Billington, *Journal of Charlotte L. Forten*, 224.

31. Glatthaar, *Forged in Battle*, 91–92; Dobak, *Freedom by the Sword*, 116.

32. "Our Duty in the Crisis," *Christian Recorder*, May 7, 1864, 73. Cain foresaw that "a brighter day is dawning for our race" due to the "moral and political revolutions" of the past several years.

33. Coffin, *Reminiscences*, 633–35.

34. Drumgoold, *Slave Girl's Story*, 33. More generally, see Blassingame, *Slave Testimony*, introduction; Hager, *Word by Word*; Andrews, *To Tell a Free Story*.

35. For Colonel Samuel Thomas's thorough report on the plantations under his jurisdiction, see Saml. Thomas to L. Thomas, June 15, 1864, in *Freedom: Wartime Genesis, Lower South*, 834–41, quotation at 838.

36. Josua Culverson to Commissioners of Plantations, Jan. 11, 1864, with endorsement by Theodore Fitler, in *Freedom: Wartime Genesis, Lower South*, 781–82. Yeatman named twenty other black lessees, including a woman "whose husband was killed by the rebels," who had leased land on which they grew cotton in 1863. See *Report on the Condition of the Freedmen*, 10.

37. *Freedom: Wartime Genesis, Lower South*, 648.

38. In response to his superior's request for information regarding the contraband tax, the chief quartermaster of the Department of Washington offered wide-ranging insights into the terms and conditions under which black men and women worked, in various settings, on behalf of the Union war effort in Washington and northern

Virginia. See Elias M. Greene to Chas. Thomas, Dec. 17, 1863, in *Freedom: Wartime Genesis, Upper South*, 315–21.

39. Taylor, *Reminiscences of My Life in Camp*, 17, 31–32. A small number of black women were enlisted into the navy during the Civil War as nurses and hospital attendants, particularly on the U.S. hospital ship *Red Rover*, which operated out of Memphis along the Mississippi River and its major tributaries. See King, "In Search of Women of African Descent," 302–9.

40. For a pioneering treatment of this phenomenon, see Hunter, *To 'Joy My Freedom*, esp. 74–98.

41. Besides the coverage in *Freedom: Wartime Genesis, Lower South*, 345–900, see Powell, *New Masters*, chaps. 1–6; Ripley, *Slaves and Freedmen*, chaps. 1–4; Rodrigue, *Reconstruction in the Cane Fields*, esp. chap. 2.

42. R. Q. Mallard et al. to Brigadier General Mercer, [Aug. 1, 1862], in *Freedom: Destruction of Slavery*, 795–98, quotations at 797.

43. For representative examples, see Johannson, *Widows by the Thousand*; and Ball, *Slaves in the Family*, 335–41. More generally, see Brewer, *Confederate Negro*; Martinez, *Confederate Slave Impressment*.

44. O. G. Eiland to President Davis, July 20, 1863, in *Freedom: Black Military Experience*, 284.

45. Behrend, "Rebellious Talk and Conspiratorial Plots," 17–52. Cf. Jordan, *Tumult and Silence at Second Creek*.

46. Eaton to Rawlins, Apr. 29, 1863, in *Freedom: Wartime Genesis, Lower South*, 692, 693.

47. A number of the published reports of superintendents of freed people's affairs are noteworthy for their comprehensiveness and insight. See especially James, *Annual Report of the Superintendent of Negro Affairs in North Carolina, 1864*; Conway, *Annual Report, Superintendent of the Bureau of Free Labor, 1864*; Conway, *Freedmen of Louisiana*; Banks, *Emancipated Labor in Louisiana*; Eaton to Levi Coffin, July 5, 1864, in Warren, *Extracts from Reports of Superintendents of Freedmen*, 49–64. See also Yeatman, *Report on the Condition of the Freedmen*; and Yeatman, *Suggestions of a Plan of Organization for Freed Labor, and the Leasing of Plantations along the Mississippi River*. Numerous reports covering individual camps as well as aggregate summaries are reproduced in *Freedom: Wartime Genesis, Lower South*, and *Freedom: Wartime Genesis, Upper South*. For a sampling of the best secondary literature, see Walker, "Corinth"; Gerteis, *From Contraband to Freedman*; Click, *Time Full of Trial*; Glymph, "This Species of Property"; Sears, *Camp Nelson, Kentucky*; Manning, *Troubled Refuge*.

48. Coffin, *Reminiscences*, 630. In 1860, the black population of Memphis consisted of 3,084 slaves and 198 free people. In Nashville, by way of contrast, where the enslaved population of 3,226 was a mere 5 percent higher, the free black population of 719 was more than 360 percent higher. Kennedy, *Population of the United States in 1860*, 467.

49. Eaton to Rawlins, Apr. 29, 1863, in *Freedom: Wartime Genesis, Lower South*, 686. The table in which these numbers appear accompanied an extensive narrative report, extracts of which appear in *Freedom: Wartime Genesis, Lower South*, 684–98. For the full report see John Eaton Jr. to Jno. A. Rawlins, Apr. 29, 1863, filed with O-328

1863, Letters Received, ser. 12, RG 94, Records of the Adjutant General, 1780s–1917, National Archives. See also the detailed comments on conditions in Memphis that the superintendent of refugee camps there submitted to the AFIC: A. Severance Fiske to Messrs. Owen, McKaye, and Howe, Aug. 31, 1863, Series 1, Item 40, AFIC Records, Harvard. At the time of Fiske's report, he estimated the number of refugees to be in excess of 3,000 persons.

50. Yeatman, *Report on the Condition of the Freedmen*, 1–2.

51. See Eaton to Jno. A. Rawlins, Apr. 29, 1863, filed with O-328 1863, Letters Received, ser. 12, RG 94, Records of the Adjutant General, 1780s–1917, National Archives. The *Anglo-African* reported frequently about developments in Memphis. See, for instance, "The Freedmen at Memphis," submitted by Rev. H. W. Cobb, [general agent of the Western Freedmen's Aid Society], June 27, 1863; "Freedmen of the Department of the Tennessee," Aug. 15, 1863; and "Emancipation Celebration in Memphis," Jan. 28, 1865.

52. Yeatman, *Report on the Condition of the Freedmen*, 4.

53. Eaton to Rawlins, Apr. 29, 1863, in *Freedom: Wartime Genesis, Lower South*, 690–91; Fiske to Messrs. Owen, McKaye, and Howe, Aug. 31, 1863, Series 1, Item 40, AFIC Records, Harvard.

54. Eaton to Rawlins, Apr. 29, 1863, filed with O-328 1863, Letters Received, ser. 12, RG 94, Records of the Adjutant General, 1780s–1917, National Archives.

55. Genl. Orders No. 41, Head Quarters 60th U.S. Cold. Inft., Feb. 3, 1865, in *Freedom: Black Military Experience*, 709.

56. John Foley to T. Harris, Jan. 11, 1865, in *Freedom: Black Military Experience*, 719.

57. S. Thomas to L. Thomas, June 15, 1864, in *Freedom: Wartime Genesis, Lower South*, 834–41; Hermann, *Pursuit of a Dream*, 43–60.

58. John Oliver to [Simeon S. Jocelyn], Nov. 25, 1862, in Ripley et al., *Black Abolitionist Papers*, 5:161. Oliver was an African American missionary affiliated with the American Missionary Association (AMA).

59. See Ferebee, *Brief History*, 6–11; Click, *Time Full of Trial*, esp. 125–51.

60. Roanoke Island N.C. to Mr. President, Mar. 9, 1865, in *Freedom: Wartime Genesis, Upper South*, 231–33, quotation at 232; Richard Etheridge and Wm. Benson to Genl. Howard, [May or June 1865], in *Freedom: Black Military Experience*, 729–30. An assistant superintendent of Negro affairs and several missionaries petitioned the commissioner of the Freedmen's Bureau for relief at the same time; see Wm. A. Green et al. to O. O. Howard, June 5, 1865, in *Freedom: Black Military Experience*, 727–28.

61. See especially Powell, *New Masters*, 84–87, 115, 119; Rose, *Rehearsal for Reconstruction*, 297–314; and Saville, *Work of Reconstruction*, 32–71.

62. Rich documentary evidence of this tension may be found in *Freedom: Wartime Genesis, Lower South*, 345–900. See also Gerteis, *From Contraband to Freedman*, 119–81.

63. John Washington described the various stages of his journey to the capital after having escaped from Fredericksburg, Virginia. See Washington, "Memorys of the Past," in Blight, *Slave No More*, 210–12. For the perspective of a black soldier, see the account of Commissary Sergeant John C. Brock, of the Forty-Third U.S. Colored Infantry, "Letter from Hanover, Va. Camp near Hanover, Va., June 5, 1864," *Christian Recorder*, July 18, 1864, 98.

64. Green, *Washington: Village and Capital*, 252–53, 273–74; Masur, *Example for All the Land*, 23–24; Sarah Emery et al. to the Honorable Senate and House of Representatives in Congress Assembled, Dec. 14, 1861, in *Freedom: Destruction of Slavery*, 176; B. B. French to Edwin M. Stanton, Feb. 13, 1862, in *Freedom: Wartime Genesis, Upper South*, 262–63; *Condition and Management of the Jail in the City of Washington*, 37th Cong., 2d Sess. (1862), S. Rep. No. 60, serial 1125, at 2–3, 6, 10, 12–13, 19, 24–27, 35–36, 39–41.

65. Testimony of D. B. Nichols before the American Freedmen's Inquiry Commission, [Apr.? 1863], in *Freedom: Wartime Genesis, Upper South*, 289.

66. Testimony of Luisa Jane Barker, [Jan. 14, 1864], in the case of Lucy Ellen Johnson, in *Freedom: Wartime Genesis, Upper South*, 308–11, quotations at 308, 310. After the war, Nichols was one of the founders of Howard University and served as one of the first three "chairs of instruction," a precursor to the position of dean. For Nichols at Howard University, see Dyson, *Founding of Howard University*, 9–11.

67. Testimony of Luisa Jane Barker, [Jan. 14, 1864], in the case of Lucy Ellen Johnson, in *Freedom: Wartime Genesis, Upper South*, 308–11, quotations at 308, 310. The attempt by Johnson's father, Fielding Lewis, to intervene is summarized in *Freedom: Wartime Genesis, Upper South*, 311n. When the enslaved Mississippi man Louis Hughes witnessed the whipping of his wife, Matilda, he too felt "powerless" to intervene. Hughes, *Thirty Years a Slave*, 99.

68. Testimony of Louis Johnson, [Jan.? 1864], in *Freedom: Wartime Genesis, Upper South*, 295–96. For other criticism, see testimony of Luisa Jane Barker, [Jan. 14, 1864], and of James I. Ferree, Georgiana Willets, and Lucy Smith, [Jan.? 1864], in *Freedom: Wartime Genesis, Upper South*, 308–11, 327–32. More generally, see Harriet Jacob's survey of camps in the Washington area in "Life among the Contrabands," *Liberator*, Sept. 5, 1862, 144.

69. Testimony of D. B. Nichols before the American Freedmen's Inquiry Commission, [Apr.? 1863], in *Freedom: Wartime Genesis, Upper South*, 289–93. On the challenging conditions in the contraband camps and the difficulties freed people had in obtaining housing, see Fry, "Activities of the Freedmen's Aid Societies," 64–104.

70. For an overview, see Reidy, "'Coming from the Shadow of the Past,'" 403–14.

71. "Letter from Sojourner Truth," *Liberator*, Dec. 23, 1864, 3.

72. Entry for Dec. 2, 1863, "Diaries of Julia Wilbur, March 1860 to July 1866," 365, accessed Mar. 15, 2018, https://www.alexandriava.gov/uploadedFiles/historic/info/civilwar/JuliaWilburDiary1860to1866.pdf. Julia Wilbur and Harriet Jacobs, who administered to the needs of the freed people at Alexandria on behalf of the Rochester Ladies' Anti-slavery Society and the New York Yearly Meeting of Friends, respectively, tangled repeatedly with Gladwin. See Yellin et al., *Harriet Jacobs Family Papers*, 2:450, 462–63, 473–75, 499–500, 504, 523–26, 532, 546, and 551–52; and "Diaries of Julia Wilbur," 269, 272, 287, 312, 317, 335, 394, 408, 438, 465, 479, 480, 516, and 528. See also Julia Wilbur to E. M. Stanton, Mar. 24, 1863, in *Freedom: Wartime Genesis, Upper South*, 280–83; and Samuel Shaw to J. R. Bigelow, June 14, 1863, in *Freedom: Wartime Genesis, Upper South*, 299–302.

73. Testimony of Georgiana Willets and Lucy Smith, [Jan.? 1864], in *Freedom: Wartime Genesis, Upper South*, 330–31. Hinton's observation appears in "Washington Correspondence," *Christian Recorder*, June 4, 1864, 89. The following month,

Julia Wilbur lamented that Congress just adjourned without having passed the Freedmen's Bureau bill and that "Old Nichols & Gladwin will continue to tyrannize over the people." See entry for July 4, 1864, "Diaries of Julia Wilbur," 438. Several months earlier the *Recorder* reported approvingly on three model villages that General Benjamin Butler had established at the farm of former Virginia governor Henry A. Wise: one for soldiers' families, one for agriculture, and one for the mechanical arts. See "The Freedmen in Gen. Butler's Department. Going the Right Way to Work," *Christian Recorder*, Feb. 13, 1864, 25.

74. "Regulations for the Government of Freedman's Village," Digital Commonwealth, accessed May 9, 2016, https://www.digitalcommonwealth.org/search /commonwealth:70796c439.

75. Testimony of D. B. Nichols before the American Freedmen's Inquiry Commission, [Apr.? 1863], in *Freedom: Wartime Genesis, Upper South*, 290.

76. Reidy, "Coming from the Shadow of the Past," 409–14. Laws also led a postwar protest regarding the payment of rents.

77. See, for instance, "Letter from James Lynch," *Christian Recorder*, Feb. 27, 1864, 33. Subscribing himself as a missionary and government superintendent, Lynch reported that in the recent sales of property for delinquent taxes in Beaufort, "The colored people, who, three years ago, were slaves, bought two-fifths of the town, or about eighteen thousand dollars' worth of property," which in some cases included "their masters' houses." Lynch also reported that the Direct Tax Commissioners placed under his direction a school-farm of 165 acres. More generally, see De Boer, "Role of Afro-Americans."

78. Turner to the AME and AMEZ Bishops, *Christian Recorder*, Oct. 1, 1864, 157. Northern black Methodists played an early and important part in providing missionary support to the freed people of the Southern states, in the process promoting the growth of truly national networks among the African American denominations, which in turn helped reinforce the sense of nationalism, both to the United States and to the larger black nationality that Robert Hamilton described. See, for instance, "Letter from Wilmington, N.C.," *Christian Recorder*, Apr. 8, 1865, 53; "Libby, Andersonville," *Christian Recorder*, Apr. 15, 1865, 58. The end of the war began an era in which African American Christians throughout the South sought autonomy from the white-controlled governance structures of the major Christian denominations. During the summer and fall of 1865, reports from all quarters of the South to the *Christian Recorder* described the contests over denominational autonomy and, with it, the disposition of the property that prewar black Methodists often purchased with their own funds.

79. Jones, *Saving Savannah*, esp. 218–20.

80. See Cecelski, *Fire of Freedom*, for details about Galloway's remarkable life and career.

81. "Emancipation Celebration in Memphis," *Anglo-African*, Jan. 28, 1865.

82. See, for instance, "Portsmouth Correspondence" and "Washington Correspondence," *Christian Recorder*, Jan. 16, 1864, 9; "Brooklyn Correspondence" and "Letter from South Carolina," *Christian Recorder*, Jan. 16, 1864, 10; "Grand Union Jubilee" (New Haven), *Christian Recorder*, Jan. 14, 1865, 5; "Celebration of Emancipation in Chester, Illinois" and "Indianapolis Correspondence," *Christian Recorder*, Jan. 28, 1865, 13.

83. Singleton, *Recollections of My Slavery Days*, 7–9, quotation at 8.

84. Hall, *Samuel Hall, 47 Years a Slave*, 21–25. This account of Hall's adventures is in the words of Orville Elder, a storekeeper from the Iowa town in which he settled. The chapter treating the confrontation with the owner is titled "A Chance for Revenge."

85. Harris to Gen. Ullman, Dec. 27, 1864, in *Freedom: Black Military Experience*, 692.

86. See Aug's. G. Bennett to Wm. L. M. Burger, Nov. 30, 1863, in *Freedom: Black Military Experience*, 389–90; Taylor, *Reminiscences of My Life in Camp*, 15–16. Black soldiers who corresponded with the *Christian Recorder* and the *Anglo-African* denounced the government's policy and practice of discriminatory pay ceaselessly, from the time it was first articulated in the summer of 1863 until long after the military appropriations bill of June 1864 established parity. For representative samples, see *Freedom: Black Military Experience*, 362–405; Redkey, *Grand Army of Black Men*, 229–48.

87. Wm. J. Brown to Honourable Secretary of War, Apr. 27, 1864, in *Freedom: Black Military Experience*, 377–78. Brown voiced sentiments akin to those voiced by Corporal James Henry Gooding, who had written to President Abraham Lincoln the previous fall asking "Are we *Soldiers*, or are we LABOURERS?" See Gooding to Lincoln, Sept. 28, 1863, in *Freedom: Black Military Experience*, 385–86. On Gooding, see Adams, *On the Altar of Freedom*.

88. On the case of Sergeant Walker, see especially the excerpt from the testimony of Lt. Col. A. G. Bennett, Jan. 11, 1864, and excerpts from the statement of Sergt. William Walker, Jan. 12, 1864, proceedings of general court-martial of Sergeant William Walker, 3rd S.C. Vols., in *Freedom: Black Military Experience*, 391–94. The quotations from Saxton appear in his endorsement, dated Dec. 11, 1863, on Wm. B. Barton to R. Saxton, Dec. 5, 1863, in *Freedom: Black Military Experience*, 390. Barton, commander of U.S. forces at Hilton Head, forwarded a petition by the commander of the Third South Carolina Volunteers asking that the government feed the men's families. "Colored men employed in the *Quartermaster's* Department receive from 10 to 25 dollars per month, with ample opportunity for the cultivation of the soil," and at the same time "receive full rations for their families thereby causing great dissatisfaction among the men of this Command."

89. Commanding general David Hunter's declaration of martial law and emancipation appears in General Orders, No. 11, Headquarters Department of the South, May 9, 1862, in *Official Records*, ser. 1, vol. 14:341; Lincoln's repudiation of Hunter's declaration of freedom and his renewed appeal on behalf of his March offer of federal assistance to any state that would promote "a gradual abolishment of slavery" appears in *Official Records*, ser. 3, vol. 2:42–43. Lincoln memorably characterized his proposal as making "common cause for a common object." "The change it contemplates," he insisted, "would come gently as the dews of heaven, not rending or wrecking anything." *Official Records*, ser. 3, vol. 2:43. Testimony of Frederick A. Eustis before the American Freedmen's Inquiry Commission, [June 1863], in *Freedom: Wartime Genesis, Lower South*, 246.

90. Pearson, *Letters from Port Royal*, 14, 56.

91. H. W. Benham to Jules de la Croix, May 6, 1862, in *Official Records*, ser. 3, vol. 2:29–30. Hunter informed General Isaac I. Stevens on May 8 that he was "authorized by the War Department to form the negroes into 'squads, companies, or otherwise,' as I may deem most beneficial to the public service," and asked Stevens's assistance in raising companies, officering them "from the most intelligent and energetic of our non-commissioned officers; men who will go into it with all their hearts." David Hunter to Isaac I. Stevens, May 8, 1862, in *Official Records*, ser. 3, vol. 2:30.

92. Edward L. Pierce to Maj. Gen. Hunter, May 11, 1862, in *Freedom: Black Military Experience*, 47–48.

93. G. M. Wells to E. L. Pierce, [May 1862], in *Freedom: Black Military Experience*, 49–50.

94. Charles P. Ware to Dear Sister [Emma Ware], Oct. 31, 1862, folder 54, box 109-1, Charles Pickard Ware Papers, MSRC-HU.

95. Edward S. Philbrick to Charles [Ware], May 1, 1863, folder 29, box 109-1, Charles Pickard Ware Papers, MSRC-HU; Pearson, *Letters from Port Royal*, 187–90, quotations at 188 and 190. Northern missionaries at Port Royal were called "Gideonites."

96. Higginson, *Army Life in a Black Regiment*, 62–129.

97. Henderson, *Speech of Hon. J. B. Henderson of Missouri, on Emancipation in Missouri*, 3. According to some estimates, Missouri's black population decreased by more than 40,000 during the war. Etcheson, *Bleeding Kansas*, 227–32, 320n83. Other estimates varied wildly: in late summer 1863, Leavenworth mayor D. R. Anthony estimated that some 5,000 "run away slaves" from Missouri had settled in Kansas, but Governor Thomas Carney could do no better than conjecture a figure of between 15,000 and 20,000. Carney suggested that his state proved attractive because its citizens "do not deem it necessary to tear negroes to pieces or hang them to lamp-posts to prevent being outstripped in any of the pursuits of life." See Anthony to S. G. Howe, n.d., and Carney to Sam'l G. Howe, Sept. 9, 1863, Series I, Items 5 and 24, AFIC Records, Harvard. See also Astor, *Rebels on the Border*, 142–43.

98. E. Smith to Honl. W. H. Seward, Jan. 6, 1863, in *Freedom: Destruction of Slavery*, 565. In March 1863, Kentucky lawmakers enacted measures providing for the arrest, confinement, and sale of alleged "runaway slaves" who attempted to live in the state under the guise of having been freed by the Emancipation Proclamation. Smith to Seward, Jan. 6, 1863, 503–5.

99. Thaddeus Stevens to Majr. Genl. Howard, Dec. 4, 1865, S97 vol. 2 1865, Letters Received, Office of the Commissioner, RG 105, Records of the Bureau of Refugees, Freedmen and Abandoned Lands, National Archives. An endorsement by an agent of the bureau in Richmond indicated that attempts to locate the children by means of notices read "in all the colored churches" proved futile. On Gettysburg, see also Peter C. Vermilyea, "The Effects of the Confederate Invasion of Pennsylvania on Gettysburg's African American Community," accessed Mar. 8, 2018, http://www.gdg.org/gettysburg%20magazine/gburgafrican.html; Ward, *Slaves' War*, 166–68. See also Johnson, *Battleground Adventures*, 183–91, for the testimony of two black eyewitnesses who managed not to be removed.

100. Martha to My Dear Husband [Richard Glover], Dec. 30, 1863, in *Freedom: Black Military Experience*, 244.

101. Rawick et al., *American Slave*, suppl. ser. 1, vol. 5, Indiana and Ohio Narratives, 236.

102. "A Voice from the South-West," *Christian Recorder*, Jan. 30, 1864, 17. Cf. Aikman, *Future of the Colored Race in America*, 3; *Memorial of the Emancipation League of Boston, Massachusetts*, 37th Cong., 3d Sess. (1862), S. Misc. Doc. No. 10, serial 1150, at 2.

103. "Emancipation Celebration at Wilmington," *Christian Recorder*, Jan. 30, 1864, 18.

104. "The Capabilities of Our Race," *Christian Recorder*, May 21, 1864, 81.

105. The 1860 census recorded 1,798 enslaved persons in Delaware and 225,483 in Kentucky. Kennedy, *Population of the United States in 1860*, 594–95.

106. James, *Life of Rev. Thomas James*, 16–23, quotations at 18, 21.

107. James, 22.

108. Wilson, *History of the Antislavery Measures*, 313.

109. Wilson, 314–28, esp. 320–23, 325–26.

110. Howard, *Black Liberation in Kentucky*, 57–87, esp. 78–80; Astor, *Rebels on the Border*, 124–31.

111. Palmer's orders aimed to relieve the city of Louisville of its growing population of black refugees. See General Orders, No. 32, Department of Kentucky, May 11, 1865, in *Freedom: Destruction of Slavery*, 619–21. "Recent events," he explained to local officials, "have disturbed, if not changed, their relations toward those who were their former masters." "What is now required is," he continued, "that their relations to the state shall be defined with reference to existing, and not past, facts. When that is done, confidence between the races will be restored . . . and prosperity will take the place of the confusion and vagrancy, which is now seen on every hand, to the alarm of all. As preliminary to this, and as preventative to vagrancy, these people must be allowed to migrate at their pleasure, and seek employment where it may be found," including across the Ohio River. Palmer, *Personal Recollections*, 232–39, quotation at 237–38. Palmer recounted the events of July 4, 1864, in *Personal Recollections*, 240–42, with the quotation regarding substantial freedom at 242. James, *Life of Rev. Thomas James*, 16–22, quotation at 22.

112. John M. Palmer to Andrew Johnson, July 29, 1865, in *Freedom: Destruction of Slavery*, 632–34; Chas. A. Roxborough et al. to Mr. President, [June 1865], in *Freedom: Destruction of Slavery*, 624–26.

113. "Wanted! A Nation!," editorial, *Anglo-African*, May 11, 1861.

114. Quoted in Litwack, *Been in the Storm So Long*, 51.

Chapter 9

1. "Perils by the Way," editorial, *Anglo-African*, Sept. 26, 1863.

2. "Perils by the Way."

3. For the proceedings of these meetings, see Foner and Walker, *Proceedings of the Black State Conventions*; and the website of the Colored Conventions Project at the University of Delaware: http://coloredconventions.org/ (accessed Mar. 8, 2018).

4. *Proceedings of the National Emigration Convention*, 25. For two recent studies that offer insightful commentary on the broad intellectual and cultural implications

of the first emancipation, see Cobb, *Picture Freedom*; and Rael, *Black Identity and Black Protest*.

5. For a superb recent exploration of such forces in the "middle border," the states touching the Ohio and Missouri Rivers, see Phillips, *Rivers Ran Backward*, esp. 15–82.

6. Sinha, *Slave's Cause*, 64–85; Rael, *Eighty-Eight Years*, 62–79; Berlin, *Long Emancipation*, 47–99; Newman, "Grammar of Emancipation," 11–25. See also Zilversmit, *First Emancipation*; McManus, *Black Bondage in the North*; Melish, *Disowning Slavery*; Nash and Soderlund, *Freedom by Degrees*; Harris, *In the Shadow of Slavery*; Hodges, *Black New Jersey*.

7. Schwalm, *Emancipation's Diaspora*, 17–23; Fehrenbacher, *Dred Scott Case*; Brooks, *Captives and Cousins*; Smith, *Freedom's Frontier*; and Downs and Masur, *The World the Civil War Made*.

8. Kantrowitz, *More Than Freedom*, offers a model case study of such developments in Boston, as does Taylor, *Frontiers of Freedom*, for Cincinnati. More generally, see Horton and Horton, *In Hope of Liberty*; Rael, *Black Identity and Black Protest*; and Reidy, "African American Struggle for Citizenship Rights."

9. "From Indianapolis, Ind.," *Christian Recorder*, May 21, 1864, 82.

10. Keckley, *Behind the Scenes*, 95–100; Lusane, *Black History of the White House*, 169–80; "Washington Correspondence," *Christian Recorder*, Nov. 29, 1862, 190, and Jan. 10, 1863, 5; Faulkner, *Women's Radical Reconstruction*, esp. 67–82. Richard H. Cain, an AME minister in Brooklyn, did not take all charitable work at face value, criticizing "teachers, editors and pastors, with good fat salaries" who were "happy in their hallucinations" about civilizing Africa or busy profiting from "the 'contraband' business." "Brooklyn Correspondence," *Christian Recorder*, May 23, 1863, 86.

11. "Washington Correspondence," *Christian Recorder*, Sept. 5, 1863, 141. Several months earlier, "a committee of ladies" had presented books to the lyceum. "Washington Correspondence," *Christian Recorder*, May 2, 1863, 69. "Washington Correspondence," *Christian Recorder*, Aug. 29, 1863, 137, references a speech by Elizabeth Butler, a protégé of Turner's, on the topic of "Benevolence to God's poor" before the Sabbath-school Association.

12. "An act to incorporate the Colored Catholic Benevolent Society," June 28, 1864, in United States, *Statutes at Large*, 13:201.

13. Masur, *Example for All the Land*, 34–38; Davis, "Pennsylvania State Equal Rights League," 614–15. For related developments in Boston, see Kantrowitz, *More Than Freedom*.

14. "Second Letter from R. H. Cain," *Christian Recorder*, Feb. 13, 1864, 25.

15. "A Trip to Hayti," *Douglass' Monthly*, May 1861, 449–50.

16. *Proceedings of the National Emigration Convention of Colored People*, 32–70, quotations at 6, 32, 43, 46–47.

17. "The Scheme of Colonization," *Christian Recorder*, Aug. 23, 1862, 135; "Washington Correspondence," *Christian Recorder*, Aug. 30, 1862, 137; Masur, *Example for All the Land*, 35–39; Masur, "African American Delegation to Abraham Lincoln," 117–44.

18. "Sketch of Liberia," *Christian Recorder*, Apr. 26, 1862, 66.

19. Joseph Enoch Williams et al. to the Honorable Senate and House of Representatives, [Apr. 1862], in *Freedom: Wartime Genesis, Upper South*, 263–65, quotation

regarding whom they represented at 263 and the "Africo-West India Islands" at 264; "District of Columbia Correspondence," *Christian Recorder*, May 17, 1862, 77. The correspondent to the *Recorder* noted that Williams had procured some of the signatures by fraud.

20. Williams et al. to the Honorable Senate and House of Representatives, [Apr. 1862], in *Freedom: Wartime Genesis, Upper South*, quotation regarding slavery at 264; others at 265.

21. *Proceedings of the National Emigration Convention of Colored People*, 26; Aikman, *Future of the Colored Race in America*, 33–35.

22. Williams et al. to the Honorable Senate and House of Representatives, [Apr. 1862], in *Freedom: Wartime Genesis, Upper South*, quotation regarding "land of our birth" at 264; "our country" at 263; "your country" at 265; and "the families of God's great world" at 264.

23. "Washington Correspondence," *Christian Recorder*, Feb. 15, 1862, 26. A superfluous comma in the original is omitted. A rich literature assesses African American nationalism and emigrationism. See especially Franklin, *Black Self-Determination*; Hahn, *Nation under Our Feet*; Harding, *There Is a River*; Miller, *Search for a Black Nationality*; Moses, *Golden Age of Black Nationalism*; Redkey, *Black Exodus*; Stuckey, *Ideological Origins of Black Nationalism*.

24. "Illinois Correspondence," *Christian Recorder*, Sept. 6, 1862, 141.

25. Richd. Yates to President Lincoln, July 11, 1862, in *Freedom: Black Military Experience*, 84–85.

26. "A Contraband's Story," *Douglass' Monthly*, March 1862, 617. J. W. Phelps to Charles C. Churchill, Aug. 11, 1861, in *Official Records*, ser. 1, vol. 4:569. The incidence of such reports increased dramatically during McClellan's 1862 Peninsula Campaign; see Brasher, *Peninsula Campaign and the Necessity of Emancipation*, 52, 76, 113–15; and, more generally, Jordan, *Black Confederates and Afro-Yankees*, esp. 222–26.

27. McKaye, *Birth and Death of Nations*, 31.

28. *Douglass' Monthly*, June 1861, 469.

29. Melish, *Disowning Slavery*; McManus, *Black Bondage in the North*.

30. The original Militia Act, dated May 2, 1792, addressed the purposes of the militia, the circumstances under which it might be mobilized, its discipline, and its pay and other amenities in relation to regular army personnel. The law was silent as to who was subject to militia service. On May 8, 1792, a separate act stated explicitly that "each and every free able-bodied white male citizen" between the ages of eighteen and forty-five in the respective states was obliged to serve. The Militia Act of February 28, 1795, superseded that of May 2, 1792. Following Fort Sumter, when Lincoln called for 75,000 volunteers referencing the 1795 act, the language regarding "combinations too powerful to be suppressed by the ordinary course of judicial proceedings, or by the powers vested in the Marshals by law" was nearly identical to that in the act of May 2, 1792. United States, *Statutes at Large*, 1:264–65, 271–74 (quotation at 271), 424–25; "Proclamation Calling Militia and Convening Congress," Apr. 15, 1861, in Basler, Pratt, and Dunlap, *Collected Works*, 4:331–32. The stipulation of the act of May 8, 1792, requiring white men to serve remained unchanged. In New Orleans, which became U.S. territory after the Louisiana Purchase in 1803, free men of mixed

European and African ancestry continued to perform militia service despite the proscriptive language of the 1792 law.

31. The renowned activist, attorney, and Episcopal priest Pauli Murray, whose grandfather served as a civilian teamster before enlisting first in the navy and then in the army, knew from family lore that "before the war was many weeks old thousands of mixed bloods [from Pennsylvania] were entering white regiments. Some never recrossed the line and others were not known in the official records as Negroes until many years later." Murray, *Proud Shoes*, 117.

32. The national press reported Reeder's story: "A Colored Soldier at Bull Run," *Anglo-African*, Sept. 21, 1861. H. Ford Douglas wrote to Frederick Douglass in January 1863 as Grant's assault on Vicksburg gathered momentum, jubilant that "the slaves are *free*!" and confident that "this war will educate Mr. Lincoln out of his idea of the deportation of the Negro, quite as fast as it has some of his other proslavery ideas with respect to employing them as soldiers." He encouraged Douglass to "finish the crowning work of your life. Go to work at once and raise a Regiment and offer your services to the Government." Douglas to Douglass, Jan. 8, 1863, in Ripley et al., *Black Abolitionist Papers*, 5:169–70. On Belcher, see Edwin Belcher to O. O. Howard, Nov. 5, 1867, B-217 Vol. 11 1867, Letters Received, Office of the Commissioner, RG 105, Records of the Bureau of Refugees, Freedmen and Abandoned Lands, National Archives; and Murray, *Proud Shoes*, 116. Algernon S. Belcher, Edwin's younger brother, served in the navy.

33. Rufus Sibb Jones to Edwin M. Stanton, May 13, 1862, in *Freedom: Black Military Experience*, 83–84. Jones reported that, having been organized for "some two years," his men were "quite Proficient in military discipline." On the Hannibal Guards, see "District of Columbia Correspondence," *Christian Recorder*, Mar. 22, 1862, 46. See also "John S. Rock, Esq.," *Christian Recorder*, Apr. 19, 1862, 62; Garnet, *Memorial Discourse*, 57. Garnet's 1843 "Address to the Slaves of the United States" had called for the use of armed rebellion to achieve freedom.

34. White to E. M. Stanton, May 7, 1862, in *Freedom: Black Military Experience*, 82–83. See Reid, *African-Canadians in Union Blue*, for a comprehensive overview of the service of the enslaved refugees and Canadian citizens in the Union's armed forces (navy as well as army) during the Civil War.

35. Murray, *Proud Shoes*, 117–18.

36. McPherson, *War on the Waters*, 135–68; Bennett, *Union Jacks*, 155–81; Ramold, *Slaves, Sailors, Citizens*, chaps. 2 and 3; Alexander, *Homelands and Waterways*, 38–88.

37. Douglass, *Narrative*, 64; Douglass, *Life and Times*, 246–48, quotation at 247.

38. Lane's First Kansas Colored Volunteers is a staple of every account of the chronicle of black soldiers during the Civil War, but see Spurgeon, *Soldiers in the Army of Freedom*, for a thorough recent study.

39. "The War," *Christian Recorder*, Aug. 16, 1862, 130. The newspaper's "Domestic Items" of the same date noted that Rhode Island's adjutant general had announced the state's intention to raise a regiment that will "consist entirely of colored citizens" (131).

40. On the war in the West generally, see Josephy, *Civil War in the American West*; Richardson, *West from Appomattox*, esp. 8–77; and Hahn, *Nation without Borders*, esp.

243–69, 280–85. For the implications of emancipation on the various peoples of the Southwest, see Brooks, *Captives and Cousins*, 331–60; Smith, *Freedom's Frontier*, 174–235; and Smith, "Emancipating Peons, Excluding Coolies," 46–74.

41. "The Call for Colored Soldiers: Will They Fight? Should They Fight?," editorial, *Christian Recorder*, Feb. 14, 1863, 25.

42. "Letter from the Recruiting Department," *Christian Recorder*, Mar. 7, 1863, 39. War Secretary Stanton had authorized Andrew to begin recruiting on the principle that the "colored volunteers are precisely like the white volunteers" with only one exception—he was "not to commission any colored men as officers." See Andrew to John Wilder, May 23, 1863, in *Freedom: Black Military Experience*, 369–70.

43. "Men of Color, to Arms!," *Douglass' Monthly*, March 1863, 801. The call was printed and distributed widely as a broadside, a copy of which is in Frederick Douglass Papers, box 28-3, folder 63, MSRC-HU. Also note the efforts of other black leaders of national stature to recruit black soldiers. See, for instance, M. R. Delany to Hon. Secry. War, Dec. 15, 1863, in *Freedom: Black Military Experience*, 101–2.

44. M. R. Delany to Mrs. Cary, Dec. 7, 1863; Lt. Col. Benj. S. Pardee to Mrs. Mary A. S. Cary, Mar. 3, 1864, box 13-1, Mary Ann Shadd Cary Papers, MSRC-HU.

45. "Indianapolis Correspondence," *Christian Recorder*, Jan. 13, 1865, 13.

46. Williams, *History of Negro Troops*, 191–205, quotation at 199. The Fifty-Fourth Massachusetts Volunteers and the Battle of Fort Wagner are staple building blocks in every account of the black military experience in the Civil War. See, for example, Quarles, *Negro in the Civil War*, 3–21; Cornish, *Sable Arm*, 154–57; *Freedom: Black Military Experience*, 519, 534–38; Burchard, *One Gallant Rush*; Trudeau, *Like Men of War*, 71–90; Blatt, Brown, and Yacovone, *Hope and Glory*. Still useful is Emilio, *History of the Fifty-Fourth Regiment*, 51–127.

47. "Letter from Soldiers," *Christian Recorder*, Dec. 26, 1863, 206. On the South Carolina units, see Higginson, *Army Life in a Black Regiment*, 280–92, quotation at 280; Taylor, *Reminiscences of My Life in Camp*, 15–16.

48. James Henry Gooding to Abraham Lincoln, Sept. 28, 1863, in *Freedom: Black Military Experience*, 386. Gooding reported that the paymaster had recently visited the regiment and offered the opinion that "on the next sitting of Congress," the matter would be resolved in favor of the soldiers. *Freedom: Black Military Experience*, 385.

49. *Freedom: Black Military Experience*, 386.

50. George Rodgers, Thomas Sipple, and Samuel Sampson to Mr. President, Aug. 1864, in *Freedom: Black Military Experience*, 680–81. The letter is in the handwriting of Nimrod Rowley, a literate member of the same regiment, who certified that these were the words of Rodgers and Sipple.

51. "Colored Troops, No. 2," *Christian Recorder*, July 11, 1863, 113; "The Third Colored Regiment Here in the North," editorial, *Christian Recorder*, July 11, 1863, 114. The following week the editor offered similar assurances that "the friends of this movement" intend to bring it before Congress for resolution expeditiously. *Christian Recorder*, July 18, 1863, 118.

52. "Brooklyn Correspondence," *Christian Recorder*, Dec. 26, 1863, 205.

53. The original letter appeared in an issue of the *Christian Recorder* that has not survived. The rejoinder by 1st Sergt. Ferdinand H. Hughes of the Twenty-Fifth U.S.

Colored Infantry (raised in Philadelphia) appears in the *Christian Recorder*, Jan. 14, 1865, 5, and that of William Paul Green of the Eleventh U.S. Colored Heavy Artillery (originally the Fourteenth Rhode Island Heavy Artillery, raised in Providence in October 1863) in the *Christian Recorder*, Feb. 4, 1865, 19.

54. "From Morris Island, S.C.," *Christian Recorder*, July 30, 1864, 125.

55. "An Important Soldier's Letter," *Christian Recorder*, June 24, 1864, 102.

56. Wilson, *History of the Antislavery Measures*, 293–312, quotations at 309 (Stevens), 299 (Wilson), and 302 (Saulsbury).

57. Wilson, 309–12. United States, *Statutes at Large*, 13:126–30, quotations at 129. Regarding bounty payments, the law capped the payment at one hundred dollars to any person of color who enlisted thereafter. It further stipulated that men who entered service in response to the president's call for volunteers of October 17, 1863, were entitled to "the same amount of bounty without regard to color," and that men already mustered into service who were free as of April 18, 1861, were "entitled to receive the pay, bounty, and clothing allowed to such persons by the laws existing at the time of their enlistment." The pattern of enlistments of black Canadians in the U.S. Army suggests that black workingmen weighed the real economic implications of military service before they enlisted in the fight to free the slaves. The annual number of volunteers from north of the border increased by more than fivefold between 1863 and 1864, with most enlistments during the latter year occurring after Congress rectified the inequality. See Reid, *African-Canadians in Union Blue*, chaps. 2, 4, and 5. On the correlation of enlistment figures with the equalization of pay between black and white soldiers, see Reid, 122–23, esp. Fig. 2.

58. United States, *Statutes at Large*, 13:327.

59. Harris, *In the Shadow of Slavery*, 270–71. See also "An Archbishop on the War," *Anglo-African*, Oct. 19, 1861. For a good general overview of these struggles, see Johnson, "Beyond Freedom," 162–82.

60. Foner, "Battle to End Discrimination," 275–80; Still, *Brief Narrative of the Struggle for the Rights of the Colored People of Philadelphia*, 8.

61. "Outrage," editorial, *Christian Recorder*, Mar. 15, 1862, 42.

62. "An Incident," editorial, *Christian Recorder*, May 2, 1863, 70.

63. In June 1862, the Philadelphia native Charlotte L. Forten, who had been living for some years in Salem, Massachusetts, reflected on having spent the winter of 1861–62 in the city at her physician's orders. "A weary winter I had there," she confided in her journal, "unable to work, and having but little congenial society, and suffering the many deprivations which all our unhappy race must suffer in the so-called 'City of Brotherly Love.' What a mockery that name is!" Entry for June 22, 1862, in Billington, *Journal of Charlotte L. Forten*, 131–32.

64. Late in 1863, William Still compiled a list of the incidents that black Philadelphians had endured in their attempt to gain access to the cars, including the death of the minister who fell from the platform. "The Passenger Cars of Philadelphia," *Christian Recorder*, Dec. 26, 1863, 206. See also Still, *Brief Narrative of the Struggle for the Rights of the Colored People of Philadelphia*, 9.

65. "The Defence of the State," editorial, *Christian Recorder*, June 20, 1863, 102; "Scattered Recollections of the Past," *Christian Recorder*, Aug. 1, 1863, 125; "The Enthusiastic Gathering of Colored Persons in Sansom St. Hall," *Christian Recorder*,

July 30, 1864, 122; "Colored People and the Philadelphia City Railroads," *Liberator*, Dec. 23, 1864, 2. See also Foner, "Battle to End Discrimination," 271–73.

66. "The Enthusiastic Gathering of Colored Persons in Sansom St. Hall," *Christian Recorder*, July 30, 1864, 122.

67. "The Enthusiastic Gathering of Colored Persons in Sansom St. Hall," *Christian Recorder*, July 30, 1864, 122.

68. "Colored People and the Philadelphia City Railroads," *Liberator*, Dec. 23, 1864, 207; Still, *Brief Narrative of the Struggle for the Rights of the Colored People of Philadelphia*, esp. 8–11.

69. "Letter from the Front," *Christian Recorder*, Mar. 18, 1865, 42. The writer noted that he had read about the change in the Philadelphia *Inquirer*. See also "Observer," who viewed segregated cars as "a stepping stone" to full access, *Anglo-African*, Jan. 7, 1865; and Foner, "Battle to End Discrimination," esp. part 2, 355–56.

70. "Letter from the Front," *Christian Recorder*, Mar. 18, 1862, 42.

71. Still, *Brief Narrative of the Struggle for the Rights of the Colored People of Philadelphia*, 21. The commentator was M. B. Lowry, a Radical Republican state senator from Erie County.

72. Entry for Sept. 14, 1862, in Billington, *Journal of Charlotte E. Forten*, 138.

73. "From San Francisco," *Anglo-African*, Jan. 2, 1864. See also Foner, "Battle to End Discrimination," part 1, 283–84; Masur, *Example for All the Land*, 100–112.

74. "Washington Correspondence," *Christian Recorder*, June 20, 1863, 101.

75. "From Washington," *Anglo-African*, Feb. 13, 1864.

76. While debating the extension of the charter for the Alexandria and Washington Railroad, Congress added a prohibition against excluding any person "on account of color," which became law on March 3, 1863. See United States, *Statutes at Large*, 12:805. On July 1, 1864, the charter authorizing the new Metropolitan Railroad Company banned "excluding any person from any car on account of color." United States, *Statutes at Large*, 13:326–31, quotation at 329. Then on March 3, 1865, an amendment to the charter of the Metropolitan Railroad prohibited "exclusion . . . on account of color" on all railroads that operated in the District of Columbia. United States, *Statutes at Large*, 536–37, quotation at 537. Also see Wilson, *History of the Antislavery Measures*, 373–76; Masur, *Example for all the Land*, 100–112.

77. Masur, 107–12.

78. Foner, "Battle to End Discrimination," part 1, 264, quoting Quarles, *Black Abolitionists*, 72.

79. Johnson, "Out of Egypt," 229. See also Schwalm, *Emancipation's Diaspora*, 64–80.

80. Statements of S. R. Curtis, Mar. 20, 1863, and of David Haywood and Sam Washington, June 27, 1863, in *Freedom: Wartime Genesis, Lower South*, 660–64.

81. Adams, *Narrative of the Life of John Quincy Adams*, 35–37.

82. Adams, quotations at 83, 85.

83. Adams, editor's introduction, 10–39.

84. See Wesley, *Negro Labor in the United States*, 87–191, for a succinct summary of the key challenges affecting black laborers, North and South, during the Civil War era.

85. Still, *Brief Narrative of the Struggle for the Rights of the Colored People of Philadelphia*, 23–24, quote on 24; "Colored People and the War: A Visit to Camp Wm. Penn," editorial, *Christian Recorder*, Oct. 1, 1864, 158.

86. Taylor, *Frontiers of Freedom*, 161, 176–77; Johnson, "Beyond Freedom," 176–77.

87. Schwalm, *Emancipation's Diaspora*, 29–31; Litwack, *North of Slavery*; McManus, *Political Abolitionism*; Dykstra, *Bright Radical Star*, 108–13. Ironically, during the 1840s, when Robert Dale Owen served in the Indiana state legislature, he advocated extending the franchise to black men. When the measure was defeated, he sponsored the law that excluded black men from settling in the state, apparently assuming that if they were denied the right to vote, they had better not live there at all. Also see Frankel, *States of Inquiry*, 226. For a compilation of relevant laws, see Douglas Harper, "Exclusion of Free Blacks," Slavery in the North, accessed Feb. 20, 2018, http://slavenorth.com/exclusion.htm.

88. "Case of Nelson (mulatto) v. The People (33 Ill. 390, Jan. 1864)," in Catterall and Hayden, *Judicial Cases*, 77–79; Johnson, "Beyond Freedom," 167–69.

89. Kantrowitz, *More Than Freedom*, 314, 317–20.

90. Alexander, *Homelands and Waterways*, 211–40; Gould, *Diary of a Contraband*, 287–97.

91. Gould, 294–97.

92. Alexander, *Homelands and Waterways*, 288–89.

93. Foner and Walker, *Proceedings of the Black State Conventions*, 2:236.

94. Foner and Walker, 2:238. The petitioners also made a shrewd appeal to ethnic politics, suggesting that the state's Republican Party would need black voters to serve as "a counterpoise . . . to this disturbing element" of "ignorant . . . voters" that was "alien alike in their birth, religion, and habits of thought." Foner and Walker, 2:237.

95. Krauthamer, *Black Slaves, Indian Masters*; Krauthamer, "Indian Territory and the Treaties of 1866," 226–48; Littlefield, *Africans and Seminoles*; Littlefield, *Cherokee Freedmen*; Yarbrough, "'Dis Land Which Jines Dat of Ole Master's'," 224–41; Yarbrough, "Reconstructing Other Southerners," 47–62; Hahn, "Slave Emancipation, Indian Peoples, and the Projects of a New American Nation-State," 307–30. Only in August 2017 was the matter of the freed people's citizenship resolved by a court order in favor of the so-called Cherokee Freedmen. See NPR, "Judge Rules That Cherokee Freedmen Have Right to Tribal Citizenship," Aug. 31, 2017, accessed Oct. 5, 2017, http://www.npr.org/sections/thetwo-way/2017/08/31/547705829/judge-rules-that-cherokee-freedmen-have-right-to-tribal-citizenship. See also Brooks, *Captives and Cousins*, 331–60; Smith, *Freedom's Frontier*, 174–235; and Smith, "Emancipating Peons, Excluding Coolies," 46–74.

96. Howard, *Autobiography*, 449–55, quotation at 455. A committee of the House of Representatives had investigated him in 1870–71 in connection with similar charges for which he was also found blameless. Recent studies of Howard and the Nez Perce include West, *Last Indian War*; and Sharfstein, *Thunder in the Mountains*.

97. Anderson, *From Slavery to Affluence*, 42–49.

98. Wm. White et al. to Dear President, July 3, 1866, in *Freedom: Black Military Experience*, 764. Punctuation was added to improve readability.

99. "The Michigan State Convention," *Anglo-African*, Jan. 23, 1864; "Our Domestic Correspondence," *Anglo-African*, Feb. 13, 1864.

100. "Brooklyn Correspondence," *Christian Recorder*, July 16, 1864, 114.

101. "The National Convention—A Reply to the Rev. R. H. Cain," *Christian Recorder*, July 30, 1864, 121; "Brooklyn Correspondence," *Christian Recorder*, 122. For an

insightful recent examination of this international context, see Doyle, *Cause of All Nations*, esp. 131–57; and Doyle, *American Civil Wars*.

102. "Brooklyn Correspondence" (Cain), *Christian Recorder*, July 16, 1864, 114; "The National Convention—A Reply to the Rev. R. H. Cain," *Christian Recorder*, July 30, 1864, 121. Minutes of the Philadelphia meeting appeared as "Our Delegates to the National Convention," *Christian Recorder*, Oct. 15, 1864, 165.

103. "The National Convention of Colored Men," *Christian Recorder*, Oct. 1, 1864, 158.

104. *Proceedings of the National Convention of Colored Men, 1864*, 9, 21, 24.

105. *Proceedings of the National Convention of Colored Men, 1864*, 33–34.

106. *Proceedings of the National Convention of Colored Men, 1864*, 41.

107. *Proceedings of the National Convention of Colored Men, 1864*, 34.

108. *Proceedings of the National Convention of Colored Men, 1864*, 42.

109. *Proceedings of the National Convention of Colored Men, 1864*, 36.

110. In its issues of October 15 and October 22, 1864, the *Anglo-African* devoted several pages, beginning on the first page, to the proceedings of the convention.

111. "The National Convention of Colored Men in America," *Christian Recorder*, Oct. 15, 1864, 166; "Grand Public Demonstration of the Colored Citizens of Bridgeport, Ct.," *Christian Recorder*, Dec. 3, 1864, 193; "Grand Ratification Meeting in Philadelphia," *Anglo-African*, Oct. 29, 1864.

112. Manning, *Troubled Refuge*, 284.

113. Taylor, *Frontiers of Freedom*, 177.

114. Dykstra, *Bright Radical Star*.

115. Johnson, "Beyond Freedom," 56–60.

116. "The New England Convention of Colored Citizens, at Boston, on the 1st Inst.," *Anglo-African*, Dec. 23, 1865.

117. "Hon. Wm. D. Kelley's Lecture," *Christian Recorder*, Apr. 1, 1865, 50.

118. Johnson, "Beyond Freedom," 66–72.

119. "The Lecture of the Future of the Colored Race in America," *Anglo-African*, Jan. 28, 1865.

120. *Proceedings of the National Convention of Colored Men, 1864*, 24–27.

121. "Brooklyn Correspondence," *Christian Recorder*, Feb. 25, 1865, 30. "Some of us are of the F. F. V's.," he quipped, referring to the First Families of Virginia. "We love our relations, 'My Maryland,' Plymouth rock, Bunker Hill."

122. "Army Correspondence from Chaplain Turner," *Christian Recorder*, Mar. 25, 1865, 45.

123. "Progress of Liberty," *Christian Recorder*, May 28, 1864, 85.

Epilogue

1. Downs, "Force, Freedom, and the Making of Emancipation," 59–65.

2. See Gregory P. Downs and Scott Nesbit, "Mapping Occupation: Force, Freedom, and the Army in Reconstruction," accessed July 19, 2016, http://mappingoccupation.org.

3. *Christian Recorder*, June 17, 1865, 95. The caption to Bond's letter appeared on a page of the newspaper that is missing from the microfilm copy in the holdings of Mother Bethel A.M.E. Church in Philadelphia.

4. "The Perils by the Way," editorial, *Anglo-African*, Sept. 26, 1863. Also see Ripley et al., *Black Abolitionist Papers*, 5:256.

5. For treatments of how awkwardly the standard applied in the West, for example, see Brooks, *Captives and Cousins*, esp. 304–68; and Smith, "Emancipating Peons, Excluding Coolies," 46–74.

6. Hahn, "Class and State in Postemancipation Societies," 75–98.

7. Richardson, *Death of Reconstruction*, 6–182, nicely analyzes the impact of the divergence between the smallholder and self-improving strains of classical republican ideology, to which most freed people subscribed, and the evolution of an industrial working class during and after the war. See also Levy, *Freaks of Fortune*, esp. chap. 4.

8. The Reconstruction Acts of March 2 and 23, 1867 (United States, *Statutes at Large*, 14:428–30; 15:2–5) extended suffrage to African American men in the former Confederate States, and the Fourteenth Amendment (1868) declared forthrightly that "Representatives shall be apportioned among the several States according to their respective numbers, counting the whole number of persons in each State, excluding Indians not taxed." United States, *Statutes at Large*, 14:358–59. For the Civil Rights Act, which became law on April 9, 1866, see United States, *Statutes at Large*, 14:27–30.

9. United States, *Statutes at Large*, 16:346. See also Edwards, *Legal History of the Civil War and Reconstruction*, 64–173.

10. Foner and Walker, *Proceedings of the Black State Conventions*.

11. *Freedmen's Bureau. Message from the President of the United States, Transmitting Report of the Commissioner of the Bureau of Refugees, Freedmen, and Abandoned Lands*, 39th Cong., 1st Sess. (1865), H. Exec. Doc. No. 11, 12.

12. Stanley, *From Bondage to Contract*.

13. See Wilson, *Black Codes*. For a concise summary of "lessons learned" between April and December 1865, see *Freedom: Land and Labor, 1865*, 910–27.

14. For Maryland, see Fuke, "Planters, Apprenticeship, and Forced Labor," 57–74, and Fields, *Slavery and Freedom on the Middle Ground*, 148–56; for North Carolina, see Scott, "Battle over the Child," 101–13. On Belcher, see Reidy, *From Slavery to Agrarian Capitalism*, 153–54.

15. *Freedom: Land and Labor, 1865*, 494–597, richly documents these "points of contention."

16. Robinson, *Bitter Fruits of Bondage*, 126.

17. See especially Kantrowitz, *More Than Freedom*.

18. Litwack, *Been in the Storm So Long*, 292–335; Sternhell, *Routes of War*, 155–94; Sternhell, "Bodies in Motion," 15–41.

19. A. P. Ketcham to O. O. Howard, Dec. 12, 1865, in *Freedom: Land and Labor, 1865*, 450–52, quotation at 451. For Howard's later reflections on this episode, see *Autobiography*, 2:237–41.

20. N. B. Forrest to O. O. Howard, Dec. 5, 1866, F230 Vol. 8 1866, Letters Received, Washington Headquarters, RG 105, Records of the Bureau of Refugees, Freedmen and Abandoned Lands, National Archives; Cohen, *At Freedom's Edge*, 67–69. Pronouncing himself ever "friendly to the race, and . . . as anxious, as any one Can be, for every possible amelioration of their Condition," Forrest hoped that the commissioner would furnish transportation to persons from the Atlantic states, where "there are

large numbers of Negroes, much in excess of the present labor wants" there. Howard demurred.

21. See Rochester Ladies' Antislavery Society, *Fifteenth Annual Report*, 13–15, quote at 15. See also Johnston, "Surviving Freedom"; Williams, "Blacks in Washington."

22. Rochester Ladies' Antislavery and Freedmen's Aid Society, *Sixteenth Annual Report*, 9.

23. The literature on the Great Migrations is extensive. For notable recent contributions, see Berlin, *Making of African America*, chap. 4; and Wilkerson, *Warmth of Other Suns*.

24. United States, *Statutes at Large*, 13:507–9. Oubre's classic, *Forty Acres and a Mule*, contains useful insights into this dynamic, especially chaps. 1 and 2.

25. Testimony of Harry McMillan before the American Freedmen's Inquiry Commission [June 1863], in *Freedom: Wartime Genesis, Lower South*, 253–54; Frazier is quoted in a clipping from the New-York *Daily Tribune*, [Feb. 13, 1865], in *Freedom: Wartime Genesis, Lower South*, 334. As the work of Julie Saville and Dylan Penningroth makes clear, however, the freed people did not desire land either as an abstraction or as a purely fungible commodity, separate from how the attributes of particular parcels might contribute to a family's subsistence and the welfare of the larger community. See Saville, *Work of Reconstruction*; Penningroth, *Claims of Kinfolk*.

26. See Rochester Ladies' Antislavery and Freedmen's Aid Society, *Sixteenth Annual Report*, 8–9.

27. "Bureau of Freedmen Refugees and Abandoned Lands. Letter from Ossabau Island, Geo.," *Anglo-African*, Dec. 23, 1865. See also Duncan, *Freedom's Shore*, chap. 1; Coulter, *Negro Legislators*, 123–24. On the importance of access to marsh and woodland for subsistence purposes, see Saville, *Work of Reconstruction*, 42–43; Swanson, *Remaking Wormsloe Plantation*, 95–128.

28. Philbrick [to Ware], Jan. 9, 1865, in Pearson, *Letters from Port Royal*, 299–301. Saville, *Work of Reconstruction*, 59–70, explores this incident, including its antebellum roots and its postwar consequences.

29. Philbrick [to Ware], Jan. 9, 1865, in Pearson, *Letters from Port Royal*, 299–301. Philbrick's comment about human nature appears in *Freedom: Wartime Genesis, Lower South*, 280; and Eustis's "great civilizer" reference is in *Freedom: Wartime Genesis, Lower South*, 246. Esup to Dear Mother, Sept. 25, 1863, folder 79, box 109-2, Charles Pickard Ware Papers, MSRC-HU. See also Saville, *Work of Reconstruction*, 60–70.

30. Bram, Moultrie, and Sampson to O. O. Howard, [Oct. 20 or 21, 1865], in *Freedom: Land and Labor, 1865*, 440.

31. Philbrick to W. C. G. [William C. Gannett, another of the New England Gideonites], Nov. 21, 1865, in Pearson, ed., *Letters from Port Royal*, 317.

32. Perhaps no other region of the Union-occupied South has benefited from the wealth of scholarship to rival that of coastal South Carolina, particularly Taylor, *Negro in South Carolina*; Rose, *Rehearsal for Reconstruction*; Williamson, *After Slavery*; Holt, *Black over White*; Foner, *Nothing but Freedom*; Saville, *Work of Reconstruction*; Penningroth, *Claims of Kinfolk*; and Schwalm, *"Hard Fight for We."* Rose brings nearly Shakespearean empathy to all the protagonists of the Port Royal Experiment, particularly Philbrick. See, for example, *Rehearsal for Reconstruction*, 308–11.

33. See uncaptioned letter from "Guerre," *Christian Recorder*, May 16, 1863, 77. The marginal tracts in Florida became part of the public lands made accessible for settlement in the Southern Homestead Act of 1866. See Oubre, *Forty Acres and a Mule*, chap. 7. Oubre characterized most of it as "palmetto swamp" (156).

34. "Baltimore Correspondence," *Christian Recorder*, Apr. 9, 1864, 57; "Washington Correspondence," *Christian Recorder*, Aug. 30, 1862, 137.

35. "Letter from a Freedman to His Old Master," in Child, *Freedmen's Book*, 265–67. See also Litwack, *Been in the Storm So Long*, 333–35.

36. Jackson, *Story of Mattie J. Jackson*, 31.

37. Coates, "Case for Reparations"; special issue on "African Americans and Movements for Reparations: Past, Present, and Future," *Journal of African American History*, 2012, esp. V. P. Franklin, "Introduction: African Americans and Movements for Reparations from Ex-Slave Pensions to the Reparations Superfund," 1–12; and Araujo, *Reparations for Slavery*.

38. For perspectives on the bureau, see Bentley, *History of the Freedmen's Bureau*; and Cimbala and Miller, *Freedmen's Bureau and Reconstruction*. Insightful biographies of Commissioner O. O. Howard include Carpenter, *Sword and Olive Branch*; and McFeely, *Yankee Stepfather*. Studies of the bureau's operations in the various states include Cimbala, *Under the Guardianship of the Nation*; Finley, *From Slavery to Uncertain Freedom*; and Crouch, *Freedmen's Bureau and Black Texans*.

39. By the closing months of the war, most Northerners had come to associate the term "refugees" with white Southerners who were displaced by the war, thousands of whom followed Sherman's forces through the Carolinas. Similarly situated black Southerners were referred to simply as "freedmen." The distinction is reflected in the title of the Bureau of Refugees, Freedmen, and Abandoned Lands.

40. Most notable among the institutions of higher education was Howard University, named in honor of Commissioner Oliver Otis Howard, who served as a trustee and as the institution's third president, from 1869 to 1874. See Howard, *Autobiography*, 2:263–445.

41. See Jones, *Soldiers of Light and Love*; Anderson, *Education of Blacks in the South*.

42. Foner, *Reconstruction*, 454–59; Trelease, *White Terror*; Downs, *After Appomattox*, esp. 211–36.

43. Calvin Holly to O. O. Howard, Dec. 16, 1865, in *Freedom: Black Military Experience*, 754–56. According to Holly's compiled service records, he was a thirty-eight-year-old farmer from LaGrange County, Tennessee, at the time of his enlistment in Company H, Fifth U.S. Colored Heavy Artillery at Urbana, Ohio, in February 1865. He was on detached duty with the Freedmen's Bureau beginning June 16, 1865. The feared insurrection scare never materialized, but the freed people's resentment against the heavy-handed tactics of the former masters did not go away, largely because the landowners proved so reluctant to abandon their violent ways. See Hahn, "'Extravagant Expectations' of Freedom"; and Hahn, *Nation under Our Feet*, chap. 4, esp. 146–59.

44. Excerpt of O. O. Howard's remarks to the American Missionary Association meeting in Hartford, Connecticut, *American Missionary* 13, no. 7 (July 1869): 155, in box 53-2, Oliver Otis Howard Papers, MSRC-HU.

45. *Charges against General Howard*, 41st Cong., 2d Sess. (1870), H. Rep. 121, serial 1438, at 20. See also Howard, *Autobiography*, 2:435–44. Two years later Howard faced similar charges in a military inquiry, which also concluded in his exoneration in 1874. See *Autobiography*, 2:445–52.

46. See Circular letter prepared by Mrs. M. A. Lipscomb with attached preamble and resolutions submitted to state convention of the Daughters of the Confederacy held at Athens GA Oct. 11–13, [1896?], Duke University Library, Digital Collections, accessed Mar. 19, 2018, http://library.duke.edu/digitalcollections/broadsides_bdsga 40391/. Resolving that the Emancipation Proclamation "violated its original compact with the slave-holding states and by force of arms deprived them of the rights of property" and that the Fourteenth Amendment constituted "a repudiation of a nation's just debt," the convention petitioned Congress to authorize payment for slave property "that was taken from owners under the emancipation proclamation."

47. Du Bois, *Black Reconstruction*, 580–636.

48. On Henry Adams and the Colonization Council, see Painter, *Exodusters*, 71–255; and Hahn, *Nation under Our Feet*, 317–63. For developments in Tennessee, see "Still Going West," quoted in *Georgia Weekly Telegraph and Messenger*, Apr. 25, 1876, 3. More generally, see Taylor, *Negro in Tennessee*, 108–23; Sanderfer, "Tennessee's Black Postwar Emigration Movements," 254–75; and Painter, *Exodusters*, esp. 108–17, on Singleton.

49. Redkey, *Black Exodus*, 170–94; Wells, *Crusade for Justice*; Olsen, *Carpetbagger's Crusade*; Hill et al., *Marcus Garvey and Universal Negro Improvement Association Papers*.

50. R. H. Cain, *Christian Recorder*, Apr. 21, 1866, 1.

51. It bears noting in this context that Cervantes spent five years as a slave in Algiers following his capture by Turkish pirates. Numerous commentators describe his enslavement as the most formative experience of his life.

Bibliography

Manuscripts

Harvard University, Houghton Library, Cambridge, Mass.
    United States American Freedmen's Inquiry Commission Records, 1862–64
Haverford College, Special Collections, Haverford, Pa.
    Julia Wilbur Papers (MC #1158) (accessed Feb. 8, 2018, at https://www.alexandriava
        .gov/uploadedFiles/historic/info/civilwar/JuliaWilburDiary1860to1866.pdf)
Howard University, Moorland-Spingarn Research Center, Washington, D.C.
    Bustill-Bowser-Asbury Family Papers
    Mary Ann Shad Cary Papers
    Frederick Douglass Collection
    George T. Downing Papers
    Oliver Otis Howard Papers
    Edward W. Kinsley Papers
    Charles W. Martin Collection
    Metropolitan A.M.E. Church Records
    Omnium Gatherum: Scrapbooks of Civil War Era Clippings
    Henry McNeal Turner Papers
    Charles Pickard Ware Papers
Library of Congress, Washington, D.C.
    Nathaniel P. Banks Papers
    Benjamin F. Butler Papers
    Abraham Lincoln Papers (online)
    James Morrison MacKaye Papers
    Carter G. Woodson Papers
National Archives and Records Administration, Washington, D.C.
    RG 15 Records of the Veterans Administration
    RG 21 Records of the District Courts of the United States
    RG 29 Records of the Bureau of the Census
    RG 45 Naval Records Collection of the Office of Naval Records and Library
    RG 46 Records of the United States Senate
    RG 52 Records of the Bureau of Medicine and Surgery
    RG 92 Records of the Office of the Quartermaster General
    RG 94 Records of the Adjutant General, 1780s–1917
    RG 105 Records of the Bureau of Refugees, Freedmen and Abandoned Lands
    RG 125 Records of the Office of the Judge Advocate General (Navy)
    RG 217 Records of the United States General Accounting Office
    RG 233 Records of the United States House of Representatives
    RG 393 Records of U.S. Army Continental Commands, 1821–1920

Government Publications

Confederate States of America

Confederate States of America. *A Digest of the Military and Naval Laws of the Confederate States, from the Provisional Congress to the End of the First Congress under the Permanent Constitution. Analytically Arranged by Capt. W. W. Lester, of the Quartermaster-General's Office, and Wm. J. Bromwell, of the Department of State, Attorneys-at-Law. To Be Continued Every Session.* Columbia, S.C.: Evans and Cogswell, 1864.

———. *Public Laws of the Confederate States of America, First Congress, 1862–1864.* Richmond, Va.: R. M. Smith, 1862–64.

United States of America

Kennedy, Joseph C. G. *Population of the United States in 1860; Compiled from the Original Returns of the Eighth Census under the Direction of the Secretary of the Interior.* Washington, D.C.: Government Printing Office, 1864.

United States. *The Statutes at Large, Treaties, and Proclamations of the United States of America.* Vol. 12. Boston: Little, Brown, 1863.

———. *The Statutes at Large, Treaties, and Proclamations of the United States of America.* Vols. 13–16. Boston: Little, Brown, 1866–71.

United States Congress. *Abstract of the Returns of the Fifth Census, Showing the Number of Free People, the Number of Slaves, the Federal Representation Numbers, and the Aggregate of Each County of Each State in the United States. Prepared from the Corrected Returns of the Secretary of State to Congress, by the Clerk of the House of Representatives.* Washington, D.C.: Duff Green, 1832.

———. *Africans in Fort Monroe Military District.* 37th Cong., 2d Sess. (1862), H. Exec. Doc. No. 85, serial 1135.

———. *Authorizing the President to Place Robert Smalls on the Retired List of the Navy.* 47th Cong., 2d Sess. (1883), H. Rep. 1887, serial 2159.

———. *Charges against General Howard.* 41st Cong., 2d Sess. (1870), H. Rep. 121, serial 1438.

———. *Condition and Management of the Jail in the City of Washington.* 37th Cong., 2d Sess. (1862), S. Rep. No. 60, serial 1125.

———. *Emancipation in the District of Columbia.* 38th Cong., 1st Sess. (1864), H. Exec. Doc. 42, serial 1189.

———. *Freedmen's Bureau. Message from the President of the United States, Transmitting Report of the Commissioner of the Bureau of Refugees, Freedmen, and Abandoned Lands.* 39th Cong., 1st Sess. (1865), H. Exec. Doc. 11.

———. *Information Relating to the Arrest and Imprisonment, by the Military Authorities in Missouri, of Soldiers Belonging to the 9th Minnesota Regiment.* 38th Cong., 1st Sess. (1864), S. Exec. Doc. No. 24.

———. *Memorial of Inhabitants of the District of Columbia, Praying for the Gradual Abolition of Slavery in the District of Columbia.* 23rd Cong., 2d sess. (1835), H. Doc. No. 140.

———. *Memorial of the Emancipation League of Boston, Massachusetts, Praying the Immediate Establishment of a Bureau of Emancipation.* 37th Cong., 3d Sess. (1862), S. Misc. Doc. No. 10, serial 1150.

———. *Message of the President of the United States Communicating a Letter Addressed to Him from a Committee of Gentlemen Representing the Freedman's Aid Societies of Boston, New York, Philadelphia, and Cincinnati, in Relation to the Freedmen under the Proclamation of Emancipation.* 38th Cong., 1st Sess. (1863), S. Exec. Doc. No. 1, serial 1176.

———. *Penitentiary in the District of Columbia.* 38th Cong., 1st Sess. (1864), H. Rep. 41, serial 1206.

———. *Report from the Secretary of State, upon the Subject of the Supposed Kidnapping of Colored Persons in the Southern States for the Purpose of Selling Them as Slaves in Cuba.* 39th Cong., 1st Sess. (1866), S. Exec. Doc. No. 30.

———. *Report of the Commissioners of Investigation of Colored Refugees in Kentucky, Tennessee, and Alabama.* 38th Cong., 2d Sess. (1865), S. Exec. Doc. No. 28.

———. *Report of the Committee on the Judiciary on the Case of William Yokum.* 38th Cong., 1st Sess. (1864), H. Rep. 118, serial 1207.

———. *Report of the Secretary of War.* 37th Cong., 2d sess. (1861), S. Exec. Doc. No. 1.

———. *Report of the Secretary of War, Communicating . . . a Copy of the Preliminary Report, and Also of the Final Report of the American Freedmen's Inquiry Commission.* 38th Cong., 1st Sess. (1864), S. Exec. Doc. 53.

———. *Testimony Taken by the Joint Select Committee on the Condition of Affairs in the Late Insurrectionary States (the Ku Klux Conspiracy).* 42d Cong., 2d Sess. (1872), S. Rep. No. 41, pts. 1–13.

United States Department of Agriculture. *Report of the Commissioner of Agriculture, 1865.* (see Daniel R. Goodloe, "Resources and Industrial Condition of the Southern States," 102–36).

United States Department of the Navy. Naval War Records Office. *Official Records of the Union and Confederate Navies in the War of the Rebellion.* 30 vols. Washington, D.C.: Government Printing Office, 1894–1922.

United States War Department. *General Orders of the War Department Embracing the Years 1861, 1862, & 1863. Adapted Specially for the Use of the Army and Navy of the United States.* Thos. M. O'Brien and Oliver Diefendorf, comps. 2 vols. New York: Derby & Miller, 1864.

———. *Revised United States Army Regulations of 1861. With an Appendix Containing the Changes and Laws Affecting Army Regulations and Articles of War to June 25, 1863.* Washington, D.C.: Government Printing Office, 1863.

———. *The War of the Rebellion: A Compilation of the Official Records of the Union and Confederate Armies.* 70 vols. Washington, D.C.: Government Printing Office, 1880–1901.

States

Hinkley, Edward Otis. *The Constitution of the State of Maryland. Reported and Adopted by the Convention of Delegates Assembled at the City of Annapolis,*

April 27th, 1864, and Submitted to and Ratified by the People on the 12th and 13th Days of October, 1864. Baltimore: John Murphy, 1864.

Missouri. State Convention. *Journal of the Missouri State Convention, Held at the City of St. Louis, January 6—April 10, 1865*. St. Louis: Missouri Democrat, 1865.

Tennessee. Legislature. *Acts and Resolutions of the Tennessee Legislature Adopted in 1861*. N.p., n.d. https://archive.org/stream/actsresolutionsoootenn#page/n53/mode/2up/search/free+negro.

Newspapers and Periodicals

Anglo-African (New York), 1861–65
Atlantic Monthly, 1863
Christian Recorder, 1861–65
Congressional Globe, 1861–65
Douglass' Monthly, 1861–63
Frank Leslie's Illustrated Newspaper, 1863
Harper's Weekly, 1861–65
Liberator, 1861–65

New Orleans Daily Crescent, April–May 1861
New Orleans Daily Picayune, April–May 1861
New Orleans Daily True Delta, April–May 1861
New-York Tribune, 1861–65
Southern Cultivator, 1861–65
Washington *Evening Star*, 1863

Collections of Electronic Resources

Ancestry.com. https://www.ancestry.com/.

Boston Public Library, Anti-Slavery (Collection of Distinction), Digital Commonwealth: Massachusetts Collections Online. https://www.digitalcommonwealth.org/.

Civil War Washington Project, University of Nebraska, Lincoln. http://www.civilwardc.org/.

Colored Conventions Project, University of Delaware. http://coloredconventions.org/.

Cornell University Library, Making of America. http://collections.library.cornell.edu/moa_new/index.html.

Duke University Library, Digital Collections. http://library.duke.edu/digitalcollections/.

Fold3.com. https://www.fold3.com/.

Freedmen and Southern Society Project, University of Maryland, College Park. http://freedmen.umd.edu/.

HathiTrust. https://www.hathitrust.org/.

Historical Society of Pennsylvania, Digital Library. http://digitallibrary.hsp.org/.

Interactive Map of Contraband Camps, History Digital Projects, Scholarly Commons, University of Pennsylvania. https://repository.upenn.edu/hist_digital/1/.

Internet Archive. https://archive.org/.

JSTOR. https://www.jstor.org/.

Library of Congress, *Born in Slavery: Slave Narratives from the Federal Writers'*

Project, 1936 to 1938. Federal Writers' Project, Slave Narrative Project. 17 vols. https://www.loc.gov/collections/slave-narratives-from-the-federal-writers -project-1936-to-1938/.

———. Chronicling America: Historic American Newspapers. https:// chroniclingamerica.loc.gov/.

National Public Radio. https://npr.org/sections/thetwo-way/.

North American Slave Narratives: Documenting the American South, University of North Carolina, Chapel Hill. http://docsouth.unc.edu/neh/texts.html.

Samuel J. May Anti-Slavery Collection, Cornell University. http://ebooks.library .cornell.edu/m/mayantislavery/browse_C.html.

Slavery in the North. http://slavenorth.com/.

University of Michigan Library, Making of America. http://quod.lib.umich.edu/m /moa/.

Published Primary Sources

Adams, John Quincy. *Narrative of the Life of John Quincy Adams, When in Slavery, and Now as a Freeman*. Harrisburg, Pa.: Sieg, Printer and Stationer, 1872. [DocSouth]

Adams, Virginia M., ed. *On the Altar of Freedom: A Black Soldier's Civil War Letters from the Front. By Corporal James Henry Gooding*. Amherst: University of Massachusetts Press, 1991.

Address and Ceremonies at the New Year's Festival to the Freedmen, on Arlington Heights; and Statistics and Statements of the Educational Condition of the Colored People in the Southern States, and Other Facts. Washington, D.C.: McGill and Weatherow, 1867.

Agassiz, Elizabeth Cary, ed. *Louis Agassiz: His Life and Correspondence*. 2 vols. Boston: Houghton Mifflin, 1885.

Aikman, William. *The Future of the Colored Race in America; Being an Article in the Presbyterian Quarterly Review, of July, 1862*. New York: Anson D. F. Randolph, 1862.

Albert, Octavia V. Rogers. *The House of Bondage or Charlotte Brooks and Other Slaves, Original and Life-Like, as They Appeared in Their Old Plantation and City Slave Life; Together with Pen-Pictures of the Peculiar Institution, with Sights and Insights into Their New Relations as Freedmen, Freemen, and Citizens*. New York: Hunt & Eaton, 1890. [DocSouth]

Aleckson, Sam. *Before the War, and after the Union, an Autobiography*. Boston: Gold Mind Publishing, [1929]. [DocSouth]

Allen, William Francis, Charles Pickard Ware, and Lucy McKim Garrison, compilers. *Slave Songs of the United States*. New York: A. Simpson, 1867.

[American Colonization Society.] *Thirty-First Annual Report of the American Colonization Society, with the Proceedings of the Board of Directors, and of the Society at Its Annual Meeting, January 18, 1848*. Washington, D.C.: C. Alexander, 1848.

American Freedman's Union Commission. *The Results of Emancipation in the United States of America*. New York: American Freedman's Union Commission, [1867].

American Freedmen's Inquiry Commission. "Final Report of the American Freedmen's Inquiry Commission to the Secretary of War," May 15, 1864. Also published in *Report of the Secretary of War, Communicating . . . a Copy of the Preliminary Report, and Also of the Final Report of the American Freedmen's Inquiry Commission*, 38th Cong., 1st Sess. (1864), S. Exec. Doc. No. 53, 25–110. Also published in *Official Records*, ser. 3: vol. 4: 289–382.

———. *Preliminary Report Touching the Condition and Management of Emancipated Refugees; Made to the Secretary of War, by the American Freedmen's Inquiry Commission, June 30, 1863*. New York: John F. Trow, 1863. Also published in *Report of the Secretary of War, Communicating . . . a Copy of the Preliminary Report, and Also of the Final Report of the American Freedmen's Inquiry Commission*, 38th Cong., 1st Sess. (1864), S. Exec. Doc. 53, 2–24. Also published in *Official Records*, ser. 3, vol. 3: 430–54.

Anderson, John Q., ed. *Brokenburn: The Journal of Kate Stone, 1861–1868*. Baton Rouge: Louisiana State University Press, 1955.

Anderson, Robert. *From Slavery to Affluence: Memoirs of Robert Anderson, Ex-Slave*. By Daisy Anderson Leonard. Steamboat Springs, Colo.: Steamboat Pilot, c. 1927 and 1967.

———. *The Life of Rev. Robert Anderson. Born the 22d Day of February, in the Year of Our Lord 1819, and Joined the Methodist Episcopal Church in 1839. This Book Shall Be Called the Young Men's Guide, or, the Brother in White*. Macon, Ga: Printed for the Author, 1892.

"April 19th, 1861. A Record of the Events in Baltimore, Md., on That Day. Conflict of the Sixth Massachusetts Regiment with Citizens." *Southern Historical Society Papers* 29 (1901): 251–69.

Aptheker, Herbert, ed. *A Documentary History of the Negro People in America*. Vol. 1. *From Colonial Times through the Civil War*. 8th paperback ed. New York: Citadel Press, 1969.

Arter, Jared Maurice. *Echoes from a Pioneer Life*. Atlanta, Ga.: A. B. Caldwell Publishing, 1922. [DocSouth]

[Ball, Charles.] *Fifty Years in Chains; Or, The Life of an American Slave*. New York: H. Dayton, 1860. [Internet Archive]

[Banks, Nathaniel P.] *Emancipated Labor in Louisiana*. N.p., 1864.

Basler, Roy P., Marion Dolores Pratt, and Lloyd A. Dunlap, eds. *The Collected Works of Abraham Lincoln*. 9 vols. New Brunswick, N.J.: Rutgers University Press, 1953–55.

Berlin, Ira, Barbara J. Fields, Thavolia Glymph, Joseph P. Reidy, and Leslie S. Rowland, eds. *The Destruction of Slavery*. Ser. 1, Vol. 1 of *Freedom: A Documentary History of Emancipation, 1861–1867*. Cambridge: Cambridge University Press, 1985.

Berlin, Ira, Barbara J. Fields, Steven F. Miller, Joseph P. Reidy, and Leslie S. Rowland. *Free At Last: A Documentary History of Slavery, Freedom, and the Civil War*. New York: New Press, 1992.

Berlin, Ira, Barbara J. Fields, Steven F. Miller, Joseph P. Reidy, and Leslie S. Rowland. *Slaves No More: Three Essays on Emancipation and the Civil War*. Cambridge: Cambridge University Press, 1992.

Berlin, Ira, Thavolia Glymph, Steven F. Miller, Joseph P. Reidy, Leslie S. Rowland, and Julie Saville, eds. *The Wartime Genesis of Free Labor: The Lower South.* Ser. 1, Vol. 3 of *Freedom: A Documentary History of Emancipation, 1861–1867.* Cambridge: Cambridge University Press, 1990.

Berlin, Ira, Steven F. Miller, Joseph P. Reidy, and Leslie S. Rowland, eds. *The Wartime Genesis of Free Labor: The Upper South.* Ser. 1, Vol. 2 of *Freedom: A Documentary History of Emancipation, 1861–1867.* Cambridge: Cambridge University Press, 1993.

Berlin, Ira, Joseph P. Reidy, and Leslie S. Rowland, eds. *The Black Military Experience.* Ser. 2 of *Freedom: A Documentary History of Emancipation, 1861–1867.* Cambridge: Cambridge University Press, 1982.

Berlin, Ira, Joseph P. Reidy, and Leslie S. Rowland, eds. *Freedom's Soldiers: The Black Military Experience in the Civil War.* Cambridge: Cambridge University Press, 1998.

Berlin, Ira, and Leslie S. Rowland, eds. *Families and Freedom: A Documentary History of African-American Kinship in the Civil War Era.* New York: New Press, 1997.

Billington, Ray Allen, ed. *The Journal of Charlotte L. Forten: A Free Negro in the Slave Era.* 1953. Reprint, New York: W. W. Norton, 1981.

Blackett, R. J. M., ed. *Thomas Morris Chester, Black Civil War Correspondent: His Dispatches from the Virginia Front.* Baton Rouge: Louisiana State University Press, 1989.

Blassingame, John W., ed. *Slave Testimony: Two Centuries of Letters, Speeches, Interviews, and Autobiographies.* Baton Rouge: Louisiana State University Press, 1977.

Blassingame, John W., et al., eds. *The Frederick Douglass Papers.* 9 vols. to date. New Haven, Conn.: Yale University Press, 1979–present.

Blight, David W. *A Slave No More: Two Men Who Escaped to Freedom, Including Their Own Narratives of Emancipation.* New York: Harcourt, 2007.

Botume, Elizabeth Hyde. *First Days amongst the Contrabands.* Boston: Lee and Shepard, 1893.

Boutwell, George S. *Speeches and Papers Relating to the Rebellion and the Overthrow of Slavery.* Boston: Little, Brown, 1867.

Brown, B. Gratz. *Immediate Abolition of Slavery by Act of Congress, Speech of B. Gratz Brown, of Missouri, Delivered in the U.S. Senate, March 8, 1864.* Washington, D.C.: H. Polkinhorn, Printer, 1864.

Browning, Orville Hickman. *Diary of Orville Hickman Browning, 1850–1881.* 2 vols. Collections of the Illinois State Historical Library, Vol. 20, Lincoln Series, Vol. 2. Edited by Theodore Calvin Pease and James G. Randall. Springfield: Trustees of the Illinois State Historical Library, 1925–31.

Bruce, H. C. [Henry Clay]. *The New Man: Twenty-Nine Years a Slave. Twenty-Nine Years a Free Man. Recollections of H. C. Bruce.* York, Pa.: P. Anstadt & Sons, 1895.

Bruner, Peter. *A Slave's Adventures toward Freedom: Not Fiction but the True Story of a Struggle.* Oxford, Ohio: n.p., n.d. [DocSouth]

Burton, Annie L. *Memories of Childhood's Slavery Days.* Boston: Ross Publishing, 1909. [DocSouth]

Butler, Benjamin F. *Autobiography and Personal Reminiscences of Major-General Benj. F. Butler: Butler's Book: A Review of His Legal, Political, and Military Career.* Boston: A. M. Thayer, 1892.

———. *Private and Official Correspondence of Gen. Benjamin F. Butler during the Period of the Civil War.* Compiled by Jessie Ames Marshall. 5 vols. Norwood, Mass.: Plimpton Press, 1917. [Internet Archive]

Campbell, Randall C., and Donald K. Pickens, eds. "'My Dear Husband': A Texas Slave's Love Letter, 1862." *Journal of Negro History* 68 (Autumn 1980): 361–64.

A Carolinian [Daniel R. Goodloe]. *Inquiry into the Causes Which Have Retarded the Accumulation of Wealth and Increase of Population in the Southern States: In Which the Question of Slavery Is Considered in a Politico-Economical Point of View.* Washington, D.C.: W. Blanchard, 1846.

Catterall, Helen Tunnicliff, and James J. Hayden, eds. *Judicial Cases concerning American Slavery and the Negro.* 5 vols. Washington, D.C.: Carnegie Institution of Washington, 1926.

Channing, William E. *Emancipation.* London: C. Fox, 1841.

Cheever, George B. *The Salvation of the Country Secured by Immediate Emancipation. A Discourse by Rev. George B. Cheever, D.D., Delivered in the Church of the Puritans, Sabbath Evening, Nov. 10, 1861.* New York: John A. Gray, 1861.

[Chesnut, Mary Boykin.] *A Diary from Dixie, as Written by Mary Boykin Chesnut.* Edited by Isabella D. Martin and Myrta Lockett Avery. New York: D. Appleton, 1906. [Internet Archive]

Child, L. Maria. *The Freedmen's Book.* Boston: Ticknor and Fields, 1866.

Clement, Samuel Spottford. *Memoirs of Samuel Spottford Clement. Relating Interesting Experiences in Days of Slavery and Freedom.* Steubenville, Ohio: Herald Printing, 1908.

Cochin, Augustin. *The Results of Emancipation.* Translated by Mary L. Booth. 2nd ed. Boston: Walker, Wise, 1863.

Coffin, Levi. *Reminiscences of Levi Coffin, the Reputed President of the Underground Railroad; Being a Brief History of the Labors of a Lifetime in Behalf of the Slave, with the Stories of Numerous Fugitives, Who Gained Their Freedom through His Instrumentality, and Many Other Incidents.* 2nd ed. Cincinnati, Ohio: Robert Clarke, 1880.

Colored Men's Council. *Constitution and By-Laws of the Colored Men's Council.* Washington, D.C.: n.p., 1866.

"Condition of the Negroes Who Came into Vicksburg with Sherman's Army, as described by Mr. N. M. Mann, Agent of the Western Sanitary Commission. Affecting Scenes and Incidents. What Is Doing, for Their Relief and Comfort." Broadside. N.p., [1864]. [Duke University Library Digital Collections]

Conway, Thomas W. *Annual Report of Thos. W. Conway, Superintendent of the Bureau of Free Labor, Department of the Gulf, to Major General Hurlbut, Commanding. For the Year 1864.* New Orleans: Printed at the Times Book and Job Office, [1865]. [Historical Society of Pennsylvania Digital Library]

———. *The Freedmen of Louisiana. Final Report of the Bureau of Free Labor,*

Department of the Gulf, to Major General E. R. S. Canby, Commanding. New Orelans: Printed at the New Orleans Times Book and Job Office, 1865.

A Cotton Manufacturer [Edward Atkinson]. *Cheap Cotton by Free Labor.* Boston: A. Williams, 1861.

Cox, S. S. *Emancipation and Its Results—Is Ohio to Be Africanized? Speech of Hon. S. S. Cox, of Ohio. Delivered in the House of Representatives, June 6, 1862.* Washington, D.C.: L. Towers, Printers, 1862.

Daly, Robert W., ed. *Aboard the USS Monitor: 1862: The Letters of Acting Paymaster William Frederick Keeler, U.S. Navy, to his Wife, Anna.* Annapolis, Md.: U.S. Naval Institute, 1964.

Davis, Garrett. *Confiscation of Rebel Property. Speech of Hon. Garrett Davis, of Kentucky, in the Senate of the United States, April 22 and 23, 1862.* [Washington, D.C.]: Printed at the Office of the Congressional Globe, [1862].

Douglass, Frederick. *Address by Hon. Frederick Douglass, Delivered in the Congregational Church, Washington, D.C., on April 16, 1883. On the Twenty-First Anniversary of Emancipation in the District of Columbia.* Washington, D.C.: n.p., 1883.

———. *Life and Times of Frederick Douglass. Written by Himself. His Early Life as a Slave, His Escape from Bondage, and His Complete History to the Present Time.* Hartford, Conn.: Park Publishing Co., 1884.

———. *My Bondage and My Freedom. Part I. Life as a Slave. Part II. Life as a Freeman.* New York: Miller, Orton & Mulligan, 1855. [DocSouth]

———. *Narrative of the Life of Frederick Douglass, An American Slave. Written by Himself.* Boston: Anti-Slavery Office, 1845. [DocSouth]

[Drayton, Daniel.] *Personal Memoir of Daniel Drayton: For Four Years and Four Months, a Prisoner (for Charity's Sake) in Washington Jail. Including a Narrative of the Voyage and Capture of the Schooner Pearl.* Boston: Bela Marsh, 1853.

Drumgoold, Kate. *A Slave Girl's Story. Being an Autobiography of Kate Drumgoold.* Brooklyn: n.p., 1898. [DocSouth]

Early, Sarah Jane Woodson. *Life and Labors of Rev. Jordan W. Early; One of the Pioneers of African Methodism in the West and South.* Nashville, Tenn.: A. M. E. Church Sunday School Union, 1894.

Eaton, John. *Grant, Lincoln, and the Freedmen: Reminiscences of the Civil War with Special Reference to the Work for the Contrabands and Freedmen of the Mississippi Valley.* New York: Longmans, Green, 1907.

Eliot, William G. *The Story of Archer Alexander. From Slavery to Freedom. March 30, 1863.* Boston: Cupples, Upham, 1885. [DocSouth]

Emancipation League of Boston. *Facts concerning the Freedmen. Their Capacity and Their Destiny. Collected and Published by the Emancipation League.* Boston: Press of Commercial Printing House, 1863.

Emilio, Luis P. *History of the Fifty-Fourth Regiment of Massachusetts Volunteer Infantry, 1863–1865.* 2nd ed. Boston: Boston Book, 1894.

Ferebee, L. R. *A Brief History of the Slave Life of Rev. L. R. Ferebee, and the Battles of Life, and Four Years of His Ministerial Life. Written from Memory, to 1882.* Raleigh, N.C.: Edwards, Broughton, 1882. [DocSouth]

First Organization of Colored Troops in the State of New York, to Aid in Suppressing the Slaveholders' Rebellion. New York: Baker & Godwin, 1864.

Fitzhugh, George. "What's to Be Done with the Negroes?" *DeBow's Review,* June 1866, 577–81.

Foner, Philip S., ed. *The Life and Writings of Frederick Douglass.* 5 vols. New York: International Publishers, 1950.

Foner, Philip S., and George E. Walker, eds. *Proceedings of the Black State Conventions, 1840–1865.* 2 vols. Philadelphia: Temple University Press, 1979–80.

Gaines, Wesley John. *African Methodism in the South; or, Twenty-Five Years of Freedom.* 1890. Reprint, Chicago: Afro-Am Press, 1969.

Garnet, Henry Highland. *A Memorial Discourse; by Rev. Henry Highland Garnet, Delivered in the Hall of the House of Representatives, Washington City, D.C., on Sabbath, February, 12, 1865.* Philadelphia: Joseph M. Wilson, 1865.

———. *The Past and the Present Condition, and the Destiny, of the Colored Race: A Discourse Delivered at the Fifteenth Anniversary of the Female Benevolent Society of Troy, N.Y., Feb. 14, 1848.* Troy, N.Y.: Steam Press of J. C. Kneeland, 1848. [Internet Archive]

Gasparin, Agénor, comte de. *The Uprising of a Great People. The United States in 1861. From the French of Count Agénor de Gasparin.* Translated by Mary L. Booth. New York: Charles Scribner, 1861.

Golden Jubilee Anniversary of the Emancipation Proclamation. Washington, D.C.: Hamilton Printing, 1913.

Goodloe, Daniel R. *Emancipation and the War: Compensation Essential to Peace and Civilization.* [Washington, D.C.?], [1861?].

———. "Resources and Industrial Condition of the Southern States." In *Report of the Commissioner of Agriculture, 1865,* 102–36.

Gould, William B., IV. *Diary of a Contraband: The Civil War passage of a Black Sailor.* Stanford, Calif.: Stanford University Press, 2002.

Greeley, Horace. *The American Conflict: A History of the Great Rebellion in the United States of America, 1860–'65.* 2 vols. Hartford: O. D. Case, 1867.

Hahn, Steven, Steven F. Miller, Susan E. O'Donovan, John C. Rodrigue, and Leslie S. Rowland, eds. *Land and Labor, 1865.* Ser. 3, Vol. 1 of *Freedom: A Documentary History of Emancipation, 1861–1867.* Chapel Hill: University of North Carolina Press, 2008.

Hall, Samuel. *Samuel Hall, 47 Years a Slave; A Brief Story of His Life before and after Freedom Came to Him.* Washington, Iowa: Journal Print, 1912. [DocSouth]

[Hammond, James H.] *Selections from the Letters and Speeches of the Hon. James H. Hammond of South Carolina.* New York: John F. Trow, 1866.

Handy, James A. *Scraps of African Methodist Episcopal History.* Philadelphia: A. M. E. Book Concern, n.d.

Hanson, J. W., ed. *The World's Congress of Religions. The Addresses and Papers Delivered before the Parliament, and an Abstract of the Congresses Held in the Art Institute, Chicago, Ill., U.S.A., August 25 to October 15, 1893 under the Auspices of the World's Columbian Exposition.* Chicago: International Pub., 1894.

Harrison, W. P., ed. and comp. *The Gospel among the Slaves: A Short Account of Missionary Operations among the African Slaves of the Southern States*. Nashville, Tenn.: Publishing House of the M. E. Church, South, 1893.

Haviland, Laura S. *A Woman's Life-Work: Labors and Experiences of Laura S. Haviland*. 4th ed. Chicago: C. V. Waite, 1887.

Hawkins, William G. (Rev.). *Lunsford Lane; or, Another Helper from North Carolina*. Boston: Crosby & Nichols, 1863. [DocSouth]

Hayden, René, Anthony E. Kaye, Kate Masur, Steven F. Miller, Susan E. O'Donovan, Leslie S. Rowland, and Stephen A. West, eds. *Land and Labor, 1866–1867*. Ser. 3, Vol. 2 of *Freedom: A Documentary History of Emancipation, 1861–1867*. Chapel Hill: University of North Carolina Press, 2013.

Heard, William Henry. *From Slavery to the Bishopric in the A. M. E. Church*. 1924. Reprint, New York: Arno Press, 1969.

[Henderson, John B.] *Speech of Hon. J. B. Henderson, of Mo., on the Confiscation of Property. Delivered in the Senate of the United States, April 8, 1862*. [Washington, D.C.]: L. Towers, [1862].

———. *Speech of Hon. J. B. Henderson of Missouri, on Emancipation in Missouri. Delivered in the Senate of the United States, January 16, 1863*. Washington: L. Towers, [1863].

Henry, Thomas W. *Autobiography of Rev. Thomas W. Henry of the A. M. E. Church*. Baltimore: n.p., 1872.

Higginson, Thomas Wentworth. *Army Life in a Black Regiment*. Boston: Fields, Osgood, 1870.

———. "Negro Spirituals." *Atlantic Monthly* 19 (June 1867): 685–94 (reprinted as chapter 9 in Higginson, *Army Life in a Black Regiment*).

Hill, Robert A., et al., eds. *The Marcus Garvey and Universal Negro Improvement Association Papers*. 11 vols. to date. Berkeley: University of California Press, 1983–2006 (vols. 1–10); Durham, N.C.: Duke University Press, 2011 (vol. 11).

Holly, James Theodore. *The Word of God, against Ecclesiastical Imperialism, Set Forth in a Letter Addressed to Bishop Daniel A. Payne, the Senior of the A. M. E. Church, by the Rt. Rev. James Theodore Holly, Bishop of Haiti*. N.p., n.d.

[Howard, Oliver Otis.] *Autobiography of Oliver Otis Howard, Major General, United States Army*. 2 vols. New York: Baker & Taylor, 1907.

Howe, S. G. *Refugees from Slavery in Canada West: Report to the Freedmen's Inquiry Commission*. Boston: Wright & Potter, Printers, 1864.

Hughes, Langston. *The Weary Blues*. New York: Alfred A. Knopf, 1926.

Hughes, Louis. *Thirty Years a Slave: The Institution of Slavery as Seen on the Plantation and in the Home of the Planter. The Autobiography of Louis Hughes*. Milwaukee, Wis.: South Side Printing, 1897.

Inaugural Ceremonies of the Freedmen's Memorial Monument to Abraham Lincoln. Washington City, April 14th, 1876. St. Louis: Levison & Blythe, 1876.

Jackson, Mattie J. *The Story of Mattie J. Jackson; Her Parentage—Experience of Eighteen Years in Slavery—Incidents during the War—Her Escape from Slavery. A True Story. Written and Arranged by Dr. L. S. Thompson, (formerly Mrs. Schutler,) As Given By Mattie*. Lawrence, Mass.: Printed at Sentinel Office, 1866. [DocSouth]

James, Horace. *Annual Report of the Superintendent of Negro Affairs in North Carolina. 1864. With an Appendix, Containing the History and Management of the Freedmen in This Department up to June 1st 1865.* Boston: W. F. Brown, 1865.

James, Thomas. *Life of Rev. Thomas James, by Himself.* Rochester, N.Y.: Post Express Printing, 1886. [DocSouth]

Jamison, Monroe F. *Autobiography and Work of Bishop M. F. Jamison, D.D. ("Uncle Joe"). Editor, Publisher, and Church Extension Secretary. A Narration of His Whole Career from the Cradle to the Bishopric of the Colored M. E. Church in America.* Nashville, Tenn.: Publishing House of the M. E. Church, South, 1912. [DocSouth]

Jay, William. *An Inquiry into the Character and Tendency of the American Colonization, and American Anti-Slavery Societies.* New York: Leavitt, Lord, 1835.

Johansson, M. Jane, ed. *Widows by the Thousand: The Civil War Letters of Theophilus and Harriet Perry, 1862–1864.* Fayetteville: University of Arkansas Press, 2000.

Johnson, Isaac. *Slavery Days in Old Kentucky. A True Story of a Father Who Sold His Wife and Four Children. By One of the Children.* N.p., 1901. [DocSouth]

Keckley, Elizabeth. *Behind the Scenes. Or, Thirty Years a Slave, and Four Years in the White House.* New York: G. W. Carleton, 1868. [DocSouth]

[Knox, George L.] *Slave and Freeman: The Autobiography of George L. Knox.* Edited by Williard B. Gatewood Jr. Louisville: University Press of Kentucky, 1979.

Laas, Virginia Jeans, ed. *Wartime Washington: The Civil War Letters of Elizabeth Blair Lee.* Urbana: University of Illinois Press, 1991.

Lane, Isaac. *Autobiography of Bishop Isaac Lane, LL.D.: With a Short History of the C.M.E. Church in America and of Methodism.* Nashville, Tenn.: Publishing House of the M.E. Church, South, 1916. [DocSouth]

Marrs, Elijah P. *Life and History of the Rev. Elijah P. Marrs, First Pastor of the Beargrass Baptist Church, and Author.* Miami, Fla.: Mnemosyne Publishing, 1969; reprint of Louisville, Ky.: Bradley & Gilbert, 1885.

Marx, Karl, and Frederick Engels. *The Civil War in the United States.* New York: International Publishers, 1937.

[McKaye, James.] *The Mastership and Its Fruits: The Emancipated Slave Face to Face with His Old Master. A Supplemental Report to Hon. Edwin M. Stanton, Secretary of War.* New York: Wm. C. Bryant, 1864.

———. *Of the Birth and Death of Nations: A Thought for the Crisis.* New York: G. P. Putnam, 1862.

McPherson, Edward. *The Political History of the United States of America, during the Great Rebellion.* Washington, D.C.: Philp and Solomons, 1865.

Mitchell, James. *Letter on the Relation of the White and African Races in the United States, Showing the Necessity of the Colonization of the Latter. Addressed to the President of the U.S.* Washington, D.C.: Government Printing Office, 1862. [Internet Archive]

M'Kim, J. Miller. *The Freedmen of South Carolina. An Address Delivered by J. Miller M'Kim, in Sansom Hall, July 9th, 1862. Together with a Letter from the Same to Stephen Colwell, Esq., Chairman of the Port Royal Relief Committee.* Philadelphia: Willis P. Hazard, 1862.

Moore, Frank, ed. *The Rebellion Record: A Diary of American Events, with Documents, Narratives, Illustrative Incidents, Poetry, etc.* 12 vols. New York: G. P. Putnam, 1861–68.

The National Celebration of Union Victories. Grand Military and Civic Procession. Mass Meeting at Union Square, New York, March 6th, 1865. New York: George F. Nesbitt, 1865. [University of Michigan, Making of America]

[National Freedman's Relief Association.] *First Annual Report of the National Freedman's Relief Association of the District of Columbia*. Washington, D.C.: M'Gill & Witherow, Printers, 1863.

Nell, Wm. C. *Colored Patriots of the American Revolution, with Sketches of Several Distinguished Colored Persons: To Which Is Added a Brief Survey of the Condition and Prospects of Colored Americans*. Boston: Robert F. Wallcut, 1855.

Newton, Alexander Herritage. *Out of the Briars; An Autobiography and Sketch of the Twenty-Ninth Regiment, Connecticut Volunteers*. Miami, Fla.: Mnemosyne Pub., 1969, c. 1910.

Nordhoff, Charles. *The Freedmen of South-Carolina: Some Account of Their Appearance, Character, Condition, and Peculiar Customs. Papers of the Day; Collected and Arranged by Frank Moore, Editor of the Rebellion Record, Diary of the American Revolution, etc, etc*. New York: Charles T. Evans, 1863.

Opinion of Attorney General Bates on Citizenship. Washington, D.C.: Government Printing Office, 1862.

Oration by Frederick Douglass Delivered on the Occasion of the Unveiling of the Freedmen's Monument in Memory of Abraham Lincoln, in Lincoln Park, Washington, D. C., April 14th, 1876. With an Appendix. Washington, D.C.: Gibson Brothers, Printers, 1876.

Owen, Robert Dale. *The Policy of Emancipation: In Three Letters to the Secretary of War, the President of the United States, and the Secretary of the Treasury*. Philadelphia: J. B. Lippincott, 1863.

———. *The Wrong of Slavery and the Right of Emancipation and the Future of the African Race in the United States*. Philadelphia: J. B. Lippincott, 1864. [HathiTrust]

[Palmer, John M.] *Personal Recollections of John M. Palmer: The Story of an Earnest Life*. Cincinnati, Ohio: Robert Clarke, 1901.

Parker, Allen. *Recollections of Slavery Times*. Worcester, Mass.: Chas. W. Burbank, 1895. [DocSouth]

Payne, D. A. *History of the African Methodist Episcopal Church*. Edited by Rev. C. S. Smith. Nashville, Tenn.: A. M. E. Sunday School Union, 1891.

———. *Recollections of Seventy Years; by Bishop Daniel Alexander Payne*. Nashville, Tenn.: Publishing House of the A. M. E. Sunday School Union, 1888.

———. *Welcome to the Ransomed, or Duties of the Colored Inhabitants of the District of Columbia*. Baltimore: Bull and Tuttle, 1862.

Pearson, Elizabeth Ware, ed. *Letters from Port Royal: Written at the Time of the Civil War*. Boston: W. B. Clarke, 1906.

[Peterson, T. B., and Brothers.] *Life and Public Services of Major-General Butler. (Benjamin F. Butler.) The Hero of New Orleans*. Philadelphia: T. B. Peterson & Brothers, 1864.

[Pierce, Edward L.] "The Contrabands at Fortress Monroe." *Atlantic Monthly* 8 (November 1861): 626–40.

———. "The Freedmen at Port Royal." *Atlantic Monthly* 12 (September 1863): 291–315.

———. *The Freedmen of Port Royal, South-Carolina. Official Reports of Edward L. Pierce.* New York: Rebellion Record, 1863.

———, ed. *Memoir and Letters of Charles Sumner.* 4 vols. Boston: Roberts Brothers, 1878–93.

Proceedings of a Convention of Colored Citizens Held in the City of Lawrence, October 17, 1866. Leavenworth, Kans.: Evening Bulletin Steam Power Printing House, 1866. [ColoredConventions.org]

Proceedings of the National Convention of Colored Men; Held in the City of Syracuse, N.Y.; October 4, 5, 6, and 7, 1864; with the Bill of Wrongs and Rights; and the Address to the American People. Boston: J. S. Rock and Geo. L. Ruffin, 1864. [ColoredConventions.org]

Proceedings of the National Emigration Convention of Colored People; Held at Cleveland, Ohio, on Thursday, Friday and Saturday, the 24th, 25th and 26th of August, 1854. Pittsburgh, Pa.: A. A. Anderson, 1854.

Putnam, Sally Brock. *Richmond during the War: Four Years of Personal Observation.* New York: G. W. Carleton, 1867.

Rankin, David C. *Diary of a Christian Soldier: Rufus Kinsley and the Civil War.* Cambridge: Cambridge University Press, 2004.

Rawick, George P., et al., eds. *The American Slave: A Composite Autobiography.* 41 vols. Westport, Conn.: Greenwood Press, 1972–79. (Series 1, 7 vols.; Series 2, 12 vols.; Supplemental Series 1, 12 vols.; Supplemental Series 2, 10 vols.)

Record of Action of the Convention Held at Poughkeepsie, N.Y., July 15th and 16th, 1863, for the Purpose of Facilitating the Introduction of Colored Troops into the Service of the United States, [1863]. [ColoredConventions.org]

Redkey, Edwin S., ed. *A Grand Army of Black Men: Letters from African-American Soldiers in the Union Army 1861–1865.* Cambridge: Cambridge University Press, 1992.

Richards, Laura E., ed. *Letters and Journals of Samuel Gridley Howe. The Servant of Humanity.* 2nd of 2 vols. Boston: Dana Estes, 1909.

Richardson, James D. *A Compilation of the Messages and Papers of the Confederacy Including the Diplomatic Correspondence, 1861–1865.* 2 vols. Nashville, Tenn.: United States Publishing, 1905.

Ripley, C. Peter, et al., eds. *The Black Abolitionist Papers.* 5 vols. Chapel Hill: University of North Carolina Press, 1985–92.

Robinson, W. [William] H. *From Log Cabin to the Pulpit. Or, Fifteen Years in Slavery.* 3rd ed. Eau Claire, Wis.: James H. Tifft, Publishing Printer, 1913. [DocSouth]

Rochester Ladies' Antislavery and Freedmen's Aid Society. *Sixteenth Annual Report.* Rochester, N.Y.: Wm. S. Falls, 1867.

Rochester Ladies' Antislavery Society. *Fifteenth Annual Report.* Rochester, N.Y.: Wm. S. Falls, 1866.

Rudd, Dan A., and Theo. Bond. *From Slavery to Wealth. The Life of Scott Bond. The Rewards of Honesty, Industry, Economy and Perseverance.* Madison, Ark.: Journal Printing, 1917. [DocSouth]

Sewell, William G. *The Ordeal of Free Labor in the British West Indies.* New York: Harper & Brothers, 1861. [Internet Archive]

[Sherman, William T.] *Memoirs of General William T. Sherman by Himself.* 2 vols. New York: D. Appleton, 1875.

Simmons, William J. *Men of Mark: Eminent, Progressive and Rising*. Cleveland: Geo. M. Rewell & Co., 1887. [DocSouth]

Singleton, William Henry. *Recollections of My Slavery Days*. Peekskill, N.Y.: Highland Democrat, 1922.

Slavery Code of the District of Columbia, Together with Notes and Judicial Decisions Explanatory of the Same. Washington, D.C.: L. Towers, 1862.

Sluby, Paul E., Sr., and Stanton L. Wormley, eds. *Diary of Charles B. Fisher*. Washington, D.C.: Columbian Harmony Society, 1983.

————, eds. *Narrative of Billy Tilghman*. Washington, D.C.: Columbian Harmony Society, 1983.

Smith, David. *Biography of Rev. David Smith, of the A. M. E. Church, Being a Complete History Embracing over Sixty Years Labor in the Advancement of the Redeemer's Kingdom on Earth*. Xenia, Ohio: Printed at the Xenia Gazette Office, 1881.

Smith, Gerald J., ed. "Reminiscences of the Civil War by J. W. Frederick." *Georgia Historical Quarterly* 59, no. 5 (Supplement 1975): 154–59.

Smith, James L. *Autobiography of James L. Smith, Including, Also, Reminiscences of Slave Life, Recollections of the War, Education of Freedmen, Causes of the Exodus, etc.* Norwich, Conn.: Press of the Bulletin, 1881. [DocSouth]

[Society for Colonizing the Free People of Colour of the United States.] *The Fourteenth Annual Report of the Society for Colonizing the Free People of Colour of the United States*. Washington, D.C.: James C. Dunn, 1831.

Still, William. *A Brief Narrative of the Struggle for the Rights of the Colored People of Philadelphia in the City Railway Cars* . . . Philadelphia: Merrihew and Son, Printers, 1867.

Stone, A. L. *Emancipation. A Discourse Delivered in Park Street Church, on Fast Day Morning, April 3, 1862*. Boston: Henry Hoyt, 1862.

Sumner, Charles. *Indemnity for the Past and Security for the Future. Speech of Hon. Charles Sumner, of Massachusetts, on His Bill for the Confiscation of Property and the Liberation of Slaves Belonging to Rebels. In the Senate of the United States, May 19, 1862*. [Washington: n.p., 1862.]

Tanner, Benjamin Tucker. *An Apology for African Methodism, by Benj. T. Tanner*. Baltimore: n.p., 1867.

Tappan, Lewis. *Immediate Emancipation: The Only Wise and Safe Mode*. New York: n.p., 1861. [Internet Archive]

Taylor, Susie King. *Reminiscences of My Life in Camp with the 33d United States Colored Troops Late 1st S. C. Volunteers*. Boston: Published by the Author, 1902. [DocSouth]

Tenney, W. J. *The Military and Naval History of the Rebellion in the United States. With Biographical Sketches of Deceased Officers*. New York: D. Appleton, 1865.

————. *A Thrilling Narrative from the Lips of the Sufferers of the Late Detroit Riot, March 6, 1863, with the Hair Breadth Escapes of Men, Women and Children, and Destruction of Colored Men's Property, Not Less than $15,000*. Detroit: Published by the Author, 1863. [DocSouth]

[Turnage, Wallace.] "Journal of Wallace Turnage." In David W. Blight. *A Slave No More: Two Men Who Escaped to Freedom, Including Their Own Narratives of Emancipation*, 213–58. New York: Harcourt, 2007.

Warren, Joseph, comp. *Extracts from Reports of Superintendents of Freedmen, Second Series, June, 1864*. Vicksburg, Miss.: Freedmen Press, 1864. [HathiTrust]

Washington, Booker T. *The Story of My Life and Work*. Toronto, Ontario: J. L. Nichols, 1901. [DocSouth]

Washington, John M. "Memorys of the Past." In David W. Blight. *A Slave No More: Two Men Who Escaped to Freedom, Including Their Own Narratives of Emancipation*, 165–212. New York: Harcourt, 2007.

Webb, William. *The History of William Webb, Composed by Himself*. Detroit: Egbert Hoekstra, Printer, 1873. [DocSouth]

Weiss, John. "The Horrors of San Domingo." *Atlantic Monthly* 10, no. 56 (June 1862): 732–54; no. 58 (August 1862): 212–27; no. 59 (September 1862): 347–58; 11, no. 65 (March 1863): 289–306. [Cornell University, Making of America]

Wells, Ida B. *Crusade for Justice: The Autobiography of Ida B. Wells*. Edited by Alfreda M. Duster. Chicago: University of Chicago Press, 1970.

Wesley, Charles H. *The Thirteenth Amendment: A Milestone in Emancipation*. Washington, D.C.: Graduate School, Howard University, 1940.

[Williams, Andrew.] "Civil War on the Kansas-Missouri Border: The Narrative of Former Slave Andrew Williams." *Kansas History* 6, no. 4 (Winter 1983–84): 237–42.

Williams, George Washington. *A History of the Negro Troops in the War of the Rebellion, 1861–1865*. New York: Harper & Brothers, 1888.

Wilson, Henry. *History of the Antislavery Measures of the Thirty-Seventh and Thirty-Eighth United-States Congresses, 1861–64*. Boston: Walker, Wise, 1864 (with a revised and updated edition in 1865).

Yacovone, Donald, ed. *A Voice of Thunder: The Civil War Letters of George E. Stephens*. Urbana: University of Illinois Press, 1997.

Yeatman, James E. *A Report on the Condition of the Freedmen of the Mississippi, Presented to the Western Sanitary Commission, December 17th, 1863*. St. Louis: Western Sanitary Commission Rooms, 1864.

———. *Suggestions of a Plan of Organization for Freed Labor, and the Leasing of Plantations along the Mississippi River, under a Bureau or Commission to Be Appointed by the Government. Accompanying a Report Presented to the Western Sanitary Commission*. St. Louis: Rooms Western Sanitary Commission, 1864.

Yellin, Jean Fagan, Joseph M. Thomas, Kate Culkin, and Scott Korb, eds. *The Harriet Jacobs Family Papers*. 2 vols. Chapel Hill: University of North Carolina Press, 2009.

Secondary Sources

Aaron, Daniel. *The Unwritten War: American Writers and the Civil War*. New York: Alfred A. Knopf, 1973.

Abruzzo, Margaret. *Polemical Pain: Slavery, Cruelty, and the Rise of Humanitarianism*. Baltimore: Johns Hopkins University Press, 2011.

Adams, Kevin, and Leonne M. Hudson, eds. *Democracy and the American Civil War: Race and African Americans in the Nineteenth Century*. Kent, Ohio: Kent State University Press, 2016.

Alexander, Adele Logan. *Homelands and Waterways: The American Journey of the Bond Family, 1846–1926*. New York: Random House, 1999.

Alexander, Michelle. *The New Jim Crow: Mass Incarceration in the Age of Colorblindness*. New York: New Press, 2010.

Anderson, Benedict. *Imagined Communities: Reflections on the Origin and Spread of Nationalism*. London: Verso, 1983.

Anderson, James D. *The Education of Blacks in the South, 1860–1935*. Chapel Hill: University of North Carolina Press, 1981.

Andrews, J. Cutler. *The North Reports the Civil War*. Pittsburgh: University of Pittsburgh Press, 1955.

Andrews, William L. *To Tell a Free Story: The First Century of Afro-American Autobiography, 1760–1865*. Urbana: University of Illinois Press, 1987.

Aptheker, Herbert. *American Negro Slave Revolts*. New York: Columbia University Press, 1943.

Araujo, Ana Luisa. *Reparations for Slavery and the Slave Trade: A Transnational and Comparative History*. London: Bloomsbury, 2017.

Arenson, Adam. *The Great Heart of the Republic: St. Louis and the Cultural Civil War*. Cambridge, Mass.: Harvard University Press, 2011.

Arenson, Adam, and Andrew R. Graybill, eds. *Civil War Wests: Testing the Limits of the United States*. Berkeley: University of California Press, 2015.

Ash, Stephen V. *Firebrand of Liberty: The Story of Two Black Regiments That Changed the Course of the Civil War*. New York: W. W. Norton, 2008.

———. *Middle Tennessee Society Transformed, 1860–1870: War and Peace in the Upper South*. Knoxville: University of Tennessee Press, 1988.

———. *When the Yankees Came: Conflict and Chaos in the Occupied South, 1861–1865*. Chapel Hill: University of North Carolina Press, 1995.

———. *A Year in the South: Four Lives in 1865*. New York: Palgrave Macmillan, 2002.

Astor, Aaron. *Rebels on the Border: Civil War, Emancipation, and the Reconstruction of Kentucky and Missouri*. Baton Rouge: Louisiana State University Press, 2012.

Aveni, Anthony F. *Empires of Time: Calendars, Clocks and Cultures*. New York: Basic Books, 1989.

Ayers, Edward L. *In the Presence of Mine Enemies: War in the Heart of America, 1859–1863*. New York: W. W. Norton, 2003.

———. *The Thin Light of Freedom: The Civil War and Emancipation in the Heart of America*. New York: W. W. Norton, 2017.

Ball, Edward. *Slaves in the Family*. New York: Farrar, Straus and Giroux, 1998.

Bancroft, Frederic. *Slave-Trading in the Old South*. Baltimore: J. H. Furst, 1931.

Baptist, Edward. *The Half Has Never Been Told: Slavery and the Making of American Capitalism*. New York: Basic Books, 2014.

Barrow, Charles Kelley, J. H. Segars, and R. B. Rosenburg, eds. *Forgotten Confederates: An Anthology about Black Southerners*. Murfreesboro, Tenn.: Southern Heritage Press, 1995.

Bartky, Ian R. *One Time Fits All: The Campaigns for Global Uniformity*. Stanford, Calif.: Stanford University Press, 2007.

———. *Selling the True Time: Nineteenth-Century Timekeeping in America*. Stanford, Calif.: Stanford University Press, 2000.

Bartlett, John. *Familiar Quotations: A Collection of Passages, Phrases, and Proverbs Traced to Their Sources in Ancient and Modern Literature.* 9th ed. Boston: Little, Brown, 1907.

Beckert, Sven. "Emancipation and Empire: Reconstructing the Worldwide Web of Cotton Production in the Age of the American Civil War." *American Historical Review* 109, no. 5 (December 2004): 1405–38.

———. *Empire of Cotton: A Global History.* New York: Alfred A. Knopf. 2014.

Behrend, Justin. "Rebellious Talk and Conspiratorial Plots: The Making of a Slave Insurrection in Civil War Natchez." *Journal of Southern History* 77, no. 1 (February 2011): 17–52.

Bell, Rudolph M., and Virginia Yans, eds. *Women on Their Own: Interdisciplinary Perspectives on Being Single.* New Brunswick, N.J.: Rutgers University Press, 2008.

Bennett, Michael J. *Union Jacks: Yankee Sailors in the Civil War.* Chapel Hill: University of North Carolina Press, 2004.

Bensel, Richard Franklin. *Yankee Leviathan: The Origins of Central State Authority in America, 1859–1877.* Cambridge: Cambridge University Press, 1990.

Bentley, George R. *A History of the Freedmen's Bureau.* Philadelphia: University of Pennsylvania Press, 1955.

Beringer, Richard D., Herman Hattaway, Archer Jones, and William N. Still Jr. *Why the South Lost the Civil War.* Athens: University of Georgia Press, 1986.

Berlin, Ira. *The Long Emancipation: The Demise of Slavery in the United States.* Cambridge, Mass.: Harvard University Press, 2015.

———. *The Making of African America: The Four Great Migrations.* New York: Viking, 2010.

———. *Many Thousands Gone: The First Two Centuries of Slavery in North America.* Cambridge, Mass.: Harvard University Press, 1998.

———. *Slaves without Masters: The Free Negro in the Antebellum South.* New York: Pantheon, 1974.

———. "Time, Space, and the Evolution of Afro-American Society in British Mainland North America." *American Historical Review* 85, no. 1 (February 1980): 44–78.

———. "Who Freed the Slaves?," In *Union and Emancipation: Essays on Politics and Race in the Civil War Era*, edited by David W. Blight and Brooks D. Simpson, 105–21. Kent, Ohio: Kent State University Press, 1997.

Bernstein, Iver. *The New York City Draft Riots: Their Significance for American Society and Politics in the Age of the Civil War.* New York: Oxford University Press, 1990.

Berry, Mary F. "Negro Troops in Blue and Gray: The Louisiana Native Guards, 1861–1863." *Louisiana History* 8 (Spring 1967): 165–90.

Berry, Stephen, ed. *Weirding the War: Stories from the Civil War's Ragged Edges.* Athens: University of Georgia Press, 2011.

Blackburn, Robin. *The American Crucible: Slavery, Emancipation and Human Rights.* London: Verso, 2011.

———. "Haiti, Slavery, and the Age of the Democratic Revolution." *William and Mary Quarterly*, 3rd ser., 63, no. 4 (October 2006): 643–74.

———. *The Making of New World Slavery: From the Baroque to the Modern, 1492–1800.* London: Verso, 1997.

———. *The Overthrow of Colonial Slavery, 1776–1848.* London: Verso, 1988.

Blair, William A., and Karen Fisher Younger, eds. *Lincoln's Proclamation: Emancipation Reconsidered.* Chapel Hill: University of North Carolina Press, 2009.

Blassingame, John W. *Black New Orleans, 1860–1880.* Chicago: University of Chicago Press, 1973.

———. "The Recruitment of Negro Troops in Maryland." *Maryland Historical Magazine* 58, no. 1 (March 1963): 20–29.

———. *The Slave Community: Plantation Life in the Antebellum South.* New York: Oxford University Press, 1972.

Blatt, Matthew H., Thomas J. Brown, and Donald Yacovone, eds. *Hope and Glory: Essays on the Legacy of the Fifty-Fourth Massachusetts Volunteer Regiment.* Amherst: University of Massachusetts Press, 2001.

Blight, David W. *Frederick Douglass' Civil War: Keeping Faith in Jubilee.* Baton Rouge: Louisiana State University Press, 1989.

———. *Race and Reunion: The Civil War in American Memory.* Cambridge, Mass.: Harvard University Press, 2001.

Blight, David W., and Jim Downs, eds. *Beyond Freedom: Disrupting the History of Emancipation.* Athens: University of Georgia Press, 2017.

Bogue, Alan G. *The Earnest Men: Republicans of the Civil War Senate.* Ithaca, N.Y.: Cornell University Press, 1961.

Boime, Albert. *The Art of Exclusion: Representing Blacks in the Nineteenth Century.* Washington, D.C.: Smithsonian Institution Press, 1990.

Boles, John B. *Jefferson: Architect of American Liberty.* New York: Basic Books, 2017.

Bosse, David. *Civil War Newspaper Maps: A Historical Atlas.* Baltimore: Johns Hopkins University Press, 1993.

Brasher, Glenn David. *The Peninsula Campaign and the Necessity of Emancipation: African Americans and the Fight for Freedom.* Chapel Hill: University of North Carolina Press, 2012.

Brewer, James H. *The Confederate Negro: Virginia's Craftsmen and Military Laborers, 1861–1865.* Durham, N.C.: Duke University Press, 1969.

Brooks, James F. *Captives and Cousins: Slavery, Kinship, and Community in the Southwest Borderlands.* Chapel Hill: University of North Carolina Press, 2003.

Brown, Christopher Leslie, and Philip D. Morgan, eds. *Arming Slaves: From Classical Times to the Modern Age.* New Haven, Conn.: Yale University Press, 2006.

Bryant, James K., II. *The 36th U.S. Colored Troops in the Civil War: A History and Roster.* Jefferson, N.C.: McFarland, 2012.

Buchanan, Thomas C. *Black Life on the Mississippi: Slaves, Free Blacks, and the Western Steamboat World.* Chapel Hill: University of North Carolina Press, 2004.

Buick, Kirsten Pai. *Child of the Fire: Mary Edmonia Lewis and the Problem of Art History's Black and Indian Subject.* Durham, N.C.: Duke University Press, 2010.

Burchard, Peter. *One Gallant Rush: Robert Gould Shaw and His Brave Black Regiment.* New York: St. Martin's Press, 1965.

Burdick, Alan. *Why Time Flies: A Mostly Scientific Investigation*. New York: Simon & Schuster, 2017.

Burgess, John W. *Reconstruction and the Constitution, 1866–1876*. New York: Charles Scribner's Sons, 1902.

Burke, Diane Mutti. *On Slavery's Border: Missouri's Small Slaveholding Households, 1815–1865*. Athens: University of Georgia Press, 2010.

Camp, Stephanie. "'I Could Not Stay There': Enslaved Women, Truancy, and the Geography of Everyday Forms of Resistance in the Antebellum Plantation South." *Slavery and Abolition* 23, no. 1 (December 2002): 1–20.

Campbell, Randolph B. *A Southern Community in Crisis: Harrison County, Texas, 1850–1880*. Austin: Texas State Historical Association, 1983.

Carpenter, John A. *Sword and Olive Branch: Oliver Otis Howard*. Pittsburgh: University of Pittsburgh Press, 1964.

Carwardine, Richard. *Lincoln: A Life of Purpose and Power*. New York: Alfred A. Knopf, 2006.

Casstevens, Frances H. *Edward A. Wild and the African Brigade in the Civil War*. Jefferson, N.C.: McFarland, 2003.

Cecelski, David S. *The Fire of Freedom: Abraham Galloway and the Slaves' Civil War*. Chapel Hill: University of North Carolina Press, 2012.

———. *The Waterman's Song: Slavery and Freedom in Maritime North Carolina*. Chapel Hill: University of North Carolina Press, 2001.

Cimbala, Paul A. *Under the Guardianship of the Nation: The Freedmen's Bureau and the Reconstruction of Georgia, 1865–1870*. Athens: University of Georgia Press, 1997.

Cimbala, Paul A., and Randall M. Miller, eds. *The Freedmen's Bureau and Reconstruction: Reconsiderations*. New York: Fordham University Press, 1999.

Cimprich, John. *Slavery's End in Tennessee, 1861–1865*. Tuscaloosa: University of Alabama Press, 1985.

Cippolo, Carlo M. *Clocks and Culture, 1300–1700*. London: Collins, 1967.

Clark, Elizabeth B. "'The Sacred Rights of the Weak': Pain, Suffering, and the Culture of Individual Rights in Antebellum America." *Journal of American History* 82 (September 1995): 463–93.

Click, Patricia C. *Time Full of Trial: The Roanoke Island Freedmen's Colony, 1862–1867*. Chapel Hill: University of North Carolina Press, 2001.

Coates, Ta-Nehisi. "The Case for Reparations." In *We Were Eight Years in Power: An American Tragedy*, 163–208. New York: One World Publishing, 2017.

Cobb, Jasmine Nichole. *Picture Freedom: Remaking Black Visuality in the Early Nineteenth Century*. New York: New York University Press, 2015.

Cobb, J. Michael. "Rehearsing Reconstruction in Occupied Virginia: Life and Emancipation at Fortress Monroe." In *Virginia at War, 1864*, edited by William C. Davis and James I. Robertson Jr., 139–57. Lexington: University Press of Kentucky, 2009.

Coddington, Ronald S. *African American Faces of the Civil War: An Album*. Baltimore: Johns Hopkins University Press, 2012.

Cohen, Michael C. "Contraband Singing: Poems and Songs in Circulation during the Civil War." *American Literature* 82, no. 2 (June 2010): 292–300.

Cohen, William. *At Freedom's Edge: Black Mobility and the Southern White Quest for Racial Control, 1861–1915.* Baton Rouge: Louisiana State University Press, 1991.

Cook, Adrian. *The Armies of the Streets: The New York City Draft Riots of 1863.* Lexington: University Press of Kentucky, 1974.

Cornish, Dudley Taylor. *The Sable Arm: Black Troops in the Union Army, 1861–1865.* New York: Longmans, Green, 1956.

Corrigan, Mary Beth. "'It's a Family Affair': Buying Freedom in the District of Columbia, 1850–1860." In *Working toward Freedom: Slave Society and Domestic Economy in the American South,* edited by Larry E. Hudson Jr., 163–91. Rochester, N.Y.: University of Rochester Press, 1994.

Coulter, E. Merton. *Negro Legislators in Georgia during the Reconstruction Period.* Athens: Georgia Historical Society, 1968.

Crosby, Alfred W. *The Measure of Reality: Quantification and Western Society, 1250–1600.* Cambridge: Cambridge University Press, 1997.

Crouch, Barry A. *The Freedmen's Bureau and Black Texans.* Austin: University of Texas Press, 1999.

Curry, Leonard P. *Blueprint for Modern America: Nonmilitary Legislation of the First Civil War Congress.* Nashville, Tenn.: Vanderbilt University Press, 1968.

Curtin, Philip D. *The Atlantic Slave Trade: A Census.* Madison: University of Wisconsin Press, 1969.

Davis, David Brion. *Inhuman Bondage: The Rise and Fall of Slavery in the New World.* New York: Oxford University Press, 2006.

———. *The Problem of Slavery in the Age of Emancipation.* New York: Alfred A. Knopf, 2014.

———. *The Problem of Slavery in the Age of Revolution, 1770–1823.* New York: Oxford University Press, 1999.

Davis, Hugh. "The Pennsylvania State Equal Rights League and the Northern Black Struggle for Legal Equality, 1864–1877." *Pennsylvania Magazine of History and Biography* 126, no. 4 (October 2002): 611–34.

Davis, Robert Scott, Jr. "A Soldier's Story: The Records of Hubbard Pryor, Forty-Fourth United States Colored Troops." *Prologue* 31, no. 4 (Winter 1999): 266–72.

Dawson, Joseph G., III. "Jefferson Davis and the Confederacy's 'Offensive-Defensive' Strategy in the U.S. Civil War." *Journal of Military History* 73, no. 2 (April 2009): 591–607.

Dean, Eric T., Jr., *Shook All Over Hell: Post-Traumatic Stress, Vietnam, and the Civil War.* Cambridge, Mass.: Harvard University Press, 1997.

De Jong, Greta. *You Can't Eat Freedom: Southerners and Social Justice after the Civil Rights Movement.* Chapel Hill: University of North Carolina Press, 2016.

Deyle, Steven. *Carry Me Back: The Domestic Slave Trade in American Life.* New York: Oxford University Press, 2005.

Dobak, William A. *Freedom by the Sword: The U.S. Colored Troops, 1862–1867.* Washington, D.C.: Center of Military History, 2011.

Downs, Gregory P. *After Appomattox: Military Occupation and the Ends of War.* Cambridge, Mass.: Harvard University Press, 2015.

———. "Force, Freedom, and the Making of Emancipation." In *Rethinking American Emancipation: Legacies of Slavery and the Quest for Black Freedom,* edited by

William A. Link and James J. Broomall, 42–68. New York: Cambridge University Press, 2016.

Downs, Gregory P., and Kate Masur. *The World the Civil War Made*. Chapel Hill: University of North Carolina Press, 2015.

Downs, Jim. "Emancipating the Evidence: The Ontology of the Freedmen's Bureau Records." In *Beyond Freedom: Disrupting the History of Emancipation*, edited by David W. Blight and Jim Downs, 160–80. Athens: University of Georgia Press, 2017.

———. *Sick from Freedom: African-American Illness and Suffering during the Civil War and Reconstruction*. Oxford: Oxford University Press, 2012.

Doyle, Don H., ed. *American Civil Wars: The United States, Latin America, Europe, and the Crisis of the 1860s*. Chapel Hill: University of North Carolina Press, 2017.

———. *The Cause of All Nations: An International History of the American Civil War*. New York: Basic Books, 2015.

Drago, Edmund L. *Black Politicians and Reconstruction in Georgia*. Baton Rouge: Louisiana State University Press, 1982.

———. "How Sherman's March through Georgia Affected the Slaves." *Georgia Historical Quarterly* 57, no. 3 (Fall 1973): 361–75.

Drescher, Seymour. *Abolition: A History of Slavery and Antislavery*. New York: Cambridge University Press, 2009.

Dubois, Laurent. *Avengers of the New World: The Story of the Haitian Revolution*. Cambridge, Mass.: Harvard University Press, 2005.

———. *Colony of Citizens: Revolution and Slave Emancipation in the French Caribbean, 1787–1804*. Chapel Hill: University of North Carolina Press, 2012.

Du Bois, W. E. Burghardt. *Black Reconstruction in America: An Essay toward a History of the Part Which Black Folk Played in the Attempt to Reconstruct Democracy in America, 1860–1880*. New York: Russell & Russell, 1935.

———. *The Suppression of the African Slave Trade to the United States of America, 1638–1870*. New York: Longmans, Green, 1904.

Duncan, Russell B. *Freedom's Shore: Tunis Campbell and the Georgia Freedmen*. Athens: University of Georgia Press, 1986.

Dunning, William Archibald. *Reconstruction: Political and Economic, 1865–1877*. New York: Harper & Brothers, 1907.

Durden, Robert F. *The Gray and the Black: The Confederate Debate on Emancipation*. Baton Rouge: Louisiana State University Press, 1972.

Dykstra, Robert R. *Bright Radical Star: Black Freedom and White Supremacy on the Hawkeye Frontier*. Cambridge, Mass.: Harvard University Press, 1993.

Dyson, Walter. *The Founding of Howard University*. Howard University Studies in History, No. 1. Washington, D.C.: Howard University Press, 1921.

Eagleman, David. *The Brain: The Story of You*. New York: Pantheon, 2015.

———. *Incognito: The Secret Lives of the Brain*. New York: Pantheon, 2011.

Eberstadt, Charles. "Lincoln's Emancipation Proclamation." *The New Colophon*. 1950, 312–56.

Edgerton, Douglas R. *Thunder at the Gates: The Black Civil War Regiments That Redeemed America*. New York: Basic Books, 2016.

Edwards, Laura F. *A Legal History of the Civil War and Reconstruction: A Nation of Rights*. Cambridge: Cambridge University Press, 2015.

Eggleston, G. K. "The Work of Relief Societies during the Civil War." *Journal of Negro History* 14, no. 3 (1929): 272–99.

Engs, Robert F. *Freedom's First Generation: Black Hampton, Virginia, 1861–1890.* 1979. Reprint, New York: Fordham University Press, 2004.

Escott, Paul D. *"What Shall We Do with the Negro?": Lincoln, White Racism, and Civil War America.* Charlottesville: University of Virginia Press, 2009.

Essah, Patience. *A House Divided: Slavery and Emancipation in Delaware, 1638–1865.* Charlottesville: University Press of Virginia, 1996.

Etcheson, Nicole. *Bleeding Kansas: Contested Liberty in the Civil War Era.* Lawrence: University Press of Kansas, 2004.

Everett, Donald E. "Ben Butler and the Louisiana Native Guards 1861–1862." *Journal of Southern History* 24 (May 1958): 202–17.

Fahs, Alice. *The Imagined Civil War: Popular Literature of the North and South, 1861–1865.* Chapel Hill: University of North Carolina Press, 2001.

Faulkner, Carol. "'A Proper Recognition of Our Manhood': The African Civilization Society and the Freedmen's Aid Movement." *Afro-Americans in New York Life and History* 24, no. 1 (January 2000): 41–62.

———. *Women's Radical Reconstruction: The Freedmen's Aid Movement.* Philadelphia: University of Pennsylvania Press, 2004.

Faulkner, William. *The Mansion.* New York: Random House, 1955.

Faust, Drew Gilpin. *This Republic of Suffering: Death and the American Civil War.* New York: Alfred A. Knopf, 2008.

Fehrenbacher, Don E. *The Dred Scott Case: Its Significance in American Law and Politics.* New York: Oxford University Press, 1978.

Ferrer, Ada. *Freedom's Mirror: Cuba and Haiti in the Age of Revolution.* Cambridge: Cambridge University Press, 2014.

Fields, Barbara J. *Slavery and Freedom on the Middle Ground, Maryland during the Nineteenth Century.* New Haven, Conn.: Yale University Press, 1985.

———. "Who Freed the Slaves?" In *The Civil War,* edited by Geoffrey Ward, with Ric Burns and Ken Burns, 146–55. New York: Alfred A. Knopf, 1990.

Fields, Karen E., and Barbara J. Fields. *Racecraft: The Soul of Inequality in American Life.* London: Verso Books, 2012.

Finley, Randy. *From Slavery to Uncertain Freedom: The Freedmen's Bureau in Arkansas, 1865–1869.* Fayetteville: University of Arkansas Press, 1996.

Fisher, David Hackett. *Albion's Seed: Four British Folkways in America.* New York: Oxford University Press, 1989.

Fleche, Andre M. *The Revolution of 1861. The American Civil War in the Age of Nationalist Conflict.* Chapel Hill: University of North Carolina Press, 2012.

Fogel, Robert William, and Stanley Engerman L. *Time on the Cross: The Economics of American Negro Slavery.* 2 vols. Boston: Little, Brown, 1974.

Follett, Richard, Eric Foner, and Walter Johnson. *Slavery's Ghost: The Problem of Freedom in the Age of Emancipation.* Baltimore: Johns Hopkins University Press, 2011.

Foner, Eric. *The Fiery Trial: Abraham Lincoln and American Slavery.* New York: W. W. Norton, 2010.

———. *Forever Free: The Story of Emancipation and Reconstruction.* New York: Alfred A. Knopf, 2005.

———. *Nothing but Freedom: Emancipation and Its Legacy*. Baton Rouge: Louisiana State University Press, 1983.

———. *Reconstruction: America's Unfinished Revolution, 1863–1877*. New York: Harper & Row, 1988.

Foner, Philip S. "The Battle to End Discrimination against Negroes on Philadelphia Streetcars (Part 1): Background and Beginning of the Battle." *Pennsylvania History* 40 (July 1973): 260–90.

———. "The Battle to End Discrimination against Negroes on Philadelphia Streetcars (Part 2): The Victory." *Pennsylvania History* 40 (October 1973): 354–79.

Ford, Bridget. *Bonds of Union: Religion, Race, and Politics in a Civil War Borderland*. Chapel Hill: University of North Carolina Press, 2016.

Fowler, John D., and David B. Parker, eds. *Breaking the Heartland: The Civil War in Georgia*. Macon, Ga.: Mercer University Press, 2011.

Fox-Genovese, Elizabeth. *Within the Plantation Household: Black and White Women of the Old South*. Chapel Hill: University of North Carolina Press, 1988.

Fox-Genovese, Elizabeth, and Eugene D. Genovese. *The Mind of the Master Class: History and Faith in the Southern Slaveholders' Worldview*. New York: Cambridge University Press, 2005.

Frankel, Oz. "The Predicament of Racial Knowledge: Government Studying the Freedmen during the Civil War." *Social Research* 70, no. 1 (Spring 2003): 45–81.

———. *States of Inquiry: Social Investigations and Print Culture in Nineteenth-Century Britain and the United States*. Baltimore: Johns Hopkins University Press, 2006.

Franklin, John Hope. *The Emancipation Proclamation*. Garden City, N.Y.: Doubleday, 1963.

———. *From Slavery to Freedom: A History of Negro Americans*. New York: Random House, 1947 (2nd ed., 1956; 3rd ed., 1967).

Franklin, V. P., ed. "African Americans and Movements for Reparations: Past, Present, and Future." Special issue, *Journal of African American History* 97, nos. 1–2 (Winter-Spring 2012).

———. *Black Self-Determination: A Cultural History of African-American Resistance*. 2nd ed. New York: Lawrence Hill, 1992.

Frazier, E. Franklin. *The Negro Family in the United States*. Chicago: University of Chicago Press, 1939.

Fredrickson, George. *The Black Image in the White Mind: The Debate on Afro-American Character and Destiny, 1817–1914*. New York: Harper & Row, 1971.

Freehling, William W. *The Road to Disunion: Volume 2: Secessionists Triumphant, 1854–1861*. New York: Oxford University Press, 2007.

Fuke, Richard Paul. *Imperfect Equality: African Americans and the Confines of White Racial Attitudes in Post-Emancipation Maryland*. New York: Fordham University Press, 1999.

———. "Planters, Apprenticeship, and Forced Labor: The Black Family under Pressure in Post-Emancipation Maryland." *Agricultural History* 62 (Fall 1988): 57–74.

Furrow, Matthew. "Samuel Gridley Howe, the Black Population of Canada West, and the Racial Ideology of the 'Blueprint for Radical Reconstruction.'" *Journal of American History* 97, no. 2 (September 2010): 344–70.

Gallagher, Gary, ed. *The Shenandoah Valley Campaign of 1862*. Chapel Hill: University of North Carolina Press, 2003.

———, ed. *The Shenandoah Valley Campaign of 1864*. Chapel Hill: University of North Carolina Press, 2006.

———. *The Union War*. Cambridge, Mass.: Harvard University Press, 2011. .

Gardner, Eric. *Black Print Unbound: The Christian Recorder, African American Literature, and Periodical Culture*. New York: Oxford University Press, 2015.

Garfield, Simon. *Timekeepers*. Edinburgh: Canongate, 2016.

Gates, Henry Louis, ed. *The Classic Slave Narratives*. New York: Penguin Press, 1987.

Genovese, Eugene D. *A Consuming Fire: The Fall of the Confederacy in the Mind of the White Christian South*. Athens: University of Georgia Press, 1998.

———. *From Rebellion to Revolution: Afro-American Slave Revolts in the Making of the Modern World*. Baton Rouge: Louisiana State University Press, 1979.

———. *Roll, Jordan, Roll: The World the Slaves Made*. New York: Random House, 1974.

Gerteis, Louis S. *Civil War St. Louis*. Lawrence: University Press of Kansas, 2001.

———. *From Contraband to Freedman: Federal Policy toward Southern Blacks, 1861–1865*. Westport, Conn.: Greenwood Press, 1973.

Gilroy, Paul. *The Black Atlantic: Modernity and Double-Consciousness*. Cambridge, Mass.: Harvard University Press, 1995.

Glatthaar, Joseph T. *Forged in Battle: The Civil War Alliance of Black Soldiers and White Officers*. New York: Free Press, 1990.

———. *The March to the Sea and Beyond: Sherman's Troops in the Savannah and Carolinas Campaigns*. New York: New York University Press, 1985.

———. *Partners in Command: The Relationships between Leaders in the Civil War*. New York: Free Press. 1994.

Gleick, James. *Time Travel: A History*. New York: Pantheon, 2016.

Glymph, Thavolia. *Out of the House of Bondage: The Transformation of the Plantation Household*. Cambridge: Cambridge University Press, 2008.

———. "This Species of Property: Female Slave Contrabands in the Civil War." In *A Woman's War: Southern Women, Civil War, and the Confederate Legacy*, edited by Edward D. C. Campbell Jr. and Kym S. Rice, 54–71. Richmond, Va.: Museum of the Confederacy, 1996.

Goodheart, Adam. *1861: The Civil War Awakening*. New York: Alfred A. Knopf, 2011.

Gordon, Lesley J., and John C. Inscoe, eds. *Inside the Confederate Nation: Essays in Honor of Emory M. Thomas*. Baton Rouge: Louisiana State University Press, 2005.

Gould, Stephen Jay. *The Mismeasure of Man*. New York: W. W. Norton, 1981.

Gray, Lewis Cecil. *History of Agriculture in the Southern United States to 1860*. 2 vols. Washington, D.C.: Carnegie Institution of Washington, 1933.

Green, Constance McLaughlin. *The Secret City: A History of Race Relations in the Nation's Capital*. Princeton, N.J.: Princeton University Press, 1962.

———. *Washington*. 2 vols. Vol. 1, *Village and Capital, 1800–1878*. Princeton, N.J.: Princeton University Press, 1962.

Grimsley, Mark. *The Hard Hand of War: Union Military Policy toward Southern Civilians, 1861–1865*. Cambridge: Cambridge University Press, 1995.

Guelzo, Allen C. *Abraham Lincoln: Redeemer President*. Grand Rapids, Mich.: William B. Erdmans Publishing, 1999.

———. *Lincoln's Emancipation Proclamation: The End of Slavery in America*. New York: Simon & Schuster, 2004.

Gutman, Herbert G. *The Black Family in Slavery and Freedom, 1750–1925*. New York: Random House, 1976.

Hager, Christopher. *Word by Word: Emancipation and the Act of Writing*. Cambridge, Mass.: Harvard University Press, 2013.

Hahn, Steven. "Class and State in Postemancipation Societies: Southern Planters in Comparative Perspective." *American Historical Review* 95, no. 1 (February 1990): 75–98.

———. "'Extravagant Expectations' of Freedom: Rumour, Political Struggle, and the Christmas Insurrection Scare of 1865 in the American South." *Past and Present* 157, no. 1 (November 1997): 122–58.

———. *A Nation under Our Feet: Black Political Struggles in the Rural South from Slavery to the Great Migration*. Cambridge, Mass.: Harvard University Press, 2003.

———. *A Nation without Borders: The United States and Its World in an Age of Civil Wars, 1830–1910*. New York: Viking, 2016.

———. *The Political Worlds of Slavery and Freedom*. Cambridge, Mass.: Harvard University Press, 2009.

———. "Slave Emancipation, Indian Peoples, and the Projects of a New American Nation-State." *Journal of the Civil War Era* 3, no. 3 (September 2013): 307–30.

Harding, Vincent. *There Is a River: The Black Struggle for Freedom in America*. New York: Vintage, 1983.

Harper, Matthew. *The End of Days: African American Religion and Politics in the Age of Emancipation*. Chapel Hill: University of North Carolina Press, 2016.

Harris, Leslie M. *In the Shadow of Slavery: African Americans in New York City, 1626–1863*. Chicago: University of Chicago Press, 2003.

Harris, Robert L., Jr. "H. Ford Douglas: Afro-American Antislavery Emigrationist." *Journal of Negro History* 62, no. 3 (July 1997): 217–34.

Harris, William C. "The Hampton Roads Peace Conference: A Final Test of Lincoln's Presidential Leadership." *Journal of the Abraham Lincoln Association* 22, no. 1 (Winter 2000): 30–61.

———. "His Loyal Opposition: Lincoln's Border State Critics." *Journal of the Abraham Lincoln Association* 32, no. 1 (Winter 2011): 1–17.

Harrold, Stanley. *Subversives: Antislavery Community in Washington, D.C., 1828–1865*. Baton Rouge: Louisiana State University Press, 2003.

Hermann, Janet Sharp. *The Pursuit of a Dream*. New York: Oxford University Press, 1981.

Hess, Earl J. *Civil War Infantry Tactics: Training, Combat, and Small-Unit Effectiveness*. Baton Rouge: Louisiana State University Press, 2015.

———. *Field Armies and Fortifications in the Civil War: The Eastern Campaigns, 1861–1864*. Chapel Hill: University of North Carolina Press, 2005.

Hinkley, N., J. A. Sherman, N. B. Phillips, M. Schioppo, N. D. Lemke, K. Beloy, M. Pizzocaro, C. W. Oates, and A. D. Ludlow. "An Atomic Clock with 10^{-18} Instability." *Science* 341, no. 6151 (2013): 1215–18.

Hodes, Martha. *Mourning Lincoln.* New Haven, Conn.: Yale University Press, 2015.

———. "Wartime Dialogues on Illicit Sex: White Women and Black Men." In *Sexual Borderlands: Constructing an American Sexual Past,* edited by Kathleen Kennedy and Sharon Rena Ullman, 115–30. Columbus: Ohio State University Press, 2003.

Hodges, Graham Russell Gao. *Black New Jersey: 1664 to the Present Day.* New Brunswick, N.J.: Rutgers University Press, 2018.

Hofstadter, Richard. *The American Political Tradition and the Men Who Made It.* New York: Alfred A. Knopf, 1948.

Hollandsworth, James G., Jr. "Looking for Bob: Black Confederate Pensioners after the War." *Journal of Mississippi History* 69, no. 4 (Winter 2007): 295–324.

———. *The Louisiana Native Guards: The Black Military Experience during the Civil War.* Baton Rouge: Louisiana State University Press, 1995.

Holt, Thomas C. *Black over White: Negro Political Leadership in South Carolina during Reconstruction.* Urbana: University of Illinois Press, 1977.

———. *The Problem of Freedom: Race, Labor, and Politics in Jamaica and Britain, 1832–1938.* Baltimore: Johns Hopkins University Press, 1992.

Holzer, Harold. *Emancipating Lincoln: The Proclamation in Text, Context, and Memory.* Cambridge, Mass.: Harvard University Press, 2012.

Holzer, Harold, Edna Greene Medford, and Frank J. Williams. *The Emancipation Proclamation: Three Views.* Baton Rouge: Louisiana State University Press, 2006.

Horton, James O., and Lois E. Horton. *In Hope of Liberty: Culture, Community, and Protest among Northern Free Blacks, 1700–1860.* New York: Oxford University Press, 1997.

Howard, Victor B. *Black Liberation in Kentucky: Emancipation and Freedom, 1862–1884.* Lexington: University Press of Kentucky, 1983.

Howe, Daniel Walker. *What Hath God Wrought: The Transformation of America, 1815–1848.* New York: Oxford University Press, 2007.

Humphreys, Margaret. *Intensely Human: The Health of the Black Soldier in the American Civil War.* Baltimore: Johns Hopkins University Press, 2008.

Hunter, Tera W. *To 'Joy My Freedom: Southern Black Women's Lives and Labors after the Civil War.* Cambridge, Mass.: Harvard University Press, 1997.

Hurt, R. Douglas. *Agriculture and the Confederacy: Policy, Productivity, and Power in the Civil War South.* Chapel Hill: University of North Carolina Press, 2015.

Irmscher, Christoph. *Louis Agassiz: Creator of American Science.* Boston: Houghton Mifflin Harcourt, 2013.

James, C. L. R. *The Black Jacobins: Toussaint L'Ouverture and the San Domingo Revolution.* London: Secker & Warburg, 1938.

Johnson, Clifton, comp. *Battleground Adventures: The Stories of Dwellers on the Scenes of Conflict in Some of the Most Notable Battles of the Civil War.* New York: Houghton Mifflin, 1915. [Internet Archive]

Johnson, Michael P. "Out of Egypt: The Migration of Former Slaves to the Midwest during the 1860s in Comparative Perspective." In *Crossing Boundaries:*

Comparative History of Black People in Diaspora, edited by Darlene Clark Hine and Jacqueline McLeod, 223–45. Bloomington: University of Indiana Press, 1999.

Johnson, Walter. *River of Dark Dreams: Slavery and Empire in the Cotton Kingdom*. Cambridge, Mass.: Harvard University Press, 2013.

———. *Soul By Soul: Life Inside the Antebellum Slave Market*. Cambridge, Mass.: Harvard University Press, 1999.

Jones, Jacqueline. *Saving Savannah: The City and the Civil War*. New York: Alfred A. Knopf, 2008.

———. *Soldiers of Light and Love: Northern Teachers and Georgia Blacks, 1865–1873*. Chapel Hill: University of North Carolina Press, 1980.

Jones, Martha S. *All Bound Up Together: The Woman Question in African American Public Culture, 1830–1900*. Chapel Hill: University of North Carolina Press, 2007.

Jordan, Ervin L., Jr. *Black Confederates and Afro-Yankees in Civil War Virginia*. Charlottesville: University Press of Virginia, 1995.

Jordan, Winthrop D. *Tumult and Silence at Second Creek: An Inquiry into a Civil War Slave Conspiracy*. Baton Rouge: Louisiana State University Press, 1993.

———. *White over Black: American Attitudes toward the Negro, 1550–1912*. Chapel Hill: University of North Carolina Press, 1968.

Josephy, Alvin M., Jr. *The Civil War in the American West*. New York: Alfred A. Knopf, 1991.

Joshi, Manoj K., and Joseph P. Reidy. "'To Come Forward and Aid in Putting Down This Unholy Rebellion': The Officers of Louisiana's Free Black Native Guard during the Civil War Era." *Southern Studies* 21 no. 3 (Fall 1982): 326–42.

Kantrowitz, Stephen. *More Than Freedom: Fighting for Black Citizenship in a White Republic, 1829–1889*. New York: Penguin Press, 2012.

Kaye, Anthony E. *Joining Places: Slave Neighborhoods in the Old South*. Chapel Hill: University of North Carolina Press, 2007.

———. "Slaves, Emancipation, and the Powers of War: Views from the Natchez District of Mississippi." In *The War Was You and Me: Civilians in the American Civil War*, edited by Joan Cashen, 60–84. Princeton, N.J.: Princeton University Press, 2002.

Kelley, Robin D. G. "'We Are Not What We Seem': Rethinking Black Working-Class Opposition in the Jim Crow South." *Journal of American History* 80, no. 1 (June 1993): 75–112.

Kendi, Ibram X. *Stamped from the Beginning: The Definitive History of Racist Ideas in America*. New York: Nation Books, 2016.

Kerr-Ritchie, Jeffrey R. *Rites of August First: Emancipation Day in the Black Atlantic World*. Baton Rouge: Louisiana State University Press, 2007.

King, Lisa Y. "In Search of Women of African Descent Who Served in the Civil War Navy." *Journal of Negro History* 83, no. 4 (Autumn 1998): 302–9.

———. "'They Called Us Bluejackets': The Transformation of Self-Emancipated Slaves from Contrabands of War to Fighting Sailors in the South Atlantic Blocking Squadron during the Civil War." *International Journal of Naval History* 1, no. 1 (Spring 2002). http://www.ijnhonline.org/wp-content/uploads/2012/01/pdf _king1.pdf.

Knowles, Scott Gabriel. *The Disaster Experts: Mastering Risk in Modern America*. Philadelphia: University of Pennsylvania Press, 2011.

Kolchin, Peter. "Reexamining Southern Emancipation in Comparative Perspective." *Journal of Southern History* 81, no. 1 (February 2015): 7–40.

Krauthamer, Barbara. *Black Slaves, Indian Masters: Slavery, Emancipation, and Citizenship in the Native American South*. Chapel Hill: University of North Carolina Press, 2013.

———. "Indian Territory and the Treaties of 1866: A Long History of Emancipation." In *The World the Civil War Made*, edited by Gregory P. Downs and Kate Masur, 226–48. Chapel Hill: University of North Carolina Press, 2015.

Kytle, Ethan J. *Romantic Reformers and the Antislavery Struggle in the Civil War Era*. New York: Cambridge University Press, 2014.

Landes, David S. *Revolution in Time: Clocks and the Making of the Modern World*. Cambridge, Mass.: Harvard University Press, 1983.

Larson, Kate Clifford. *Bound for the Promised Land: Harriet Tubman, Portrait of an American Hero*. New York: One World, 2004.

Leech, Margaret. *Reveille in Washington 1861–1865*. New York: Harper & Brothers, 1941.

LeFloria, Talitha L. *Chained in Silence: Black Women and Convict Labor in the New South*. Chapel Hill: University of North Carolina Press, 2015.

Levine, Bruce. *Confederate Emancipation: Southern Plans to Free and Arm Slaves during the Civil War*. Oxford: Oxford University Press, 2006.

———. *The Fall of the House of Dixie: The Civil War and the Social Revolution That Transformed the South*. New York: Random House, 2013.

Levy, Jonathan. *Freaks of Fortune: The Emerging World of Capitalism and Risk in America*. Cambridge, Mass.: Harvard University Press, 2012.

Link, William A., and James J. Broomall, eds. *Rethinking American Emancipation: Legacies of Slavery and the Quest for Black Freedom*. New York: Cambridge University Press, 2016.

Littlefield, Daniel F., Jr. *Africans and Seminoles: From Removal to Emancipation*. Westport, Conn.: Greenwood Press, 1977.

———. *The Cherokee Freedmen: From Emancipation to American Citizenship*. Westport, Conn.: Greenwood Press, 1978.

Litwack, Leon F. *Been in the Storm So Long: The Aftermath of Slavery*. New York: Alfred A. Knopf, 1979.

———. *North of Slavery: The Negro in the Free States, 1790–1860*. Chicago: University of Chicago Press, 1961.

Logan, Rayford W. *The Diplomatic Relations of the United States with Haiti, 1776–1891*. Chapel Hill: University of North Carolina Press, 1941.

———. *Howard University: The First Hundred Years, 1867–1967*. New York: New York University Press, 1969.

———. "Some New Interpretations of the Colonization Movement." *Phylon* 4, no. 4 (4th Qtr. 1943): 328–34.

Long, Gretchen. *Doctoring Freedom: The Politics of African American Medical Care in Slavery and Emancipation*. Chapel Hill: University of North Carolina Press, 2012.

Lonn, Ella. "Extent and Importance of Federal Naval Raids on Salt-Making in Florida." *Florida Historical Society Quarterly* 10, no. 4 (April 1932): 167–84.

——. *Salt as a Factor in the Confederacy.* New York: Columbia University Press, 1933.

Lovejoy, Paul E. "'Freedom Narratives' of Transatlantic Slavery." *Slavery & Abolition* 32, no. 1 (March 2011): 91–107.

Lundstrom, John B. *One Drop in a Sea of Blue: The Liberators of the Ninth Minnesota.* St. Paul: Minnesota Historical Society Press, 2012.

Lusane, Clarence. *The Black History of the White House.* New York: City Lights, 2010.

MacKethan, Lucinda H. "Reading Marlboro Jones: A Georgia Slave in Civil War Virginia." In *Virginia's Civil War,* edited by Peter Wallenstein and Bertram Wyatt Brown, 165–75. Charlottesville: University of Virginia Press, 2005.

Maddex, Jack P., Jr. "Proslavery Millennialism: Social Eschatology in Antebellum Southern Calvinism." *American Quarterly* 31, no. 1 (Spring 1979): 46–62.

Magness, Phillip W. "James Mitchell and the Mystery of the Emigration Office." *Journal of the Abraham Lincoln Association* 32 (September 2011): 50–62.

Manning, Chandra. *Troubled Refuge: Struggling for Freedom in the Civil War.* New York: Alfred A. Knopf, 2016.

——. *What This Cruel War Was Over: Soldiers, Slavery, and the Civil War.* New York: Alfred A. Knopf, 2007.

——. "Working for Citizenship in Civil War Contraband Camps." *Journal of the Civil War Era* 4, no. 2 (June 2014): 172–204.

Marten, James. *The Children's Civil War.* Chapel Hill: University of North Carolina Press, 1998.

Martin, Jonathan D. *Divided Mastery: Slave Hiring in the American South.* Cambridge, Mass.: Harvard University Press, 2004.

Martin, Waldo. *The Mind of Frederick Douglass.* Chapel Hill: University of North Carolina Press, 1984.

Martinez, Jaime Amanda. *Confederate Slave Impressment in the Upper South.* Chapel Hill: University of North Carolina Press, 2013.

Massey, Mary Elizabeth. *Refugee Life in the Confederacy.* Baton Rouge: Louisiana State University Press, 1964.

Masur, Kate. "The African American Delegation to Abraham Lincoln: A Reappraisal." *Civil War History* 56, no. 2 (June 2010): 117–44.

——. *An Example for All the Land: Emancipation and the Struggle over Equality in Washington, D.C.* Chapel Hill: University of North Carolina Press, 2010.

——. "'A Rare Phenomenon of Philological Vegetation': The Word 'Contraband' and the Meanings of Emancipation in the United States." *Journal of American History* 93, no. 4 (March 2007): 1050–84.

Masur, Louis P. "Liberty Is a Slow Fruit: Lincoln the Deliberate Emancipator." *The American Scholar* (Autumn 2012). https://theamericanscholar.org/liberty-is-a-slow-fruit/#.VKrEUSvF-oM.

——. *Lincoln's Hundred Days: The Emancipation Proclamation and the War for the Union.* Cambridge, Mass.: Belknap Press of Harvard University Press, 2012.

Mathisen, Erik. *The Loyal Republic: Traitors, Slaves, and the Remaking of Citizenship in Civil War America*. Chapel Hill: University of North Carolina Press, 2018.

McCrossen, Alexis. *Marking Modern Times: A History of Clocks, Watches, and Other Timekeepers in American Life*. Chicago: University of Chicago Press, 2013.

McCurry, Stephanie. *Confederate Reckoning: Power and Politics in the Civil War South*. Cambridge, Mass.: Harvard University Press, 2010.

———. *Masters of Small Worlds: Yeoman Households, Gender Relations, and the Political Culture of the Antebellum South Carolina Low Country*. New York: Oxford University Press, 1995.

McFeely, William S. *Yankee Stepfather: General Oliver Otis Howard and the Freedmen*. New Haven, Conn.: Yale University Press, 1968.

McManus, Edgar J. *Black Bondage in the North*. Syracuse, N.Y.: Syracuse University Press, 1973.

———. *A History of Negro Slavery in New York*. Syracuse, N.Y.: Syracuse University Press, 1966.

McManus, Michael J. *Political Abolitionism in Wisconsin, 1840–1861*. Kent, Ohio: Kent State University Press, 1998.

McPherson, James M. *The Abolitionist Legacy: From Reconstruction to the NAACP*. Princeton, N.J.: Princeton University Press, 1975.

———. *Battle Cry of Freedom: The Civil War Era*. Oxford: Oxford University Press, 1988.

———. *The Negro's Civil War: How American Negroes Felt and Acted during the War for the Union*. New York: Pantheon, 1965.

———. *Ordeal by Fire: The Civil War and Reconstruction*. New York: McGraw-Hill, 1982.

———. *The Struggle for Equality: Abolitionists and the Negro in the Civil War and Reconstruction*. Princeton, N.J.: Princeton University Press, 1992.

———. *War on the Waters: The Union and Confederate Navies, 1861–1865*. Chapel Hill: University of North Carolina Press, 2012.

———. "Who Freed the Slaves?" *Proceedings of the American Philosophical Society* 139, no. 1 (March 1995): 1–10.

McWhiney, Grady, and Perry D. Jamieson. *Attack and Die: Civil War Military Tactics and the Southern Heritage*. University: University of Alabama Press, 1982.

Medford, Edna Greene. *Lincoln and Emancipation*. Edwardsville: Southern Illinois University Press, 2015.

Melish, Joanne Pope. *Disowning Slavery: Gradual Emancipation and "Race" in New England, 1780–1860*. Ithaca, N.Y.: Cornell University Press, 1998.

Melton, Maurice. *"The Best Station of Them All": The Savannah Squadron, 1861–1865*. Tuscaloosa: University of Alabama Press, 2012.

Messner, William F. *Freedmen and the Ideology of Free Labor in Louisiana, 1862–1865*. Lafayette: Center for Louisiana Studies, University of Southwestern Louisiana, 1978.

Middleton, Stephen. "The Fugitive Slave Crisis in Cincinnati, 1850–1860: Resistance, Enforcement, and Black Refugees." *Journal of Negro History* 72, no. 1/2 (Winter/Spring 1987): 20–32.

Milburn, Page. "The Emancipation of the Slaves in the District of Columbia." *Records of the Columbia Historical Society* 16 (1913): 96–119.

Miller, Edward A., Jr. "Garland H. White: Black Army Chaplain." *Civil War History* 43, no. 3 (September 1997): 201–18.

Miller, Floyd J. *The Search for a Black Nationality: Black Emigration and Colonization, 1787–1863*. Urbana: University of Illinois Press, 1975.

Mitchell, Mary Niall. *Raising Freedom's Child: Black Children and Visions of the Future after Slavery*. New York: New York University Press, 2008.

Mohr, Clarence L. *On the Threshold of Freedom: Masters and Slaves in Civil War Georgia*. Baton Rouge: Louisiana State University Press, 1986.

Moses, Wilson Jeremiah. *The Golden Age of Black Nationalism, 1850–1925*. New York: Oxford University Press, 1978.

Murray, Pauli. *Proud Shoes: The Story of an American Family*. 2nd ed. New York: Harper & Row, 1978.

Nash, Gary B., and Jean R. Soderlund. *Freedom by Degrees: Emancipation in Pennsylvania and Its Aftermath*. New York: Oxford University Press, 1991.

Nelson, Bernard H. "Confederate Slave Impressment Legislation, 1861–1865." *Journal of Negro History* 31, no. 4 (October 1946): 392–410.

———. "Legislative Control of the Southern Free Negro, 1861–1865." *Catholic Historical Review* 32 (April 1946): 28–46.

Nelson, Megan Kate. "The Pleasures of Civil War Ruins." In *Weirding the War: Stories from the Civil War's Ragged Edges*, edited by Stephen Berry, 36–53. Athens: University of Georgia Press, 2011.

———. *Ruin Nation: Destruction and the American Civil War*. Athens: University of Georgia Press, 2012.

Newman, Richard. "The Grammar of Emancipation: Putting Final Freedom in Context." In *Beyond Freedom: Disrupting the History of Emancipation*, edited by David W. Blight and Jim Downs, 11–25. Athens: University of Georgia Press, 2017.

Noll, Mark A. *The Civil War as a Theological Crisis*. Chapel Hill: University of North Carolina Press, 2006.

Newmark, Jill L. "Face to Face with History." *Prologue, Quarterly of the National Archives and Records Administration* 41, no. 3 (Fall 2009): 22–25.

Oakes, James. *Freedom National: The Destruction of Slavery in the United States, 1861–1865*. New York: W. W. Norton, 2013.

———. *The Radical and the Republican: Frederick Douglass, Abraham Lincoln, and the Triumph of Antislavery Politics*. New York: W. W. Norton, 2007.

Ochs, Stephen J. *A Black Patriot and a White Priest: André Cailloux and Claude Paschal Maistre in Civil War New Orleans*. Baton Rouge: Louisiana State University Press, 2000.

O'Donovan, Susan Eva. *Becoming Free in the Cotton South*. Cambridge, Mass.: Harvard University Press, 2007.

Ogle, Vanessa. "Whose Time Is It? The Pluralization of Time and the Global Condition, 1870s–1940s." *American Historical Review* 118, no. 5 (December 2013): 1376–1402.

Olsen, Otto H. "Abraham Lincoln as Revolutionary." *Civil War History* 24 (1978): 213–24.

———. *Carpetbagger's Crusade: The Life of Albion Winegar Tourgée*. Baltimore: Johns Hopkins University Press, 1965.

———. "Historians and the Extent of Slave Ownership in the Southern United States." *Civil War History* 18, no. 2 (June 1972): 101–16.

Oubre, Claude F. *Forty Acres and a Mule: The Freedmen's Bureau and Black Land Ownership*. Baton Rouge: Louisiana State University Press, 1978.

Pacheco, Josephine F. *The Pearl: A Failed Slave Escape on the Potomac*. Chapel Hill: University of North Carolina Press, 2005.

Painter, Nell Irvin. *Exodusters: Black Migration to Kansas after Reconstruction*. New York: W. W. Norton, 1976.

Pancoast, Elinor, and Anne E. Lincoln, *The Incorrigible Idealist: Robert Dale Owen in America*. Bloomington, Ind.: Principia Press, 1940.

Parrish, William E. *Turbulent Partnership: Missouri and the Union, 1861–1865*. Columbia: University of South Carolina Press, 1963.

Penningroth, Dylan C. *The Claims of Kinfolk: African American Property and Community in the Nineteenth-Century South*. Chapel Hill: University of North Carolina Press, 2003.

Peterson, Merrill D. *Lincoln in American Memory*. New York: Oxford University Press, 1994.

Phillips, Christopher. *The Rivers Ran Backward: The Civil War and the Remaking of the American Middle Border*. New York: Oxford University Press, 2016.

Poe, Ryan M. "The Contours of Emancipation: Freedom Comes to Southwest Arkansas." *Arkansas Historical Quarterly* 70, no. 2 (Summer 2011): 109–30.

Powell, Lawrence N. *The Accidental City: Improvising New Orleans*. Cambridge, Mass.: Harvard University Press, 2012.

———. *New Masters: Northern Planters during the Civil War and Reconstruction*. New Haven, Conn.: Yale University Press, 1980.

Pritchett, Jonathan B. "Quantitative Estimates of the United States Interregional Slave Trade, 1820–1860." *Journal of Economic History* 61, no. 2 (June 2001): 467–75.

Pybus, Cassandra. *Epic Journeys of Freedom: Runaway Slaves of the American Revolution and Their Global Quest for Liberty*. New York: Beacon, 2006.

Quarles, Benjamin. *Black Abolitionists*. New York: Oxford University Press, 1969.

———. *Lincoln and the Negro*. New York: Oxford University Press, 1962.

———. *The Negro in the Civil War*. Boston: Little, Brown, 1953.

Quarstein, John V. *Big Bethel: The First Battle*. Charleston, S.C.: History Press, 2011.

Rable, George C. *Civil Wars: Women and the Crisis of Southern Nationalism*. Urbana: University of Illinois Press, 1989.

———. *Fredericksburg! Fredericksburg!* Chapel Hill: University of North Carolina Press, 2002.

———. *God's Almost Chosen Peoples: A Religious History of the American Civil War*. Chapel Hill: University of North Carolina Press, 2010.

Raboteau, Albert J. *Slave Religion: The "Invisible Institution" in the Antebellum South*. New York: Oxford University Press, 1978.

Rael, Patrick. *Black Identity and Black Protest in the Antebellum North*. Chapel Hill: University of North Carolina Press, 2002.

————. *Eighty-Eight Years: The Long Death of Slavery in the United States, 1777–1865*. Athens: University of Georgia Press, 2015.

Ramold, Steven J. *Slaves, Sailors, Citizens: African Americans in the Union Navy*. DeKalb: Northern Illinois University Press, 2001.

Rawick, George P. *From Sundown to Sunup: The Making of the Black Community*. Westport, Conn.: Greenwood Press, 1972.

Redkey, Edwin S. *Black Exodus: Black Nationalist and Back-to-Africa Movements, 1890–1910*. New Haven, Conn.: Yale University Press, 1969.

Regosin, Elizabeth. *Freedom's Promise: Ex-Slave Families and Citizenship in the Age of Emancipation*. Charlottesville: University Press of Virginia, 2002.

Reid, Richard M. *African Canadians in Union Blue: Volunteering for the Cause in America's Civil War*. Kent, Ohio: Kent State University Press, 2015 [originally published in 2014].

————. *Freedom for Themselves: North Carolina's Black Soldiers in the Civil War Era*. Chapel Hill: University of North Carolina Press, 2008.

Reidy, Joseph P. "The African American Struggle for Citizenship Rights in the Northern United States during the Civil War. In *Civil War Citizens: Race, Ethnicity, and Identity in America's Bloodiest Conflict*, edited by Susannah J. Ural, 213–36. New York: New York University Press, 2010.

————. "Black Men in Navy Blue during the Civil War." *Prologue: Quarterly of the National Archives and Records Administration* 33, no. 3 (Fall 2001): 155–67.

————. "'Coming from the Shadow of the Past': The Transition from Slavery to Freedom at Freedmen's Village, 1863–1900." *Virginia Magazine of History and Biography* 95, no. 4 (October 1987): 403–28.

————. *From Slavery to Agrarian Capitalism in the Cotton Plantation South: Central Georgia, 1800–1880*. Chapel Hill: University of North Carolina Press, 1992.

————. "States of Dependence and Independence in Civil War Georgia." In *Breaking the Heartland: The Civil War in Georgia*, edited by John D. Fowler and David B. Parker, 46–66. Macon, Ga.: Mercer University Press, 2011.

————. "The Winding Path to Freedom under the District of Columbia's Emancipation Act of April 16, 1862." *Washington History* 26, no. 1 (Fall 2014): 12–18.

Richards, Leonard L. *Who Freed the Slaves?: The Fight over the Thirteenth Amendment*. Chicago: University of Chicago Press, 2015.

Richardson, Heather Cox. *The Death of Reconstruction: Race, Labor, and Politics in the Post-Civil War North, 1865–1901*. Cambridge, Mass.: Harvard University Press, 2001.

————. *West from Appomattox: The Reconstruction of America after the Civil War*. New Haven, Conn.: Yale University Press, 2007.

Ripley, C. Peter. *Slaves and Freedmen in Civil War Louisiana*. Baton Rouge: Louisiana State University Press, 1976.

Rivers, Larry Eugene. *Rebels and Runaways: Slave Resistance in Nineteenth-Century Florida*. Urbana: University of Illinois Press, 2012.

Robinson, Armstead L. *Bitter Fruits of Bondage: The Demise of Slavery and the Collapse of the Confederacy, 1861–1865*. Charlottesville: University of Virginia Press, 2011.

———. "In the Shadow of Old John Brown: Insurrection Anxiety and Confederate Mobilization, 1861–1863." *Journal of Negro History* 65, no. 4 (Autumn 1980): 279–97.

———. "'Plans Dat Comed from God': Institution Building and the Emergence of Black Leadership in Reconstruction Memphis." In *Toward a New South? Studies in Post-Civil War Southern Communities,* edited by Orville Vernon Burton and Robert C. McMath Jr., 71–102. Westport, Conn.: Greenwood Press, 1972.

Rodrigue, John C. *Reconstruction in the Cane Fields: From Slavery to Free Labor in Louisiana's Sugar Parishes, 1862–1880.* Baton Rouge: Louisiana State University Press, 2001.

Roediger, David. *Seizing Freedom: Slave Emancipation and Liberty for All.* London: Verso, 2014.

Roland, Charles P. *Louisiana Sugar Plantations during the American Civil War.* Leiden, Netherlands: E. J. Brill, 1957.

Rollins, Richard, ed. *Black Southerners in Gray: Essays on Afro-Americans in Confederate Armies.* Redondo Beach, Calif.: Rank and File Publications, 1994.

Rose, Willie Lee. *Rehearsal for Reconstruction: The Port Royal Experiment.* Indianapolis: Bobbs-Merrill, 1964.

Rothman, Adam. *Beyond Freedom's Reach: A Kidnapping in the Twilight of Slavery.* Cambridge, Mass.: Harvard University Press, 2015.

Rubin, Anne Sarah. *A Shattered Nation: The Rise and Fall of the Confederacy, 1861–1868.* Chapel Hill: University of North Carolina Press, 2005.

———. *Through the Heart of Dixie: Sherman's March and American History.* Chapel Hill: University of North Carolina Press, 2014.

Samito, Christian G. *Becoming American under Fire: Irish Americans, African Americans, and the Politics of Citizenship during the Civil War Era.* Ithaca, N.Y.: Cornell University Press, 2009.

Sanderfer, Selena. "Tennessee's Black Postwar Emigration Movements, 1866–1880." *Tennessee Historical Quarterly* 73, no. 4 (Winter 2014): 254–79.

Savage, Kirk. *Standing Soldiers, Kneeling Slaves: Race, War, and Monument in Nineteenth-Century America.* Princeton, N.J.: Princeton University Press, 1997.

Saville, Julie. *The Work of Reconstruction: From Slave to Wage Laborer in South Carolina, 1860–1870.* Cambridge: Cambridge University Press, 1994.

Sears, Stephen W. *Gettysburg.* New York: Houghton Mifflin, 2003.

Schecter, Barnet. *The Devil's Own Work: The Civil War Draft Riots and the Fight to Reconstruct America.* New York: Walker, 2005.

Schermerhorn, Calvin. *The Business of Slavery and the Rise of American Capitalism, 1815–1860.* New Haven, Conn.: Yale University Press, 2015.

Schwalm, Leslie. *Emancipation's Diaspora: Race and Reconstruction in the Upper Midwest.* Chapel Hill: University of North Carolina Press, 2009.

———. *"A Hard Fight for We": Women's Transition from Slavery to Freedom in South Carolina.* Urbana: University of Illinois Press, 1997.

———. "'Overrun with Free Negroes': Emancipation and Wartime Migration in the Upper Midwest." *Civil War History* 50, no. 2 (June 2004): 145–74.

Schwartz, Harold. *Samuel Gridley Howe: Social Reformer, 1801–1876.* Cambridge, Mass.: Harvard University Press, 1956.

Scott, Rebecca J. "The Battle over the Child: Child Apprenticeship and the Freedmen's Bureau in North Carolina." *Prologue: Quarterly of the National Archives and Records Administration* 10, no. 2 (Summer 1978): 101–13.

———. *Degrees of Freedom: Louisiana and Cuba after Slavery*. Cambridge, Mass.: Harvard University Press, 2005.

———. *Slave Emancipation in Cuba: The Transition to Free Labor, 1860–1899*. Princeton, N.J.: Princeton University Press, 1985.

Scott, Rebecca J., and Jean M. Hébrard. *Freedom Papers: An Atlantic Odyssey in the Age of Emancipation*. Cambridge, Mass.: Harvard University Press, 2012.

Sears, Richard D. *Camp Nelson, Kentucky: A Civil War History*. Louisville: University Press of Kentucky, 2002.

Segars, J. H., and Charles Kelly Barrow. *Black Southerners in Confederate Armies: A Collection of Historical Accounts*. Gretna, La.: Pelican Publishing, 2007.

Shaffer, Donald R. *After the Glory: The Struggles of Black Civil War Veterans*. Lawrence: University Press of Kansas, 2004.

Sharfstein, Daniel J. *Thunder in the Mountains: Chief Joseph, Oliver Otis Howard, and the Nez Perce War*. New York: W. W. Norton, 2017.

Siddali, Silvana R. *From Property to Person: Slavery and the Confiscation Acts, 1861–1862*. Baton Rouge: Louisiana State University Press, 2005.

Sinha, Manisha. *The Slave's Cause: A History of Abolition*. New Haven, Conn.: Yale University Press, 2016.

Skocpol, Theda. *Protecting Soldiers and Mothers: The Political Origins of Social Policy in the United States*. Cambridge, Mass.: Harvard University Press, 1992.

Smith, Mark M. "Counting Clocks, Owning Time: Detailing and Interpreting Clock and Watch Ownership in the American South, 1739–1865." *Time & Society* 3, no. 3 (October 1994): 321–39.

———. *Mastered by the Clock: Time, Slavery, and Freedom in the American South*. Chapel Hill: University of North Carolina Press, 1997.

———. "Old South Time in Comparative Perspective." *American Historical Review* 101, no. 5 (December 1996): 1432–69.

Smith, Stacy L. "Emancipating Peons, Excluding Coolies: Reconstructing Coercion in the American West." In *The World the Civil War Made*, edited by Gregory P. Downs and Kate Masur, 46–74. Chapel Hill: University of North Carolina Press, 2015.

———. *Freedom's Frontier: California and the Struggle over Unfree Labor, Emancipation, and Reconstruction*. Chapel Hill: University of North Carolina Press, 2013.

Spraggins, Tinsley Lee. "Mobilization of Negro Labor for the Department of Virginia and North Carolina, 1861–1865." *North Carolina Historical Review* 24, no. 2 (April 1947): 160–97.

Spurgeon, Ian Michael. *Soldiers in the Army of Freedom: The 1st Kansas Colored, the Civil War's First African American Combat Unit*. Norman: University of Oklahoma Press, 2014.

Stampp, Kenneth M. *The Peculiar Institution: Slavery in the Ante-Bellum South*. New York: Alfred A. Knopf, 1956.

Stanley, Amy Dru. *From Bondage to Contract: Wage Labor, Marriage and the Market in the Age of Slave Emancipation*. New York: Cambridge University Press, 1998.

———. "Instead of Waiting for the Thirteenth Amendment: The War Power, Slave Marriage, and Inviolate Human Rights." *American Historical Review* 115, no. 3 (June 2010): 732–65.

———. "Slave Emancipation and the Revolutionizing of Human Rights." In *The World the Civil War Made*, edited by Gregory P. Downs and Kate Masur, 269–303. Chapel Hill: University of North Carolina Press, 2015.

Stauffer, John. *Giants: The Parallel Lives of Frederick Douglass and Abraham Lincoln*. New York: Twelve, 2008.

Steiner, Paul E. *Medical History of a Civil War Regiment: Disease in the Sixty-Fifth United States Colored Infantry*. Clayton, Mo.: Institute of Civil War Studies, 1977.

Sternhell, Yael A. "Bodies in Motion and the Making of Emancipation." In *Rethinking American Emancipation: Legacies of Slavery and the Quest for Black Freedom*, edited by William A. Link and James J. Broomall, 15–41. Cambridge: Cambridge University Press, 2015.

———. *Routes of War: The World of Movement in the Confederate South*. Cambridge, Mass.: Harvard University Press, 2012.

Stuckey, Sterling. *The Ideological Origins of Black Nationalism*. Boston: Beacon Press, 1972.

Sugrue, Thomas J. *The Origins of the Urban Crisis: Race and Inequality in Postwar Detroit*. Princeton, N.J.: Princeton University Press, 1996.

Swanson, Drew A. *Remaking Wormsloe Plantation: The Environmental History of a Lowcountry Landscape*. Athens: University of Georgia Press, 2012.

Tadman, Michael. *Speculators and Slaves: Masters, Traders, and Slaves in the Old South*. Madison: University of Wisconsin Press, 1989.

Taylor, Alrutheus A. *The Negro in South Carolina during the Reconstruction*. Washington, D.C.: Associated Publishers, 1924.

———. *The Negro in Tennessee, 1865–1880*. Washington, D.C.: Associated Publishers, 1941.

———. *The Negro in the Reconstruction of Virginia*. Washington, D.C.: Associated Publishers, 1926.

Taylor, Amy Murrell. "How a Cold Snap in Kentucky Led to Freedom for Thousands: An Environmental Story of Emancipation." In *Weirding the War: Stories from the Civil War's Ragged Edges*, edited by Stephen Berry, 191–214. Athens: University of Georgia Press, 2011.

Taylor, Nikki M. *Frontiers of Freedom: Cincinnati's Black Community, 1862–1868*. Athens: Ohio University Press, 2004.

Taylor, Quintard. *In Search of the Racial Frontier: African Americans in the American West, 1528–1990*. New York: W. W. Norton, 1998.

Thomas, Emory M. *The Confederacy as a Revolutionary Experience*. Englewood Cliffs, N.J.: Prentice Hall, 1971.

Thompson, Shirley Elizabeth. *Exiles at Home: The Struggle to Become American in Creole New Orleans*. Cambridge, Mass.: Harvard University Press, 2009.

Tomblin, Barbara Brooks. *Bluejackets and Contrabands: African Americans and the Union Navy*. Lexington: University Press of Kentucky, 2009.

Tomich, Dale W. *Through the Prism of Slavery: Labor, Capital, and World Economy*. Lanham, Md.: Rowman and Littlefield, 2004.

Tomich, Dale W., ed. *The Politics of the Second Slavery*. Albany: State University of New York Press, 2016.

Trelease, Alan W. *White Terror: The Ku Klux Klan Conspiracy and Southern Reconstruction*. New York: Harper & Row, 1971.

Trimpop, Rüdiger M. *The Psychology of Risk Taking Behavior*. Amsterdam: North-Holland, 1994.

Troutman, Phillip. "Grapevine in the Slave Market: African American Geopolitical Literacy and the 1841 *Creole* Revolt." In *The Chattel Principle: Internal Slave Trades in the Americas*, edited by Walter Johnson, 203–33. New Haven, Conn.: Yale University Press, 2004.

Trudeau, Noah Andre. *Like Men of War: Black Troops in the Civil War, 1862–1865*. Boston: Little, Brown, 1998.

Ural, Susannah J., ed. *Civil War Citizens: Race, Ethnicity, and Identity in America's Bloodiest Contest*. New York: New York University Press, 2010.

Valuska, David. *The African American in the Union Navy*. New York: Garland Publishers, 1993.

Vandiver, Frank. *Plowshares into Swords: Josiah Gorgas and Confederate Ordnance*. Austin: University of Texas Press, 1952.

Varon, Elizabeth R. *Appomattox: Victory, Defeat, and Freedom at the End of the Civil War*. New York: Oxford University Press, 2014.

Voegeli, V. Jacque. *Free but Not Equal: The Midwest and the Negro during the Civil War*. Chicago: University of Chicago Press, 1968.

———. "A Rejected Alternative: Union Policy and the Relocation of Southern 'Contrabands' at the Dawn of Emancipation." *Journal of Southern History* 69, no. 4 (November 2003): 765–90.

Vorenberg, Michael. *Final Freedom: The Civil War, the Abolition of Slavery, and the Thirteenth Amendment*. Cambridge: Cambridge University Press, 2001.

Wagandt, Charles L. "The Army versus Maryland Slavery, 1862–1864," *Civil War History* 10, no. 2 (June 1964): 141–48.

———. *A Mighty Revolution: Negro Emancipation in Maryland, 1862–1864*. Baltimore: Johns Hopkins University Press, 1964.

Walker, Cam. "Corinth: The Story of a Contraband Camp." *Civil War History* 20, no. 1 (March 1974): 5–22.

Walker, Clarence E. *A Rock in a Weary Land: The African Methodist Episcopal Church during the Civil War and Reconstruction*. Baton Rouge: Louisiana State University Press, 1982.

Walker, James W. St. G. *The Black Loyalists: The Search for a Promised Land in Nova Scotia and Sierra Leone, 1783–1870*. Toronto: University of Toronto Press, 1992.

Wallenstein, Peter, and Bertram Wyatt-Brown, eds. *Virginia's Civil War*. Charlottesville: University of Virginia Press, 2005.

Ward, Andrew. *The Slaves' War: The Civil War in the Words of Former Slaves*. New York: Houghton Mifflin, 2008.

Washington, John E. *They Knew Lincoln*. New York: E. P. Dutton, 1942.

Wax, Darold D. "Robert Ball Anderson, Ex-Slave, A Pioneer in Western Nebraska, 1884–1930." *Nebraska History* 64 (1983): 163–92.

Weeks, Stephen B. "Anti-Slavery Sentiment in the South; with Unpublished Letters from John Stuart Mill and Mrs. Stowe." *Publications of the Southern History Association* 2, no. 1 (April 1898): 87–130.

Weigley, Russell F. *A Great Civil War: A Military and Political History, 1861–1865.* Bloomington: Indiana University Press, 2000.

Wells, Cheryl A. *Civil War Time: Temporality and Identity in America, 1861–1865.* Athens: University of Georgia Press, 2005.

Wesley, Charles H. *The Collapse of the Confederacy.* Washington, D.C.: Associated Publishers, 1937.

———. "The Employment of Negroes as Soldiers in the Confederate Army." *Journal of Negro History* 4, no. 3 (July 1919): 239–53.

———. *Negro Labor in the United States, 1850–1925: A Study in American Economic History.* New York: Vanguard Press, 1927.

West, Elliott. *The Last Indian War: The Nez Perce Story.* New York: Oxford University Press, 2009.

Wiggins, William. *O Freedom! Afro-American Emancipation Celebrations.* Knoxville: University of Tennessee Press, 1987.

Wiley, Bell I. *Southern Negroes, 1861–1865.* New Haven, Conn.: Yale University Press, 1938.

Wilkerson, Isabel. *The Warmth of Other Suns: The Epic Story of America's Great Migration.* New York: Random House, 2010.

Williams, Eric. *Capitalism and Slavery.* Chapel Hill: University of North Carolina Press, 1944.

Williams, David. *Bitterly Divided: The South's Inner Civil War.* New York: New Press, 2013.

———. *I Freed Myself: African American Self-Emancipation in the Civil War Era.* Cambridge: Cambridge University Press, 2014.

Williams, Heather Andrea. *Help Me to Find My People: The African American Search for Family Lost in Slavery.* Chapel Hill: University of North Carolina Press, 2012.

Williams, Kidada E. *They Left Great Marks on Me: African American Testimonies of Racial Violence from Emancipation to World War I.* New York: New York University Press, 2012.

Williams, Teresa Crisp, and David Williams. "'The Women Rising': Cotton, Class, and Confederate Georgia's Rioting Women." *Georgia Historical Quarterly* 86, no. 1 (Spring 2002): 49–83.

Williamson, Joel. *After Slavery: The Negro in South Carolina during Reconstruction, 1861–1877.* Chapel Hill: University of North Carolina Press, 1965.

Willis, Deborah, and Barbara Krauthamer. *Envisioning Emancipation: Black Americans and the End of Slavery.* Philadelphia: Temple University Press, 2013.

Wills, Eric. "The Forgotten: The Contraband of America and the Road to Freedom." *Preservation,* May/June 2011. http://www.preservationnation.org/magazine/2011 /may-june/the-forgotten.html.

Wilson, Douglas L. *Honor's Voice: The Transformation of Abraham Lincoln.* New York: Alfred A. Knopf, 1998.

———. *Lincoln's Sword: The Presidency and the Power of Words.* New York: Alfred A. Knopf, 2007.

Wilson, Keith P. *Campfires of Freedom: The Camp Life of Black Soldiers during the Civil War*. Kent, Ohio: Kent State University Press, 2002.

Wilson, Theodore Brantner. *The Black Codes of the South*. University: University of Alabama Press, 1965.

Winkle, Kenneth J. "Emancipation in the District of Columbia." Civil War Washington, accessed July 18, 2018, at http://civilwardc.org/interpretations/narrative/emancipation.php.

———. "Mining the Compensated Emancipation Petitions." Civil War Washington, accessed July 18, 2018, at http://civilwardc.org/interpretations/narrative/mining.php.

Winters, John D. *The Civil War in Louisiana*. Baton Rouge: Louisiana State University Press, 1963.

Witt, John Fabian. *Lincoln's Code: The Laws of War in American History*. New York: Free Press, 2012.

Woodman, Harold D. *King Cotton & His Retainers; Financing & Marketing the Cotton Crop of the South, 1800–1925*. Lexington: University of Kentucky Press, 1968.

Woodson, Carter G. *A Century of Negro Migration*. Washington, D.C.: Association for the Study of Negro Life and History, 1918.

———. *The Education of the Negro Prior to 1861: A History of the Education of the Colored People of the United States from the Beginning of Slavery to the Civil War*. New York: Knickerbocker Press, 1915.

———. *The Negro in Our History*. Washington, D.C.: Associated Publishers, 1922.

———, ed. *The Mind of the Negro as Reflected in Letters Written during the Crisis, 1800–1860*. Washington, D.C.: Association for the Study of Negro Life and History, 1926.

Woodson, Carter G., and Charles H. Wesley. *The Story of the Negro Retold*. Washington, D.C.: Associated Publishers, 1935.

Woodward, C. Vann. *Origins of the New South, 1877–1913*. Baton Rouge: Louisiana State University Press, 1951.

Yacovone, Donald. *Freedom's Journey: African American Voices of the Civil War*. Chicago: Lawrence Hill Books, 2004.

Yarbrough, Fay A. "'Dis Land Which Jines Dat of Ole Master's': The Meaning of Citizenship for the Choctaw Freedpeople." In *Civil War Wests: Testing the Limits of the United States*, edited by Adam Arenson and Andrew R. Graybill, 224–41. Berkeley: University of California Press, 2015.

———. "Reconstructing Other Southerners: The Aftermath of the Civil War in the Cherokee Nation." In *Democracy and the American Civil War: Race and African Americans in the Nineteenth Century*, edited by Kevin Adams and Leonne M. Hudson, 47–62. Kent, Ohio: Kent State University Press, 2016.

Zakim, Michael, and Gary J. Kornblith. *Capitalism Takes Command: The Social Transformation of Nineteenth-Century America*. Chicago: University of Chicago Press, 2012.

Zilversmit, Arthur. *The First Emancipation: The Abolition of Slavery in the North*. Chicago: University of Chicago Press, 1967.

Unpublished Theses and Dissertations

Davidson, Roger A. "A Question of Loyalty: The Potomac Flotilla and Civil Insurrection in the Chesapeake Region." PhD diss., Howard University, 2000.

De Boer, Clara Merritt. "The Role of Afro-Americans in the Origin and Work of the American Missionary Association, 1839–1877." PhD diss., Rutgers University, 1973.

Fry, Gladys Marie. "The Activities of the Freedmen's Aid Societies in the District of Columbia, 1860–1870." MA thesis, Howard University, 1954.

Johnson, David Miles. "Beyond Freedom: The Black North, 1863–1883." PhD diss., University of California, Berkeley, 2007.

Johnston, Allan John. "Surviving Freedom: The Black Community of Washington, D.C., 1860–1880." PhD diss., Duke University, 1980.

King, Lisa Y. "Wounds That Bind: A Comparative Study of the Role Played by Civil War Veterans of African Descent in Community Formation in Massachusetts and South Carolina, 1865–1915." PhD diss., Howard University, 1999.

Williams, Melvin Roscoe. "Blacks in Washington, D.C., 1860–1870." PhD diss., Johns Hopkins University, 1975.

Index

Note: Figures are indicated by page numbers in *italics*.

320–24, 442n76; wage, 121, 263,
434n86. *See also* "Black Codes";
"Black Laws"
disease, 114, 275, 281, 384n95
District of Columbia. *See* Washington,
D.C.
Diven, Alexander S., 41
Divine Providence, 24, 94, 250, 392n70
domestic institutions. *See* institutions,
domestic
domestic workers. *See* house servants
Douglas, H. Ford, 98–99, 311, 329,
389n42, 439n32
Douglas, Stephen A., 104
Douglass, Frederick, 2, 7; on American
government, 90; on Confederate
victory, 92; Douglas and, 389n42,
439n32; and Emancipation Proclama-
tion, 29, 32; on future of nation, 94;
Haiti and, 307; on Lincoln, 4–5;
military service and, 101–2, 315; at
National Convention of Colored Men,
331; slave narrative of, 44; on super-
natural influence, 107; on watches,
366n2
Douglass, Lewis H., 52
Downing, George T., 307, 336
draft, military, 295–97
Draper, A. G., 416n61
Drayton, Daniel, 182
Dred Scott decision, 232
Drumgoold, James, 108
Drumgoold, Kate, 108, 277
Du Bois, W. E. B., 10–11, 12, 18, 354
Duff Green's Row, 286
Dumas, Francis E., 169, 405n22
Dunning, William Archibald, 10
Du Pont, Samuel F., 84, 203–4

Eaton, John, 72, 81, 167, 255–56, 275,
282–83, 421n32
economic self-sufficiency, 325–26
Edisto Island, South Carolina, 112,
178–79, 348–49, 407n47, 408n51
education, 102, 103, 167, 240, 271, 323, 331,
351

election: of 1856, 134; of 1860, 90, 133–34,
138, 231; of 1864, 76, 77, 99, 266,
383n71; of 1869 (New York), 335; of
1875 (Mississippi), 353; of 1876, 353; of
2008, 98; black voters in, 333
Eliot, Thomas D., 260–61
Eliot, William Greenleaf, 2, 274
Ellis, Josephine, 404n89
emancipation: in British West Indies,
234–36, 419n15; citizenship and,
303–4; compensated, 249, 388n32,
389n41; expansion of, 342–43; family
and, 267–68, 301; gradual, 104–5, 303;
home and, 246–47, 269–70, 301–2; in
Northern states, 236–37, 419n18; in
Saint-Domingue, 234; Sewell on, 235,
236, 264; social order and, 91; and
spirit of age, 233–34; in Washington,
D.C., 182–86, 247–48, 410n74
Emancipation (Nast), *268*
Emancipation League, 251, 254–55,
423n64
Emancipation Proclamation, 5, 27, 28–33,
362n14; Border Slave States and, 29,
297–98; exemptions under, 8, 34–37,
73–74, 148, 292; Marx on, 389n38;
military service and, 73, 314–15;
Turner on, 114
Emancipation Proclamation, The
(Franklin), 11–12
emigration, 45, 250, 307–9, 354. *See also*
colonization
employment, 174, 219, 243, 341, 344.
See also labor; military service,
African American
enfranchisement, 236, 259–60, 303,
328–29, 333–35
enslaved people: abandoned, 164; in
Border Slave States, 156–57; as capital,
339; employment of, 220–21; feeding
of, 164; in military labor, 64–71, 70–71,
75, 200–201; in naval service, 71–72;
population numbers, 15, 130; sheltering
of, 164; in Tennessee, 73–74. *See also*
freedom seeker(s)
Esup (freedman), 177, 347–48

marriage, interracial: fears of, 248–49, 326–27

Marrs, Elijah, 46, 138

Marshal, Robert, 185, 186–87

Marx, Karl, 389n38

Mary Ann (slave), 169–70

Maryland, 51, 82, 125, 155, 166, 185–90, 341–42. *See also* Annapolis; Baltimore

Mastership and Its Fruits, The: The Emancipated Slave Face to Face with His Old Master (McKaye), 265, 352

Maximilian I, 122

Mayo, William D., 56–57

McClellan, George B., 15, 48, 69–70, 73, 91, 145, 178, 199, 313, 381n46, 438n26

McComb, Morris, 394n92

McCormick, Alexander, 185, 187–90

McKaye, James, 117–18, 152, 253, 254, 257, 261, 265, 310, 352, 427n112

McKim, J. Miller, 252, 414n30

McLean, Wilmer, 144

McMillan, Harry, 346

Meade, George G., 76, 221

"Memorial Discourse," 7

memory, historical, 6

Memphis, Tennessee, 292

"Men of Color, to Arms!" (Douglass), 315

Meridian, Mississippi, 76, 86, 115–16, 168, 180–81

metaphors: for change, 96–97; seasonal, 59; temporal, 24, 94, 104

Mexican-American War, 90

Mexico, 233, 392n75

Michigan, 43, 329–30, 333

Middle Passage, 201

Midwest, 43, 98–99, 147, 180, 248–49, 250, 311, 324, 340. *See also specific states*

military draft, 295–97

military hospital, 190–93

military labor, 62–67, 68–71, 75, 200–201, 219, 278–79

military service, African American, 82–83, 100–102, 157–58, 309–16, 376n98, 377n106, 384n92, 397n121; black officers, 50–51, 53–57, 377nn99–102; citizenship and, 51–52, 293–94,

329–30; Confederate, 118–22; military labor, 257–58, 294–96; prisoners of war, 52–53, 374n86, 375n89, 390n56; unequal pay, 53, 316–19, 376n91. *See also* impressment; naval service

Militia Act: 1792, 51, 202, 438n30; 1794, 51; 1795, 438n30; 1862, 42, 53, 294, 313, 370n35, 372n55

Miller, Joseph, 50, 83–84, 300

Miller, Virginia Ann, 186

Minnesota, 333

minstrelsy, 18, 42

missionaries, 33, 115, 291, 308–9, 433nn77–78. *See also* American Missionary Association

Mississippi River, 204–5

mistresses, 16, 67, 163, 169–70

Mitchel, Ormsby M., 98, 145

Mobile, Alabama, 169

mobility, 14, 343, 396n108. *See also* "refugeeing"

Montgomery, Benjamin, 179–80

Montgomery, Isaiah, 180

Montgomery, James, 85, 96, 217, 388n30

Montgomery Bus Boycott, 37

More, Thomas, 54

Mortar Flotilla, 71–72

Moultrie, Ishmael, 348

Murray, Pauli, 439n31

Mussey, Reuben D., 99

Napoleonic wars, 137

narratives, slave, 43–44, 277

Nast, Thomas, 122, *123*, 267–68, *268*

National Anti-Slavery Standard, 236

National Association for the Advancement of Colored People (NAACP), 10

national convention movement, black, 330

National Convention of Colored Citizens, 233

National Convention of Colored Men, 330–33

National Emigration Convention, 303, 307

National Equal Rights Convention, 340

National Equal Rights League, 332–33
National Freedmen's Relief Association, 102
nationalism, 63, 355
nationalist, 270
Native Americans, 314, 328–29
Native Guard, 54–55
nativism, 8, 255
nature: time and, 59. *See also* seasons
naval service, African American, 158–59, 202, 204–5, 207–13, *212*, 313, 413n26. *See also* military service, African American
Negro in the Civil War, The (Quarles), 11
Nell, William C., 420n19
New England, 236, 237, 304
New England Convention of Colored Citizens, 334
New Hampshire, 419n18
New Jersey, 43, 99, 237, 304
New Orleans, Louisiana, 34–35, 72, 148–49, 169, 204–5, 376n95, 438n30
newspapers, 18–19, 43, 44, 45–48. *See also specific papers*
New York, 236, 237; draft riots, 110–12,
New York Herald, 172
New York Times, 235
New York World, 236
Nichols, Danforth B., 286–91, 421n32, 422n34
Nichols, Joseph, 367n5
Ninety-Fifth Illinois Volunteer Infantry, 98–99, 311
Ninety-Ninth New York Volunteer Infantry, 218
Ninety-Ninth U.S. Colored Infantry, 157, 403n89
Norfolk, Virginia, 34
North: Confederate supporters in, 92; as destination for freedom seekers, 17, 28, 220; emancipation in, 236–37, 419n18; free people of color in, 42, 43, 110, 325; individualism in, 227; supremacy of, 338–39; violence against African Americans in, 110
North Carolina, 341–42

Northcross, W. E., 108
Northwest Ordinance, 43, 266, 304
Northwest Territory, 304, 326

Obama, Barack, 98
Ohio, 43, 248–49, 333
Ohio River, 125, 201, 203
Oliver, John, 34, 174, 216–17, 291, 369n23
"On Matrimony" (Burke), 306
On to Liberty (Kaufman), *248*
Ordeal of Free Labor in the British West Indies, The (Sewell), 235–36, 264, 420n24
ordnance manufacturing, 165–66
O'Sullivan, Timothy, *247*
Owen, Robert Dale, 8, 98, 179, 252–54, 257, 261–62, 267, 398n128, 425n84, 426nn104–5, 443n87

Palmer, John M., 300–301, 436n111
Panic of 1873, 339
Parker, John, 215–16
Parker, Theodore, 424n69
Parks, Rosa, 162
patriarchy, 91, 228
pay, unequal, for black soldiers, 53, 57, 294, 317–18
Payne, Daniel Alexander, 392n70
Payton, James, 409n71
Pendleton, George H., 261
Peninsula Campaign, 91, 178, 313, 438n26
Pennsylvania, 419n18
Perry, Fannie, 149–51
Perry, Harriet, 149–50, 402n68
Perry, Levin, 150–51
Perry, Norfleet, 149–51
Perry, Theophilus, 149–51, 402n68
personhood, 269
Phelps, John W., 72, 121, 406n32
Phelps, S. L., 207
Philadelphia, Pennsylvania, 320–21, 323
Philadelphia Ledger, 94
Philbrick, Edward S., 295, 347, 348–49
Philippines, 6
Phillips, Wendell, 9, 232, 386n11
photography, 101–4, *103*

Rousseau, Lovell H., 36, 171
Rowland, Leslie S., 12
Rowley, Nimrod, 121, 440n50
runaway slaves. *See* freedom seeker(s)
Russell, LeBaron, 241, 421n28, 423n64
Russia, 109, 234, 252, 386n7, 392n75

sailors, 203–4
St. Catherine's Island, Georgia, 347, 354
Saint-Domingue, 27, 195, 234, 366n2
St. Helena Island, South Carolina, 178
St. Mary, USS, 210–11
Sampson, Yates, 348
Sanborn, Franklin B., 424n69
"Saturday Club," 253
Saulsbury, Willard, 319
Savannah, Georgia, 77–78
Saxton, Rufus, 33, 122, 178, 179, 294, 421n32
Scott, Charlotte, 2
Scott, Robert, 213
Scott, William, 171–72
Scott, Winfield, 136, *136*, 400n36
SCSA. *See* Social, Civil, and Statistical Association (SCSA)
Sea Islands (South Carolina), 33–34, 70, 174–79, 243–46, 345, 369n21, 407n46, 407n47
seasonal changes, 24, 59, 82
seasons: freedom seekers and, 60–61, 61–62; metaphors with, 59; military operations and, 59, 62–63, 76–77, 78–79
secession: and abolition in Washington, D.C., 182–83; Northern support of, 92; revolution and, 90; slavery and, 6
Second North Carolina Colored Volunteers, 416n61
Second South Carolina Colored Volunteers, 85–86
"Secret Six," 251, 424n69
Seddon, James A., 141, 374n86
segregation, 320–24, 442n76
self-sufficiency, 325–26
serfdom, in Russia, 109, 234, 392n75
Seventh New York Militia, 95
Seventh U.S. Colored Infantry, 55

Seventy-Eighth U.S. Colored Infantry, 318
Sewall, S. E., 423n65
Seward, William H., 1, 31, 266
Sewell, William G., 235–36, 264–65, 419n15, 420n24
sexual assault, 276
Seymour, Horatio, 121, 313, 397n122
Shadd Cary, Mary Ann, 315
Shaw, Robert Gould, 52, 86, 316, 327
Shaw Guards, 327
Sherman, John, 40
Sherman, Thomas W., 47, 67, 174, 420n20
Sherman, William T., 8, 40, 75, 76–77, 77–78, 99, 125, 199, 225, 387n20
Sierra Leone, 337
Simmes, Laura, 138
Singleton, William Henry, 293
Sisters of the Visitation of Georgetown, 182
Sixty-Fifth U.S. Colored Infantry, 384n95
Slack, Charles W., 327
slave narratives, 23, 43–44
slavery: families and, 227–28; returns to, 112–17, 391n60; secession and, 6; space and, 162–63
Slavery & Abolition (journal), 13
slaves. *See* enslaved people
slave trade: internal, 131–32; interstate, 51, 131, 148, 413n18; water and, 201
Small, Hannah, 414n30
Small, Robert (a.k.a. Robert Smalls), 161, 203–4, 274, 321, 414n30
Smallwood, James, 337
Smith, E. Kirby, 151, 153, 298
Smith, George E., 56
Smith, Gerrit, 424n69
Smith, John A., 1
Social, Civil, and Statistical Association (SCSA): Pennsylvania, 320, 334–35; Washington, D.C., 306–7
socialism, 90
social order, 91
"Song of the Negro Boatmen" (Whittier), 206